CHILTON'S

REPAIR & TUNE-UP GUIDE

MERCEDES-BENZ 1974-84

All U.S. and Canadian models of 190E • 190D • 230 • 240D • 280 • 280C 280CE • 280E • 280S • 280SE • 300D • 300CD • 300SD • 300TD • 380SE 380SEC • 380SEL • 380SL • 380SLC • 450SE • 450SEL • 450SL • 450SLC 500SEC • 500SEL • 6.9

Senior Vice President	Ronald A. Hoxter
Publisher and Editor-In-Chief	Kerry A. Freeman, S.A.E.
Executive Editors	Dean F. Morgantini, S.A.E., W. Calvin Settle, Jr., S.A.E.
Managing Editor	Nick D'Andrea
Special Products Manager	Ken Grabowski, A.S.E., S.A.E.
Senior Editors	Jacques Gordon, Michael L. Grady, Debra McCall, Kevin M. G. Maher, Richard J. Rivele, S.A.E., Richard T. Smith, Jim Taylor, Ron Webb
Project Managers	Martin J. Gunther, Will Kessler, A.S.E., Richard Schwartz
Production Manager	Andrea Steiger
Product Systems Manager	Robert Maxey
Director of Manufacturing	Mike D'Imperio

CHILTON BOOK COMPANY

SAFETY NOTICE

Proper service and repair procedures are vital to the safe, reliable operation of all motor vehicles, as well as the personal safety of those performing repairs. This book outlines procedures for servicing and repairing vehicles using safe, effective methods. The procedures contain many NOTES, CAUTIONS and WARNINGS which should be followed along with standard safety procedures to eliminate the possibility of personal injury or improper service which could damage the vehicle or compromise its safety.

It is important to note that repair procedures and techniques, tools and parts for servicing motor vehicles, as well as the skill and experience of the individual performing the work vary widely. It is not possible to anticipate all of the conceivable ways or conditions under which vehicles may be serviced, or to provide cautions as to all of the possible hazards that may result. Standard and accepted safety precautions and equipment should be used when handling toxic or flammable fluids, and safety goggles or other protection should be used during cutting, grinding, chiseling, prying, or any other process that can cause material removal or projectiles.

Some procedures require the use of tools specially designed for a specific purpose. Before substituting another tool or procedure, you must be completely satisfied that neither your personal safety, nor the performance of the vehicle will be endangered.

Although information in this guide is based on industry sources and is as complete as possible at the time of publication, the possibility exists that the manufacturer made later changes which could not be included here. While striving for total accuracy, Chilton Book Company cannot assume responsibility for any errors, changes, or omissions that may occur in the compilation of this data.

PART NUMBERS

Part numbers listed in this reference are not recommendations by Chilton for any product by brand name. They are references that can be used with interchange manuals and aftermarket supplier catalogs to locate each brand supplier's discrete part number.

ACKNOWLEDGMENTS

The Chilton Book Company expresses its appreciation to Mercedes-Benz of North America, Inc., Montvale, New Jersey; and Mercedes-Benz Parts Depot East, Training Facility, Teaneck, New Jersey.

Photographs by Kerry A. Freeman

Published in Radnor, Pennsylvania, 19089 by Chilton Book Company

Manufactured in the United States of America
22nd Printing, December 1998

Chilton's Repair & Tune-Up Guide: Mercedes-Benz 1974–84
ISBN 0-8019-7463-1 pbk.
Library of Congress Catalog Card No. 83-45305

CONTENTS

1 General Information and Maintenance

1 How to Use this Book
2 Tools and Equipment
11 Routine Maintenance and Lubrication
51 How To Buy A Used Car

2 Tune-Up and Performance Maintenance

54 Tune-Up Procedures
56 Gasoline Engine Tune-Up Specifications
58 Diesel Engine Tune-Up Specifications

3 Engine and Engine Rebuilding

84 Engine Electrical System
86 Engine Service and Specifications

4 Emission Controls and Fuel System

135 Emission Control System and Service
164 Fuel System

5 Chassis Electrical

180 Heater and Accessory Service
183 Instrument Panel Service
189 Lights, Fuses and Flashers

6 Clutch and Transmission

193 Manual Transmission
197 Clutch
199 Automatic Transmission

7 Drive Train

206 Driveshaft and U-Joints
207 Rear Axle

8 Suspension and Steering

211 Front Suspension
224 Rear Suspension
230 Steering

9 Brakes

234 Brake Specifications
237 Front Brakes
243 Rear Brakes

10 Troubleshooting

248 Problem Diagnosis

11

281 Mechanic's Data
283 Index

156 Chilton's Fuel Economy and Tune-Up Tips

252 Chilton's Body Repair Tips

Quick Reference Specifications For Your Vehicle

Fill in this chart with the most commonly used specifications for your vehicle. Specifications can be found in Chapters 1 through 3 or on the tune-up decal under the hood of the vehicle.

Tune-Up

Firing Order ____________________

Spark Plugs:

Type ____________________

Gap (in.) ____________________

Point Gap (in.) ____________________

Dwell Angle (°) ____________________

Ignition Timing (°) ____________________

Vacuum (Connected/Disconnected) ____________________

Valve Clearance (in.)

Intake ____________________ **Exhaust** ____________________

Capacities

Engine Oil (qts)

With Filter Change ____________________

Without Filter Change ____________________

Cooling System (qts) ____________________

Manual Transmission (pts) ____________________

Type ____________________

Automatic Transmission (pts) ____________________

Type ____________________

Front Differential (pts) ____________________

Type ____________________

Rear Differential (pts) ____________________

Type ____________________

Transfer Case (pts) ____________________

Type ____________________

FREQUENTLY REPLACED PARTS

Use these spaces to record the part numbers of frequently replaced parts.

PCV VALVE	OIL FILTER	AIR FILTER
Manufacturer ________	Manufacturer ________	Manufacturer ________
Part No. ________	Part No. ________	Part No. ________

General Information and Maintenance

1

HOW TO USE THIS BOOK

Chilton's Repair and Tune-Up Guide for the Mercedes Benz is intended to teach you more about the inner workings of your automobile and save you money in its upkeep. The first two chapters will be the most used, since they contain maintenance and tune-up information and procedures. The following chapters concern themselves with the more complex systems. Operating systems from engine through brakes are covered to the extent that we feel the average do-it-yourselfer should get involved. Chilton's Mercedes-Benz won't explain rebuilding the differential or transmission for the simple reason that the expertise required and the investment in special tools make this task uneconomical. We will tell you how to change your own brake pads and shoes, replace points and plugs, and many more jobs that will save you money, give you personal satisfaction, and help you avoid problems.

A secondary purpose of this book is as a reference for owners who want to understand their cars, or their mechanics, better. In this case, no tools at all are required.

Before removing any bolts, read through the entire procedure. This will give you the overall view of what tools and supplies will be required. There is nothing more frustrating than having to walk to the bus stop on Monday morning because you were short one metric bolt during your Sunday afternoon repair. So read ahead and plan ahead.

The sections begin with a brief discussion of the system and what it involves, adjustments, maintenance, removal and installation procedures and repair or overhaul procedures. When repair is considered to be out of your league, we tell you how to remove the part and then how to install the new or rebuilt replacement. In this way you at least save the labor costs. Backyard repair of such components as the alternator are just not practical.

"CAUTIONS," "WARNINGS" and "NOTES" will be provided where appropriate to help prevent you from injuring yourself or damaging your car. Consequently, you should always read through the entire procedure before beginning the work so as to familiarize yourself with any special problems which may occur during the given procedure. Since no number of warnings could cover every possible situation, you should work slowly and try to envision what is going to happen in each operation ahead of time.

When it comes to tightening things, there is generally a slim area between too loose to properly seal or resist vibration and so tight as to risk damage or warping. When dealing with major engine parts, or with any aluminum component, it pays to buy a torque wrench and go by the recommended figures. When reference is made in this book to the "right side" or the "left side" of the car, it should be understood that the positions are always to be viewed from the front seat. This means that the left side of the car is the driver's side and the right side is the passenger's side. This will hold true throughout the book, regardless of how you might be looking at the car at the time. Safety is always the most important rule. Constantly be aware of the dangers involved in working on an automobile and take the proper precautions. Use jackstands when working under a raised vehicle. Don't smoke or allow an exposed flame to come near the battery or any part of the fuel system. Always use the proper tool and use it correctly; bruised knuckles and skinned fingers aren't a mechanic's standard equipment. Always take your time and be patient; once you have some experience and gain confidence, working on your car will become an enjoyable hobby.

TOOLS AND EQUIPMENT

It would be impossible to catalog each tool that you would need to perform each or any operation in this book. It would also not be wise for the amateur to rush out and buy an expensive set of tools on the theory that he may need one of them at some time. The best approach is to proceed slowly, gathering together a good quality set of those tools that are used most frequently. Don't be misled by the low cost of bargain tools. It is far better to spend a little more for better quality. Forged wrenches, 10 or 12 point sockets and fine tooth ratchets are by far preferable to their less expensive counterparts. As any good mechanic can tell you, there are few worse experiences than trying to work on a car or truck with bad tools. Your monetary savings will be far outweighed by frustration and mangled knuckles.

Begin accumulating those tools that are used most frequently; those associated with routine maintenance and tune-up.

You will find that almost every nut and bolt on your Mercedes-Benz is metric. In addition to the normal assortment of screwdrivers and pliers you should have the following tools for routine maintenance jobs:

1. Metric sockets, also a 13⁄16 in. spark plug socket. If possible, buy various length socket drive extensions. One break in this department is that the metric sockets available in the U.S. will all fit the ratchet handles and extensions you may already have (1⁄4, 3⁄8, and 1⁄2 in. drive).
2. Jackstands—for support;
3. Band wrench—for oil filters;
4. Oil filler spout—for pouring oil;
5. Grease gun—for chassis lubrication;
6. Hydrometer—for checking the battery;
7. A container for draining oil;
8. Many rags for wiping up the inevitable mess.

In addition to these items there are several others which are not absolutely necessary, but handy to have around. These include a transmission funnel and filler tube, a drop light on a long cord, and adjustable wrench and a pair of slip joint pliers.

An more advanced set of tools, suitable for tune-up work, can be drawn up easily. While the tools are slightly more sophisticated, they need not be outrageously expensive. The key to these purchases is to make them with an eye towards adaptability and wide range. A basic list of tune-up tools could include:

1. Tachometer/dwell meter;
2. Spark plug gauge and gapping tool;
3. Feeler gauges for valve and point adjustment.
4. Timing light.

A tachometer/dwell meter will ensure accurate tune-up work on cars without electronic ignition. The choice of a timing light should be made carefully. A light which works on the DC current supplied by the car battery is the best choice; it should have a xenon tube for brightness. Since most later models have an electronic ignition system, the timing light should have an inductive pickup which clamps around the No. 1 spark plug cable (the timing light illustrated has one of these pickups).

In addition to these basic tools, there are several other tools and gauges which, though not particularly necessary for basic tune-up work, you may find to be quite useful. These include:

1. A compression gauge. The screw-in type is slower to use but eliminates the possibility of a faulty reading due to escaping pressure;
2. A manifold vacuum gauge;
3. A test light;
4. A combination volt/ohmmeter;
5. An induction meter, used to determine whether or not there is current flowing through a wire. An extremely helpful tool for electrical troubleshooting.

Finally, you will find a torque wrench necessary for all but the most basic of work. The beam-type models are perfectly adequate. The new click-type (breakaway) torque wrenches are more accurate, but are also much more expensive and must be periodically recalibrated.

Special Tools

There are many Mercedes-Benz special tools. Occasionally, it is possible to use a substitute, but in most cases, the tool was designed to perform a specific function and should be used. Special tools (other than those preceded by 000, 001 or 700) can be ordered only through a Mercedes-Benz dealer. Other tools are available commercially.

Special tool numbers are broken down as follows:

Ex—115 589 07 33 00

115 vehicle type for which tool was developed

000 }
001 } commercially available special tool

700 Special tool manufactured in U.S.

The rest of the numbers identify the design group, tool type and whether it is part of a set or an individual tool.

SERVICING YOUR CAR SAFELY

It is virtually impossible to anticipate all of the hazards involved with automotive maintenance

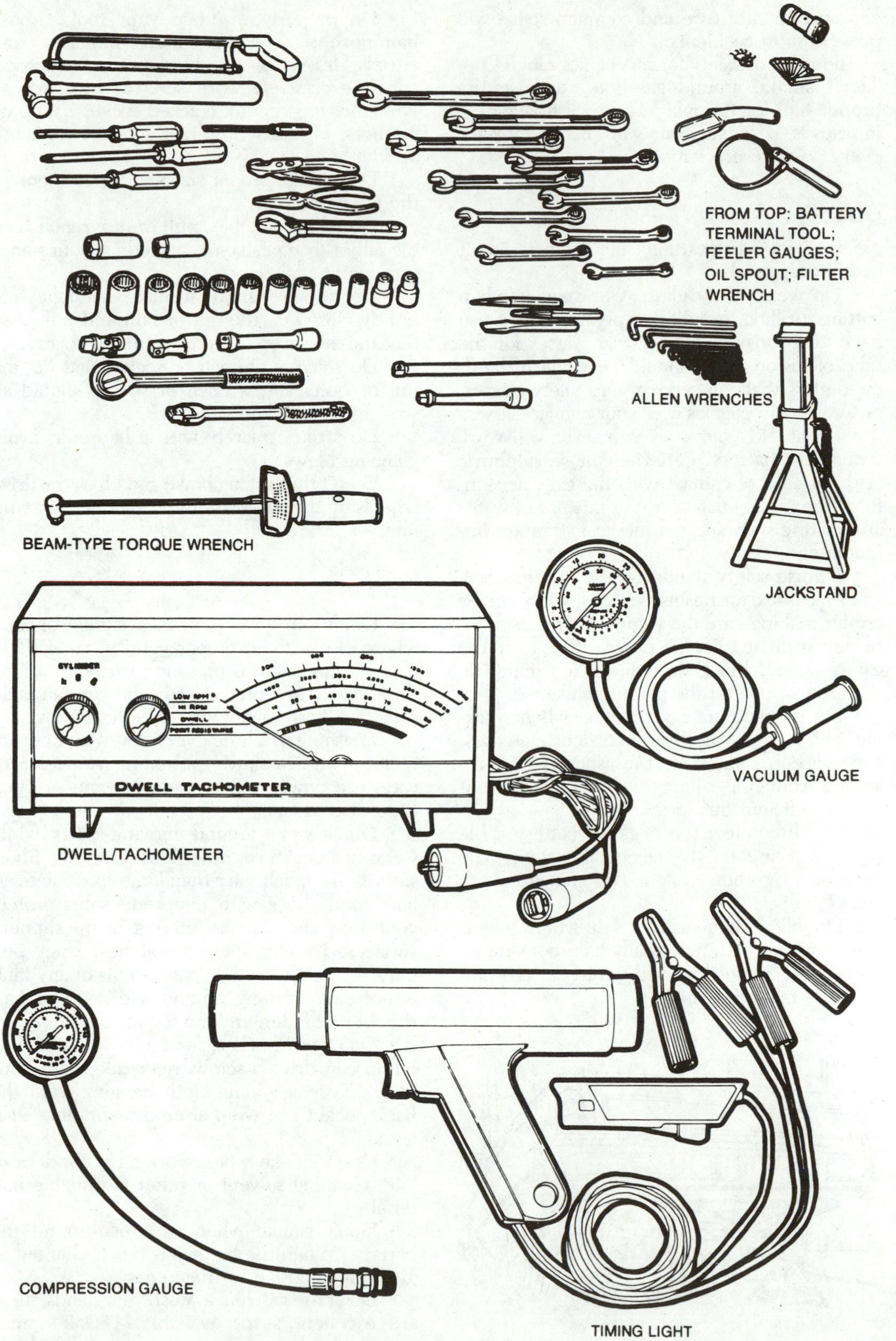

You need only a basic assortment of hand tools and test instruments for most maintenance and repair jobs

and service, but care and common sense will prevent most accidents.

The rules of safety for mechanics range from "don't smoke around gasoline," to "use the proper tool for the job." The trick to avoiding injuries is to develop safe work habits and take every possible precaution.

Dos

- Do keep a fire extinguisher and first aid kit within easy reach.
- Do wear safety glassess or goggles when cutting, drilling, grinding or prying, even if you have 20-20 vision. If you wear glasses for the sake of vision, they should be made of hardened glass that can serve also as safety glasses, or wear safety goggles over your regular glasses.
- Do shield your eyes whenever you work around the battery. Batteries contain sulphuric acid. In case of contact with the eyes or skin, flush the area with water or a mixture of water and baking soda and get medical attention immediately.
- Do use safety stands for any undercar service. Jacks are for raising vehicles; safety stands are for making sure the vehicle stays raised until you want it to come down. Whenever the car is raised, block the wheels remaining on the ground and set the parking brake.
- Do use adequate ventilation when working with any chemicals or hazardous materials. Like carbon monoxide, the asbestos dust resulting from brake lining wear can be poisonous in sufficient quantities.
- Do disconnect the negative battery cable when working on the electrical system. The secondary ignition system can contain up to 40,000 volts.
- Do follow manufacturer's directions whenever working with potentially hazardous materials. Both brake fluid and antifreeze are poisonous if taken internally.

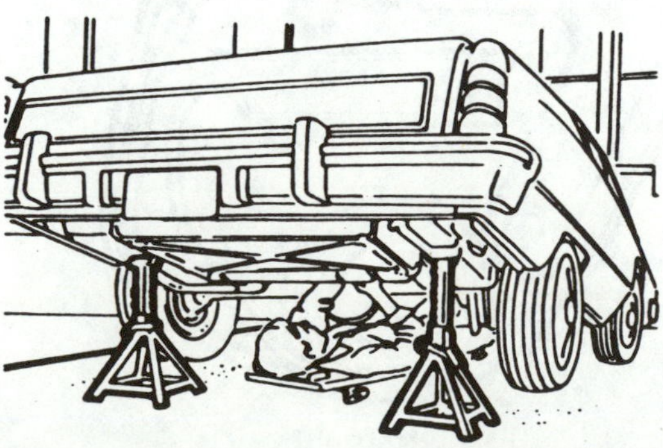

Always support the car securely with jackstands; never use cinder blocks, tire changing jacks or the like

- Do properly maintain your tools. Loose hammerheads, mushroomed punches and chisels, frayed or poorly grounded electrical cords, excessively worn screwdrivers, spread wrenches (open end), cracked sockets, slipping ratchets, or faulty droplight sockets can cause accidents.
- Do use the proper size and type of tool for the job being done.
- Do when possible, pull on a wrench handle rather than push on it, and adjust your stance to prevent a fall.
- Do be sure that adjustable wrenches are tightly closed on the nut or bolt and pulled so that the face is on the side of the fixed jaw.
- Do select a wrench or socket that fits the nut or bolt. The wrench or socket should sit straight, not cocked.
- Do strike squarely with a hammer; avoid glancing blows.
- Do set the parking brake and block the drive wheels if the work requires the engine running.

Don'ts

- Don't run an engine in a garage or anywhere else without proper ventilation—EVER! Carbon monoxide is poisonous; it takes a long time to leave the human body and you can build up a deadly supply of it in your system by simply breathing in a little every day. You may not realize you are slowly poisoning yourself. Always use power vents, windows, fans or open the garage doors.
- Don't work around moving parts while wearing a necktie or other loose clothing. Short sleeves are much safer than long, loose sleeves; hard-toed shoes with neoprene soles protect your toes and give a better grip on slippery surfaces. Jewelry such as watches, fancy belt buckles, beads or body adornment of any kind is not safe working around a car. Long hair should be hidden under a hat or cap.
- Don't use pockets for toolboxes. A fall or bump can drive a screwdriver deep into your body. Even a wiping cloth hanging from the back pocket can wrap around a spinning shaft or fan.
- Don't smoke when working around gasoline, cleaning solvent or other flammable material.
- Don't smoke when working around the battery. When the battery is being charged, it gives off explosive hydrogen gas.
- Don't use gasoline to wash your hands; there are excellent soaps available. Gasoline may contain lead, and lead can enter the body through a cut, accumulating in the body until you are very ill. Gasoline also removes all the

natural oils from the skin so that bone dry hands will suck up oil and grease.

• Don't service the air conditioning system unless you are equipped with the necessary tools and training. The refrigerant, R-12, is extremely cold when compressed, and when released into the air will instantly freeze any surface it contacts, including your eyes. Although the refrigerant is normally non-toxic, R-12 becomes a deadly poisonous gas in the presence of an open flame. One good whiff of the vapors from burning refrigerant can be fatal.

HISTORY

The history of Mercedes-Benz cars is steeped in a tradition of engineering excellence and performance. Mercedes-Benz cars have no peer for quality, craftsmanship engineering safety and performance.

While the name Mercedes-Benz is familiar to most Americans, few are aware that the firm is the world's oldest automobile manufacturer. Two mechanical engineers, Gottlieb Daimeler and Karl Benz, share the credit for simultaneously inventing the automobile. It was 1886, 22 years before Henry Ford's Model T, when they brought their revolutionary machines to life.

The name Mercedes was adopted in 1901, when a wealthy businessman Emil Jellinek, agreed to buy one entire year's production, on the condition that the car be named after his daughter, Mercedes. In 1906, a license to reproduce Mercedes automobiles in the United States was granted to the Daimler Manufacturing Company, operating at the site of the Steinway Piano Company, 939 Steinway Avenue, Long Island City, New York. The idea was to duplicate the 45 horsepower, 1906 Mercedes in the United States. Since the royalty paid for this privilege would have been less than the import duty to buy a European Mercedes, the American Mercedes became a bargain at $7500, almost $3000 less than the "Foreign" Mercedes. Unfortunately, shortly after production began, a fire destroyed the factory and the dreams of an American Mercedes.

In 1926, the firms of Daimler and Benz merged and the familiar Mercedes-Benz emblem was created from the 3-pointed star of Mercedes and the circular symbol of Benz.

To this day, Daimler-Benz has remained a company ruled by engineers, who follow the basic rule that "form is determined by function." Over 90 years of engineering "firsts" attest to their reputation for engineering excellence.

1886—Karl Benz is granted patent number 37435 for the "Patent Motorcar" on January 29. The public introduction took place on July 3, 1886.

1894—The first automobile race in the world is won by a car with a Daimler engine.

1895—The first automobile race in the U.S. is won by Benz.

1931—Mercedes-Benz pioneers the use of 4-wheel independent suspension.

1936—The first diesel engine production car is introduced (260D).

1954—Fuel injection is pioneered on the 300SL Gullwing.

1975—World's first 5-cylinder diesel passenger car (300D)

1978—World's first turbocharged 5-cylinder passenger car (300SD)

The firm's two concessions to tradition are the upright, honeycomb design radiator grille, used since 1901 on every sedan bearing the name "Mercedes," and the use of numbers (and sometimes letters) in place of names. It has been more than 40 years since Daimler-Benz made a car designated by a name instead of numbers. In their ultralogical, though sometimes confusing system, the number refers to the engine displacement in liters. Thus, the engine in the 450SEL displaces 4.5 liters; the engine in the 300D displaces 3.0 liters, and so forth. The exception to this is when a larger engine is installed in the same body at a later date. The most recent example of this was in 1978, when the 6.9 liter V8 was made available in the 450SEL. The number 6.9 (designating the engine displacement in liters) is simply tacked on the end, making it a 450SEL 6.9, though it is called simply, the "6.9." The letters, if any, usually apply to the chassis and can be deciphered as follows:

- S—Sports Model
- E—Einspritz (German for fuel injection)
- L—Long (when used on sedans)
- SL—Super Leicht (German for Super Light) when used on sports cars
- D—Diesel
- T—Station wagon (Touring and transport)
- C—Coupe

In addition to pioneering such technical advances as fuel injected engines and the first diesel powered car, Mercedes-Benz has played a prominent role in racing. No other car manufacturer can match Mercedes' record of over 4400 competition victories—a long string stretching back to history's first auto race from Paris to Rouen in 1894. In the pursuit of land speed records, Mercedes-Benz has been equally successful. The legendary Blitzen Benz was the world's fastest automobile from 1911 to 1924, and a 1938 Mercedes-Benz record of 271.5 mph still stands as the highest speed ever recorded on a highway.

More recently, in April of 1978, a Mercedes-Benz C-111/III established 9 world speed marks while averaging 195.398 mph/14.7 mpg for 12 hours, on a test track in Italy. The most amazing part of the record, however, is that it was set by a car powered by a turbocharged, 5-cylinder diesel, similar to the engine in the 300SD, but with about twice the horsepower.

In 1968, Mercedes-Benz introduced the "New Generation" of Mercedes-Benz cars. These new sedans, the 220D/8, 220/8, 230/8 and the 250/8, share the same new body style and represent a nine year advance in automotive design (the preceding models were first introduced in 1959). The new bodies featured a sharply sloping hood with decreased frontal area, to insure a smoother flow of air over the car, greater glass area and a squared off rear deck. These new features combine to give the cars a look that is clean and simple, and at the same time, classic. The smaller sedans were followed by the 280 series and the 300 series, all the way up to the 300SEL 6.3 in 1970. All bodies share the same basic concept of clean and timeless styling.

The 350 SLC (450SLC in 1973) marked an important change in the coupe design philosophy of Mercedes-Benz. Previous coupe designs had been derived from the contemporary sedan models but the 350 and 450SLC models are based on the new "wedge" body, resulting in a vehicle which combines sports car performance with luxurious looks and comfort. The 350 and 450SLC replace the coupe and convertible sedan models which were built until 1971. The introduction of the 350 and 450SL and SLC models was followed by the introduction of the 450SE and 450SEL in 1973. These cars share the wedge body design with the newer SL and SLC series. The 450SE and 450SEL use the 4.5 liter DOHC V-8 used in the 450SL and 450SLC. The front axle is a modified design taken from the rotary engined test vehicle, the C-111.

1974 Mercedes-Benz models remained basically unchanged from those in 1973. The next new car to come along was the 280S, introduced in 1975. Basically, the 280S combined the chassis of the 450SE and SEL with the DOHC, 6-cylinder engine from the 280 and 280C models. Best described as an economical luxury car, it filled a gap between the smaller coupes and larger sedans.

In 1977, the 280S became the 280SE and the 280 became the 280E, both cars using a fuel injected version of the twin cam 6-cylinder. In addition, the first completely new Mercedes intermediate sedans since 1968 were introduced. The 240D, 300D, 230 and 280E received a scaled down version of the W123 "wedge" body used by the 450 sedans and sports cars. Also incorporated on the new intermediate sedans was the "zero-offset" front end from the larger sedans.

Late in 1977, the 6.9, successor to the 300SEL 6.3 was introduced. In all, less than 1000 of these high performance sedans were made and the entire production was bought before they were even made. Technically these were 1978 models, but to those who coughed up more than $44,000 for what may be the world's finest (certainly, the fastest) sedan, it wouldn't have mattered if they were 1977 models.

For years, the use of diesel engines was confined to large trucks. Even today, that remains the popular image of the diesel—a smoke belching, rumbling monster that didn't go very fast, but would last forever. This image of the diesel was bolstered by the occasional glimpse of a stately Mercedes diesel laboring away from a stop light. These glimpses only reinforced our view of the diesel as reliable, but slow (and ignored the fact that owners of these types of cars *habitually* drove as though they were on a journey to somewhere disagreeable). Today, the diesel has suddenly emerged as a possible alternative to the conventional spark-ignition engine.

1978 also saw the introduction of the 300CD, the coupe version of the 5-cylinder 300D introduced in 1975. This also shared the W123 chassis and body of the other intermediate sedans. But the introduction of the 300SD far overshadowed it. The 300SD is the world's first turbocharged diesel sedan, a full size car capable of more than 100 mph with an average fuel consumption of better than 26 miles per gallon. Mercedes-Benz has long been a leader in the field of diesel technology and the 300SD joins the 240D, 300D and 300SD, representing more than half of the Mercedes-Benz sales in the United States. Clearly the reputation of the diesel car is changing from one of a smoke-belching monster to that of an engine capable of powering a full-size car with good performance and economy.

The 1979 300TD marks another milestone in Mercedes-Benz history. "Estate cars" and "shooting brakes" based on various Mercedes models have been assembled by numerous custom body builders, but this is the first station wagon actually produced by Mercedes-Benz. The modern station wagon evolved from the original "shooting brake," a large open vehicle intended to carry members of hunting parties around the grand estates of Europe. In truth, Karl Benz (one of the founders of Daimler-Benz, the parent company) produced an 8-seater "shooting brake" in 1894,, but it has not been until recently that there has been any interest in a Mercedes wagon. The result is the 300TD, a full-size station wagon powered by the 5-cylinder diesel engine from the 300D, combining the added load capacity and functionalism of a wagon with the handling, comfort and fuel economy of a sedan. The EPA estimates that the 300TD will deliver 23 mpg (city) and 28 mpg (highway).

The 1980 model line-up continued virtually unchanged from 1979. The only significant event was the passing from the line of the 6.9, one of the fastest and best handling sedans in the world, a victim of limited sales and its less than tolerable effect on CAFE (Corporate Average Fuel Economy).

In 1981, the 380SL/380SLC and 380SEL replaced the 450SL and 450SEL respectively. The 380SL and SLC models were basically the same vehicle with a new 3.8 liter V-8 engine. But, the 380SEL, along with the 300SD, were built on the newly redesigned W126 chassis. The new chassis and bodywork retained the classic Mercedes-Benz styling and comfort, while further reducing fuel consumption through reduced vehicle weight and improved aerodynamics. At the same time, the normally-aspirated 5 cylinder diesel engine in the 300TD was replaced by the turbocharged version, and the designation changed to the 300TD Turbodiesel.

The following year, 1982, was a year of refining the model line-up. The 280E and 280CE were dropped from the model line, but the major change was the installation of the turbocharged diesel engine in all diesel models except for the 240D. This brought the number of turbocharged Mercedes-Benz diesel models to four, at a time when diesel sales in the U.S. were reaching a peak, and not coincidentally, diesels were accounting for nearly 2/3 of all Mercedes-Benz U.S. sales. The 3.0 liter, 5 cylinder oil-burner had established itself, not only as a clean, efficient and tractable powerplant for even large sedans, but also as one of the best diesel engines in the world. It still accounts for nearly half of all Mercedes-Benz' U.S. sales at a time when the bottom has fallen out of the U.S. diesel market. The year 1982 also saw the introduction of the 380SEC, which was to replace the 380SLC. Mechanically identical to the 380SEL, the big coupe was marked by the flowing, graceful lines that have been a hallmark of Mercedes-Benz coupes for 20 years. Not since the days of the 280SE coupe and convertible, had the company been able to lay claim to one of the world's most beautifully sculpted cars.

The model line remained intact, with only minor mechanical changes, until 1984, when four new models were introduced.

The 240D was dropped entirely, and its place taken by an entirely new series, the first all-new Mercedes-Benz cars in 10 years. The 190 cars represent a new era of Mercedes-Benz passenger cars, offering a smaller than traditional model, with lower fuel consumption than any existing Mercedes-Benz model, along with ride and handling comparable to that of the S-class cars. The path to fuel economy was through the power train, aerodynamics, and reduced weight. The 190E 2.3 uses an all new 4 cylinder gasoline engine and the 190D 2.2 uses an all new 4 cylinder, normally aspirated diesel engine. Both models are available with 5 speed manual transmissions or 4 speed automatic transmissions. Both cars have a low drag coefficient (cd) of .35 and weigh more than 600 pounds less than the 240D.

Roadholding is excellent and traditional Mercedes-Benz design parameters—the chassis must be capable of holding the road at any speed the engine can produce—are upheld. In short, it is left to the forthcoming 16-valve Cosworth head, installed on the 190E in Europe to allow the car to live up to its potential.

The 380SEL was dropped, but the 380SE remains as a gasoline powered alternative to the 300SD. The 500SEL and 500SEC take their place at the top of the Mercedes-Benz line. Since the introduction of the 5.0 liter gasoline V8 in Europe, these cars have been finding their way to the U.S. even in U.S. emissions trim. The 5.0 liter gasoline engine makes the sedan and coupe significantly faster than their 3.8 liter cousins and fills a niche for a high-priced, high-performance car for those accustomed to serious motoring.

SERIAL NUMBER IDENTIFICATION

Since Mercedes-Benz design is a continuous process of evolution and development, the newest developments are put into production as soon as they are available, rather than waiting for a new model year. While arbitrary cut-off chassis numbers are chosen each year to designate the onset of a "new" model year, it does not necessarily mean that a 1974 car, for example, is radically different from a 1976 car.

Especially it does not mean that an "old" 1974 car is obsolete.

All this is great for the owner, but it presents a problem when ordering parts. The solution is found in the comprehensive Daimler-Benz identification plates, found in various places, but usually under the hood and on the door posts. Consulting the illustration pertaining to your model, find the location of the chassis number plate, type plate and engine number. With these numbers, plus other sub-system numbers, you'll have all the information you need to identify your car.

When ordering parts, give the complete chassis or engine number, plus the number of the concerned area. The engine and chassis numbers are quite complicated, but each is a 6-digit number divided by a decimal point. The 3 digits to the left of the decimal point identify the basic chassis or engine, and the 3 digits to the right identify specific modifications. This is the reason you have to give the entire identifying number when ordering parts. The Model/Engine identification chart gives a picture of the model/engine/chassis combinations that have been imported to the U.S. that are covered by this book. Some models, of course began production before 1974 (the first year this book covers). For space reasons, these models are covered in another book, *CHILTON'S Mercedes-Benz 1968–73 Repair & Tune-Up Guide.*

NOTE: *Be careful with the model designations. Just because the same number is used to identify a car, it does not mean components are necessarily the same. For example, the 300CD and 300SD do not share the same chassis design, nor do the 280CE and 280SE.*

Location of Identification Data

SERIAL NUMBERS

Refer to the accompanying illustrations for the location of all important data concerning your car. The chassis number will usually appear something like this:

107.044-12-00001

By referring to the engine/vehicle identification chart, the 107.044 identifies the car as a 450SL or 450SLC. The middle number will always be either a "10" or "12". 10 indicates a manual transmission (240D only since 1974 until the introduction of the 5 speed 190 in 1984) and a 12 indicates an automatic transmission. The rest of the numbers are a sequential serial number. Various other numbers are located throughout the vehicle, but the most important are the transmission number and the emission control plate.

TRANSMISSION NUMBER

Manual transmission serial numbers are located on a pad on the left side of the transmission. Only two models covered in this book use a manual transmission, the 240D and the new 190 series. Automatic transmission serial numbers are located on a plate attached to the drivers side of the transmission.

1. Certification tag (left door pillar)
2. Identification tag (left window post)
3. Chassis no.
4. Body no. and paintwork no.
5. Engine no.

Location of important information on 240D, 230, 280, 280C and 300D models through 1976

1. Catalyst and certification tag (left door pillar)
2. Identification tag (left window post)
3. Chassis no.
4. Body no. and paintwork no.
5. Engine no. on rear engine block
6. Emission control information

Location of important information on 1977 and later models (except those shown)

1. Catalyst and certification tag (left door pillar)
2. Identification tag (left window post)
3. Chassis no.
4. Body no. and paintwork no.
5. Engine no. on rear engine block
6. Emission control.information

Location of important information on the 450SL, 450SLC and 380SL

EMISSION CONTROL INFORMATION PLATE

The type of emission control system, model year and important tune-up data can be found on the Emission Control Information Plate, which is attached to the crossmember above the radiator. Beginning with 1977 models, there is also a plate attached to the drivers side door pillar, which tells whether the vehicle is equipped with a catalytic converter. The type of emission system can also be identified by the color coding of the plate.

Engine/Vehicle Identification

Model	Chassis Type	Engine Type	No. of Cyls	Engine Description: Fuel, Fuel Delivery, Valve Gear, Displacement	Production Years
190D	201.122	601.921	4	Diesel, Fuel Inj., DHC, 2197 cc	1984
190E	201.024	102.961	4	Gas, Fuel Inj., OHC, 2299 cc	1984
230	115.017	115.951	4	Gas, Carb., OHC, 2307 cc	1974–76
	123.023	115.954	4	Gas, Carb., OHC, 2307 cc	1977–78
240D	115.117	616.916	4	Diesel, Fuel Inj., OHC, 2404 cc	1974–76
	123.123	616.912	4	Diesel, Fuel Inj., OHC, 2404 cc	1977–83
280	114.060	110.921	6	Gas, Carb., DOHC, 2746 cc	1973–76
280C	114.073	110.921	6	Gas, Carb., DOHC, 2746 cc	1973–76
280E	123.033	110.984 ①	6	Gas, Fuel Inj., DOHC, 2746 cc	1977–81
280CE	123.053	110.984 ①	6	Gas, Fuel Inj., DOHC, 2746 cc	1978–81
280S	116.020	110.922	6	Gas, Carb., DOHC, 2746 cc	1975–76
280SE	116.024	110.985 ①	6	Gas, Fuel Inj., DOHC, 2746 cc	1977–80
300D	115.114	617.910	5	Diesel, Fuel Inj., OHC, 3005 cc	1975–76
	123.130	617.912	5	Diesel, Fuel Inj., OHC, 2998 cc ②	1977–81
	123.133	617.952	5	Diesel, Turbo., Fuel Inj., OHC, 2998 cc	1982–84
300CD	123.150	617.912	5	Diesel, Fuel Inj., OHC, 2998 cc ②	1978–81
	123.153	617.952	5	Diesel, Turbo., Fuel Inj., OHC, 2998 cc	1982–84
300SD	116.120	617.950	5	Diesel, Turbocharged, Fuel Inj., 2998 cc	1978–80
	126.120	617.951	5	Diesel, Turbocharged, Fuel Inj., 2998 cc	1981–84
300TD	123.190	617.912	5	Diesel, Fuel Inj., OHC, 2998 cc	1979–80
	123.190	617.953	5	Diesel, Turbocharged, Fuel Inj., 2998 cc	1981–84
380SE	126.032	116.963	8	Gas, Fuel Inj., OHC, 3839 cc	1984
380SEL	126.033	116.961	8	Gas, Fuel Inj., OHC, 3839 cc	1981–83
380SL	107.045	116.960	8	Gas, Fuel Inj., OHC, 3839 cc	1981–84
380SLC	107.025	116.960	8	Gas, Fuel Inj., OHC, 3839 cc	1981–82
380SEC	126.043	116.963	8	Gas, Fuel Inj., OHC, 3839 cc	1982–83
450SE	116.032	117.983	8	Gas, Fuel Inj., DOHC, 4520 cc	1973–75
	116.032	117.986 ①	8	Gas, Fuel Inj., DOHC, 4520 cc	1976
450SEL	116.033	117.983	8	Gas, Fuel Inj., DOHC, 4520 cc	1973–75
	116.033	117.986 ①	8	Gas, Fuel Inj. DOHC, 4520 cc	1976–80
450SL	107.044	117.982	8	Gas, Fuel Inj., DOHC, 4520 cc	1973–75
	107.044	117.985 ①	8	Gas, Fuel Inj., DOHC, 4520 cc	1976–80
450SLC	107.024	117.982	8	Gas, Fuel Inj., DOHC, 4520 cc	1973–75
	107.024	117.985 ①	8	Gas, Fuel Inj., DOHC, 4520 cc	1976–80
500SEC	126.044	117.963	8	Gas, Fuel Inj., OHC, 4973 cc	1984
500SEL	126.037	117.963	8	Gas, Fuel Inj., OHC, 4973 cc	1984
6.9	116.036	100.985 ①	8	Gas, Fuel Inj., DOHC, 6836 cc	1978–79

NOTE: *Production years given since inception, but only 1974–79 models are covered.*
Engine designations are as follows: C = 1982, D = 1983, E = 1984
DMB 2.4D6-J501-2.4 liter Diesel
DMB 3.0D9-J508-3.0 liter Turbodiesel
DMB 3.8V6-FSE8-3.8 liter V8 (380SEL/SEC)
DMB 3.8V6-FSL6-3.8 liter V8 (380 SEL)
① Air flow controlled fuel injection (Bosch K-Jetronic®)
② 1977–78: 3005 cc

1 Certification Tag (left door pillar)
2 Identification Tag (left window post)
3 Chassis No.
4 Engine No.
5 Body No. and Paintwork No.
6 Emission Control Tag
7 Information Tag
California version
Vacuum line routing for emission control system
8 Emission Control Tag
Catalyst Information

Location of important information on the 380SE, 500SEC and 500SEL

1 Certification Tag (left door pillar)
2 Identification Tag (left window post)
3 Chassis No.
4 Engine No.
5 Body No. and Paintwork No.
6 Information Tag
California version
Vacuum line routing for emission control system
7 Emission Control Tag
8 Emission Control Tag
Catalyst Information

Location of important information on the 300TD

ROUTINE MAINTENANCE

Routine maintenance is the self-explanatory term used to describe the sort of periodic work necessary to keep a car in safe and reliable working order. A regular program aimed at monitoring essential systems ensures that the car's components are functioning correctly (and will continue to do so until the next inspection, one hopes), and can prevent small problems from developing into major headaches. Routine maintenance also pays off big dividends in keeping major repair costs at a minimum, extending the life of the car, and enhancing resale value, should you ever desire to part with your Mercedes.

1 Certification Tag (left door pillar)
2 Identification Tag (left window post)
3 Chassis No.
4 Engine No.
5 Body No. and Paintwork No.
6 Information Tag California version Vacuum line routing for emission control system
7 Emission Control Tag
8 Emission Control Tag Catalyst Information

Location of important information on the 190D and 190E

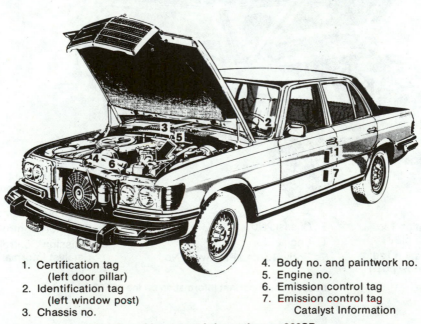

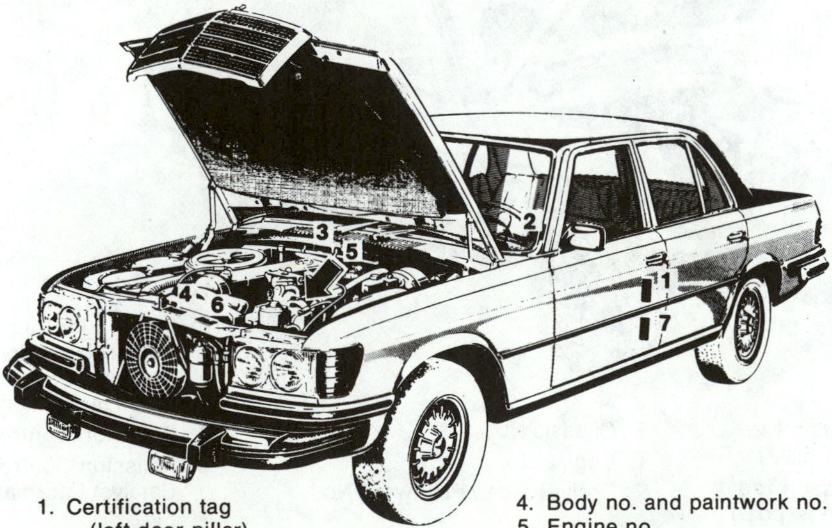

1. Certification tag (left door pillar)
2. Identification tag (left window post)
3. Chassis no.
4. Body no. and paintwork no.
5. Engine no.
6. Emission control tag
7. Emission control tag Catalyst Information

Location of important information on 300SD

A very definite maintenance schedule is provided by Mercedes-Benz, and must be followed, not only to keep the new car working properly. The "Maintenance Intervals" chart in this chapter outlines the routine maintenance which must be performed according to intervals based on accumulated mileage. Your car also came with a maintenance schedule provided by Mercedes-Benz. Adherence to these schedules will result in a longer life for your car, and will, over the long run, save you money and time.

Location of manual transmission number

Location of emission control information plate (1) and catalyst plate (2)

Transmission Applications

Model	Automatic Transmission	Manual Transmission
190D	W4A 020	GL68/20A-5
190E	W4A 020	GL68/20B-5
230	W4B 025	—
240D (thru '80)	W4B 025	G-76/18C(4-spd.)
240D ('81 and later)	W4B 025	GL68/20A(4-spd.)
280, 280C, 280E, 280CE	W4B 025	—
280S, 280SE	W4B 025	—
300D, 300CD, 300TD	W4B 025	—
300D Turbo, 300CD Turbo	W4A 040	—
300TD Turbo 1981–83	W4A 040	—
300SD 1978–80	W4B 025	—
300SD 1981–83	W4A 040	—
380SL, 380SLC, 380SEL, 380SEC, 380SE	W4A 040	—
450SE, 450SEL, 450SL, 450SLC	W3A 040	—
500SEL, 500SEC	W4A 040	—
6.9	W3B 050	—

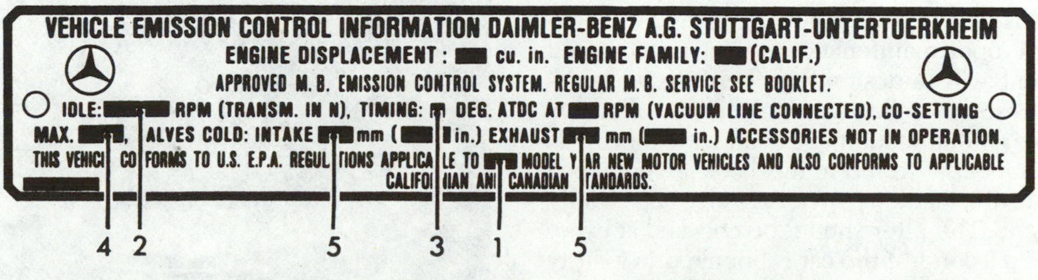

1. Model year designation
2. Idle speed
3. Idle ignition timing at rpm.
4. CO value at idle
5. Valve clearance

A typical emission control information plate reveals the emission system, model year and critical tune-up data. Tune-up data on this plate takes precedence over any other information

The checks and adjustments in the following sections generally require only a few minutes of attention every few weeks; the services to be performed can be easily accomplished in a morning. The most important part of any maintenance program is regularity. The few minutes or occasional morning spent on these seemingly trivial tasks will forestall or eliminate major problems later.

Special Lubricants

AUTOMATIC LEVEL CONTROL

Mercedes-Benz recommends that only the following fluids be used in the automatic level control unit:

- Aral 1010 (must be used on 6.9)
- Gasolin 1010
- Shell Tellus T 17
- Shell Aero Fluid 4

RECOMMENDED ENGINE OILS (INCLUDING DIESEL)

There are many high quality engine oils available, but the following are particularly recommended for Mercedes-Benz engines, providing the greatest engine life and the best service. Only multi-viscosity oils are listed, and the appropriate viscosity should be chosen according to anticipated ambient temperatures. All oils are available in the U.S. unless otherwise noted:

- Castrol GTX 2 (Canada only)
- Mobiloil Special
- Mobiloil Super
- Mobil Delvac Special
- Quaker State Super Blend
- Quaker State Deluxe
- Pennzoil Z-7 Multi-Vis
- Sum Motor Oil 3800-X Series
- Texaco Havoline
- Valvoline All Climate HD
- Valvoline XLD

Air Cleaner

An air cleaner is used to keep air-borne dirt and dust out of the air flowing through the engine. Proper maintenance is vital, as a clogged element will undesirably richen the fuel mixture, restrict air flow and power, and allow excessive contamination of the oil with abrasives.

All models covered in this book are equipped with a disposable, paper cartridge air cleaner element. The filter should be checked at every tune-up (sooner if the car is operated in a dusty area). Loose dust can sometimes be removed by striking the filter against a hard surface several times or by blowing through it with compressed air (never more than 70 psi).

To remove the filter, unscrew the nut(s) (if so equipped), lift off the housing cover and remove the filter element. Many models may also have three or four thumb latches which will also have to be released before removing the housing cover. Before installing the original or the replacement filter, wipe out the inside of the housing with a clean lint-free rag or paper towel soaked in kerosene. Install the paper air cleaner filter, seat the top cover on the bottom housing and tighten the nut(s). Clip on the thumb latches if so equipped.

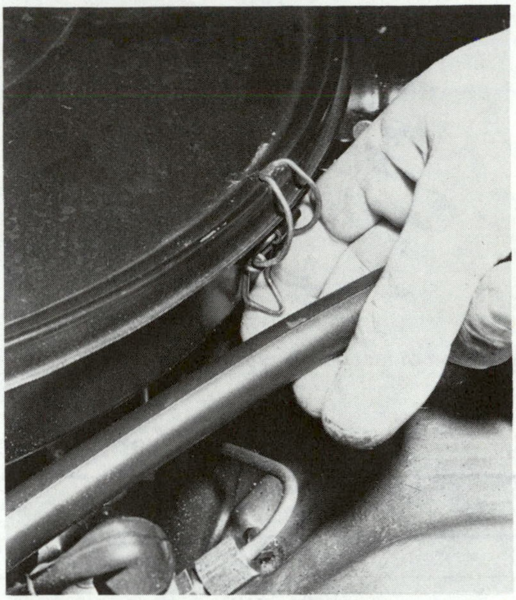

Unsnap the clips around the outside of the air filter housing

Remove the air cleaner cover. Some models require a wrench; others have a wing nut

Remove the paper element from the housing (diesel shown)

Flame Guard Element

1974 gasoline engine models use a flame guard element in the crankcase ventilation system. On V-8's and 4-cylinder engines, the element is located in the rocker cover; on 6-cylinder engines it is located in the air filter housing.

1. On V8's and 4-cylinder engines remove the crankcase breather hose from the air cleaner housing or rocker arm cover.
2. Remove the flame guard element with pliers.
3. Clean the element with gasoline and allow it to thoroughly air dry.
4. Reinstall the element with the long wire element facing inward, toward the air cleaner housing or engine.

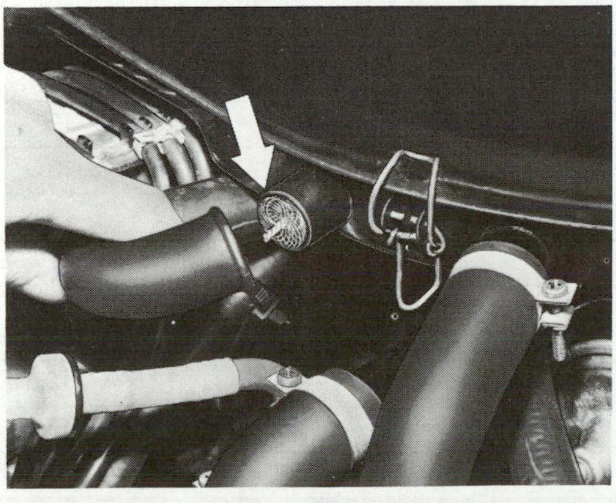

Flame guard element—6 cylinder engines

Flame guard element—4 cylinder engines

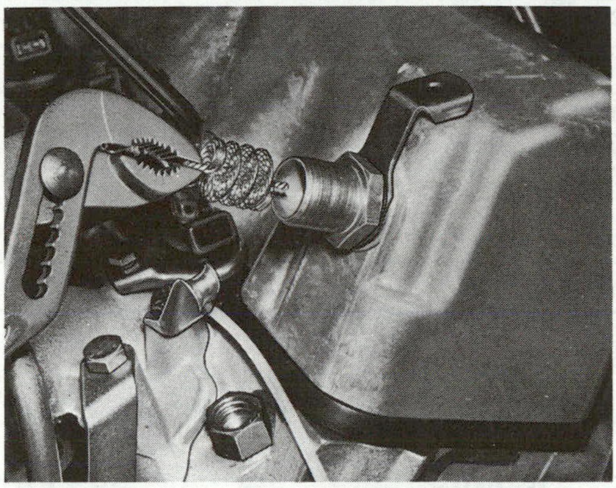

Flame guard element—V8 engines

Battery

SPECIFIC GRAVITY (EXCEPT "MAINTENANCE FREE" BATTERIES)

At least once a year, check the specific gravity of the battery. It should be between 1.20 and 1.26 at room temperature.

The specific gravity can be checked with the use of an hydrometer, an inexpensive instrument available from many sources, including auto parts stores. The hydrometer has a squeeze bulb at one end and a nozzle at the other. Battery electrolyte is sucked into the hydrometer until the float is lifted from its seat. The specific gravity is then read by noting the position of the float. Generally, if after charging, the specific gravity between any two cells varies more than 50 points (.050), the battery is bad and should be replaced.

It is not possible to check the specific gravity in this manner on sealed ("maintenance free") batteries. Instead, the indicator built into the top of the case must be relied on to display any signs of battery deterioration. If the indicator

Maintenance Intervals (All Figures in Thousands of Miles)

Model(s)	Automatic Trans Fluid Check & Refill	Automatic Trans Fluid Change	Engine Oil Check* & Refill	Engine Oil ** Change	Oil Filter Change	Coolant Check Level	Coolant Renew	Paper Element Air Filter Clean	Paper Element Air Filter Change	Inj Pump Oil Check	Clutch Master Cylinder Fluid Check	Manual Trans Oil Check
1974												
230	10	30	1	5	5	5	24	10	①	—	10	10
240D	10	30	1	3	3	5	24	10	①	10	—	—
280, 280C	10	30	1	5	5	5	24	10	①	—	—	—
450SE, 450SEL, 450SL, 450SLC	10	30	1	5	5	5	24	10	①	—	—	—
1975–76												
230	6	25	1	6	6	5	24	12.5	①	—	—	—
240D, 300D	6	25	1	3	3	5	24	12.5	①	3	6	12.5
All others	6	25	1	6	6	5	24	12.5	①	—	—	—
1977 and later												
190D, 240D, 300D, 300CD, 300SD, 300TD	6	30	1	5	5	5	24	12.5	①	12.5	3	15
230,280E, 280CE	6	30	1	6	6	5	24	12.5	①	—	—	—
6.9	6	30	1	12.5	12.5	5	24	12.5	①	—	—	—
All others	6	30	1	7.5	7.5	5	24	12.5	①	—	—	15

Maintenance Intervals (All Figures in Thousands of Miles) (cont.)

Model(s)	Power Steering Fluid Check	Manual Steering Oil Check	Rear Axle Oil Check	Level Control Fluid Check	Brake Fluid Level Check	Fuel Filter Element	Fuel Filter Fuel Pump Strainer	Carburetor Damper Fluid Check	Flame Guard Element Clean	Drive Belts Check/ Adjust	Body Lubrication
1974											
230	10	10	10	—	10	—	30	10	10	10	10
240D	10	10	10	—	10	30	30	—	—	10	10
280, 280C	10	10	10	—	10	30	30	—	10	10	10
450SE, 450SEL, 450SL, 450SLC	10	—	10	—	10	30	—	—	10	10	10
1975–76											
230	6	—	12.5	—	6	—	25	6	—	12.5	12.5
240D, 300D	6	—	12.5	—	6	25	25	—	—	12.5	12.5
All others	6	—	12.5	12.5	6	25	—	—	—	12.5	12.5
1977 and Later											
240D, 300D, 300CD, 300TD	—	—	6	6	6	30	30	—	—	12.5	12.5
230, 280E, 280CE	6	—	6	—	6	37.5	37.5	6	—	12.5	12.5
6.9	6	—	6	6	6	37.5	—	—	—	12.5	12.5
All others	6	—	6	6	6	30	—	—	—	12.5	12.5

① Replace as necessary —Not Applicable

is dark, the battery can be assumed to be OK. If the indicator is light, the specific gravity is low, and the battery should be charged or replaced.

CABLES AND CLAMPS

Once a year, the battery terminals and the cable clamps should be cleaned. Loosen the clamps and remove the cables, negative cable first. On batteries with posts on top, the use of a puller specially made for the purpose is recommended. These are inexpensive, and available in auto parts stores. Side terminal battery cables are secured with a bolt.

Clean the cable clamps and the battery terminal with a wire brush, until all corrosion, grease, etc. is removed and the metal is shiny. It is especially important to clean the inside of the clamp thoroughly, since a small deposit of foreign material or oxidation will prevent a sound electrical connection and inhibit either starting or charging. Special tools are available for cleaning these parts, one type for conventional batteries and another type for side terminal batteries.

Before installing the cables, loosen the battery hold-down clamp or strap, remove the battery and check the battery tray. Clear it of any debris, and check it for soundness. Rust should be wire brushed away, and the metal given a coat of anti-rust paint. Replace the battery and tighten the hold-down clamp or strap securely, but be careful not to overtighten, which will crack the battery case.

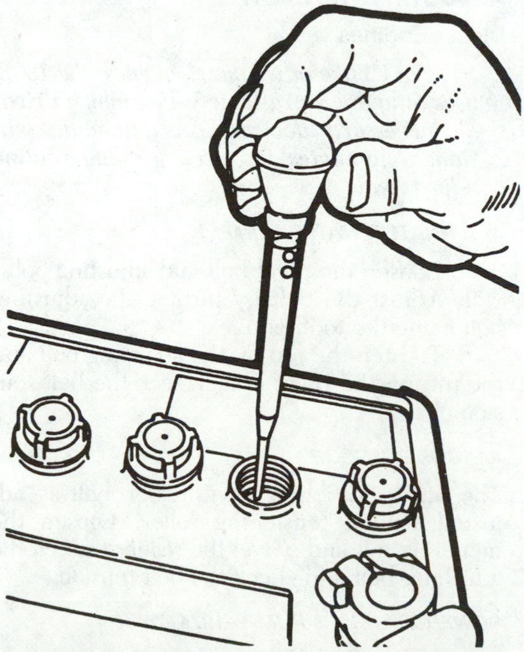

Specific gravity can be checked with an hydrometer

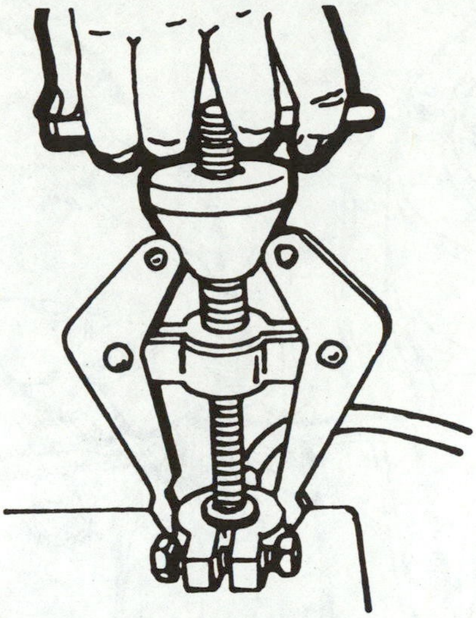

Pullers make clamp removal easier

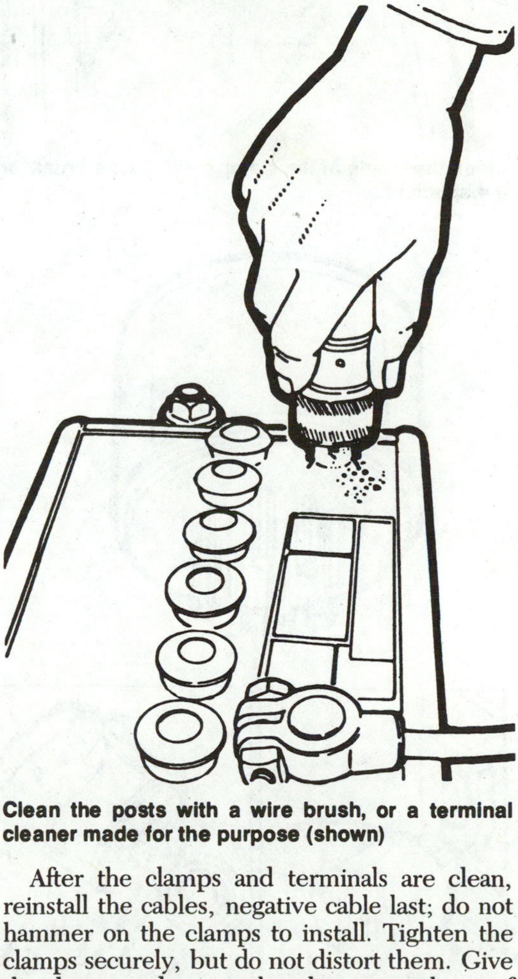

Clean the posts with a wire brush, or a terminal cleaner made for the purpose (shown)

After the clamps and terminals are clean, reinstall the cables, negative cable last; do not hammer on the clamps to install. Tighten the clamps securely, but do not distort them. Give the clamps and terminals a thin external coat of grease after installation, to retard corrosion.

Check the cables at the same time that the terminals are cleaned. If the cable insulation is

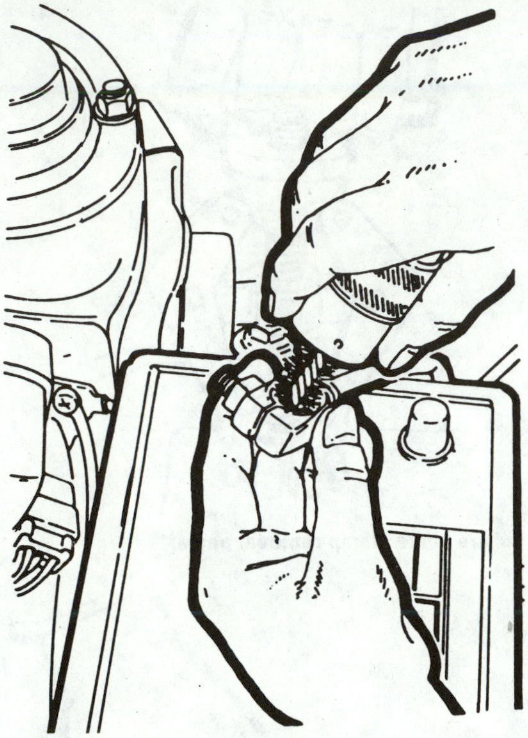

Clean the inside of the clamps with a wire brush, or the special tool

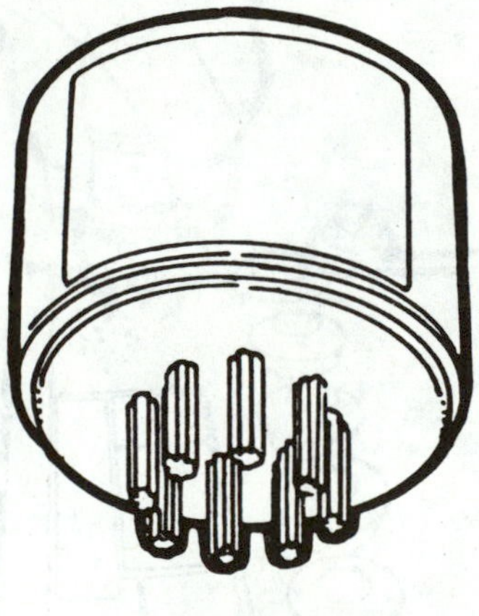

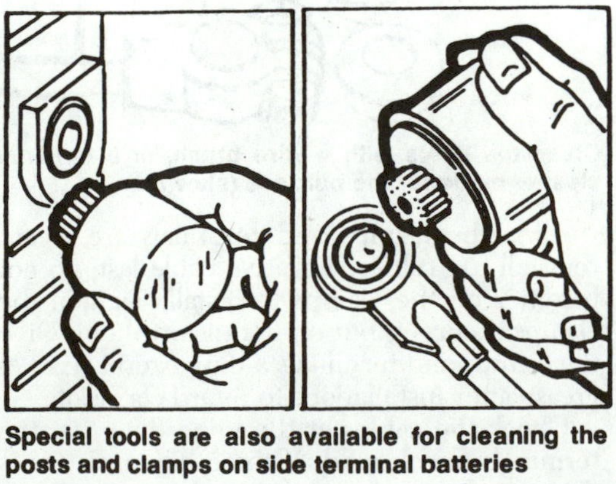

Special tools are also available for cleaning the posts and clamps on side terminal batteries

cracked or broken, or if the ends are frayed, the cable should be replaced with a new cable of the same length and gauge.

NOTE: *Keep flame or sparks away from the battery; it gives off explosive hydrogen gas. Battery electrolyte contains sulphuric acid. If you should splash any on your skin or in your eyes, flush the affected area with plenty of clear water; if it lands in your eyes, get medical help immediately.*

REPLACEMENT

When it becomes necessary to replace the battery, select a battery with a rating equal to or greater than the battery originally installed. Deterioration, embrittlement and just plain aging of the battery cables, starter motor, and associated wires makes the battery's job harder in successive years. The slow increase in electrical resistance over time makes it prudent to install a new battery with a greater capacity than the old.

Drive Belts

CHECKING

All Models

Drive belts should be checked for wear, cracks and fraying and if necessary, replaced. Under a pressure of approximately 15 lbs. (strong thumb pressure), the deflection at the middle of the longest span should be as listed in the chart below.

ADJUSTING TENSION

Diesel Engines

NOTE: *Unlike other diesel engines, the 190D uses only one extra-wide V-belt which drives all necessary devices. An automatic tensioner eliminates the need for any routine adjustment.*

ALTERNATOR/WATER PUMP

1. Loosen the pivot bolt and adjusting bolt.
2. Adjust the belt by turning the adjusting bolt along the toothed rack.
3. Tighten the nut on the adjusting bolt and the nut on the pivot bolt. Check the belt tension.

A/C COMPRESSOR

The air conditioning compressor belt is adjusted with a tensioning roller. Loosen the mounting nut and swivel the roller. Tighten the attaching bolt and check the belt tension.

POWER STEERING PUMP—1974–76

1. Loosen the bolts at the front and rear of the pump.

Drive Belt Deflection (in.)

Driven Components	Diesel Engines 4 and 5 Cylinder	Gasoline Engines 4 and 6 Cylinder	Gasoline Engine 8 Cylinder
Alternator & water pump	½	½	—
Alternator	—	—	½
Water pump & power steering pump	—	—	½
Power steering pump	½ ①	¼	—
Refrigerant compressor	½	½	¼
Vacuum pump	½	½	—
Air pump	½	½	½
Air compressor	—	—	½
Comfort hydraulic pump	—	—	¼

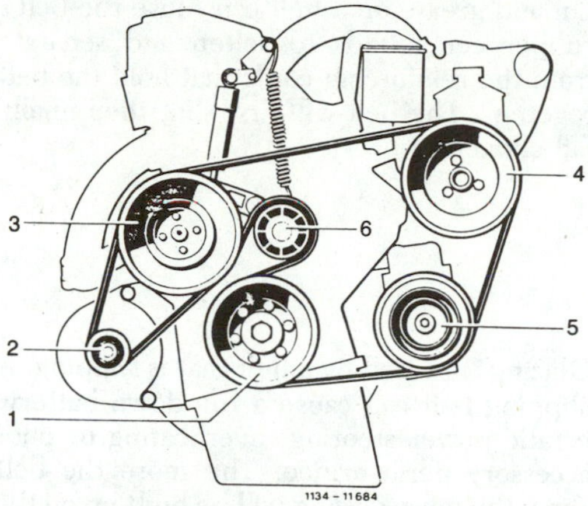

1. Crankshaft pulley
2. Alternator pulley
3. Coolant pump pulley
4. Power steering pump pulley
5. Air conditioning compressor pulley
6. Tensioning pulley

The 190D uses an automatic adjuster, no adjustment is necessary

Alternator adjustment on diesel engines. Loosen the pivot bolt (3,4) and adjusting bolt (1). Turn the hex nut (2) to adjust

Checking drive belt tension—all models

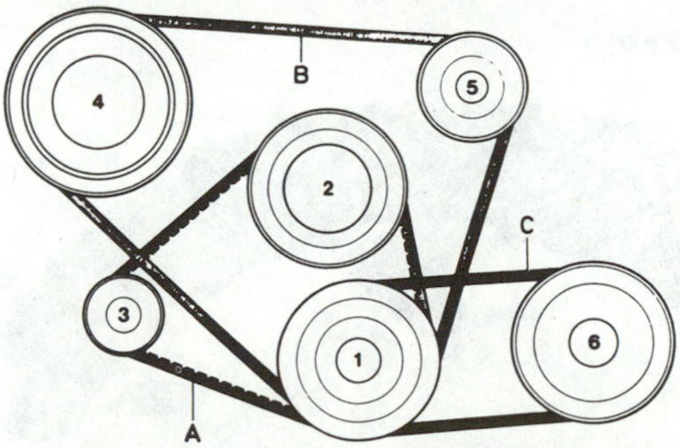

1. Crankshaft
2. Water pump
3. Alternator
4. Refrigerant compressor
5. Tensioning roller
6. Power steering pump

Drive belt arrangement—diesel engines

2. Pry the pump outward to tighten the belt. Do not pry on the pump housing.

3. Tighten the screws and check the belt tension.

HOW TO SPOT WORN V-BELTS

V-Belts are vital to efficient engine operation—they drive the fan, water pump and other accessories. They require little maintenance (occasional tightening) but they will not last forever. Slipping or failure of the V-belt will lead to overheating. If your V-belt looks like any of these, it should be replaced.

Cracking or weathering

This belt has deep cracks, which cause it to flex. Too much flexing leads to heat build-up and premature failure. These cracks can be caused by using the belt on a pulley that is too small. Notched belts are available for small diameter pulleys.

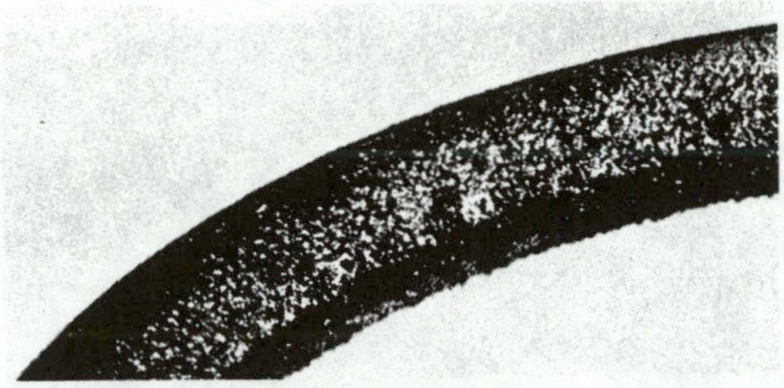

Softening (grease and oil)

Oil and grease on a belt can cause the belt's rubber compounds to soften and separate from the reinforcing cords that hold the belt together. The belt will first slip, then finally fail altogether.

Glazing

Glazing is caused by a belt that is slipping. A slipping belt can cause a run-down battery, erratic power steering, overheating or poor accessory performance. The more the belt slips, the more glazing will be built up on the surface of the belt. The more the belt is glazed, the more it will slip. If the glazing is light, tighten the belt.

Worn cover

The cover of this belt is worn off and is peeling away. The reinforcing cords will begin to wear and the belt will shortly break. When the belt cover wears in spots or has a rough jagged appearance, check the pulley grooves for roughness.

Separation

This belt is on the verge of breaking and leaving you stranded. The layers of the belt are separating and the reinforcing cords are exposed. It's just a matter of time before it breaks completely.

A/C compressor adjustment on diesel engine. Loosen the screw (1) and swivel the roller (2)

Power steering pump adjustment on 1974–76 diesel engine. Loosen the bolts (1,2) and lever the pump outwards

POWER STEERING PUMP—1977 AND LATER

1. Loosen the nut on the mounting stud and the nuts on the adjusting bolts.
2. Tighten the belt tension using the adjusting screw. Check the tension and tighten the pivot and mounting bolts.

V8 Engines

WATER PUMP/POWER STEERING PUMP

1. Loosen the 3 attaching screws.
2. Loosen the pivot bolt slightly.
3. Adjust the belt tension by pushing the power steering pump outwards. Starting in 1975, adjust the belt by turning the hex headed toothed lockwasher.
4. Tighten the pivot and attaching bolts. Check the belt tension. If the belt is still in good shape but cannot be adjusted, the attaching bolt (2) can be removed and reinstalled in another hole. If you do this, be sure you replace the belt in the original hole when you replace the belt.

Loosen the mounting bolts and adjust belt tension with the adjusting bolt

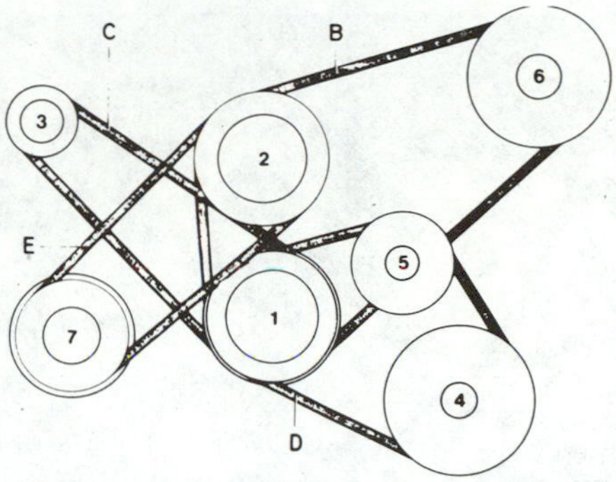

1. Crankshaft
2. Water pump
3. Alternator
4. Refrigerant compressor
5. Tensioning roller
6. Power steering pump
7. Air pump

Drive belt arrangement—1974–V8 engines

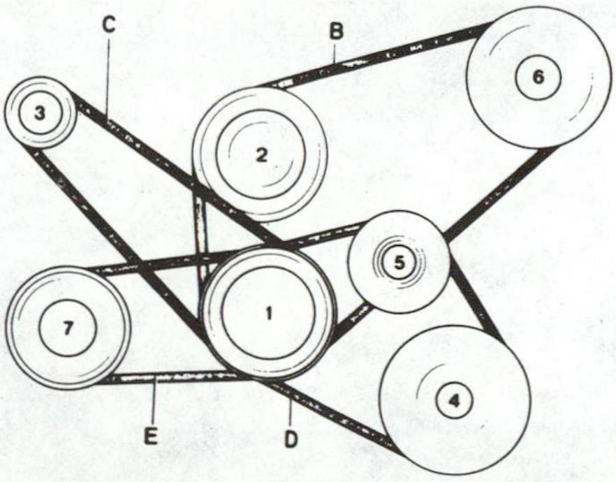

1. Crankshaft
2. Water pump
3. Alternator
4. Refrigerant compressor
5. Tensioning roller
6. Power steering pump
7. Air pump

Drive belt arrangement—1975 and later V8 engines

ALTERNATOR

There are 2 types of adjustments on the alternator. Early types use a threaded rod and later

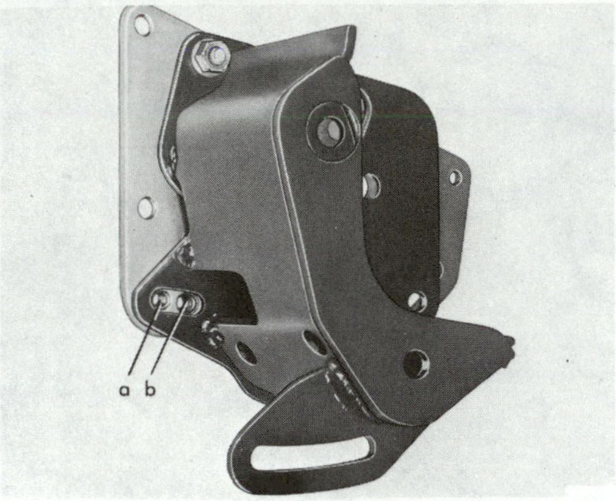

If adjustment is impossible, the bolt can be moved from hole "a" to hole "b"

Early V8 alternator adjustment. Loosen the attaching bolts (6,8) and adjust with adjusting nut (7) after loosening the locknut (5)

Later V8 alternator adjustment. Loosen the attaching bolts (1,2) and adjust with bolt (3)

models use a hex-headed, toothed washer.

1. On early models, loosen the 2 pivot bolts and the lockwasher. Turn the adjusting nut on the threaded rod to adjust the belt tension. Check the tension and tighten the locknut and pivot bolts.

2. On later models, loosen the pivot and attaching bolts. Adjust the tension by turning the hex-headed, toothed washer. Check the belt tension and tighten the mounting and adjusting bolts.

A/C COMPRESSOR

The air conditioning compressor belt is adjusted by means of a tensioning roller (idler pulley). Loosen the idler pulley mounting bolt and swivel the roller to adjust the belt tension. Tighten the mounting nut and check the belt tension.

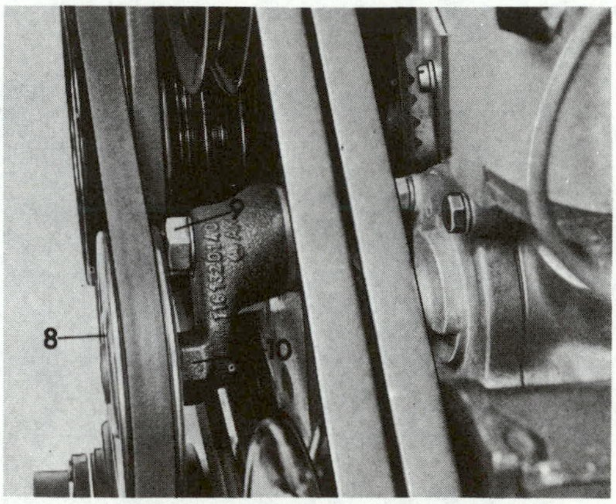

A/C compressor adjustment. Loosen the attaching bolt (9) and tensioner roller bolt (8)

AIR PUMP

1. Loosen the top mounting bolt at the front and rear of the air pump.

2. Slightly loosen the pivot bolt at the bottom of the air pump. Push the pump outwards by hand, until the belt tension is correct. Do not pry on the pump housing.

3. Tighten the mounting and pivot bolts.

Air pump adjustment on V8's. Loosen at bolts (1,2,3)

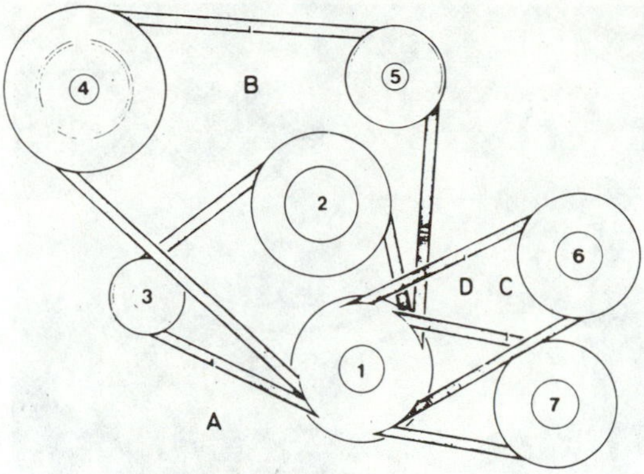

1. Crankshaft
2. Water pump
3. Alternator
4. Refrigerant compressor
5. Tensioning roller
6. Power steering pump
7. Air pump
8. Vacuum pump

Arrangement of drive belts on 230

230

ALTERNATOR

1. Loosen the attaching bolt at the bottom of the alternator. Loosen the adjusting bolt at the top.
2. Adjust the belt tension by turning the hex-headed, toothed washer.
3. Tighten the adjusting bolt and pivot bolt. Check the belt tension.

Alternator belt on 230. Loosen bolts (1,3,4). Adjust with bolt (2)

A/C COMPRESSOR

1. Loosen the attaching screw behind the idler pulley.
2. Swivel the idler pulley to adjust the belt and tighten the mounting bolt.
3. Recheck the belt tension.

A/C compressor adjustment. Loosen bolt (1) and tighten with roller (2)

POWER STEERING PUMP—1974

1. Loosen the 2 mounting bolts and lever the pump outwards to tighten the belt. Do not pry on the pump housing.
2. Tighten the attaching bolts and check the belt tension.

Loosen attaching screws (1,2) and lever power steering pump outward

POWER STEERING PUMP—1975–76

On 1975 models, you'll have to swing the evaporative canister aside and remove the battery and tray to allow access.

1. Loosen the mounting bolts at the top and bottom.
2. Locate the adjusting nut at the rear of the power steering pump carrier. Loosen the lock-nut on the adjusting bolt.
3. Turn the adjusting bolt to adjust the belt tension and tighten the locknut and mounting nuts.
4. Check the belt tension and be sure there is sufficient clearance for the power steering pump supply line.

Power steering pump on 1975–76 230. Loosen 2 attaching bolts and adjust with adjusting screw (5) after loosening locknut (4)

Vacuum pump on 230. Loosen attaching screws (1,2) and swivel pump outward

POWER STEERING PUMP—1977–78

1. Loosen the mounting nut and bolt on the face of the pump.
2. To adjust the belt, loosen the hex-headed, toothed adjusting nut and bolt and turn the bolt.
3. Tighten the adjusting bolt/nut and the mounting nut and blt. Check the belt tension.

VACUUM PUMP

1. Loosen the attaching bolts at the top and bottom.
2. Adjust the belt by swivelling the vacuum pump outward.
3. Tighten the attaching screws and check the belt tension.

Air pump adjustment. Loosen bolts (1,2,3). Tighten with toothed adjusting bolt on the bottom of the pump (1975 and later) or pry pump outward (prior to 1975)

AIR PUMP—1975–76

1. To allow access to the air pump adjustment on 1975 models, pull the evaporative canister aside and remove the battery and tray.
2. Loosen the mounting nuts and adjust the belt tension with the threaded adjusting rod. Tighten the attaching screws and check the belt tension.
3. Replace the battery, battery tray and evaporative canister.

AIR PUMP—1977–78

1. Loosen the mounting bolts and the nut on the rear of the hex-headed adjusting bolt.
2. To adjust the belt tension, turn the hex-headed, toothed lockwasher.
3. Check the belt tension and tighten the mounting nuts and nut on the rear of the adjusting bolt.

The battery, tray and evaporative canister must be moved to adjust air pump and power steering pump on 230

6-Cylinder Engine

ALTERNATOR

1. Loosen the upper (adjusting) bolt and the lower (pivot) bolts.

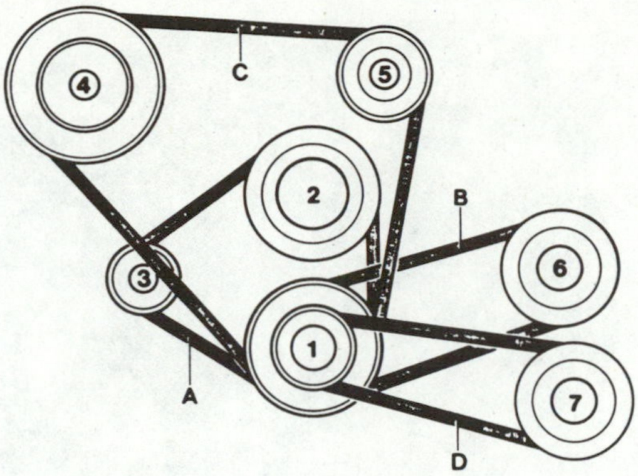

1. Crankshaft
2. Water pump
3. Alternator
4. Refrigerant compressor
5. Tensioning roller
6. Power steering pump
7. Air pump

Arrangement of drive belts on 6-cylinder engines. On 1974–76 models, the air pump is below the power steering pump

Alternator adjustment on 6-cylinder engines. Loosen the pivot bolt (arrow) and adjusting nut (2). Adjust the tension at either end (1 or 3) of the adjusting bolt

2. Models through 1976, and 1977 and later air conditioned models can be adjusted at either end of the upper bolt. One end is a hex-headed, toothed washer and the other end is 6 mm square. All other models are adjusted with the hex-headed toothed washer.

3. Tighten the upper and lower nuts/bolts and check the belt tension.

POWER STEERING PUMP—1974–76

Loosen the adjusting (lower) bolt and pry the power steering pump outward to tighten the belt. Tighten the adjusting bolt and check the belt tension.

POWER STEERING PUMP—1977–81

1. Loosen the attaching (pivot) bolt on the face of the pump.

Loosen the adjusting bolt (1) and lever the power steering pump outward on 1974–76 6-cylinder models

On 1977 and later 6-cylinder engines, loosen the pivot bolt and the toothed adjuster (2,3)

2. Loosen the nut behind the toothed adjusting bolt.

3. Turn the hex-headed toothed lockwasher to adjust the belt.

4. Tighten the nut and pivot bolt and check the belt tension.

A/C COMPRESSOR

The air conditioning compressor is adjusted at the idler pulley. Loosen the center screw of the idler pulley and adjust the belt tension with the adjusting screw. Tighten the center screw to 12 ft. lbs.

AIR PUMP

Loosen the adjusting bolt and adjust the belt tension by prying the air pump outward. Do not pry on the air pump housing. Tighten the adjusting bolt and check the belt tension.

6.9

POWER STEERING PUMP

1. Loosen the attaching bolts and nuts.

2. Loosen the nut behind the toothed adjuster.

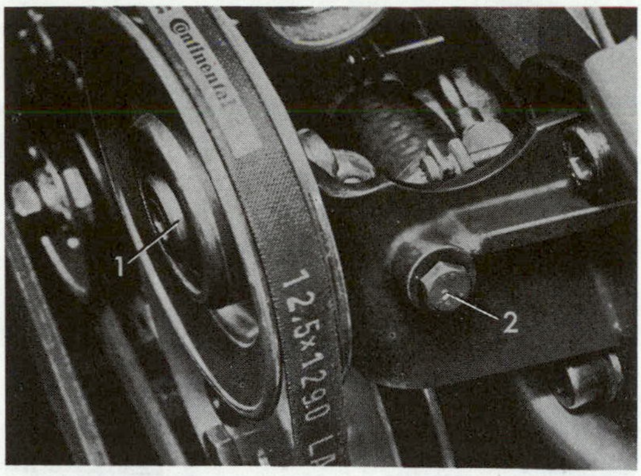

Adjust the A/C compressor on 6-cylinder engines by loosening the Allen screw (1) and turning the adjusting bolt (2)

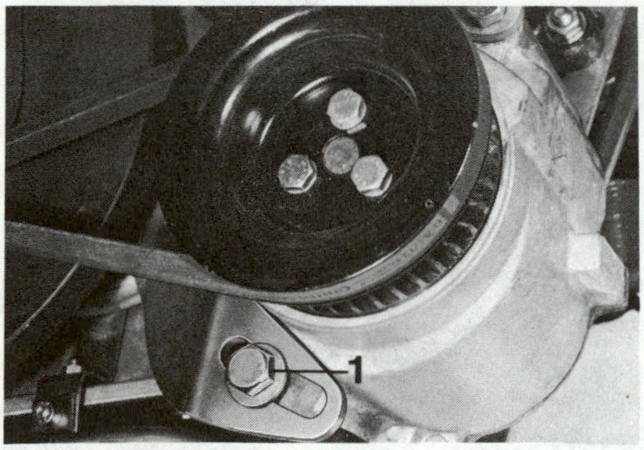

On 6-cylinder engines, adjust the air pump by loosening the adjusting bolt (1) and lever the pump outward

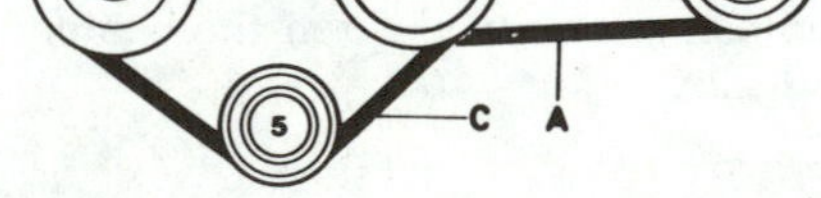

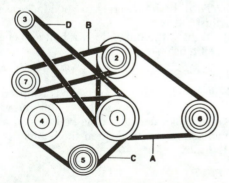

1. Crankshaft
2. Water pump
3. Alternator
4. Refrigerant compressor
5. Tensioning roller
6. Power steering pump

Arrangements of drive belts on 6.9

3. Adjust the belt tension by turning the hex-headed, toothed washer. Tighten the adjusting nut and mounting bolts.
4. Check the belt tension.

On the 6.9, adjust the power steering pump with the toothed adjuster (4), after loosening the attaching bolts (not shown) and the adjuster nut (3)

AIR PUMP

Loosen the attaching bolt and adjust the belt tension with the adjusting screw. Tighten the attaching bolt and check the belt tension.

A/C COMPRESSOR

Loosen the pivot bolt and the bolt in front of the toothed adjuster. Turn the hex-headed toothed adjuster to adjust belt tension. Tighten the adjusting bolt and attaching bolt. Check the belt tension.

ALTERNATOR

Loosen the upper and lower nuts on the adjusting and pivot bolts. Tighten the belt by turning the toothed washer and retighten the nuts. Check the belt tension.

On the 6.9 air pump, loosen the attaching bolt (1) and adjust the belt tension with the adjusting bolt (2)

Adjust the A/C compressor belt tension on the 6.9 after loosening the attaching bolts (1,2). The adjuster is (3)

Adjust the alternator belt tension on the 6.9, with the toothed adjuster, after loosening the attaching bolts (1,2)

Hoses

Upper and lower radiator hoses and all heater hoses should be checked for deterioration, leaks and loose hose clamps every 15,000 miles. To remove the hoses:

1. Drain the radiator as detailed later in this chapter.
2. Loosen the hose clamps at each end of the hose to be removed.
3. Working the hose back and forth, slide it off its connection and then install a new hose if necessary.
4. Position the hose clamps at least ¼ in. from the end of the hose and tighten them.

NOTE: *Always make sure that the hose clamps are beyond the bead and placed in the center of the clamping surface before tightening them.*

Air Conditioning

This book contains no repair or maintenance procedures for the air conditioning system. It is recommended that any such repairs be left to the experts, who are well aware of the hazards and who have the proper equipment.

CAUTION: *The compressed refrigerant used in the air conditioning system expands into the atmosphere at a temperature of −21.7° F or lower. This will freeze any surface, including your eyes, that it contacts. In addition, the refrigerant decomposes into a poisonous gas in the presence of flame. Do not open or disconnect any part of the air conditioning system.*

A lot of A/C problems can be avoided by simply running the air conditioner at least once a week, regardless of the season. Simply let the system run for at least 5 minutes a week (even in the winter), and you'll keep the internal parts lubricated as well as preventing the hoses from hardening.

KEEP THE CONDENSER CLEAR

Periodically inspect the front of the condenser for bent fins or foreign material (dirt, bugs, leaves, etc.). If any cooling fins are bent, straighten them carefully with needlenosed pliers. You can remove any debris with a stiff bristle brush.

CHECK THE REFRIGERANT LEVEL

If you suspect the A/C system is low on refrigerant, (air is not as cold as normal), there is a check you can make. Normally, it is located in the head of the receiver/drier. The receiver/drier is a large metal cylinder that looks something like a fire extinguisher, usually in front of the grille. Once you've found it, wipe it clean and proceed as follows:

1. Place the automatic transmission in Park or the manual transmission in Neutral. Set the parking brake.
2. Run the engine at a fast idle (about 1500 rpm) either with the help of a friend, or by temporarily readjusting the idle speed screw.
3. Set the controls for maximum cold with the blower on high.
4. Locate the sight glass.
5. With the engine and the air conditioning system running, look for the flow of refrigerant through the sight glass. If the air conditioner is working properly, you'll be able to see a continuous flow of clear refrigerant through the sight glass, with perhaps an occasional bubble at very high temperatures.
6. Cycle the air conditioner on and off to make sure what you are seeing is clear refrigerant. Since the refrigerant is clear, it is possible to mistake a completely discharged system for one that is fully charged. Turn the system off and watch the sight glass. If there is refrigerant in the system, you'll see bubbles during

HOW TO SPOT BAD HOSES

Both the upper and lower radiator hoses are called upon to perform difficult jobs in an inhospitable environment. They are subject to nearly 18 psi at under hood temperatures often over 280°F., and must circulate nearly 7500 gallons of coolant an hour—3 good reasons to have good hoses.

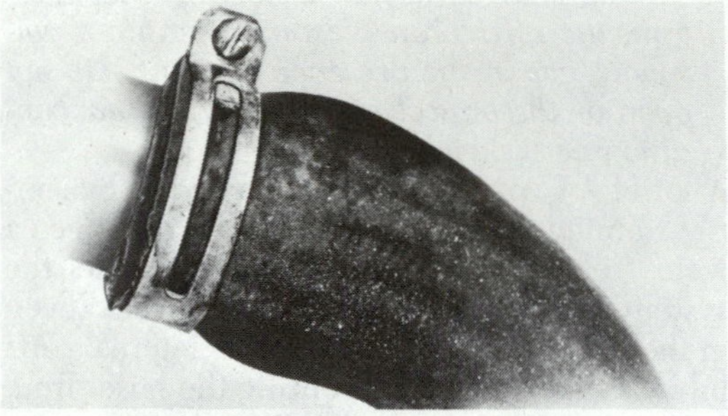

Swollen hose

A good test for any hose is to feel it for soft or spongy spots. Frequently these will appear as swollen areas of the hose. The most likely cause is oil soaking. This hose could burst at any time, when hot or under pressure.

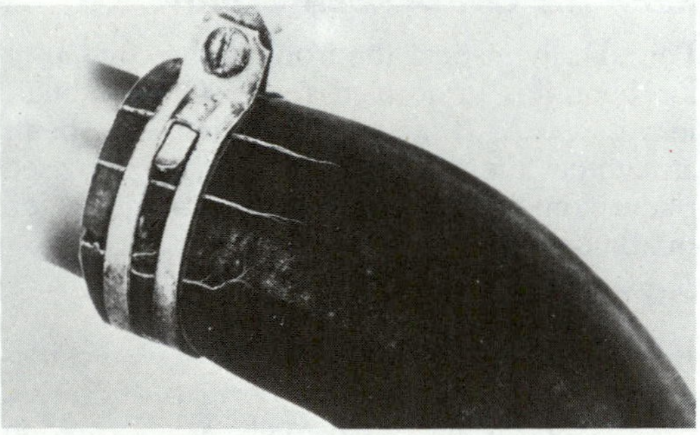

Cracked hose

Cracked hoses can usually be seen but feel the hoses to be sure they have not hardened; a prime cause of cracking. This hose has cracked down to the reinforcing cords and could split at any of the cracks.

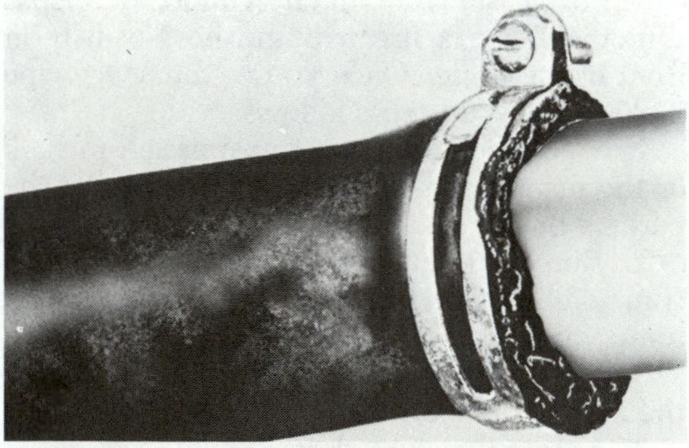

Frayed hose end (due to weak clamp)

Weakened clamps frequently are the cause of hose and cooling system failure. The connection between the pipe and hose has deteriorated enough to allow coolant to escape when the engine is hot.

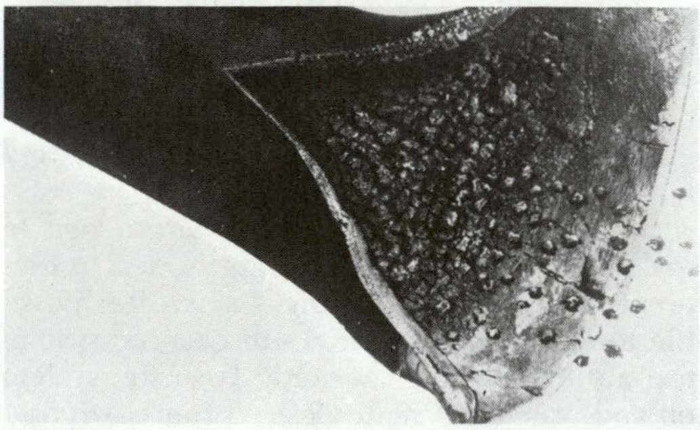

Debris in cooling system

Debris, rust and scale in the cooling system can cause the inside of a hose to weaken. This can usually be felt on the outside of the hose as soft or thinner areas.

The A/C sight glass (arrow) is located on the receiver/drier. On 450 models, the receiver/drier is in front of the radiator support, next to the fan. On other models, the receiver/drier is in one of the front corners of the engine compartment behind the headlight and the sight glass is on top of the receiver/drier

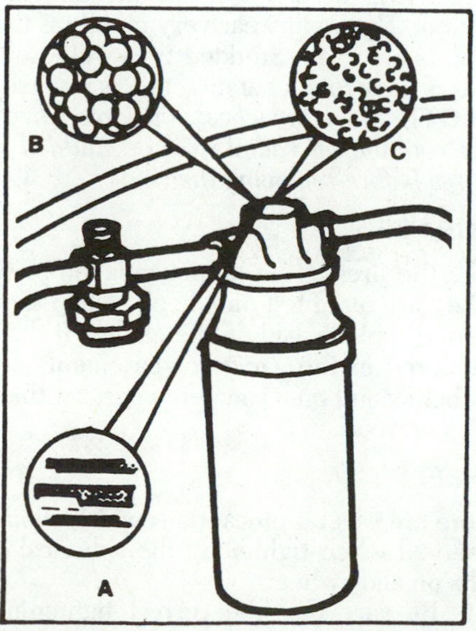

Oil streaks (A) constant bubbles (B) or foam (C) indicate there is not enough refrigerant in the system. Occasional bubbles during initial operation is normal. A clear sight glass indicates a proper charge of refrigerant or no refrigerant at all, which can be determined by the presence of cold air at the outlets in the car. If the glass is clouded with a milky white substance, have the receiver/drier checked professionally

the off cycle. If you observe no bubbles when the system is running, and the air flow from the unit in the car is delivering cold air, everything is OK.

7. If you observe bubbles in the sight glass while the system is operating, the system is low on refrigerant. Have it checked by a professional.

8. Oil streaks in the sight glass are an indication of trouble. Most of the time, if you see oil in the sight glass, it wi'l appear as a series of streaks, although occasionally it may be a solid stream of oil. In either case, it means that part of the charge has been lost.

Tires and Wheels

Tires should be checked weekly for proper air pressure. A chart, located either in the glove compartment or on the driver's or passenger's door, gives the recommended inflation pressures. Maximum fuel economy and tire life will result if the pressure is maintained at the highest figure given on the chart (usually located on the fuel tank filler lid). Pressures should be

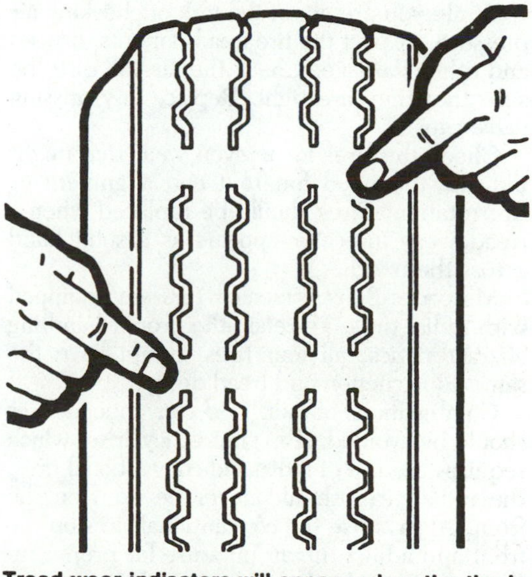

Tread wear indicators will appear when the tire is worn out

Tread depth can be checked with an inexpensive gauge

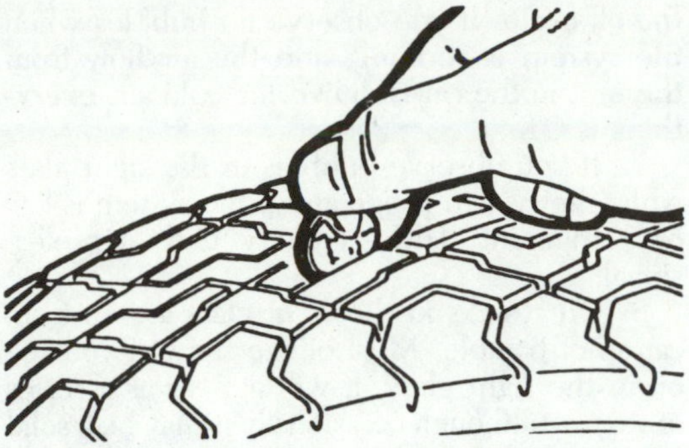

A penny works as well as anything for checking tire tread depth; when you can see the top of Lincoln's head, it's time for a new tire

checked before driving since pressure can increase as much as six pounds per square inch (psi) due to heat buildup. It is a good idea to have your own accurate pressure gauge, because not all gauges on service station air pumps can be trusted. When checking pressures, do not neglect the spare tire. Note that some spare tires require pressures considerably higher than those used in the other tires.

While you are about the task of checking air pressure, inspect the tire treads for cuts, bruises and other damage. Check the air valves to be sure that they are tight. Replace any missing valve caps.

Check the tires for uneven wear that might indicate the need for front end alignment or tire rotation. Tires should be replaced when a tread wear indicator appears as a solid band across the tread.

Mercedes-Benz passenger cars are equipped with radial tires. To retain the proper handling characteristics, all four tires should have the same construction and tread design.

Combinations of radial and conventional tires should be avoided. If an emergency arises which requires the use of radial and conventional tires, the radial tires should never be used on the front. Always use the conventional tires on the front and adjust the air pressure for proper inflation. Mercedes-Benz stresses that using radial tires on the front and conventional tires on the rear is extremely dangerous.

New tires (regardless of construction) should always be mounted on the front to maintain normal handling. After new tires are installed, it is advisable to drive at moderate speeds for the first 60 miles.

When buying new tires, give some thought to the following points, especially if you are considering a switch to larger tires or a different profile series:

1. All four tires must be of the same construction type. This rule should not be violated. Radial, bias, and bias-belted tires must not be mixed unless in extreme emergency.
2. The wheels should be the correct width for the tire. Tire dealers have charts of tire and rim compatibility. A mismatch will cause sloppy handling and rapid tire wear. The tread width should match the rim width (inside bead to inside bead) within an inch. For radial tires, the rim width should be 80% or less of the tire (not tread) width.
3. The height (mounted diameter) of the new tires can change speedometer accuracy, engine speed at a given road speed, fuel mileage, acceleration, and ground clearance. Tire manufacturers furnish full measurement specifications.
4. The spare tire should be usable, at least for short distance and low speed operation, with the new tires.
5. There shouldn't be any body interference when loaded, on bumps, or in turns.

TIRE ROTATION

Tire rotation is recommended every 6,000 miles or so, to obtain maximum tire wear. The pattern you use depends on whether or not your car has a usable spare. Radial tires should not be cross-switched (from one side of the car to the other); they last longer if their direction of rotation is not changed. Snow tires sometimes have directional arrows molded into the side of the carcass; the arrow shows the direction of rotation. They will wear very rapidly if the rotation is reversed. Studded tires will lose their studs if their rotational direction is reversed.

NOTE: *Mark the wheel position or direction of rotation on radial tires or studded snow tires before removing them.*

STORAGE

Store the tires at the proper inflation pressure if they are mounted on wheels. Keep them in a cool dry place, laid on their sides. If the tires are stored in the garage or basement, do not let them stand on a concrete floor; set them on strips of wood.

WHEELS

There are several precautions which should be observed when tightening the spherical collar bolts on alloy wheels.

1. Be sure that the correct tightening sequence is followed. It doesn't matter where you start, but a criss-cross tightening sequence should be used.
2. The correct torque for the spherical collar bolts is 72 ft. lbs.
3. Only the spherical collar bolts should be used for the disc wheels (light alloy and steel wheels).

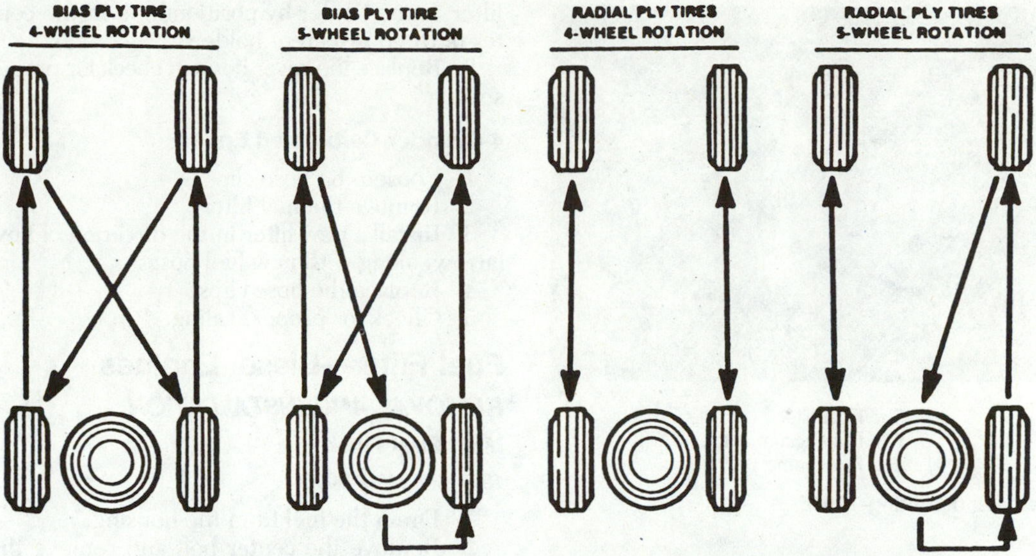

Tire rotation diagrams; note that radials should not be cross-switched

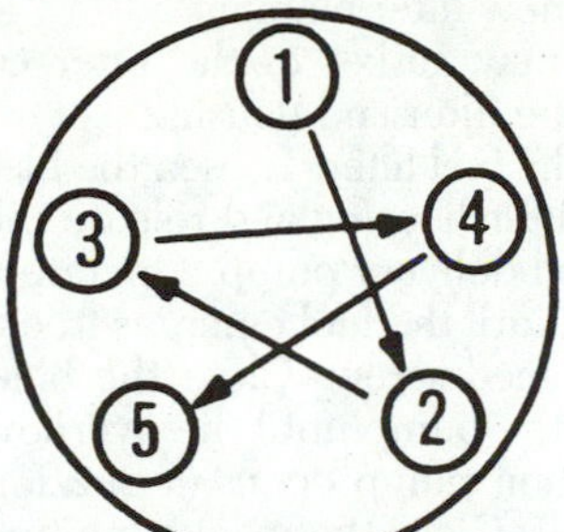

All wheels should be tightened in a criss-cross pattern

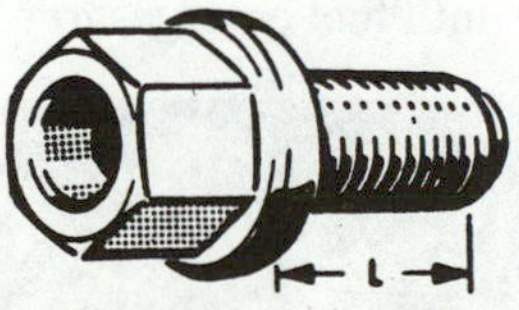

Bolts used with steel wheels. L = approx. 0.8 in.

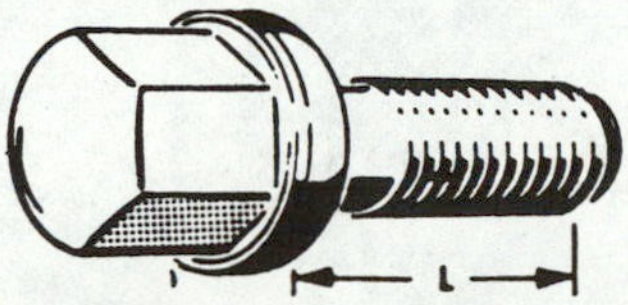

Bolts used with light alloy wheels. L = approx. 1.2 in.

4. Do not use an air gun to tighten the spherical collar bolts. These should only be tightened with a torque wrench.
5. The tightening torque is for cold wheels. If the wheels are tightened when warm, be sure that they are not tightened to the full torque. As soon as the wheels have cooled, torque them to the correct specification.

Fuel Filter—Gasoline Engines

REMOVAL AND INSTALLATION

6-Cylinder Carbureted Engines

The fuel filter is located in the carburetor housing. Put some rags under the fuel return valve to absorb the inevitable gasoline spillage.

1. Unscrew the fuel return valve and plug it at the carburetor.
2. Remove the fuel filter.
3. Renew the gasket at the seal plug.
4. Install a new filter. Check for leaks.

6-cylinder carburetor fuel filter

Fuel Injected Engines—All Models

Two types of filter are used, one on the electronically controlled fuel injection and the other on the CIS fuel injection. Both are located between the rear axle and the fuel tank.

1. Unscrew the cover box.
2. Remove the pressure hoses.

55. Fuel filter
57. Fuel accumulator
65. Fuel pump

Fuel filter mounting—190E

Fuel filter on 1974–75 V8

Fuel filter on 1976 and later V8 and fuel injected 6-cylinder

3. Loosen the attaching screws and remove the filter. Remove the connecting plug from the old filter and install it on a new filter using a new gasket.
4. Install a new filter in the direction of flow.
5. Replace the attaching screws.
6. Install the pressure hoses.
7. On 1976 and later models, install the fuel filter in the holder by positioning it in the center of the transparent holder.
8. Replace the cover box and check for proper sealing.

4-Cylinder Carbureted Engine

1. Loosen the hose clips.
2. Remove the fuel filter.
3. Install a new filter in the direction of flow (arrow) along with new fuel hoses.
4. Replace the hose clips.
5. Check for proper sealing.

Fuel Filter—Diesel Engines

REMOVAL AND INSTALLATION

Main Fuel Filter

1974–76 240D, 300D

1. Drain the fuel from the housing.
2. Remove the center bolt and remove the filter housing and filter.
3. Wash the filter housing in clean diesel fuel and install a new filter element.
4. Use a new gasket in the filter cap and reassemble the filter and housing.
5. Bleed the fuel filter. Loosen the bleed bolt on the fuel filter housing and release the manually operated delivery pump. Operate the delivery pump until the fuel emerges free of bubbles at the bleed screw. Close the bleed bolt and operate the pump until the overflow valve on the injection pump opens (a buzzing noise will be heard). Close the manual pump before starting the engine. To bleed the injection pump on 4-cylinder diesels, loosen the bleed screw on the injection pump and keep pumping the hand pump until fuel emerges free of bubbles.

Remove the main diesel fuel filter after removing the center attaching bolt. The bleed screw is (2)

Some diesel injection pumps have a manually operated delivery pump (1)

NOTE: *The 190D uses a self-bleeding fuel pump, therefore the hand pump has been eliminated. No bleeding is necessary.*

1977 AND LATER DIESELS

Loosen the center attaching bolt and remove the filter cartridge downward. Lubricate the new filter gasket with clean diesel fuel and install a new filter cartridge.

To bleed the fuel filter, see Step 5 of the previous procedure.

Diesel Prefilter

Diesel engines use a prefilter in addition to the main fuel filter, since even the most minute particle of dirt will clog the injection system. The prefilter is located in the line just before it enters the injection pump.

To replace it, simply unscrew the clamps on each end and remove the old filter. Install a new filter and bleed the system (see Main Fuel Filter).

Diesel engines use a prefilter in addition to the main fuel filter. The arrow indicates the hand operated delivery pump

Fuel Pump Strainer (Carbureted Engines)

Plunger type fuel pumps on carbureted engines use a strainer located behind the cover.

1. Disconnect and plug the fuel line at the pump.
2. Remove the center screw and remove the cover. A small amount of fuel will run out.
3. Replace the strainer, gasket, screw and aluminum washer, all of which are part of the replacement kit.
4. Replace the cover. There are assembly marks on the cover and fuel pump body.
5. Reconnect the fuel line. Start the engine and check for leaks.

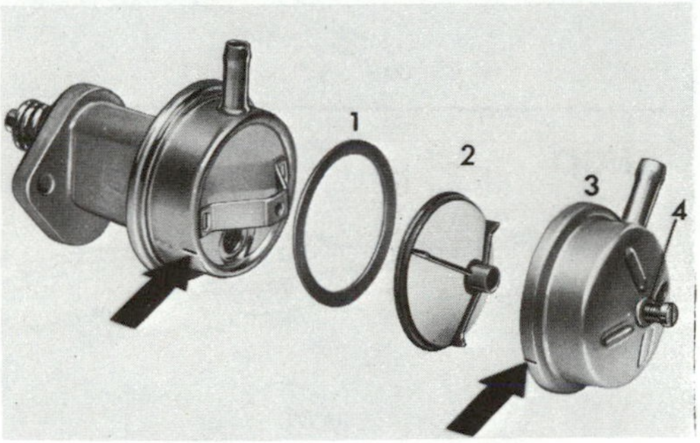

1. Gasket
2. Strainer (filter)
3. Cover
4. Screw

Fuel pump strainer used with carbureted engines. When assembling use the matchmarks (arrows)

Windshield Wipers

For maximum effectiveness and longest element life, the windshield and wiper blades should be kept clean. Dirt, tree sap, road tar and so on will cause streaking, smearing and blade deterioration if left on the glass. It is advisable to wash the windshield carefully with a commercial glass cleaner at least once a month. Wipe off the rubber blades with the wet rag afterwards. Do not attempt to move the wipers back and forth by hand; damage to the motor and drive mechanism will result.

If the blades are found to be cracked, broken or torn, they should be replaced immediately. Replacement intervals will vary with usage, although ozone deterioration usually limits blade life to about one year. If the wiper pattern is smeared or streaked, or if the blade chatters across the glass, the blades should be replaced. It is easiest and most sensible to replace them in pairs.

There are basically three different types of wiper blade refills, which differ in their method of replacement. One type has two release but-

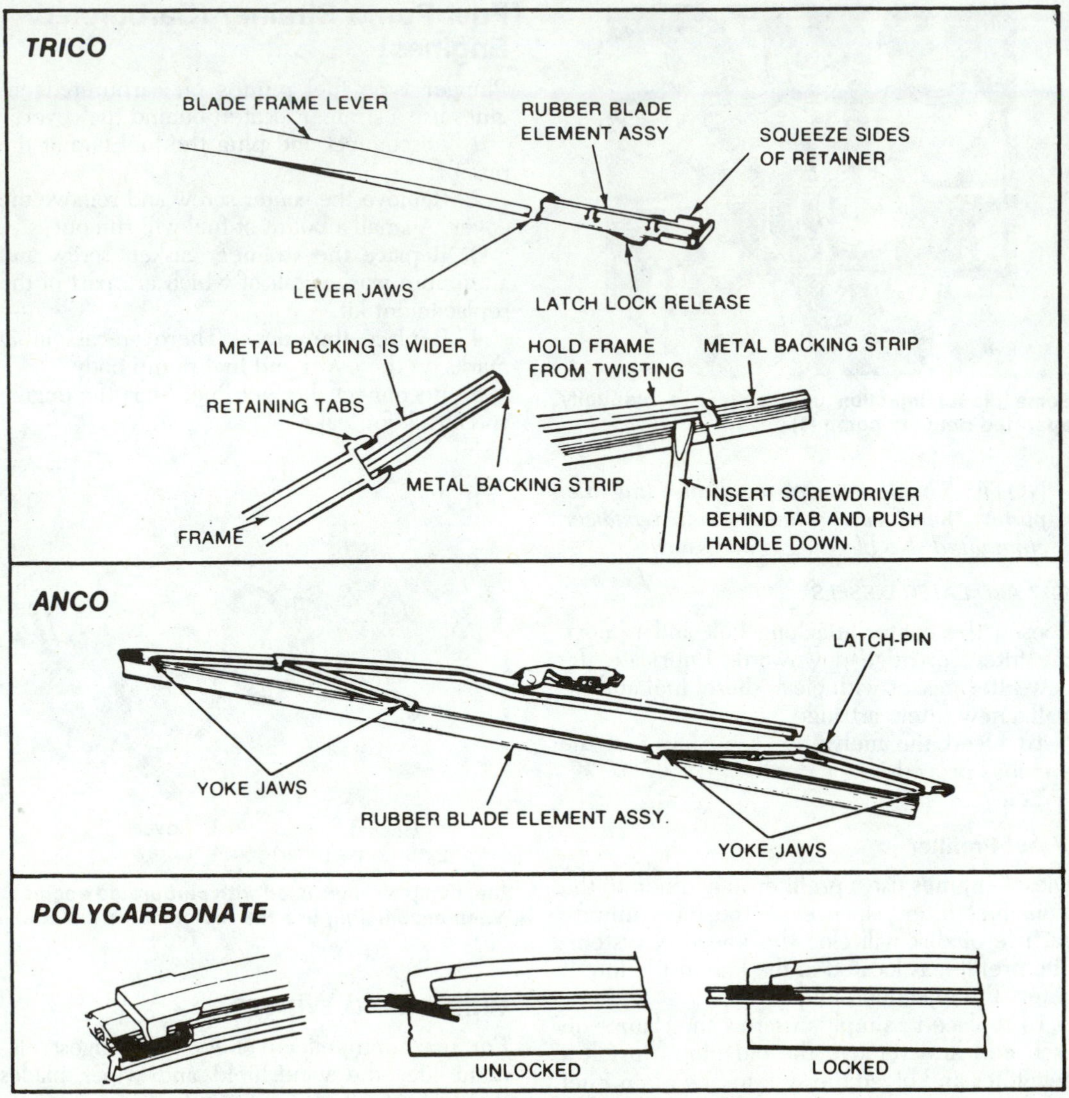

The three types of wiper element retention

tons, approximately one-third of the way up from the ends of the blade frame. Pushing the buttons down release a lock and allows the rubber blade to be removed from the frame. The new blade slides back into the frame and locks in place.

The second type of refill has two metal tabs which are unlocked by squeezing them together. The rubber blade can then be withdrawn from the frame jaws. A new one is installed by inserting it into the front frame jaws and sliding it rearward to engage the remaining frame jaws. There are usually four jaws; when installing, be certain that the refill is engaged in all of them. At the end of its travel, the tabs will lock into place on the front jaws of the wiper blade frame.

The third type is a refill made from polycarbonate. The refill has a simple locking device at one end which flexes downward out of the groove into which the jaws of the holder fit, allowing easy release. By sliding the new refill through all the jaws and pushing through the slight resistance when it reaches the end of its travel, the refill will lock into position.

Regardless of the type of refill used, make sure that all of the frame jaws are engaged as the refill is pushed into place and locked. The metal blade holder and frame will scratch the glass if allowed to touch it.

FLUIDS AND LUBRICANTS

Oil and Fuel Recommendations

Mercedes-Benz is constantly testing and analyzing fuels and lubricants in an effort to determine which lubricants and fuels are suitable and provide the best service in their vehicles. The recommended fluids and their applications are published by Mercedes-Benz under the title "Specifications for Service Products". It is impossible to detail, in this book, those materials which are suitable at any given time, since the publication is constantly revised and updated by Mercedes-Benz.

In general, most any high quality material is suitable for the particular application, with the exceptions noted below.

OIL

The SAE (Society of Automotive Engineers) grade number indicates the viscosity of the engine oil and thus its ability to lubricate at a given temperature. The lower the SAE grade number, the lighter the oil; the lower the viscosity, the easier it is to crank the engine in cold weather.

Oil viscosities should be chosen from those oils recommended for the lowest anticipated temperatures during the oil change interval.

Multi-viscosity oils (10W–30, 20W–50 etc.) offer the important advantage of being adaptable to temperature extremes. They allow easy starting at low temperatures, yet they give good protection at high speeds and engine temperature. This is a decided advantage in changeable climates or in long distance touring.

The API (American Petroleum Institute) designation indicates the classification of engine oil used under certain given operating conditions. Only oils designated for use "Service SE" should be used. Oils of the SE type perform a variety of functions inside the engine in addition to their basic function as a lubricant. Through a balanced system of metallic detergents and polymeric dispersants, the oil prevents the formation of high and low temperature deposits and also keeps sludge and particles of dirt in suspension. Acids, particularly sulfuric acid, as well as other byproducts of combustion, are neutralized. Both the SAE grade number and the API designation can be found on top of the oil can.

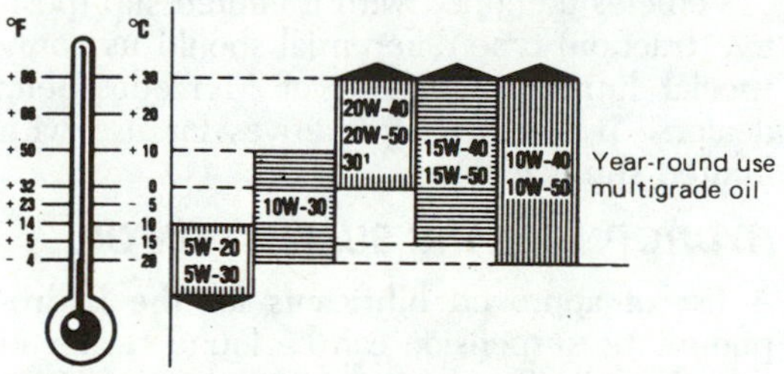

SAE 40 may be used if ambient temperatures constantly exceed +30° C (+86° F).

Oil viscosity selection chart—gasoline engines

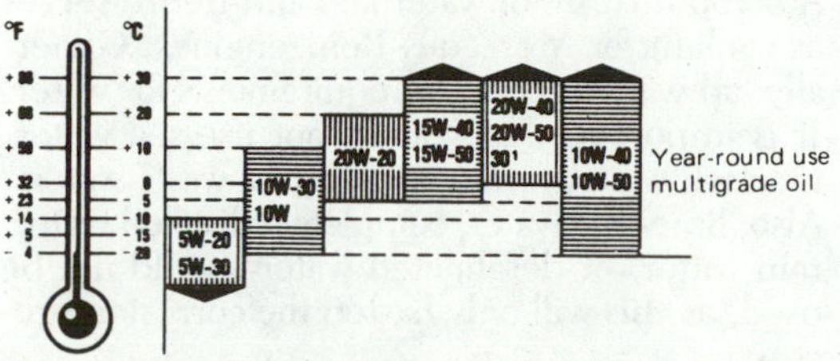

SAE 40 may be used if ambient temperatures constantly exceed +30° C (+86° F).

Oil viscosity selection chart—diesel engines

Diesel engines also require SE engine oil. In addition, the oil must qualify for a CC rating. The API has a number of different diesel engine ratings, including CB, CC and CD. Any of these other oils are fine as long as the designation CC appears on the can along with them. Do not use oil labeled only SE or only CC. Both designations must always appear together.

For recommended oil viscosities, refer to the chart.

NOTE: *As of late 1980, the API has come out with a new designation of motor oil, SF. Oils designated for use "Service SF" are equally acceptable in your pre-'80 car and should be used exclusively in 1981 and later models.*

CAUTION: *Non-detergent or straight mineral oils should not be used in your car.*

SYNTHETIC OIL

There are many excellent synthetic and fuel-efficient oils currently available that can provide better gas mileage, longer service life, and in some cases better engine protection. These benefits do not come without a few hitches, however—the main one being the price of synthetic oils, which is three or four times the price per quart of conventional oil.

Synthetic oil is not for every car and every type of driving, so you should consider your engine's condition and your type of driving. Also, check your car's warranty conditions regarding the use of synthetic oils.

Both brand new engines and older, high mileage engines are the wrong candidates for synthetic oil. The synthetic oils are so slippery that they can prevent the proper break-in of new engines; most manufacturers recommend that you wait until the engine is properly broken in (5,000 miles) until using synthetic oil. Older engines with wear have a different problem with synthetics: they "use" (consume during operation) more oil as they age. Slippery synthetic oils get past these worn parts easily—if your engine is "using" conventional oil, it will use synthetics much faster. Also, if your car is leaking oil past old seals you'll have a much greater leak problems with synthetics.

Consider your type of driving. If most of your accumulated mileage is high speed, highway type driving, the more expensive synthetic oils may be of benefit. Extended highway driving gives the engine a chance to warm up, accumulating less acids in the oil and putting less stress on the engine over the long run. Under these conditions, the oil change interval can be extended (as long as your oil filter can last the extended life of the oil) up to the advertised mileage claims of the synthetics. Cars with synthetic oils may show increased fuel economy in highway driving, due to less internal friction. However, many automotive experts agree that 50,000 miles is too long to keep any oil in your engine.

Cars used under harder circumstances, such as stop-and-go, city type driving, short trips, or extended idling, should be serviced more frequently. For the engines in these cars, the much greater cost of synthetic or fuel-efficient oils may not be worth the investment. Internal wear increases much quicker on these cars, causing greater oil consumption and leakage.

NOTE: *The mixing of conventional and synthetic oils is not recommended. If you are using synthetic oil, it might be wise to carry two or three quarts with you no matter where you drive, as not all service stations carry this type of lubricant.*

FUELS

Gasoline

The fuel requirement (octane rating) for your vehicle is listed in the owner's manual or available from any Mercedes-Benz dealer. In general, since 1974, Mercedes-Benz engines are designed to run on regular gasoline or regular unleaded gasoline if a converter is used. In the event that a fuel of the proper octane rating is not available, the timing can be retarded but this is as an emergency measure only. The proper fuel should be obtained as quickly as possible and the timing should be reset to specifications as soon as possible.

NOTE: *If the timing has been retarded because of low octane fuel, the car should not be driven at high speeds.*

Diesel

Use only commercially available No. 2 or No. 1 diesel fuel. Mercedes-Benz does not recommend the use of marine diesel fuel or heating oil.

At very low temperatures, the viscosity of No. 2 summer diesel fuel may become insufficient (the fuel will not adequately flow); winter diesel fuel should be unaffected as low as approximately 0°F.

If summer diesel fuel clogs at low winter temperatures, a specified percentage of kerosene can be mixed with No. 2 summer diesel fuel to improve its viscosity.

Add kerosene according to the following table, but keep the percentage of kerosene to a minimum since a loss of engine power will likely result. At no time should the % of kerosene exceed 50%. Regular gasoline can be substituted for kerosene, but the amount should not exceed 30%, and it is not recommended to dilute No. 1 diesel fuel.

Ambient Temperature (°F)	% No. 2 Summer Diesel Fuel	% Kerosene
+32 to +14	70	30
+14 to +5	50	50

AUTOMATIC TRANSMISSION FLUID

Since 1974, all Mercedes-Benz automatic transmissions have been of the torque converter type. All use DEXRON® B, Type B fluid, of which there are many high quality brands available.

REAR AXLE LUBRICANT

There are many high quality gear lubricants available for use with standard type differentials. Just be sure that the lubricant is specified SAE 90 viscosity for hypoid gears.

Vehicles equipped with a limited slip (positive traction) type differential should use only special lubricant available at Mercedes-Benz dealers. It has special additives for use with limited slip rear axles.

HYDROPNEUMATIC SUSPENSION OIL

A list of approved lubricants for the hydropneumatic suspension can be found earlier in this chapter. The 6.9 can use only Aral 1010, available from dealerships.

ENGINE COOLANT

A 50/50 mixture of water and anti-freeze serves as coolant for Mercedes-Benz engines. Generally tap water meets the requirements for water. It is important that you do not use sea water, brackish water, brine, or industrial waste waters. Also, lime-free water, completely distilled water, rain water, or desalinated water should not be used, as this will only hasten the corrosion process.

Consult the back of this book for the proper mixture of antifreeze and water to protect your engine to a given temperature. In addition, an

Capacities

Year	Model	Cooling System (qts)	Crankcase Engine (qts)▲ With Filter	Crankcase Engine (qts)▲ Without Filter	Transmission (pts) Manual	Transmission (pts) Automatic	Drive Axle (pts)	Steering Gear (pts) Pwr	Steering Gear (pts) Man	Level Control (qts)
1984	190E	9.0	4.8	4.3	3.2	11.6	1.5	1.0	—	—
1984	190D	9.0	6.3	5.8	3.2	11.6	1.5	1.0	—	—
1974–78	230	10.5	5.8	5.3	—	11.5	②	3.0	5/8	—
1974–76	240D	10.5	6.3	5.3	3.4	11.5	②	3.0	5/8	—
1977–83	240D	10.5	6.3	5.3	3.4	11.5	②	3.0	5/8	—
1973–76	280, 280C	11.5	6.3	5.8	—	12.3	②	3.0	—	—
1977–81	280E, 280CE	11.5	6.3	5.8	—	12.3	2.1	3.0	—	—
1975–76	280S	11.5	6.3	5.8	—	12.3	2.1	3.0	—	—
1977–80	280SE	11.5	6.3	5.8	—	12.3	2.1	3.0	—	—
1975–76	300D	11.7	6.8	5.8	—	11.5	③	3.0	—	—
1977–81	300D, 300CD	11.7	6.8	5.3	—	11.5	2.1	3.0	—	—
1982–84	300D, 300CD	13.2	8.0	6.3	—	13.2	2.2	3.0	—	—
1978–80	300SD, 300TD	12.7	6.8	5.3	—	11.5	2.1	3.0	—	6.2④
1981–84	300SD, 300TD	13.2	8.0	6.3	—	13.2	2.2	3.0	—	3.7
1981	380SL, SLC, SEL	13.7	8.5	8.0	—	13.0	2.7	⑤	—	—
1982–84	380SL, 380SE	13.2	8.5	8.0	—	16.2	2.7	3.0	—	—
1982–83	380SEL, 380SEC	13.2	8.5	8.0	—	13.0	2.7	2.5	—	—
1974–80	450SE, 450SEL, 450SL, 450SLC	16.0	8.5	8.0	—	16.5	①	3.0	—	6.2④
1984	500SEC, 500SEL	13.7	8.5	8.0	—	16.2	2.8	2.6	—	—
1978–79	6.9	16.0	11.5	10.5	—	16.5	2.7	3.0	—	6.2④

▲Add approximately ½ quart if equipped with additional oil cooler
—Not Applicable
① 450SL, 450SLC—2.7 pts
450SE 450SEL—3.0 pts
② See text: 1st version—2.4 pts
2nd version—2.1 pts
③ 1975–76—1st version—2.4 pts
2nd version—2.1 pts } See Text
④ Approximately 1 qt between dipstick maximum and minimum marks
⑤ 380SEL—2.5
380SL, 380SLC—3.0

emulsifying corrosion inhibitor should be used (add a can of corrosion inhibitor every time you change the coolant). This is to combat the effects of rust, scale, and other deposits which tend to reduce the cooling properties of the coolant due to poor heat conductivity.

Engine

OIL LEVEL CHECK

Every time you stop for fuel, check the engine oil as follows:

1. Park the car on level ground.

2. When checking the oil level it is best for the engine to be at operating temperature, although checking the oil immediately after stopping will lead to a false reading. Wait a few minutes after turning off the engine to allow the oil to drain back into the crankcase.

3. Open the hood and remove the dipstick from the engine. Generally, the dipstick is located on the front of the engine near the distributor (230 and 6-cylinder engines), on the right side of the engine, near the exhaust manifold (190E), on the front of the engine near the battery (V-8's) or at the front on the right-hand side (diesel engines).

Remove the engine oil dipstick (300D shown). The engine oil dipstick usually has a round ring at the top (arrow)

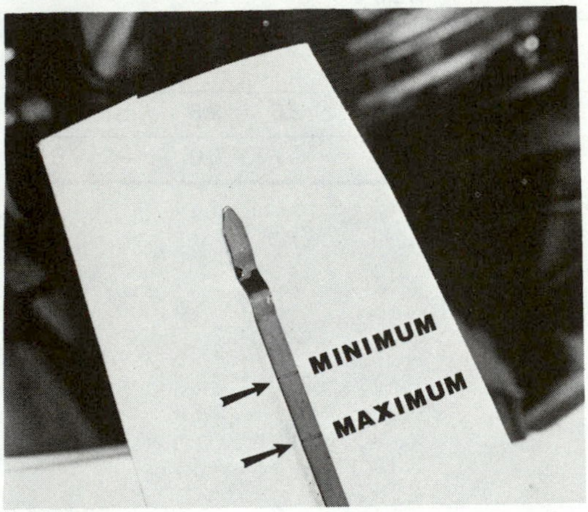

Check the engine oil level on the dipstick. It should be between the marks

4. Pull the dipstick out again and, holding it horizontally, read the oil level. The oil should be between the "upper (maximum)" and "lower (minimum)" marks on the dipstick. If the oil is below the "lower" mark, add oil of the proper viscosity through the capped opening on the top of the cylinder head cover (on the 6.9, add oil through the oil supply tank opening). See the "Oil and Fuel Recommendations" chart in this chapter for the proper viscosity and rating of oil to use.

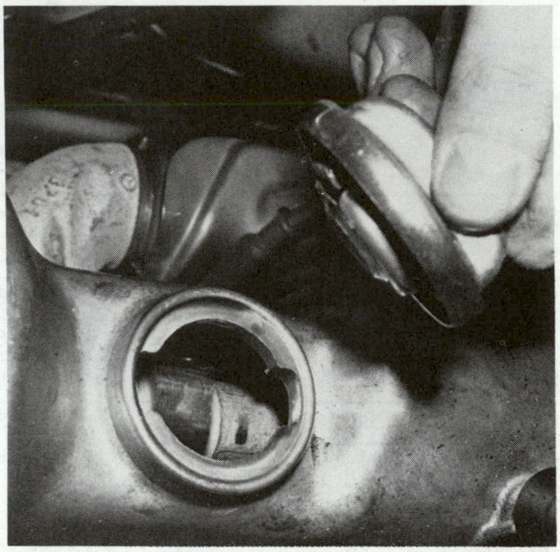

Add oil through the capped opening on the valve cover (except 6.9). On the 6.9, add oil to the oil reservoir

5. Replace the dipstick and check the oil level again after adding any oil. Be careful not to overfill the crankcase. Approximately one quart of oil will raise the level from the "lower" to the "upper." Excess oil will generally be consumed at an accelerated rate.

OIL AND FILTER CHANGE

The oil should be changed approximately every 6,000 miles.

The oil drain plug is located on the bottom of the oil pan (bottom of the engine, underneath the car).

The mileage figures given here and in the chart are the Mercedes-Benz recommended intervals assuming normal driving and conditions. If your car is being used under dusty, polluted or off-road conditions, change the oil and filter more frequently than specified. The same goes for cars driven in stop-and-go traffic or only for short distances. Always drain the oil after the engine has been running long enough to bring it to normal operating temperature. Hot oil will flow easier and more contaminents will be removed along with the oil than if it were drained cold. To change the oil and filter:

Gasoline Engines—Except 190E

1. Run the engine until it reaches normal operating temperature.
2. Jack up the front of the car and support it on safety stands.
3. From under the car, loosen but do not remove the oil drain plug. The drain plug may be a conventional hex head plug or an allen head type.

4. Position a pan, sufficient to hold all of the oil, under the drain hole.

5. Slowly unscrew the drain plug with your fingers and at the same time push the drain plug threads against the threads in the drain hole. This will prevent hot oil from leaking past the threads while the plug is being removed. The 6.9 has an oil supply tank; opening the cap will speed the draining process.

CAUTION: *The engine oil will be very hot. Be careful to stay out of the way as the oil drains out of the engine.*

6. As the drain plug comes to the end of the threads, quickly remove it from the hole allowing the oil to escape. By using this method you can also avoid having to reach into a pan full of warm, dirty oil, to retrieve the drain plug.

7. If so equipped, drain the oil from the oil cooler in the same manner.

8. Carefully unscrew the oil filter bowl. This is done by holding the filter bowl and unscrewing the long bolt which holds it. *Be careful, since there will still be oil in the filter bowl.*

9. Empty the filter bowl, wash it out, and blow it dry.

10. Throw the old filter element away.

11. Check the condition of the sealing ring and renew it if necessary.

12. Note the position of the pressure spring. This must be installed properly when the filter is assembled.

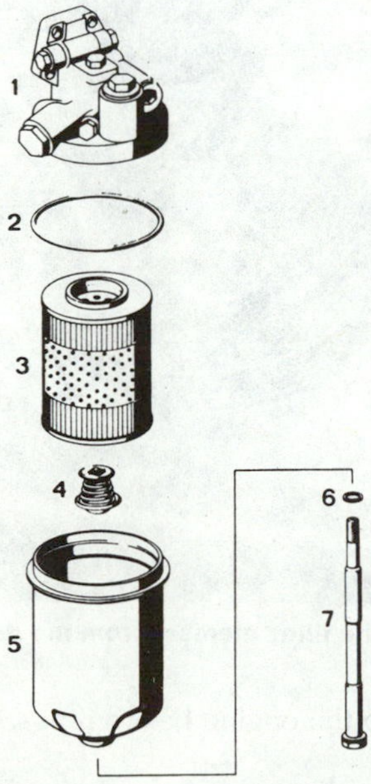

1. Upper filter housing
2. Rubber ring
3. Filter element
4. Spring
5. Lower filter housing
6. Washer
7. Bolt

Oil filter—6.9

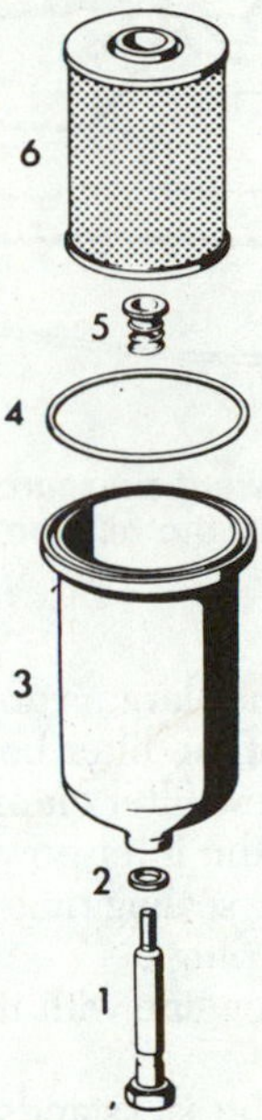

1. Bolt
2. Washer
3. Lower filter housing
4. Rubber ring
5. Spring
6. Filter element

Oil filter—overhead cam 6-cylinder engines

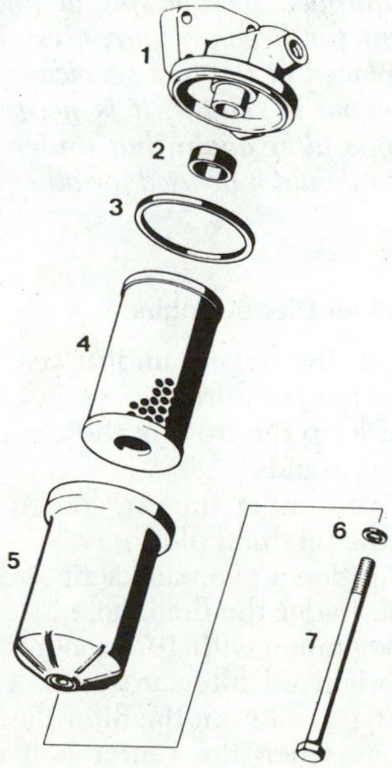

1. Upper filter housing
2. Spacer
3. Rubber sealing ring
4. Filter element
5. Filter housing
6. Washer
7. Bolt

Oil filter—4 cylinder engines (except 190E)

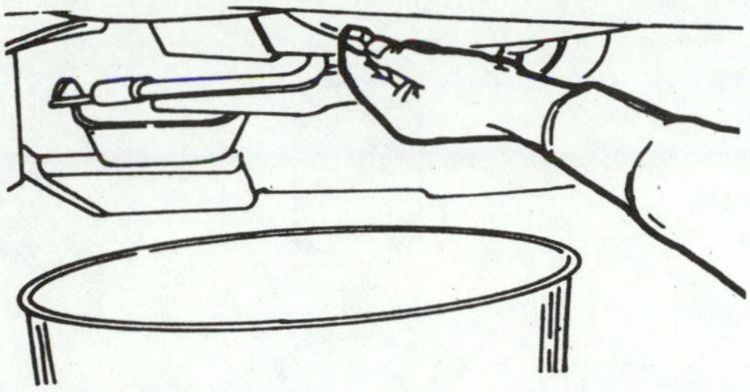

By keeping an inward pressure on the drain plug as you unscrew it, the oil won't escape past the threads

13. Renew the large rubber sealing ring around the top of the filter bowl.
14. Insert a new filter element into the filter bowl and install the filter bowl.
15. Install new sealing rings on all drain plugs and reinstall the plugs.
16. Refill the engine with the proper amount of oil.
17. Remove the jackstands and position the car on a level surface again.
18. Run the engine and check for leaks.

CAUTION: *Do not run the engine above idle speed until it has built up oil pressure, indicated when the oil light goes out.*

19. Turn off the engine, wait several minutes for the oil to drain into the crankcase, and check the oil level.

NOTE: *All new Mercedes-Benz automobiles are equipped with a special finepore filter element for break-in purposes. This should be replaced at the first service inspection. If the engine is rebuilt, it is necessary to use this type filter again, but under no circumstances should it be used for other than break-in.*

190E and all Diesel Engines

1. Run the engine until it reaches normal operating temperature.
2. Jack up the front of the car and support it on safety stands.
3. From under the car, loosen but do not remove the oil drain plug.
4. Position a pan, sufficient size to hold all of the oil, under the drain hole.
5. Beginning with 1977 models, 2 versions of an upright oil filter are used. On the first (earlier) type, oil from the filter flows back into the engine when the center bolt is removed about 2 in. On the 2nd (later) version, the oil will run back when the cover is removed. On these later versions, the cover is attached by 2 bolts instead of a center bolt (except the 190E which has only 1 center bolt).

In either case the oil should be allowed to drain into the engine before removing the drain plug.

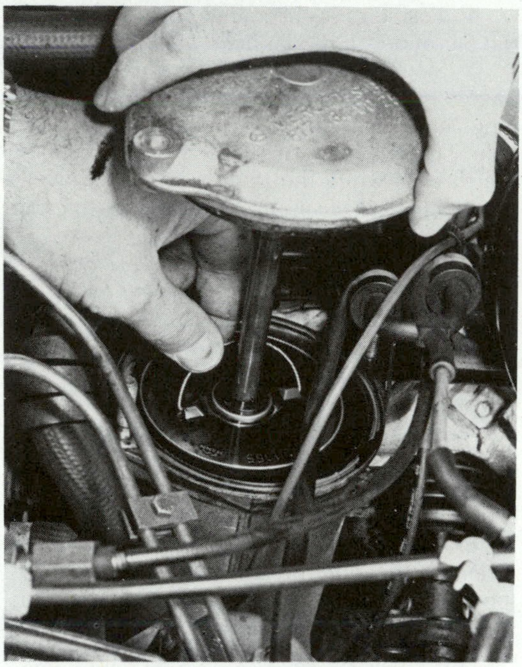

Remove the 2 bolts and lift the cover up, allowing the oil to drain back

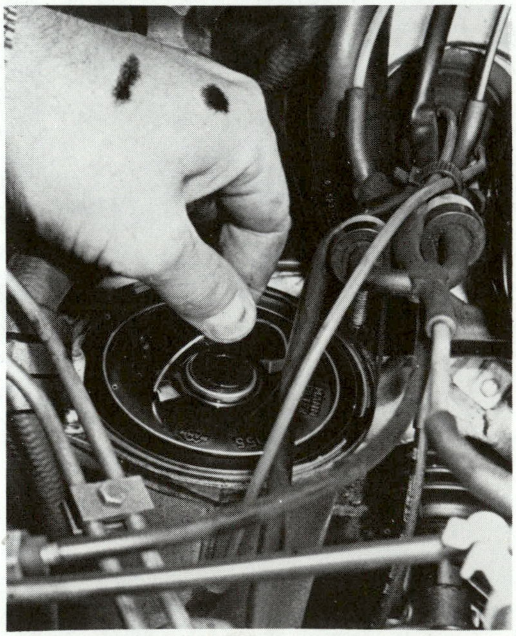

Remove the filter element from the diesel engine

6. Slowly unscrew the drain plug with your fingers and at the same time push the drain plug threads against the threads in the drain hole. This will prevent hot oil from leaking past the threads while the plug is being removed.

CAUTION: *The engine oil will be very hot.*

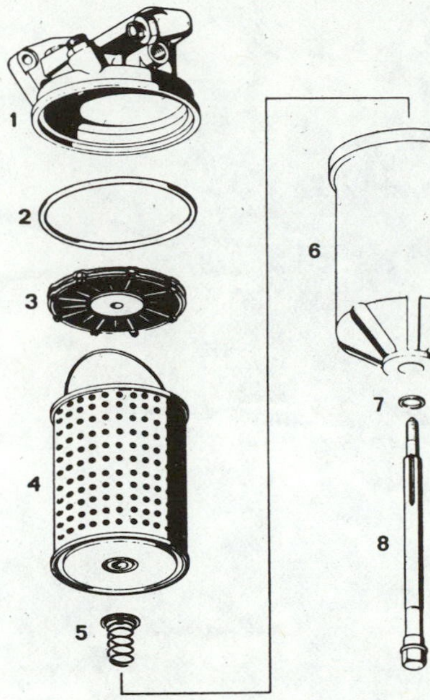

1. Upper housing
2. Rubber sealing ring
3. Filter screen
4. Filter element
5. Spring
6. Lower filter housing
7. Washer
8. Bolt

Diesel engine fuel filter—up to 1976. Later models use the upright oil filter

The flow screen (arrows) should be installed as shown

Be careful to stay out of the way as the oil drains out of the engine.

7. As the drain plug comes to the end of the threads, quickly remove it from the hole allowing the oil to escape. By using this method you can also avoid having to reach into a pan full of warm, dirty oil to retrieve the drain plug.

8. If so equipped, drain the oil from the oil cooler in the same manner.

9. On 1976 and earlier models carefully unscrew the oil filter bowl. This is done by holding the filter bowl and unscrewing the long bolt which holds it. Be careful, since there is still oil in the filter bowl.

10. On 1977 and later models, remove the cover, and lift out the filter element using the wire handle.

11. On 1976 and earlier models, empty the filter bowl, wash it out, and blow it dry.

12. Throw the old element away.

13. Check the condition of the sealing ring and renew if necessary.

14. Note the position of the pressure spring. This must be installed properly when the filter is assembled. *The upright filter with 2 attaching nuts (1 on the 190E) uses no pressure spring.*

15. Using pliers, wash out the fine mesh filter element in gasoline and blow it dry with low air pressure. 1977 and later models use no fine mesh filter.

16. Renew the large rubber sealing ring.

17. Install a new filter cartridge and the fine mesh filter (if so equipped). It is important that the filter be installed as shown. 1977 and later models use no fine mesh filter. Install the top to the housing.

NOTE: *At the first prescribed maintenance job (200–600 miles) the break-in filter is to be replaced with the service filter and the full flow fine mesh filter supplied.*

18. Renew the drain plug sealing rings and tighten the drain plugs.

19. Fill the engine with the proper amount of oil.

20. Remove the car from the jackstands and position the car on a level surface.

21. Run the engine and check for leaks.

CAUTION: *Do not run the engine above idle speed until it has built up oil pressure, indicated when the oil light goes out.*

22. Turn the engine off and wait several minutes for the oil to drain into the crankcase. Check the oil level.

Transmission

FLUID LEVEL CHECK

Manual Transmission

The transmission oil level should be checked at the recommended intervals or sooner. Since there is no dipstick, the level is checked at the filler and drain plugs. In the event that a major loss of oil is found, the problem should be found and corrected immediately.

Check the level when the fluid is hot. You'll need a 14 mm Allen socket to remove the plug. If fluid is needed use ATF, Type A, Suffix A.

1. With the car parked on a level surface, remove the filler plug (upper arrow in illustration) from the side of the transmission housing.

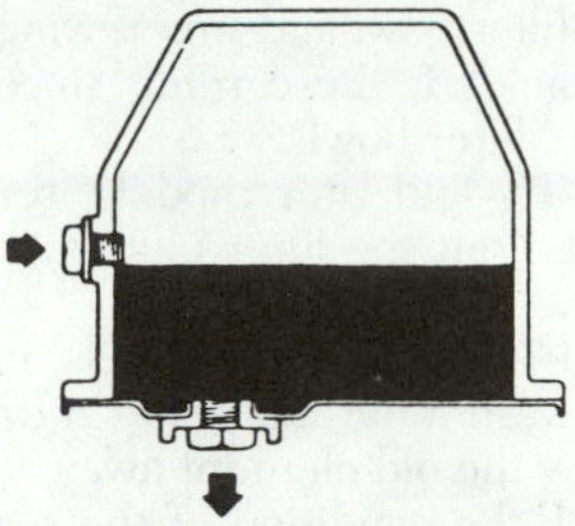

Manual transmission oil level should be up to the bottom of the filler (upper) plug hole

2. If the lubricant begins to trickle out of the hole, there is enough. Otherwise, carefully insert your finger (watch out for sharp threads) and check to see if the oil is up to the edge of the hole.

CAUTION: *Prolonged and repeated skin contact with used engine oil, with no effort to remove the oil, may be harmful. Always follow these simple precautions when handling used motor oil:*

- *Avoid prolonged skin contact with used motor oil.*
- *Remove oil from skin by washing thoroughly with soap and water or waterless hand cleaner. Do not use gasoline, thinners or other solvents.*
- *Avoid prolonged skin contact with oil-soaked clothing.*

3. If not, add oil through the hole until the level is at the edge of the hole. Most gear lubricants come in a plastic squeeze bottle with a nozzle, making additions simple. You can also use a common everyday kitchen baster.

4. Replace the filler plug, run the engine and check for leaks.

Automatic Transmission

Too little or too much fluid will impair the proper operation of the automatic transmission. The fluid level should be checked regularly (see "Maintenance Intervals") by using the transmission dipstick, which is accessible through the engine compartment. During this check, the car should be on a level surface and the engine and transmission should be at normal operating temperature.

1. Apply the parking brake.
2. Move the selector lever into the Park position.
3. Run the engine at normal operating temperature.
4. Remove the dipstick and wipe it with a clean, lint-free rag.

NOTE: *Some automatic transmissions have a clamp lock that must be released; others do not.*

The automatic transmission dipstick is located at the rear of the engine compartment. Some models have a small lever that must be unlocked to remove the dipstick

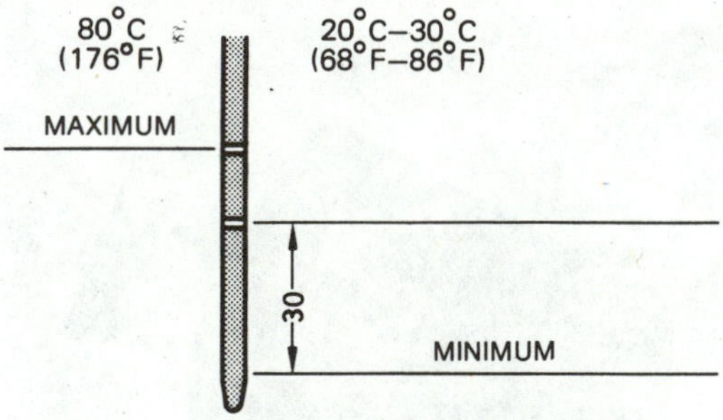

Fluid level of automatic transmissions. The minimum fluid level of all transmission covered by this book is 30 mm (1⅛ in.) below the mark on the dipstick

Add automatic transmission fluid through the dipstick tube

5. Insert the dipstick, remove it again, and read the fluid level.

6. With a correct fluid level and a warm transmission, the fluid level should be at the upper marking or at least between the two marks.

The fluid level will change with temperature. The "min" and "max" marks on the dipstick apply when the fluid is hot, after 5 minutes driving. When the fluid is cold, the fluid level will be approximately 1 in. below the minimum mark.

7. Additional oil (use only Dexron B) can be added through the dipstick guide (engine running) by using a funnel. Be careful not to add too much fluid. As a rough guide, there is approximately 0.3 quart between the maximum and minimum dipstick markings.

Bottom view of the automatic transmission showing (1) filler pipe, (2) converter drain plug and (3) bottom pan

DRAIN AND REFILL

Manual Transmission

The manual transmission oil should be changed at least every 25,000–30,000 miles. To change, proceed as follows:

1. The oil must be hot before it is drained. If the car is driven until the engine is at normal operating temperature, the oil should be hot enough.
2. Remove the filler plug to provide a vent.
3. The drain plug is on the bottom of the transmission. Place a large container underneath the transmission and remove the plug.
4. Allow the oil to drain completely. Clean off the plug and replace it using a new washer. Tighten it until it is just snug.
5. Fill the transmission with the proper lubricant. Use a plastic squeeze bottle with a long nozzle; or you can use a squeeze bulb or a kitchen baster to squirt the oil in. Refer to the "Capacities" chart for the proper amount of oil to put in.
6. The oil level should come up to the top of the filler hole.
7. Replace the filler plug, drive the car for a few minutes, stop, and check for any leaks.

Automatic Transmission

Before attempting to drain the transmission fluid, be sure that the vehicle is on level ground and that the transmission is at normal operating temperature. The engine should be shut off.

1. Drain the fluid from the transmission either by removing the filler pipe under the transmission or by removing the drain plug.
2. Observe the same safety precautions as are listed for "Engine Oil Changes," regarding hot oil and safety.
3. When all the fluid is drained, remove the transmission oil pan. Be sure the filler pipe is disconnected.
4. Replace the oil filter, making sure that all bolts are tightened. The oil filter should not be cleaned, but replaced with a new one.

CAUTION: *The filter may have oil remaining in it.*

5. Clean the inside of the pan with a clean lint-free rag.
6. Install the oil pan.
7. Install the filler pipe or drain plug using new washers or gaskets in each case.
8. Insert a funnel with a fine mesh strainer into the dipstick tube and add a large portion (not all) of the transmission oil capacity. This should be done with the engine stopped.
9. Start the engine and run it at idle speed with the selector lever in Park. Gradually add the remaining fluid. Do not overfill the transmission.
10. Check the oil level with the transmission at operating temperature.
11. Be sure to remove any excess fluid.

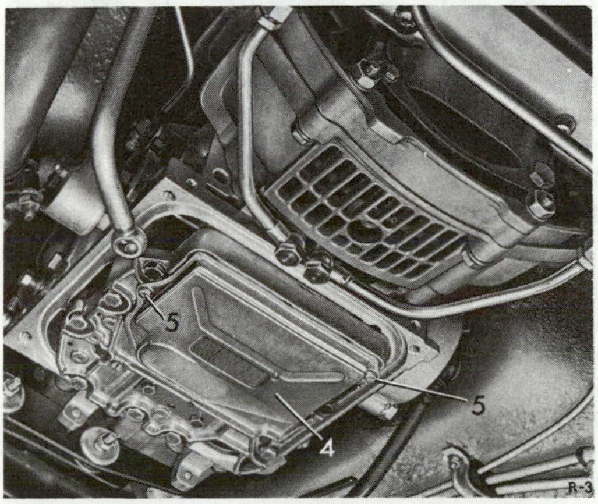

Bottom view of automatic transmission with pan removed

Rear Axle

FLUID LEVEL CHECK

The rear axle lubricant should be checked at the interval specified in the chart, or sooner.

1. Before checking the rear axle lubricant level, be sure that the vehicle is on level ground.
2. Slowly unscrew the drain plug from the oil filler hole (upper hole). You will need a 14mm hex allen wrench. If the lubricant level is satisfactory, lubricant will begin to seep past the threads of the plug. If lubricant does not seep past the threads, remove the plug entirely. The lubricant level should be up to the bottom of the filler hole. If not, lubricant can be added through the filler hole by using a pressure gun. Add only enough lubricant to bring the level to the bottom edge of the filler hole.

   NOTE: *Rear axles without limited slip may use any high quality SAE 90 hypoid gear oil. The limited slip differential can be filled only with special Limited Slip Special lubricant available at Mercedes-Benz dealers. Identification of this type differential is by a plate attached to the rear axle housing, reading "Achtung Spezial—Öl Sperr-differential." (Caution! Special oil—limited slip differential.)*
3. Replace the oil filler plug.

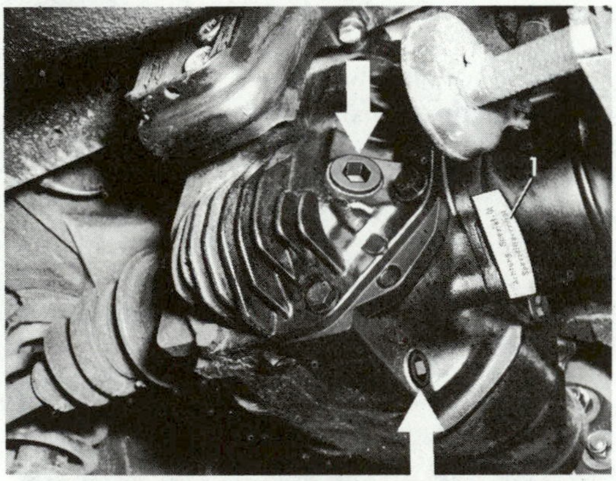

Check the rear axle fluid level at the upper (fill) plug. Bottom plug is the drain plug and (1) is the special tag designating a limited slip rear axle

DRAIN AND REFILL

The rear axle need not be drained regularly, but if desired, the car must be on a level surface with the weight on the wheels or with the axle tubes supported by jackstands. This is necessary to prevent oil from entering the axle tubes.

1. Remove the bottom drain plug and loosen the top drain plug.
2. After the fluid has drained, replace the bottom drain plug using a new washer.
3. Refill the unit with the specified lubricant. Be sure that the proper lubricant is used. Consult the "Oil and Fuel Recommendations" section.
4. Replace the top plug using a new washer. The fluid level should be at the top of the oil filler opening.

Coolant

LEVEL CHECK

Dealing with the cooling system can be a dangerous matter unless the proper precautions are observed. It is best to check the coolant level in the radiator when the engine is cold. This is done by removing the radiator cap and seeing that the coolant reaches the mark on the bottom of the filler neck. On later models, the cooling system has, as one of its components, an expansion tank. As long as the coolant is visible above the "Low" mark on the tank, the level is satisfactory. Always be certain that the filler caps on both the radiator and the reservoir are tightly closed.

In the event that the coolant level must be checked when the engine is warm on engines without the expansion tank, place a thick rag over the radiator cap and slowly turn the cap counterclockwise until it reaches the first detent. Allow all the hot steam to escape. This will allow the pressure in the system to drop

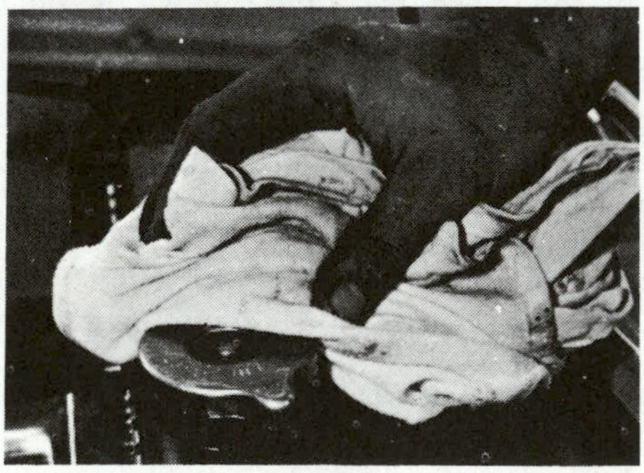

If the engine is hot, cover the radiator cap with a rag

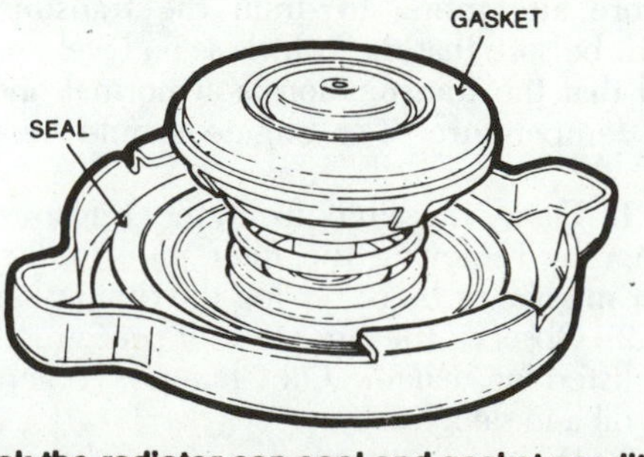

Check the radiator cap seal and gasket condition

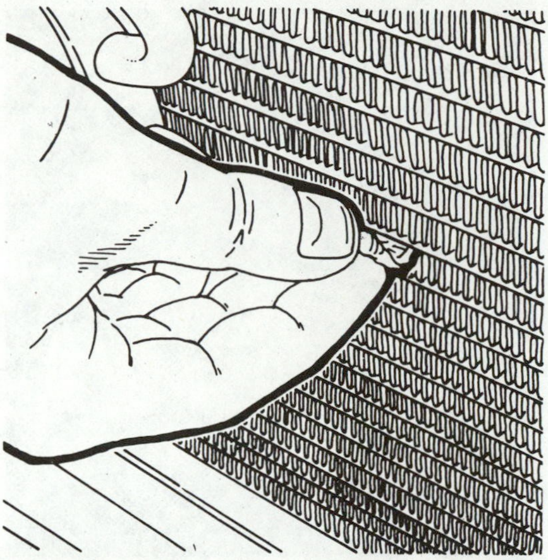

Clean the radiator fins of any debris which impedes air flow

gradually, preventing an explosion of hot coolant. When the hissing noise stops, remove the cap the rest of the way.

If the coolant level is low, add equal amounts of ethylene glycol-based antifreeze and clean water. On models without an expansion tank, add coolant through the radiator filler neck. Fill the expansion tank to the "Full" level on cars with that system.

CAUTION: *Never add cold coolant to a hot engine unless the engine is running, to avoid cracking the engine block.*

If the coolant level is chronically low or rusty, refer to Chapter 10 for diagnosis of the problem.

The radiator hoses and clamps and the radiator cap should be checked at the same time as

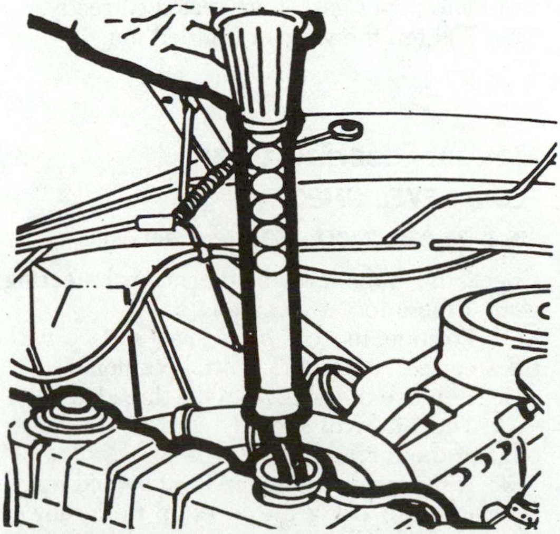

The freezing protection rating can be checked with an antifreeze tester

the coolant level. Hoses which are brittle, cracked, or swollen should be replaced. Clamps should be checked for tightness (screwdriver tight only—do not allow the clamp to cut into the hose or crush the fitting). The radiator cap gasket should be checked for any obvious tears, cracks, or swelling, or any signs of incorrect seating in the radiator neck.

Check the freezing protection rating at least once a year, preferably just before the winter sets in. This can be done with an antifreeze tester (most service stations will have one on hand and will probably check it for you, if not, they are available at an auto parts store). Maintain a protection rating of at least −20°F (−29°C) to prevent engine damage as a result of freezing and to assure the proper engine operating temperature.

DRAIN SYSTEM, FLUSH AND REFILL

The cooling system should be drained, thoroughly flushed and then refilled at least every 25,000–30,000 miles. This should be done with the engine cold.

1. Remove the radiator cap and the expansion tank cap (if so equipped).

On models with a plastic expansion tank, the level should be at the mark on the reservoir (arrow)

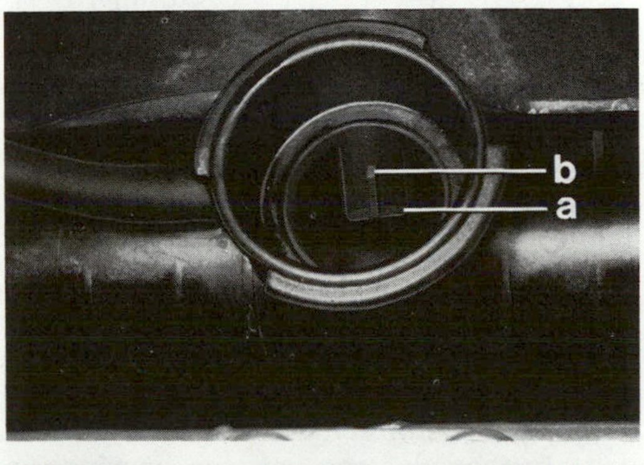

1977 and later models (except 450, 280SE and 300SD) have a plastic tab in the radiator neck. a = minimum, b = maximum

2. With the caps removed, run the engine until the upper radiator hose is hot. This means that the thermostat is open and the coolant is flowing through the system.

3. With the engine stopped, open the radiator drain cock located at the bottom of the radiator, and (to speed the draining) the engine block drain on the right-hand side. Before opening the radiator drain, it is a good idea to soak it for a few minutes with penetrating oil to loosen it. The radiator can also be emptied by siphoning, using the type of siphon used for pilfering gasoline, or coolant can be drained by removing the lower radiator hose.

NOTE: *Do not attempt to siphon coolant by sucking on the end of a hose. The coolant is poisonous and can cause death or serious illness if swallowed.*

4. Completely drain the coolant, and close the drain cocks. Add clean water until the system is filled.

5. Repeat Steps 3 and 4 several times until the drained liquid is nearly colorless.

6. Tighten the drain valve and then fill the radiator with a 50/50 mixture of ethylene glycol and water.

7. With the radiator cap still removed, run the engine until the upper radiator hose is hot. Add coolant if necessary, replace the caps and check for any leaks.

Brake Master Cylinder

FLUID LEVEL CHECK

The brake master cylinder is attached to the brake booster which is located on the firewall (driver's side). To check the fluid level, proceed as follows.

1. Clean the area around the cap since even minute particles of dirt can cause a malfunction of the system.

2. Remove the top from the reservoir and check to see that the fluid is up to the marks stamped in the reservoir.

3. Add fluid, if necessary, to bring the level up to the marks.

NOTE: *Use only a high quality brake fluid. Mercedes-Benz recommends ATE Blue Original brake fluid. In countries where this is difficult to obtain, use only fluid which meets or exceeds SAE J 1703B standards. This will be marked on the container.*

CAUTION: *Do not allow brake fluid to contact the vehicle paintwork because brake fluid acts as a solvent.*

4. Replace the reservoir cap, making sure that the ventilation bore in the top is not blocked.

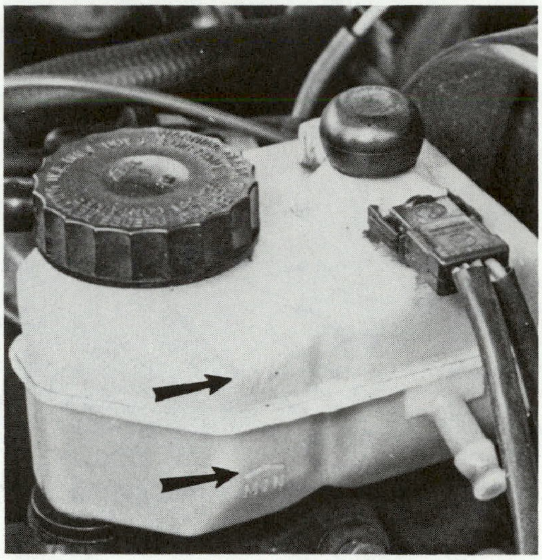

The maximum and minimum marks (arrows) are molded into the master cylinder reservoir

Power Steering Pump Reservoir

FLUID LEVEL CHECK

Check the level of the fluid in the power steering reservoir at the interval specified in the chart.

1. Position the car on a level surface and center the steering gear.

2. Loosen the wing nut or knurled nut and remove the reservoir cover.

3. With the fluid at operating temperature, the fluid should reach to the mark stamped in the reservoir. If not, add sufficient automatic transmission fluid (ATF) to bring the level up to the mark.

4. Replace the cover and be sure that the cover and paper gasket are seated correctly.

5. Tighten the wing or knurled nut.

Manual Steering Gear

FLUID LEVEL CHECK

1974–76 230, 240D, 300D and 280 Only

Check the fluid level of the manual steering gear at the interval specified.

1. Position the car on a level surface with the steering gear in the central position.

2. Remove the plug from the threaded hole.

3. The oil level should reach to the lower edge of the threaded hole.

4. If not, add enough SAE 90 hypoid transmission oil to bring the level up to the lower edge of the hole.

5. Replace the plug.

The fluid level in the power steering pump should reach the mark (arrow) cast or stamped into the side of the reservoir

Hydro-Pnuematic Suspension Reservoir

FLUID LEVEL CHECK

450 Series Sedans, 300TD and 6.9 Only

The hydro-pneumatic suspension uses a special oil. See the list of approved oils in the beginning of this chapter.

The car should be level and the engine warm.

1. Remove the cover from the oil reservoir. The reservoir is located at the driver's side front corner of the engine compartment.
2. Remove the dipstick and wipe it clearn.
3. Reinsert the dipstick and read the oil level. It should be between the maximum and minimum marks on the dipstick. There is about 2 pts between the "max" and "min" levels.

Remove the plug (40) to check the fluid level in the manual steering gear

Clutch Master Cylinder

FLUID LEVEL CHECK

Some models use a separate clutch master cylinder, located next to the brake master cylinder. Other models, use the brake master cylinder as a reservoir and have a separate line leading to the clutch master cylinder.

If your car has a common reservoir, refer to the section on checking the fluid level in the brake master cylinder, in this chapter. If your car has a separate reservoir, the level should be maintained at the mark on the plastic reservoir.

Regardless of which type you have, clean the ventilation bore in the cap.

Check the fluid level in the hydropneumatic suspension reservoir (2) with the dipstick (2a). a and b are the maximum and minimum marks

Carburetor Damper Reservoir

FLUID LEVEL CHECK

230 Only

Up to 1976 models, use ATF in the carburetor damper. Beginning with 1977 models, use ATF in the winter and engine oil in the summer.

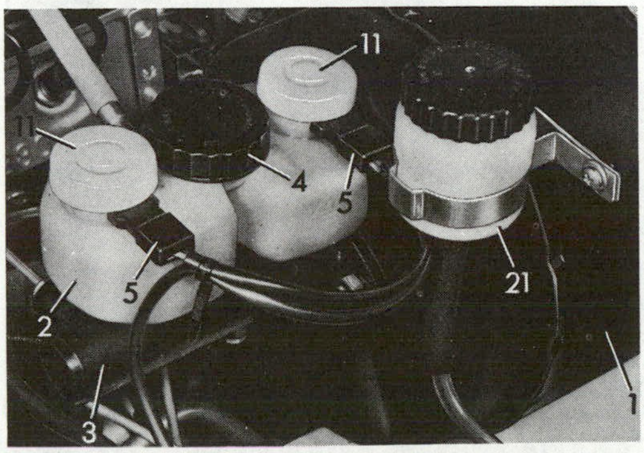

Some 240D's have a separate clutch master cylinder (21)

Some carburetor models use an oil reservoir and some do not. If no reservoir is used, unscrew and remove the damper. The oil level should be at the upper edge of the piston pin. If a reservoir is used, the oil level should be as specified (see illustration).

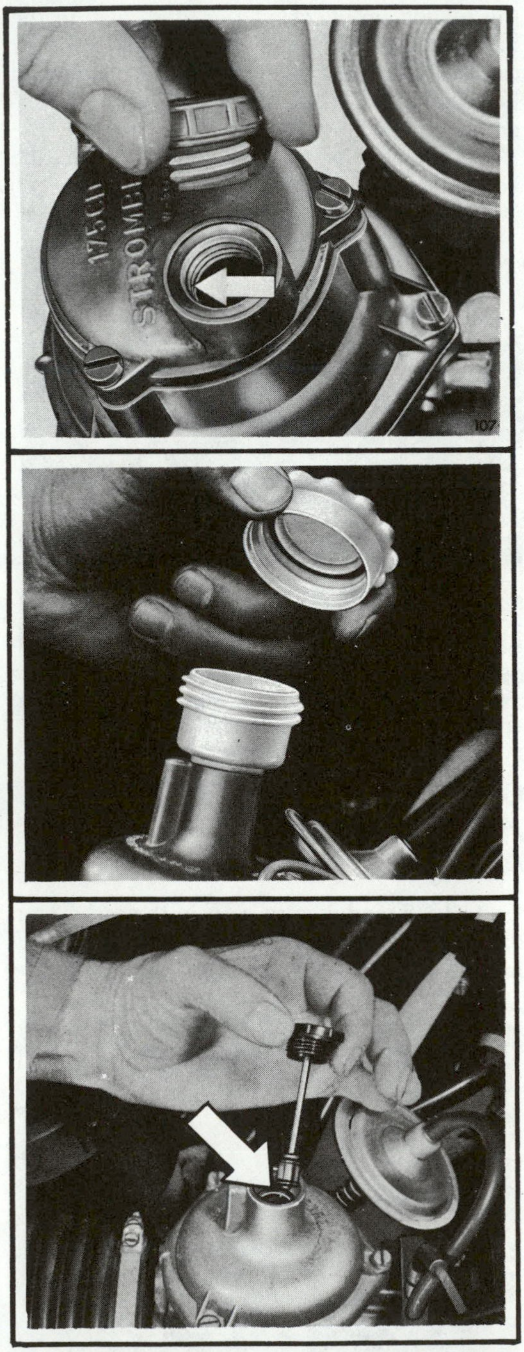

There are 3 different ways to check oil level in the Stromberg carburetor used on 230 models. Your carburetor will look like one of these

Injection Pump

FLUID LEVEL CHECK

Diesel Engines Only

1. Screw out the check screw.
2. If there is too much oil, allow the oil to drain as far as the check bore.
3. If no oil flows from the check bore, unscrew the filter and add engine oil up to the check bore.

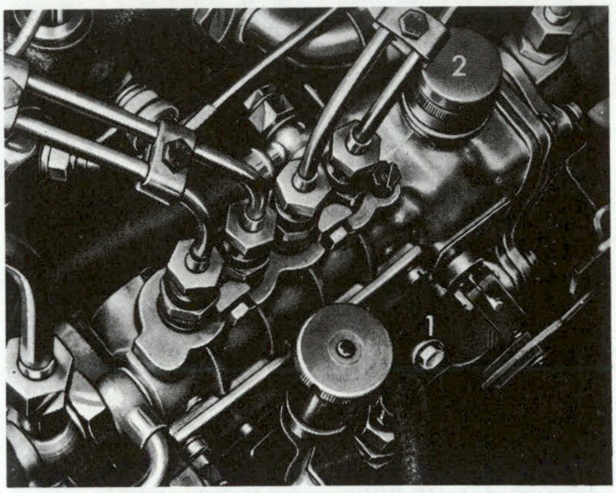

Check the oil level in the injection pump at the plug (1). If necessary, add engine oil at opening (2)

CHASSIS GREASING

It is not necessary to lubricate the chassis of models covered in this book. Development and use of long term lubricants has made this unnecessary.

BODY LUBRICATION

The following points should be lubricated with multipurpose, lithium base chassis grease. The door hinges require the use of a grease gun; at other points, lubricant can be applied on the end of your finger.

Other points on the body should be lubricated with engine oil.

TOWING

All Models

For towing, the vehicle has a tow ring at the front of the chassis side member. A similar ring is provided at the rear for attaching a tow rope. It goes without saying that these tow rings are for emergency use and for short distances only. A strong, flexible, woven fabric strap should be used. Never use a steel cable or rope.

CAUTION: *Whenever a vehicle is towed, for any reason, great care should be used.*

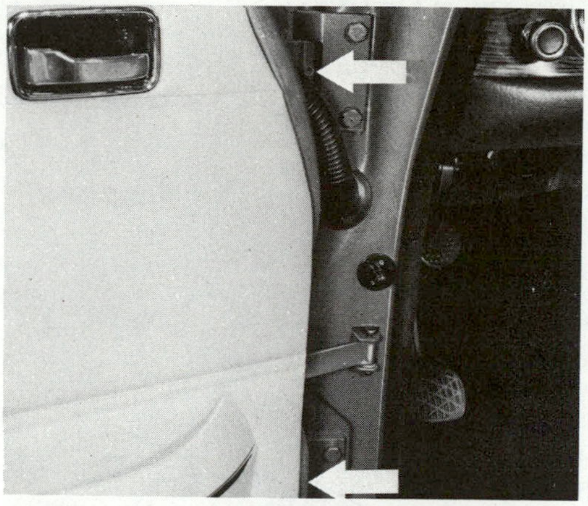

Front door hinges (chassis grease)

Hood hinges (engine oil)

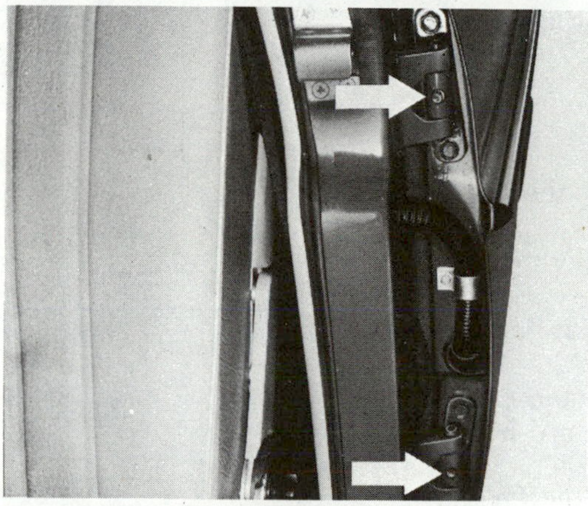

Rear door hinges (chassis grease)

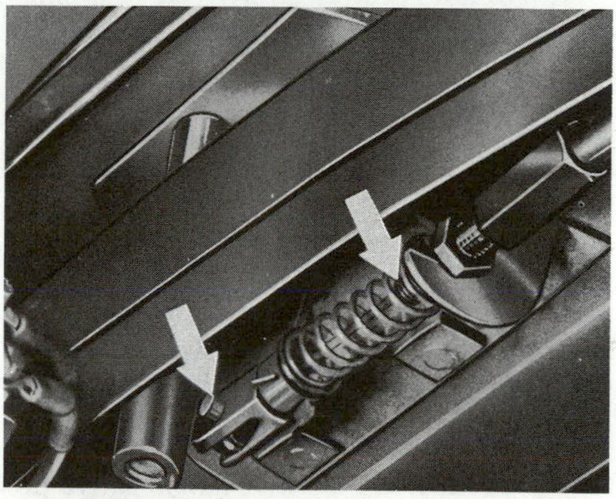

Hood release (engine oil)

Door tumbler locks (chassis grease)

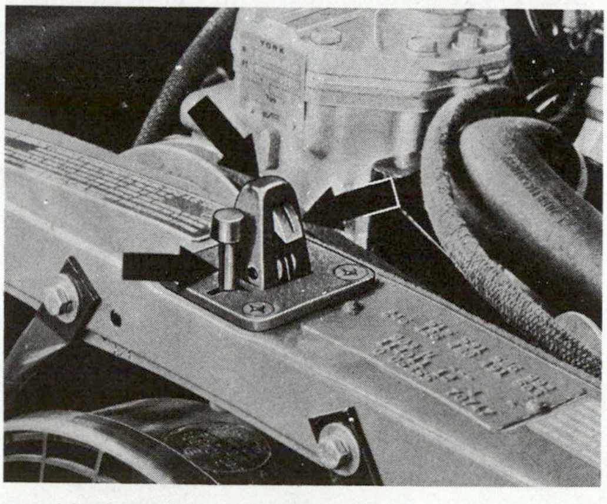

Hood lock on frame (engine oil)

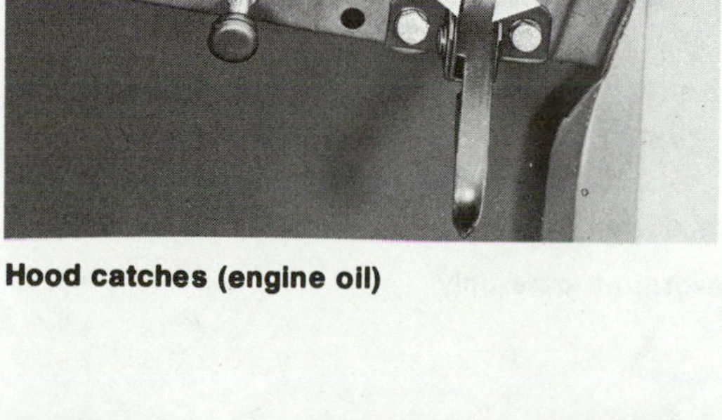

Hood catches (engine oil)

WHEEL BEARINGS

Refer to Chapter 9 for wheel bearing service, adjustment and repacking.

JUMP STARTING A DEAD BATTERY

The chemical reaction in a battery produces explosive hydrogen gas. This is the safe way to jump start a dead battery, reducing the chances of an accidental spark that could cause an explosion.

Jump Starting Precautions

1. Be sure both batteries are of the same voltage.
2. Be sure both batteries are of the same polarity (have the same grounded terminal).
3. Be sure the vehicles are not touching.
4. Be sure the vent cap holes are not obstructed.
5. Do not smoke or allow sparks around the battery.
6. In cold weather, check for frozen electrolyte in the battery.
7. Do not allow electrolyte on your skin or clothing.
8. Be sure the electrolyte is not frozen.

Jump Starting Procedure

1. Determine voltages of the two batteries; they must be the same.
2. Bring the starting vehicle close (they must not touch) so that the batteries can be reached easily.
3. Turn off all accessories and both engines. Put both cars in Neutral or Park and set the handbrake.
4. Cover the cell caps with a rag—do not cover terminals.
5. If the terminals on the run-down battery are heavily corroded, clean them.
6. Identify the positive and negative posts on both batteries and connect the cables in the order shown.
7. Start the engine of the starting vehicle and run it at fast idle. Try to start the car with the dead battery. Crank it for no more than 10 seconds at a time and let it cool off for 20 seconds in between tries.
8. If it doesn't start in 3 tries, there is something else wrong.
9. Disconnect the cables in the reverse order.
10. Replace the cell covers and dispose of the rags.

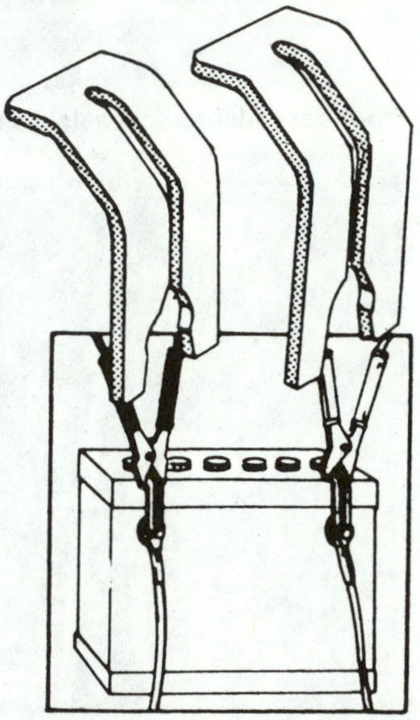

Side terminal batteries occasionally pose a problem when connecting jumper cables. There frequently isn't enough room to clamp the cables without touching sheet metal. Side terminal adaptors are available to alleviate this problem and should be removed after use.

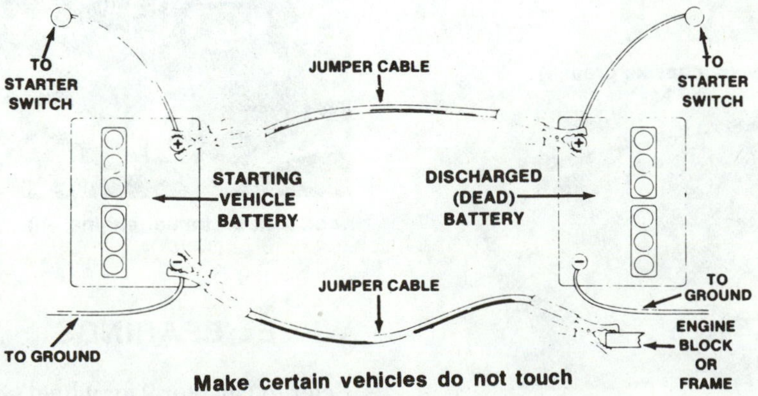

Make certain vehicles do not touch

This hook-up for negative ground cars only

Vehicles equipped with manual transmissions should be towed in Neutral and vehicles with automatic transmissions should be towed with the selector lever in Neutral. The towing speed should never exceed 30 miles per hour.

CAUTION: *On vehicles with a damaged front end, the driveshaft must be disconnected to ensure that cooling water does not enter the transmission fluid or that the transmission is no longer lubricated due to an interrupted oil circuit.*

JACKING AND HOISTING

The bumper jack supplied with the car should never be used for any service operation other than tire changing. NEVER get under the car while it is supported by the tire changing jack. Always block the wheels when changing tires.

The service operations in this book often require that one end of the car, or both, be raised and supported safely. The best arrangement is a vehicle hoist. A hydraulic floor jack is not often found in the home garage, but there are reasonable and safe substitutes. Small hydraulic, screw, or scissors jacks are satisfactory for raising the car. Heavy wooden blocks or adjustable jackstands should be used to support the car while it is being worked on.

NOTE: *Concrete blocks are not recommended. They may break if the load is not evenly distributed.*

Drive-on trestles or ramps are a handy and safe way to raise the car. These can be bought or constructed from suitable heavy timbers or steel.

In any case, it is always best to spend a little extra time to make sure that the car is lifted and supported safely.

When raising the vehicle with the jack supplied, be sure to position the chocks which are supplied in the vehicle's trunk.

Position the chocks as follows:

1. On level ground, place one chock in front of the wheel and one chock behind the wheel on the opposite side from which you are working.
2. On a grade, place one chock behind the front and rear wheels on the opposite side of the jack.
3. On vehicles with a manual transmission, place the transmission in Low gear. On vehicles with an automatic transmission, place the selector lever in Park.
4. Always be sure to set the parking brake firmly.
5. Always position the vehicle jack vertically.

In a shop, the vehicle is best lifted with a pit jack or cross-head jack. To lift the car with a pit jack, the jack should be under the front and rear axle. This also applies to floor jacks.

HOW TO BUY A USED CAR

Many people believe that a two or three year old used car is a better buy than a new car. This may be true; the new car suffers the heaviest depreciation in the first two years, but is not old enough to present a lot of costly repair problems. Whatever the age of the used car you might want to buy, this section and a little patience will help you select one that should be safe and dependable.

Tips

1. First decide what model you want, and how much you want to spend.
2. Check the used car lots and your local newspaper ads. Privately owned cars are usually less expensive, however you will not get a warranty that, in most cases, comes with a used car purchased from a lot.
3. Never shop at night. The glare of the lights make it easy to miss faults on the body caused by accident or rust repair.
4. Try to get the name and phone number of the previous owner. Contact him/her and ask about the car. If the owner of the lot refuses this information, look for a car somewhere else.

A private seller can tell you about the car and maintenance. Remember, however, there's no law requiring honesty from private citizens selling used cars. There is a law that forbids the tampering with or turning back the odometer mileage. This includes both the private citizen and the lot owner. The law also requires that the seller or anyone transferring ownership of the car must provide the buyer with a signed statement indicating the mileage on the odometer at the time of transfer.

5. Write down the year, model and serial number before you buy any used car. Then dial 1-800-424-9393, the toll free number of the National Highway Traffic Safety Administration, and ask if the car has ever been included on any manufacturer's recall list. If so, make sure the needed repairs were made.
6. Use the "Used Car Checklist" in this section and check all the items on the used car you are considering. Some items are more important than others. You know how much money you can afford for repairs, and, depending on the price of the car, may consider doing any needed work yourself. Beware, however, of trouble in areas that will affect operation, safety

or emission. Problems in the "Used Car Checklist" break down as follows:

1–8: Two or more problems in these areas indicate a lack of maintenance. You should beware.

9–13: Indicates a lack of proper care, however, these can usually be corrected with a tune-up or relatively simple parts replacement.

14–17: Problems in the engine or transmission can be very expensive. Walk away from any car with problems in both of these areas.

7. If you are satisfied with the apparent condition of the car, take it to an independent diagnostic center or mechanic for a complete check. If you have a state inspection program, have it inspected immediately before purchase, or specify on the bill of sale that the sale is conditional on passing state inspection.

8. Road test the car—refer to the "Road Test Checklist" in this section. If your original evaluation and the road test agree—the rest is up to you.

Used Car Checklist

NOTE: *The numbers on the illustrations refer to the numbers on this checklist.*

1. *Mileage:* Average mileage is about 12,000 miles per year. More than average mileage may indicate hard usage. 1975 and later catalytic converter equipped models may need converter service at 50,000 miles.

2. *Paint:* Check around the tailpipe, molding and windows for overspray indicating that the car has been repainted.

3. *Rust:* Check fenders, doors, rocker panels, window moldings, wheelwells, floorboards, under floormats, and in the trunk for signs of rust. Any rust at all will be a problem. There is no way to check the spread of rust, except to replace the part or panel.

4. *Body appearance:* Check the moldings, bumpers, grille, vinyl roof, glass, doors, trunk lid and body panels for general overall condition. Check for misalignment, loose holdown clips, ripples, scratches in glass, welding in the trunk, severe misalignment of body panels or ripples may indicate crash work.

5. *Leaks:* Get down and look under the car. There are no normal "leaks," other than water from the air conditioning condenser.

6. *Tires:* Check the tire air pressure. A common trick is to pump the tire pressure up to make the car roll easier. Check the tread wear, open the trunk and check the spare too. Uneven wear is a clue that the front end needs alignment. See the troubleshooting chapter for clues to the causes of tire wear.

7. *Shock absorbers:* Check the shock absorbers by forcing downward sharply on each corner of the car. Good shocks will not allow the car to bounce more than twice after you let go.

8. *Interior:* Check the entire interior. You're looking for an interior condition that agrees with the overall condition of the car. Reasonable wear is expected, but be suspicious of new seatcovers on sagging seats, new pedal pads, and worn armrests. These indicate an attempt to cover up hard use. Pull back the carpets and look for evidence of water leaks or flooding. Look for missing hardware, door handles, control knobs, etc. Check lights and signal operations. Make

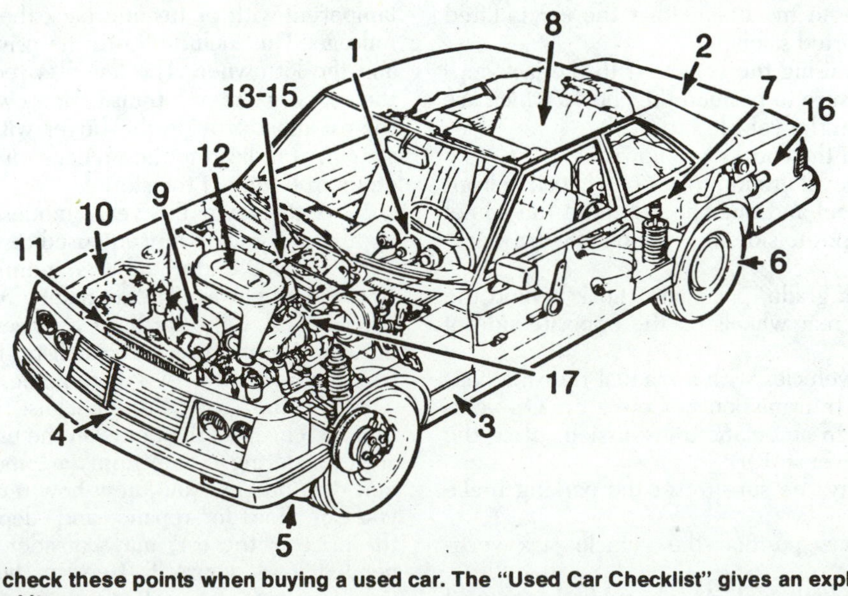

You should check these points when buying a used car. The "Used Car Checklist" gives an explanation of the numbered items

sure all accessories (air conditioner, heater, radio, etc.) work. Check windshield wiper operation.

9. *Belts and Hoses:* Open the hood and check all belts and hoses for wear, cracks or weak spots.

10. *Battery:* Low electrolyte level, corroded terminals and/or cracked case indicate a lack of maintenance.

11. *Radiator:* Look for corrosion or rust in the coolant indicating a lack of maintenance.

12. *Air filter:* A dirty air filter usually means a lack of maintenance.

13. *Ignition Wires:* Check the ignition wires for cracks, burned spots, or wear. Worn wires will have to be replaced.

14. *Oil level:* If the oil level is low, chances are the engine uses oil or leaks. Beware of water in the oil (cracked block), excessively thick oil (used to quiet a noisy engine), or thin, dirty oil with a distinct gasoline smell (internal engine problems).

15. *Automatic Transmission:* Pull the transmission dipstick out when the engine is running. The level should read "Full," and the fluid should be clear or bright red. Dark brown or black fluid that has distinct burnt odor, signals a transmission need of repair or overhaul.

16. *Exhaust:* Check the color of the exhaust smoke. Blue smoke indicates, among other problems, worn rings; black smoke can indicate burnt valves or carburetor problems. Check the exhaust system for leaks; it can be expensive to replace.

17. *Spark Plugs:* Remove one of the spark plugs (the most accessible will do). An engine in good condition will show plugs with a light tan or gray deposit on the firing tip. See the color Tune-Up tips section for spark plug conditions.

Road Test Check List

1. *Engine Performance:* The car should be peppy whether cold or warm, with adequate power and good pickup. It should respond smoothly through the gears.

2. *Brakes:* They should provide quick, firm stops with no noise, pulling or brake fade.

3. *Steering:* Sure control with no binding, harshness, or looseness and no shimmy in the wheel should be expected. Noise or vibration from the steering wheel when turning the car means trouble.

4. *Clutch (Manual Transmission):* Clutch action should give quick, smooth response with easy shifting. The clutch pedal should have about 1–1½ inches of free-play before it disengages the clutch. Start the engine, set the parking brake, put the transmission in first gear and slowly release the clutch pedal. The engine should begin to stall when the pedal is one-half to three-quarters of the way up.

5. *Automatic Transmission:* The transmission should shift rapidly and smoothly, with no noise, hesitation, or slipping.

6. *Differential:* No noise or thumps should be present. Differentials have no "normal" leaks.

7. *Driveshaft, Universal Joints:* Vibration and noise could mean driveshaft problems. Clicking at low speed or coast conditions means worn U-joints.

8. *Suspension:* Try hitting bumps at different speeds. A car that bounces has weak shock absorbers. Clunks mean worn bushings or ball joints.

9. *Frame:* Wet the tires and drive in a straight line. Tracks should show two straight lines, not four. Four tire tracks indicate a frame bent by collision damage. If the tires can't be wet for this purpose, have a friend drive along behind you and see if the car appears to be traveling in a straight line.

Tune-Up and Performance Maintenance

2

TUNE-UP PROCEDURES

In order to extract the full measure of performance and economy from your engine it is essential that it be properly tuned at regular intervals. A regular tune-up will keep your Mercedes' engine running smoothly and will prevent the annoying minor breakdowns and poor performance associated with an untuned engine.

A complete tune-up should be performed every 15,000 miles or twelve months, whichever comes first. This interval should be halved if the car is operated under severe conditions, such as trailer towing, prolonged idling, continual stop and start driving, or if starting or running problems are noticed. It is assumed that the routine maintenance described in Chapter 1 has been kept up, as this will have a decided effect on the results of a tune-up. All of the applicable steps of a tune-up should be followed in order, as the result is a cumulative one.

If the specifications on the tune-up sticker in the engine compartment of your Mercedes-Benz disagree with the "Tune-Up Specifications" chart in this chapter, the figures on the sticker must be used. The sticker often reflects changes made during the production run.

Spark Plugs

Spark plugs ignite the air and fuel mixture in the cylinder as the piston reaches the top of the compression stroke. The controlled explosion that results forces the piston down, turning the crankshaft and the rest of the drive train.

The average life of a normal, non-platinum tipped spark plug is 15,000 miles. This is, however, dependent on a number of factors: the mechanical condition of the engine; the type of fuel; the driving conditions; and the driver.

When you remove the spark plugs, check their condition. They are a good indicator of the condition of the engine. It is a good idea to remove the spark plugs every 6,000 miles to keep an eye on the mechanical state of the engine.

A small deposit of light tan or gray material (or rust red with unleaded fuel) on a spark plug that has been used for any period of time is to be considered normal. Any other color, or abnormal amounts of deposit, indicates that there is something amiss in the engine.

The gap between the center electrode and the side or ground electrode can be expected to increase not more than 0.001 in. every 1,000 miles under normal conditions.

When a spark plug is functioning normally or, more accurately, when the plug is installed in an engine that is functioning properly, the plugs can be taken out, cleaned, regapped, and reinstalled in the engine without doing the engine any harm.

When, and if, a plug fouls and begins to misfire, you will have to investigate, correct the cause of the fouling, and either clean or replace the plug.

There are several reasons why a spark plug will foul and you can learn which is at fault by just looking at the plug. A few of the most common reasons for plug fouling, and a description of the fouled plug's appearance, are listed in the "Color Insert," which also offers solutions to the problems.

Spark plugs suitable for use in your Mercedes' engine are offered in a number of different heat ranges. The amount of heat which the plug absorbs is determined by the length of the lower insulator. The longer the insulator, the hotter the plug will operate; the shorter the insulator, the cooler it will operate. A spark plug that absorbs (or retains) little heat and remains too cool will accumulate deposits of lead, oil, and carbon, because it is not hot enough to burn them off. This leads to fouling and consequent mis-

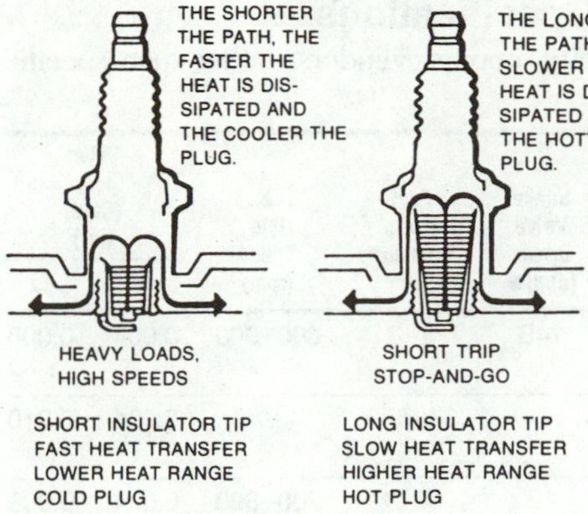

Spark plug heat range

firing. A spark plug that absorbs too much heat will have no deposits, but the electrodes will burn away quickly and, in some cases, pre-ignition may result. Pre-ignition occurs when the spark plug tips get so hot that they ignite the fuel/air mixture before the actual spark fires. This premature ignition will usually cause a pinging sound under conditions of low speed and heavy load. In severe cases, the heat may become high enough to start the fuel/air mixture burning throughout the combustion chamber rather than just to the front of the plug. In this case, the resultant explosion will be strong enough to damage pistons, rings, and valves.

In most cases the factory recommended heat range is correct; it is chosen to perform well under a wide range of operating conditions. However, if most of your driving is long distance, high speed travel, you may want to install a spark plug one step colder than standard. If most of your driving is of the short trip variety, when the engine may not always reach operating temperature, a hotter plug may help burn off the deposits normally accumulated under those conditions.

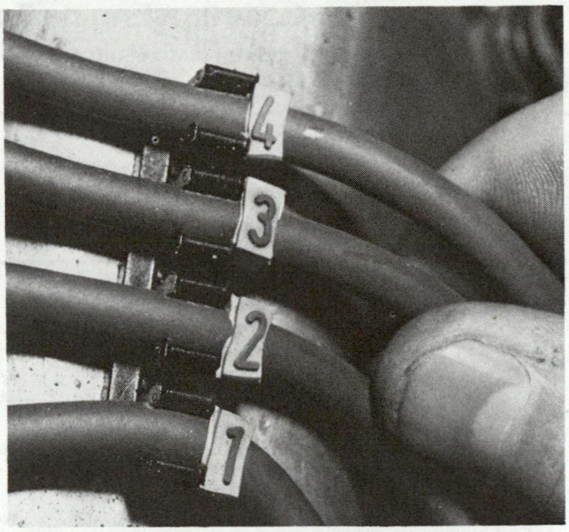

Most Mercedes-Benz engines have rubber rings around the spark plug wire showing the cylinder number

The plugs wires are also numbered at the distributor cap, since it is usually impossible to follow the wires once they disappear inside the protective harness

REMOVAL

Spark plugs should be removed, inspected and regapped or replaced one at a time to avoid confusion. Make a mental note of the location of each plug to analyze possible problems.

1. Raise the hood and locate all of the spark plugs.
2. The spark plug leads on most Mercedes-Benz engines are numbered at the cap and on the wire by small yellow rings. If the spark plug wires are not numbered by cylinder, mark each wire with a small piece of masking tape.
3. Grasp each wire by the rubber boot. Pull the wires from the spark plugs one at a time. If the wires do not come off readily, remove them with a slight twisting motion. Never pull the wires off by the wires themselves.
4. Blow out the recesses around the spark plugs to remove accumulated dirt. This is especially necessary with the overhead cam 6-cylinder engine.
5. Using a spark plug socket and extension (if necessary), loosen the spark plug a few turns.
6. Blow out the accumulated dirt again or, if compressed air is not available, wipe the dirt away with a clean cloth. The object is not to allow any foreign material to enter the cylinder.

Gasoline Engine Tune-Up Specifications

When analyzing compression test results, look for uniformity among cylinders, rather than specific pressures.

		Spark Plugs							Valve Clear* (Cold) (in.)	
Year	Model	Type	Gap (in.)	Distributor Point Dwell (deg)	Ignition Timing (deg) ①	Intake Valve Opens (deg)●	Fuel Pump Pressure (psi)	▲ Idle Speed (rpm)	In	Ex
1974	230	N9Y	0.024	47–53	10B w/vacuum	14B	2–3	800–900	0.004	0.008
	280, 280C	N9Y	0.024	34–40	4A w/vacuum	②	3.5–5.0	④	0.004	0.010
	450SE, 450SEL	N9Y	0.024	30–34	5A w/vacuum	4B	30 ③	700–800	0.004	0.008
	450SL, 450SLC	N9Y	0.024	30–34	5A w/vacuum	4B	30 ③	700–800	0.004	0.008
1975	230	N9Y	0.024	47–53	10B w/o vacuum	14B	2–3	800–900	0.004	0.008
	280, 280C, 280S	N9Y	0.024	34–40	7B w/vacuum	7B	3.5–5.0	800–900	0.004	0.010
	450SE, 450SEL	N9Y	0.024	30–34	TDC w/vacuum	⑤	30 ③	700–800	0.004	0.008
	450SL, 450SLC	N9Y	0.024	30–34	TDC w/vacuum	⑤	30 ③	700–800	0.004	0.008
1976	230	N9Y	0.024	47–53	10B w/o vacuum	14B	2–3	800–900	0.004	0.008
	280, 280C, 280S	N9Y	0.024	34–40	7B w/vacuum	7B	3.5–5.0	800–900	0.004	0.010
	450SE, 450SEL	N9Y	0.024	Elec.	TDC w/vacuum	⑥	75–84 ③	700–800	Hyd.	Hyd.
	450SL, 450SLC	N9Y	0.024	Elec.	TDC w/vacuum	⑥	75–84 ③	700–800	Hyd.	Hyd.
1977	230	N10Y	0.028	46–53	10B w/vacuum	14B	2–3	850	0.004	0.008
	280E	N10Y	0.028	Elec.	TDC w/vacuum	7B	75–84 ③	800	0.004	0.010
	280SE	N10Y	0.028	Elec.	TDC w/vacuum	7B	75–84 ③	800	0.004	0.010
	450SE, 450SEL	N10Y	0.028	Elec.	TDC w/vacuum	⑥	75–84 ③	750	Hyd.	Hyd.
	450SL, 450SLC	N10Y	0.028	Elec.	TDC w/vacuum	⑥	75–84 ③	750	Hyd.	Hyd.
1978–79	230	N10Y	0.032	Elec.	10B w/vacuum	14B	2–3	850	0.004	0.008
	280E, 280CE, 280SE	N10Y	0.032	Elec.	TDC w/vacuum	7B	75–84 ③	800	0.004	0.010
	450SEL	N10Y	0.032	Elec.	TDC w/vacuum	⑥	75–84 ③	750	Hyd.	Hyd.
	450SL, 450SLC	N10Y	0.032	Elec.	TDC w/vacuum	⑥	75–84 ③	750	Hyd.	Hyd.
	6.9	N10Y	0.032	Elec.	TDC w/vacuum	⑦	75–84 ③	600	Hyd.	Hyd.

Gasoline Engine Tune-Up Specifications (cont.)

When analyzing compression test results, look for uniformity among cylinders, rather than specific pressures.

Year	Model	Spark Plugs Type	Spark Plugs Gap (in.)	Distributor Point Dwell (deg)	Ignition Timing (deg) ①	Intake Valve Opens (deg)●	Fuel Pump Pressure (psi)	▲ Idle Speed (rpm)	Valve Clear* (Cold) (in.) In	Valve Clear* (Cold) (in.) Ex
1980	280E, 280CE, 280SE	N10Y	0.032	Elec.	10B	7B	⑨	700–800	0.004	0.010
	450SEL	N10Y	0.032	Elec.	5B	⑩	⑨	600–700	Hyd.	Hyd.
	450SL, 450SLC	N10Y	0.032	Elec.	5B	⑩	⑨	600–700	Hyd.	Hyd.
1981	280E, 280CE	N10Y	0.032	Elec.	10B	7B	⑨	700–800	0.004	0.010
	380SEL	N10Y	0.032	Elec.	5B	24A	⑨	500	Hyd.	Hyd.
	380SL, 380SLC	N10Y	0.032	Elec.	5B	24A	⑨	500	Hyd.	Hyd.
1982	380SL	N10Y	0.032	Elec.	5B	24A	⑨	500–600	Hyd.	Hyd.
	380SEL	N10Y	0.032	Elec.	5B	24A	⑨	500–600	Hyd.	Hyd.
	380SEC	N10Y	0.032	Elec.	5B	24A	⑨	500–600	Hyd.	Hyd.
1983–84	190E	S12YC	0.032	Elec.	5B	⑧	77–80	700–800	Hyd.	Hyd.
	380SE	N10Y	0.032	Elec.	TDC w/o vacuum	24A	⑨	500–600	Hyd.	Hyd.
	380SL	N10Y	0.032	Elec.	TDC w/o vacuum	24A	⑨	500–600	Hyd.	Hyd.
	380SEL	N10Y	0.032	Elec.	TDC w/o vacuum	24A	⑨	500–600	Hyd.	Hyd.
	380SLC	N10Y	0.032	Elec.	TDC w/o vacuum	24A	⑨	500–600	Hyd.	Hyd.
	500SEC	N10Y	0.032	Elec.	TDC w/o vacuum	⑩	⑨	600–700	Hyd.	Hyd.
	500SEL	N10Y	0.032	Elec.	TDC w/o vacuum	⑩	⑨	600–700	Hyd.	Hyd.

CAUTION: *If the specifications listed above differ from those on the tune-up decal in the engine compartment, use those listed on the tune-up decal.*

NOTES: 1. On transistor ignitions, only a transistorized dwell meter can be used. Transistor ignitions are recognizable by the "Blue" ignition coil, 2 series resistors and the transistor switchgear.

2. To counteract wear of the fiber contact block, adjust the dwell to the lover end of the range.

A After Top Dead Center
B Before Top Dead Center
w/vacuum—vacuum advance connected
w/o vacuum—advance disconnected
*Below 0°F; increase valve clearance by 0.002 in.
—Not Available
▲ In Drive
● Timing for test measurements @ 2mm valve lift
① —At idle
② —11B—Federal; 6B—California
③ —Injection pump pressure
④ 750–900 Federal; 700–900 California
⑤ Right-side camshift—3° BTDC
Left-side camshaft—5° BTDC
⑥ Right-side camshaft—4.5° BTDC
Left-side camshaft—6.5° BTDC
⑦ Right-side camshaft—12° BTDC
Left-side camshaft—10° BTDC
⑧ New timing chain: 17A
Used timing chain (12,000 miles): 18A
⑨ Approx. 1 quart in 30 seconds
⑩ Right-side camshaft—20° ATDC
Left-side camshaft—22° ATDC

% CO at Idle (With or Without Air Injection) (Gasoline Engines Only)

Model	1974	1975	1976	1977	1978–79
230	0.4–1.5 without	0.4–1.5 without	0.4–1.5 without	0.4–2.0 with	0.4–2.0 with
280 280C, 280S	max. 1.5 with	max. 1.0 without	max. 1.0 without	—	—
280E, 280CE, 280SE	—	—	—	0.4–2.0 without	0.4–2.0 without
450SE, 450SEL, 450SL, 450SLC	0.5–2.0 max. 1.0 with (Calif.)	max. 1.5 without	0.2–1.5 without	①	①
6.9	—	—	—	—	②

—Not Applicable
① California 0.2–2.0 without
Federal 0.2–2.0 with
Federal high altitude 0.2–2.0 with
② Federal and California 0.2–2.0 without
Federal high altitude 0.2–1.2 without

Diesel Engine Tune-Up Specifications

Model	Valve Clearance (cold) ① Intake (in.)	Valve Clearance (cold) ① Exhaust (in.)	Intake Valve Opens (deg)	Injection Pump Setting (deg)	Injection Nozzle Pressure (psi) New	Injection Nozzle Pressure (psi) Used	Idle Speed (rpm) ②	Cranking Compression Pressure (psi)
190D	Hyd.	Hyd.	⑤	15A	1564–1706	1422–1706	700–800	284–327
240D (4-cylinder) '74–'81	0.004	0.016	13.5B	24B	1564–1706	1422–1706	750–800	284–327
240D 4-cylinder '82–'83	0.004	0.016	13.5B	24B	1564–1706	1422–1706	700–800	284–327
300D, 300CD, 300TD (5-cylinder, non-turbo)	0.004	0.012	13.5B	24B ④	1635–1750 ③	1422	700–800	284–327
300SD, 300TD (5-cylinder, turbo) '77–'81	0.004	0.014	13.5B	24B ④	1958–2074	1740	650–850	284–327
300D 300CD 300SD 300TD (5-cylinder, turbo) '82–'84	0.004	0.014	13.5B	24B ④⑦	1958–2074	1740	650–850 ⑥	284–327

B Before Top Dead Center
① In cold weather (below 5°F.), increase valve clearance 0.002 in.
② Manual transmission in Neutral; Automatic in Drive.
③ Difference in opening pressure on injection nozzles should not exceed 71 psi.
④ The injection pump is in start of delivery position when the mark on the pump camshaft is aligned with the mark on the injection pump flange.
⑤ New timing chain—11A
Used timing chain (12,000 miles)— 12A
⑥ 1984—700-800

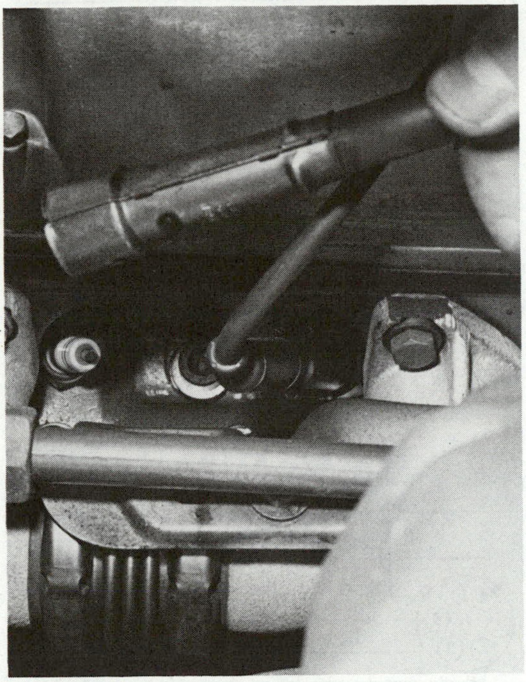
Remove the plug wires by pulling on the boot

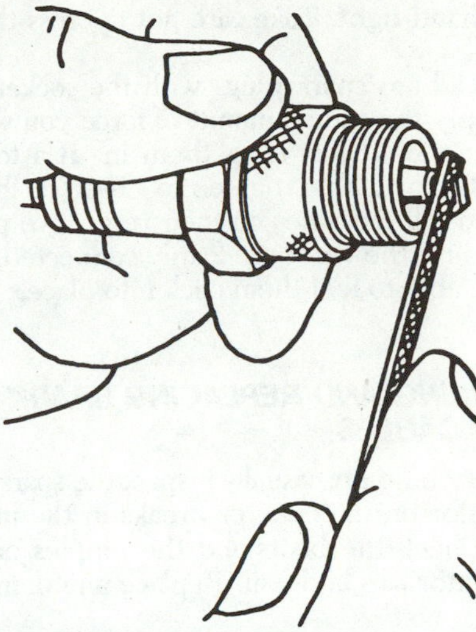
Plugs in good condition can be filed and re-used

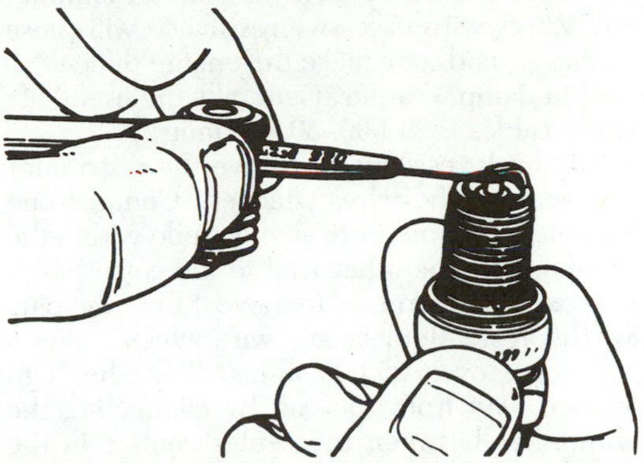
Always use a wire gauge to check the electrode gap

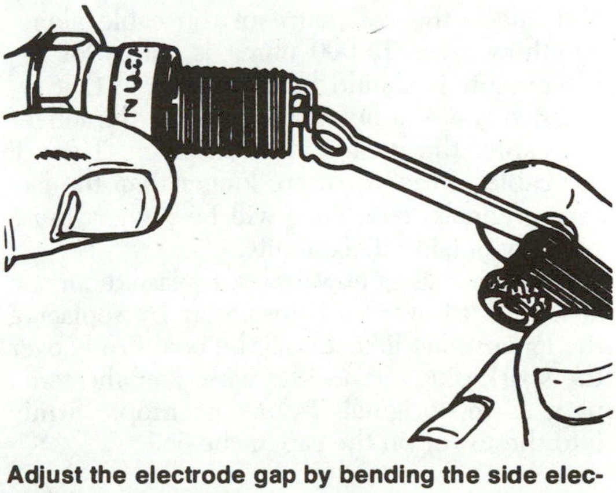
Adjust the electrode gap by bending the side electrode

7. Unscrew the plug the rest of the way and remove it from the engine.

INSPECTION

Check the plugs for deposits and wear. If they are not going to be replaced, clean the plugs thoroughly. Remember that any kind of deposit will decrease the efficiency of the plug. Plugs can be cleaned on a spark plug cleaning machine, which can sometimes be found in service stations, or you can do an acceptable job of cleaning with a stiff brush. If the plugs are cleaned, the electrodes must be filed flat. Use an ignition points file, not an emery board or the like, which will leave deposits. The electrodes must be filed perfectly flat with sharp edges; rounded edges reduce the spark plug voltage by as much as 50%.

Check spark plug gap before installation. The ground electrode (the L-shaped one connected to the body of the plug) must be parallel to the center electrode and the specified size wire gauge (see "Tune-Up Specifications") should pass through the gap with a slight drag. Always check the gap on new plugs, too; they are not always set correctly at the factory. Do not use a flat feeler gauge when measuring the gap, because the reading will be inaccurate. Wire gapping tools usually have a bending tool attached. Use that to adjust the side electrode until the proper distance is obtained. *Absolutely never bend the center electrode.* Also, be careful not to bend the side electrode too far or too often; it may weaken and break off within the engine, requiring removal of the cylinder head to retrieve it.

INSTALLATION

1. Lubricate the threads of the spark plugs with a drop of oil. Install the plugs and tighten

them hand-tight. Take care not to cross-thread them.

2. Tighten spark plugs with the socket. Do not apply the same amount of force you would use for a bolt; just snug them in. If a torque wrench is available, tighten to 11–15 ft. lbs.

3. Install the wires on their respective plugs. Make sure the wires are firmly connected. You will be able to feel them click into place.

CHECKING AND REPLACING SPARK PLUG CABLES

At every tune-up, visually inspect the spark plug cables for burns, cuts, or breaks in the insulation. Check the boots and the nipples on the distributor cap and coil. Replace any damaged wiring.

Every 36,000 miles or so, the resistance of the wires should be checked with an ohmmeter. Wires with excessive resistance will cause misfiring, and may make the engine difficult to start in damp weather. Generally the useful life of the cables is 36,000–50,000 miles.

To check resistance, remove the distributor cap, leaving the wires attached. Connect one lead of an ohmmeter to an electrode within the cap; connect the other lead to the corresponding spark plug terminal (remove it from the plug for this test). Replace any wire which shows a resistance over 25,000 ohms. Test the high tension lead from the coil by connecting the ohmmeter between the center contact in the distributor cap and either of the primary terminals of the coil. If resistance is more than 25,000 ohms, remove the cable from the coil and check the resistance of the cable alone. Anything over 15,000 ohms is cause for replacement. It should be remembered that resistance is also a function of length; the longer the cable, the greater the resistance. Thus, if the cables on your car are longer than the factory originals, resistance will be higher, quite possibly outside these limits.

When installing new cables, replace them one at a time to avoid mixups. Start by replacing the longest one first. Install the boot firmly over the spark plug. Route the wire over the same path as the original. Insert the nipple firmly into the tower on the cap or the coil.

FIRING ORDER

To avoid confusion, spark plug wires should be replaced one at a time. Distributor terminal position may differ slightly from that which is illustrated. The notch cut into the rim of the distributor body always indicates No. 1 cylinder.

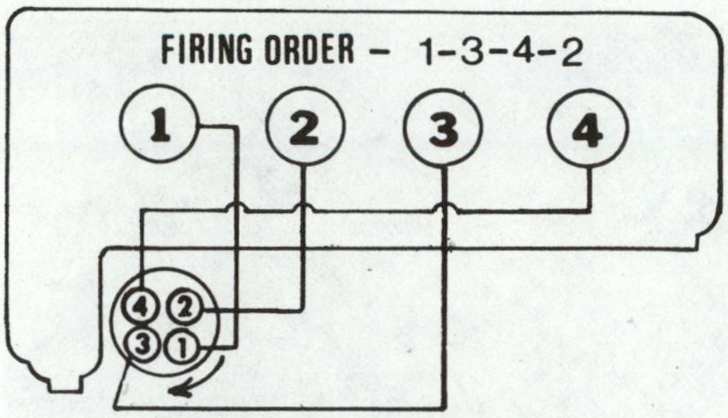

Firing order—4 cylinder gasoline engines

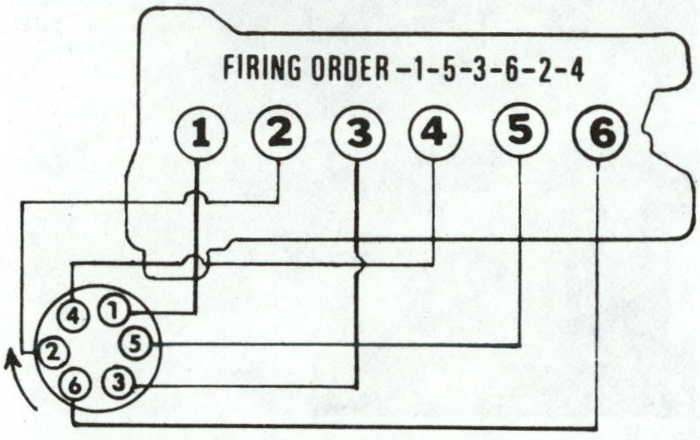

Firing order—6 cylinder gasoline engines

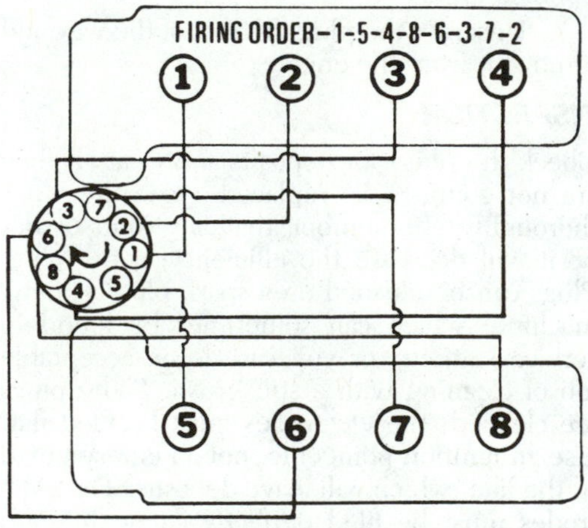

Firing order—8 cylinder gasoline engines

Breaker Points and Condenser

NOTE: *The diesel engine has no distributor so there are no breaker points or condensers to replace. Also, 1976 and later V-8's, 1977 and later 6-cylinder engines and 1977 and later 4-cylinder engines use a breakerless, electronic ignition which has no breaker points.*

The points function as a circuit breaker for the primary circuit of the ignition system. The ignition coil must boost the 12 volts of electrical pressure supplied by the battery to as much as 25,000 volts in order to fire the plugs. To do this, the coil depends on the points and the condenser to make a clean break in the primary circuit.

The coil has both primary and secondary circuits. When the ignition is turned on, the battery supplies voltage through the coil and onto the points. The points are connected to ground, completing the primary circuit. As the current passes through the coil, a magnetic field is created in the iron center core of the coil. When the cam in the distributor turns, the points open, breaking the primary circuit. The magnetic field in the primary circuit of the coil then collapses and cuts through the secondary circuit windings around the iron core. Because of the physical principle called "electromagnetic induction," the battery voltage is increased to a level sufficient to fire the spark plugs.

When the points open, the electrical charge in the primary circuit tries to jump the gap created between the two open contacts of the points. If this electrical charge were not transferred elsewhere, the metal contacts of the points would start to change rapidly.

The function of the condenser is to absorb excessive voltage from the points when they open and thus prevent the points from becoming pitted or burned.

If you have ever wondered why it is necessary to tune-up your engine occasionally, consider the fact that the ignition system must complete the above cycle each time a spark plug fires. On a four-cylinder, four-cycle engine, two of the four plugs must fire once for every engine revolution. If the idle speed of your engine is 800 revolutions per minute (800 rpm), the breaker points open and close two times for each revolution. For every minute your engine idles, your points open and close 1,600 times ($2 \times 800 = 1,600$). And that is just at idle. What about at 60 mph?

There are two ways to check breaker point gap: with a feeler gauge or with a dwell meter. Either way you set the points, you are adjusting the amount of time (in degrees of distributor rotation) that the points will remain open. If you adjust the points with a feeler gauge, you are setting the maximum amount the points will open when the rubbing block on the points is on a high point of the distributor cam. When you adjust the points with a dwell meter, you are measuring the number of degrees (of distributor cam rotation) that the points will remain closed before they start to open as a high point of the distributor cam approaches the rubbing block of the points.

If you still do not understand how the points function, take a friend, go outside, and remove the distributor cap from your engine. Have your friend operate the starter (make sure that the transmission is not in gear) as you look at the exposed parts of the distributor.

There are two rules that should always be followed when adjusting or replacing points. *The points and condenser are a matched set; never replace one without replacing the other. If you change the point gap or dwell of the engine, you also change the ignition timing. Therefore, if you adjust the points, you must also adjust the timing.*

IGNITION SYSTEM PRECAUTIONS

Mercedes-Benz has determined that some transistorized switching units have been damaged due to improper handling during service and maintenance work. The following precautions should be observed when working with transistorized switching units.

1. Do not shut off a running engine by shorting terminal 15 of the ignition coil to ground or the transistorized switching unit will be destroyed.
2. Do not steam clean or apply water pressure to transistorized switching units, fuel injection control units, or ignition components, since water may enter these and short them.
3. Do not assume that transistor switching units are defective without checking the plug terminals. The plug terminals are frequently corroded because the rubber boot was not properly seated. In addition, the terminals can become corroded even if the rubber boot is properly seated. Mercedes-Benz recommends that all contacts be cleaned before assuming that a transistorized switching unit is defective.

INSPECTION AND CLEANING

The breaker points should be inspected and cleaned at 6,000 mile intervals. To do so, perform the following steps:

1. Disconnect the high-tension lead from the coil.
2. Unsnap the two distributor cap retaining clips and lift the cap straight up. Leave the leads connected to the cap and position it out of the way.
3. Remove the rotor and dust cover by pulling them straight up.
4. Place a screwdriver against the breaker points and pry them open. Examine their condition. If they are excessively worn, burned, or pitted, they should be replaced.
5. Clean the distributor cap and rotor with alcohol. Inspect the cap terminals for looseness and corrosion. Check the rotor tip for excessive burning. Inspect both cap and rotor for cracks. Replace either if they show any of the above signs of wear or damage.
6. Check the operation of the centrifugal advance mechanism by turning the rotor clock-

wise. Release the rotor; it should return to its original position. If it doesn't, check for binding parts.

7. If the points do not require replacement, proceed with the adjustment section below. Otherwise perform the point and condenser replacement procedures.

REPLACEMENT

1. Raise the hood and locate the distributor. Remove the rubber or plastic cover (if equipped).

2. Release the clips on the side of the distributor cap and remove the cap. Lay it aside.

3. Remove the rotor and dust shield from the distributor shaft. The rotor only fits one way.

4. Some distributors have a protective cover installed over the points, which must be removed.

5. Remove the distributor contact holder by removing the screw or screws. Some models also have a snap-ring on the bearing contact lever, which must also be removed. Pry the wire from the connecting terminal or loosen the screw at the terminal and remove the wire from the connecting terminal.

6. Disconnect the condenser wire and remove the condenser from its bracket. The condenser screw is located on the outside of the distributor.

7. Before installing new points, clean the contact surfaces by squeezing them against a clean matchbook cover. This will remove any film or grease. Also be sure the point contact faces are aligned. If not, bend the fixed contact arm so that the points align and close squarely.

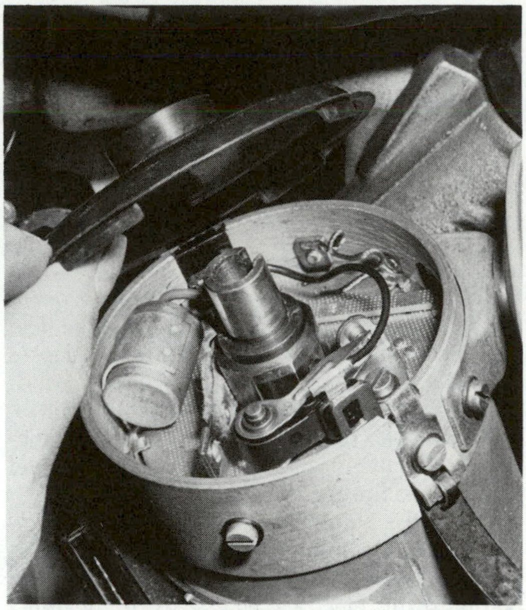

Remove the rotor and dust shield

The condenser attaching screw is located on the outside of the distributor housing

Remove the distributor cap

8. Lightly coat the rubbing arm of the contact breaker with high temperature multipurpose grease. It is no longer necessary to lubricate the felt pad.

9. Install a new condenser and connect the wire.

10. Install a new contact set or sets into the distributor.

11. Install the hold-down screw(s) or the snap-rings on the bearing pins of the contact plate.

1. Condenser
2. Point set
3. Point set attaching screw
4. Vacuum advance unit
5. Adjusting lugs and notch in breaker plate
6. Point gap (must be on the high point of the distributor cam to measure)
7. Notch in distributor rim indicating no. 1 cylinder

Internal view of breaker point type distributor

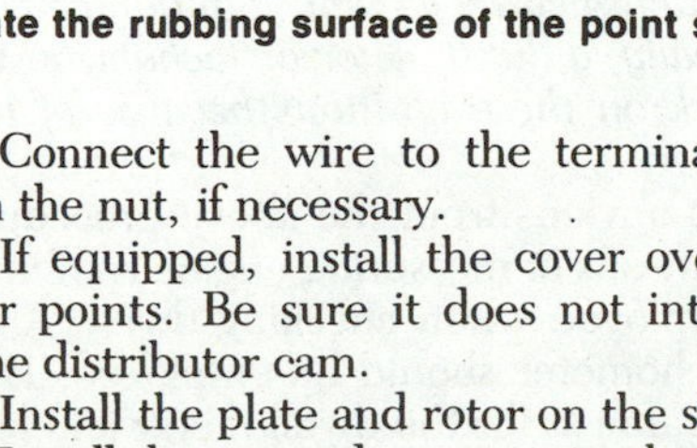

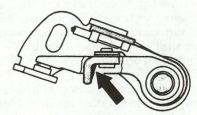

Lubricate the rubbing surface of the point set

12. Connect the wire to the terminal and tighten the nut, if necessary.

13. If equipped, install the cover over the breaker points. Be sure it does not interfere with the distributor cam.

14. Install the plate and rotor on the shaft.

15. Install the cap and secure it in place with the clips.

16. Check the dwell angle and ignition timing. Adjust if necessary.

ADJUSTMENT WITH A FEELER GAUGE

Perform the gap adjustment procedure whenever new points are installed, or as part of routine maintenance. If you are adjusting an old

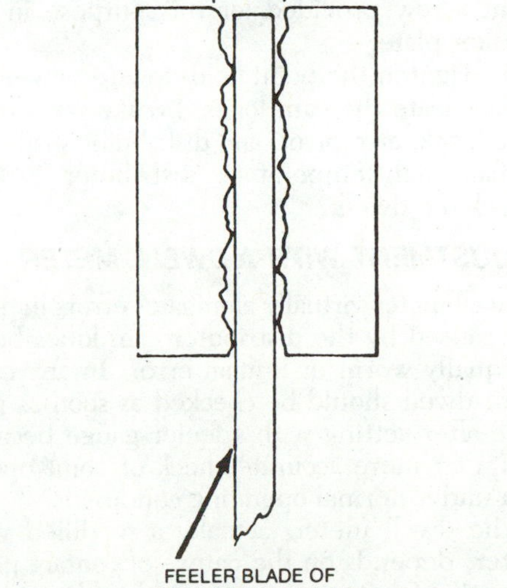

The feeler gauge method of checking point gap is less accurate than the dwell meter method

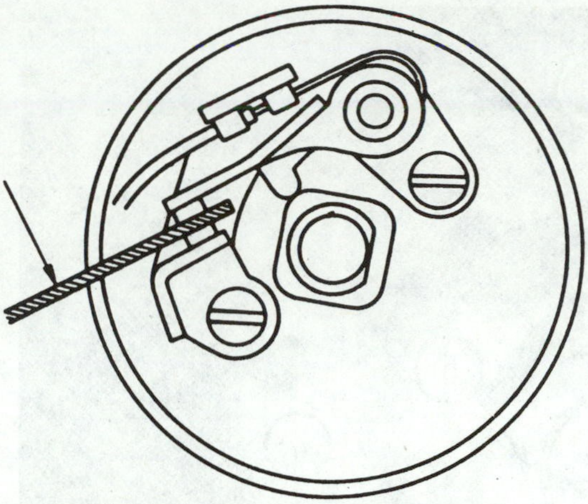

The arrow indicates the feeler gauge used to check the point gap

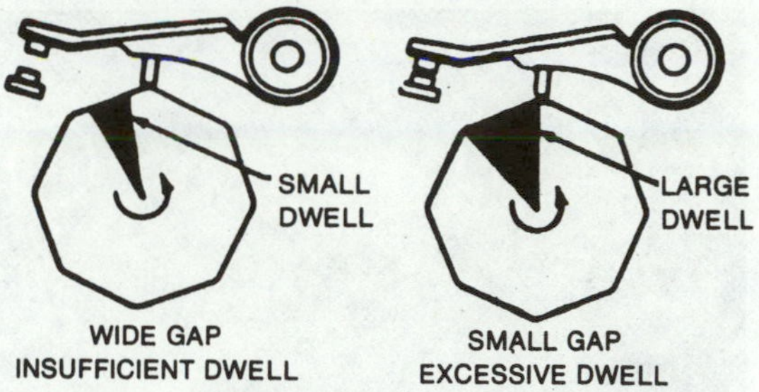

Dwell is a function of point gap

set of points, you *must* check the dwell as well, since the feeler gauge is really only accurate with a new point set.

1. Rotate the engine by hand or by using a remote starter switch, so that the rubbing block is on the high point of the cam lobe.
2. Insert a feeler gauge between the points; a slight drag should be felt.
3. If no drag is felt or if the feeler gauge cannot be inserted at all, loosen, but do not remove, the point hold-down screw.
4. Insert a screwdriver into the adjustment slot. Rotate the screwdriver until the proper point gap is attained. The point gap is increased by rotating the screwdriver counterclockwise and decreased by rotating it clockwise. On some models it is possible to adjust the point gap by means of an eccentric adjustment screw provided for this purpose in the breaker plate.
5. Tighten the point hold-down screw.

Lubricate the cam lobes, breaker arm, rubbing block, arm pivot, and distributor shaft with special high-temperature distributor grease. Check the dwell.

ADJUSTMENT WITH A DWELL METER

A dwell meter virtually eliminates errors in point gap caused by the distributor cam lobes being unequally worn, or human error. In any case, point dwell should be checked as soon as possible after setting with a feeler gauge because it is a far more accurate check of point operation under normal operating conditions.

The dwell meter, actually a modified voltmeter, depends on the nature of contact point operation for its usefulness. In this electro-mechanical system, a fiber block slides under tension, over a cam (see illustrations). The angle (in black) that the block traverses on the cam, during which time current is made available to the coil primary winding, is an inverse function of point gap. In other words, the wider the gap, the smaller the "dwell" (expressed in degrees); the closer the gap, the greater the "dwell."

Because the fiber block wears down gradually in service, it is a good practice to set the dwell on the low side of any dwell range (smaller number of degrees) given in specifications. As the block wears, the dwell becomes greater (toward the center of the range) and point life is increased between adjustments.

To connect the dwell meter, switch the meter to the six-, four- or eight-cylinder range, as the case may be, and connect one lead to ground. The other lead should be connected to the coil distributor terminal (the one having the wire going to contact points). Follow the manufacturer's instructions if they differ from those listed. Zero the meter, start the engine and gradually allow it to assume normal idle speed. (See "Tune-Up Specifications.") The meter should agree with the specifications. Any excessive variation in dwell indicates a worn distributor shaft or bushings, or perhaps a worn distributor cam or breaker plate.

NOTE: *Up until 1976 (V8), 1977 (6-cylinder) or 1977 (4-cylinder), Mercedes-Benz engines use transistorized ignitions. These can be identified by a "blue" ignition coil. Occassionally, a dwell meter or tachometer will not work on these ignitions because of internal design.*

It is obvious from the above procedure that some means of measuring engine rpm must also be employed when checking dwell. An external tachometer should be employed. Hook-up is the same as for the dwell meter and both can be used in conjunction. Most commercial dwell meters have a tachometer scale built in and switching between them is possible.

NOTE: *Diesel engines, 1976 and later V8's, 1977 and later 6-cylinder engines and 1977 and later 4-cylinder engines have no provision for adjusting dwell.*

1. The dwell angle should be measured at idle speed.

The ignition coil (arrow) is usually located on or near the fender. The protective plastic cover must be removed to make dwell meter connections

2. Raise the hood and connect a dwell meter/tachometer.
3. Start the engine and allow it to reach normal idle speed. Read the dwell angle from the meter on the appropriate scale.
4. If the dwell angle is not according to specifications, remove the distributor cap and adjust the dwell angle. Reduce the point gap if the dwell angle is too small, or increase the contact point gap if the dwell angle is too large.
5. To actually adjust the point gap, stop the engine and loosen the hold-down screw and insert a screwdriver between the lugs on the breaker plate. Move the plate to the desired location. Tighten the hold-down screw. On some models it is possible to adjust the point gap by means of the eccentric screw provided for this purpose in the breaker plate.
6. Recheck the dwell angle and adjust the gap again if it is still not satisfactory. Repeat the process until the dwell angle is as specified.

Ignition Timing

Ignition timing is the measurement in degrees of crankshaft rotation of the instant the spark plugs in the cylinders fire, in relation to the location of the piston, while the piston is on its compression stroke.

NOTE: *Diesel engines use no distributor, so they require no ignition timing adjustment.*

Ignition timing is adjusted by loosening the distributor locking device and turning the distributor in the engine.

Ideally, the air/fuel mixture in the cylinder will be ignited (by the spark plug) and just beginning its rapid expansion as the piston passes top dead center (TDC) of the compression stroke. If this happens, the piston will be beginning the power stroke just as the compressed (by the movement of the piston) and ignited (by the spark plug) air/fuel mixture starts to expand. The expansion of the air/fuel mixture will then force the piston down on the power stroke and turn the crankshaft.

It takes a fraction of a second for the spark from the plug to completely ignite the mixture in the cylinder. Because of this, the spark plug must fire before the piston reaches TDC, if the mixture is to be completely ignited as the piston passes TDC. This measurement is given in degrees (of crankshaft rotation) *before* the piston reaches *top dead center* (BTDC). If the ignition timing setting for your engine is seven degrees (7°) BTDC, this means that the spark plug must fire at a time when the piston for that cylinder is 7° before top dead center of its compression stroke. However, this only holds true while your engine is at idle speed.

As you accelerate from idle, the speed of your engine (rpm) increases. The increase in rpm means that the pistons are now traveling up and down much faster. Because of this, the spark plugs will have to fire even sooner if the mixture is to be completely ignited as the piston passes TDC. To accomplish this, the distributor incorporates means to advance the timing of the spark as engine speed increases.

The distributor in your Mercedes-Benz has two means of advancing the ignition timing. One is called centrifugal advance and is actuated by weights in the distributor. The other is called vacuum advance and is controlled by that larger circular housing on the side of the distributor.

In addition, some distributors have a vacuum-retard mechanism which is contained in the same housing on the side of the distributor as the vacuum advance. The function of this mechanism is to retard the timing of the ignition spark under certain engine conditions. This causes more complete burning of the air/fuel mixture in the cylinder and consequently lowers exhaust emissions.

Because these mechanisms change ignition timing, it is necessary to disconnect and plug the one or two vacuum lines from the distributor when setting the basic ignition timing.

If ignition timing is set too far advanced (BTDC), the ignition and expansion of the air/fuel mixture in the cylinder will try to force the piston down the cylinder while it is still traveling upward. This causes engine "ping," a sound which resembles marbles being dropped into an empty tin can. If the ignition timing is too far retarded (after, or ATDC), the piston will have already started down on the power stroke when the air/fuel mixture ignites and expands. This will cause the piston to be forced down only a portion of its travel. This will result in poor engine performance and lack of power.

Ignition timing adjustment is checked with a timing light. This instrument is connected to the number one (No. 1) spark plug of the engine. The timing light flashes every time an electrical current is sent from the distributor, through the No. 1 spark plug wire, to the spark plug. The vibration damper or balancing plate are marked with a timing pointer and a timing scale. When the timing pointer is aligned with the mark (pin) on the timing scale, the piston in No. 1 cylinder is at TDC of its compression stroke. With the engine running, and the timing light aimed at the timing pointer and timing scale, the stroboscopic flashes from the timing light will allow you to check the ignition timing setting of the engine. The timing light flashes every time the spark plug in the No. 1 cylinder of the engine fires. Since the flash from the timing light makes the crankshaft pulley seem stationary for a moment, you will be able to read the exact position of the piston in the No. 1 cylinder on the timing scale on the front of the engine.

There are three basic types of timing light available. The first is a simple neon bulb with two wire connections (one for the spark plug and one for the plug wire, connecting the light in series). This type of light is quite dim, and must be held closely to the marks to be seen, but it is inexpensive. The second type of light operates from the car battery. Two alligator clips connect to the battery terminals, while a third wire connects to the spark plug with an adapter. This type of light is more expensive, but the zenon bulb provides a nice bright flash which can even be seen in sunlight. The third type replaces the battery source with 110 volt house current. Some timing lights have other functions built into them, such as dwell meters, tachometers, or remote starting switches. These are convenient, in that they reduce the tangle of wires under the hood, but may duplicate the functions of tools you already have.

If your Mercedes has electronic ignition, you should use a timing light with an inductive pickup. This pickup simply clamps onto the No. 1 plug wire, eliminating the adapter. It is not susceptible to crossfiring or false triggering, which may occur with a conventional light, due to the greater voltages produced by electronic ignition.

CHECKING AND ADJUSTMENT

All Engines (Except Diesels)

1. Warm-up the engine. Connect a tachometer and check the engine idle speed to be sure that it is within the specification given in the "Tune-Up Specifications" chart at the beginning of the chapter.
2. If the timing marks are difficult to see use a dab of paint or chalk to make them more visible.
3. Connect a timing light according to the manufacturer's instructions.
4. Disconnect the vacuum line(s) from the distributor vacuum unit. Plug it (them) with a pencil or golf tee(s).
5. Be sure that the timing light wires are clear of the fan and start the engine.

   CAUTION: *Keep fingers, clothes, tools, hair, and leads clear of the spinning engine fan. Be sure that you are running the engine in a well-ventilated area.*
6. Allow the engine to run at the specified idle speed with the gearshift in Neutral with manual transmission and Drive (D) with automatic transmission.

   CAUTION: *Be sure that the parking brake is set and that the front wheels are blocked to prevent the car from rolling forward, especially when Drive is selected with an automatic.*

The typical vibration damper is marked like this (note the pin)

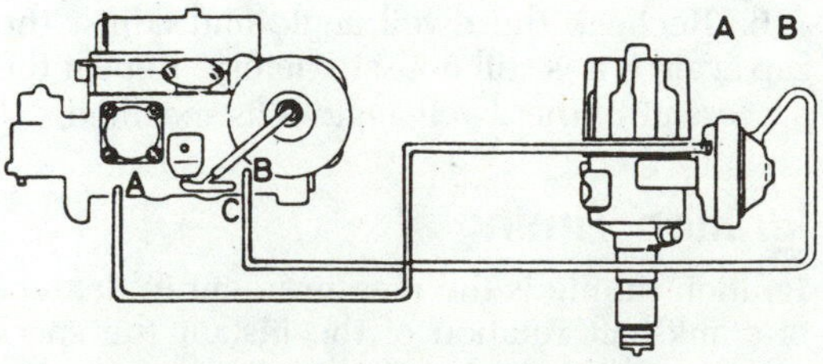

A. Vacuum connection (retard) (white)
B. Vacuum connection (advance) (red)
C. Vacuum connection to vacuum governor and fuel return valve

Disconnect and plug both vacuum connections on carbureted 280, 280C and 280S engines

7. Point the timing light at the mark indicated previously. With the engine at idle, timing should be at the specification given on the "Tune-Up Specifications" chart at the beginning of the chapter.

NOTE: *The balancer on some engines has two timing scales. If in doubt as to which scale to use, rotate the crankshaft (in the direction of rotation only) until the distributor rotor is aligned with the notch on the distributor housing (No. 1 cylinder). In this position, the timing pointer should be at TDC on the proper timing scale.*

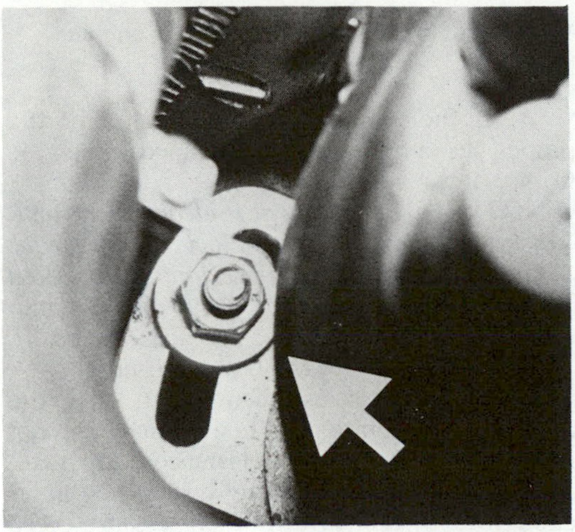

The distributor is held in place by a clamp bolt (arrow) on the side

To adjust the ignition timing, loosen the clamp bolt slightly and rotate the distributor. Turning the distributor counterclockwise advances the timing, and clockwise retards the timing

8. If the timing is not at the specification, loosen the pinch-bolt at the base of the distributor just enough so that the distributor can be turned. Turn the distributor to advance or retard the timing as required. Once the proper marks are seen to align with the timing light, timing is correct.

9. Stop the engine and tighten the pinch-bolt. Start the engine and recheck timing. Stop the engine; disconnect the tachometer and timing light. Connect the vacuum line(s) to the distributor vacuum unit.

Valve Clearance

The valve clearance can be checked with a feeler gauge on a hot or cold engine. Be sure to consult the illustrations of valve placement; the clearance on intake and exhaust valves is different.

Valve lash is one factor which determines how far the intake and exhaust valves will open into the cylinder.

If the valve clearance is too large, part of the lift of the camshaft will be used up in removing the excessive clearance, thus the valves will not be opened far enough. This condition has two effects, the valve train components will emit a tapping noise as they take up the excessive clearance, and the engine will perform poorly, since the less the intake valves open, the smaller the amount of air/fuel mixture admitted to the cylinders will be. The less the exhaust valves open, the greater the back-pressure in the cylinder which prevents the proper air/fuel mixture from entering the cylinder.

If the valve clearance is too small, the intake and exhaust valves will not fully seat on the cylinder head when they close. When a valve seats on the cylinder head it does two things; it seals the combustion chamber so none of the gases in the cylinder can escape and it cools itself by transferring some of the heat it absorbed from the combustion process through the cylinder head and into the engine cooling system. Therefore, if the valve clearance is too small, the engine will run poorly (due to gases escaping from the combustion chamber), and the valves will overheat and warp (since they cannot transfer heat unless they are touching the seat in the cylinder head).

NOTE: *While all valve adjustments must be as accurate as possible, it is better to have the valve adjustment slightly loose than slightly tight, as burnt valves may result from overly tight adjustments.*

ADJUSTMENT

4 and 6-Cylinder Gasoline Engines

NOTE: *The 190E has hydraulic valve clearance compensation. No adjustment is either possible or necessary.*

The valve clearance is measured between the sliding surface of the rocker arm and the heel of the camshaft lobe. The highest point of the camshaft lobe should be at a 90° angle to the sliding surface of the rocker arm.

NOTE: *Prior to rotating the 6 cyl. engine manually, disconnect the transmitter ignition distributor plug (green) from the switching unit.*

1. Remove the air vent hose and air cleaner from the valve cover. Remove the spark plugs. This makes it easier to crank the engine by hand.
2. Remove the valve cover and gasket.
3. Note the position of the intake and exhaust valves.
4. Rotate the crankshaft with a socket wrench on the crankshaft pulley bolt until the heel of the camshaft lobe is perpendicular to the sliding surface of the rocker arm.

NOTE: *Do not rotate the engine using the camshaft sprocket bolt. The strain will distort the timing chain tensioner rail. Always rotate the engine in the direction of normal rotation only.*

5. Some models have holes in the vibration damper plate to assist in crankshaft rotation. In this case, a screwdriver can be used to carefully rotate the crankshaft.
6. To measure the valve clearance, insert a feeler blade of the specified thickness between the heel of the camshaft lobe and the sliding surface of the rocker arm. The clearance is correct if the blade can be inserted and withdrawn with a very slight drag.
7. If adjustment is necessary, it can be done by turning the ball pin head at the hex collar. If the clearance is too small, increase it by turning the ball pin head in. If the clearance is too large, decrease it by turning the ball pin head out.

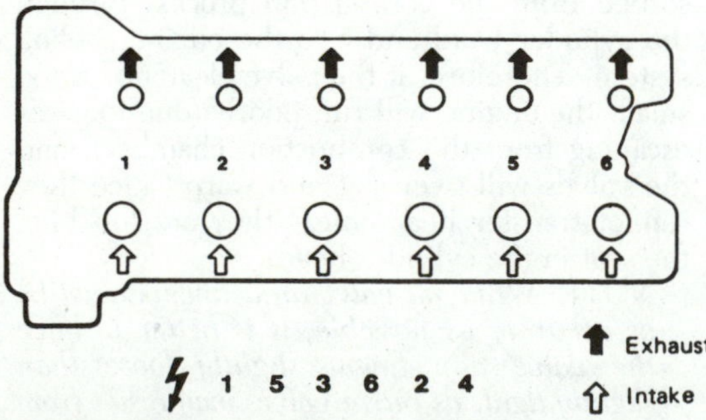

Valve locations—6-cylinder engines

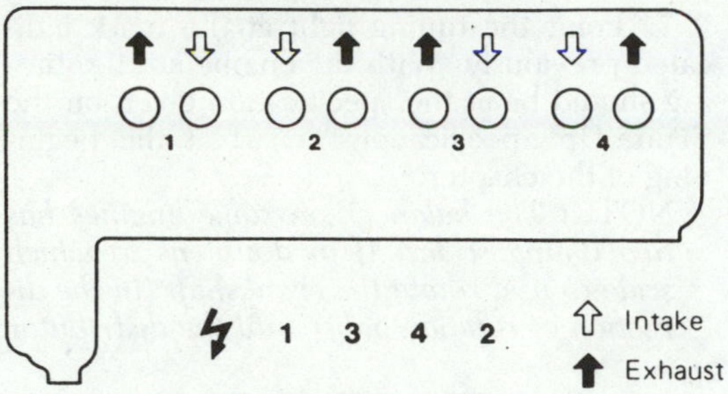

Valve locations—4-cylinder gasoline engine

8. If the adjuster turns too easily or the proper clearance cannot be obtained, check the torque of the adjuster.

NOTE: *This adjustment is ideally made with a special adaptor ("crow's foot") and a torque wrench. The shape of the adaptor is dictated by the need for accurate torque readings and, by using it, the torque wrench can be directly aligned with the ball pin head.*

If the torque is less than 14.8 ft. lbs., the adjuster will vibrate and the clearance will not remain as set. If the valve clearance is too small, and the ball pin head cannot be screwed in far enough to correct it, a thinner pressure piece should be installed in the spring retainer. To

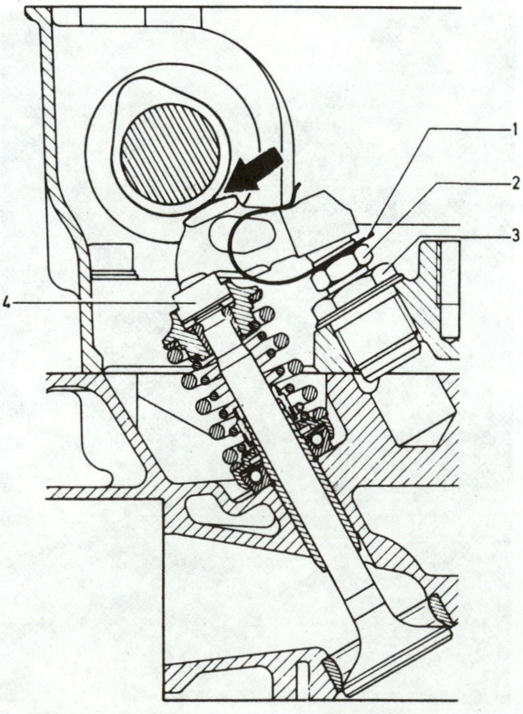

1. Tensioning spring
2. Adjusting nut
3. Threaded bushing
4. Thrust piece

On 6-cylinder engines, measure the valve clearance at arrow

Adjusting the valves on the 4 (except 190E) and 6 cylinder engines (6 cylinder shown)

replace the pressure piece, the rocker arm must be removed. See Chapter 3 for this operation.

9. After all the valves have been checked and adjusted, install the valve cover. Be sure that the gaskets are seated properly. It is best to use a new gasket whenever the valve cover is removed.

NOTE: *Two types of triangular rubber gaskets are used on 6-cylinder DOHC engines, but only the later type with 3 notches are supplied for service.*

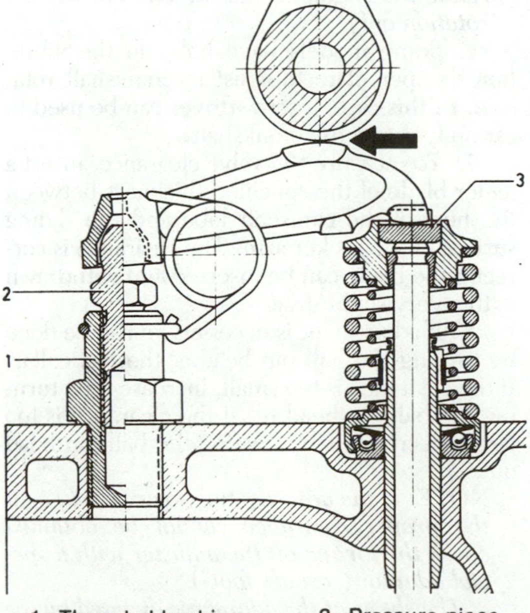

1. Threaded bushing
2. Adjusting nut
3. Pressure piece

Measure valve clearance at the arrow—4 cyl. (except 190)

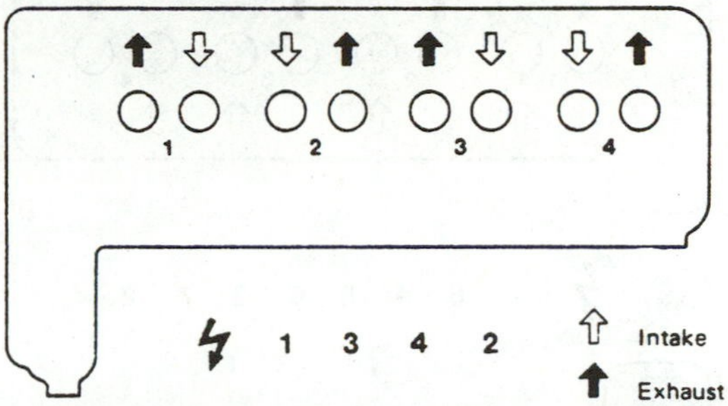

Valve arrangement—4 cylinder engines (except 190E)

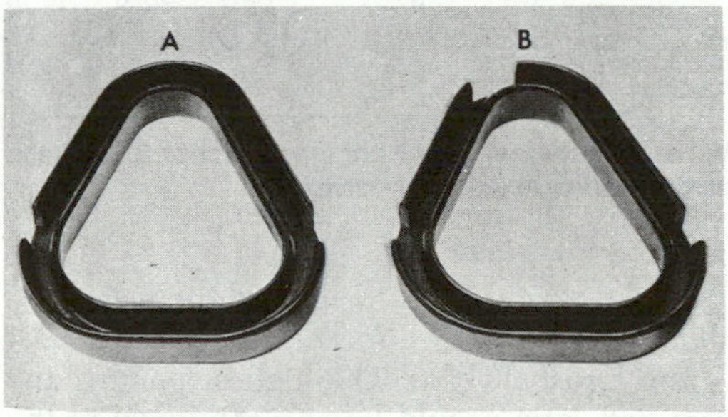

A. Spark plug holes 1, 3, 5 (early models)
B. Spark plug holes 1–5 (later models)

Two types of gaskets are used on DOHC 6-cylinder engines

10. Install the spark plugs.

11. Reconnect the air vent line to the valve cover and install the air cleaner, if removed.

12. Run the engine and check for leaks at the rocker arm cover.

V-8 Engines

NOTE: *1976 and later V-8 engines use hydraulic valve lifters that require no periodic adjustment.*

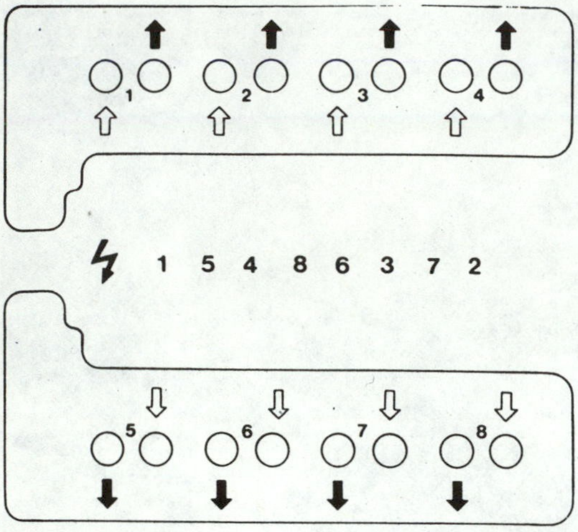

Valve locations—6.9 V8. Black arrows indicate exhaust valves.

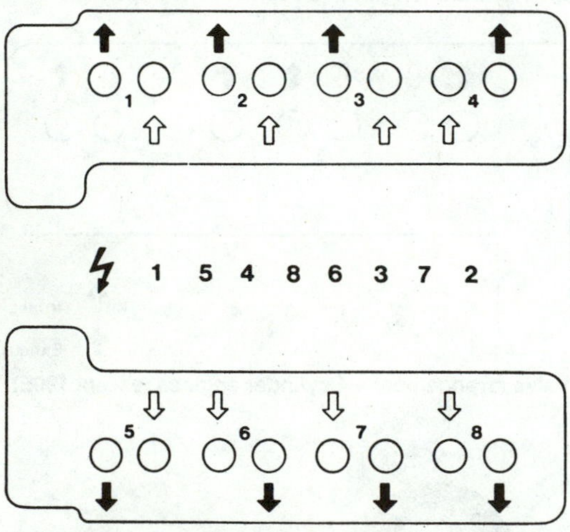

Valve arrangement—V8 engines (except 6.9). Black arrows indicate exhaust valves

Valve clearance is measured between the sliding surface of the rocker arm and the heel of the camshaft lobe. The highest point of the camshaft lobe should be at a 90° angle to the sliding surface of the rocker arm.

1. Loosen the venting line and disconnect the regulating linkage. Remove the valve cover.
2. Disconnect the cable from the ignition coil.
3. Identify all of the valves as intake or exhaust.
4. Beginning with No. 1 cylinder, crank the engine with the starter to position the heel of the camshaft approximately over the sliding surface of the rocker arm.
5. Rotate the crankshaft by using a socket wrench on the crankshaft pulley bolt until the heel of the camshaft lobe is perpendicular to the sliding surface of the rocker arm.

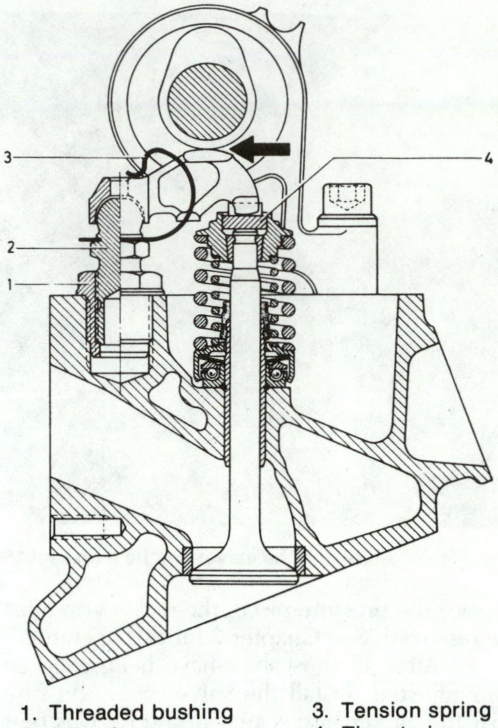

1. Threaded bushing
2. Adjusting nut
3. Tension spring
4. Thrust piece

Measure valve clearance on 1975 and earlier V8's at arrow. 1977 and later V8's require no periodic valve adjustment

NOTE: *Do not rotate the engine using the camshaft sprocket bolt. The strain will distort the timing chain tensioner rail. Always rotate the engine in the direction of normal rotation only.*

6. Some models have holes in the vibration damper plate to assist in crankshaft rotation. In this case, a screwdriver can be used to carefully rotate the crankshaft.
7. To measure the valve clearance, insert a feeler blade of the specified thickness between the heel of the camshaft lobe and the sliding surface of the rocker arm. The clearance is correct if the blade can be inserted and withdrawn with a very slight drag.
8. If adjustment is necessary, it can be done by turning the ball pin head at the hex collar. If the clearance is too small, increase it by turning the ball pin head in. If the clearance is too large, decrease it by turning the ball pin head out.

NOTE: *If the adjuster turns very easily or if the proper clearance cannot be obtained check the torque on the adjuster with a special adaptor ("crow's foot").*

The shape of the adapter is dictated by the need for accurate torque readings and, by using it, the torque wrench can be directly aligned with the ball pin head.

A valve adjusting wrench (crow's foot) is required to accurately measure torque on all models

9. When the ball pin head is turned, if the torque is less than 14.4 ft. lbs., either the adjusting screw, the threaded bolt, or both will have to be replaced. If the valve clearance is too small, and the ball pin head cannot be screwed in far enough to correct it, a thinner pressure piece should be installed in the spring retainer. To replace the pressure piece, the rocker arm must be removed. See Chapter Three for this operation.

10. Install the regulating linkage, valve cover gasket, and valve cover. Be sure the gasket is seated properly.

11. Connect the cable to the coil, the venting line and the regulating linkage. Run the engine and check for leaks at the valve cover.

Diesel Engines

NOTE: *The 190D utilizes hydraulic valve clearance compensators. No adjustment is either necessary or possible.*

1. Remove the valve cover and note the position of the intake and exhaust valves.

2. Turn the engine with a socket and breaker bar on the crankshaft pulley or by using a remote starter, hooked to the battery (+) terminal and the large, uppermost starter solenoid terminal. Due to the extremely high compression pressures in the diesel engine, it will be considerably easier to use a remote starter. If a remote starter is not available, the engine can be bumped into position with the normal starter.

NOTE: *Do not turn the engine backwards or use the camshaft sprocket bolt to rotate the engine.*

Before the valve cover can be removed from a diesel engine, the regulating linkage must be unbolted from the valve cover

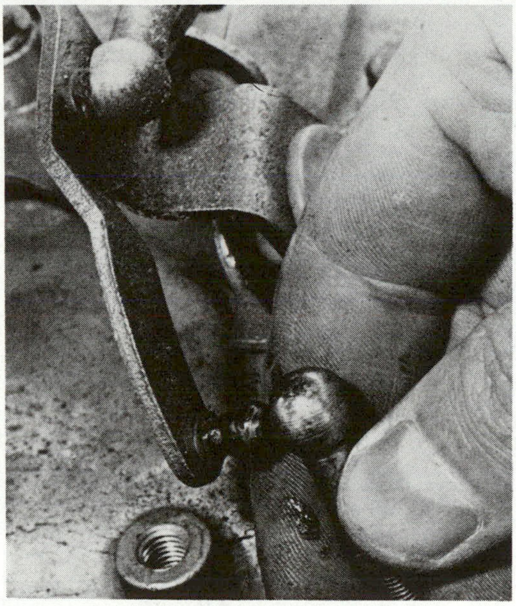

Unsnap the ball sockets to disengage the regulating linkage

3. Measure the valve clearance when the heel of the camshaft lobe is directly over the sliding surface of the rocker arm. The lobe of the camshaft should be vertical to the surface of the rocker arm. The clearance is correct when the specified feeler gauge can be pulled out with a very slight drag.

4. To adjust the clearance, loosen the cap nut while holding the hex nut. Adjust the valve clearance by turning the hex nut.

5. After adjustment hold the cap nut and lock

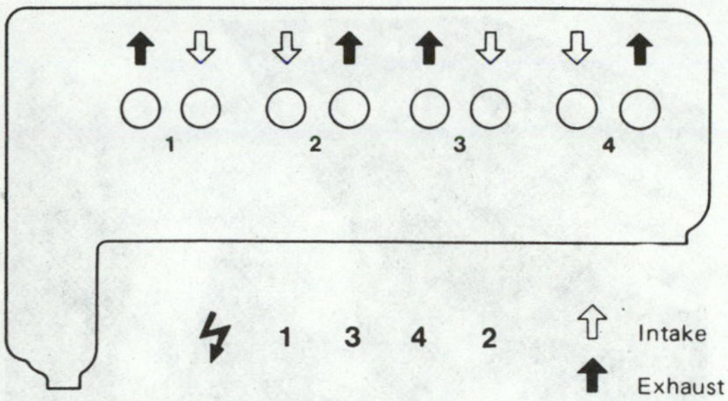

Valve arrangement—4-cylinder diesels

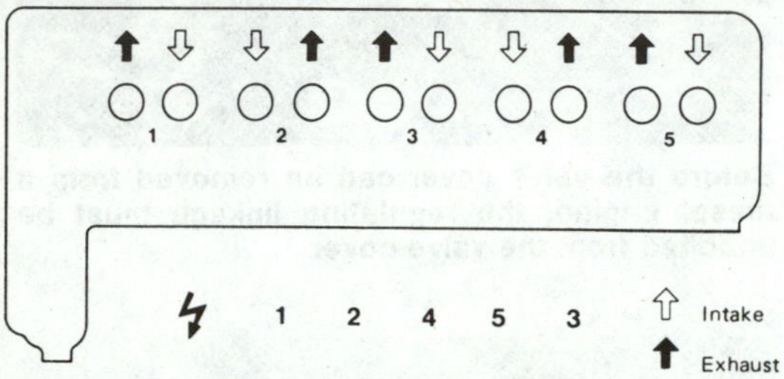

Valve arrangement—5-cylinder diesels

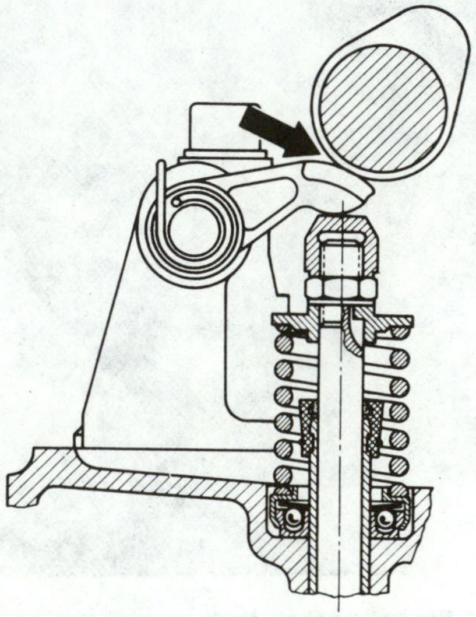

Measure valve clearance on diesel engines at arrow

7. Capnut
8. Locknut
14. Holding wrench
16. Adjusting wrench

Adjusting valve clearance on diesel engine

it in place with the nex nut. Recheck the clearance.

6. Check the gasket and install the rocker arm cover.

Idle Speed

The adjustments given here are intended to include only those which would be performed in the course of a normal tune-up, after the spark plugs, dwell angle, and ignition timing have been adjusted. Obviously, there are other adjustments which can and should be made for various reasons. These can be found in Chapter Four. The following chart gives the applications of various carburetors.

Carburetor Applications

Model	Year	Carburetor
230	1973–78	1 Stromberg 175 CDT
280 280C	1973–76 1973–76	1 Solex 4A1

NOTE: *Idle speed and fuel mixture are best set with a CO meter to comply with federal emission regulations. Follow the instructions that are packaged with the meter.*

CATALYTIC CONVERTER PRECAUTIONS

With the exception of diesels, most Mercedes-Benz cars are equipped with catalysts. The following points should be adhered to:

1. Use only unleaded gas.
2. Maintain the engine at the specified intervals.
3. Avoid running the engine with an excessively rich mixture. Do not run the engine excessively on fast idle.
4. Prolonged warm-up after a cold start should be avoided.
5. Do not check exhaust emissions over a long period of time without air injection.
6. Do not alter the emission control system in any way.

CARBURETORS

Stromberg 175 CDT

1. Turn off the heater and A/C and run the vehicle to normal operating temperature.

2. Check the throttle valve for ease of operation.
3. Connect a tachometer. Adjust the idle speed to specifications with the idle speed adjusting screw.
4. See whether the idle speed stop is resting against the throttle valve lever and not against the vacuum governor. Set the vacuum governor back if required.
5. If an exhaust gas analyzer (CO meter) is available, check the exhaust gas for percentage of CO. On 1975–76 models, check CO without air injection. Disconnect and plug the centerline from the blue switch-over valve. On 1977 models, be sure the wheel for altitude compensation is set properly.
6. Remove the plug in the exhaust gas tapping pipe and connect a tester to the hose.
7. If required, adjust the CO by means of the adjusting screw. Loosen the locknut while simultaneously holding the nozzle screw and turning the fuel shutoff valve. Accelerate a brief instant after each adjustment of the idle speed and fuel control screw to stabilize the mixture.
8. Check the idle speed again and adjust with the idle speed adjusting screw, if required.

Idle speed adjusting screw (8)—1973–75 230

Idle speed adjusting screw (8)—1975–76 230

Idle speed adjusting screw (147)—1977 and later 230

Adjust idle CO by turning the idle shut-off valve (38) on 1974–76 230

CO adjustment—1977 and later 230

9. Adjust the control linkage as follows:
   a. On vehicles with a manual transmission, attach the control rod and adjust it so that the roller rests in the gate lever without binding. The control lever is equipped with right and left hand threads.
   b. On vehicles with an automatic transmission, run the engine at idle speed. Set

the control rod so that it can be attached with no binding.

Solex 4A 1

1. The idle speed adjustment on this carburetor is made with the air cleaner installed and the crankcase breather connected.
2. Warm the engine to normal operating temperature. Do not adjust the idle after the engine has been driven very far or the engine will be too hot.
3. Check the throttle valve shaft for binding.
4. Adjust the idle speed to specifications with the idle speed adjusting screw. This should be done with a tachometer installed. Be sure that the idle speed stop is on the throttle valve lever and not on the vacuum governor. Loosen the spring of the vacuum governor, if necessary, by altering the setting of the adjusting nut.
5. If a CO meter is available, check the CO content of the exhaust gas without air injection. To cancel air injection, disconnect the red vacuum line (1974) or blue-violet line (1975–76). Follow the manufacturer's directions for use. If necessary, turn both mixture control screws to the right against the stop. Turn both screws simultaneously to the left until the CO percentage is within specifications. Turning the screws out will give a richer mixture and turning the screws in will give a leaner mixture.
6. Check the idle speed again until both the idle speed and CO percentage of the exhaust gas are as specified.

Disconnect air injection at arrow on carbureted 6-cylinder engines. See text for more details

FUEL INJECTION

Gasoline Engines

1974–75

Adjustment should be made with the air conditioner off and transmission in park.

1. Run the engine to normal operating temperature. The idle speed should not be adjusted immediately after hard driving for extended periods of time or when extremely hot Be sure the cruise control cable is attached free of tension.
2. Remove the air cleaner.
3. Disconnect the connecting rod from the valve connection and check to be sure that the throttle valve closes completely without binding.
4. Reattach the connecting rod so that it does not bind.
5. Connect a tachometer and adjust the idle speed to specifications with the idle speed air screw.
6. Check the exhaust gas content with a CO meter. On 1975 cars, check the CO without air injection. Pull the plug from the oil temperature switch on the right-hand wheel well and ground it to cancel air injection. If necessary, adjust the CO content with the adjusting screw on the control unit. Turning the screw clockwise will give a richer mixture, while turning

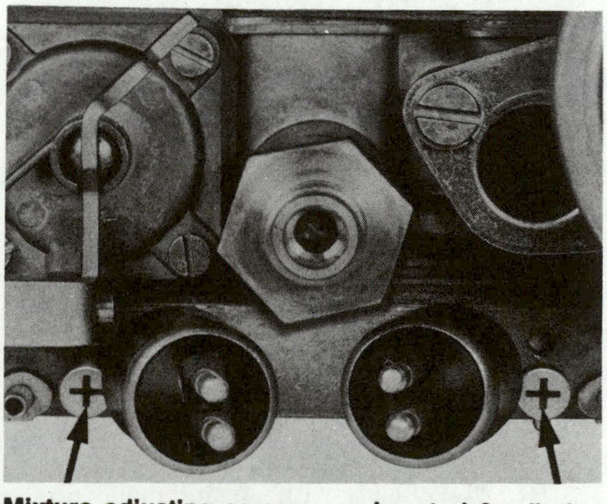

Mixture adjusting screws—carbureted 6-cylinder engines

On 1973–75 V8's, disconnect air injection at connector (arrow)

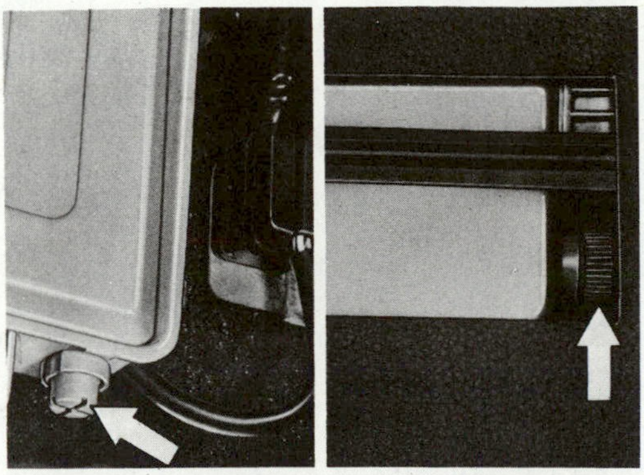

Idle mixture adjustment on 1974–75 V8 engines is performed at the control box

Idle speed adjustment on 1974–75 V8 engines is performed at the idle air screw (arrow)

the screw counterclockwise will give a leaner mixture.

7. On 450SL and 450SLC, the control unit can be reached after removing the inner lining below the glove-box. On others, the control unit adjusting screw is behind a piece of trim on the right front kick panel.

8. Check and, if necessary, readjust the idle speed.

9. Install the air cleaner. Check the idle speed and exhaust emissions values and readjust if necessary.

10. Remove the tachometer.

11. Adjust the regulating linkage (on cars with a gate lever) so that the roller in the gate lever rests free in the gate. Move the transmission lever to Drive and switch on the A/C. Move the power steering to full lock. Adjust the speed so the engine runs smoothly.

1976–79

The mechanical fuel injection is the airflow controlled type known as Bosch K-Jetronic®. The idle speed should be adjusted with the air conditioner off and the transmission in Park.

1. Connect a tachometer

2. Be sure the cruise control cable is connected to the regulating lever with no binding or kinking.

3. Run the engine to normal operating temperature.

4. Be sure the throttle valve rests against the idle speed stop.

5. Set the idle speed to specifications with the idle air screw.

6. If possible, check the CO level.

All 1976 engines—Check CO without air injection. Disconnect the blue/purple vacuum line at the blue thermal valve and plug the opening at the thermal valve to stop air injection.

1977–79 models—Disconnect the hose at the exhaust back pressure line and connect the CO tester to the line. On Federal V-8 engines, check CO with air injection connected. On all others, disconnect the blue/purple vacuum line from the blue thermal valve and plug the thermo valve to cancel air injection.

7. Adjust the CO valve by unscrewing the plug and inserting the special adjusting tool (allen wrench). Turn the screw in to richen the mixture and out to lean the mixture.

8. Accelerate briefly and check the speed and CO again.

Adjust the idle speed on 1976–79 V8 engines at the idle air screw (arrow)

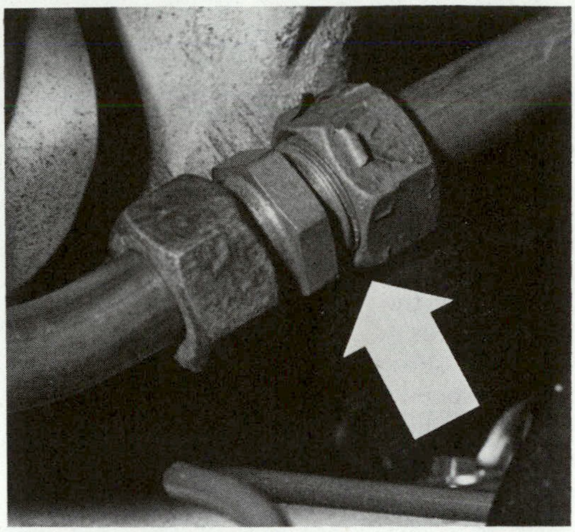

CO tap on 1976–79 V8 engines

An Allen wrench is necessary to adjust the idle mixture on 1976–79 V8 engines

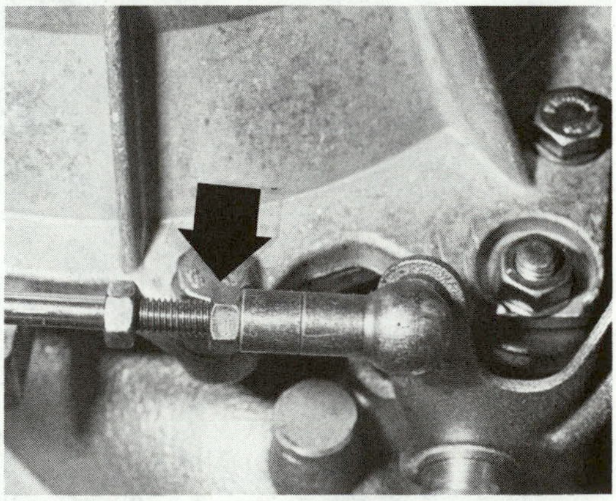

Regulating lever adjustment on 1976–79 V8 engines

9. Reconnect the vacuum lines and check the CO value again. It should be below the specified value.
10. Adjust the regulating lever so that the roller rests in the gate lever without binding. Put the transmission in Drive and turn on the A/C. Turn the wheels to full lock and adjust the idle speed so the engine runs smoothly.

1980 6 CYLINDER AND V8

1. Connect a tachometer and remote oil temperature gauge.
2. Run the engine to approximately 176°F oil temperature.
3. The automatic transmission should be in Park and the A/C off.
4. Be sure the throttle valve lever rests against the idle stop.
5. Adjust the Bowden cable with the adjusting screw so there is no tension against the throttle valve lever.
6. Check the idle speed. If necessary, adjust with the idle air adjustment screw.

1981 6 CYLINDER

1. Run the engine to normal operating temperature (167°–185° oil temperature) and connect a tachometer.
2. The automatic transmission should be in Park and A/C off.
3. Be sure the throttle valve lever rests against the idle speed stop.
4. Be sure the cruise control actuating rod rests against the idle speed stop. Disconnect the connecting rod and push the lever of the actuating lever clockwise to the idle speed position.
5. Reconnect the connecting rod; make sure that the actuating element is approximately .04 in. from the idle speed stop. Adjust this clearance with the pull rod.
6. Check and adjust the idle speed. Idle speed is adjusted at the idle speed air screw.

Idle speed adjusting screw—1980 and later V8 engines

1981–84

These engines have electronically controlled idle speed, using a solenoid connected to terminals 1 and 5 of the control unit.

Diesel Engines

1973–80 (EXCEPT 1980 300 SD)

Since the diesel engine has no ignition distributor or ignition coil there is no way to connect an external tachometer to measure idle speed. While using the built-in tachometer on the dash is not the most accurate way, the only other possibility is to set the idle speed by ear.

1. On models before 1977, turn the knob on the instrument panel completely clockwise. Turn it again counterclockwise. The travel before the idle speed is raised should not exceed about ½ turn. If required, adjust the travel with the nut.
2. On 1977–80 models, turn the knob on the instrument panel completely clockwise and check the distance between the adjusting ring and the specially shaped spring. It should be approximately .04 in.
3. With the engine stopped, depress the accelerator pedal while turning the idle knob counterclockwise.
4. Start the engine. The idle should be 1000–1100 rpm. Adjust this with the adjusting screw, but do not exceed 1100 rpm.
5. On 1977–80 models, be sure the special spring is installed correctly.
6. Run the engine to operating temperature.
7. Turn the idle adjusting knob on the dash fully to the right.

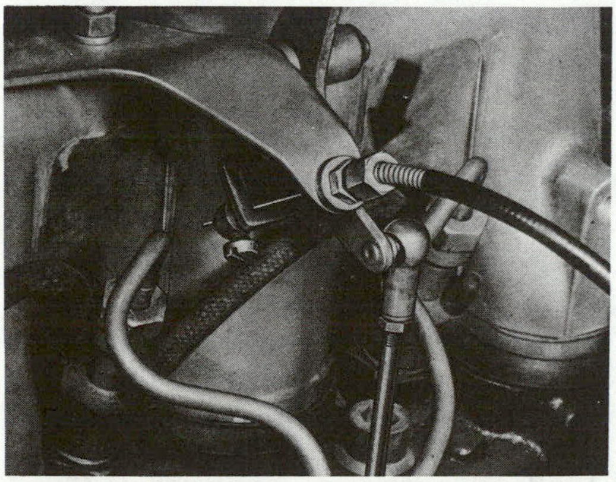

Adjusting nut for dashboard idle speed knob

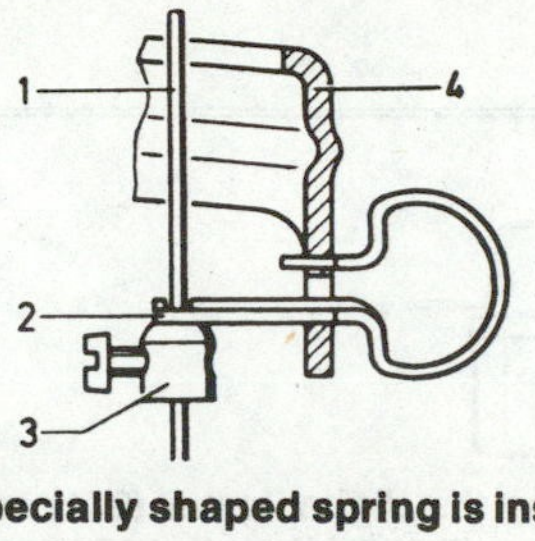

Be sure the specially shaped spring is installed as shown

Diesel engine idle speed adjustment on the 240D

Diesel engine idle speed adjustment—300D, 300CD

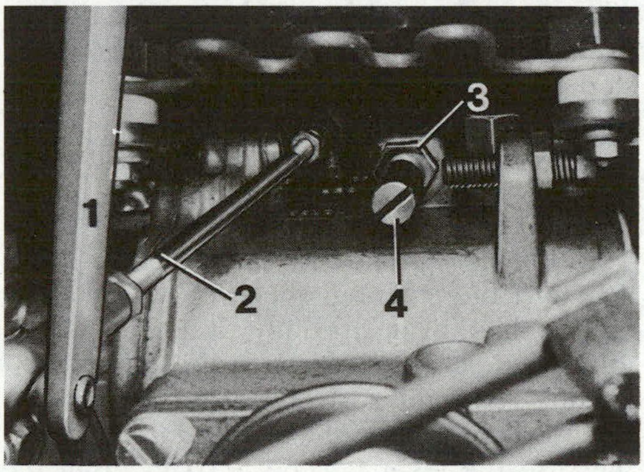

Diesel engine idle speed adjustment—1976 and later

8. Disconnect the regulating rod and adjust the idle speed with the idle speed adjusting screw. 1977–80 models have a locknut on the idle speed adjusting screw.
9. Reconnect the regulating rod.

1980 300SD AND 1981–84 DIESELS EXCEPT 1982–83 240D AND 1984 190D

1. Run the engine to normal operating temperature.

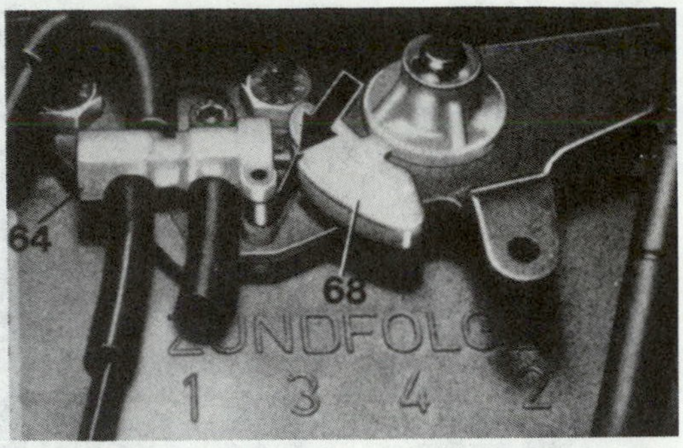

Clearance between the cam and actuator on the switchover valve—1980 and later diesels (except turbos)

2. On normally aspirated engines, turn the idle speed adjuster on the dash completely to the right.
3. Disconnect the pushrod at the angle lever.
4. Check the idle speed. Adjust by loosening the locknut and adjusting the idle speed screw. Tighten the locknut.
5. On all except Turbodiesels, adjust the pushrod so that a clearance of approximately 0.2 in. exists between the cam on the lever and the actuator on the switchover valve. The lever on the fuel injection pump must rest against the idle stop.
6. On all models except the 1981 turbodiesel, depress the stop lever as far as possible. The cruise control Bowden cable should be free of tension against the angle lever. Use the adjusting screw to alter the tension. Let go of the stop lever. The Bowden cable should have a slight amount of play.
7. On turbodiesels, adjust the pushrod so that the roller in the guide lever rests free of tension against the stop.
8. Put the automatic transmission in Drive and turn the steering wheel to full lock. The engine should run smoothly. If not, adjust the idle speed. Disconnect the cruise control connecting rod, and push the lever clockwise to the idle stop. Attach the connecting rod, making sure the lever is about 0.04 in. from the idle speed stop.

CAUTION: *If the engine speed is adjusted higher, it will be above the controlled idle speed range of the governor and the engine can increase in speed to maximum rpm.*

1982–83 240D

1. Run the engine to normal operating temperature.
2. Turn the idle speed adjuster knob on the dashboard completely to the right.
3. Disconnect the pushrod at the operating lever.
4. Move the guide lever to the idle speed position. Set the edge of the guide lever at the mark (arrow) on the cap.
5. Check, and if necessary, adjust the idle speed. Use the idle speed adjusting screw.
6. Attach the pushrod to the injection pump lever so that the rod is free of tension when the lever is against the idle speed stop.
7. Check to be sure the cruise control rods are free of tension.
8. Move the automatic transmission into Drive. Turn on the A/C and turn the wheels to full lock. The engine should run smoothly. Adjust the idle speed if necessary.

1984 190D

NOTE: *Testing the idle speed on the 190D will require two special tools. A digital tester (Sun-1019, 2110 or All-Test 3610-MB) and a TDC impulse transmitter; not commonly available tools. Without these two special tools, idle speed adjustment is impossible and should not be attempted.*

1. Run the engine until it reaches normal operating temperature.
2. Connect the digital tester and the TDC impulse transmitter as indicated in the illustration.
3. Check all linkages for ease of operation.

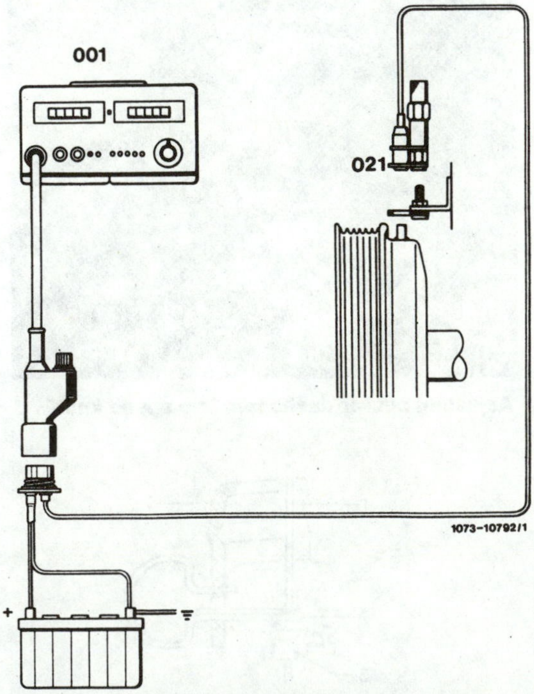

Connecting the digital tester (001) and the TDC impulse transmitter (021) on the 190D

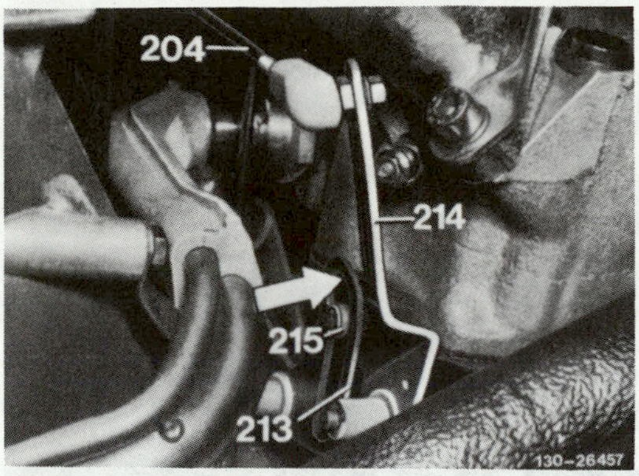

Throttle linkage on the 190D

Loosen the locknut (4A) and turn the vacuum control unit (4) to adjust the idle speed on the 190D

4. Disconnect the pushrod (204) from the adjusting lever (214).

5. Start the engine and check the idle speed. If required, adjust by loosening the locknut on the vacuum control unit and turning the unit itself in or out.

6. After the idle speed is correct, tighten the vacuum control unit locknut and reconnect the pushrod so that it is tension free when the lever is against the idle speed stop.

7. Switch on all auxiliary power accessories and check that the engine continues to run smoothly. Readjust the idle speed if necessary.

8. Disconnect the two special tools and turn off the engine.

Engine and Engine Rebuilding

3

UNDERSTANDING BASIC ELECTRICITY

Understanding the basic theory of electricity makes electrical troubleshooting much easier. Several gauges are used in electrical troubleshooting to see inside the circuit being tested. Without a basic understanding, it will be difficult to understand testing procedures.

Electricity is the flow of electrons—hypothetical particles thought to constitute the basic "stuff" of electricity. In a comparison with water flowing in a pipe, the electrons would be the water. As the flow of water can be measured, the flow of electricity can be measured. The unit of measurement is amperes, frequently abbreviated "amps." An ammeter will measure the actual amount of current flowing in the circuit.

Just as the water pressure is measured in units such as pounds per square inch, electrical pressure is measured in volts. When a voltmeter's two probes are placed on two "live" portions of an electrical circuit with different electrical pressures, current will flow through the voltmeter and produce a reading which indicates the difference in electrical pressure between the two parts of the circuit.

While increasing the voltage in a circuit will increase the flow of current, the actual flow depends not only on voltage, but on the resistance of the circuit. The standard unit for measuring circuit resistance is an ohm, measured by an ohmmeter. The ohmmeter is somewhat similar to an ammeter, but incorporates it own source of power so that a standard voltage is always present.

An actual electric circuit consists of four basic parts. These are: the power source, such as a generator or battery; a hot wire, which conducts the electricity under a relatively high voltage to the component supplied by the circuit; the load, such as a lamp, motor, resistor, or relay coil; and the ground wire, which carries the current back to the source under very low voltage. In such a circuit the bulk of the resistance exists between the point where the hot wire is connected to the load, and the point where the load is grounded. In an automobile, the vehicle's frame, which is made of steel, is used as a part of the ground circuit for many of the electrical devices.

Remember that, in electrical testing, the voltmeter is connected in parallel with the circuit being tested (without disconnecting any wires) and measures the difference in voltage between the locations of the two probes; that the ammeter is connected in series with the load (the circuit is separated at one point and the ammeter inserted so it becomes a part of the circuit); and the ohmmeter is self-powered, so that all the power in the circuit should be off and the portion of the circuit to be measured contacted at either end by one of the probes of the meter.

For any electrical system to operate, it must make a complete circuit. This simply means that the power flow from the battery must make a complete circle. When an electrical component is operating, power flows from the battery to the component, passes through the component causing it to perform its function (lighting a light bulb) and then returns to the battery through the ground of the circuit. This ground is usually (but not always) the metal part of the car on which the electrical component is mounted.

Perhaps the easiest way to visualize this is to think of connecting a light bulb with two wires attached to it to your car battery. The battery in your car has two posts (negative and positive). If one of the two wires attached to the light bulb was attached to the negative post of the battery and the other wire was attached to the positive post of the battery, you would have a complete circuit. Current from the battery would flow out one post, through the wire attached to it and then to the light bulb, where it would pass through causing it to light. It would then leave the light bulb, travel through the other wire, and return to the other post of the battery.

The normal automotive circuit differs from this simple example in two ways. First, instead of having a return wire from the bulb to the battery, the light bulb returns the current to the battery through the chassis of the vehicle. Since the negative battery cable is attached to the chassis and the chassis is made of electrically conductive metal, the chassis of the vehicle can serve as a ground wire to complete the circuit. Secondly, most automotive circuits contain switches to turn components on and off.

Some electrical components which require a large amount of current to operate also have a relay in their circuit. Since these circuits carry a large amount of current, the thickness of the wire in the circuit (gauge size) is also greater. If this large wire were connected from the component to the control switch on the instrument panel, and then back to the component, a voltage drop would occur in the circuit. To prevent this potential drop in voltage, an electromagnetic switch (relay) is used. The large wires in the circuit are connected from the car battery to one side of the relay, and from the opposite side of the relay to the component. The relay is normally open, preventing current from passing through the circuit. An additional, smaller, wire is connected from the relay to the control switch for the circuit. When the control switch is turned on, it grounds the smaller wire from the relay and completes the circuit. When the control switch is turned on, it grounds the smaller wire from the relay. If you were to disconnect the light bulb (from the previous example of a lightbulb being connected to the battery by two wires) from the wires and touch the two wires together (please take our word for this; don't try it), the result will be a shower of sparks. A similar thing happens (on a smaller scale) when the power supply wire to a component or the electrical component itself becomes grounded before the normal ground connection for the circuit. To prevent damage to the system, the fuse for the circuit blows to interrupt the circuit—protecting the components from damage. Because grounding a wire from a power source makes a complete circuit—less the required component to use the power—the phenomenon is called a short circuit. The most common causes of short circuits are: the rubber insulation on a wire breaking or rubbing through to expose the current carrying core of the wire to a metal part of the car, or a shorted switch.

Some electrical systems on the car are protected by a circuit breaker which is, basically, a self-repairing fuse. When either of the above-described events takes place in a system which is protected by a circuit breaker, the circuit breaker opens the circuit the same way a fuse does. However, when either the short is removed from the circuit or the surge subsides, the circuit breaker resets itself and does not have to be replaced as a fuse does.

The final protective device in the chassis electrical system is a fuse link. A fuse link is a wire that acts as a fuse. It is connected between the starter relay and the main wiring harness for the car. This connection is under the hood, very near a similar fuse link which protects the engine electrical system. Since the fuse link protects all the chassis electrical components, it is the probable cause of trouble when none of the electrical components function, unless the battery is disconnected or dead.

Electrical problems generally fall into one of three areas:

1. The component that is not functioning is not receiving current.
2. The component itself is not functioning.
3. The component is not properly grounded.

Problems that fall into the first category are by far the most complicated. It is the current supply system to the component which contains all the switches, relays, fuses, etc.

The electrical system can be checked with a test light and a jumper wire. A test light is a device that looks like a pointed screwdriver with a wire attached to it. It has a light bulb in its handle. A jumper wire is a piece of insulated wire with an alligator clip attached to each end.

If a light bulb is not working, you must follow a systematic plan to determine which of the three causes is the villain.

1. Turn on the switch that controls the inoperable bulb.
2. Disconnect the power supply wire from the bulb.
3. Attach the ground wire on the test light to a good metal ground.
4. Touch the probe end of the test light to the end of the power supply wire that was disconnected from the bulb. If the bulb is receiving current, the test light will go on.

NOTE: *If the bulb is one which works only when the ignition key is turned on (turn signal), make sure the key is turned on.*

If the test light does not go on, then the problem is in the circuit between the battery and the bulb. As mentioned before, this includes all the switches, fuses, and relays in the system. Turn to the wiring diagram and find the bulb on the diagram. Follow the wire that runs back to the battery. The problem is an open circuit between the battery and the bulb. If the fuse is blown and, when replaced, immediately blows again, there is a short circuit in the system which must be located and repaired. If there is a switch in the system, bypass it with a jumper wire. This is done by connecting one end of the jumper wire to the power supply wire into the switch and the other end of the jumper wire to the wire coming out of the switch. Again, consult the wiring diagram. If the test light lights with the jumper wire installed, the switch or whatever was bypassed is defective.

NOTE: *Never substitute the jumper wire for the bulb, as the bulb is the component required to use the power from the power source.*

5. If the bulb in the test light goes on, then the current is getting to the bulb that is not working in the car. This eliminates the first of the three possible causes. Connect the power supply wire and connect a jumper wire from the bulb to a good metal ground. Do this with the switch which controls the bulb turned on, and also the ignition switch turned on if it is required for the light to work. If the bulb works with jumper wire installed, then it has a bad ground. This is usually caused by the metal area on which the bulb mounts to the car being coated with some type of foreign matter.

6. If neither test located the source of the trouble, then the light bulb itself is defective.

The above test procedure can be applied to any of the components of the chassis electrical system by substituting the component that is not working for the light bulb. Remember that for any electrical system to work, all connections must be clean and tight.

Battery and Starting System

The battery is the first link in the chain of mechanisms which work together to provide cranking of the automobile engine. In most modern cars, the battery is a lead-acid electrochemical device consisting of six two-volt (2-V) subsections connected in series so the unit is capable of producing approximately 12 V of electrical pressure. Each subsection, or cell, consists of a series of positive and negative plates held a short distance apart in a solution of sulfuric and water. The two types of plates are of dissimilar metals. This causes a chemical reaction to be set up, and it is this reaction which produces current flow from the battery when its positive and negative terminals are connected to an electrical appliance such as a lamp or motor. The continued transfer of electrons would eventually convert the sulfuric acid in the electrolyte to water, and make the two plates identical in chemical composition. As electrical energy is removed from the battery, its voltage output tends to drop. Thus, measuring battery voltage and battery electrolyte composition are two ways of checking the ability of the unit to supply power. During the starting of the engine, electrical energy is removed from the battery. However, if the charging circuit is in good condition and the operating conditions are normal, the power removed from the battery will be replaced by the generator (or alternator) which will force electrons back through the battery, reversing the normal flow, and restoring the battery to its original chemical state.

The battery and starting motor are linked by very heavy electrical cables designed to minimize resistance to the flow of current. Generally, the major power supply cable that leaves the battery goes directly to the starter, while other electrical system needs are supplied by a smaller cable. During the starter operation, power flows from the battery to the starter and is grounded through the car's frame and the battery's negative ground strap.

The starting motor is a specially designed, direct current electric motor capable of producing a very great amount of power for its size. One thing that allows the motor to produce a great deal of power is its tremendous rotating speed. It drives the engine through a tiny piston gear (attached to the starter's armature), which drives the very large flywheel ring gear at a greatly reduced speed. Another factor allowing it to produce so much power is that only intermittent operation is required of it. Thus, little allowance for air circulation is required, and the windings can be built into a very small space.

The starter solenoid is a magnetic device which employs the small current supplied by the starting switch circuit of the ignition switch. This magnetic action moves a plunger which mechanically engages the starter and electrically closes the heavy switch which connects it to the battery. The starting switch circuit consists of the starting switch contained within the ignition switch, a transmission neutral safety switch or clutch pedal switch, and the wiring necessary to connect these with the starter solenoid or relay.

A pinion, which is a small gear, is mounted to a one-way drive clutch. This clutch is splined to the starter armature shaft. When the ignition switch is moved to the "start" position, the solenoid plunger slides the pinion toward the flywheel ring gear via a collar and spring. If the teeth on the pinion and flywheel match properly, the pinion will engage the flywheel immediately. If the gear teeth butt one another, the spring will be compressed and will force the gears to mesh as soon as the starter turns far enough to allow them to do so. As the solenoid plunger reaches the end of its travel, it closes the contacts that connect the battery and starter and then the engine is cranked.

As soon as the engine starts, the flywheel ring gear begins turning fast enough to drive the pinion at an extremely high rate of speed. At this point, the one-way clutch begins allowing the pinion to spin faster than the starter shaft so that the starter will not operate at excessive speed. When the ignition switch is released from the starter position, the solenoid is de-energized, and a spring contained within the solenoid assembly pulls the gear out of mesh and interrupts the current flow to the starter.

Some starters employ a separate relay, mounted away from the starter, to switch the motor and solenoid current on and off. The relay thus replaces the solenoid electrical switch, but does not eliminate the need for a solenoid mounted on the starter used to mechanically engage the starter drive gears. The relay is used to reduce the amount of current the starting switch must carry.

The Charging System

The automobile charging system provides electrical power for operation of the vehicle's ignition and starting systems and all the electrical accessories. The battery serves as an electrical surge or storage tank, storing (in chemical form) the energy originally produced by the engine-driven generator. The system also provides a means of regulating generator output to protect the battery from being overcharged and to avoid excessive voltage to the accessories.

The storage battery is a chemical device incorporating parallel lead plates in a tank containing a sulfuric acid-water solution. Adjacent plates are slightly dissimilar, and the chemical reaction of the two dissimilar plates produces electrical energy when the battery is connected to a load such as the starter motor. The chemical reaction is reversible, so that when the generator is producing a voltage (electrical pressure) greater than that produced by the battery, electricity is forced into the battery, and the battery is returned to its fully charged state.

The vehicle's generator is driven mechanically, through V belts, by the engine crankshaft. It consists of two coils of fine wire, one stationary (the "stator"), and one movable (the "rotor"). The rotor may also be known as the "armature," and consists of fine wire wrapped around an iron core which is mounted on a shaft. The electricity which flows through the two coils of wire (provided initially by the battery in some cases) creates an intense magnetic field around both rotor and stator, and the interaction between the two fields creates voltage, allowing the generator to power the accessories and charge the battery.

There are two types of generators; the earlier is the direct current (DC) type. The current produced by the DC generator is generated in the armature and carried off the spinning armature by stationary brushes contacting the commutator. The commutator plates, which are separated from one another by a very short gap, are connected to the armature circuits so that current will flow in one direction only in the wires carrying the generator output. The generator stator consists of two stationary coils of wire which draw some of the output current of the generator to form a powerful magnetic field and create the interaction of fields which generates the voltage. The generator field is wired in series with the regulator.

Newer automobiles use alternating current generators because they are more efficient, can be rotated at higher speeds, and have fewer brush problems. In an alternator, the field rotates while all the current produced passes only through the stator windings. The brushes bear against continuous slip rings rather than a commutator. This causes the current produced to periodically reverse the direction of its flow. Diodes (electrical one-way switches) block the flow of current from traveling in the wrong direction. A series of diodes is wired together to permit the alternating flow of the stator to be converted to a pulsating, but unidirectional flow at the alternator output. The alternator's field is wired in series with the voltage regulator.

The regulator consists of several circuits. Each circuit has a core, or magnetic coil of wire, which operates a switch. Each switch is connected to ground through one or more resistors. The coil of wire responds directly to system voltage. When the voltage reaches the required level, the magnetic field created by the winding of wire closes the switch and inserts a resistance into the generator field circuit, thus reducing the output. The contacts of the switch cycle open and close many times each second to precisely control voltage.

While alternators are self-limiting as far as maximum current is concerned, DC generators employ a current regulating circuit which responds directly to the total amount of current flowing through the generator circuit rather than to the output voltage. The current regulator is similar to the voltage regulator except that all system current must flow through the energizing coil on its way to the various accessories.

SAFETY PRECAUTIONS

Observing these precautions will ensure safe handling of the electrical system components, and will avoid damage to the vehicle's electrical system:

A. Be *absolutely* sure of the polarity of a booster battery before making connections. Connect the cables positive to positive, and negative to negative. Connect positive cables first and then make the last connection to a ground on the body of the booster vehicle so that arching cannot ignite hydrogen gas that may have accumulated near the battery. Even momentary connection of a booster battery with the polarity reserved will damage alternator diodes.

B. Disconnect both vehicle battery cables before attempting to charge a battery.

C. Never ground the alternator or generator output or battery terminal. Be cautious when using metal tools around a battery to avoid creating a short circuit between the terminals.

D. Never ground the field circuit between the alternator and regulator.

E. Never run an alternator or generator without load unless the field circuit is disconnected.

F. Never attempt to polarize an alternator.

G. Keep the regulator cover in place when taking voltage and current limiter readings.

H. Use insulated tools when adjusting the regulator.

I. Whenever DC generator-to-regulator wires have been disconnected, the generator *must* be repolarized. To do this with an externally grounded, light duty generator, momentarily place a jumper wire between the battery terminal and the generator terminal of the regulator. With an internally grounded heavy duty unit, disconnect the wire to the regulator field terminal and touch the regulator battery terminal with it.

ENGINE ELECTRICAL

Distributor

REMOVAL AND INSTALLATION

The removal and installation procedures for all distributors on Mercedes-Benz vehicles are basically similar. However, certain minor differences may exist from model to model.

1. The distributor (on most models) is located on the front of the engine.
2. Remove the dust cover, distributor cap, cable plug connections, and vacuum line.
3. Rotating the engine in the direction of normal rotation, crank it around until the markings on the distributor rotor and distributor housing are aligned.
4. The engine can be cranked with a socket wrench on the balancer bolt or with a small prybar inserted in the balancer.
5. Matchmark the distributor body and the engine so that the distributor can be returned to its original position. White paint can be used for this purpose. The notch on the rim of the distributor housing indicates No. 1 cylinder.
6. Remove the distributor hold-down bolt and withdraw the distributor from the engine.

NOTE: *Do not crank the engine while the distributor is removed.*

7. To install the distributor, reverse the removal instructions. Insert the distributor so that the matchmarks on the distributor and engine are aligned.
8. Tighten the clamp bolt and check the dwell angle and ignition timing.

Electronic Ignition Distributor

TESTING

All Except 1981 6 Cyl. and 1984 4 Cyl.

1. Check the screw type plug terminals and the plug wires.
2. With the ignition ON, a primary current of about 8 amps will flow continuously through the system.
3. Check the input voltage at the terminal block. Terminal 15 should show 4.5 volts and terminal 1 should show 05–2.0 volts. If the voltage at terminal 1 is excessive, replace the switching unit.
4. If there is no spark but terminal 1 voltage is OK, check the armature resistance (terminal 7 and 31d). Resistance should be 450–750 ohms.
5. Test the pick-up coil resistance. There should be infinite resistance between terminal 7 and ground.
6. Check the armature and pick-up coil for mechanical damage. An air gap should exist between them.

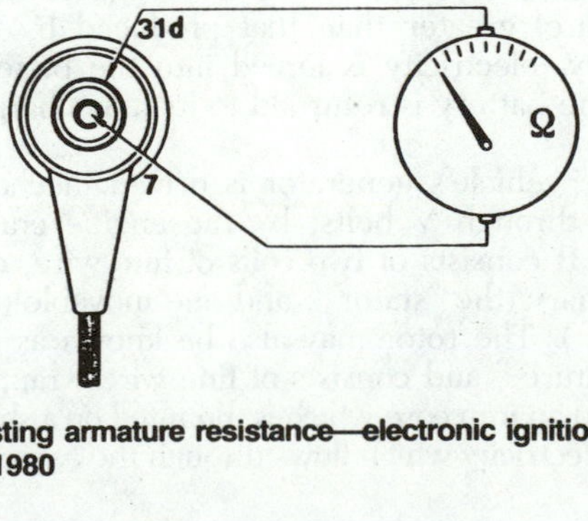

Testing armature resistance—electronic ignition prior to 1980

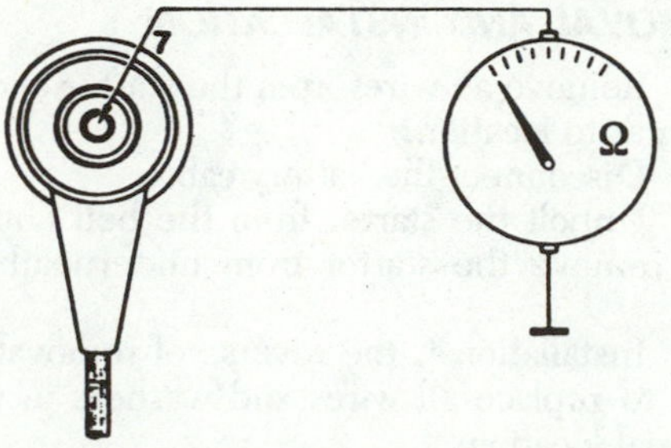

Testing pick-up coil resistance—electronic ignition prior to 1980

7. Check the dwell angle. Even though it cannot be adjusted, it should be 25–39° at 1400–1500 rpm.

8. If the armature and pick up coil are functioning, replace the switching unit. If the armature and pick-up coil indicate no damage, replace the switching unit. If the armature or pick-up coil are defective, replace the distributor.

1981 6 Cylinder

This engine uses a new breakerless transistorized ignition system with no preresistance and no current flow unless the engine is running. The new system consists of ignition coil, distributor, harness and switching unit. Do not replace the coil with a previously used coil. Also, see the ignition system precautions given previously.

1. Test the voltage between bushing 5 of the diagnosis plug and ground with the ignition ON. Nominal battery voltage should be indicated. If not, test the voltage via the ignition switch. If voltage is correct, go to Step 2.

2. Test the voltage between bushing 4 and 5 of the diagnosis plug socket. Zero voltage should be indicated. If voltage is more than 0.1 volt, switch off the ignition immediately. Renew the switching unit. Check the pressure relief plug in the ignition coil and the ohmic value of the ignition coil between terminals 1 and 15. If the pressure relief plug has popped out or the resistance is not .7Ω, replace the ignition coil.

3. Test the dwell angle. It should be 7–25°. If more than 25°, replace the switching unit. If no reading or the reading is correct, go to Step 4.

4. Disconnect the green control line from the switching unit and test the resistance between terminals 3 and 7. Resistance should be 500–700ohms. If the resistance is wrong, pull the green cable from the distributor and see if there are 500–700 ohms present at the connector plugs. If so, replace the green cable. If not, replace the distributor.

5. Remove the green cable from the control unit. There should be 200 kΩ between terminals 3 or 7 and ground. If not, disconnect the green cable from the distributor and test the resistance between any of the plugs and ground. If 200 kΩ are not present, replace the distributor.

1984 4 Cylinder

The electronic ignition system on the 190E differs from the previous systems with the addition of a small switching unit.

NOTE: *The base plate on this switching unit serves as a heat sink; periodic cleaning will ensure proper heat flow between it and the wheel arch.*

The ignition coil and all testing procedures are similar to those given for the 1981 6 cylinder engine.

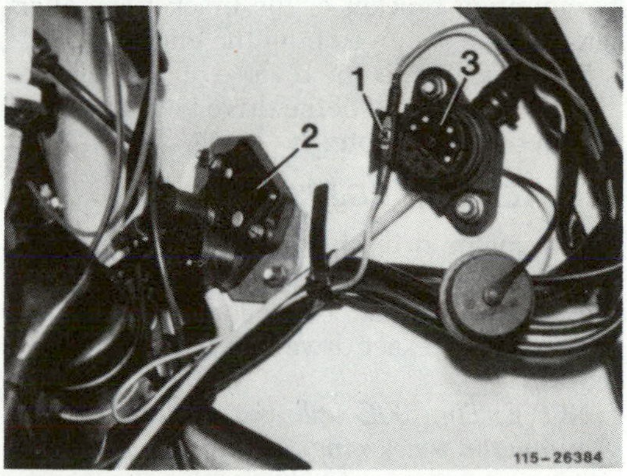

The switching unit (2), cable connector (1) and diagnostic socket (3) distinguish the 190E electronic ignition from that of the 1981 6 cylinder

Alternator

Since 1968, all Mercedes-Benz cars imported into the United States use 12 volt alternators, sometimes in conjunction with the transistor (electronic) ignition system.

PRECAUTIONS

Some precautions that should be taken into consideration when working on this, or any other, AC charging system are as follows:

1. Never switch battery polarity.
2. When installing a battery, always connect the grounded terminal first.
3. Never disconnect the battery while the engine is running.
4. If the molded connector is disconnected from the alternator, do not ground the hot wire.
5. Never run the alternator with the main output cable disconnected.
6. Never electric weld around the car without disconnecting the alternator.

7. Never apply any voltage in excess of battery voltage during testing.

8. Never "jump" a battery for starting purposes with more than 12 volts.

REMOVAL AND INSTALLATION

The alternator is located on the left or right-hand side, usually down low. Because of the location, it is sometimes easier to remove the alternator from below the vehicle. The following is a general procedure for all models.

1. Locate the alternator and disconnect and tag all wires.
2. Loosen the adjusting (pivot) bolt or the adjusting mechanism and swing the alternator in toward the engine.
3. Remove the drive belt from the alternator pulley.
4. The alternator can now be removed from its mounting bracket or the bracket and alternator can be removed from the engine.
5. Installation is the reverse of removal.
6. Re-tension all of the drive belts that were loosened. See Chapter 1.

BELT TENSION ADJUSTMENT

All alternator drive belts should be tensioned to the specified deflection under thumb pressure at the middle of its longest span. See Chapter 1 for exact drive belt adjustment procedures.

NOTE: *The 190D utilizes a single V-belt with automatic tensioning. No adjustment is necessary.*

Starter

All Mercedes-Benz passenger cars are equipped with 12-volt Bosch electric starters of various rated outputs. The starter motor is actually nothing but a simple series-wound electric motor of high torque output, fitted with a drive pinion and a device to mesh the pinion with the flywheel ring gear. The carrier, which is connected to the pinion through the overrunning clutch, runs in splines machined in the armature shaft. When the armature rotates, these splines force the pinion into mesh. When the engine starts, the overrunning (one-way) clutch releases the pinion and the unit disengages. The starter is actuated and the pinion engaged by an electric solenoid mounted on top of the starter motor.

When removing the starter, note the exact position of all wires and washers, since they should be installed in their original locations. On some models it may be necessary to also position the front wheels to the left or right to provide working clearance.

REMOVAL AND INSTALLATION

1. Remove all wires from the starter and tag them as to location.
2. Disconnect the battery cable.
3. Unbolt the starter from the bell housing and remove the starter from underneath the car.
5. Installation is the reverse of removal. Be sure to replace all wires and washers in their original locations.

Battery

The battery is located in the engine compartment and can be easily removed by disconnecting the battery cables and removing the hold-down clamp.

ENGINE MECHANICAL

Engine Removal and Installation

NOTE: *In all cases, Mercedes-Benz engines and transmissions are removed as a unit.*

CAUTION: *Air conditioner lines should not be indiscriminately disconnected without taking proper precautions. It is best to swing the compressor out of the way while still connected to its hoses. Never do any welding around the compressor—heat may cause an explosion. Also, the refrigerant, while inert at normal room temperature, breaks down under high temperature into hydrogen fluoride and phosgene (among other products), which are highly poisonous.*

190D, 190E, 230, 240D, 300D, 300CD, 300TD, AND 300SD

Remove the engine/transmission as a unit.

1. Remove the hood, then drain the cooling system and disconnect the battery.
2. Remove the fan shroud, radiator, and disconnect all heater hoses and oil cooler lines. Plug all openings to keep out dirt.
3. Remove the air cleaner and all fuel, vacuum and oil hoses.

Swing the A/C compressor aside. Leave lines connected. Disconnect all other fluid lines and hoses. Plug all openings to keep out dirt.

4. Remove the viscous coupling and fan and disconnect the carburetor choke cable (if so equipped).
5. On diesel engines, disconnect the idle control and starting cables. On the 300SD, loosen the oil filter cover slightly. Siphon off the power steering fluid and disconnect the hoses.
6. On all engines, disconnect the accelerator linkage.

Battery and Starter Specifications

All cars use 12 volt, negative ground electrical systems

Engine Model	Battery AMP Hour Capacity	Starter: Lock Test Amps	Lock Test Volts	Lock Test Torque (ft/lbs)	No Load Test Amps	No Load Test Volts	No Load Test RPM	Brush Spring Tension (oz)	Min Brush Length (in.)
All w/Diesel Engine	88	650–750	9.0	1000–1200	80–95	12	7500–8500	NA	NA
All w/Gas Engine	66	290–300	9.0	1600–1800	50–70	12	9000–11000	NA	.05

NA—Not specified by manufacturer

General Gasoline Engine Specifications

Year Model	Engine Model	Engine Displacement (cc)	Carburetor Type	Horsepower @ rpm	Torque @ rpm (ft lbs)	Bore x Stroke (mm)	Compression Ratio	Firing Order
190E	M102	2299	Fuel Injection	113 @ 5000	133 @ 3500	95.50 x 80.25	8.0:1	1342
230	M115	2307	Stromberg 175 CDT	95 @ 4800 ③	128 @ 2500 ④	93.75 x 83.6	8.0:1	1342
280S (1975–76)	M110	2746	Solex 4-bbl	120 @ 4800	143 @ 2800	86.00 x 78.80	8.0:1	153624
280, 280C (1974–76)	M110	2746	Solex 4-bbl	120 @ 4800	143 @ 2800	86.00 x 78.80	8.0:1	153624
280E, 280CE (1977–79) 280SE (1977–79)	M110	2746	Fuel Injection	142 @ 5750 ⑤	149 @ 4600 ⑥	86.00 x 78.80	8.0:1	153624
380SE, 380SEC, 380SEL, 380SL, 380SLC	M116	3839	Fuel Injection	155 @ 4750	196 @ 2750	88.0 x 78.9	8.3:1	15486372
1974 450SE 450SEL 450SL 450SLC	M117	4520	Fuel Injection	190 @ 4750 ①	240 @ 3000 ②	92.00 x 85.00	8.0:	15486372
1975–79 450SE 450SEL 450SL 450SLC	M117	4520	Fuel Injection	180 @ 4750	220 @ 3000	92.00 x 85.00	8.0:1	15486372
450SEL 6.9	M100	6834	Fuel Injection	250 @ 4000	360 @ 2500	107.00 x 95.00	8.0:1	15486372
500SEC, 500SEL	M117	4973	Fuel Injection	184 @ 4500	247 @ 2000	96.5 x 85.0	8.0:1	1548672

① California—180 @ 4750
② California—232 @ 3000
③ 1975 California—85 @ 4800
④ 1975–77 California—122 @ 2500
⑤ 1977 and later California—137 @ 5750
⑥ 1977 and later California—142 @ 4600

General Diesel Engine Specifications

Car Model	Engine Model	Engine Displacement (cc)	Fuel Delivery	Horsepower @ rpm	Torque @ rpm (ft. lbs.)	Bore x Stroke (mm)	Compression Ratio	Firing Order
190D	OM601	2197	Fuel Injection	72 @ 4200	96 @ 2800	87.0 x 92.4	22.0:1	1342
240D	OM616	2404	Fuel Injection	62–67 @ 4000	97 @ 2400	91.0 x 92.4	21:1	1342
300D ('77–'81) 300CD ('78–'81) 300TD ('79–'80)	OM617	3005 ①	Fuel Injection	77–83 @ 4000	115–120 @ 2400	91.0 x 92.4 ②	21:1	12453
300 TD Turbo ('81–'84) 300D ('82–'84) 300CD ('82–'84)	OM617	2998	Fuel Inj. Turbo-charged	120 @ 4350 ③	170 @ 2400 ④	90.0 x 92.4	21:1 ⑤	12453
300SD	OM617	2998	Fuel Inj. Turbo-charged	110–120 @ 4200 ③	168–170 @ 2400 ④	90.9 x 92.4	21:1 ⑤	12453

NOTE: *Horsepower may vary depending on year and application.*
① 1979 and later: 2998
② 1979 and later: 90.0 x 92.4
③ 1984: 123 @ 4350
④ 1984: 184 @ 2400
⑤ 1984: 21.5:1

7. Disconnect all ground straps and electrical connections. Tag each wire for easy reassembly.
8. Detach the gearshift linkage and the exhaust pipes.
9. Loosen the steering relay arm and pull it down out of the way, along with the center steering rod and hydraulic steering damper.
10. The hydraulic engine shock absorber should be removed.
11. Remove the hydraulic line from the clutch housing and the oil line connectors from the automatic transmission.
12. Unbolt the clutch slave cylinder from the bellhousing after removing the return spring.
13. Remove the exhaust pipe bracket attached to the transmission and place a wood-padded jack under the bellhousing, or place a cable sling under the oil pan, to support the engine. On turbocharged models, disconnect the exhaust pipes at the turbo charger.
14. Mark the position of the rear engine support and unbolt the two outer bolts, then remove the top bolt at the transmission and pull the support out.
15. Disconnect the speedometer cable and the front driveshaft U-joint. Push the driveshaft back and wire it out of the way.
16. Unbolt the engine mounts on both sides and, on four-cylinder engines, the front limit stop.
17. Unbolt the power steering fluid reservoir and swing it out of the way; then, using a chain hoist and cable, lift the engine and transmission upward and outward. An angle of about 45° will allow the car to be pushed backward while the engine is coming up.
18. Reverse the procedure to install, making sure to bleed the hydraulic clutch, power steering, power brakes and fuel system.

V-8 ENGINES

NOTE: *Removal of a V-8 engine equipped with air conditioning, requires disconnecting the air conditioning system. This should only be done by an air conditioning specialist. Take the car to an air conditioning specialist to have the system discharged prior to engine removal.*

1. Remove the hood. On the 380 SEC, the hood can be tilted back 90° and does not need to be removed.
2. Drain the cooling system.
3. Remove the radiator and fan shroud.
4. Remove the cable plug from the temperature switch.
5. Remove the battery, battery frame and air filter.

Valve Specifications

Car Model	Engine Displacement (cc)	Seat Angle (deg)	Spring Test Pressure (mm @ KP)	Stem Diameter (mm)	
				Intake	Exhaust
190E	2299	45	30.5 @ 85.96–91.98	7.97	8.96
190D	2197	45	27 @ 73.42–78.52	7.97	8.96
230	2307	45 + 15′	39 @ 36 ①	8.948–8.970	10.918–10.940
240D	2404	30 + 15′	38.4 @ 23–26.4	9.920–9.905	9.918–9.940
280, 280C, 280CE, 280E, 280S, 290SE	2746	45 + 15′	84–92 @ 30.5	8.950–8.970	③
300D, 300CD, 300TD, 300SD	3005 ②	30 + 15′	38.4 @ 23–26.4	9.920–9.940	9.918–9.940
380SE 380SL 380SLC 380SEL 380SEC	3839	45	30.5 @ 88 ①	8.955–8.970	8.935–8.960
450SL 450SLC 450SEL	4520	45 + 15′	42 @ 29.5–32.5 ①	8.955–8.970	10.940–10.960
500SEC 500SEL	4973	45 + 15′	30.5 @ 88 ①	8.955–8.970	8.935–8.960
6.9	6834	45 + 15′	44.5 2.3	8.948–8.970	11.932–11.950

① Outer spring—the spring should be installed so that the close coils are in contact with the cylinder head
② 1979 and later: 2998
③ Thru 1979: 10.940–10.960
1980 and later: 8.940–8.960
④ 1980 and later: 28.0

6. Drain the power steering reservoir and windshield washer reservoir.
7. Disconnect and plug the high pressure and return lines on the power steering pump.
8. Detach the fuel lines from the fuel filter, pressure regulator, and pressure sensor.
9. If equipped, loosen the line to the supply and anti-freeze tanks. On models so equipped, disconnect the lines to the hydropneumatic suspension.
10. Disconnect the cables from the ignition coil and transistor ignition switchbox.
11. Disconnect the brake vacuum lines.
12. Detach the cable connections for the following:
   a. venturi control unit
   b. temperature sensor
   c. distributor
   d. temperature switch
   e. cold starting valve
   f. speedometer inductance transmitter (380 series only)
13. Remove the regulating shaft by pushing it in the direction of the firewall.
14. Disconnect the thrust and pullrods.
15. Disconnect the heater lines.
16. Detach the lines to the oil pressure and temperature gauges.
17. Remove the ground strap from the vehicle.
18. Detach the cables from the alternator, terminal bridge, and battery. Remove the battery.
19. On the 6.9, remove the oil line shield and disconnect the oil lines between the oil pan and oil reservoir.
20. Position a lifting sling on the engine and take up the slack in the chain.
21. Remove the left-hand engine mount and loosen the hex nut on the right-hand mount.
22. Remove the exhaust system. Remove the connecting rod chain on the rear level control valve and loosen the torsion bar slightly. Raise the vehicle slightly at the rear and remove the exhaust system in a rearward direction.

Valve Timing Specifications▲

Model	Camshaft Code Number●	Intake Valve		Exhaust Valve	
		Opens ATDC*	Closes ABDC*	Opens BBDC*	Closes BTDC*
190D	05	11/12	17/18	28/27	15/14
190E	20①, 21②	17/18	11/12	17.5/16.5	12/11
230	05	14	20	22	12
240D	02, 06③	11.5/13.5	13.5/15.5	21/19	19/17
280, 280C ('74 Fed.)	30④, 33④	11	15	22	24
280, 280C ('74 Calif.)	25④, 24④	6	21	30	13
280, 280C, 280E, 280CE, 280S, 280SE ('75 and later)	64④, 71④	7	21	30	12
300D ('75–'81), 300CD ('78–'81), 300SD ('78–'79), 300TD ('79–'80)	00, 08③	11.5/13.5	13.5/15.5	21/19	19/17
300D ('82–'84), 300CD ('82–'84), 300SD ('80–'84), 300TD ('81–'84)	05③	9/11	15/17	27/25	16/14
380SEL, 380SL, 38SLC	62/63, 68/69 L R L R	L-24 R-22	L-7.5 R-5.5	L-4 R-6	L-12.5 R-14.5
380SE, 380SEC	70/71 L R	L-16 R-14	L-15 R-13	L-16 R-18	L-17 R-19
450SE, 450SEL, 450SL, 450SLC ('74)	52/53 L R	4	14	30	16
450SE ('75–'76) 450SEL, 450SL, 450SLC ('75–'77)	54/55, 56/57 L R L R	5	21	25	5
450SEL, 450SL, 450SLC ('78–'80)	00/01 L R	L-6.5 R-4.5	L-18.5 R-16.5	L-23 R-25	L-8 R-10
500SEC, 500SEL	08/09 L R	L-22 R-20	L-21 R-19	L-10 R-12	L-15 R-17
6.9	36/37 L R	L-12 R-10	L-25 R-23	L-32 R-34	L-19 R-21

▲Taken at 2mm valve lift
●Camshaft code number is stamped into rear face of camshaft
*When numbers are separated by a slash, first figure is for new timing chain and second figure is for a used timing chain (approx. 20,000 km). When no slash is used, the figure is for a new timing chain.
L—Left
R—Right
ATDC—After Top Dead Center
ABDC—After Bottom Dead Center
BBDC—Before Bottom Dead Center
BTDC—Before Top Dead Center
① Camshaft with 32mm bearing diameter (standard)
② Camshaft with 32.5mm bearing diameter (repair version)
③ Camshaft made of chilled cast iron
④ 1st figure: exhaust camshaft
2nd figure: intake camshaft

23. Disconnect the handbrake cable.
24. Remove the shield plate from the transmission tunnel.
25. Place a block of wood between the transmission and cross yoke so the engine will not sag, when the rear mount is removed.
26. Loosen the driveshaft intermediate bearing and the driveshaft slide.
27. Support the transmission with a jack.
28. Mark the installation of the crossmember and remove the crossmember. Remove the rear engine carrier with the engine mount.
29. Unbolt the front U-joint flange on the transmission and push it back. Do not loosen the clamp nut on the intermediate bearing. Support the driveshaft.
30. Disconnect the speedometer shaft, shift rod, control pressure rod, regulating linkage (on

Crankshaft and Connecting Rod Specifications

(All measurements are given in millimeters)

Car Model	Engine Displace (cc)	Engine Model	Crankshaft				Connecting Rod		
			Main Brg. Journal Dia.	Main Brg. Oil Clearance	Shaft End-Play	Thrust on No.	Journal Diameter	Oil Clearance	Side Clearance
190D 190E	2197 2299	OM601 M102	57.960– 57.965	0.031– 0.073	0.100– 0.250	①	47.950– 47.965	0.031– 0.073	N.A.
230	2307	M115	69.955– 69.965	0.045– 0.065	0.100– 0.240	①	51.955– 51.965	0.035– 0.055	0.110– 0.260
240D	2404	OM616	69.955– 69.965	0.045– 0.065	0.100– 0.240	①	51.955– 51.965	0.035– 0.055	0.110– 0.260
280E, 280 280CE, 280C 280SE, 280S	2746	M110	59.96– 59.95	0.03– 0.07	0.10– 0.24	①	47.95– 47.96	0.15– 0.50	0.11– 0.23
300D, 300CD, 300TD, 300SD	3005 ②	OM617	69.955– 69.965	0.045– 0.065	0.100– 0.240	①	51.955– 51.965	0.035– 0.055	0.110– 0.260
380SE 380SEL 380SL 380SLC 380SEC	3839	M116	63.950– 63.965	0.045– 0.065	0.100– 0.240	①	47.945– 47.965	0.045– 0.065	0.220– 0.359
450SL 450SLC 450SEL	4520	M117	63.955– 63.965	0.035– 0.075	0.100– 0.240	①	51.955– 51.965	0.035– 0.065	0.220– 0.380
500SEC 500SEL	4973	M117	63.950– 63.965	0.045– 0.065	0.100– 0.240	①	47.945– 47.965	0.045– 0.065	0.220– 0.359
6.9	6836	M100	69.945– 69.965	0.045– 0.065	0.100– 0.240	①	54.940– 54.600	0.045– 0.065	0.220– 0.359

N.A. Not Available
① Center main on 5 main bearing engines; rear main on 7 main bearing engines; 3rd from front on 300D (5-cylinder)
② 1979 and later: 2998

automatic transmissions), kickdown switch cable, starter lockout switch cable, and the cable for the back-up light switch.

31. Remove the front engine mounting bolt and remove the engine at approximately a 45° angle.

32. Installation is the reverse of removal. Lower the engine until it is behind the front axle carrier. Place a jack under the transmission and lower the engine into its compartment. While lowering the engine, install the right-hand shock mount.

Fill the engine with all required fluids and start the engine. Check for leaks.

280, 280C, 280E, 280CE, 280SE, 280S

1. Scribe alignment marks on the hood hinges and remove the hood. Drain the coolant from the radiator and block.
2. Remove the radiator.
3. Disconnect the lines from the vacuum pump.

1. U-joint flange 2. U-joint plate 3. Wooden block
Supporting a V8 engine

Torque Specifications

(All reading in ft. lbs.)

Car Model	Engine Model	Cylinder Head Bolts	Rod Bearing Bolts	Main Bearing Bolts	Crankshaft Pulley Bolt	Flywheel to Crankshaft Bolts	Cam Sprocket Bolt(s)	Exhaust Manifold Bolts
190D	OM601	⑦ ①	⑧	65	195–239	⑨	33	N.A.
190E	M102	⑩ ①	⑨	65	195–239	⑨	58	N.A.
230	M115	58	①	58 ③	151–158	①	18	18–21
240D	OM616	65 ⑬	①	65	151–158	①	18	18–21
280E, 280 280CE, 280C 280SE, 280S	M110	58	①	58	206–226	①	58	N.A.
300D, 300CD 300TD, 300SD	OM617	65 ⑬	①	65	195–240	①	18	18–21
380SE 380SL 380SEL 380SLC 380SEC	M116	⑫	30–37 ①	⑤	289	①	74	N.A.
450SL 450SLC 450SEL	M117	⑪	①	④	180–194	①	36	18–21
500SEC 500SEL	M117	⑫	①	④	180–194	①	36	18–21
6.9	M100	65	①	⑤	289	①	72	N.A.

N.A. Not Available at time of publication
① See text
② With cold engine; cylinder head bolts should be tightened in at least 3 stages
③ 65 on M115 engines
④ M 10 bolts—37 ft. lbs.
M 12 bolts—72 ft. lbs.
⑤ M 10 bolts—43 ft. lbs
M 12 bolts—58 ft. lbs.
⑥ Tighten to 22 ft. lbs. then to 45 ft. lbs. in proper sequence. After 10 mins. loosen and tighten again to 45 ft. lbs.
⑦ M 10 bolts: 1st step—18 ft. lbs.
2nd step—29 ft. lbs.
Setting time—10 min.
3rd step—90° torquing angle
4th step—90° torquing angle
M 8 bolts: 18 ft. lbs.
⑧ 1st step: 22–25 ft. lbs.
2nd step: 90–100° torquing angle
⑨ 1st step: 22–29 ft. lbs.
2nd step: 90–100° torquing angle
⑩ M 12 bolts: 1st step—29 ft. lbs.
2nd step—51 ft. lbs.
Setting time—10 min.
3rd step—90° torquing angle
4th step—90° torquing angle
M 8 bolts: 18 ft. lbs.
⑪ 1st step: 22 ft. lbs.
2nd step: 44 ft. lbs.
setting time: 10 min.
3rd step: warm engine, loosen bolts and retighten to 44 ft. lbs.
⑫ 1st step: 22 ft. lbs.
2nd step: 44 ft. lbs.
setting time: 10 min.
3rd step: loosen bolts and retighten to 44 ft. lbs.
⑬ All vehicles manufactured after Feb. 1979:
1st step:—29 ft. lbs.
2nd step—51 ft. lbs.
setting time—10 min.
3rd step—90° torquing angle
4th step—90° torquing angle

4. On vehicles with air conditioning, remove the compressor and place it aside.

CAUTION: *Do not remove the refrigerant lines from the compressor. Physical harm could result.*

5. Disconnect and tag all electrical connections from the engine.

6. Disconnect all coolant and vacuum lines from the engine.

7. Disconnect and plug the pressure oil lines from the power steering pump, after draining the pump reservoir.

8. Remove the accelerator linkage control rod by pulling off the lock-ring and pushing the shaft in the direction of the firewall.

9. Loosen and remove the exhaust pipes from the manifold and transmission supports.

10. Disconnect the transmission linkage and all other connections.

11. Loosen the front right (driving direc-

tion) shock absorber from the front axle carrier.

12. Remove the left-hand engine shock absorber from the engine mount.

13. Attach a lifting device to the engine and tension the cables.

14. Unbolt the engine and transmission mounts and remove the engine at a 45° angle.

15. Installation is the reverse of removal. Be sure to check all fluids and fill or top up as necessary. Check all adjustments on the engine.

Rocker Arms and Shafts

REMOVAL AND INSTALLATION

Diesel Engines

Rocker arms on diesel engines can only be removed as a unit with the respective rocker arm blocks.

NOTE: *The 1984 190D does not use rocker arms. The camshaft acts directly on the hydraulic valve tappet.*

1. Detach the connecting rod for the venturi control unit from the bearing bracket lever and remove the bearing bracket from the rocker arm cover.

2. Remove the air vent line from the rocker arm cover and remove the rocker arm cover.

3. Remove the stretchbolts from the rocker arm blocks and remove the blocks with the rocker arms. Turn the crankshaft in each case so that the camshaft does not put any load on the rocker arms.

NOTE: *Turn the crankshaft with a socket wrench on the crankshaft pulley bolt. Do not rotate the engine by turning the camshaft sprocket.*

4. Before installing the rocker arms, check the sliding surfaces of the ball cup and rocker arms. Replace any defective parts.

5. To install, assemble the rocker arm blocks and insert new stretchbolts.

6. Tighten the stretchbolts. In each case, position the camshaft so that there is no load on the rocker arms. See the previous NOTE.

7. Check to be sure that the tension clamps have engaged with the notches of the rocker arm blocks.

8. Adjust the valve clearance.

9. Reinstall the rocker arm cover, air vent line, and bearing bracket for the reverse lever. Attach the connecting rod for the venturi control unit to the reversing lever.

10. Make sure that during acceleration, the control cable can move freely without binding.

11. Start the engine and check the rocker arm cover for leaks.

Gasoline Engines—All Except 190E

NOTE: *1976 and later V8's use hydraulic valve lifters.*

A tool similar to that shown is the best way to depress the valve spring

Before removing the rocker arm(s), be sure that they are identified as to their position relative to the camshaft lobe. They should be installed in the same place as they were before disassembly.

Be very careful removing the thrust pieces. They can easily fall into the engine.

1. Remove the rocker arm cover or covers.

2. Force the clamping spring out of the notch in the top of the rocker arm. Slide it in an outward direction across the ball socket or the rocker arm.

NOTE: *Turn the engine over each time to relieve any load from the rocker arm.*

3. On V8 models, the clamping spring must be forced from the adjusting screw with a small prybar.

4. Force the valve down to remove load from the rocker arm.

NOTE: *Don't depress the spring too far. When the piston is up as it should be, the valve will hit the piston. As the spring goes down the thrust piece will fall off into the engine.*

5. Lift the rocker arm from the ball pin and remove the rocker arm.

6. To install the rocker arm(s), force the rocker arm down until the rocker arm and its ball socket can be installed in the top of the ball pin.

7. Install the rocker arms.

8. Slide the clamping spring across the ball socket of the rocker arm until it rests in the notch of the rocker arm.

9. On V8 models, engage the clamping spring into the recess of the adjusting screw.

10. Check and, if necessary, adjust the valve clearance.

11. After completion of the adjustment, check to be sure that the clamping springs are correctly seated.

12. Install the rocker arm cover and connect any hoses or lines that were disconnected.

13. Run the engine and check for leaks at the rocker arm cover.

190E

Rocker arms on this engine are individually mounted on rocker arm shafts that fit into either side of the camshaft bearing brackets.

1. Remove the cylinder head cover. The cover on the 190E is removed with the spark plug wires and distributor cap still connected.

2. Tag each rocker arm and shaft so that they are identified as to their position relative to the camshaft. They should always be installed in the same place as they were before disassembly.

3. The rocker arm shaft is held axially and rotationally by a bearing bracket fastening bolt. Remove the bolt on the side of the bearing bracket that allows access to the exposed end of the rocker shaft.

4. Thread a bolt (M8) into the end of the rocker arm shaft and slowly ease the shaft out of the bearing bracket.

CAUTION: *Support the rocker arm/lifter assembly while removing the shaft so it will not drop onto the cylinder head.*

NOTE: *Carefully forcing the valve down with a small prybar will remove the load on the hydraulic valve tappet and ease the removal of the shaft. Don't depress the spring too far. When the piston is up as it should be, the valve will hit the piston. As the spring goes down the thrust piece will fall off into the engine.*

To remove the rocker shaft on the 190E, thread a bolt into the hole (D). On installation, the dished groove (arrow) must always line up with the mounting bolt shank

5. Replace the bearing bracket bolt and tighten it to 11 ft. lbs. (15 Nm) until ready to replace the rocker shaft.

6. To install, position the rocker arm between the two bearing brackets and slide the shaft into place.

NOTE: *The circular groove on the end of the rocker shaft must line up with the mounting bolt shank to ensure proper positioning.*

7. Replace the bearing bracket mounting bolt.

8. Repeat Steps 3–7 for all remaining rocker arm/shaft assemblies. Turn the engine over each time to relieve any load from the rocker arm.

9. Replace the cylinder head cover.

Intake Manifold

REMOVAL AND INSTALLATION

V8 Engine

1. Partially drain the coolant.
2. Remove the air cleaner.
3. Disconnect the regulating linkage and remove the longitudinal regulating shaft.
4. Pull off all cable plug connections.
5. Disconnect and plug the fuel lines on the pressure regulator and starting valve.
6. Unscrew the nuts on the injection valves and set the injection valves aside.
7. Remove the 16 attaching bolts from the intake manifold.

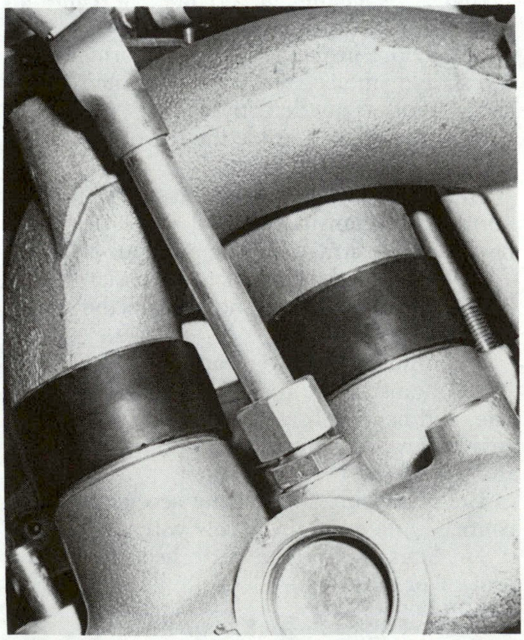

Replace the rubber connecting pieces on the intake manifold, anytime the manifold is removed

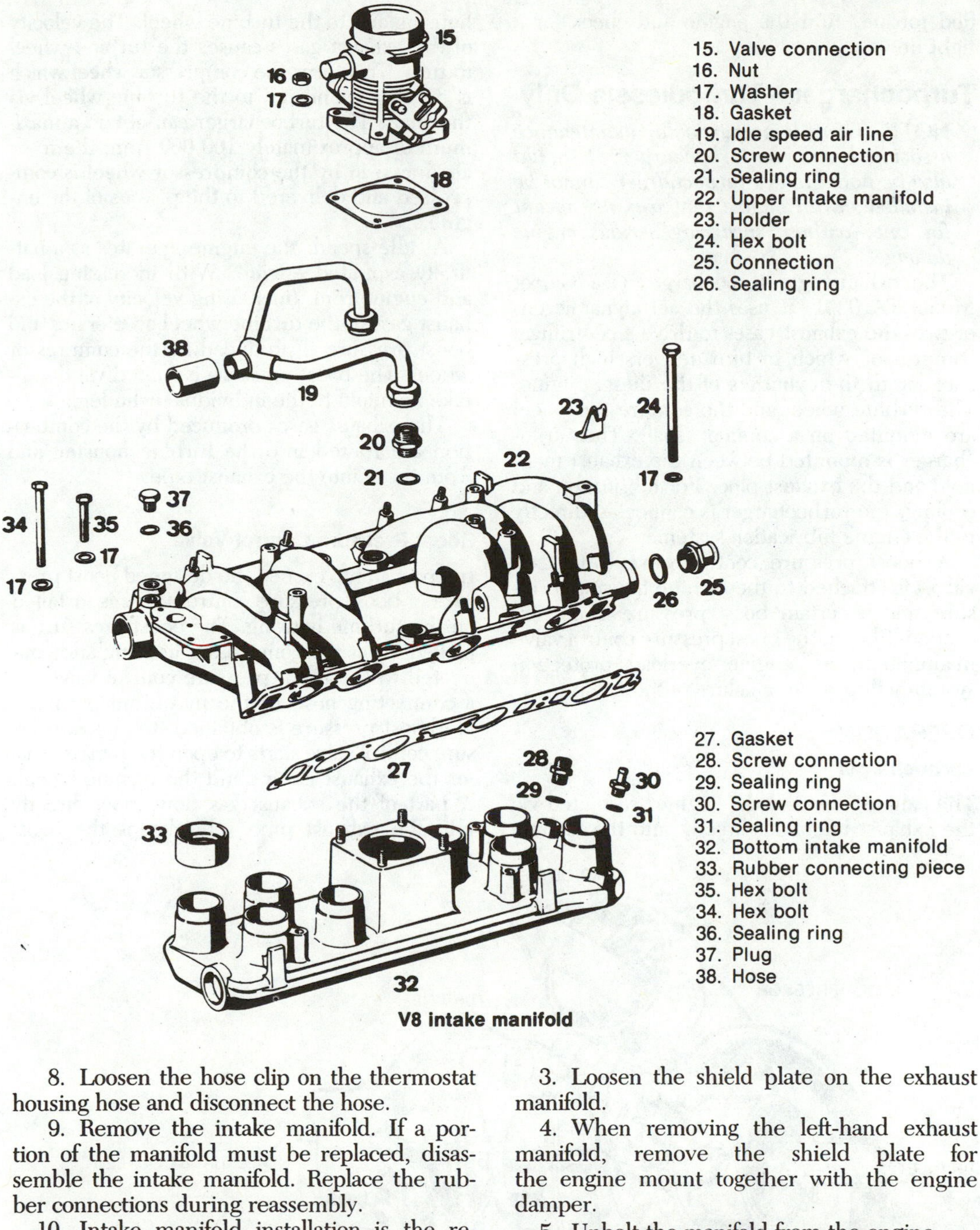

V8 intake manifold

8. Loosen the hose clip on the thermostat housing hose and disconnect the hose.

9. Remove the intake manifold. If a portion of the manifold must be replaced, disassemble the intake manifold. Replace the rubber connections during reassembly.

10. Intake manifold installation is the reverse of removal. Replace all seals and gaskets. Adjust the linkage and idle speed.

Exhaust Manifold

REMOVAL AND INSTALLATION

V8 Engine

1. Unbolt the exhaust pipes from the manifolds.

2. Disconnect the rubber mounting ring from the exhaust system.

3. Loosen the shield plate on the exhaust manifold.

4. When removing the left-hand exhaust manifold, remove the shield plate for the engine mount together with the engine damper.

5. Unbolt the manifold from the engine.

6. Pull the manifolds off of the mounting studs by turning the left-hand exhaust manifold forward and down and removing it upward. Remove the right-hand manifold down and toward the rear.

7. Installation is the reverse of removal. Replace all gaskets and nuts. Mount the flanged gaskets between the exhaust manifold and the cylinder head with their flat sides toward the exhaust manifold.

8. Tighten all nuts evenly and to the speci-

fied torque. Run the engine and check for a tight fit.

Turbocharger—Turbodiesels Only

NOTE: *There is no particular maintenance associated with the turbocharger. It should also be noted that a turbocharger cannot be installed on an engine that was not meant for one, without incurring serious engine damage.*

The exhaust gas turbocharger is a Garret Model TA 0301. It uses the aerodynamic energy of the exhaust gases to drive a centrifugal compressor which in turn delivers high pressure air to the cylinders of the diesel engine. The turbine wheel and the compressor wheel are mounted on a common shaft. The turbocharger is mounted between the exhaust manifold and the exhaust pipe. For lubrication and cooling, the turbocharger is connected directly to the engine lubrication system.

A boost pressure control valve (wastegate valve) is attached to the turbine housing to insure that a certain boost pressure is not exceeded. Should the boost pressure control valve malfunction, an engine overload protection system will prevent a failure of the engine.

OPERATION

Turbocharger

The exhaust gases of the engine are routed via the exhaust manifold directly into the turbine housing and to the turbine wheel. The velocity of the exhaust gases causes the turbine wheel to turn. This turns the compressor wheel which is directly connected to the turbine wheel via the shaft. The turbocharger can obtain a maximum of approximately 100,000 rpm; the fresh air drawn in by the compressor wheel is compressed and delivered to the pistons of the engine.

At idle speed, the engine operates as a naturally aspirated engine. With increasing load and engine rpm, (increasing velocity of the exhaust gases), the turbine wheel accelerates and boost pressure is produced by the compressor wheel. The boost pressure is routed via the intake manifold to the individual cylinders.

The exhaust gases produced by the combustion are routed into the turbine housing and from there into the exhaust pipe.

Boost Pressure Control Valve

In order not to exceed the designed boost pressure, a boost pressure control valve is installed on the turbine housing. The boost presssure is picked up at the compressor housing and connected to the boost pressure control valve via a connecting hose. If the maximum permissible boost pressure is obtained, the boost pressure control valve starts to open the bypass canal for the exhaust gas around the turbine wheel. A part of the exhaust gas flows now directly into the exhaust pipe. This keeps the boost

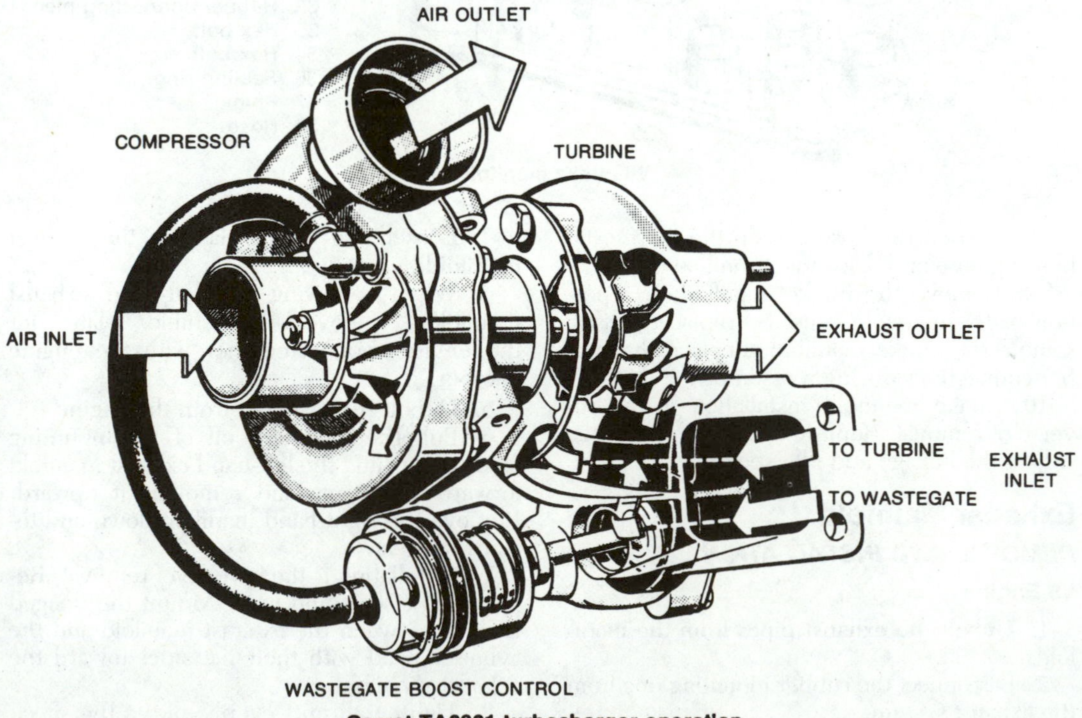

Garret TA0301 turbocharger operation

pressure constant and prevents it from increasing beyond its designed limits.

REMOVAL AND INSTALLATION

1. Remove the air filter.
2. Disconnect the electrical cable from the temperature switch.
3. Loosen the lower hose clamp on the air duct that connects the air filter with the compressor housing.
4. Remove the vacuum line and crankcase breather pipe.
5. Remove the air filter and air intake duct.
6. Disconnect the oil line at the turbocharger.
7. Remove the air filter mounting bracket.
8. Disconnect the turbocharger at the exhaust flange..
9. Disconnect and remove the pipe bracket on the automatic transmission.
10. Push the exhaust pipe rearward.
11. Remove the mounting bracket at the intermediate flange.
12. Unbolt and remove the turbocharger.
13. Remove the intermediate flange and oil return line at the turbocharger.
14. Installation is the reverse of removal. Before installing the turbocharger, install the oil return line and intermediate flange. Install the flange gasket between the turbocharger and exhaust manifold with the reinforcing bead toward the exhaust manifold.

Use only heatproof nuts and bolts and fill a new turbocharger with ¼ pint of engine oil through the engine oil supply bore before operating.

1. Mounting bracket
2. Intermediate flange
3. Turbocharger

Remove the mounting nuts (arrow) to remove the turbocharger

Cylinder Head

REMOVAL AND INSTALLATION

4 and 5-Cylinder Engines

In order to perform a valve job or to inspect cylinder bores for wear, the head must be removed. While this may seem fairly straightforward, some caution must be observed to ensure that valve timing is not disturbed.

1. Drain the radiator and remove all hoses and wires (tag all wires).
2. Remove the camshaft cover and associated throttle linkage, then press out the spring

Troubleshooting the Turbocharger

To properly evaluate the turbocharger, the full throttle stop, maximum no-load engine rpm. start of delivery and opening the pressure of the injection nozzles must be within specifications.

Complaint	Probable Cause	Remedy
Poor engine performance	Boost pressure too low	1. Clean air filter and check air intake shroud and duct for obstructions. 2. Check turbocharger for leaks at following points: Between exhaust manifold and turbine housing; tighten nuts. Between compressor housing discharge and intake manifold. Between intake or exhaust manifold and cylinder head. 3. Check pressure line between intake manifold and aneroid compensator. 4. Check fuse no. 4 or the black/red wire at the switchover valve for breaks or loose connection. 5. The boost pressure control valve (waste gate) on the turbocharger should close. If not, replace the turbocharger.
Engine surges at full load	Boost pressure control valve does not open.	Check the connecting hose between the compressor housing and waste gate. If the hose is leaking or has a kink, replace the hose. If the hose is OK, replace the turbocharger.

ENGINE OVERHAUL

Most engine overhaul procedures are fairly standard. In addition to specific parts replacement procedures and complete specifications for your individual engine, this chapter also is a guide to accepted rebuilding procedures. Examples of standard rebuilding practice are shown and should be used along with specific details concerning your particular engine.

Competent and accurate machine shop services will ensure maximum performance, reliability and engine life. Procedures marked with the symbol shown above should be performed by a competent machine shop, and are provided so that you will be familiar with the procedures necessary to a successful overhaul.

In most instances it is more profitable for the do-it-yourself mechanic to remove, clean and inspect the component, buy the necessary parts and deliver these to a shop for actual machine work.

On the other hand, much of the rebuilding work (crankshaft, block, bearings, pistons, rods, and other components) is well within the scope of the do-it-yourself mechanic.

Tools

The tools required for an engine overhaul or parts replacement will depend on the depth of your involvement. With a few exceptions, they will be the tools found in a mechanic's tool kit (see Chapter 1). More in-depth work will require any or all of the following:

- a dial indicator (reading in thousandths) mounted on a universal base
- micrometers and telescope gauges
- jaw and screw-type pullers
- scraper
- valve spring compressor
- ring groove cleaner
- piston ring expander and compressor
- ridge reamer
- cylinder hone or glaze breaker
- Plastigage®
- engine stand

Use of most of these tools is illustrated in this chapter. Many can be rented for a one-time use from a local parts jobber or tool supply house specializing in automotive work.

Occasionally, the use of special tools is called for. See the information on Special Tools and the Safety Notice in the front of this book before substituting another tool.

Inspection Techniques

Procedures and specifications are given in this chapter for inspecting, cleaning and assessing the wear limits of most major components. Other procedures such as Magnaflux and Zyglo can be used to locate material flaws and stress cracks. Magnaflux is a magnetic process applicable only to ferrous materials. The Zyglo process coats the material with a flourescent dye penetrant and can be used on any material. Check for suspected surface cracks can be more readily made using spot check dye. The dye is sprayed onto the suspected area, wiped off and the area sprayed with a developer. Cracks will show up brightly.

Overhaul Tips

Aluminum has become extremely popular for use in engines, due to its low weight. Observe the following precautions when handling aluminum parts:

- Never hot tank aluminum parts (the caustic hot-tank solution will eat the aluminum)
- Remove all aluminum parts (identification tag, etc.) from engine parts prior to hot-tanking.
- Always coat threads lightly with engine oil or anti-seize compounds before installation, to prevent seizure.
- Never over-torque bolts or spark plugs, especially in aluminum threads.

Stripped threads in any component can be repaired using any of several commercial repair kits (Heli-Coil, Microdot, Keenserts, etc.)

When assembling the engine, any parts that will be in frictional contact must be prelubed to provide lubrication at initial start-up. Any product specifically formulated for this purpose can be used, but engine oil is not recommended as a pre-lube.

When semi-permanent (locked, but removable) installation of bolts or nuts is desired, threads should be cleaned and coated with Loctite® or other similar, commercial non-hardening sealant.

Repairing Damaged Threads

Several methods of repairing damaged threads are available. Heli-Coil® (shown here), Keenserts® and Microdot® are among the most widely used. All involve basically the same principle—drilling out stripped threads, tapping the hole and installing a prewound insert—making welding, plugging and oversize fasteners unnecessary.

Two types of thread repair inserts are usually supplied—a standard type for most Inch Coarse, Inch Fine, Metric Coarse and Metric Fine thread sizes and a spark plug type to fit most spark plug port sizes. Consult the individual manufacturer's catalog to determine exact applications. Typical thread repair kits will contain a selection of prewound threaded inserts, a tap (corresponding to the outside diameter threads of the insert) and an installation tool. Spark plug inserts usually differ because they require a tap equipped with pilot threads and a combined reamer/tap section. Most manufacturers also supply blister-packed thread repair inserts separately in addition to a master kit containing a variety of taps and inserts plus installation tools.

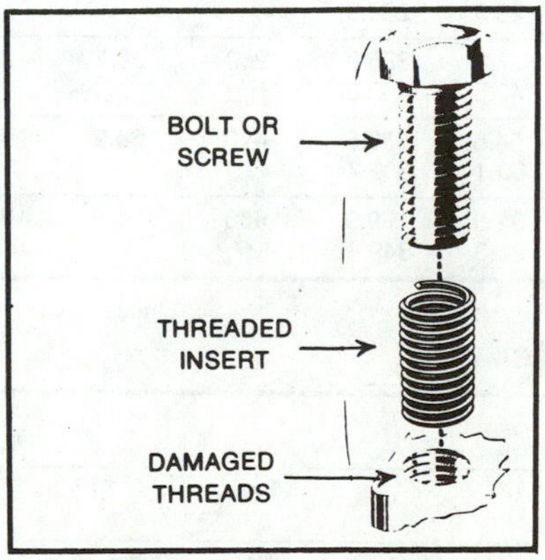

Damaged bolt holes can be repaired with thread repair inserts

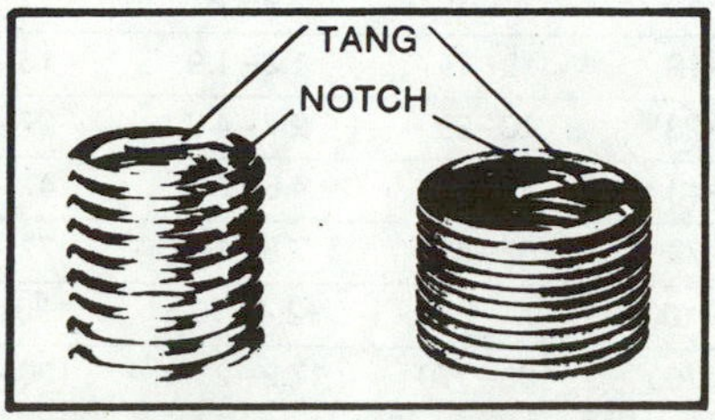

Standard thread repair insert (left) and spark plug thread insert (right)

Before effecting a repair to a threaded hole, remove any snapped, broken or damaged bolts or studs. Penetrating oil can be used to free frozen threads; the offending item can be removed with locking pliers or with a screw or stud extractor. After the hole is clear, the thread can be repaired, as follows:

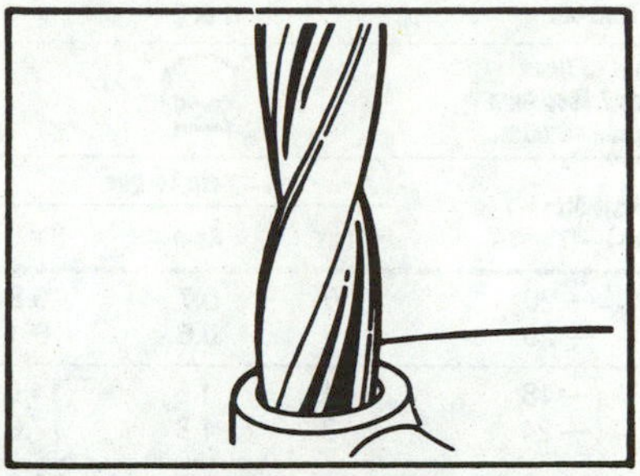

Drill out the damaged threads with specified drill. Drill completely through the hole or to the bottom of a blind hole

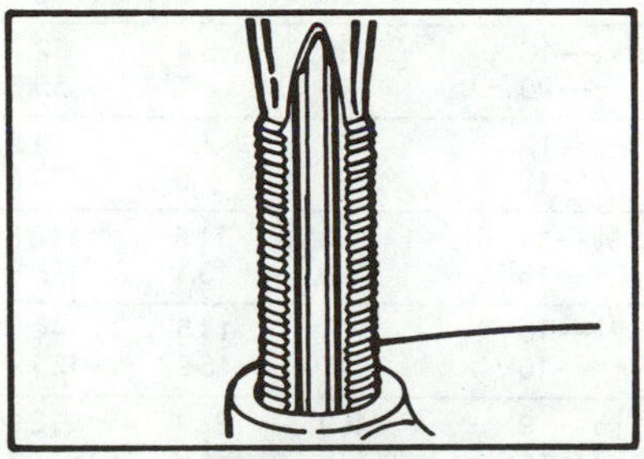

With the tap supplied, tap the hole to receive the thread insert. Keep the tap well oiled and back it out frequently to avoid clogging the threads

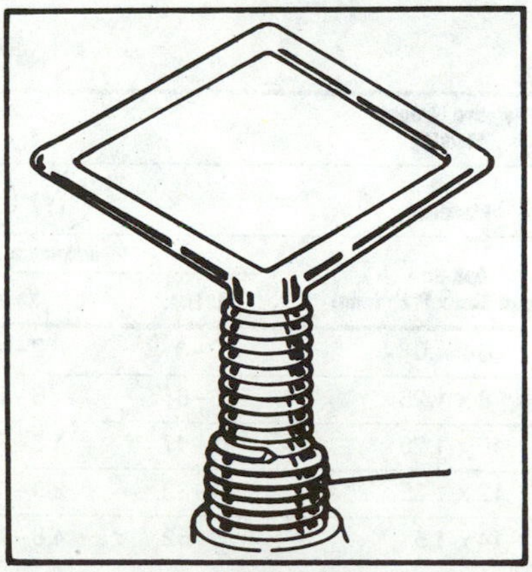

Screw the threaded insert onto the installation tool until the tang engages the slot. Screw the insert into the tapped hole until it is ¼–½ turn below the top surface. After installation break off the tang with a hammer and punch

Standard Torque Specifications and Fastener Markings

In the absence of specific torques, the following chart can be used as a guide to the maximum safe torque of a particular size/grade of fastener.

- There is no torque difference for fine or coarse threads.
- Torque values are based on clean, dry threads. Reduce the value by 10% if threads are oiled prior to assembly.
- The torque required for aluminum components or fasteners is considerably less.

U.S. Bolts

SAE Grade Number	1 or 2			5			6 or 7		
Number of lines always 2 less than the grade number.									
	Maximum Torque			Maximum Torque			Maximum Torque		
Bolt Size (Inches)—(Thread)	Ft./Lbs.	Kgm	Nm	Ft./Lbs.	Kgm	Nm	Ft./Lbs.	Kgm	Nm
¼—20	5	0.7	6.8	8	1.1	10.8	10	1.4	13.5
—28	6	0.8	8.1	10	1.4	13.6			
5/16—18	11	1.5	14.9	17	2.3	23.0	19	2.6	25.8
—24	13	1.8	17.6	19	2.6	25.7			
⅜—16	18	2.5	24.4	31	4.3	42.0	34	4.7	46.0
—24	20	2.75	27.1	35	4.8	47.5			
7/16—14	28	3.8	37.0	49	6.8	66.4	55	7.6	74.5
—20	30	4.2	40.7	55	7.6	74.5			
½—13	39	5.4	52.8	75	10.4	101.7	85	11.75	115.2
—20	41	5.7	55.6	85	11.7	115.2			
9/16—12	51	7.0	69.2	110	15.2	149.1	120	16.6	162.7
—18	55	7.6	74.5	120	16.6	162.7			
⅝—11	83	11.5	112.5	150	20.7	203.3	167	23.0	226.5
—18	95	13.1	128.8	170	23.5	230.5			
¾—10	105	14.5	142.3	270	37.3	366.0	280	38.7	379.6
—16	115	15.9	155.9	295	40.8	400.0			
⅞— 9	160	22.1	216.9	395	54.6	535.5	440	60.9	596.5
—14	175	24.2	237.2	435	60.1	589.7			
1— 8	236	32.5	318.6	590	81.6	799.9	660	91.3	894.8
—14	250	34.6	338.9	660	91.3	849.8			

Metric Bolts

Relative Strength Marking	4.6, 4.8			8.8		
Bolt Markings						
	Maximum Torque			Maximum Torque		
Bolt Size Thread Size x Pitch (mm)	Ft./Lbs.	Kgm	Nm	Ft./Lbs.	Kgm	Nm
6 x 1.0	2–3	.2–.4	3–4	3–6	.4–.8	5–8
8 x 1.25	6–8	.8–1	8–12	9–14	1.2–1.9	13–19
10 x 1.25	12–17	1.5–2.3	16–23	20–29	2.7–4.0	27–39
12 x 1.25	21–32	2.9–4.4	29–43	35–53	4.8–7.3	47–72
14 x 1.5	35–52	4.8–7.1	48–70	57–85	7.8–11.7	77–110
16 x 1.5	51–77	7.0–10.6	67–100	90–120	12.4–16.5	130–160
18 x 1.5	74–110	10.2–15.1	100–150	130–170	17.9–23.4	180–230
20 x 1.5	110–140	15.1–19.3	150–190	190–240	26.2–46.9	160–320
22 x 1.5	150–190	22.0–26.2	200–260	250–320	34.5–44.1	340–430
24 x 1.5	190–240	26.2–46.9	260–320	310–410	42.7–56.5	420–550

CHECKING ENGINE COMPRESSION

A noticeable lack of engine power, excessive oil consumption and/or poor fuel mileage measured over an extended period are all indicators of internal engine wear. Worn piston rings, scored or worn cylinder bores, blown head gaskets, sticking or burnt valves and worn valve seats are all possible culprits here. A check of each cylinder's compression will help you locate the problems.

As mentioned in the "Tools and Equipment" section of Chapter 1, a screw-in type compression gauge is more accurate than the type you simply hold against the spark plug hole, although it takes slightly longer to use. It's worth it to obtain a more accurate reading. Follow the procedures below for gasoline and diesel-engined cars.

Gasoline Engines

1. Warm up the engine to normal operating temperature.
2. Remove all spark plugs.

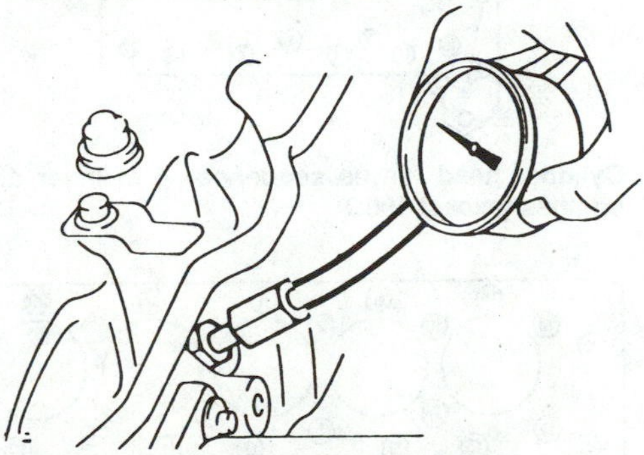

The screw-in type compression gauge is more accurate

3. Disconnect the high-tension lead from the ignition coil.
4. On carbureted cars, fully open the throttle either by operating the carburetor throttle linkage by hand or by having an assistant "floor" the accelerator pedal. On fuel-injected cars, disconnect the cold start valve and all injector connections.
5. Screw the compression gauge into the No. 1 spark plug hole until the fitting is snug.

NOTE: *Be careful not to crossthread the plug hole. On aluminum cylinder heads use extra care, as the threads in these heads are easily ruined.*

6. Ask an assistant to depress the accelerator pedal fully on both carbureted and fuel-injected cars. Then, while you read the compression gauge, ask the assistant to crank the engine two or three times in short bursts using the ignition switch.
7. Read the compression gauge at the end of each series of cranks, and record the highest of these readings. Repeat this procedure for each of the engine's cylinders. Compare the highest reading of each cylinder to the compression pressure specifications in the "Tune-Up Specifications" chart in Chapter 2. The specs in this chart are maximum values.

A cylinder's compression pressure is usually acceptable if it is not less than 80% of maximum. The difference between each cylinder should be no more than 12–14 pounds.

8. If a cylinder is unusually low, pour a tablespoon of clean engine oil into the cylinder through the spark plug hole and repeat the compression test. If the compression comes up after adding the oil, it appears that that cylinder's piston rings or bore are damaged or worn. If the pressure remains low, the valves may not be seating properly (a valve job is needed), or the head gasket may be blown near that cylinder. If compression in any two adjacent cylinders is low, and if the addition of oil doesn't help the compression, there is leakage past the head gasket. Oil and coolant water in the combustion chamber can result from this problem. There may be evidence of water droplets on the engine dipstick when a head gasket has blown.

Diesel Engines

Checking cylinder compression on diesel engines is basically the same procedure as on gasoline engines except for the following:

1. A special compression gauge adaptor suitable for diesel engines (because these engines have much greater compression pressures) must be used.
2. Remove the injector tubes and remove the injectors from each cylinder.

NOTE: *Don't forget to remove the washer underneath each injector; otherwise, it may get lost when the engine is cranked.*

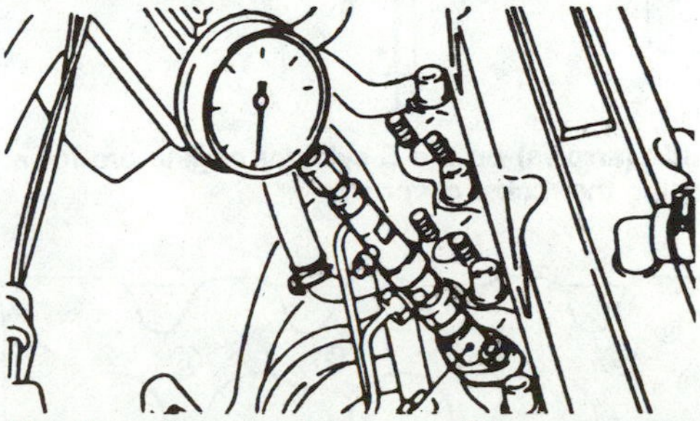

Diesel engines require a special compression gauge adaptor

3. When fitting the compression gauge adaptor to the cylinder head, make sure the bleeder of the gauge (if equipped) is closed.
4. When reinstalling the injector assemblies, install new washers underneath each injector.

clamp from the notch in the rocker arm (all except 190 series).

NOTE: *The cylinder head cover on the 190E is removed with the spark plug cables and distributor cap still attached to it.*

3. Push the clamp outward over the ball cap of the rocker, then depress the valve with a large screwdriver and lift the rocker arm out of the ball pin head (all except 190 series).

4. Remove the rocker arm supports (all except 190 series) and the camshaft sprocket nut.

5. On all 5 cyl. engines and the 190E, the rockers and their supports must be removed together.

6. Using a suitable puller, remove the camshaft sprocket, after having first marked the chain, sprocket and cam for ease in assembly.

7. Remove the sprocket and chain and wire it out of the way.

CAUTION: *Make sure the chain is securely wired so that it will not slide down into the engine.*

8. Unbolt the manifolds and exhaust header pipe and push them out of the way.

9. Then loosen the cylinder head hold-down bolts in the reverse order of that shown in torque diagrams for each model. It is good practice to loosen each bolt a little at a time, working round the head, until all are free. This prevents unequal stresses in the metal.

10. Reach into the engine compartment and gradually work the head loose from each end by rocking it. Never, under any circumstances, use a screwdriver between the head and block to pry, as the head will be scarred badly and may be ruined.

11. Installation is the reverse of removal.

NOTE: *All diesel engines manufactured after 2/79 utilize cylinder head "stretch" bolts. These bolts undergo a permenant stretch each time they are tightened. When a maximum length is reached, they must be scrapped and replaced with new bolts. When tightening the head bolts on these engines, be sure to follow the steps listed under "Torque Specifications" exactly. Maximum stretch lengths are as follows:*

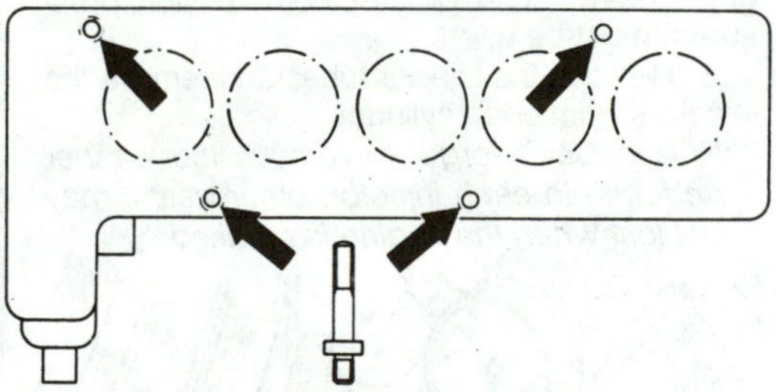

Studs (arrows) on the 5 cylinder engine are for attaching the rocker cover

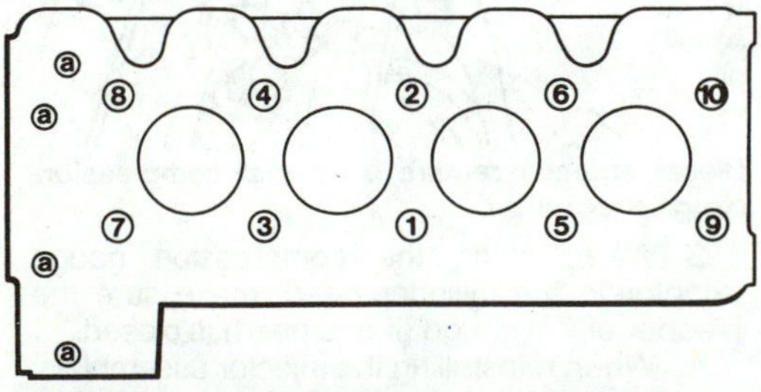

Cylinder head torque sequence—190E (bolts "a" are tightened to 25 Nm)

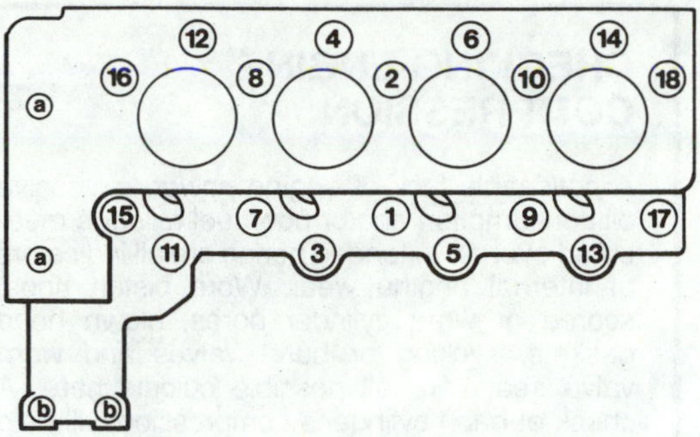

Cylinder head torque sequence—190D (bolts "a" and "b" are tightened to 25 Nm)

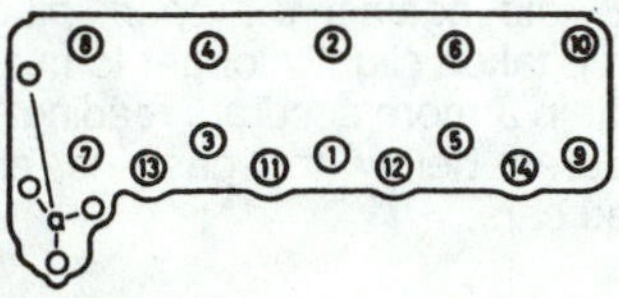

Cylinder head torque sequence—4 cylinder gasoline engines (except 190E)

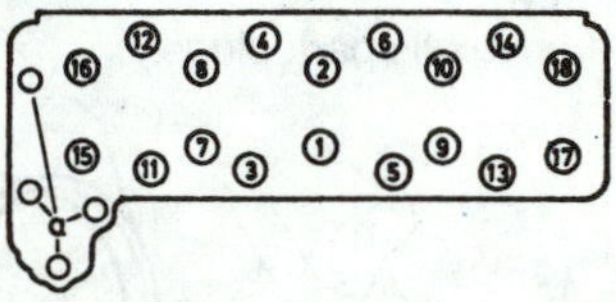

Cylinder head torque sequence—4 cylinder diesel engines (except 190D)

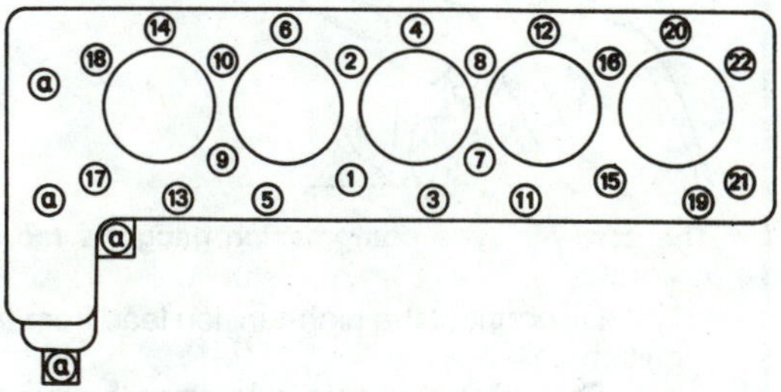

Cylinder head torque sequence—5 cylinder engines (bolts marked "a" are tightened with a Hek bit)

Model	Length when new (mm)	Maximum (mm)
190E	119	122
190D	80	83.6
	102	105.6
	115	118.6
240D, 300D, 300CD, 300SD, 300TD	104	105.5
	119	120.5
	144	145.5

Under no circumstances may the older type cylinder head bolts be exchanged with the newer "stretch" bolts.

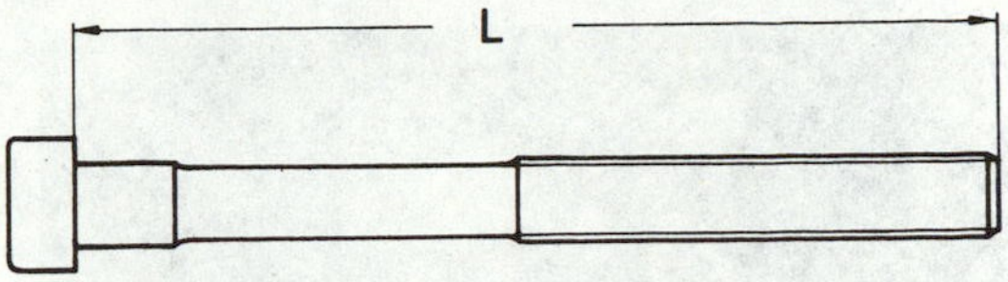

Cylinder head bolt stretch is measured at "L"

V8 Engines

NOTE: *Before removing the cylinder head from a V8, be sure you have the 4 special tools necessary to torque the head bolts; without them it will be impossible. Do not confuse the left and right-hand head gas-*

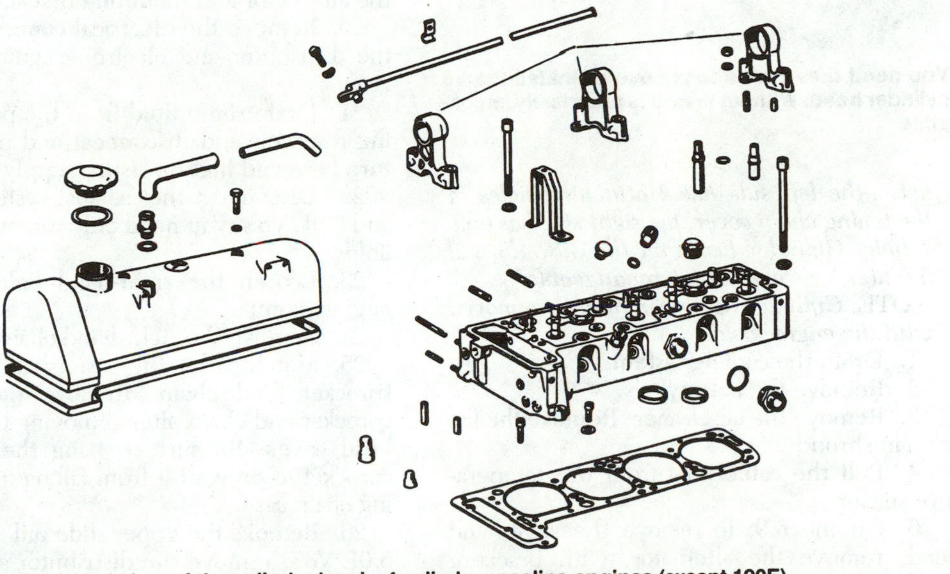

Exploded view of the cylinder head—4 cylinder gasoline engines (except 190E)

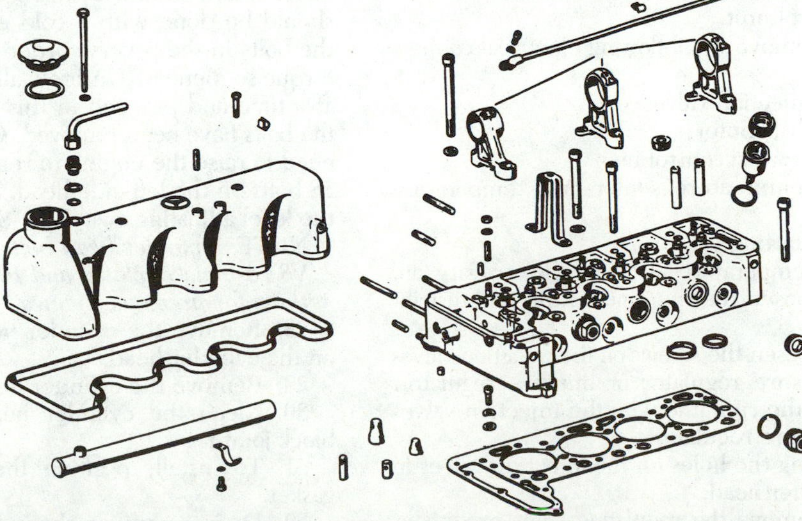

Exploded view of the cylinder head—4 cylinder diesel engines (except 190D); 5 cylinder engines similar

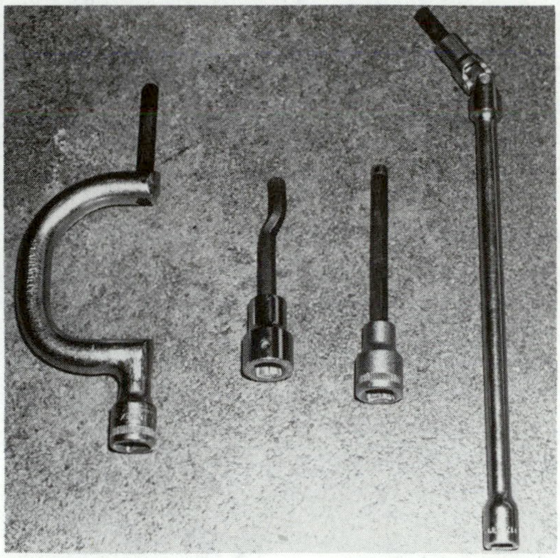

You need these tools to remove or install the V8 cylinder head. Without them it is practically impossible

kets—the left side has 2 attaching holes in the timing chain cover, the right side has only 1 hole. Cylinder heads on the 3.8, 4.5 and 5.0 liter V8's are not interchangeable.

NOTE: *Cylinder heads can only be removed with the engine cold.*

1. Drain the cooling system.
2. Remove the battery.
3. Remove the air cleaner. Remove the fan and fan shroud.
4. Pull the cable plug from the temperature sensor.
5. On the 6.9, to remove the right-hand head, remove the alternator (with bracket), windshield washer reservoir and bracket and automatic transmission dipstick tube.
6. Detach the vacuum hose from the venturi control unit.
7. Remove the following electrical connections:
   a. injection valves
   b. distributor
   c. venturi control unit
   d. temperature sensor and temperature switch
   e. starting valve
   f. temperature switch for the auxiliary fan.
8. Loosen the ring line on the fuel distributor.
9. Loosen the screws on the injection valves and pressure regulator or mixture regulator. Remove the ring line with the injection valves and pressure regulator.
10. Plug the holes for the injection valves in the cylinder head.
11. Remove the regulating shaft by disconnecting the pull rod and the thrust rod.
12. Remove the ignition cable plug.
13. Loosen the heating connection on the intake manifold.
14. Loosen the vacuum connection for the central lock at the transmission.
15. Remove the oil filler tube from the right-hand cylinder head and remove the temperature connector.
16. Remove the oil pressure gauge line from the left-hand cylinder head.
17. Loosen the coolant connection on the intake manifold.
18. Remove the intake manifold. This is not necessary on 3.8L and 5.0L V8's although the bolts must still be removed.
19. Loosen the alternator belt and remove the alternator and mounting bracket.
20. Remove the electrical connections from the distributor and electronic ignition switchgear.
21. Drain some fluid from the power steering reservoir and disconnect and plug the return hose and high pressure supply line.
22. Disconnect the exhaust system. On 3.8 and 5.0L V8's, you need only remove the manifolds.
23. Loosen the right-hand holder for the engine damper.
24. Remove the right-hand chain tensioner.
25. Matchmark the camshaft, camshaft sprocket, and chain. Remove the camshaft sprocket and chain after removing the cylinder head cover. Be sure to hang the chain and sprocket to prevent it from falling into the timing chain case.
26. Remove the upper slide rail. On 3.8 and 5.0L V8's, remove the distributor and remove the inner slide rail on the left cylinder head. Remove the rail after the camshaft sprocket.
27. Unscrew the cylinder head bolts. This should be done with a cold engine. Unscrew the bolts in the reverse order of the illustrated torque sequences. Unscrew all the bolts a little at a time and proceed in this manner until all the bolts have been removed. On the 6.9, you'll need to raise the engine to remove No. 12 and 18 bolts on the left-side head. To do this, place the level adjusting switch at "S" (first notch).

   NOTE: *Cylinder head bolts on 3.8 and 5.0L V8's are nickel plated and 10 mm longer than those for previous engines.*
28. Remove the cylinder head. Do not pry on the cylinder head.
29. Remove the cylinder head gasket.
30. Clean the cylinder head and cylinder block joint faces.
31. To install, position the cylinder head gasket.
32. Do not confuse the cylinder head gaskets. The left-hand head has two attaching holes

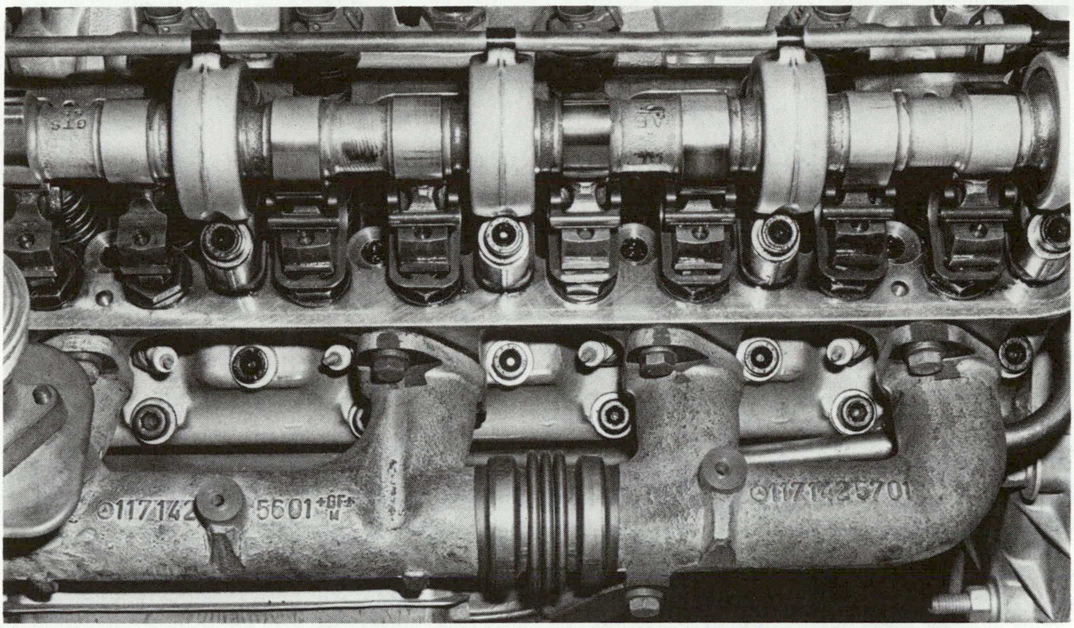

Be careful removing the cylinder head bolts on a V8. The inner row of cam bolts are the only bolts not holding the head on. Note the angle of the bolts

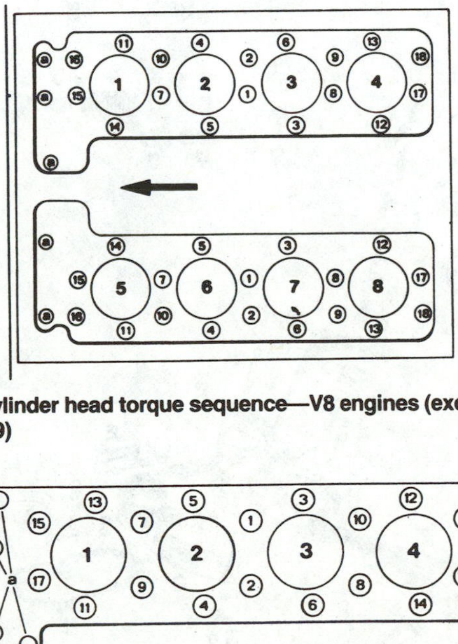

Cylinder head torque sequence—V8 engines (except 6.9)

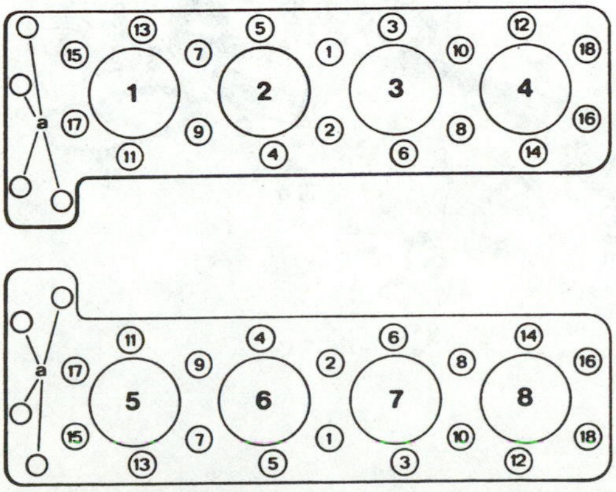

6.9 V8 cylinder head

in the timing chain cover while the right-hand head has three.

33. Install the cylinder head and torque the bolts according to the illustrated torque sequence.

34. Further installation is the reverse of removal. On 3.8 and 5.0L V8's, insert the rear cam bearing cylinder head bolt before positioning the cylinder head. Also, install the exhaust manifolds only after the cylinder head bolts have been tightened. The camshaft sprocket should be installed so that the flange faces the camshaft. Check the valve clearance and fill the engine with oil. Top up the power steering tank and bleed the power steering system.

35. Run the engine and check for leaks.

6-Cylinder DOHC Engine

NOTE: *Two people are best for this job. The head must be removed STRAIGHT up. The 2 bolts in the chain case are removed with a magnet.*

To install use 2 pieces of wood ½ in. × 1½ in. × 9 in. to lay the head on while aligning the bolt holes. The exhaust camshaft gear bolt is 0.2 in. shorter.

1. Completely drain the cooling system.
2. Remove the air filter.
3. Remove the radiator.
4. Remove the rocker arm cover.
5. Remove the battery. Remove the idler

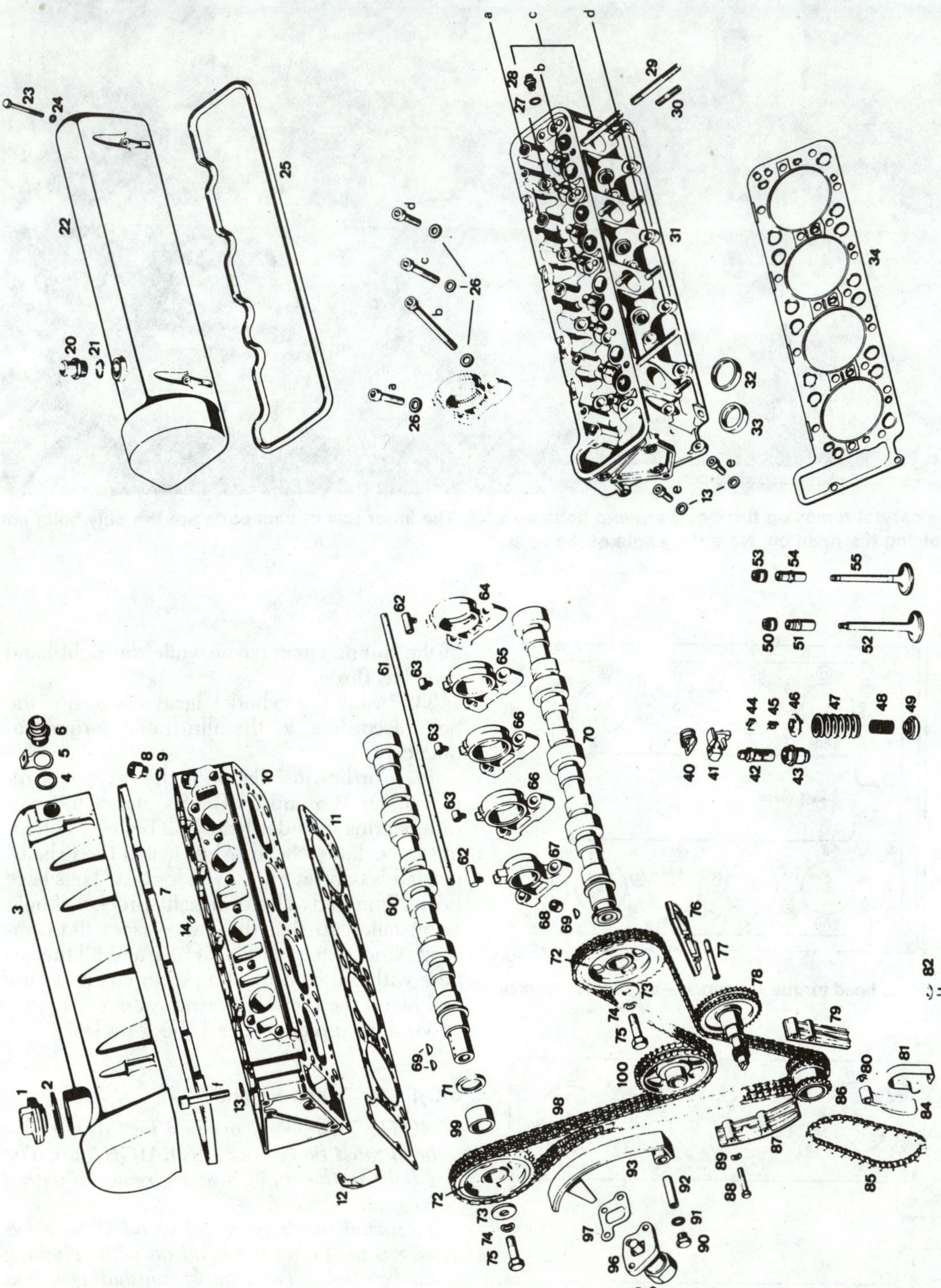

V8 engine cylinder head

Right cylinder head 1–14

1. Filler plug
2. Sealing ring
3. Cylinder head cover
4. Sealing ring
5. Holder for cable to injection valves
6. Connection
7. Valve cover gasket
8. Connection to temperature sensor
9. Sealing ring
10. Cylinder head
11. Cylinder head gasket
12. Cable holder
13. 5 Washers
14. 4 Hollow dowel pins

Left cylinder head 20–34

20. Connection
21. Sealing ring
22. Cylinder head cover
23. 8 Screws
24. 8 Sealing rings
25. Cylinder head cover gasket
26. 36 Washers
27. Sealing ring
28. Screw connection oil pressure gauge
29. 3 Studs
30. 13 Studs
31. Cylinder head
32. Valve seat ring—intake
33. Valve seat ring—exhaust
34. Cylinder head gasket

Cylinder head bolts (mm)

a. 10 M 10 × 50 (camshaft bearing fastening bolts)
b. 10 M 10 × 155
c. 18 M 10 × 80
d. 8 M 10 × 55
e. 4 M 8 × 30
f. 1 M 8 × 70

Valve arrangement 40–55

40. Tensioning spring
41. Rocker arm
42. Adjusting screw
43. Threaded bushing
44. Thrust piece
45. Valve cone piece
46. Valve spring retainer
47. Outer valve spring
48. Inner valve spring
49. Rotator
50. Intake valve seal
51. Exhaust valve guide
52. Intake valve
53. Exhaust valve seal
54. Exhaust valve guide
55. Exhaust valve

Engine timing 60–100

60. Right camshaft
61. Oil pipe (external lubrication) Oil pipe to camshaft bearing
62. Connecting piece
63. Connecting piece
64. Camshaft bearing-flywheel end
65. Camshaft bearing 4
66. Camshaft bearing 2 and 3
67. Camshaft bearing-cranking end
68. 5 hollow dowel pins
69. Spring washer
70. Left camshaft
71. Compensating washer
72. Camshaft gear
73. Camshaft gear washer
74. Spring washer
75. Bolt
76. 3 Slide rails
77. 6 Bearing bolts
78. Distributor drive gear
79. Guide rail
80. Lockwasher
81. Spring—chain tensioner, oil pump
82. Washer
83. Screw
84. Clamp
85. Single roller chain (oil pump drive)
86. Crankshaft gear
87. Slide rail
88. 4 screws
89. 4 spring washers
90. Plug
91. Sealing ring
92. Bearing bolt
93. Tensioning lever
94. 2 Bolts
95. 2 Spring washers
96. Chain tensioner
97. Gasket
98. Double roller chain
99. Spacer ring
100. Idler gear

pulley and the holding bracket for the compresser.

6. Remove the compressor and bracket and lay it aside without disconnecting any of the lines.

CAUTION: *Disconnecting any of the refrigerant lines could result in physical harm.*

7. Unbolt the cover from the camshaft housing.

8. Disconnect the heated water line from the carburetor, the vacuum line on the starter housing, and the distributor vacuum line.

9. Disconnect all electrical connections, water lines, fuel lines, and vacuum lines which are connected to the cylinder head. Tag these for reassembly.

10. Remove the regulating linkage shaft.

11. Remove the EGR line between the exhaust return valve and the exhaust pipe.

12. Disconnect and plug the oil return line at the cylinder head.

13. At the thermostat housing, loosen the hose which passes between the thermostat housing and the water pump. Unscrew the bypass line on the water pump.

14. Loosen the oil dipstick tube from the clamp and bend it slightly sidewards.

15. Unbolt the exhaust pipes from the ex-

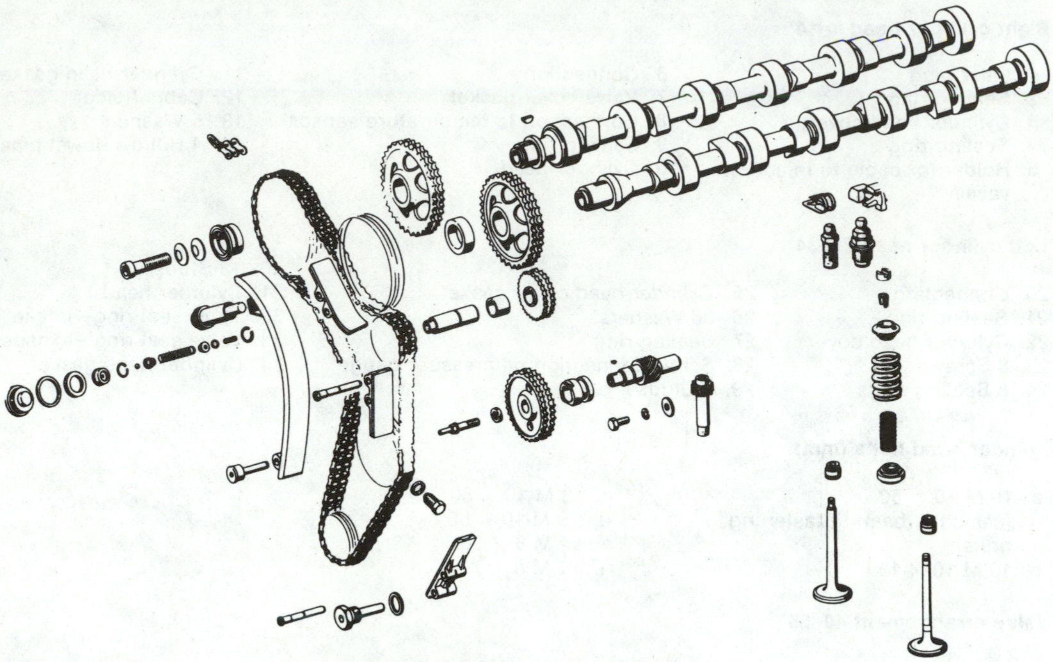

DOHC camshaft and related parts

Remove the camshaft cover

haust manifolds and bracket on the transmission.

16. Force the tension springs out of the rocker arm with a small prybar.

17. Remove all of the rocker arms.

18. Crank the engine to TDC. This can be done with a socket wrench on the crankshaft pulley bolt. The marks on the camshaft sprockets and bearing housings must be aligned.

19. Hold the camshafts and remove the bolt which holds each camshaft gear to the camshaft.

20. Remove the upper slide rail. Knock out the bearing bolts with a puller.

21. Remove the chain tensioner.

22. Push both camshafts toward the rear and remove the camshafts' sprockets.

23. Remove the spacer sleeves on both camshafts. The sleeves are located in front of the camshaft bearings.

24. Remove the guide wheel by unscrewing the plug and removing the bearing bolt.

25. Lift off the timing chain and suspend the chain from the hood with a piece of wire. Pull out the guide gear.

26. Remove the slide rail in the cylinder head by removing the bearing pin with a puller.

27. Loosen the cylinder head bolts in small increments, using the reverse order of the tightening sequence. This should be done on a

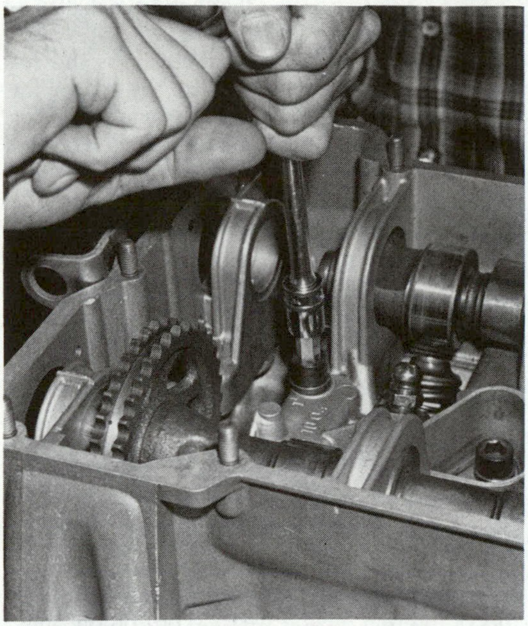

An allen wrench is required to remove cylinder head bolts

cold engine to prevent the possibility of head warpage.

28. Pull out the two bolts in the chain case with a magnet. Be careful not to drop the washers.

29. Pull up on the timing chain and force the tensioning rail toward the center of the engine.

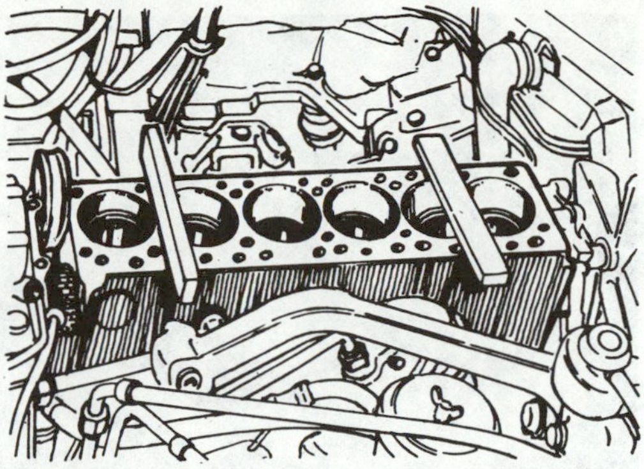

Fabricated tools for installing 6-cylinder head

30. Lift the cylinder head up in a vertical direction.

NOTE: *Mercedes-Benz recommends two people for this job.*

31. Remove the cylinder head gasket and clean the joint faces of the block and head.

32. To install, cut two pieces of wood ½ in. × 1-½ in. × 9-½ in. Lay one piece upright between cylinders 1 and 2; lay the other flat between cylinders 5 and 6.

33. Install the cylinder head in an inclined position so that the timing chain and tensioning rail can be inserted.

34. Lift the cylinder head at the front and remove the front piece of wood toward the exhaust side. Carefully lower the cylinder head until the bolt holes align.

35. Lift the head at the rear so that the board

Several people are normally required to remove the cylinder head

While the head is removed from a 6-cylinder engine, always replace this rubber hose, whether it needs it or not; it is impossible to replace with the cylinder head installed

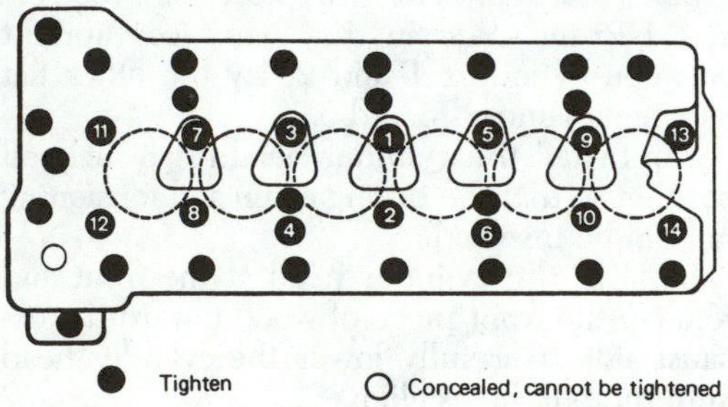

6-cylinder gasoline cylinder head and camshaft housing

The marks on the camshaft and bearing housing must align on DOHC 6 cylinder engines when the engine is at TDC

can be moved toward the exhaust side. Carefully lower the cylinder head until all the bolt holes align.

36. Tighten the cylinder head bolts in gradual steps until they are fully tightened. Follow the torque sequence illustrated.

37. Check to be sure that both camshafts rotate freely after the bolts are tight.

38. The remainder of installation is the reverse of removal. Be sure that the spacer for the camshaft gear with the engaging lugs for the vacuum pump drive gear is installed on the exhaust side. Also, the washers for the bolts attaching the camshaft gears to the camshafts must be installed with the domed side against the head of the bolt.

39. Note that the attaching bolt for the exhaust camshaft gear is 0.2 in. shorter.

40. Be sure to adjust the valve clearance and fill the cooling system. Run the engine and check for leaks.

CHECKING ENGINE COMPRESSION

Gasoline Engines Only

A noticeable lack of engine power, excessive oil consumption and/or poor fuel mileage measured over an extended period are all indicators of internal engine wear. Worn piston rings, scored and worn cylinder bores, blown head gaskets, sticking or burnt valves and worn valve seats are all possible culprits here. A check of each cylinder's compression will help you locate the problems.

As mentioned in the "Tools and Equipment" section of Chapter 1, a screw-in compression gauge is more accurate than the type you simply hold against the spark plug hole, although it takes slightly longer to use (it's worth it). To check compression:

1. Warm the engine up to operating temperature.
2. Remove spark plugs.
3. Disconnect the high tension wire from the ignition coil.
4. Screw the compression gauge into the No. 1 spark plug hole until the fitting is snug. Be very careful not to crossthread the hole, as most heads are aluminum.
5. Fully open the throttle either by operating the carburetor throttle linkage by hand, or on fuel injected cars having an assistant "floor" the accelerator pedal.
6. Ask your assistant to crank the engine a few times using the ignition switch.
7. Record the highest reading on the gauge, and compare it to the compression specifications. The specs listed are maximum, and a cylinder is usually acceptable if its compression is within about 20 pounds of maximum.
8. Repeat the procedure for the remaining cylinders, recording each cylinder's compression. The difference between each cylinder should be no more than 14 pounds. If a cylinder is unusually low, pour a tablespoon of clean engine oil into the cylinder through the spark

plug hole and repeat the compression test. If the compression comes up after adding the oil, it appears that that cylinder's piston rings or bore are damaged or worn. If the pressure remains low, the valves may not be seating properly (a valve job is needed) or the head gasket may be blown near that cylinder.

CLEANING AND INSPECTION

Carefully chip carbon away from the valve heads, combustion chambers and ports by using a chisel made of hardwood. Remove the remaining deposits with a stiff wire brush or a wire brush attachment for a hand drill.

NOTE: *Always make sure that the deposits are actually removed, rather than just burnished.*

Clean the remaining cylinder head components in an engine cleaning solvent. Do not remove the protective coating from the valve springs.

CAUTION: *As most Mercedes-Benz cylinder heads are made out of aluminum, NEVER 'hot tank' the cylinder head as is a common process with cast iron heads.*

Place a straight-edge across the gasket surface of the cylinder head. Using feeler gauges, determine the clearance at the center of the straight-edge. If warpage exceeds .003 in. in a 6 in. span, or .006 in. over the total length the cylinder head will require resurfacing.

NOTE: *If warpage exceeds the manufacturer's tolerance for material removal, the cylinder head must be replaced.*

Cylinder head resurfacing should be performed by a reputable machine shop in your area.

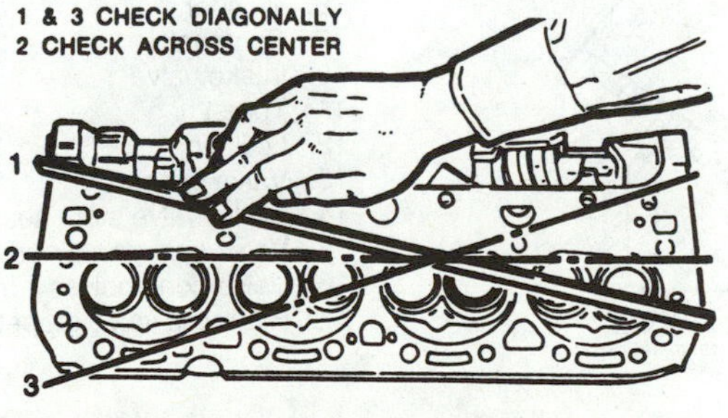

Check the cylinder head for warpage

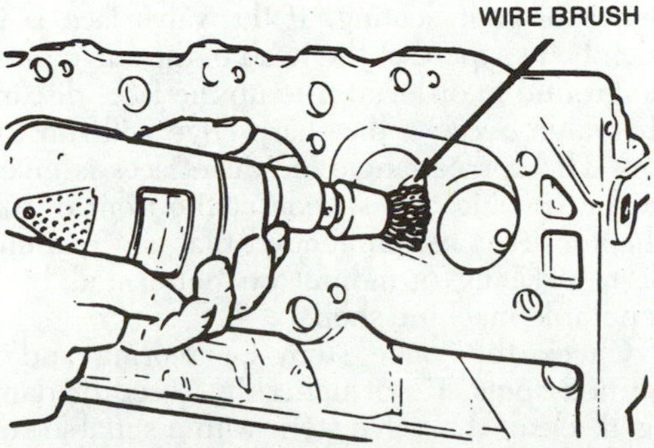

Remove the carbon from the cylinder head with a wire brush and electric drill

Valves and Springs

REMOVAL AND INSTALLATION

1. Remove the cylinder head. Remove the rocker arms and shafts (all except 190D). Remove the camshaft (190D only).

On gasoline engines only:

2. Using a valve spring compressor, compress the spring and remove the valve cone halves (be careful not to lose the two valve cone halves).
3. Remove the spring retainer and then lift out the spring.
4. Pry off the valve stem oil seal and lift out the lower spring seat (thrust ring). Remove the valve through the bottom of the cylinder head.

NOTE: *Then removing the valve stem seal and the thrust ring, a small screwdriver and a magnet may come in handy.*

On the 190D:

5. Remove the hydraulic valve tappet with Special Tool #601 589 05 33 00. After the tappet has been removed, follow the procedures detailed for gasoline engines.

On all other diesel engines:

6. Position an open-end wrench on the valve spring retainer; while holding the retainer, unscrew the capnut with a valve adjusting wrench.

NOTE: *A second valve adjusting wrench will be required to hold the counternut while loosening the capnut.*

7. Loosen and remove the counternut.
8. Lift out the valve spring and lower spring seat. Remove the valve through the bottom of the cylinder head.

On all engines:

9. Inspect the valve and spring. Clean the valve guide with a cotton swab and solvent. Inspect the valve guide and seat and check the valve guide-to-stem clearance.
10. Lubricate the valve stem and guide with engine oil. Install the valve into the cylinder head through the bottom and position the lower spring seat (thrust ring).
11. Lubricate the valve stem oil seal with engine oil, slide it down over the stem and then install it into position over the spring seat.

NOTE: *When installing seals, always ensure that a small amount of oil is able to pass the seal so as to lubricate the valve guides; otherwise, excessive wear may result.*

NOTE: *Intake and exhaust valve stem seals on the 190 series engines are not interchangeable.*

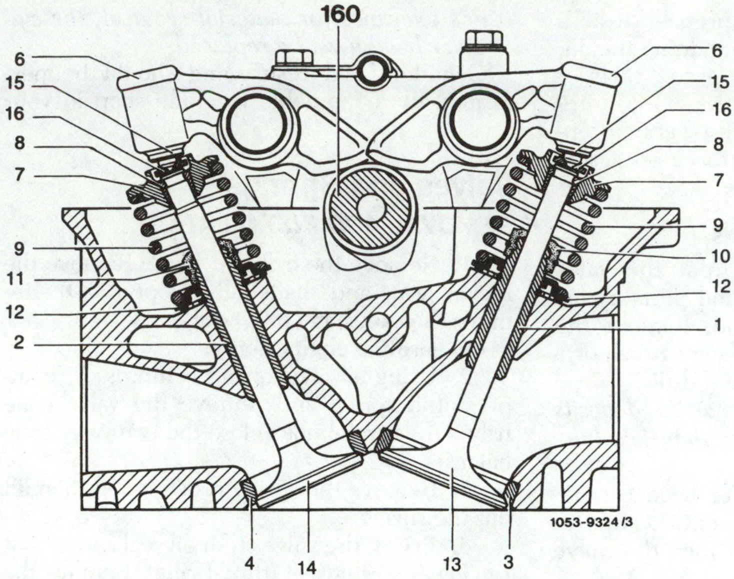

1. Intake valve guide
2. Exhaust valve guide
3. Intake valve seat ring
4. Exhaust valve seat ring
5. Camshaft
6. Rocker arm
7. Valve spring retainer
8. Valve cone halves
9. Valve spring
10. Intake valve stem seal
11. Exhaust valve stem seal
12. Thrust ring
13. Intake valve
14. Exhaust valve
15. Hydraulic valve tappet
16. Ball socket

Valve train on the 190E

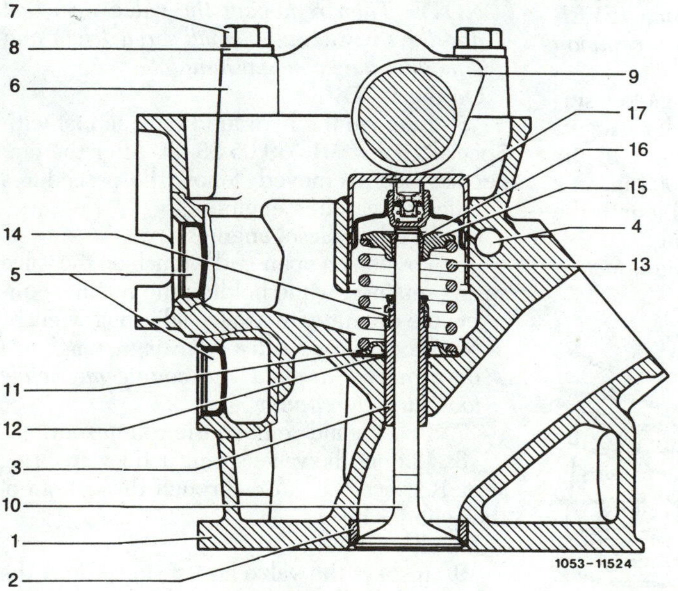

1. Cylinder head
2. Intake valve seat ring
3. Intake valve guide
4. Oil passage
5. Sheet metal plug
6. Bearing cap
7. Screw M 8 x 45
8. Washer
9. Camshaft
10. Intake valve
11. Thrust ring
12. Lock ring
13. Valve spring
14. Intake valve stem seal
15. Valve spring retainer
16. Valve cone halves
17. Hydraulic valve tappets

Valve train on the 190D (intake shown, exhaust similar)

12. Position the valve spring onto the spring seat with the tight coils facing the cylinder head.

13. Install the spring retainer. On all diesel engines (except 190D), the lug on the retainer must be seated in the groove on the valve stem.

14. Further installation is the reverse of the removal procedures detailed previously for the individual engine groups.

NOTE: *Tap the installed valve stem lightly with a rubber mallet to ensure a proper fit.*

INSPECTION

Inspect the valve faces and seats (in the cylinder head) for pits, burned spots and other evidence of poor seating. If the valve face is in such bad shape that the head of the valve must be ground in order to true up the face, discard the valve because the sharp edge will run too hot. The correct angle for valve faces is given in the specification section at the front of this chapter. It is recommended that any reaming or resurfacing (grinding) be performed by a reputable machine shop.

Check the valve stem for scoring and/or burned spots. If not noticably scored or damaged, clean the valve stem with a suitable solvent to remove all gum and varnish. Clean the valve guides using a suitable solvent and an ex-

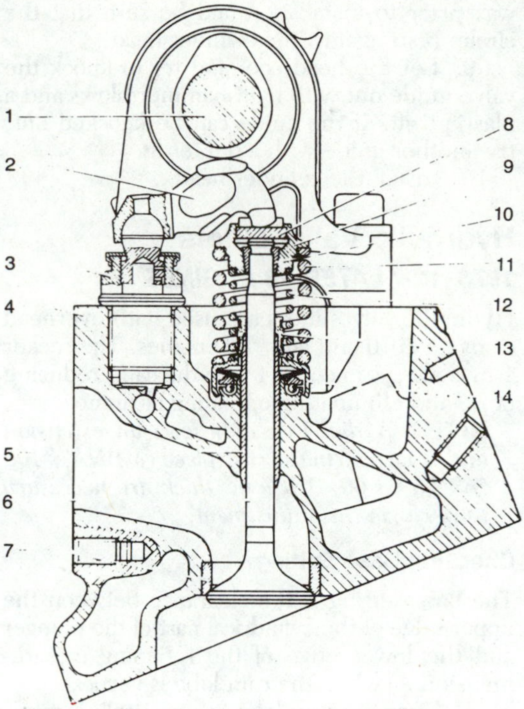

1. Camshaft
2. Rocker arm
3. Hydraulic valve clearance compensating element
4. Cylinder head
5. Valve guide
6. Exhaust valve
7. Valve seat ring
8. Thrust piece
9. Valve spring retainer
10. Valve keeper
11. Outer valve spring
12. Inner valve spring
13. Valve stem seal
14. Rotocap

Valve train on the 3.8 V8 (other V8 engines similar)

panding wire-type valve guide cleaner (generally available at a local automotive supply store). If you have access to a dial indicator for measuring valve stem-to-guide clearance, mount it so that the stem of the indicator is at a 90° angle to the valve stem and as close to the valve guide as possible. Move the valve off its seat slightly and measure the valve guide-to-stem clearance by rocking the valve back and forth so that the stem actuates the dial indicator. Measure the valve stem using a micrometer, and compare to specifications in order to determine whether the stem or the guide is responsible for the excess clearance. If a dial indicator and

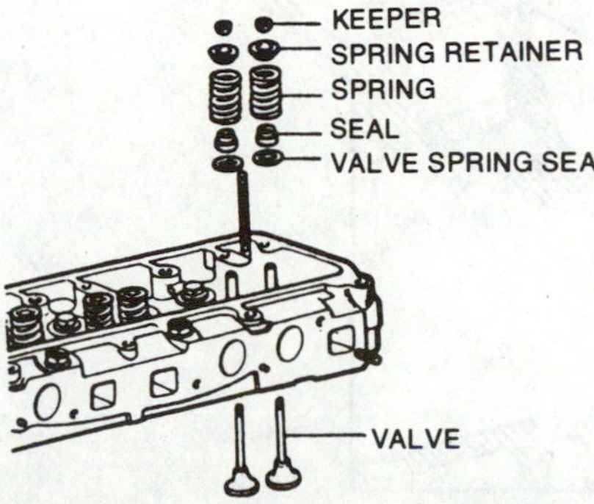

Typical valve and related components

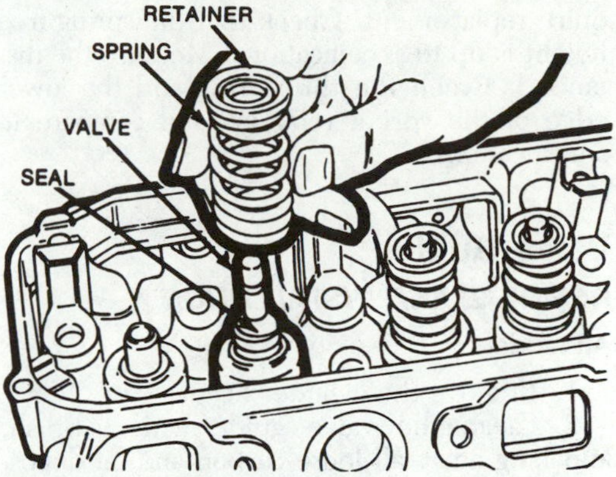

Installing the valve

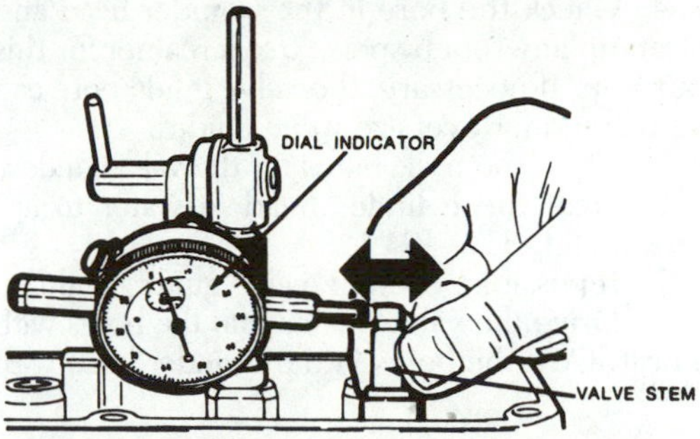

Check the valve stem-to-guide clearance

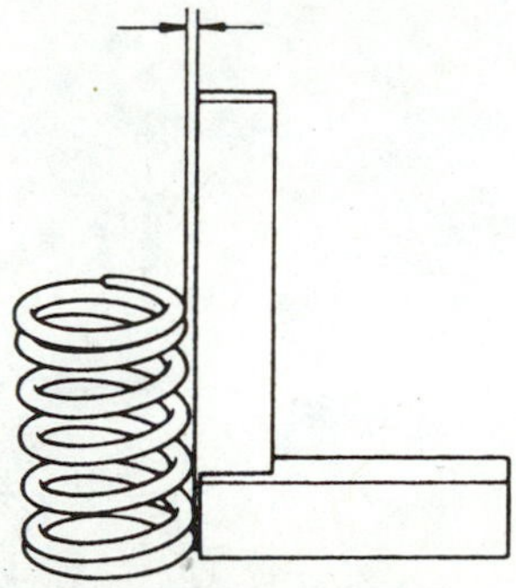

Checking the valve spring for squareness

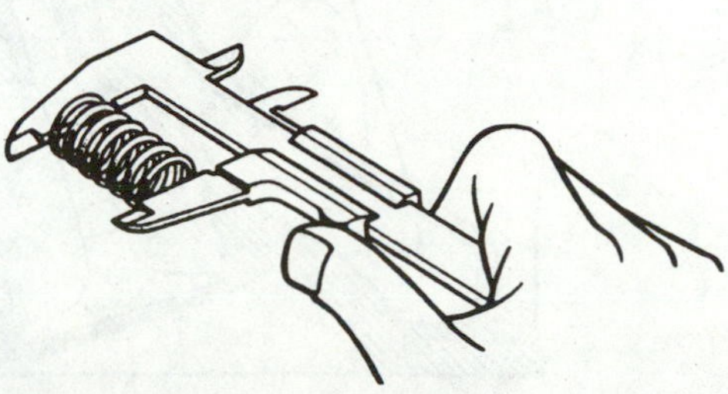

Checking the spring free height

a micrometer are not available, take the cylinder head and valves to a reputable machine shop.

Using a steel square, check the squareness of the valve spring. If the spring is out of square more than the maximum allowable, it will require replacement. Check that the spring free height is up to specifications. Measure the distance between the thrust ring and the lower edge of the spring retainer, and compare to specifications.

Valve Guides

REMOVAL AND INSTALLATION

All Models

1. Remove the cylinder head.
2. Clean the valve guide with a brush, knocking away all loose carbon and oil deposits.
3. Knock out the old valve guide with a drift.
4. Check the bore in the cylinder head and clean up any rough spots. Use a reamer for this purpose. If necessary, the valve guide bore can be reamed for oversize valve guides.
5. Clean the basic bores for the valve guides.
6. Heat the cylinder head in water to approximately 176–194°F.
7. If possible, cool the valve guides slightly.
8. Drive the valve guides into the bores with a drift. Coat the bores in the cylinder head with wax prior to installation and be sure that the circlip rests against the cylinder head.
9. Let the head cool and try to knock the valve guide out with light hammer blows and a plastic drift. If the guide can be knocked out, try another guide with a tighter fit.
10. Install the cylinder head.

Hydraulic Valve Lifters

1976 AND LATER V8 ENGINES

Hydraulic valve lifters are used with overhead cams on 1976 and later V8 engines. The rocker arm is always in contact with the cam, reducing noise and eliminating operating clearance.

NOTE: *A dial indicator with an extension and a measuring thrust piece (MBNA #100 589 16 63 00, 0.187 in. thick are necessary to perform this adjustment.*

Checking Base Setting

The base setting is the clearance between the upper edge of the cylindrical part of the plunger and the lower edge of the retaining cap (dimension A) when the cam lobe is vertical.

1. Turn the cam lobe to a vertical position.
2. Attach a dial indicator and tip extension and insert the extension through the bore in the rocker arm onto the head plunger. Preload the dial indicator by 2 mm and zero the instrument.
3. Depress the valve with a valve spring

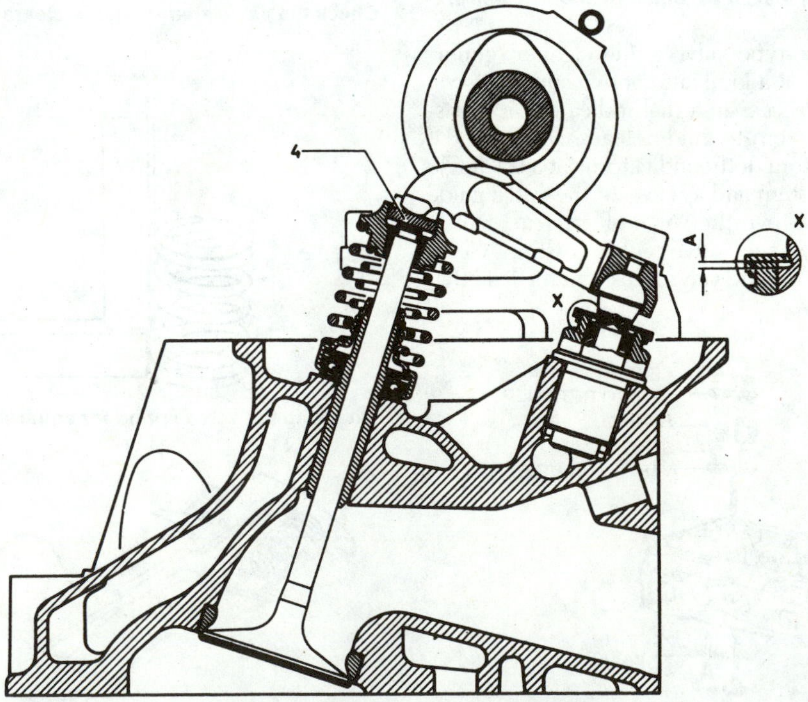

Cutaway view of hydraulic valve lifter

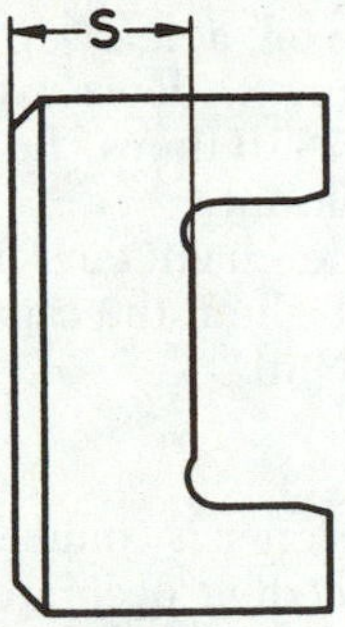

Measuring the thrust piece

compressor. The lift on the dial indicator should be 0.028–0.075 in.

4. If the lift is excessive, the base setting can be changed by installing a new thrust piece.
5. Remove the dial indicator.
6. Remove the rocker arm.
7. Remove the thrust piece and insert the measuring disc.
8. Install the rocker arm and repeat Steps 1–3.
9. Select a thrust piece according to the table. If the measure value 0–0.002 in. and the 0.2146 in. thrust piece will not give the proper base setting, use the 0.2883 in. thrust piece.

Selective Thrust Pieces

Measured Value (in.)	Thrust Piece Thickness (S) (in.)
0–0.002	0.2146/0.2283
0.002–0.034	0.2008
0.035–0.066	0.1870
0.067–0.099	0.1732
0.099–0.131	0.1594
above 0.131	0.1457

10. Remove the dial indicator and the rocker arm. Install the selected thrust piece.
11. Reinstall the rocker arm and dial indicator and repeat Steps 1–3.

REMOVAL AND INSTALLATION

Temporarily removed valve lifters must be reinstalled in their original locations. When replacing worn rocker arms, the camshaft must also be replaced. If the rocker arm, or hydraulic lifter is replaced, check the base setting.

Remove the rocker arm and unscrew the valve lifter with a 24 mm socket.

Timing Chain Tensioner

REMOVAL AND INSTALLATION

4 and 5-Cylinder Engines

There are 2 kinds of timing chain tensioners. One uses an O-ring seal and the other a flat

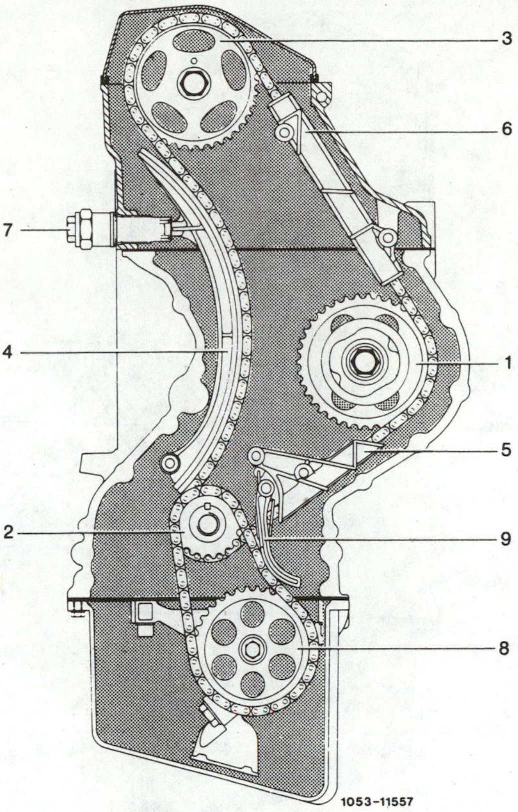

1. Injection timing advance mechanism
2. Crankshaft sprocket
3. Camshaft sprocket
4. Tensioning rail
5. Slide rail
6. Slide rail
7. Chain tensioner
8. Oil pump drive gear
9. Tensioning lever, chain, oil pump drive

Timing chain assembly—190D

gasket. Do not install a flat gasket on a tensioner meant to be used with an O-ring.

Chain tensioners should be replaced as a unit if defective.

1. Drain the coolant. If the car has air conditioning, disconnect the compressor and mounting bracket and lay it aside. Do not disconnect the refrigerant lines.

On diesel engines, drain the coolant from the block.

2. Remove the thermostat housing.
3. Loosen and remove the chain tensioner. Be careful of loose O-rings. On the 190 series you must first remove the tensioner capnut and then the tension spring. The tensioner body can now be unscrewed with an Allen wrench.
4. Check the O-rings or gasket and replace if necessary.
5. To fill the chain tensioner, place the tensioner (pressure bolt down) in a container of

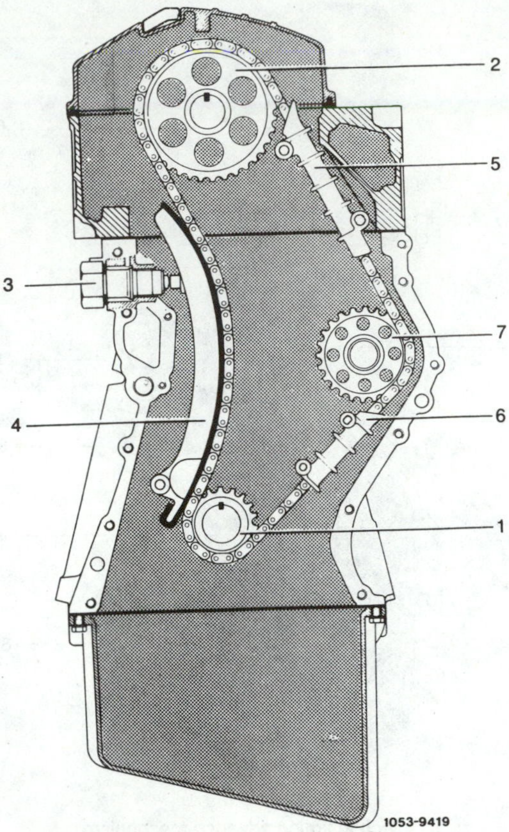

1. Crankshaft sprocket
2. Camshaft sprocket
3. Chain tensioner
4. Tensioning rail
5. Slide rail
6. Slide rail
7. Idler gear

Timing chain assembly—190E

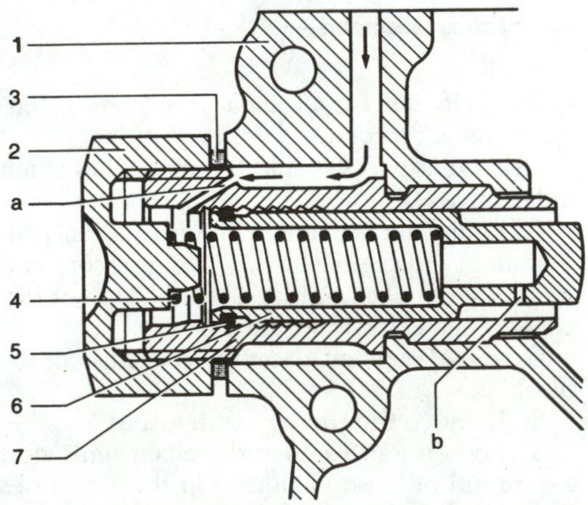

1. Crankcase
2. Cap nut
3. Seal ring
4. Compression spring
5. Detent spring
6. Thrust pin
7. Chain tensioner housing
a. Supply hole 1.1 mm dia.
b. Orifice 1.2 mm dia.

Cross section of the timing chain tensioner—190E (190D similar)

SAE 10 engine oil, at least up to the flat flange. Using a drill press, depress the pressure bolt slowly, about 7–10 times. Be sure this is done slowly and uniformly.

6. Install the chain tensioner. Tighten the bolts evenly. Tighten the capnut on the 190 to 51 ft. lbs. (70 Nm).

V8 Engines

The chain tensioner is connected to the engine oil circuit. Bleeding occurs once oil pressure has been established and the tensioner is filling with oil.

Since December of 1974, a venting hole has been installed in the tensioner to prevent oil foaming. If you have a lot of timing chain noise, use this type of tensioner, which is identified by a white paint dot on the cap.

Service procedures for tensioners and rails on the different V8's are all similar. Arrangement and shape and size of parts however, is slightly different.

1. On California models, disconnect the line from the tensioner.

The inside bolt (arrow) on the V8 chain tensioner can only be reached by inserting a long, straight allen key underneath the exhaust manifold

2. Remove the attaching bolts and remove the tensioner. The inside bolts will probably require a long, straight 6 mm allen key to bypass the exhaust manifold. It is a tight fit.

3. Place the tensioner vertically in a container of engine oil. Operate the pressure bolt to fill the tensioner. After filling, it should permit compression very slowly under considerable force. If not, replace the tensioner with a new unit.

4. Install the tensioner and tighten the bolts evenly.

6-Cylinder Engines

1. On A/C vehicles, remove the battery. Unbolt the refrigerant compressor and lay it aside. Do not disconnect the refrigerant lines.

2. Remove the plug with a 17 mm allen key.

3. Tighten the threaded ring and loosen the ball seat ring.

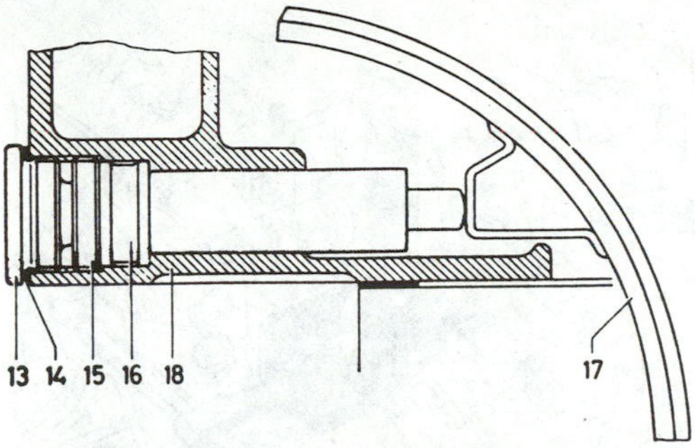

13. Closing plug
14. Sealing ring
15. Threaded ring
16. Chain tensioner
17. Tensioning rail
18. Cylinder head

6-cylinder timing chain tensioner

Remove the plug with a 17 mm allen key

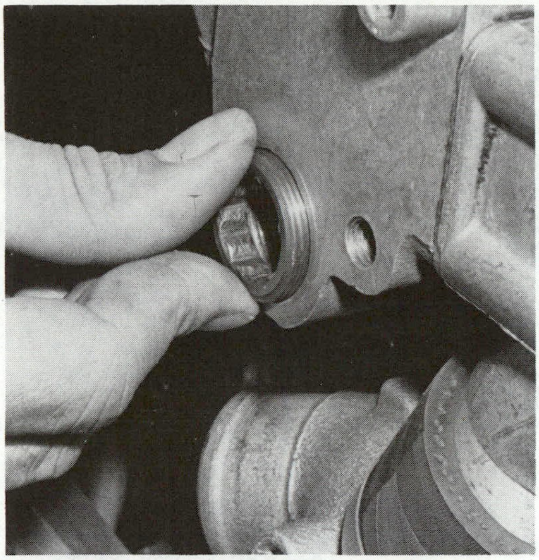

Remove the threaded plug

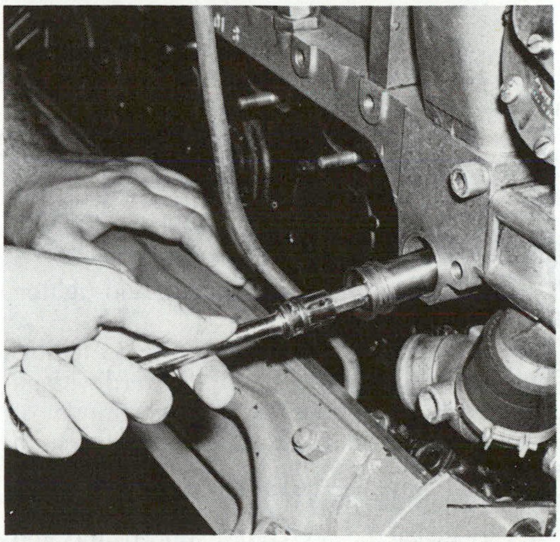

Remove the chain tensioner with a 10 mm allen key

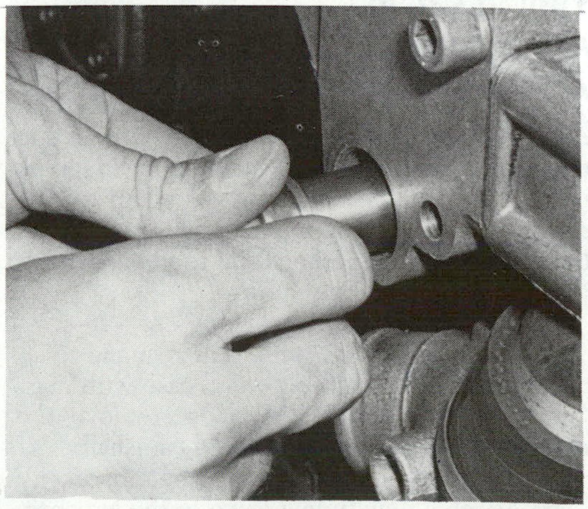

Install the chain tensioner

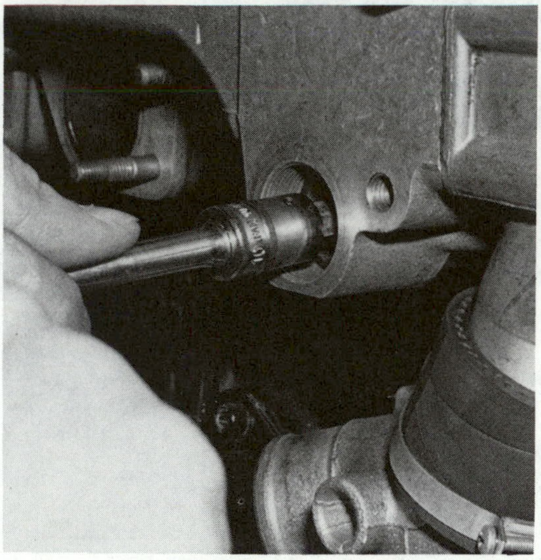

Tighten the tensioner until it "clicks"

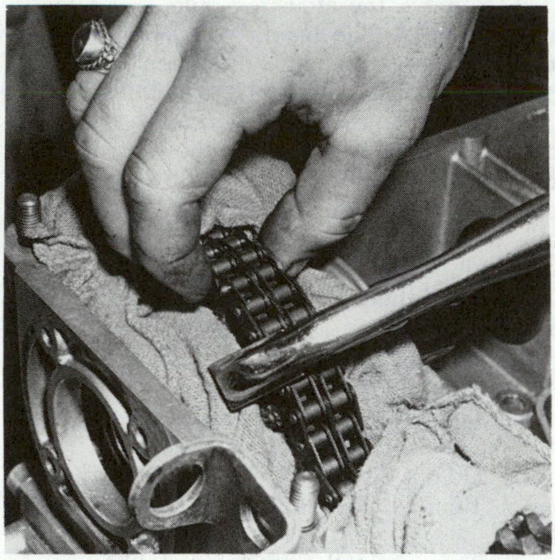

Clamp the chain to the gear and cover the opening with rags

4. Remove the threaded ring.
5. Remove the chain tensioner with a 10 mm allen key.
6. Be sure the tight side of the chain is tight.
7. Compress the tensioner and install the chain tensioner with a 10 mm allen key. Do not bump the allen key or the tensioner will release.
8. Screw in the threaded ring and tighten it to 44 ft. lbs.
9. Tighten the ball seat ring to 18 ft. lbs. The pressure bolt should jump forward with an audible clock. If it does not, the assembly must be removed and the installation repeated until it does click.
10. Install the plug.
11. Reinstall the A/C compressor, battery and air cleaner.

Timing Chain

REPLACEMENT

All Models

An endless timing chain is used on production engines, but a split chain with a connecting link is used for service. The endless chain can be separated with a "chain-breaker". Only one mast link (connecting link) should be used on a chain.

1. Remove the spark plugs.
2. Remove the valve cover(s).
3. Clamp the chain to the cam gear and cover the opening of the timing chain case with rags. On 6-cylinder and V8 engines, remove the rocker arms from the right-hand camshaft.
4. Separate the chain with a chain breaker.
5. Attach a new timing chain to the old chain with a master link.

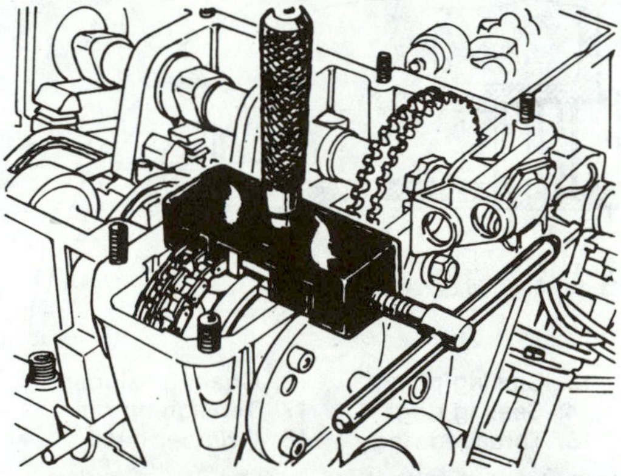

Remove the link with a chain breaker

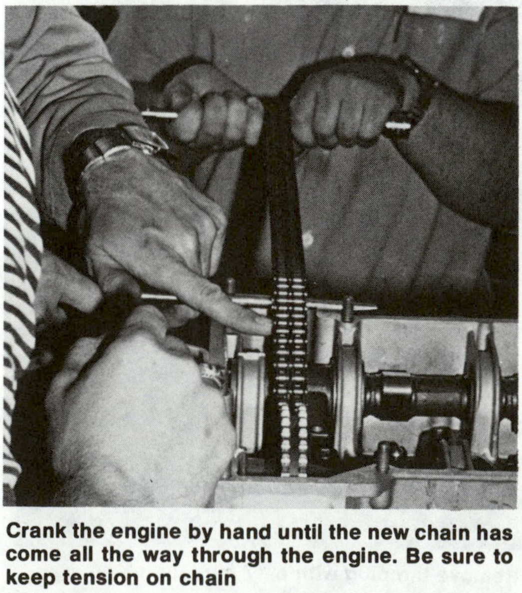

Crank the engine by hand until the new chain has come all the way through the engine. Be sure to keep tension on chain

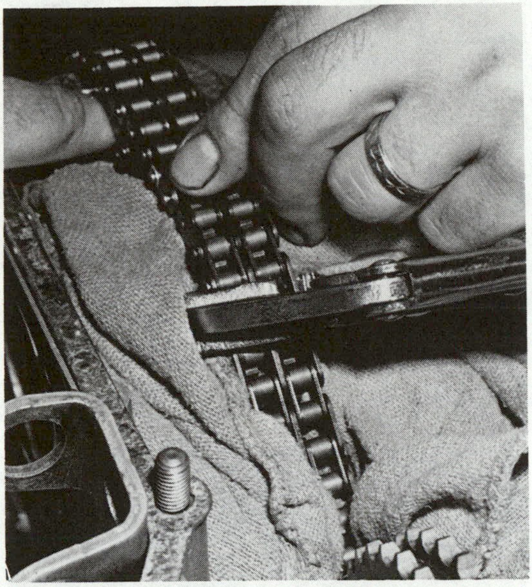

Clamp the chain again, cover the opening and remove the old chain from the master link. Connect both ends of the new chain

6. Using a socket wrench on the crankshaft, slowly rotate the engine in the direction of normal rotation. Simultaneously, pull the old chain through until the master link is uppermost on the camshaft sprocket. Be sure to keep tension on the chain throughout this procedure.
7. Disconnect the old timing chain and connect the ends of the new chain with the master link. Insert the new connecting link from the rear, so that the lockwashers can be seen from the front.
8. Rotate the engine until the timing marks align. Check the valve timing. Once the new chain is assembled, rotate the engine (by hand) through at least one complete revolution to be sure everything is OK. See valve timing for illustrations.

Camshaft

REMOVAL AND INSTALLATION

4 and 5-Cylinder Engines

EXCEPT 190D and 190E

When the camshaft is replaced, be sure the rocker arms are also replaced.

1. Remove the valve cover.
2. Remove the chain tensioner.
3. Remove the rocker arms.
4. Set the crankshaft at TDC for No. 1 cylinder and be sure that the camshaft timing marks are aligned.
5. Hold the camshaft and loosen the cam gear bolt. Remove the cam gear and wire it securely so that the chain does not loose tension nor slip down into the chain case.
6. Remove the camshaft.
7. Installation is the reverse of removal. Be sure to check that the valve timing marks align when No. 1 cylinder is at TDC. Check the valve clearance.

190D AND 190E

NOTE: *On the 190E it is always a good idea to replace the rocker arms and shafts whenever the camshaft is replaced.*

1. Remove the valve cover.
2. Remove the chain tensioner.
3. On the 190E, remove the rocker arms and shafts.
4. Set the crankshaft at TDC for the No. 1 piston and make sure that the timing marks on the camshaft are in alignment.
5. Using a 24mm open-end wrench, hold the rear of the camshaft (flats are provided) and then loosen and remove the camshaft retaining bolt. Carefully slide the gear and chain off the shaft and wire them securely so they won't slip down into the case.

NOTE: *Be careful not to lose the woodruff key while removing the gear on the 190E.*

6. The camshaft is secured on the cylinder head by means of the bearing caps. Remove them and keep them in their proper order. Each cap is marked by a number punched into its side; this number must match the number cast into the cylinder head.

CAUTION: *When removing the bearing caps on the 190D, always loosen the center two first and then move on to the outer ones.*

7. Remove the camshaft.
8. Installation is in the reverse order of removal. Always make sure that the No. 1 cylinder is at TDC and all timing marks are aligned. Tighten the bearing caps to 15 ft. lbs. (21 Nm) on the 190E and 18 ft. lbs. (25 Nm) on the 190D. The camshaft gear retaining bolt should be tightened to 58 ft. lbs. (80 Nm) on the 190E and 33 ft. lbs. (45 Nm) on the 190D.

On the 190E, the mark (arrow) on the camshaft collar (B) must always be aligned

NOTE: *Be certain not to forget the woodruff key on the 190E.*

6-Cylinder Engines

With the engine installed in the car, the camshafts can only be removed together with the camshaft housing. If a new camshaft is installed, be sure to use new rocker arms.

1. Remove the refrigerant compressor but do not disconnect the refrigerant lines.
2. Remove the battery.
3. Remove the vacuum pump from the right-hand cylinder head.
4. Drain the coolant and remove the water hoses.
5. Remove the rocker arm cover.
6. Remove the cover from the front of the camshaft housing.
7. Remove the rocker arm springs.
8. Remove the rocker arms.
9. Crank the engine around in the normal direction of rotation (using the crankshaft bolt) until No. 1 piston is at TDC, the pointer aligns with the TDC mark on the crankshaft pulley and the camshaft timing marks are aligned.
10. Hold the camshaft(s) and loosen the camshaft bolts.

Remove the vacuum pump and camshaft cover

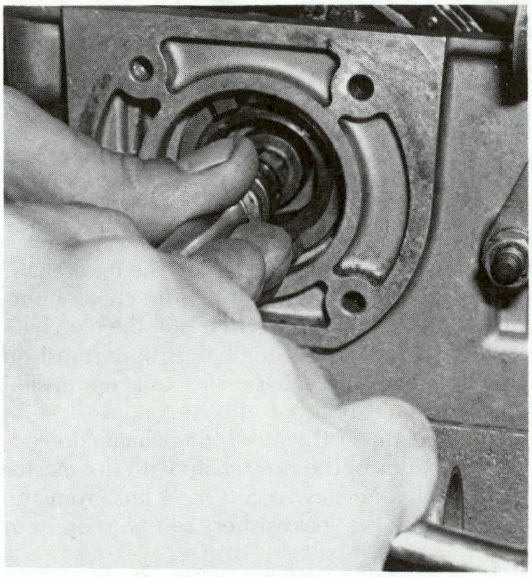

Loosen the camshaft bolts

Remove the rocker arm springs, rocker arms and thrust pieces

Using a puller, remove the pins from the slide rails and remove the slide rails

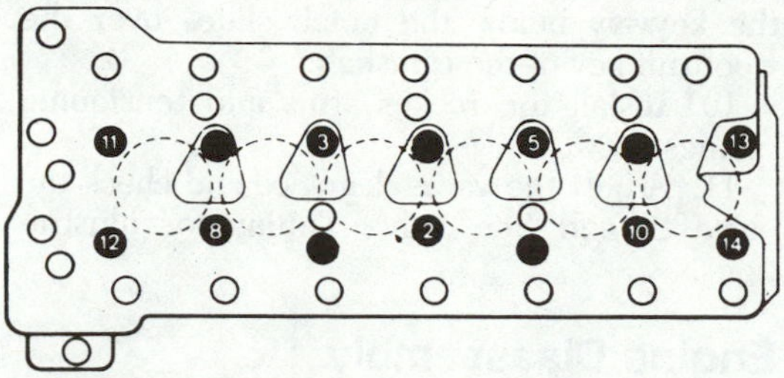

○ Unscrew M 8 bolts
① Unscrew cylinder head bolts in reverse order
● Do not loosen bolts

Bolts to be removed during camshaft housing removal

NOTE: *Wire the camshaft gears up so that tension applied to the chain. The chain must not be allowed to slip off the camshaft or crankshaft gears.*

11. Remove the chain tensioner.
12. Remove the slide rail from the camshaft housing. You'll need a small puller for this.
13. Loosen the cover at the right-hand rear side of the camshaft housing and push the right-hand camshaft toward the rear. Remove the camshaft gear.
14. Loosen the camshaft housing retaining bolts. Do not loosen the 5 lower cylinder head bolts or the 2 M8 bolts.
15. Remove the camshaft housing with the camshafts.
16. Remove the rear covers from the camshaft housing.
17. Hold the left-hand camshaft and loosen the attaching bolt.
18. Push the camshaft rearward and remove the camshaft gear. Remove the spacer from the intake camshaft.
19. Remove both camshafts from the housing.
20. Oil the bearings and install the intake camshaft (left-hand) with cam gear and spacer. Use retaining bolt and washer (not springs).
21. Install the exhaust (right-hand) camshaft. Do not install the gear until the housing is installed.
22. Install the rear camshaft covers. Do not tighten the one on the right-hand side.
23. Install the camshaft housing.
24. Lubricate the bolts and tighten them in 3 stages:
    - Starting with Bolt #2, tighten to 30 ft. lbs.
    - Starting with Bolt #2, tighten to 44 ft. lbs.
    - Starting with Bolt #1, tighten to 67 ft. lbs. First, slightly loosen the 5 lower cylinder head bolts.
25. When you are finished torquing the camshaft housing bolts, torque the cylinder head bolts. When all bolts have finally been tightened, the camshafts should rotate easily and freely.

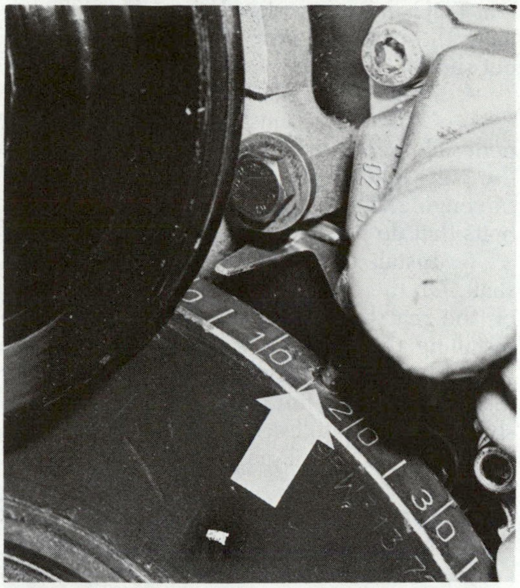

If 2 timing scales are used, the TDC scale is the one with the pin (arrow)

26. Install the righthand camshaft gear. Be sure the cam timing is accurate and the engine is set at TDC on No 1 cylinder.

CAUTION: *Some engines have a scale for BDC as well as one for TDC. The TDC mark is next to the pin in the blancer.*

27. Install the timing chain rail.
28. Install the rockers and tension springs. Adjust the valves.
29. Crank the engine by hand and check the valve timing.
30. Tighten the camshaft gear bolts to 59 ft. lbs.
31. Install the chain tensioner.
32. Install the camshaft rear housing covers (if not already done) and the vacuum pump.
33. Install the rocker covers.

V8 Engines

Experience shows that the right-hand camshaft is always the first one to require replacement. When the V8 camshaft is removed, keep the pedestals with the camshaft. In particular, make sure that the 2 left-hand rear cam pedestals are not swapped. The result will be no oil pressure. Always replace the oil gallery pipe with the camshaft.

1. Remove the valve cover.
2. Remove the tensioning springs and rocker arms.
3. Using a wrench on the crankshaft pulley, crank the engine around until No. 1 piston

is at TDC on compression. Using some stiff wire, hang the camshaft gear so that the chain will not slip off the gears.

4. Remove the camshaft gear.

5. Unbolt the camshaft, camshaft bearing pedestals and the oil pipe. Note the angle of the bolts holding the cam bearing pedestals to the engine. The inner row of bolts are the only bolts that do not hold the head to the block.

6. Install the bearing pedestals and camshaft. On the left-hand camshaft, the outer bolt on the rear bearing must be inserted prior to installing the bearings or it will not clear the power brake unit. Tighten the bolts from the inside out. When finished tightening, the camshaft should rotate freely.

7. Check the oil pipes for obstructions and replace if necessary.

8. When installing the oil pipes, also check the 3 inner connecting pipes.

9. Install the compensating washer so that the keyway below the notch slides over the woodruff key of the camshaft.

10. Install the rocker arms and tensioning springs.

11. Adjust the valve clearance and check the valve timing. See Valve Timing for illustrations.

Check the oil pipes (arrow) on a V8 engine

Install the compensating washer so the keyway below the notch slides over the woodruff key

Engine Disassembly

ALL MODELS

NOTE: *This procedure is general and intended to apply to all Mercedes-Benz engines. It is suggested however, that you be entirely familiar with Mercedes-Benz engines and be equipped with the numerous special tools before attempting an engine rebuild. If at all in doubt concerning any procedure, refer the job to a qualified dealer. While this may be more expensive, it will probably produce better results in the end.*

1. Remove the engine and support it on an engine stand or other suitable support.

2. Set the engine at TDC and matchmark the timing chain and timing gear(s). Be sure the timing marks align. Remove the cylinder head(s) and gasket(s).

3. Remove the oil pan bolts, the pan, and, on most models, the lower crankcase section.

4. Remove the oil pump.

5. Matchmark the connecting rod bearing caps to identify the proper cylinder for reassembly. Matchmark the sides of the connecting rod and the side of the bearing cap for proper alignment. Pistons should bear an arrow indicating the front. If not, mark the front of the piston with an arrow with magic marker. Also

Remove the oil pump (6-cylinder shown)

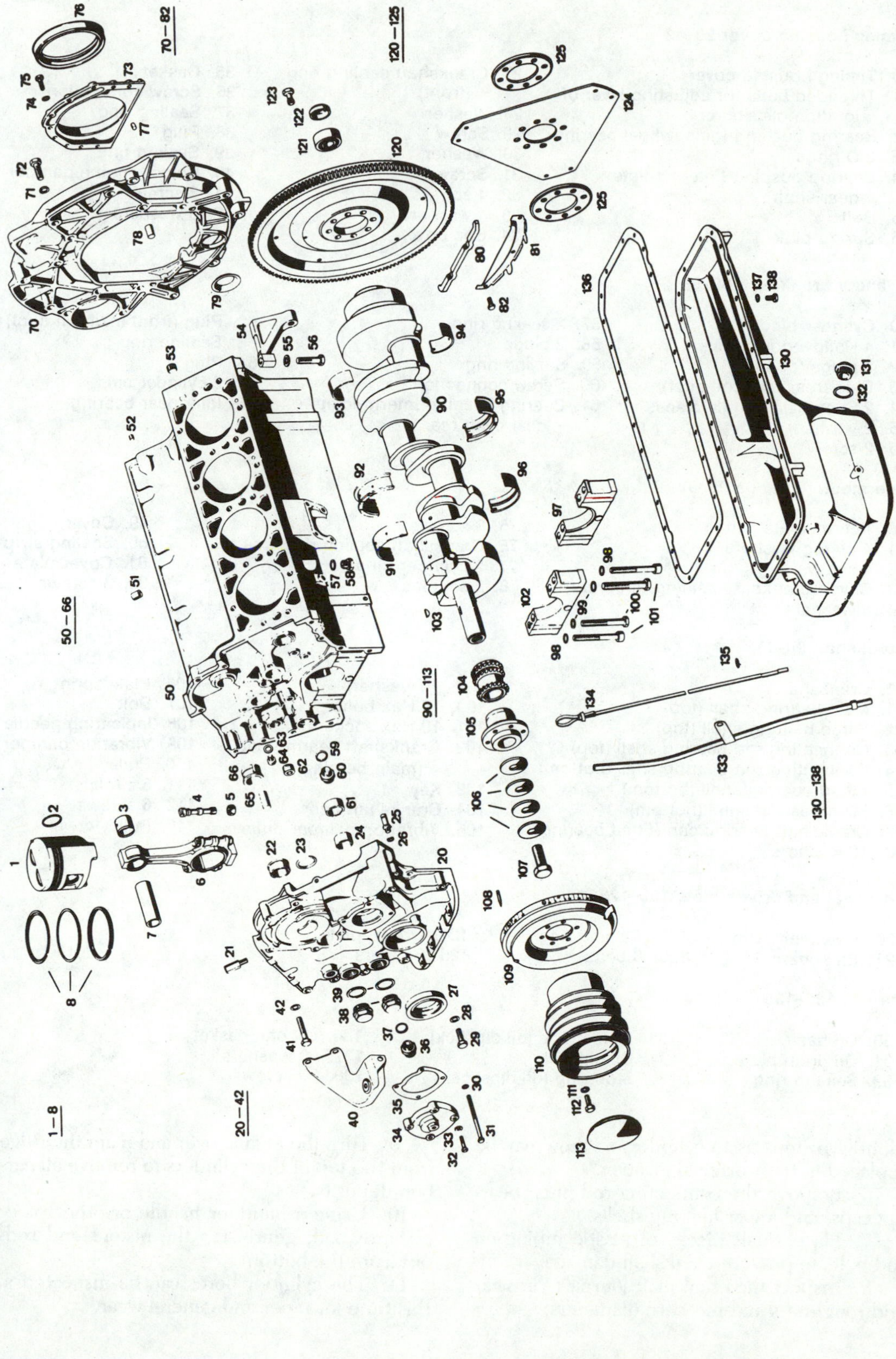

V8 engine block and crankshaft

Piston and connecting rod 1–8

1. Piston
2. Circlip
3. Connecting rod bearing
4. Connecting rod bolt
5. Nut
6. Connecting rod
7. Wrist pin
8. Piston rings

Timing housing cover 20–42

20. Timing housing cover
21. Threaded bolts for adjusting lever of ignition distributor
22. Bearing bushing (guidewheel bearing)
23. 2 O-rings
24. Bearing bushing (intermediate gear shaft)
25. Bolt
26. Spring plate
27. Crankshaft sealing ring (front)
28. Washer
29. Screw
30. Washer
31. Screw
32. 4 screws
33. 4 washers
34. End cover
35. Gasket
36. Screw connection
37. Sealing ring
38. Plug
39. Sealing ring
40. Holder-engine damper
41. 6 screws
42. 6 washers

Cylinder crankcase 50–66

50. Cylinder block
51. 4 Hollow dowel pins
52. 3 plugs (oil duct)
53. Plug (rear main oil duct)
54. 2 Supporting angle pieces
55. 2 washers
56. 2 screws
57. 2 sealing rings
58. 2 plugs
59. Sealing ring
60. Screw connection
61. Bearing bushing intermediate gear shaft rear
62. Plug (front main oil duct)
63. Sealing ring
64. Plug
65. 2 cylinder pins
66. Idler gear bearing

Intermediate flange 70–82

70. Intermediate flange
71. 4 spring washers
72. 4 screws
73. Cover (crankcase sealing ring, rear)
74. 8 washers
75. 3 screws
76. Crankshaft sealing ring (rear)
77. 2 cylinder pins
78. 2 set pins
79. Cover
80. Sealing strip
81. Cover plate
82. 3 screws

Crankshaft 90–113

90. Crankshaft
91. Main bearing shell (top)
92. Fitted bearing shell (top)
93. Connecting rod bearing shell (top)
94. Connecting rod bearing shell (bottom)
95. Fitted bearing shell (bottom)
96. Main bearing shell (bottom)
97. Crankshaft bearing cap (fitted bearing)
98. 10 washers
99. 10 washers
100. 10 Hex bolts
101. 10 Hex socket bolts
102. Crankshaft bearing cap (main bearing)
103. Key
104. Crankshaft gear
105. Vibration damper pulley
106. Plate springs
107. Bolt
108. Indicating needle
109. Vibration damper
110. Pulley
111. 6 circlips
112. 6 screws
113. Pulley cover

Flywheel and driven plate 120–125

120. Flywheel
121. Ball bearing
122. Closing ring
123. 8 bolts
124. Driven plate
125. Spacers

Oil pan 130–138

130. Oil pan
131. Oil drain plug
132. Sealing ring
133. Guide tube (oil dipstick)
134. Oil dipstick
135. Stop-ring (oil dipstick)
136. Oil pan gasket
137. 30 washers
138. 30 screws

identify pistons as to cylinder, so they may be replaced in their original location.

6. Remove the connecting rod nuts, bearing caps, and lower bearing shells.

7. Place small pieces of plastic tubing on rod bolts to prevent crankshaft damage.

8. Inspect the crankshaft journals for nicks and roughness and measure diameters.

9. Turn the engine over and ream the ridge from the top of the cylinders to remove all carbon deposits.

10. Using a hammer handle or other piece of hardwood, gently tap the pistons and rods out from the bottom.

11. The cylinder bores can be inspected at this time for taper and general wear.

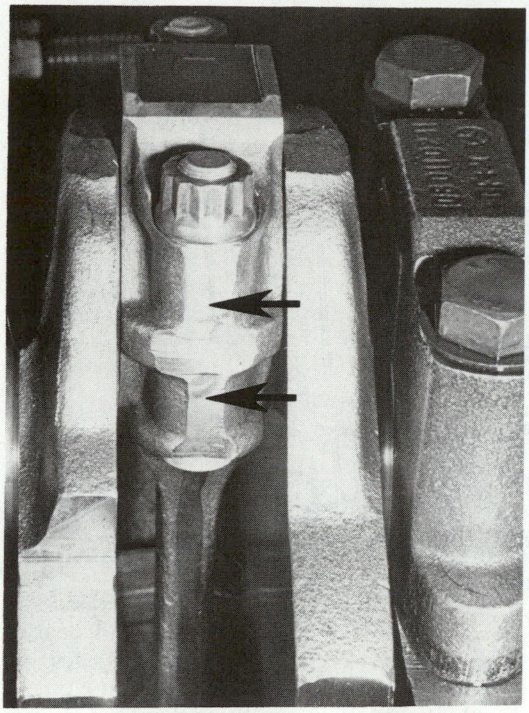

Match mark the connecting rod bearing caps

Pistons normally are marked with an arrow (A) indicating front and a weight or size marking (B)

12. Check the pistons for proper size and inspect the ring grooves. If any rings are cracked, it is almost certain that the grooves are no longer true, because broken rings work up and down. It is best to replace any such worn pistons.

13. The pistons, wrist pins, and connecting rods may be marked with a color dot assembly code. If a color code is present, only parts having the same color may be used together.

14. If the cylinders are bored, make sure the machinist has the pistons beforehand—cylinder bore sizes are nominal and the pistons must be individually fitted to the block. Maximum piston weight deviation in any one engine is 4 grams.

15. The flywheel and crankshaft are balanced together as a unit. Matchmark the location of the flywheel relative to the crankshaft and remove the flywheel. Stretch bolts are used on some newer flywheels and can be identified by their "hourglass" shape. Once used, they should be discarded and replaced at assembly.

16. Remove the water pump, alternator, and fuel pump, if not done previously.

17. Unbolt and remove the vibration damper and crankshaft pulley. On certain models,

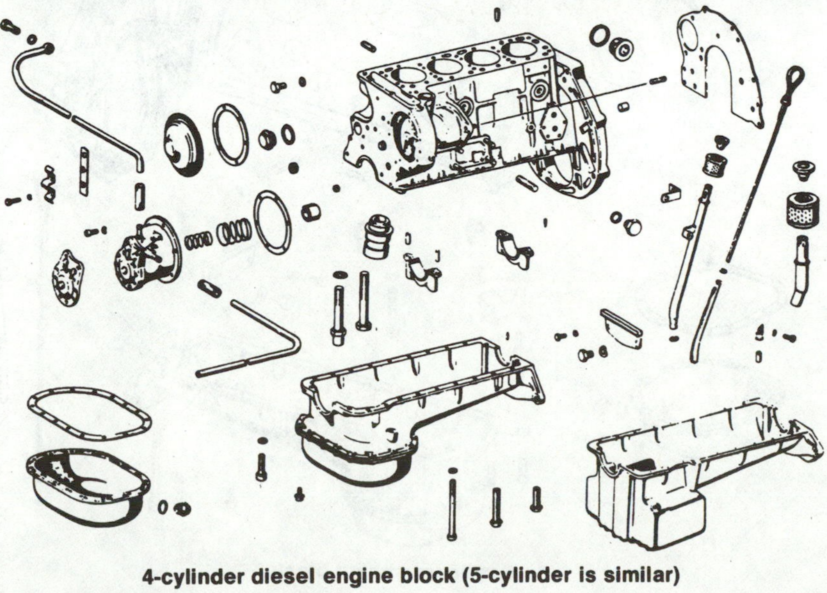

4-cylinder diesel engine block (5-cylinder is similar)

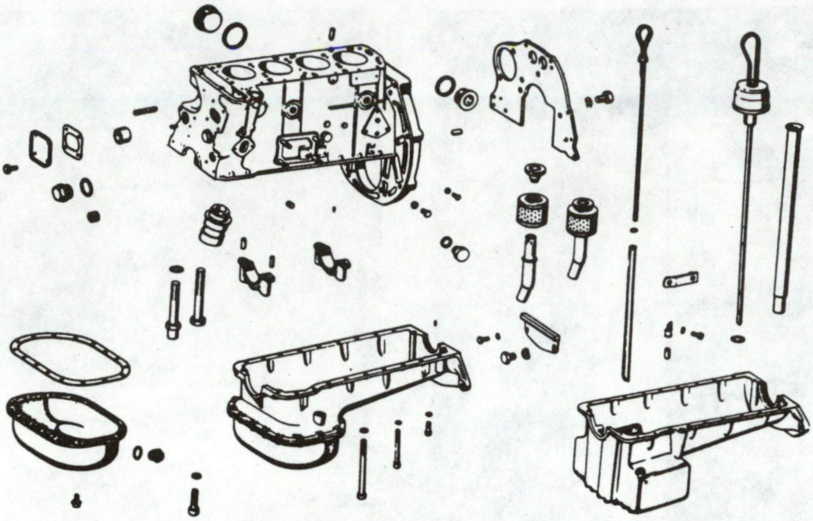

4-cylinder gas engine block

it is necessary to clamp the vibration damper with C-clamps before removing the bolts. Otherwise, the vibration damper may come apart.

18. Remove the timing chain tensioner and chain cover.

19. Matchmark the position of the timing chain on the timing gear of the crankshaft.

20. Matchmark the main bearing caps for number and position in the block. It is important that they are installed in their original positions. Most bearing caps are numbered for position. Remove the bearing caps.

21. Lift the crankshaft out of the block in a forward direction.

22. With the block completely disassembled, inspect the water passages and bearing webs for cracks. If the water passages are plugged with rust, they can be cleaned out by boiling the block at a radiator shop.

CAUTION: *Aluminum parts must not be boiled out because they will be eroded by chemicals.*

23. Measure piston ring end gap by sliding a new ring into the bore and measuring. Measure the gap at the top, bottom, and midpoint of piston travel and correct by filing or grinding the ring ends.

24. To check bearing clearances, use Plasti-

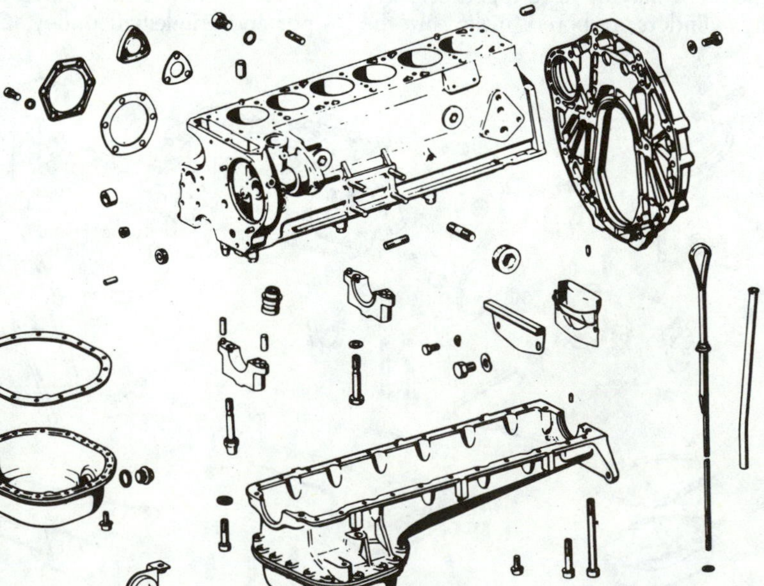

6-cylinder engine block

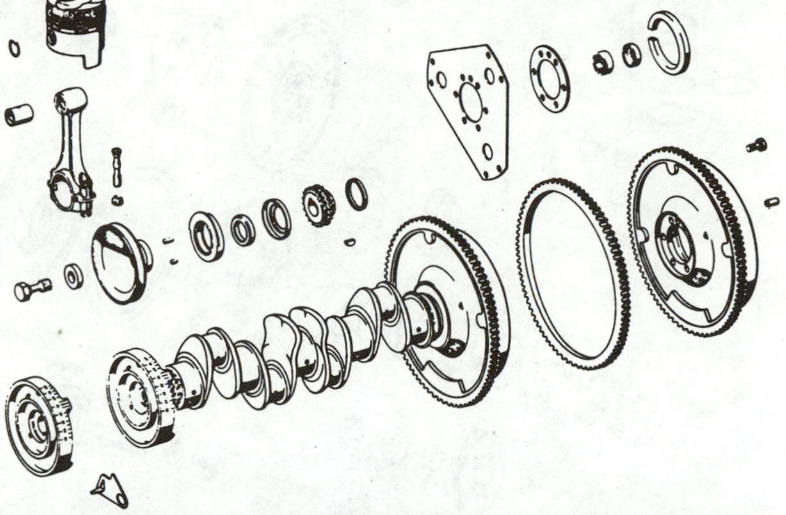

4-cylinder diesel crankshaft (5-cylinder similar)

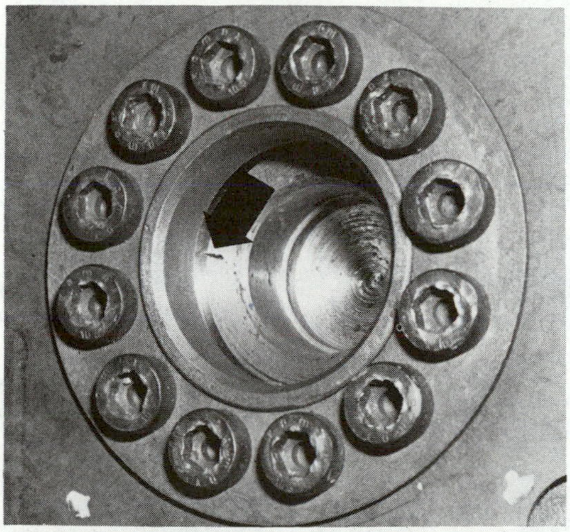

Before removing the flywheel, mark its position. It should be returned to its original position

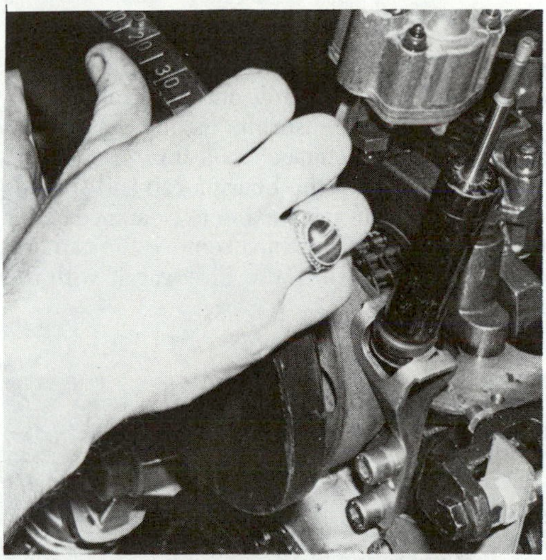

Remove the vibration damper (V8 shown)

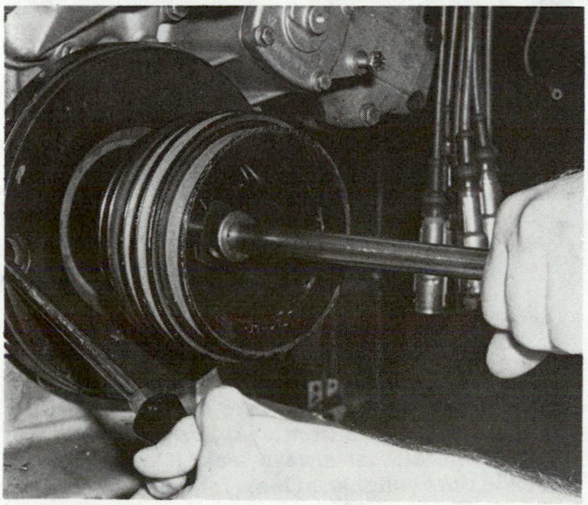

Unbolt and remove the crankshaft pulley (V8 shown)

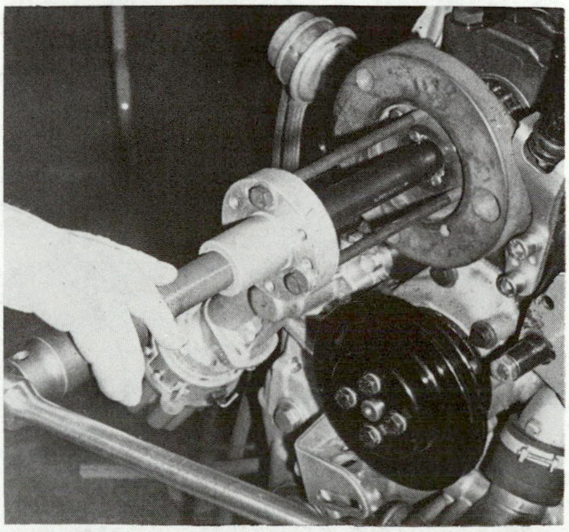

Remove the vibration aamper (6-cylinder shown)

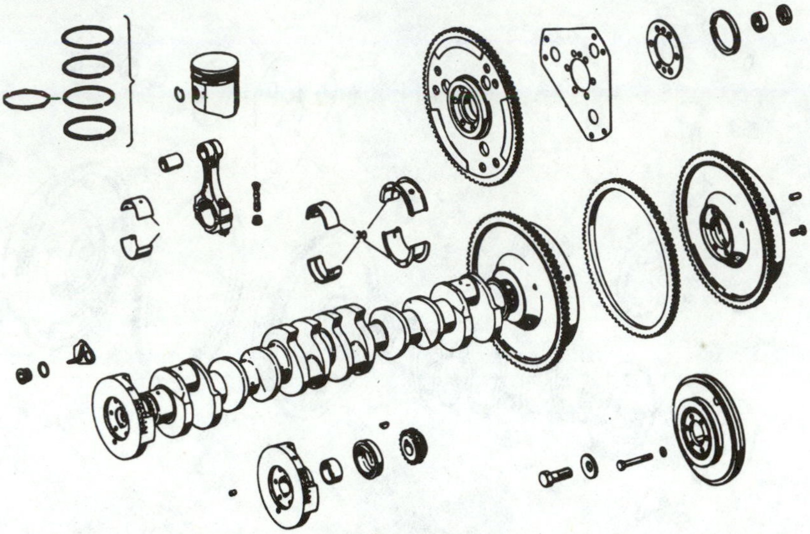

6-cylinder crankshaft (4-cylinder similar)

gage® inserted between the bearing and the crankshaft journal. Blow out all crankshaft oil passages before measuring; torque the bolts to specification. Plastigage® is a thin plastic strip that is crushed by the bearing cap and spreads out an amount in proportion to clearance. After torquing the bearing cap, remove the cap and compare the width of the Plastigage® with the scale.

NOTE: *Do not rotate the crankshaft. Bearing shells of various thicknesses are available and should be used to correct clearance; it may be necessary to machine the crankshaft journals undersize to obtain the proper oil clearance.*

CAUTION: *Use of shim stock between bearings and caps to decrease clearance is not a good practice.*

On V8 models, dress the inside of the vibration damper hub before reinstalling. This will allow you to "feel" the key when installing. On early models, the key extends only ⅓ of the length of the keyway; on later models, ½ the length of the keyway

On 6 cylinder engines, always replace the thrust piece (arrow) if the front seal is replaced. If you don't it will almost always leak. If a new thrust piece is not available, at least remove it and turn it around. This provides a new surface for the seal because the seal does not ride on the centerline of the thrust piece

25. Check crankshaft end-play using a feeler gauge.

26. When installing new piston rings, ring grooves must be cleaned out, preferably using a special groove cleaner, although a broken ring will work as well. After installing the rings, check ring side clearance.

Engine Assembly

ALL MODELS

1. Assemble the engine using all new gaskets and seals, and make sure all parts are properly lubricated. Bearing shells and cylinder walls must be lubricated with engine oil before assembly. Make sure no metal chips remain in the cylinder bores or the crankcase.

2. To install the piston and rod, turn the engine right side up and insert the rod into the cylinder. Clamp the rings to the piston, with their gaps equally spaced around the circumference, using a piston ring compressor. Gently tap the piston into the bore, using a hammer handle or similar hard wood, making sure the rings clear the edge.

NOTE: *Pistons on the 3.8 and 5.0L V-8's are installed with the arrow facing in the driving direction.*

3. Torque the rod and main caps to specification and try to turn the crankshaft by hand. It should turn with moderate resistance, not spin freely or be locked up. Stretch bolts are used for the connecting rods. These bolts are tightened by angle of rotation rather than by use of a torque wrench. Make sure the stretch section diameter is greater than 0.35 in. (−0.003 in.). Remove the bolt from the rod and measure the diameter at the point normally covered by the rod; it should be at least 0.31 in. For reasons of standardization, the angle of rotation for all the screw connections tightened according to angle of rotation has been set to 90° + 10°. Initially, the bolts should be torqued to 22–25 ft. lbs., then 90° past that point.

NOTE: *The bearing shells on the 3rd main bearing of the 190E series engines are fitted with thrust washers. The thrust washers in the bearing cap have two locating tabs to keep them from rotating. During assembly the grooves in the washers should face the crankcase thrust surfaces.*

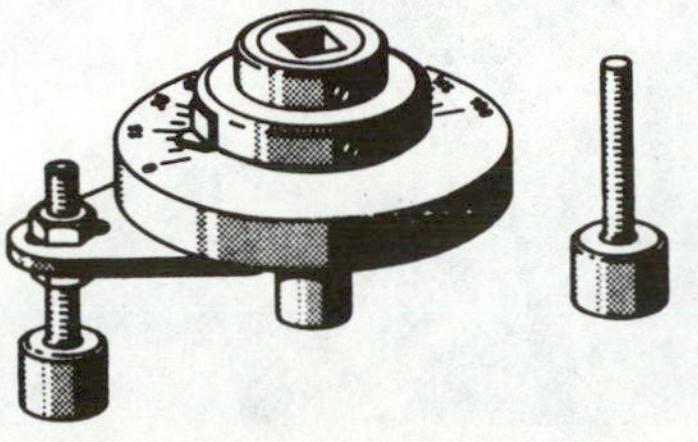

Tools for torqueing by angle rotation

Torqueing the connecting rod bolts by angle of rotation

Check the connecting rod bolts by angle of rotation

4. Disassemble the oil pump and check the gear backlash. Place a straightedge on the cover and check for warpage. Deep scoring on the cover usually indicates that metal or dirt particles have been circulating through the oil system. Covers can be machined, but it is best to replace them if damaged.

5. Install the oil pump.

6. Install the oil pan and lower crankcase and tighten the bolts evenly all around, then turn the engine right side up and install the cylinder head gasket and head. Make sure the gasket surfaces are clean before installation—a small dirt particle could cause gasket failure. Tighten

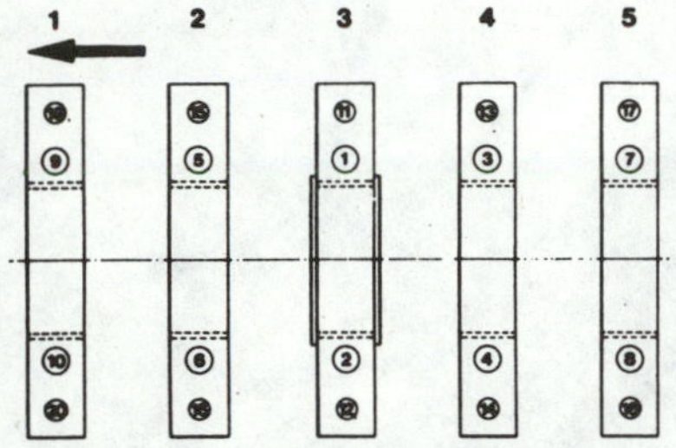

V8 engine main bearing torque sequence

the cylinder heat bolts in sequence to insure against distortion. Don't forget the small bolts at the front of the head.

7. Install the engine into the vehicle.

NOTE: *It is a good practice to use a good break-in oil after an engine overhaul. Be sure that all fluids have been replaced and perform a general tune-up. Check the valve timing.*

Valve Timing

Ideally, this operation should be performed by a dealer, who is equipped with the necessary tools and knowledge to do the job properly.

ALL ENGINES EXCEPT DIESEL

Checking valve timing is too inaccurate at the standard tappet clearance, therefore timing values are given for an assumed tappet clearance of 0.4 mm. The engines are not measured at 0.4 mm but rather at 2 mm.

1. To check timing, remove the rocker arm cover and spark plugs. Remove the tensioning springs. On the 6-cylinder engine install the testing thrust pieces. Eliminate all valve clearance.

2. Set up a degree wheel on the crankshaft pulley or cam shaft pulley.

NOTE: *If the degree wheel is attached to the camshaft as shown, valves read from it must be doubled.*

3. A pointer must be made out of a bent section of 3/16 in. brazing rod or coathanger wire, and attached to the engine.

4. With a 22 mm wrench on the crankshaft pulley, turn the engine, in the direction of rotation, until the TDC mark on the vibration damper registers with the pointer and the distributor rotor points to the No. 1 cylinder mark on the housing. The camshaft timing marks should also align at this point.

NOTE: *Due to design of the chain tensioner on V-8 engines, the right side of the chain travels farther than the left side. This means the right-side camshaft is approximately 7° retarded compared to the left-side, and both marks on each side will not simultaneously align.*

5. Turn the loosened degree wheel until the pointer lines up with the 0° (OT) mark, then tighten it in this position.

6. Continue turning the crankshaft in the direction of rotation until the camshaft lobe of the associated valve is vertical (i.e., points away from the rocker arm surface). To take up tappet clearance, insert a feeler gauge thick enough to raise the valve slightly from its seat between the rocker arm cone and the pressure piece.

7. Attach the indicator to the cylinder head so that the feeler rests against the valve spring retainer of No. 1 cylinder intake valve. Preload the indicator at least 0.008 in. then set to zero, making sure the feeler is exactly perpendicular on the valve spring retainer. It may be necessary to bleed down the chain tensioner at this time to facilitate readings.

8. Turn the crankshaft in the normal direction of rotation, again using a wrench on the

The valve timing marks must align (6-cylinder shown)

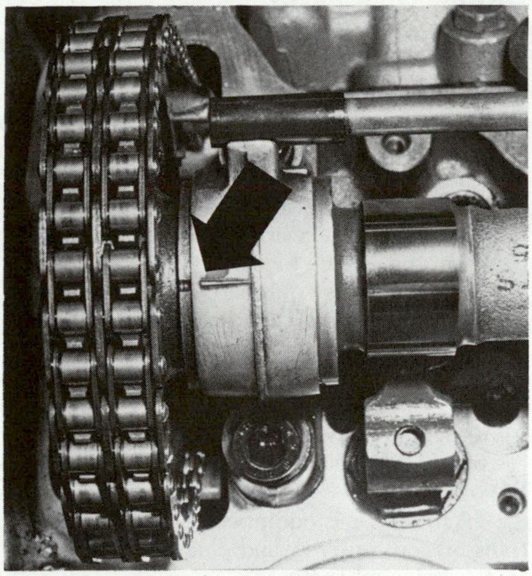

The V8 timing marks on the left-hand cam

crankshaft pulley, until the indicator reads 0.016 in. less than zero reading.

9. Note the reading of the degree wheel at this time, remembering to double the reading if the wheel is mounted to the camshaft sprocket.

10. Again turn the crankshaft until the valve is closing and the indicator again reads 0.016 in. less than zero reading. Make sure, at this time, that preload has remained constant, then note the reading of the degree wheel. The difference between the two degree wheel readings is the timing angle (number of degrees the valve is open) for that valve.

Note that the timing marks on the right-hand cam do not exactly align. This is because the timing chain travels farther on the right side than on the left

11. The other valves may be checked in the same manner, comparing them against each other and the opening values given in the "Specifications." It must be remembered that turning the crankshaft contrary to the normal direction of rotation results in inaccurate readings and damage to the engine.

12. If valve timing is not to specification, the easiest way of bringing it in line is to install an offset woodruff key in the camshaft sprocket. This is far simpler than replacing the entire timing chain, and it is the factory-recommended way of changing valve timing provided the timing chain is not stretched too far or worn out. Offset keys are available in the following sizes:

Offset	Part No.	For a Correction at Crankshaft of
2° (0.7 mm)	621 991 04 67	4°
3° 20′ (0.9 mm)	621 991 02 67	6½°
4° (1.1 mm)	621 991 01 67	8°
5° (1.3mm)	621 991 00 67	10°

13. The woodruff key must be installed with the offset toward the "right", in the normal direction of rotation, to effect advanced valve opening; toward the "left" to retard.

14. Advancing the intake valve opening too much can result in piston and/or valve damage (the valve will hit the piston). To check the clearance between the valve head and the piston, the crankshaft must be positioned at 5° ATDC (on intake stroke). The procedure is essentially the same as for measuring valve timing.

15. As before, the dial indicator is set to zero after being preloaded, then the valve is depressed until it touches the top of the piston. As the normal valve head-to-piston clearance is approximately 0.035 in., you can see that the dial indicator must be preloaded at least 0.042 in. so there will be enough movement for the feeler.

If the clearance is much less than 0.035 in., the cylinder head must be removed and checked for carbon deposits. If none exist, the valve seat must be cut deeper into the head. Always set the ignition timing after installing an offset key.

ENGINE COOLING

Mercedes-Benz passenger car engines are all equipped with closed, pressurized, water cooling systems. Care should be exercised when dealing with the cooling system Always turn the radiator cap to the first notch and allow the

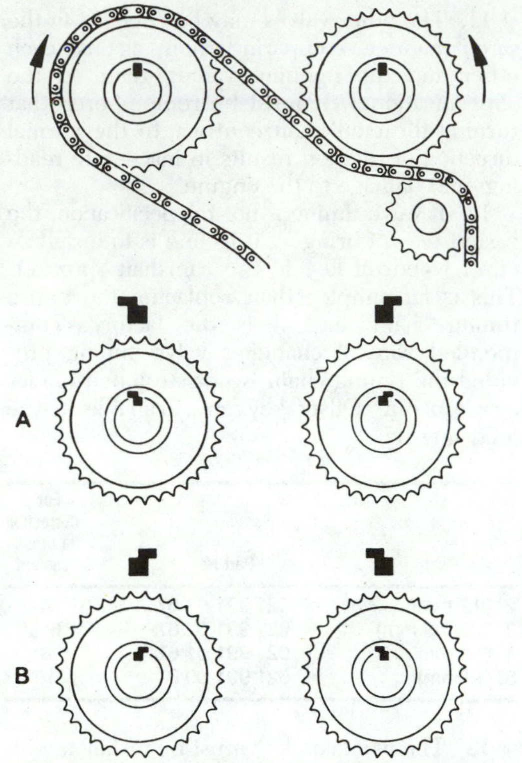

With installation position "A" opening begins earlier
With installation position "B" opening begins later

Offset woodruff keys for 6-cylinder engine

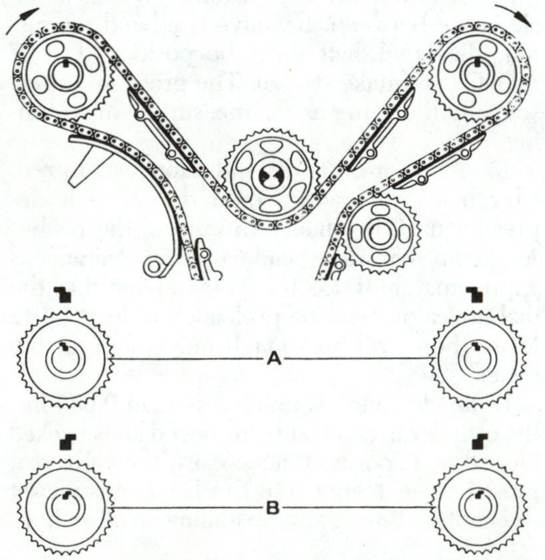

Vith installation position "A" opening begins earlier
Nith installation position "B" opening begins later

Offset woodruff keys for V8 engine

pressure to decrease before completely removing the cap. An audible hiss indicates that pressure is being released from the system.

Radiator

REMOVAL AND INSTALLATION

All Models

1. Remove the radiator cap.
2. Unscrew the radiator drain plug and drain the coolant from the radiator. If all of the coolant in the system is to be drained, move the heater controls to "warm" and open the drain cocks on the engine block.
3. If the car is equipped with an oil cooler, drain the oil from the cooler.
4. If equipped, loosen the radiator shell.
5. Loosen the hose clips on the top and bottom radiator hoses and remove the hoses from the connections on the radiator.
6. Unscrew and plug the bottom line on the oil cooler.
7. If the car is equipped with an automatic transmission, unscrew and plug the lines on the transmission oil cooler.
8. Disconnect the right-hand and left-hand rubber loops and pull the radiator up and out of the body. On 450 SL and SLC models, push the retaining springs toward the fenders to remove the radiator from the shell.
9. Inspect and replace any hoses which have become hardened or spongy.
10. Install the radiator shell and radiator (if the shell was removed) from the top and connect the top and bottom hoses to the radiator.
11. Bolt the shell to the radiator.
12. Attach the rubber loops or position the retaining springs as applicable.
13. Position the hose clips on the top and bottom hoses.
14. Attach the lines to the oil cooler.
15. On cars with automatic transmissions, connect the lines to the transmission oil cooler.
16. Move the heater levers to the "warm" position and slowly add coolant, allowing air to escape.
17. Check the oil level and fill if necessary. Run the engine for about one minute at idle with the filler neck open.
18. Add coolant to the level specified in Chapter One. Install the radiator cap and turn it until it seats in the second notch. Run the engine and check for leaks.

Water Pump

REMOVAL AND INSTALLATION

All Except V8

1. Drain the water from the radiator.
2. Loosen the radiator shell and remove the radiator.
3. Remove the fan with the coupling and set it aside in an upright position.

4. Loosen the belt around the water pump pulley and remove the belt.
5. Remove the bolts from the harmonic balancer and remove the balancer and pulley.
6. Unbolt and remove the water pump.
7. Installation is the reverse of removal. Tighten the belt and fill the cooling system.

V8 Models

1. Drain the water from the radiator and block.
2. Remove the air cleaner.
3. Loosen and remove the power steering pump drive belt.
4. Disconnect the upper water hose from the radiator and thermostat housing.
5. Remove the fan and coupling.
6. Remove the bottom water hose from the water pump housing.
7. Remove the hose from the intake (top) connection from the water pump.
8. Set the engine at TDC. Matchmark the distributor and engine and remove the distributor. Crank the engine with a socket wrench on the crankshaft pulley bolt or with a screwdriver inserted in the balancer. Crank in the normal direction of rotation only.
9. Turn the balancer so that the recesses provide access to the mounting bolts. Remove the mounting bolts. Rotate the engine in the normal direction of rotation only.
10. Remove the water pump.
11. Clean the mounting surfaces of the water pump and block.
12. Installation is the reverse of removal. Always use a new gasket. Set the engine at TDC and install the distributor so that the distributor rotor points to the notch on the distributor housing. Fill the cooling system and check and adjust the ignition timing.

Thermostat

REMOVAL AND INSTALLATION

4 and 5-Cylinder Engines

The thermostat housing is a light metal casting attached directly to the cylinder head, except on the 190D where it is attached to the side of the water pump housing.

1. Open the radiator cap and depressurize the system.
2. Open the radiator drain cock and partially drain the coolant. Drain enough coolant to bring the coolant level below the level of the thermostat housing.
3. Remove the bolts on the thermostat housing cover and remove the cover.
4. Note the installation position of the thermostat and remove the thermostat.

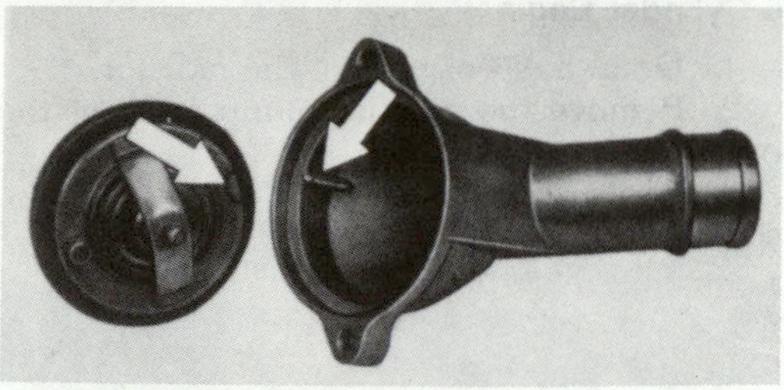

Aligning the thermostat on the 190D

5. Installation is the reverse of removal. Be sure that the thermostat is positioned with the ball valve at the highest point and that the bolts are tightened evenly against the seal. On the 190D, the recess in the thermostat casing should be located above the lug in the thermostat housing.
6. Refill the cooling system and check for leaks.

V8 Engines

1. Drain the coolant from the radiator and block.
2. Remove the air cleaner.
3. Disconnect the battery and remove the alternator. Usually this need not be done on V8 Engines.
4. Unscrew the housing cover on the side of the water pump and remove the thermostat. Note that the thermostat used on 4.5 liter V8 models differs from the one used on other models by a different positioning of the ball valve.
5. If a new thermostat is to be installed, always install a new sealing ring.
6. Installation is the reverse of removal. Be sure to tighten the screws on the housing cover evenly to prevent leaks. Refill the cooling system and check for leaks.

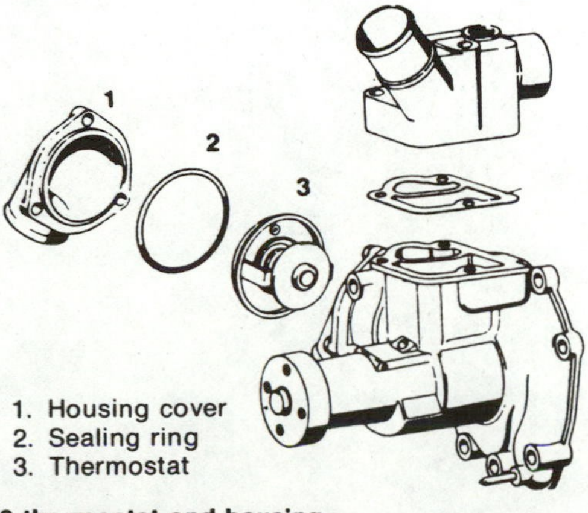

V8 thermostat and housing

6-Cylinder Engines

1. Drain the coolant from the radiator.
2. Remove the vacuum pump and put the pump aside.
3. Remove the three bolts on the thermostat housing.
4. Remove the cover and the thermostat.
5. Installation is the reverse of removal. Install the thermostat so that the ball valve is at the highest point. Refill the cooling system.

Emission Controls and Fuel Systems

4

EMISSION CONTROLS

Beginning in 1968, various modifications were incorporated on Mercedes-Benz engines to meet Federal emissions control regulations. Since 1968, these modifications have been continually updated and improved.

The following emission controls were used on 1968 carbureted engines.

1. Modifications to the Manifold Air-Oxidation System.
2. Changes to the ignition timing and distributor advance curves to provide better combustion in the middle rpm ranges.
3. A Port Burning System, which uses a belt driven pump to force in air directly behind the exhaust valves, creating an afterburning effect.
4. Modified carburetor jets to provide a leaner carburetor mixture.

Fuel injected engines required no modifications in 1968.

In 1971, the design of the combustion chambers was changed and the spark plugs were set deeper on 6-cylinder engines. Better cooling is accomplished by adding more cooling jackets. All 4 and 6-cylinder engines are equipped with a Fuel Evaporation Control System.

In 1972, the engine compression ratio was reduced to 8.0:1 on all engines except the diesel. Automatic transmission shift points were modified. The fuel evaporation control system remained unchanged, although the evaporation control valve was redesigned and relocated under the rear seat.

The fuel evaporation system remained unchanged in 1973, but the 2-way valves previously used were replaced by switchover valves that are identical in appearance. To be able to distinguish the function of the individual valves, the covers are color coded according to valve function, as follows:

- WHITE—advanced ignition valve
- RED—retarded ignition valve
- GRAY—throttle opening valve
- BROWN—exhaust gas recycling (EGR) valve.

NOTE: *It is important that the vacuum line always be connected to the center connection, whether it is on the top or the bottom.*

1974

Design and function of the system remains basically unchanged from 1973, except for the addition of an air pump on 280, 280C and 450 California models.

It is impossible to list test procedures for all the various switches and valves in this book, so only basic tests and results appear here.

The following tests should be performed on a warm engine at normal operating temperature, and should be performed in the sequence listed. Be sure to check the fuses if a malfunction is suspected.

230

Ignition changeover is accomplished through vacuum and oil temperature. Vacuum retard is only activated during acceleration, while vacuum advance is activated under the following conditions:

1. Oil temperature below 77°F.
2. Oil temperature above 77°F and engine speed above 2000 rpm.

The throttle valve is also opened slightly during coasting, through a vacuum governor on the carburetor.

Exhaust gas is being recycled by the EGR valve under the following conditions:

1. Oil temperature above 77°F. up to 3600 rpm.

Exhaust gas recirculation is not effective under the following conditions:

1. Oil temperature above 77°F up to 3600
2. Speed above 3600 rpm.

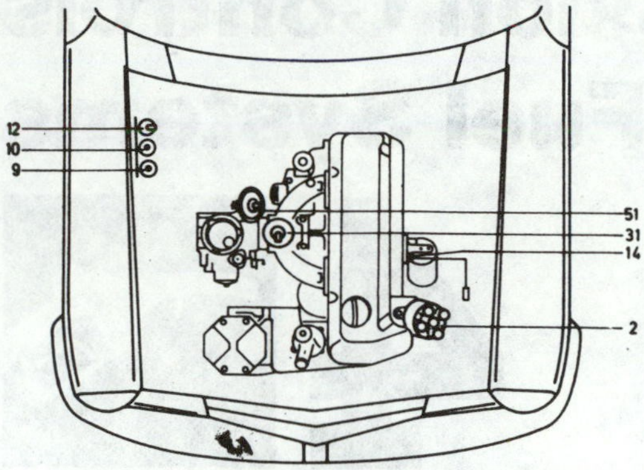

2. Ignition distributor
9. Switch-over valve, ignition
10. Switch-over valve, throttle valve lift
12. Switch-over valve, EGR
14. 77° F temperature switch
31. EGR valve
51. Vacuum governor

1974 230 emission control component location

Testing the System

77°F. TEMPERATURE SWITCH

1. Disconnect the plug to the temperature switch in the oil filter housing and ground it. The engine rpm should increase, indicating that vacuum advance is present.

2. Increase the engine speed to about 2500 rpm and remove the red vacuum line at the distributor. The engine rpm should drop slightly, indicating that vacuum advance is no longer present.

If the results are not as specified, check the connections of the vacuum lines. The blue line from the carburetor should go to the center port of the red switchover valve and the red line should go from the outer port of the switchover valve to the distributor.

EGR SWITCHOVER VALVE

1. Place your hand over the brown EGR switchover valve. It may be necessary to remove the valve to isolate its operation. Increase the engine speed. The valve should be felt to switch.

2. If it does not function, check the voltage at the plug. If no voltage is measured at the plug, below 3600 rpm, replace the rpm relay.

EGR VALVE

1. Connect the EGR valve directly to intake manifold vacuum with the blue vacuum line. The engine should run poorly or stall, indicating that the valve is open.

2. If the speed does not change, remove the valve and connect it to vacuum. The valve stem should lift from its seat. Remove exhaust deposits from the valve with a 10 mm drill and blow it clean with compressed air.

VACUUM GOVERNOR

1. Connect a tachometer and increase engine speed to about 2500 rpm and release the throttle slowly. The vacuum governor should pop out above 2000 rpm and retract below 1800 rpm.

If not, check the vacuum lines. The blue line should connect the center port of the gray switchover valve. The gray line should connect the vacuum governor and the outer port of the switchover valve.

2. If the vacuum lines are connected properly, remove the relay box plug and connect terminals 2 and 8. With the ignition ON, the switchover valve should click. If the switchover valve functions properly, the relay box is defective.

280 AND 280C (FEDERAL)

An ignition changeover is installed to retard or advance the ignition. Ignition is retarded under the following conditions:

1. When the oil temperature is above 62°F. and coolant temperature is below 212°F.

2. Engine speed is below 3200 rpm. Ignition retard is negated under the following conditions:

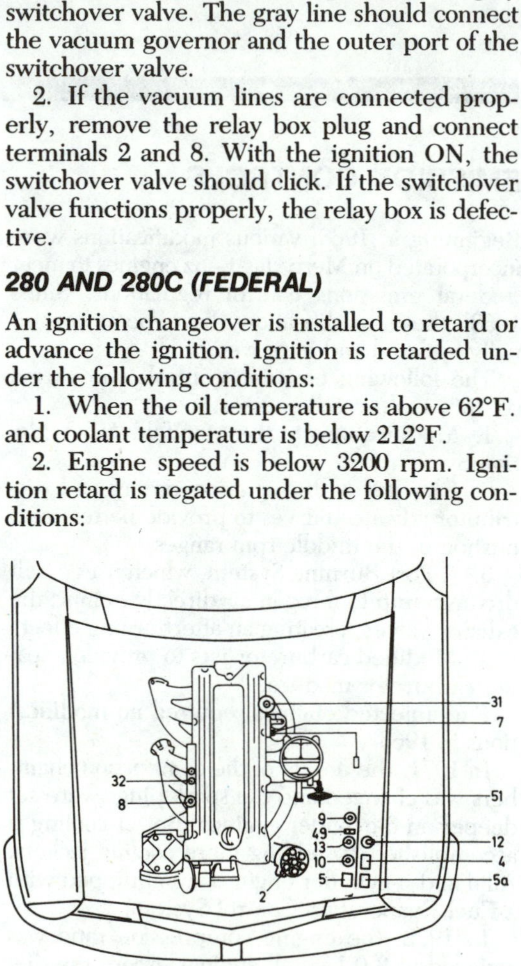

2. Distributor
4. RPM relay
5. Relay box (8 prong)
5a. Relay box (12 prong)
7. 62° F temperature switch
8. 212° F temperature switch
9. Ignition switch-over valve
10. Throttle valve lift switch-over valve
12. EGR switch-over valve
13. Vacuum switch
31. EGR valve
32. 149° F temperature switch
49. Connection at relay support
51. Vacuum governor

1974 280, 280C Federal emission control component location

1. Oil temperature below 62°F.
2. Coolant temperature above 212°F.
3. Engine speed above 3200 rpm and oil temperature above 62°F, and coolant temperature below 212°F.
4. When shifting into fourth gear.
5. When switching on the air conditioner.
6. With vacuum between 0 and 2.8 psi.

A throttle positioner is installed which will open the throttle slightly when the oil temperature is above 62°F., when the coolant temperature is below 212°F., and when engine speed exceeds 200 rpm.

Exhaust gases are recycled when engine oil temperature is above 62°F., when coolant temperature is below 212°F., and when manifold vacuum is between 0 and 2.8 psi, up to 3200 rpm.

Testing the System

IGNITION TIMING

1. Check the ignition timing. It should be as specified.
2. If not, check all vacuum connections and the temperature switches before adjusting the timing.

62°F. TEMPERATURE SWITCH

1. Disconnect the plug of the relay box.
2. Connect a voltmeter to terminals 5 and 8.
3. The voltmeter should indicate 0 volts when the oil temperature is above 62°F.

212°F. TEMPERATURE SWITCH

1. Disconnect the plug from the relay box.
2. Connect a test lamp to terminals 4 and 8.
3. Switch on the ignition.
4. The test lamp should light when coolant temperature is above 212°F.

THROTTLE POSITIONER

1. Connect a tachometer to the engine.
2. Start the engine and increase the speed to approximately 2500 rpm.
3. Release the accelerator linkage and observe the tachometer. At speeds above 1800 rpm, the adjusting screw should rest against the actuating lever. At speeds below 1800 rpm, the adjusting screw should be off the actuating lever.

RPM SWITCH

Use only a voltmeter to test the rpm switch.

1. Disconnect the plug of the switch valve and connect a voltmeter.
2. Start the engine and increase speed.
3. The voltmeter should indicate about 13 volts, above 2000 rpm.
4. Decrease speed below about 1800 rpm and the voltmeter should read approximately 0 volts.

EGR SWITCH VALVE

1. Disconnect the plug from the switch valve and connect a tachometer.
2. Connect a voltmeter and increase rpm.
3. The voltmeter should read about 13 volts up to 3200 rpm.

149°F. TEMPERATURE SWITCH

1. Disconnect the plug from the relay box and connect a voltmeter to terminals 6 and 8.
2. The voltmeter should indicate approximately 13 volts above 149°F.

VACUUM SWITCH

1. Disconnect the plug from the relay box and connect a voltmeter to terminals 7 and 8.
2. Idle the engine.
3. The voltmeter should indicate 0 volts.
4. Disconnect the vacuum line from the switch. The voltmeter should now indicate about 13 volts.

EGR RPM SWITCH

1. Disconnect the plug from the relay box.
2. Connect a voltmeter to terminals 1 and 3.
3. Start the engine and increase speed.
4. The voltmeter should indicate 0 volts up to approximately 3200 rpm. Beyond that, voltage should be about 13 volts.
5. When rpm decreases, the voltmeter should return to 0 volts at about 2800 rpm.

EGR VALVE

1. Start the engine and run it at idle.
2. Remove the lower, brown vacuum line from the EGR switchover valve and connect it to the carburetor in place of the blue vacuum line.
3. If the EGR valve is working, the engine will idle roughly or stop running. If the engine does not do one or the other, replace the EGR valve.
4. Do not forget to replace the vacuum lines.

280 AND 280C (CALIFORNIA ONLY)

The California system for these cars is a modification of the Federal system. A Saginaw air pump is used and a reactor with injection tubes is used in place of an exhaust manifold.

Testing the System

62°F. TEMPERATURE SWITCH

1. Disconnect and ground the plug to the switch in the oil filter housing. The engine rpm should increase. If not disconnect the relay box plug and connect terminals 2 and 10. With the

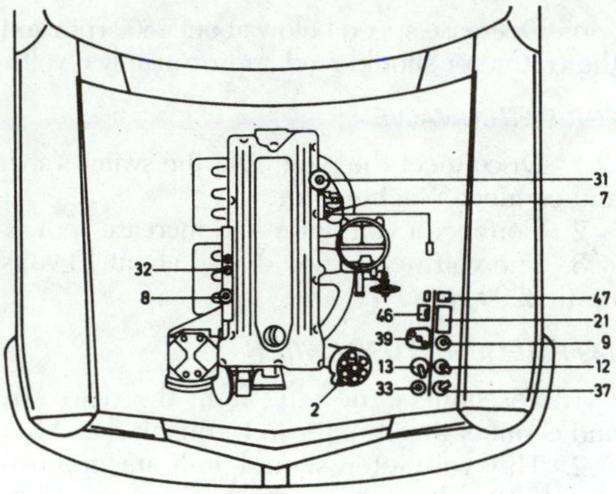

2. Distributor
7. 62° F temperature switch
8. 212° F temperature switch
9. Switchover valve, ignition
12. Switchover valve, EGR
13. Vacuum switch
21. Relay box
31. EGR valve
32. 149° F temperature switch
33. Switchover valve, air injection
37. Switchover valve, fuel evaporation system
39. Charcoal canister
46. Resistor for automatic choke
47. Relay for resistor, automatic choke

1974 280, 280C California emission control component location

ignition ON the valve should click. If the valve clicks, replace the relay box.

212°F. TEMPERATURE SWITCH

1. Unplug and ground the temperature switch. The engine should increase and the auxiliary should run. If not, replace the relay box.

RELAY BOX VOLTAGE

1. Turn the air conditioner ON. The engine speed should not drop. If the engine speed decreases, remove the relay box plug and connect a voltmeter to terminals 3 and 8 of the plug. If less than 13 volts is present, replace the relay box, or, if no voltage is present, check the air conditioner circuit.

VACUUM SWITCHOVER VALVE

1. Remove the vacuum line from the top of the switchover valve and remove the blue line from the vacuum switch. The engine speed should increase. A voltmeter should read 13 volts between terminals 11 and 2 of the relay box plug with the engine running. Remove the vacuum line from the vacuum switch. No voltage should be present. If both readings are correct, replace the relay box.

EGR VALVE AND VACUUM SWITCHOVER VALVE

1. Remove the blue vacuum line from the vacuum switch. The engine should run poorly or stall.

2. Unplug the brown vacuum line at the connection on the firewall and connect it to the vacuum line for air conditioning. The engine should run poorly or stall. If the switchover valve and EGR valve are functioning, replace the relay box.

ANTI-BACKFIRE VALVE

1. Disconnect the center hose on the air filter. There should be no air flow. If the switchover valve clicks by bridging terminals 1 and 2 of the relay box plug, the anti-backfire valve must be replaced.

AIR INJECTION SWITCHOVER VALVE

1. Increase engine speed slowly to above 3450 rpm. The air flow should stop in the injection line at about 3450 rpm.

AUTOMATIC CHOKE RELAY

1. Disconnect the plug to the 62°F. temperature switch in the oil filter housing and ground the switch. The automatic choke resistor relay should click. Voltage at the switch should be about 13 volts. If none is present, replace the relay box.

FLOAT CHAMBER VENT VALVE

1. Shut the engine OFF. Disconnect the gray vacuum line at the float chamber vent valve on the carburetor. No vacuum should be present. Reconnect the line.

2. Start the engine and remove the line again. A hissing sound should indicate the presence of vacuum. If no vacuum is present, remove the float chamber vent valve. With the vacuum lines connected, turn the ignition ON and OFF. The valve stem should move in and out. If not, replace the vent valve diaphragm.

CHARCOAL CANISTER PURGE VALVE

1. Remove the thin center hose from the charcoal canister and close the end of the hose with your finger. Increase engine speed to more than 2000 rpm. At idle, slight vacuum should be felt, increasing with engine speed. If not, the purge valve should be replaced, or there is a restriction in the line.

450SL, 450SLC, 450SE, 450SEL (FEDERAL)

A two-way valve is installed in the vacuum line between the venturi control unit and the distributor. Ignition timing is retarded when the two-way valve is not energized, and advanced

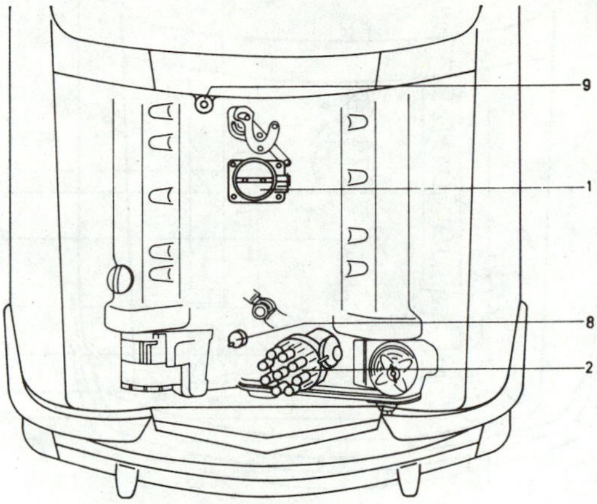

1. Throttle valve
2. Distributor
3. Throttle valve housing
8. 212° F temperature switch
9. Ignition switch-over valve

1974 V8 Federal emission control component location

when the valve is energized (circuit completed to ground). The valve is controlled by a 212°F. temperature switch in the thermostat housing, which activates the valve above coolant temperatures of 212°F.

A fuel shut-off solenoid cuts off the delivery of fuel under the following conditions:

1. Accelerator pedal is in the idling position.
2. Engine speed is above 1500 rpm, determined by an electronic control unit. There is no fuel shut-off when coolant temperature is below −4°F.

Testing the System

IGNITION CHANGEOVER DEVICE

1. Connect a timing light and check the timing at idle. It should be as specified.
2. Ground the connection of the 212°F. temperature switch. The ignition timing should advance by 15° and engine speed should increase by about 300 rpm.
3. Check the oil pressure switch. This can only be done on the road or on a dynamometer. Connect a test lamp to the B+ terminal and terminal 87 of the relay. Disconnect the relay. Above a speed of 40 mph, the test lamp should light. Below approximately 30 mph, the light should go out.
4. Check the 212°F. switch by connecting a test lamp to the B+ terminal and to the switch. At a coolant temperature above 212°F., the light should come on.
5. If there is no ignition changeover and the oil pressure switch is working, check the following:
   a. Fuse No. 6 in the main fuse box.
   b. All vacuum and electrical connections on the two-way valve.
   c. The two-way valve. Switch on the ignition and ground the oil pressure switch. This should energize the two-way valve.
   d. The relay. Connect a test lamp to the plug of the two-way valve. Switch on the ignition and ground the 212°F. temperature switch. The relay is working if the lamp lights.

450SL, SLC AND 450SE, SEL (CALIFORNIA ONLY)

The California system is a refinement of the Federal system and closely resembles it, with an added air pump.

Testing the System

212°F. TEMPERATURE SWITCH

1. Unplug the temperature switch and ground it. The engine rpm should increase and the auxiliary fan should run on the 450SE and 450SEL. If not, connect terminals 3 and 4 of the relay box plug. With the ignition ON, the switchover valve should click. If not, replace the relay.
2. Switch ON the air conditioning. The engine rpm should rise slightly. If the engine rpm does not increase, check the air conditioning. If the air conditioning works, replace the relay.

EGR

1. Remove the air filter top cover and check that exhaust gas is emitted from the recirculation line in the throttle valve housing. If no exhaust is emitted into the throttle valve housing, clean the throttle housing and EGR line.

DIVERTER CONTROL VALVE

1. Remove the air filter housing and lay it aside without unplugging the warm air sensor. Disconnect the brown vacuum line at the diverter control valve. Increase the rpm to over 2000 and release the throttle linkage. Vacuum should be present at the port of the diverter valve only when the throttle linkage is released. A hissing sound should be heard.
2. If no vacuum is present, replace the diverter valve.

CO CONTENT

1. Check the CO content of the exhaust gas. It should be a maximum of 1.0% WITH OR WITHOUT air injection. To check the CO, remove the air filter housing and lay it aside without unplugging the warm air sensor. Disconnect the brown vacuum line at the diverter valve and connect this to the vacuum supply line for the cruise control actuator.
2. If the CO content varies with or without air injection, check the brown vacuum line to

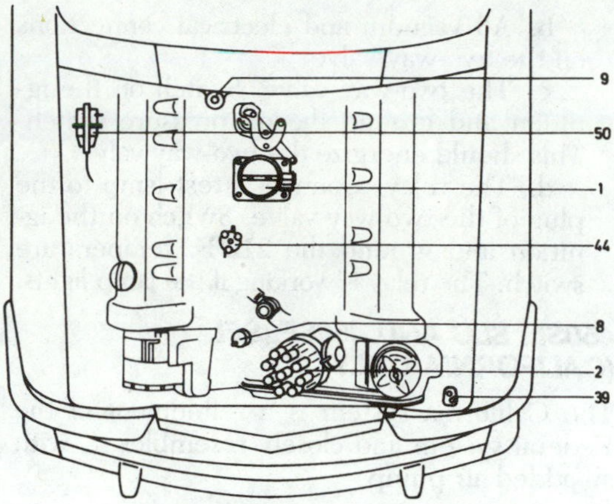

1. Throttle valve
2. Distributor
8. 212° F temperature switch
9. Switch-over valve, ignition
39. Charcoal canister
44. Diverter control valve
50. Actuator, cruise control

1974 450SE, SEL California emission control component location

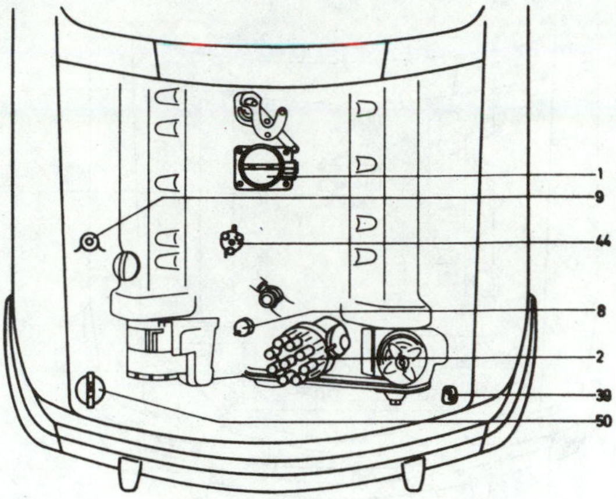

1. Throttle valve
2. Distributor
8. 212° F temperature switch
9. Switch-over valve, ignition
39. Charcoal canister
44. Diverter control valve
50. Actuator, cruise control

1974 450SL, SLC California emission control component location

the diverter valve for tightness. Also check the diverter valve.

CHARCOAL CANISTER PURGE VALVE

See this test under "280 and 280C (California Only)." The 1975 emission control equipment closely resembles that for 1974. The 230 (California only) and all other gasoline engines are equipped with catalysts. These models must be operated only with unleaded gasoline.

All of the following tests should be made in the specified sequence with the engine at operating temperature.

As of 1975, the base color of vacuum lines for emission control is white. Lines originating at a vacuum source have only one color stripe. These lines are connected to the center connection of the switchover valve of the same color. Lines terminating at a vacuum operated device have 2 color stripes. Purple is always the second color. The lines are connected to the outer connection of the switchover valve of the same color.

Switchover valve filter caps are color coded as follows:

- RED—Valve for ignition advance
- GRAY—Valve for throttle lift
- BROWN—Valve for EGR
- BLUE—Valve for air injection

230

Testing the System

77° F. TEMPERATURE SWITCH

1. Disconnect the temperature switch plug and ground the switch. The engine rpm should increase.

2. If not, check the vacuum line connections.

3. Unplug the relay box and connect terminals 7 and 1; an audible click should be heard. If not, replace the relay box.

4. Disconnect and ground the temperature switch. Place your hand over the air pump muffler. A light air flow should be present.

5. If no air flow is present, check the vacuum line connections (see Step 2).

6. Disconnect the plug from the relay box and connect terminals 6 and 7. The blue switchover valve should click. If not, replace the switchover valve. If the valve does click, the relay is defective.

RPM SWITCH

1. Increase engine speed to about 2500 rpm and remove the red/purple vacuum line from the distributor. The engine speed should drop slightly. Below about 2000 rpm, there should be 13 volts at the switch. If there is less than

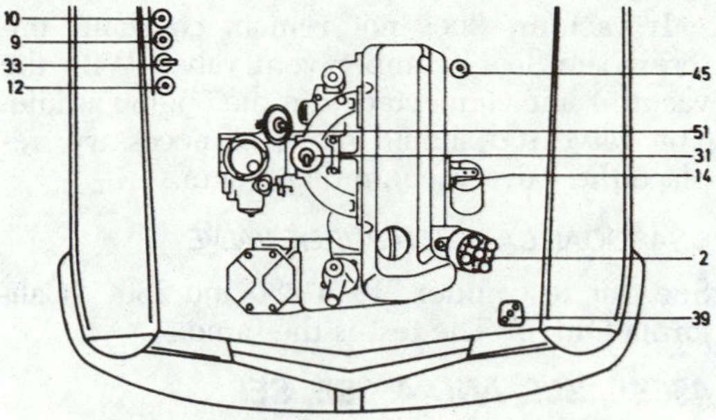

2. Distributor
9. Switch-over valve, ignition (red)
10. Switch-over valve, throttle lift (gray)
12. Switch-over valve, EGR (brown)
14. 77° F temperature switch
31. EGR valve
33. Switch-over valve, air injection (blue)
45. Muffler (air filter for noise suppression)
51. Vacuum control, throttle lift

1975–76 230 emission control component location

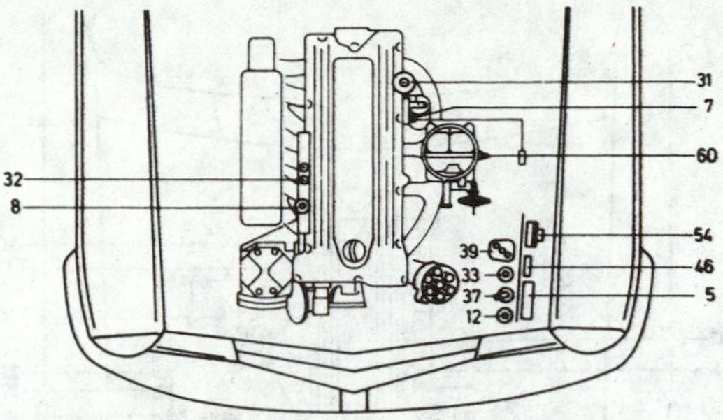

5. Relay box
7. 62° F temperature switch
8. 212° F temperature switch
12. Switch-over valve, EGR (brown)
31. EGR valve
32. 149° F temperature switch
33. Switch-over valve, air injection (blue)
37. Switch-over valve, fuel evaporation control system (green)
39. Charcoal canister
46. Resistor, automatic choke cover
54. Vacuum booster
60. Venturi connection

1975–76 280, 280C, emission control component location

11 volts, temporarily replace the rpm relay or relay box and repeat the test.

EGR SWITCHOVER VALVE

1. Disconnect the brown vacuum line at the carburetor and brown/purple vacuum line at the carburetor. Blow into the brown vacuum line and simultaneously increase the rpm to about 3600. At idle, air can be blown through the line, while above 3600, no air should pass.

EGR VALVE

1. Connect the EGR valve to intake manifold vacuum. Disconnect the red line at the carburetor and the brown/purple line at the carburetor. Connect both lines together. The engine should run poorly or stall. If not be sure that the valve stem is moving and if not, replace the valve. If the valve works, clean the EGR valve with a 10 mm drill.

VACUUM GOVERNOR

1. Increase the engine speed to about 2500 rpm and release the throttle slowly. At the same time watch the vacuum control on the carburetor. It should pop out above 2000 rpm and retract below 1800 rpm. If not, remove the plug from the relay box and connect terminals 2 and 7. With the ignition ON, the valve should click audibly. If it does, replace the relay box.

280, 280C AND 280S

The system remains basically unchanged except for different color coding of vacuum lines and addition of a catalytic converter in all states.

Testing the System

EGR

1. Remove the brown/purple vacuum line from the EGR valve and turn the ignition ON. Blow air into the line. Place the gear selector in a driving position (not N or P). The line should be closed.

2. Remove the brown vacuum line on the carburetor and the green line on the carburetor. Connect the brown line in place of the green line. Start the engine and place the gear selector in a driving position (not N or P).

3. The engine should run roughly or stall. If not, either the vacuum booster or the EGR valve is at fault.

AIR INJECTION

1. Remove the air injection hose at the air filter (center hose) and run the engine at idle. There should be no air flow present. If air is discharged at idle, replace the diverter valve.

62° F. TEMPERATURE SWITCH

1. Disconnect the plug from the switch in the oil filter housing and ground the switch. Air flow in the injection line should cease. If it does not, disconnect the plug from the blue switchover valve and connect a voltmeter. Disconnect and ground the temperature switch. Turn the ignition ON; the voltmeter should read about 12 volts. If no voltage is present, replace the relay box.

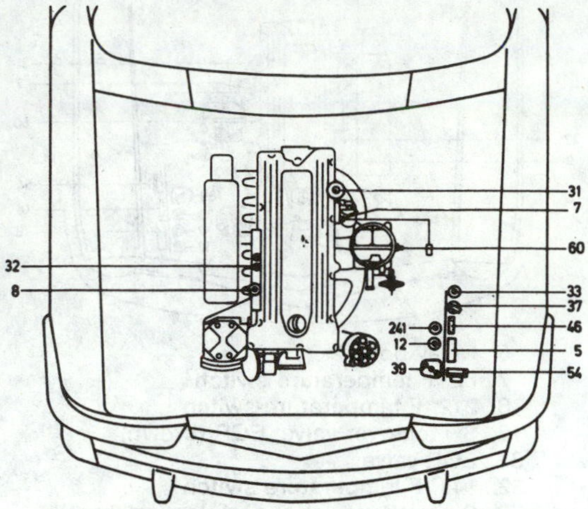

5. Relay box
7. 62° F temperature switch
8. 212° F temperature switch
12. Switch-over valve, EGR (brown)
31. EGR valve
32. 149° F temperature switch
33. Switch-over valve, air injection (blue)
37. Switch-over valve, fuel evaporation control system (green)
39. Charcoal canister
46. Resistor, automatic choke cover
54. Vacuum booster
60. Venturi connection

1975–76 280S emission control component location

AUTOMATIC CHOKE RESISTOR

1. Connect a voltmeter to the resistor outlet (top connection) and to ground. Disconnect the plug of the 62°F. temperature switch and connect it to ground. Disconnect the plug of the 149°F. temperature switch and turn the ignition ON. With the 62° switch grounded, the voltmeter should read about 7–8 volts. If the ground is interrupted, it should read about 12 volts.

2. If the voltage is not as specified, check the relay box. Connect a voltmeter to the input of the resistor (lower connection) and to ground. Ground the plug of the 62° temperature switch and the voltmeter should read about 12 volts. If not, replace the relay box.

FLOAT CHAMBER VENT VALVE

1. Connect a vacuum gauge to the green/purple vacuum line to the float chamber vent valve. Start the engine and briefly accelerate. The vacuum should build up and remain constant. With the ignition OFF, the vacuum should drop to zero.

2. If no vacuum is present, connect a voltmeter to the switchover valve. About 13 volts should be present, and the valve should click audibly.

If vacuum does not remain constant, unscrew the float chamber vent valve. With the vacuum line connected, run the engine at idle. The valve rod should move. If necessary, replace the valve vacuum diaphragm.

CHARCOAL CANISTER PURGE VALVE

See this test under "1974 280 and 280C (California Only)." The test is the same.

450SL, SLC AND 450SE, SEL

This system is basically the same as the 1974 system with the addition of a dual diaphragm distributor and catalytic converter.

Testing the System

212°F. TEMPERATURE SWITCH

See this test under "1974 450SL, SLC and 450SE, SEL." It is identical, except for color coding.

VACUUM CONTROL UNIT

1. Remove the yellow/purple and red/purple vacuum lines from the vacuum control on the distributor. The engine rpm should increase slightly. Connect the yellow/purple vacuum line to the upper connection of the vacuum control unit. The engine speed should increase slightly. If not, replace the vacuum control unit.

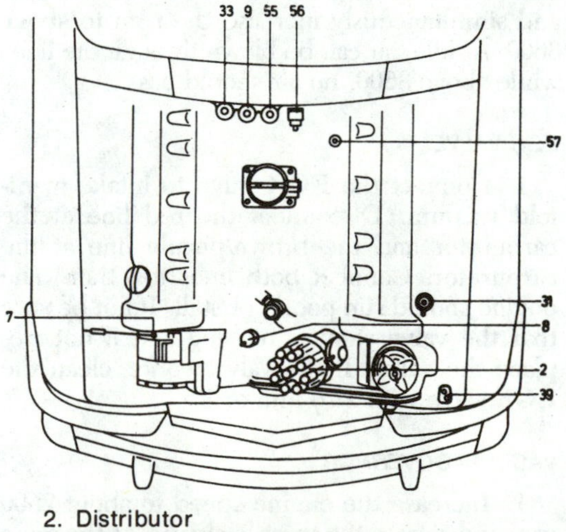

2. Distributor
7. 62° F (17° C) temperature switch
8. 202° F (100° C) temperature switch
9. Switch-over valve, ignition retard (yellow)
31. EGR valve
33. Switch-over valve, air injection (blue)
39. Charcoal canister
55. Switch-over valve, EGR/ ignition advance (red)
56. Vacuum control switch
57. 104° F (40° C) temperature switch

1975 450SE, SEL emission control component location

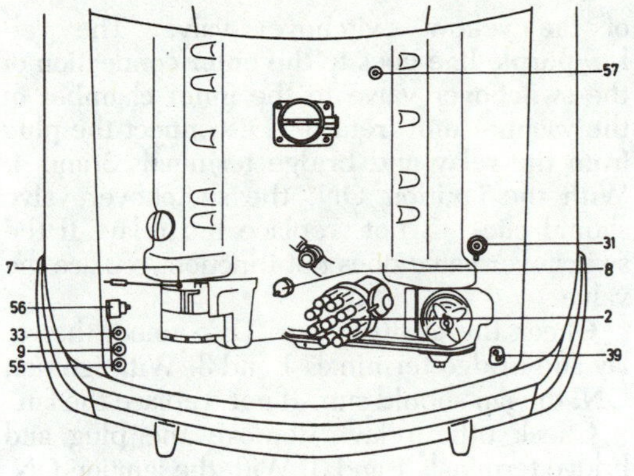

2. Distributor
7. 62° F (17° C) temperature switch
8. 202° F (100° C) temperature switch
9. Switch-over valve, ignition retard (yellow)
31. EGR valve
33. Switch-over valve, air injection (blue)
39. Charcoal canister
55. Switch-over valve, EGR/ ignition advance (red)
56. Vacuum control switch
57. 104° F (40° C) temperature switch

1975 450SL, SLC emission control component location

EGR SWITCHOVER VALVE

1. Remove the red/purple vacuum line at the EGR valve. Connect a vacuum gauge to the red/purple line and to the red connection of the EGR valve. Run the engine at idle and increase the rpm to 2500. At idle, the gauge should show no vacuum. At higher rpm, there should be some vacuum.

2. If not, shut the engine OFF and turn the ignition to ON. Remove the plug from the 104°F. temperature switch. The switchover valve should click. If it does not click, replace the switchover valve with a new one and repeat the test. If it still does not click, replace the relay.

EGR VACUUM CONTROL SWITCH

1. Remove the brown/purple vacuum line from the EGR valve. Connect a vacuum gauge to the brown/purple line and to the bottom of the EGR valve. Start the engine and increase speed to 2500 rpm. At idle, the gauge should show no vacuum. During acceleration, vacuum should be present for a brief period until engine rpm stabilizes at a higher speed.

2. If no vacuum can be measured and the vacuum lines are correctly attached, the vacuum control switch is defective.

EGR VALVE

1. Remove the yellow/purple vacuum line from the vacuum control unit on the distributor. Disconnect the vacuum lines from the EGR valve. With a vacuum test line, connect the yellow/purple line with the upper, and then the lower connection of the EGR valve. The engine should run roughly or stall in both operating phases of the EGR valve.

3. If the engine does not run roughly or stall, the EGR valve should be replaced.

CO EXHAUST GAS CONTENT

1. Run the engine at idle. Test the CO content of the exhaust gas. Disconnect the plug for the 62°F. temperature switch and ground it with a test cable. Measure the CO again without air injection. The CO content should change noticeably.

2. If it does not change noticeably, disconnect and ground the 62° temperature switch. The blue switchover valve should click. If it doesn't, replace the switchover valve.

3. If the switchover valve functions, remove the air filter on the diverter valve. Disconnect and ground the 62° temperature switch. Air should exit from the diverter valve. If there is no air flow, replace the diverter valve and repeat the test. Also, check the air pump and air pump drive belt tension.

CHARCOAL CANISTER PURGE VALVE

See this test under "1974 280 and 280C (California Only)."

1976

The 1976 emission control system is close to the system used in 1975. Catalytic converters are used on all engines, but the 450 series cars have the catalysts installed on the exhaust manifold. Due to Federal regulations, the routing of the fuel evaporation lines has been changed.

230

See the 1975 230 Emission Control System.

280, 280C, 280S

See the 1975 280, 280C and 280S Emission Control System.

450SE, 450SEL, 450SL, 450SLC

These cars with the M117 engine use one emission system for the entire U.S. market, including California.

The base color of the vacuum lines is opaque (white). Lines originating at a vacuum source have only one color stripe; lines terminating at a vacuum source have 2-color stripes. Purple is always the second color.

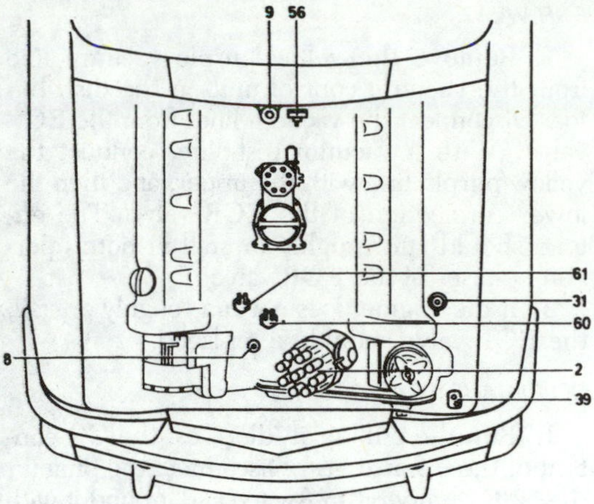

2. Distributor
8. 212° F temperature switch
9. Switch-over valve, ignition retard (yellow)
31. EGR valve
39. Charcoal canister
56. Vacuum control switch
60. 104° F thermo-vacuum valve (black)
61. 63° F thermo-vacuum valve (blue)

1976 450SE, SEL, 450SL, SLC emission control component location

Thermo vacuum valves are used to control the ignition changeover, EGR and air injection. They are color coded:

Black—104°F. valve
Blue—63°F. valve

The retard side of the vacuum control unit is only activated when the coolant is below 212°F. during deceleration with the A/C off. The advance side of the vacuum control unit is activated when temperatures at the thermo-valve are 104°F. or above and the advance is determined by the position of the throttle plate.

The EGR valve works in 2 stages. The first stage (small amount) takes place with coolant temperature above 104°F. There is no EGR with coolant temperature below 86°F.

The second (larger) stage of EGR occurs during acceleration with coolant temperature above 140°F. and vacuum less than 7.9 in./Hg.

Air injection takes place above 62°F. and is cancelled below 50°F. (coolant temperatures).

Testing the System

IGNITION CHANGEOVER SWITCH

Unplug and ground the temperature switch. The engine rpm should increase and the auxiliary fan should operate.

If the engine speed does not increase, check the vacuum lines. The yellow line from the throttle valve housing should go to the center of the yellow switchover valve. The yellow/purple line goes to the outer connection of the switchover valve to the inner chamber of the vacuum unit (retard). Disconnect the plug from the relay and bridge terminals 3 and 4. With the ignition ON, the switchover valve should click. If not, replace the relay. If the switchover valve does not function, replace the valve.

Check the auxiliary fan. Disconnect the relay and bridge terminals 1 and 3. With ignition ON; the fan should run. If not, replace the fan.

Check othe relay. Remove the plug and bridge terminals 1 and 3. With the ignition ON, the fans hould run. If so, replace the relay.

IGNITION RETARD RELAY

Switch on the A/C. The engine rpm should increase slightly. If not, check that the A/C is operating. If the A/C is operating, replace the relay.

IGNITION ADVANCE

Remove the yellow/purple and red/purple vacuum lines from the distributor. The engine speed should increase slightly. Connect the yellow/purple vacuum line to the upper connection at the vacuum diaphragm. The engine speed should increase.

If not, replace the 2-way vacuum diaphragm.

EGR SWITCHOVER VALVE

Remove the red/purple vacuum line at the EGR valve. Connect a vacuum gauge to the red/purple line and run the engine at idle. Increase speed to 2500 rpm. At idle, the gauge should show no vacuum; at 2500 rpm, vacuum should be present.

If no vacuum is indicated, check the line connections. The red line from the red connection at the throttle valve housing should go to the angular connection of the thermovacuum valve. The red/purple line should be attached to the vertical connection at the thermo-vacuum valve, to the red connection of the vacuum control switch and red connection of the EGR valve.

Check the 104°F. thermo-vacuum valve. It should open if the surrounding temperature is above 104°F. It should close below 86°F. If the valve is not functioning properly, check the bore of the throttle housing vacuum connection.

VACUUM CONTROL SWITCH

Remove the brown/purple vacuum line from the EGR valve. Connect a vacuum gauge between the line and the bottom of the EGR valve. Increase engine speed to 2500 rpm. At idle, vacuum should not be present. During acceleration, vacuum should be present briefly until the rpm stabilizes. If no vacuum is present, check the vacuum lines. The red/purple line should be connected to the red connection at the vacuum control switch, the white line to the center of the vacuum control switch and the red/purple line to the brown control switch connection. If vacuum still is not present, replace the control switch.

EGR VALVE

Disconnect the yellow/purple line from the distributor diaphragm. Disconnect both vacuum lines at the EGR valve. Connect the yellow/purple line with the upper, then the lower connection of the EGR valve. The engine should run rough or stall in both cases. If not, replace the EGR valve.

DIVERTER VALVE

Run the engine at idle. Connect a CO tester. Note the reading. Remove the blue/purple vacuum line from the blue thermo-valve and note the reading again. It should change noticeably.

If not, check the vacuum lines. The blue line runs to the angular connection on the blue thermo-vacuum valve. The blue/purple line goes to the vertical connection of the same valve.

Check the diverter valve. Remove the muffler on the valve. Disconnect the blue/purple vacuum line at the blue thermo-vacuum valve. Air should flow from the diverter valve. If there is no air flow, replace the diverter valve. If necessary, check the drive belt tension.

CHARCOAL CANISTER

Remove the thin hose from the charcoal canister. Cover the hose opening with your finger or connect a vacuum gauge. Slowly increase rpm to 2500. At idle, a small amount of vacuum should be present, and vacuum should increase with engine speed.

If no vacuum is present at idle, check the purge line to the intake manifold. Disconnect the charcoal canister hose at the purge valve and clean it by blowing through with compressed air in the direction of the intake manifold. Replace the purge valve if necessary.

If vacuum does not increase at idle, check the vacuum at the purge valve. Disconnect the white vacuum line at the purge valve. Connect a vacuum gauge or close the line with a finger. Increase engine speed. At idle, there should be no vacuum. With increasing engine speed, vacuum should increase. If vacuum is present, replace the purge valve. If no vacuum is present, blow through the line towards the throttle valve housing.

1977

The following tests should be performed in the order given with the engine at normal operating temperature.

230

Testing the System

EGR

1. Run the engine at idle speed.
2. Remove the brown vacuum line at the carburetor and the gray vacuum line at the intake manifold. Connect the brown line at the intake manifold.
3. The engine should run roughly or stall. If the rpm does not change, check the vacuum line connections. Check for leaks and blow through the vacuum connection on the carburetor.
4. Check the thermo-vacuum valve (blue plastic portion and "50AB5" stamped in metal housing). Remove the brown/purple vacuum line and race the engine. Vacuum must be present at the open connection when accelerating.
5. Check the EGR valve. Remove the EGR valve. Connect the brown/purple vacuum line to the EGR valve and slowly increase engine rpm. Cover the bores in the intake manifold. The valve stem should lift from its seat; if not replace the EGR valve with a new one.

AIR INJECTION

1. Connect a CO tester to the test connection and remove the vacuum hose from the

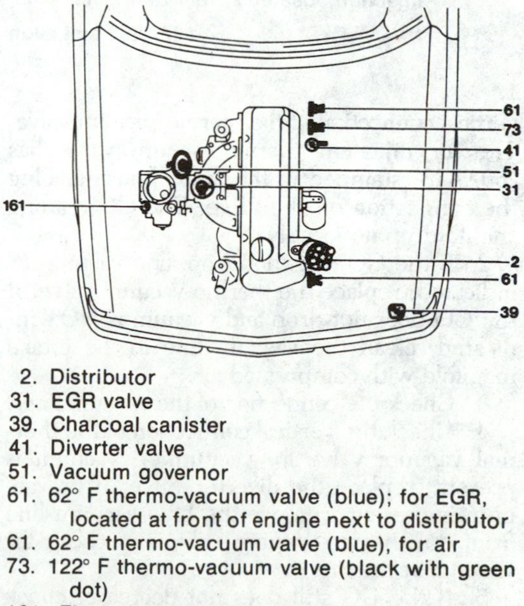

2. Distributor
31. EGR valve
39. Charcoal canister
41. Diverter valve
51. Vacuum governor
61. 62° F thermo-vacuum valve (blue); for EGR, located at front of engine next to distributor
61. 62° F thermo-vacuum valve (blue), for air
73. 122° F thermo-vacuum valve (black with green dot)
161. Float chamber vent valve

1977–79 230 emission control component location

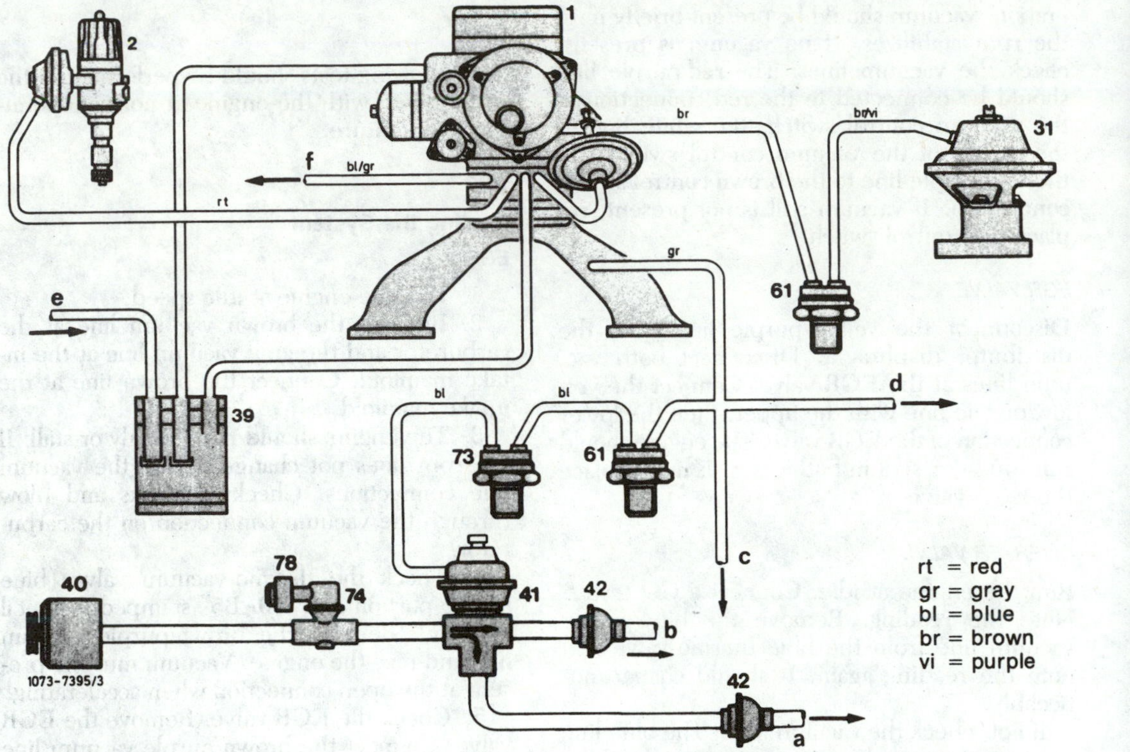

1. Carburetor
2. Distributor
31. EGR valve
39. Charcoal canister
40. Air pump
41. Diverter valve
42. Check valve
61. 62° F thermo-vacuum valve (blue), for EGR, located at front of engine next to distributor
61. 62° F thermo-vacuum valve (blue), for air injection, located at rear of engine
73. Thermo-vacuum valve 50° C/122° F
74. Pressure relief valve
78. Air filter for noise suppression

a. To cylinder head
b. To catalyst
c. Air conditioning
d. Central locking system
e. Fuel tank ventilation connection
f. To air filter

1977 230 emission control schematic

vertical connection of the thermo-vacuum valve. The air injection thermo-vacuum valve has "50AA13" stamped in the metal housing. Plug the connection on the valve. The CO reading should drop noticeably.

2. If the CO does not drop, and vacuum IS indicated, replace the thermo-vacuum valve. If the CO does not drop and vacuum is NOT indicated, clean the vacuum line to the intake manifold with compressed air.

3. Check the connection of the vacuum lines.

4. Check the vertical connection of the thermal vacuum valve for vacuum. If vacuum is present, replace the diverter valve. If no vacuum is present, remove the blue vacuum line from the thermo-vacuum valve and check for vacuum at the line.

5. If the CO still does not decrease, check that the thermo-vacuum valve is open; if not, replace the valve.

NOTE: *Below approximately 120° F., the valve should be open; above that, it should be closed.*

THROTTLE VALVE LIFT

1. Remove the vacuum hose from the vacuum governor on the carburetor. The idle speed should increase. Reconnect the hose. The idle speed should decrease.

2. If the rpm does not increase, check the connection of the hose. Check the hose for leaks.

3. Run the engine at idle. Remove the vacuum line on the carburetor; the idle speed should increase. If not, replace the vacuum governor.

FUEL EVAPORATION CONTROL SYSTEM

1. Remove the solenoid plug from the float chamber vent valve. Reconnect the solenoid; it should click audibly.

2. If the solenoid does not click, turn on the ignition and connect a test lamp to the plug. The test lamp should light with the ignition ON. If not, check the proper fuse. If the lamp still does not light, replace the solenoid.

3. Remove the middle purge hose to the carburetor from the charcoal canister and cover the hose opening with your finger. Slowly increase engine speed to over 2000 rpm. At idle no vacuum should be present. As engine speed increases, vacuum should increase. If no vacuum is present as the engine speed increases, check the connection of the purge hose. Check the hose for leaks and clean it out with compressed air.

4. On 1978–79 models remove the hose from the purge valve and repeat the test. If vacuum is present, replace the purge valve.

280E AND 280SE (FEDERAL)

Testing the System

The following tests should be performed with the engine at idle speed, at operating temperature and in the order listed.

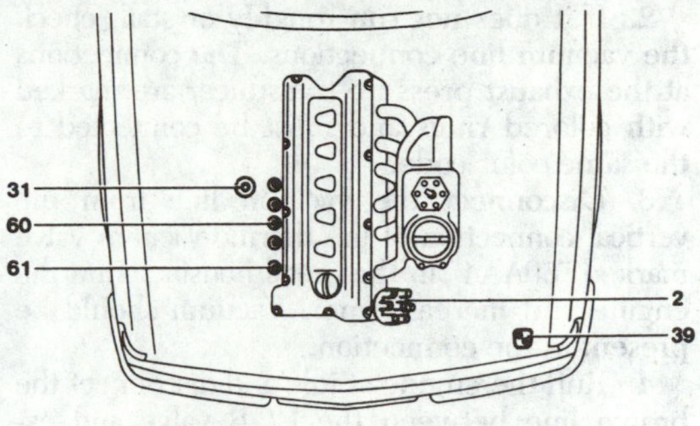

2. Distributor
31. EGR valve
39. Charcoal canister
60. 104° F thermo-vacuum valve
61. 62° F thermo-vacuum valve

1977–79 280E, 280CE, 280SE Federal emission control component location

EGR

1. Remove the brown vacuum line from the EGR valve and slowly increase engine rpm. At about 1200 rpm, the engine should run roughly or stall.

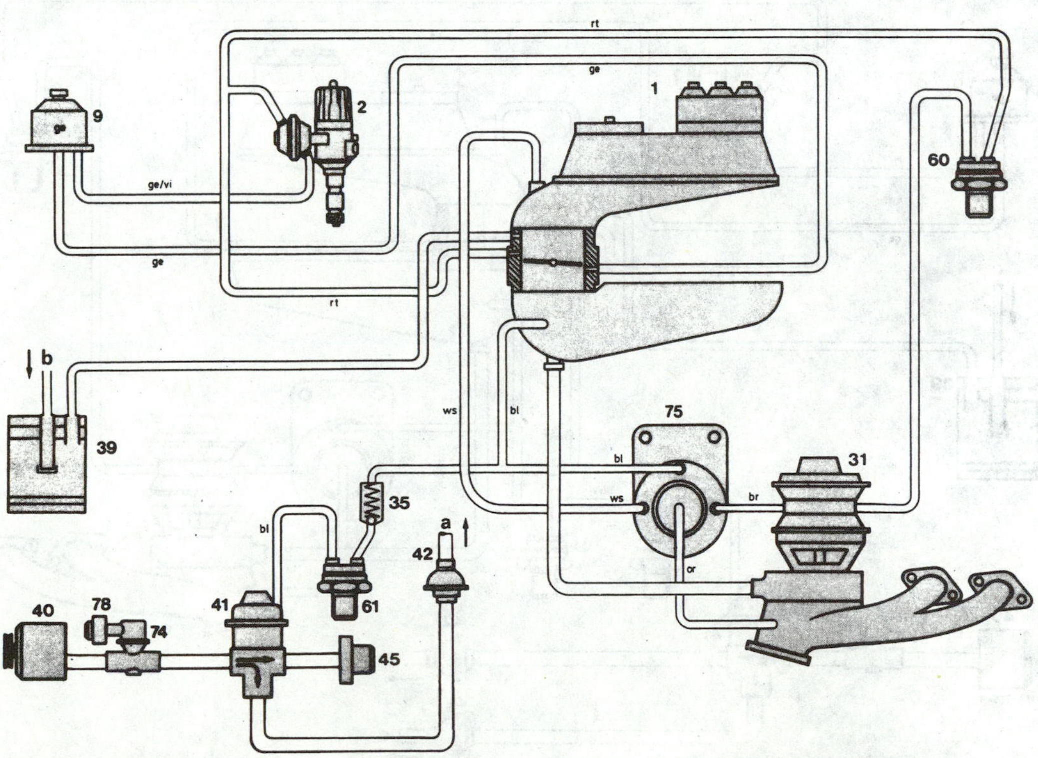

1. Mixture regulator assembly
2. Ignition distributor
9. Ignition switch-over valve
31. EGR valve
35. Check valve
39. Charcoal canister
40. Air pump
41. Diverter valve
42. Check valve
45. Muffler (air filter)
60. 104° F thermo-vacuum valve
61. 62° F thermo-vacuum valve
74. Pressure relief valve
75. Exhaust pressure transducer
78. Muffler (air filter)
a. Air injection line
b. Connection, fuel tank vent

1977 280E, 280SE Federal emission control schematic

2. If it does not run roughly or stall, check the vacuum line connections. The connections at the exhaust pressure transducer are marked with colored rings and must be connected to the same color code.

3. Disconnect the vacuum line from the vertical connection of the thermo-vacuum valve marked "50AA4" in the metal housing. Run the engine and increase rpm. Vacuum should be present at the connection.

4. Run the engine at idle and disconnect the brown line between the EGR valve and exhaust pressure transducer. Cover the line with your finger; vacuum must be present at idle. If not, replace the exhaust pressure transducer.

5. Run the engine at idle and remove both vacuum lines from the EGR valve. Connect the brown line to the connection on the red/purple line on the EGR valve. The engine should run roughly or stall. If not, replace the EGR valve.

AIR INJECTION

1. Connect a CO tester to the exhaust back pressure line. Remove and plug the vacuum

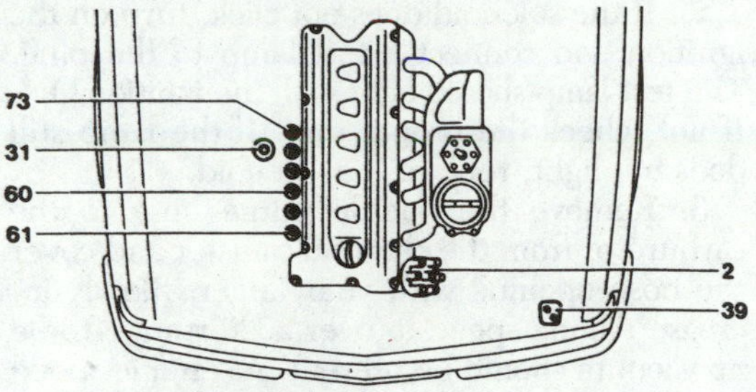

2. Distributor
31. EGR valve
39. Charcoal canister
60. 104° F thermo-vacuum valve
61. 62° F thermo-vacuum valve
73. 122° F thermo-vacuum valve

1977–79 280E, 280CE, 280SE California emission control component location

hose from the vertical connection at the thermo-vacuum valve. The CO should increase.

2. If not, check the vacuum line connections. The (large) cap end connection of the

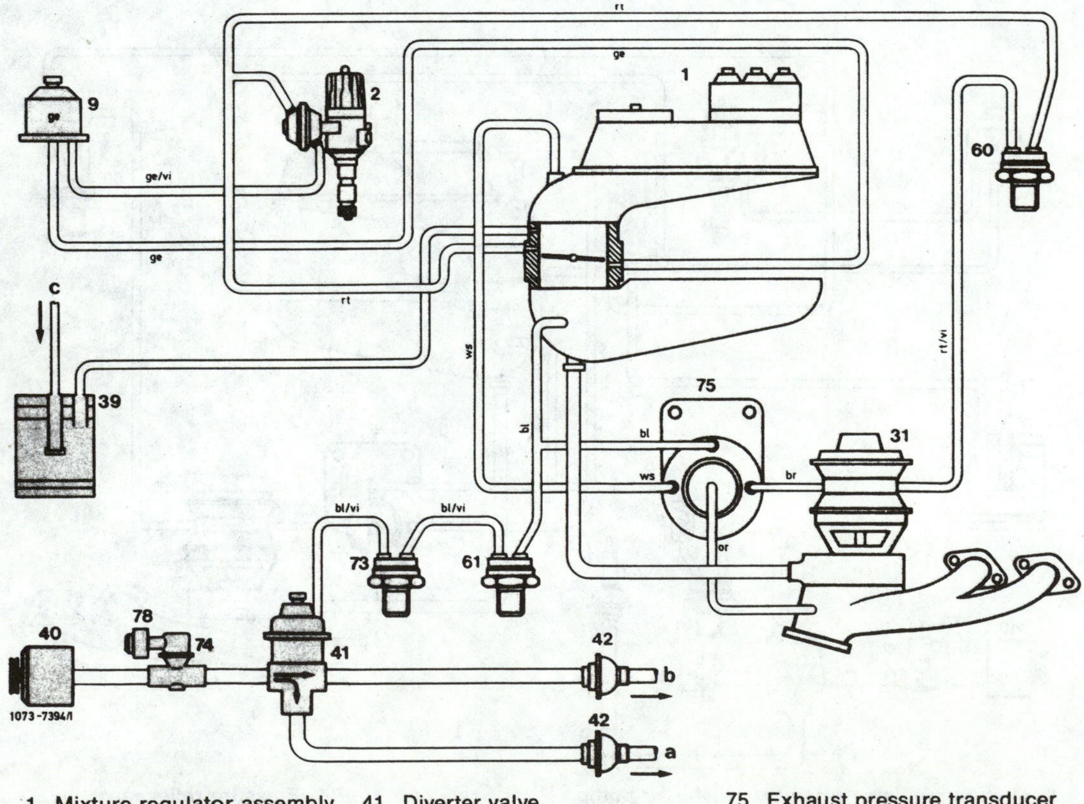

1. Mixture regulator assembly
2. Ignition distributor
9. Ignition switch-over valve
31. EGR valve
39. Charcoal canister
40. Air pump
41. Diverter valve
42. Check valve
60. 104° F thermo-vacuum valve
61. 62° F thermo-vacuum valve
73. 122° F thermo-vacuum valve
74. Pressure relief valve
75. Exhaust pressure transducer
78. Muffler (air filter)
a. Air injection line, cylinder head
b. Air injection line, between catalysts
c. Connection, fuel tank vent

1977 280E, 280SE California emission control schematic

check valve must face the intake manifold (Federal only).

3. Remove the blue vacuum line from the thermo-vacuum valve and cover it with your finger. Vacuum must be present at idle; if not, check for leaks and clean the line with compressed air.

4. If vacuum is present, check the thermo-vacuum valve and replace if necessary.

5. Disconnect the blue/purple line from the thermo-vacuum valve marked "50AB5" on the metal housing. Run the engine. Vacuum should be present at the vertical connection. If not, replace the diverter valve.

FUEL EVAPORATION CONTROL SYSTEM

1. Remove the black purge line from the charcoal canister. Cover the opening with your finger and increase rpm to over 2000 rpm. No vacuum should be present at idle and vacuum should increase with engine speed. If not, check the vacuum line connections, check for leaks and clean the line with compressed air.

280E AND 280SE (CALIFORNIA)

Testing the System

EGR

See 280E and 280SE (Federal).

AIR INJECTION

1. Connect a CO tester to the exhaust pressure transducer. Remove the vacuum line from the vertical connection of the 122°F thermo-vacuum valve and connect it to the vertical connection of the 62°F thermo-vacuum valve. The CO should drop.

2. If not, check the vacuum line connections.

3. Run the engine at idle and check for vacuum at the vertical connection of the 62°F thermo-vacuum valve. If vacuum is present, replace the diverter valve.

If no vacuum is present, remove the blue line from the 62°F. thermo-vacuum valve and check for vacuum at the valve. If vacuum is present, replace the thermo-vacuum valve. If no vacuum is present, remove the line from the intake manifold and clean it with compressed air.

4. If the CO still does not drop, check the 122°F. thermo-vacuum valve. It will have "50AA13" stamped in the metal housing. Above 122°F., the valve is closed and no vacuum should be present at the vertical connection. Below 122°F., vacuum should be present at the vertical connection. If these conditions are not met, replace the valve.

FUEL EVAPORATION CONTROL SYSTEM

See 280E and 280SE (Federal).

450SL, 450SLC, 450SEL (FEDERAL)

Testing the System

The following tests should be performed with the engine running at normal operating temperature in the order given.

EGR

1. Remove the brown line at the EGR valve and slowly increase engine speed. Above 1200 rpm, the engine should run roughly or stall. If not check the vacuum line connections.

2. Check the thermo vacuum valve with "50AA4" stamped in the metal housing (104°F valve). Remove the red/purple line from the

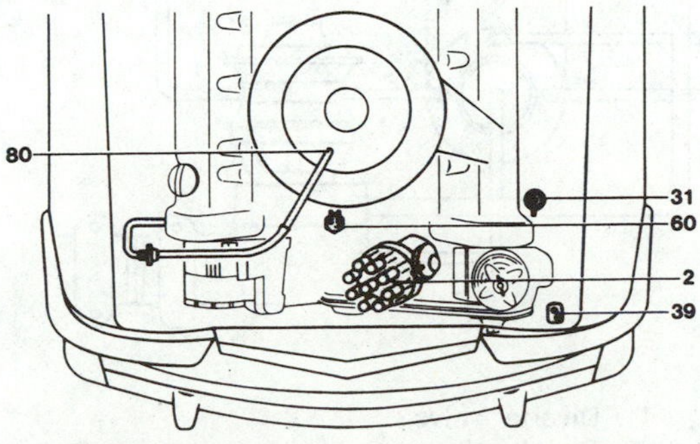

2. Distributor
31. EGR valve
39. Charcoal canister
60. 104° F thermo-vacuum valve (black)
80. Suction hose to aspirator/check valve

1977–80 4.5 V8 Federal emission control component location

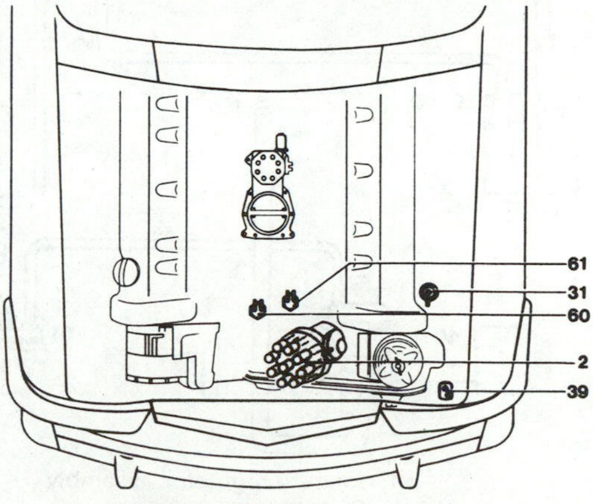

2. Distributor
31. EGR valve
39. Charcoal canister
60. 104° F thermo-vacuum valve (black)
61. 62° F thermo-vacuum valve (blue)

1977–80 4.5 V8 California emission control component location

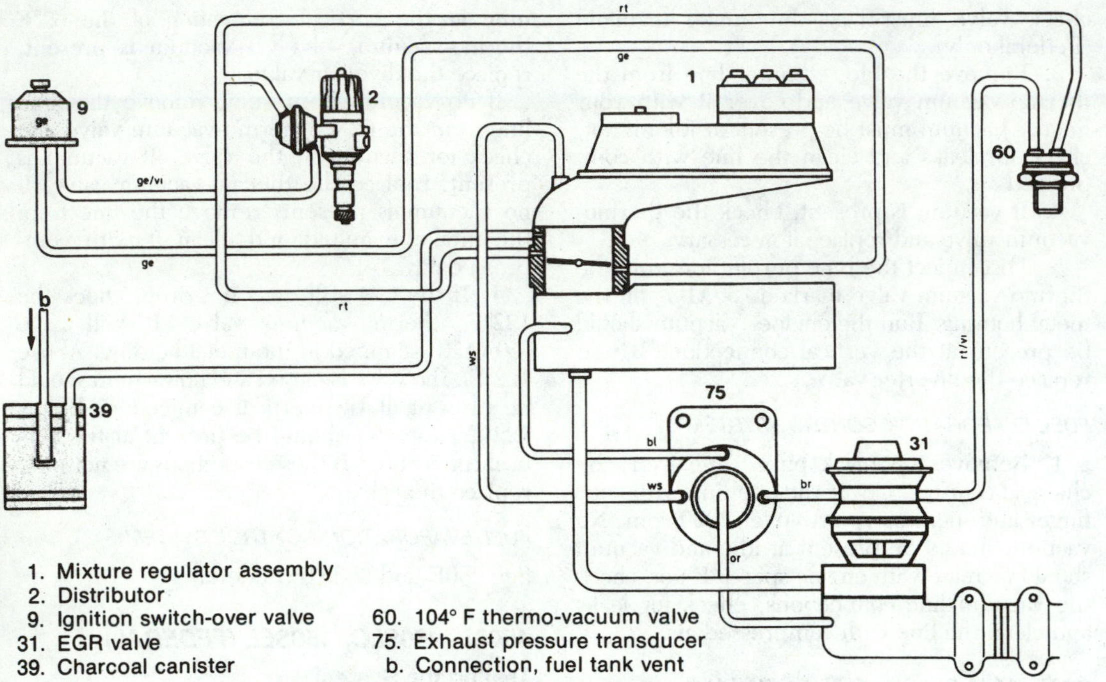

1. Mixture regulator assembly
2. Distributor
9. Ignition switch-over valve
31. EGR valve
39. Charcoal canister
60. 104° F thermo-vacuum valve
75. Exhaust pressure transducer
b. Connection, fuel tank vent

1977 4.5 V8 Federal emission control schematic

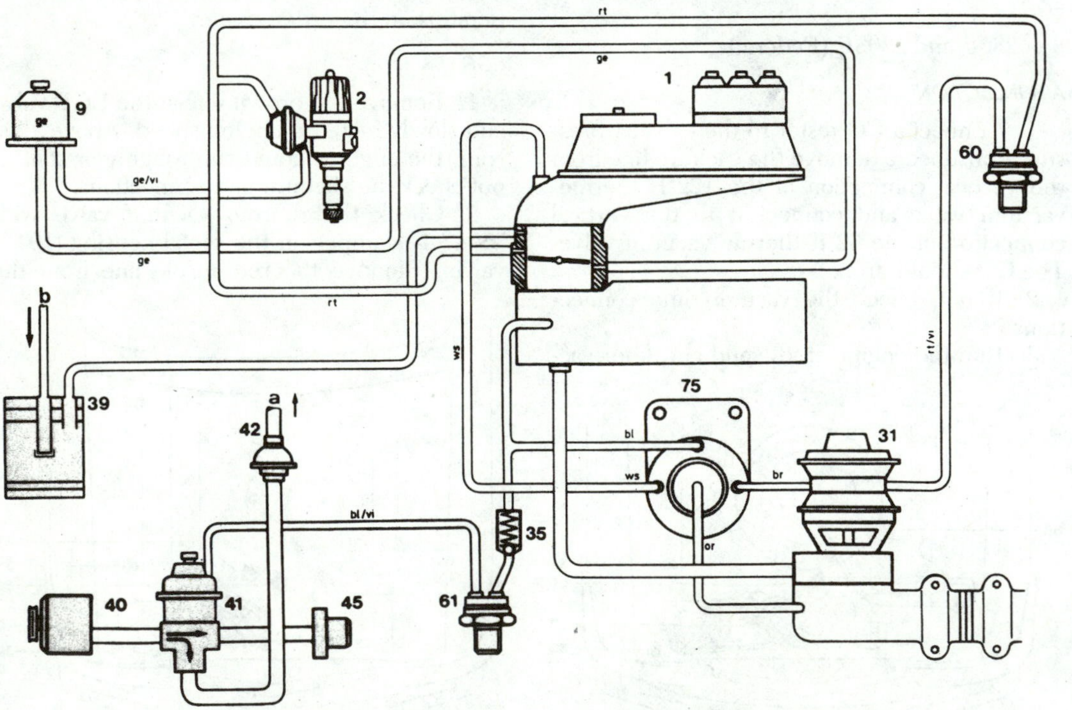

1. Mixture regulator assembly
2. Distributor
9. Ignition switch-over valve
31. EGR valve
35. Vacuum check valve
39. Charcoal canister
40. Air pump
41. Diverter valve
42. Check valve
60. 104° F thermo-vacuum valve
61. 62° F thermo-vacuum valve
75. Exhaust pressure transducer
a. Air injection line to cylinder head
b. Fuel tank vent connection

1977 4.5 V8 California emission control schematic

vertical connection, run the engine and accelerate briefly. Vacuum should be present at the vertical connection.

3. Run the engine at idle and remove the brown vacuum line at the EGR valve. If no vacuum is present at idle, replace the exhaust pressure transducer.

4. Run the engine at idle and remove both lines from the EGR valve. Connect the brown line to the connection for the red/purple line. The engine should run roughly or stall. If not, replace the EGR valve.

AIR INJECTION

1. Remove the suction hose from the aspirator/check valve in the air cleaner and cover with your finger. Vacuum should be present and a suction noise should be audible. If no vacuum is present, replace the aspirator/check valve.

FUEL EVAPORATION CONTROL SYSTEM

See this test under 280E and 280SE (Federal).

450SL, 450SLC, 450SEL (CALIFORNIA) AND 6.9

Testing the System

EGR

See 450SL, 450SLC, 450SEL (Federal).

AIR INJECTION

1. Connect a CO tester to the exhaust gas back pressure line and remove the blue/purple vacuum line from the vertical connection of the 62°F thermo-vacuum valve. Plug the connection. The CO should increase.

2. If not, check the vacuum line connections. The check valve must be installed with the larger (cap) end toward the intake manifold.

3. Remove the vacuum line from the angular connection of the 62°F thermo-vacuum valve and cover the valve with your finger. If no vacuum is present at idle, check the lines for leaks and clean the vacuum pick-up bore with compressed air.

4. If vacuum is prsent, check the thermo-vacuum valve and replace if necessary.

5. The thermo-vacuum valve can be identified by the "50AB5" stamped in the metal body. Remove the blue/purple vacuum line, run the engine at idle and accelerate briefly. Vacuum should be present at the vertical connection; if not, replace the diverter valve.

FUEL EVAPORATION CONTROL SYSTEM

See this test under 280E and 280SE (Federal).

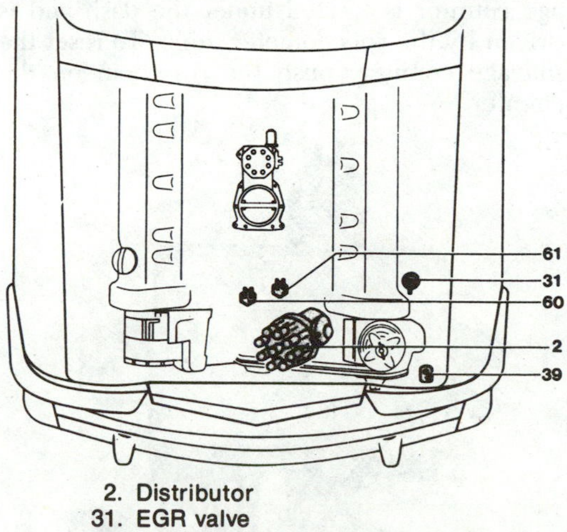

2. Distributor
31. EGR valve
39. Charcoal canister
60. 104° F thermo-vacuum valve
61. 62° F thermo-vacuum valve

1977 6.9 emission control component location

1978–79

The emission control system for 1978–79 models is very similar in components and operation to the 1977 version.

230

Perform the following tests in the order given with the engine at idle at normal operating temperature.

Testing the System

See the 1977 230 procedures for "Testing the System."

280E, 280CE, 280SE (FEDERAL)

Perform the following tests in the order given with the engine at normal operating temperature and idling.

Testing the System

See the 1977 280E and 280SE (Federal) procedures for "Testing the System."

280E, 280CE, 280SE (CALIFORNIA)

Perform the following tests in the order given with the engine at idle and at normal operating temperature.

Testing the System

See the procedures under "Testing the System" for 1977 280E and 280SE California models.

450SL, 450SLC, 450SEL (FEDERAL)

Perform the following tests in the order given with the engine idling at normal operating temperature.

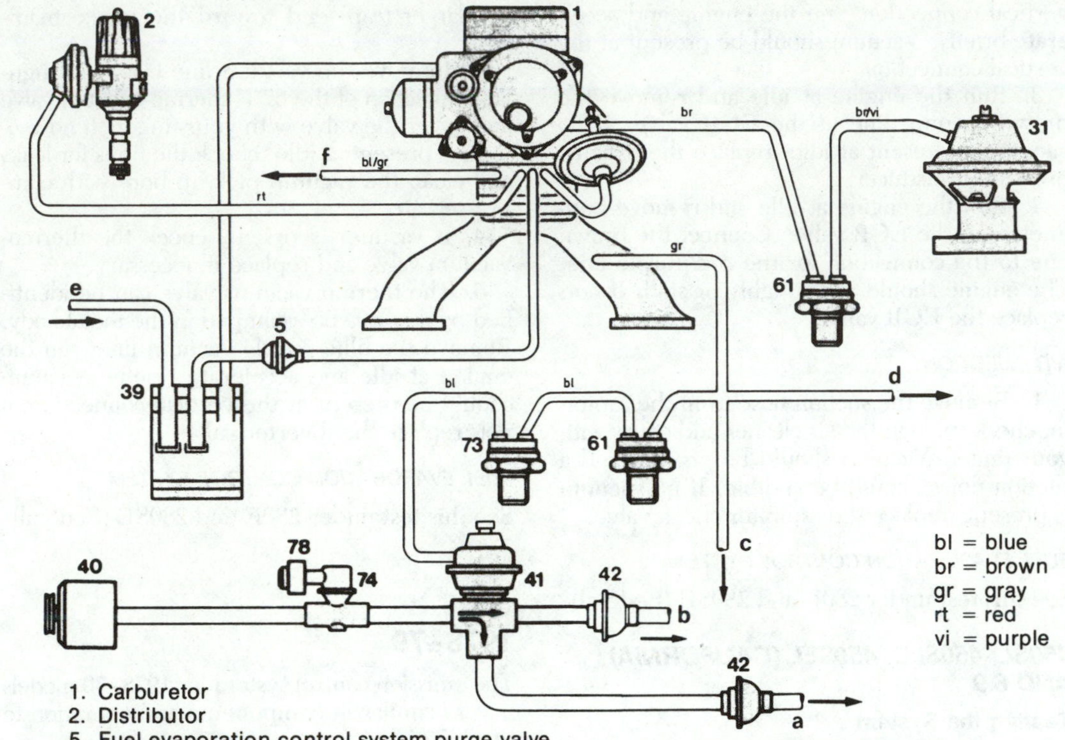

1. Carburetor
2. Distributor
5. Fuel evaporation control system purge valve
31. EGR valve
39. Charcoal canister
40. Air pump
41. Diverter valve
42. Check valve
61. 62° F thermo-vacuum valve (blue), for EGR, located at front of engine next to distributor
61. 62° F thermo-vacuum valve (blue), for air injection, located at rear of engine
73. 122° F thermo-vacuum valve
74. Pressure relief valve
78. Air filter for noise suppression
a. To cylinder head
b. To catalyst
c. Air conditioning
d. Central locking system
e. Fuel tank ventilation connection
f. To air filter

1978 230 emission control schematic components. Location same as 1977

Testing the System

See the procedures for "Testing the System" under 1977 450SL, 450SLC, 450SEL (Federal) models.

450SL, 450SLC, 450SEL (CALIFORNIA) AND 6.9

Perform the following tests in the order given with the engine idling at normal operating temperature.

Testing the System

See the procedures for "Testing the System" under 1977 450SL, 450SLC, 450SEL (California) and 6.9 models.

CATALYST REPLACEMENT WARNING INDICATOR

A warning light in the instrument cluster comes on at 37,500 mile intervals, indicating that the catalyst should be replaced. The catalyst mileage counter is located under the dash and is driven by the speedometer cable. To reset the mileage counter, push the reset pin on the counter.

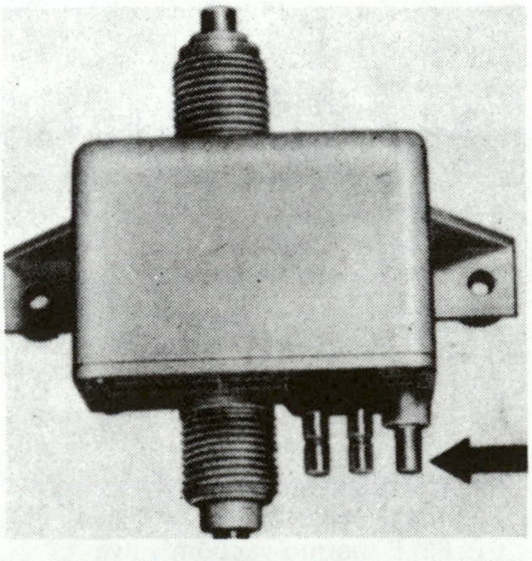

Catalyst elapsed mileage indicator reset button (arrow)

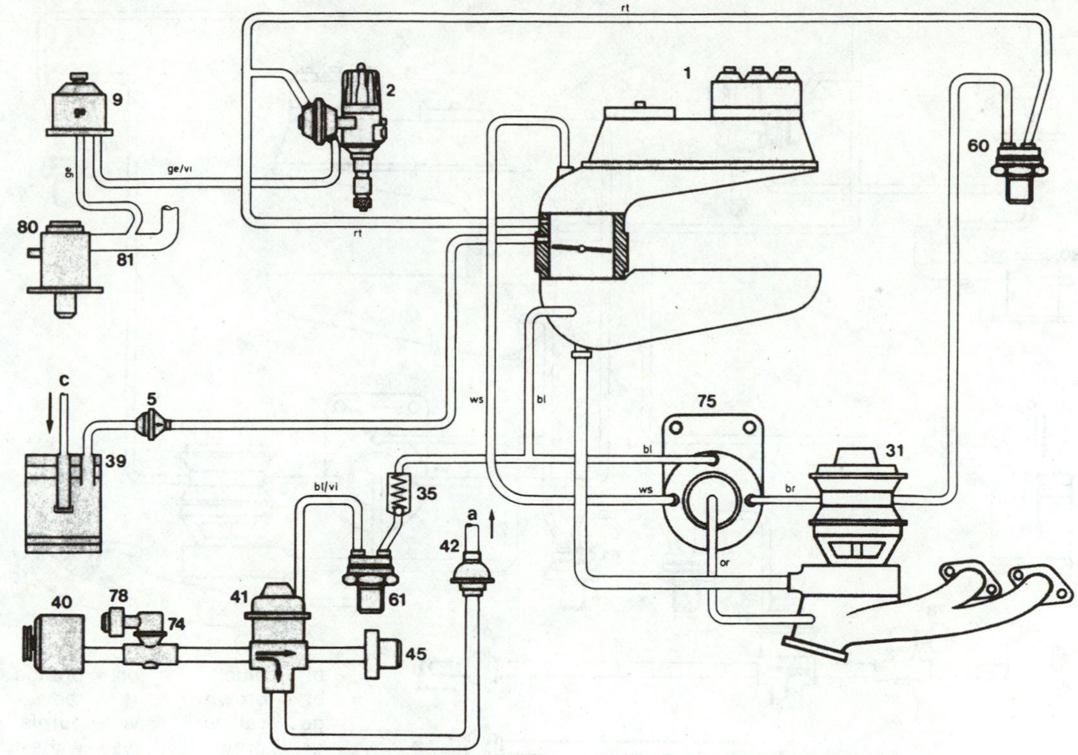

1. Mixture regulator assembly
2. Ignition distributor
5. Purge valve
9. Ignition switch-over valve
31. EGR valve
39. Charcoal canister
40. Air pump
41. Diverter valve
42. Check valve
60. 104° F thermo-vacuum valve
61. 62° F thermo-vacuum valve
73. 122° F thermo-vacuum valve
74. Pressure relief valve
75. Exhaust pressure transducer
78. Muffler (air filter)
80. Auxiliary air valve
81. Shaped hose

a. Air injection line, cylinder head
b. Fuel tank vent connection

1978–79 280E, 280CE, 280SE Federal emission control schematic component. Location same as 1977

1980

6-CYLINDER ENGINES

The base color of the emission control vacuum lines is white. Colored stripes identify various functions:

- Advanced timing = red
- Retarded timing = yellow/purple
- Air injection = blue

A Lambda oxygen sensor control system ensures a constant air fuel ratio of approximately 14.5:1. The oxygen sensor is screwed into the front part of the exhaust pipe to constantly monitor the oxygen content of the exhaust gases. An electronic control unit, located behind the kick panel, receives input from a throttle valve switch and oil temperature switch to maintain an ideal fuel mixture in conjunction with the 3-way catalyst. The oxygen sensor must be replaced every 30,000 miles (light on the dash warns driver).

An air injection system is used, the components of which are very similar to those used in 1979.

Testing the System

A special test adaptor that connects to the electronic control unit plug and a special test meter that connects to the adaptor are necessary to properly test the emission system. Do not attempt to try and test electrical components of the system with an ordinary volt-ohmmeter.

The only tests that can be performed without special equipment are as follows:

AIR INJECTION VACUUM TEST

1. Pull the Y-fitting from the angled connections at the thermo-vacuum valves and check for vacuum at the Y-fitting. If no vacuum is present, clean the connection at the intake manifold with compressed air.

2. Be sure the fitting and connecting lines are not plugged. If vacuum is present, the

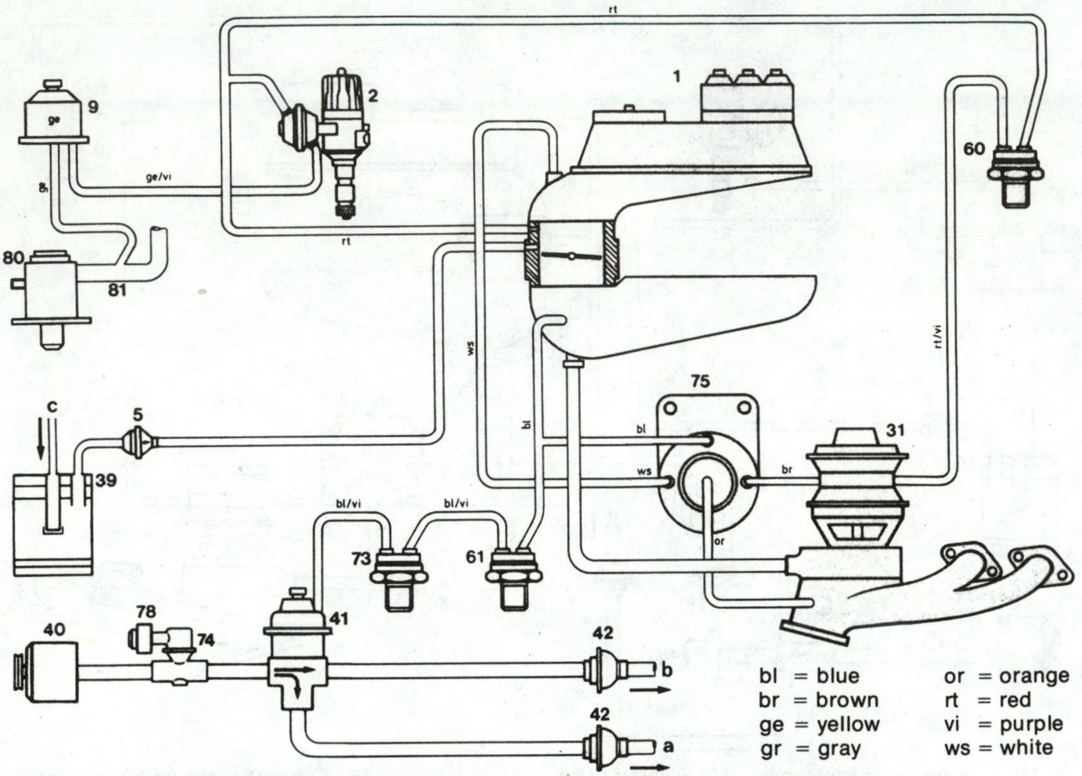

1. Mixture regulator assembly
2. Ignition distributor
5. Purge valve
9. Ignition switch-over valve
31. EGR valve
39. Charcoal canister
40. Air pump
41. Diverter valve
42. Check valve
60. 104° F thermo-vacuum valve
61. 62° F thermo-vacuum valve
73. 122° F thermo-vacuum valve
74. Pressure relief valve
75. Exhaust pressure transducer
78. Muffler (air filter)
80. Auxiliary air valve
81. Shaped hose
a. Air injection line, cylinder head
b. Air injection line, between catalysts
c. Fuel tank vent connection

1978–79 280E, 280CE, 280SE California emission control schematic component. Location same as 1977

thermo-vacuum valves should be open. If the valves are open, replace the diverter valve.

FUEL EVAPORATION CONTROL SYSTEM

1. Remove the purge line from the charcoal canister (connected to the throttle valve housing) and block it with your finger. Slowly increase the engine speed to more than 2000 rpm.
2. There should be no vacuum at idle, but vacuum should increase with rpm.
3. If vacuum does not increase with rpm, test the purge line connection and purge valve. The purge line must be connected to the throttle valve housing, and must not leak. Clean out the throttle valve housing with compressed air. If vacuum is still not present, remove the purge line from the front of the purge valve. If vacuum is present, replace the purge valve.

V8 ENGINES

Color coding of the vacuum lines is identical to the 6-cylinder engines and operation of the Lambda oxygen sensor control system is the same as 6-cylinder engines.

Air injection uses a shut-off valve in a special shaped hose between the air filter and the aspirator valve, which is in the air injection line leading to the cylinder head.

Primary, underfloor and catalyst/muffler combination catalytic converters are used, depending on application.

The fuel evaporation control system is identical to the 1979 system.

Testing the System

A special test adapter that connects to the electronic control unit plug and a special test meter that connects to the adapter are necessary to properly test the emission control system. Do not attempt to try and test electrical components of the system with an ordinary voltohmmeter.

The only tests that can be performed without special equipment are as follows:

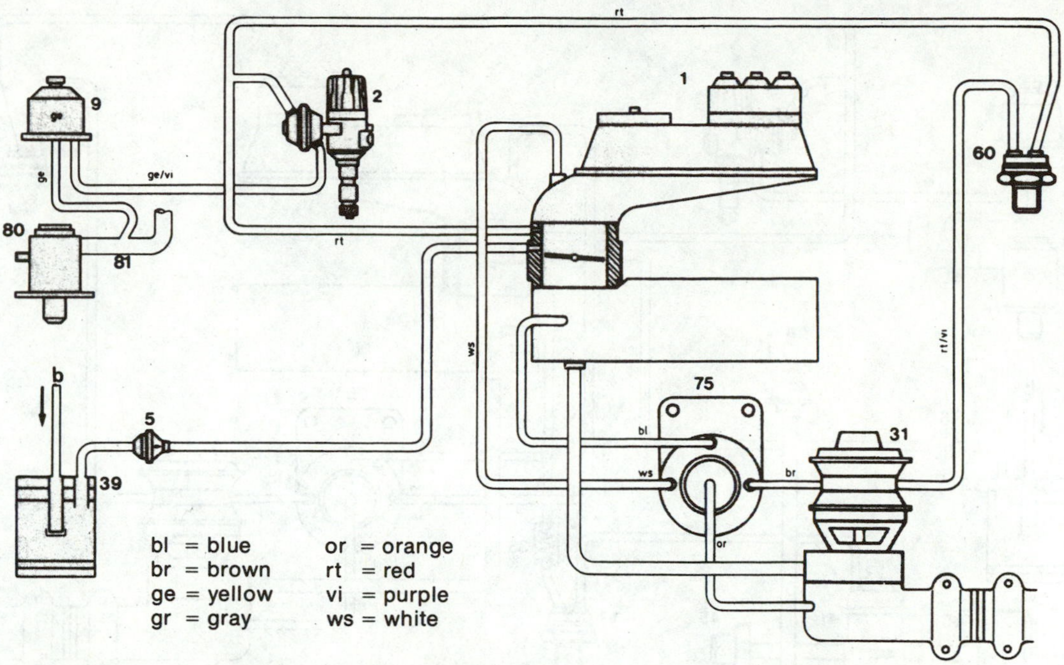

1. Mixture regulator assembly
2. Distributor
5. Purge valve
9. Ignition switch-over valve
31. EGR valve
39. Charcoal canister
60. 104° F thermo-vacuum valve
75. Exhaust pressure transducer
80. Auxiliary air valve
81. Shaped hose
b. Fuel tank vent connection

1978–79 4.5 V8 Federal emission control schematic component. Location same as 1977

FREQUENCY VALVE

1. With the engine idling at normal operating temperature, place your hand on the frequency valve.

2. Operation of the frequency valve can be felt. If not replace the valve.

AIR INJECTION

1. Idle the engine and remove the specially shaped hose from the air shut-off valve. A suction sound should be audible.

2. If there is no suction sound, check the vacuum lines and vacuum supply. Check the blue line connected to the air shut-off valve. Disconnect the line at the air shut-off valve. If vacuum is not present, clean out the vacuum connection at the throttle valve housing.

3. If vacuum is present at the air shut-off valve, remove the valve. If the suction sound is still audible, replace the air shutoff valve. If no suction sound could be heard at the air shut-off valve, replace the aspirator valve.

1981–84

6-CYLINDER ENGINES

The emission control system is the same as 1980, with two exceptions. The air pump intake is connected to the clean side of the air cleaner. A rubber scoop inside the air cleaner facilitates air intake. The second change is that the fuel evaporation control purge system is controlled by a thermo valve and is effective only at temperatures above 122°F.

Color coding of the vacuum lines is as follows:

Device	Color of Line Originating at a Vacuum Source	Color of Line Terminating at a Vacuum Operated Device
Ignition advance	Red	
Ignition retard	Yellow	
Air injection	Blue	Blue/purple
Fuel evaporation thermo valve	Black	Black/purple

Lines originating at a vacuum source have only one color stripe; lines terminating at a vacuum operated device have 2 color stripes and purple is always the second color.

Testing the System

See "Testing the System" under 1980.

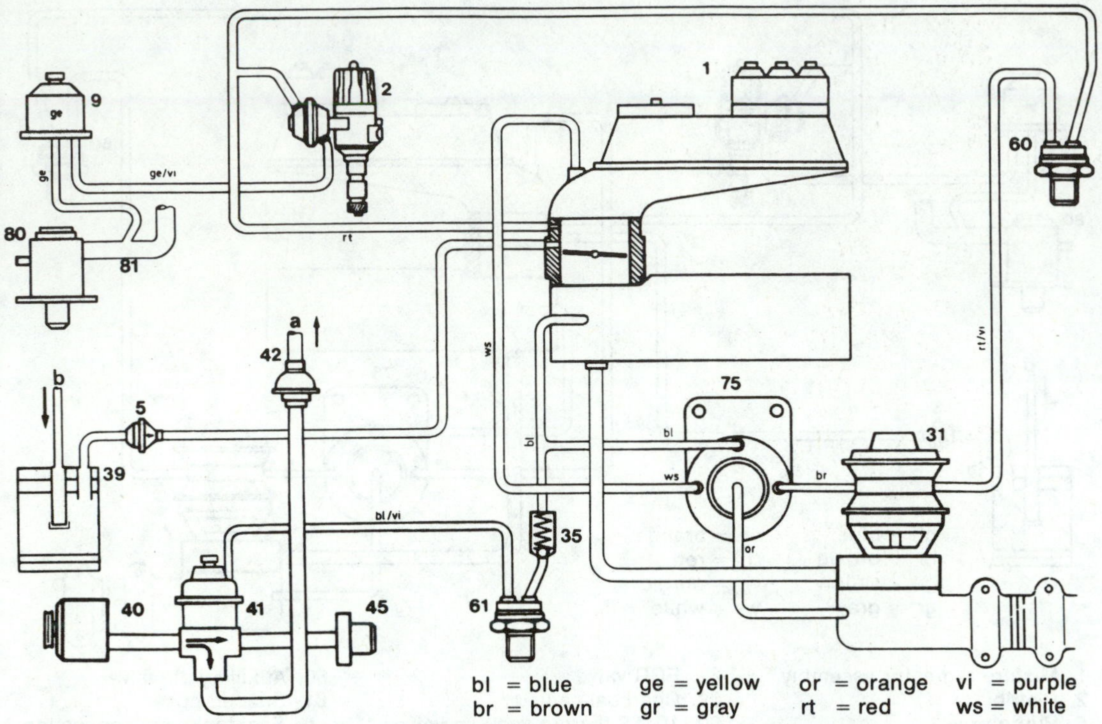

bl = blue ge = yellow or = orange vi = purple
br = brown gr = gray rt = red ws = white

1. Mixture regulator assembly
2. Distributor
5. Purge valve
9. Ignition switch-over valve
31. EGR valve
35. Vacuum check valve
39. Charcoal canister
40. Air pump
41. Diverter valve
42. Check valve
60. 104° F thermo-vacuum valve
61. 62° F thermo-vacuum valve
75. Exhaust pressure transducer
80. Auxiliary valve
81. Shaped hose
a. Air injection line to cylinder head
b. Fuel tank vent connection

1978–79 V8 Federal emission control schematic component. Location same as 1977

V8 ENGINES

Color coding of the vacuum lines is identical to the 6-cylinder engines. Operation of the Lambda oxygen sensor control system is the same as 1980. Only the oxygen sensor itself has been modified for production reasons. All models in 1983 are equipped with a standardized O_2 sensor, with a new plug connection. The plug is no longer below the vehicle, but inside the passenger compartment, accessible after removing the control unit cover plate. The air pump is a maintenance-free vane type pump, similar in operation to the 1980 system. Three-way-catalysts have been slightly modified dimensionally, but operate the same as those in 1980. The fuel evaporation control system is the same as 1980, except that the purge system is controlled by a thermo valve that allows purge only at coolant temperatures below approximately 122°F.

Testing the System

See "Testing the System" under 1980.

ELECTRONIC IDLE SPEED CONTROL

1981–82

1. The engine should be at operating temperature with the ignition ON.
2. Pull the plug from the idle speed adjuster and check the voltage. If 12 volts are present, go to Step 4.
3. If there is no voltage, pull the plug from the control unit and check the voltage between terminals 2 and 4 (arrows). There should be approximately 12 volts. If there is no voltage, check the voltage supply and replace any defective parts. If 12 volts are present, check the wires from the plug of the idle speed adjuster and the control unit plug (black/yellow wire to terminal 5 of the control unit and the black wire to terminal 1 of the control unit). If there are infinite ohms, replace the wire. If there are 0 ohms, connect the coupling to the control unit and measure the voltage at the idle speed adjuster. If there are 0 volts, replace the control unit.
4. Check the control unit. With the engine

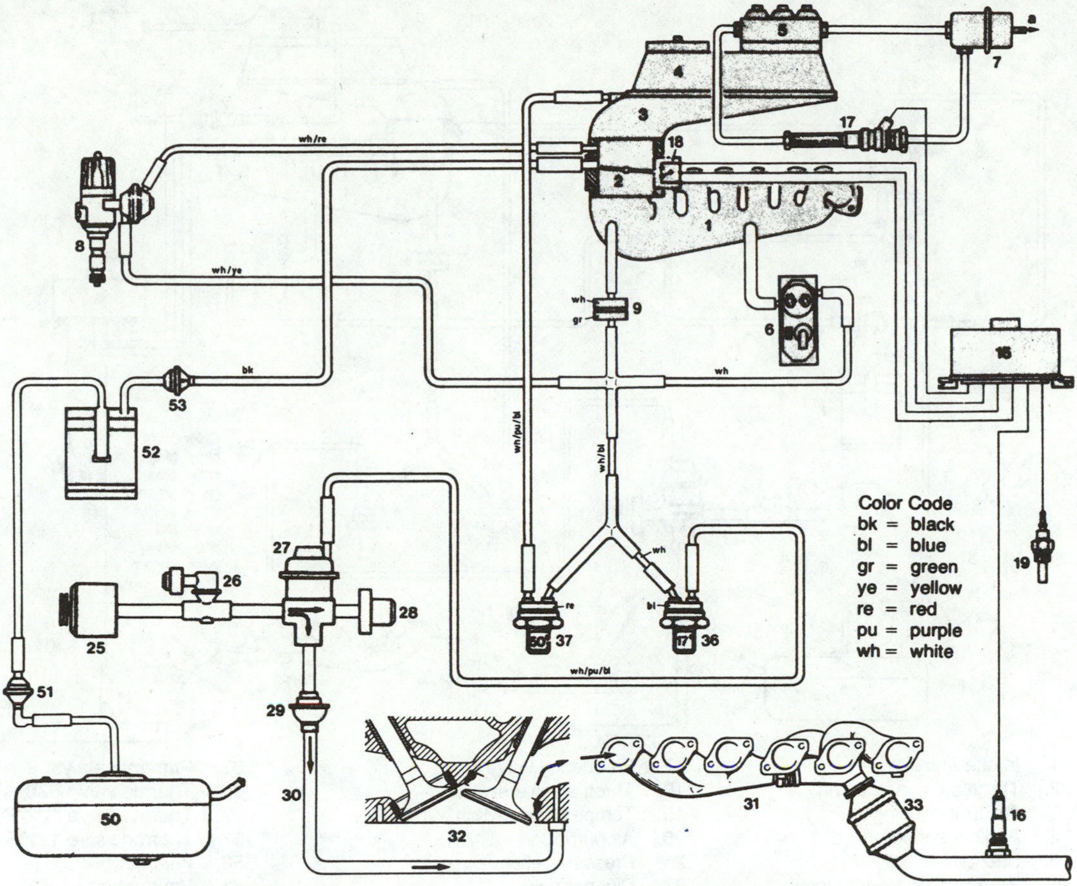

1. Intake manifold
2. Throttle valve housing
3. Air duct housing
4. Air flow sensor
5. Fuel distributor
6. Warm-up enrichment compensator
7. Pressure damper
8. Ignition distributor
9. Restricting orifice
15. Electronic control unit
16. Oxygen sensor
17. Frequency valve
18. Throttle valve switch
19. Temperature switch, oil 60°F
25. Air pump
26. Pressure relief valve
27. Diverter valve
28. Muffler (air filter)
29. Check valve
30. Air injection line
31. Exhaust manifold
32. Cylinder head
33. Primary catalyst
36. Thermo-vacuum valve 63°F
37. Thermo-vacuum valve 122°F
50. Fuel tank
51. Vent valve
52. Charcoal canister
53. Purge valve
a. Leak-off connection

Emission control schematic—1980 6 cylinder engines

idling at operating temperature, connect the plug to the idle speed adjuster so that you can check voltage at the plug. If there are 4–6 volts, go to Step 5. If there are no volts, replace the control unit.

5. Check the idle speed adjuster. Idle the engine and pull the plug from the coolant temperature switch. Bridge the terminals. The idle speed should increase. If not, apply battery voltage to the idle speed adjuster (for no more than 5 seconds). If the speed drops or the engine stops, replace the control unit. If the idle speed does not drop, replace the idle speed adjuster.

1983–84

The electronic idle speed control system has been slightly modified. A new control unit on V-8's, processes the following inputs:

- Engine speed (rpm)
- Idle and partial load
- Engine oil temperature
- Transmission shift lever position
- Engagement of A/C compressor

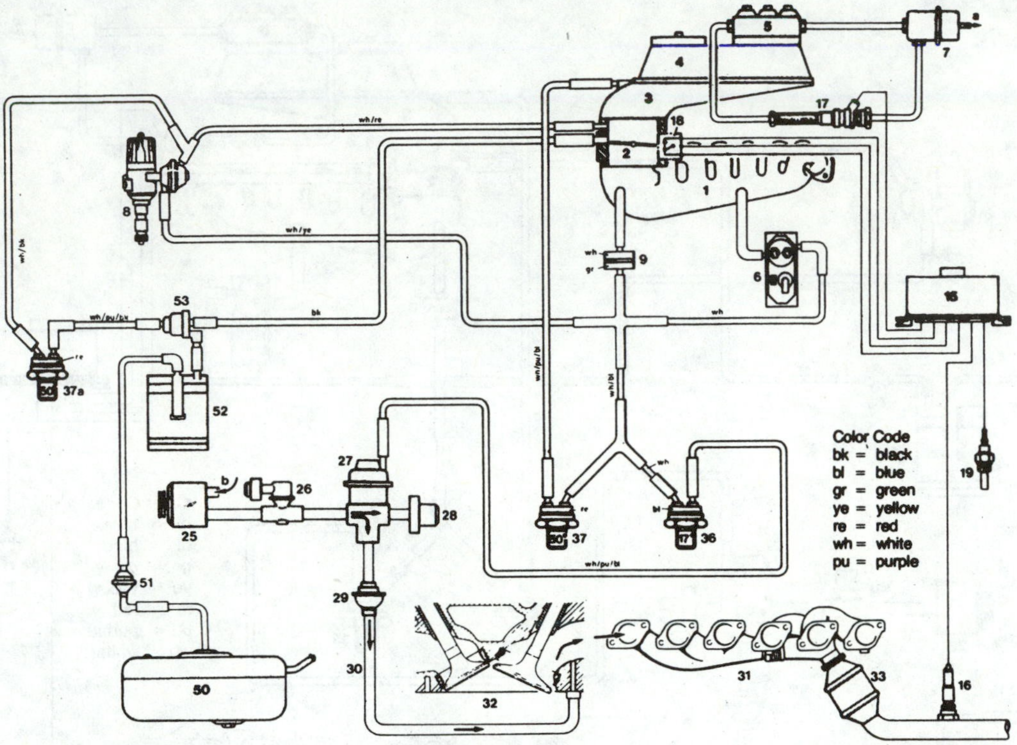

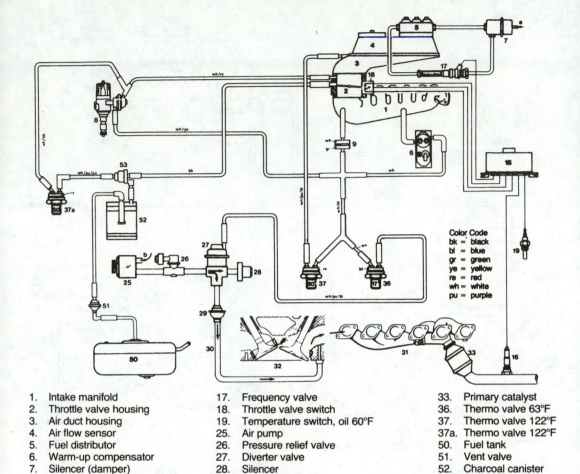

1.	Intake manifold	17.	Frequency valve	33.	Primary catalyst
2.	Throttle valve housing	18.	Throttle valve switch	36.	Thermo valve 63°F
3.	Air duct housing	19.	Temperature switch, oil 60°F	37.	Thermo valve 122°F
4.	Air flow sensor	25.	Air pump	37a.	Thermo valve 122°F
5.	Fuel distributor	26.	Pressure relief valve	50.	Fuel tank
6.	Warm-up compensator	27.	Diverter valve	51.	Vent valve
7.	Silencer (damper)	28.	Silencer	52.	Charcoal canister
8.	Ignition distributor	29.	Check valve	53.	Purge valve
9.	Orifice	30.	Air injection line		
15.	Control unit	31.	Exhaust manifold		a. Leak-off condition
16.	Oxygen sensor	32.	Cylinder head		b. from the air cleaner

Emission control schematic—1981 6 cylinder engines

The signal for engine rpm is controlled by the oil temperature switch, which also sends a signal to the Lambda system control unit at the same time.

The A/C compressor has a time delay relay in place of the relay used in '82. Through the relay, voltage is supplied to the idle speed control unit prior to engagement of the compressor clutch. The idle speed solenoid will already be maintaining sufficient rpm when the clutch is engaged.

When the automatic transmission shift lever is in P or N, the starter lockout is closed and the solenoid is ground. When the shift lever is in a driving position, the starter lockout switch is open and the idle speed is lowered.

This new version of the electronic control unit cannot be used on older model vehicles.

Troubleshooting

ENGINE STALLS OR WILL NOT START

1. Turn the ignition on and off. The idle speed control valve switch on and off noticeably (audibly).

2. If not, remove the valve and see if the aperture is open. If not, follow the Idle Speed Control Test.

ENGINE SURGES OR SHAKES AT IDLE

1. Perform the Idle Speed Control Test.

IDLE SPEED TOO HIGH OR LOW, ENGINE STALLS

1. Disconnect the plug from the idle speed control valve and reconnect it.

2. The idle speed should increase to about 1500 rpm.

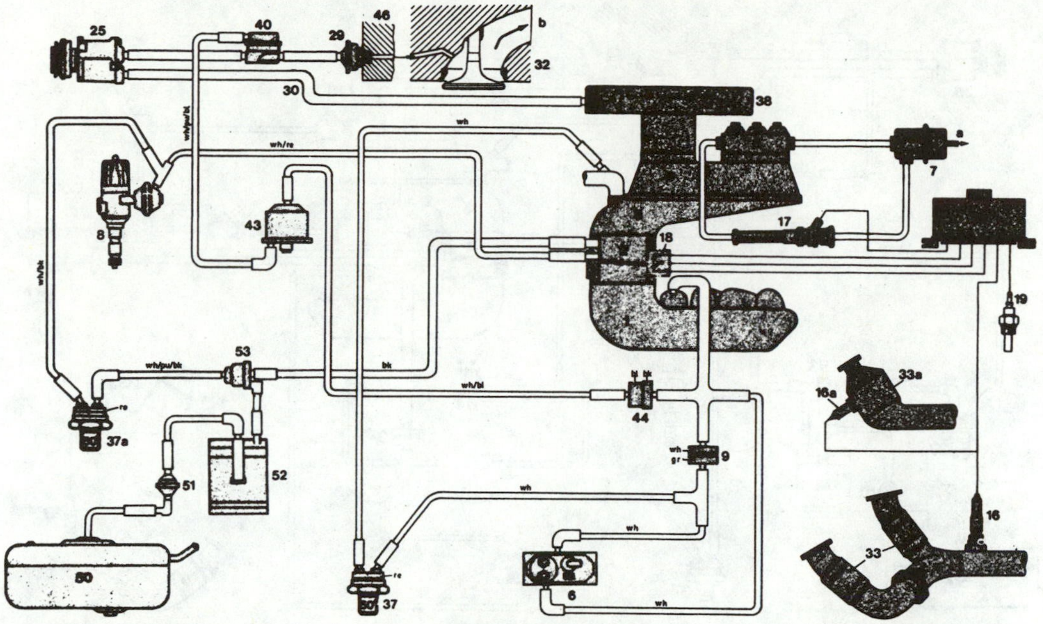

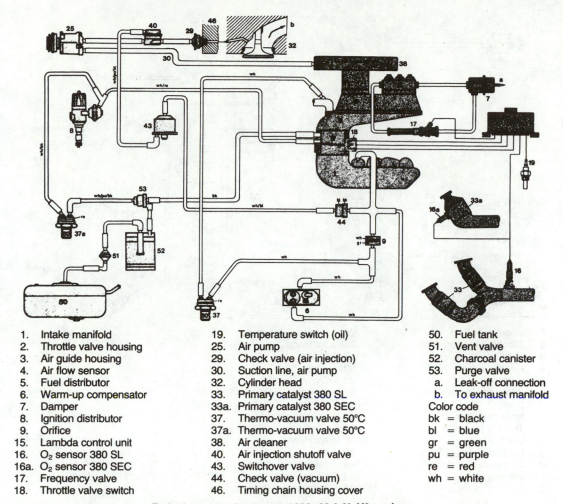

1. Intake manifold
2. Throttle valve housing
3. Air guide housing
4. Air flow sensor
5. Fuel distributor
6. Warm-up compensator
7. Damper
8. Ignition distributor
9. Orifice
15. Lambda control unit
16. O_2 sensor 380 SL
16a. O_2 sensor 380 SEC
17. Frequency valve
18. Throttle valve switch
19. Temperature switch (oil)
25. Air pump
29. Check valve (air injection)
30. Suction line, air pump
32. Cylinder head
33. Primary catalyst 380 SL
33a. Primary catalyst 380 SEC
37. Thermo-vacuum valve 50°C
37a. Thermo-vacuum valve 50°C
38. Air cleaner
40. Air injection shutoff valve
43. Switchover valve
44. Check valve (vacuum)
46. Timing chain housing cover
50. Fuel tank
51. Vent valve
52. Charcoal canister
53. Purge valve
a. Leak-off connection
b. To exhaust manifold

Color code
bk = black
bl = blue
gr = green
pu = purple
re = red
wh = white

Emission control system—1982–83 3.8L V8 engines

3. If no change in idle speed occurs, replace the control valve.

4. Put the transmission in a driving gear. The idle speed should drop to about 500 rpm. If not, perform the Idle Speed Control Test.

IDLE SPEED TO HIGH, ENGINE AT NORMAL TEMPERATURE

1. Disconnect the plug from the temperature switch.

2. If the engine rpm drops with the automatic transmission in P or N, replace the temperature switch. If the engine rpm does not drop, perform the Idle Speed Control Test.

Idle Speed Control Test

CHECK VOLTAGE TO CONTROL VALVE

1. Turn the ignition on and off.

2. The idle speed control valve should switch on and off audibly.

3. If it does not, turn the ignition on and disconnect the plug at the idle speed control valve and see if voltage is present. If it is, replace the valve.

4. If no voltage is present, disconnect the plug on the control unit and check battery voltage between pins 2 (positive) and 4 (negative). If no voltage is present, check the power supply according to the wiring diagram.

5. If there is voltage at pins 2 and 4, bridge pins 1 and 2 and 4 and 5 simultaneously for a maximum of 5 seconds. The idle speed valve should switch audibly.

6. If the valve switches, replace the control unit.

7. If the valve does not switch, check the black and the black/yellow wires to the idle speed valve for continuity and repair if necessary.

CHECK IDLE AND PART LOAD

A special M-B test cable is necessary for this test. The engine should be running at idle (with accessories turned off) at normal operating

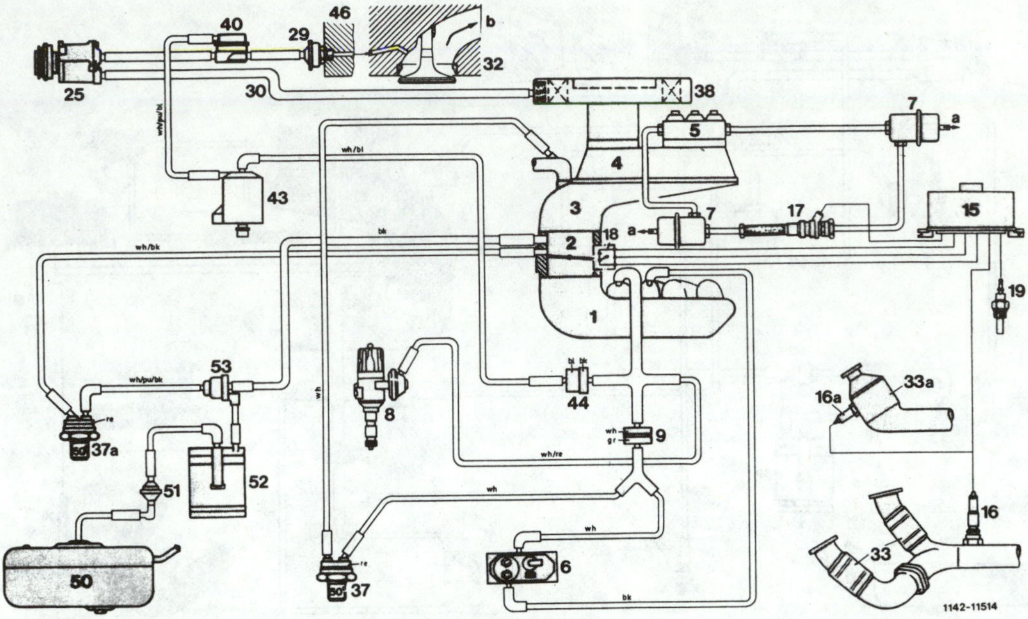

1. Intake manifold
2. Throttle valve housing
3. Air guide housing
4. Air flow sensor
5. Fuel distributor
6. Warm-up compensator
7. Damper
8. Ignition distributor
9. Throttle (orifice)
15. Control unit
16. O_2-sensor (model 107)
16a. O_2-sensor (model 126)
17. Frequency valve
18. Throttle valve switch
29. Temperature switch 16°C, oil
25. Air pump
29. Check valve (Air injection)
30. Intake line
32. Cylinder head
33. Primary catalyst (model 107)
33a. Primary catalyst (model 126)
37. Thermovalve 50°C
37a. Thermovalve 50°C
38. Air cleaner
40. Air shutoff valve
43. Switchover valve
44. Check valve (vacuum)
46. Timing housing cover
50. Fuel tank
51. Vent valve unit
53. Purge valve

a. Leak connection
b. To exhaust manifold

bk = black
bl = blue
gr = green
pu = purple
re = red
wh = white

Emission control system—1984 V8 engines

19. Temperature switch, 16 °C oil
21. Control unit, electronic idle speed control
23. Idle speed adjuster

a To terminal (a), automatic climate control
b To ignition/starter switch, terminal 50
c To lambda control unit, terminal 6
d To lambda control unit, terminal 7
e To relay, Lambda control with excess voltage protection
f To coolant temperature switch 42 °C

Wire color code
bl = blue
br = brown
ge = yellow
gn = green
gr = grey
rt = red
sw = black
vi = purple
ws = white

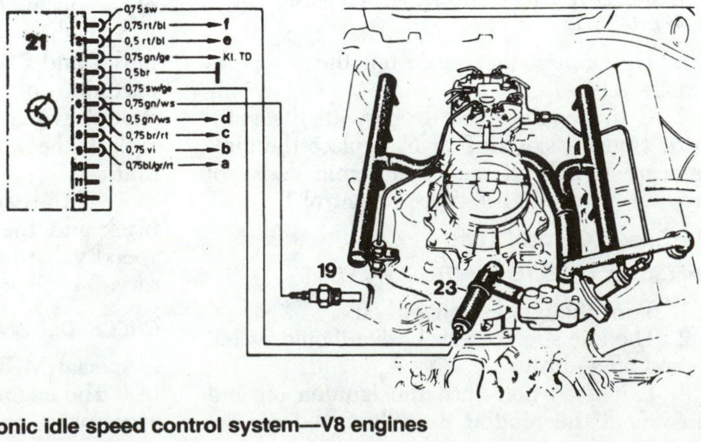

Electronic idle speed control system—V8 engines

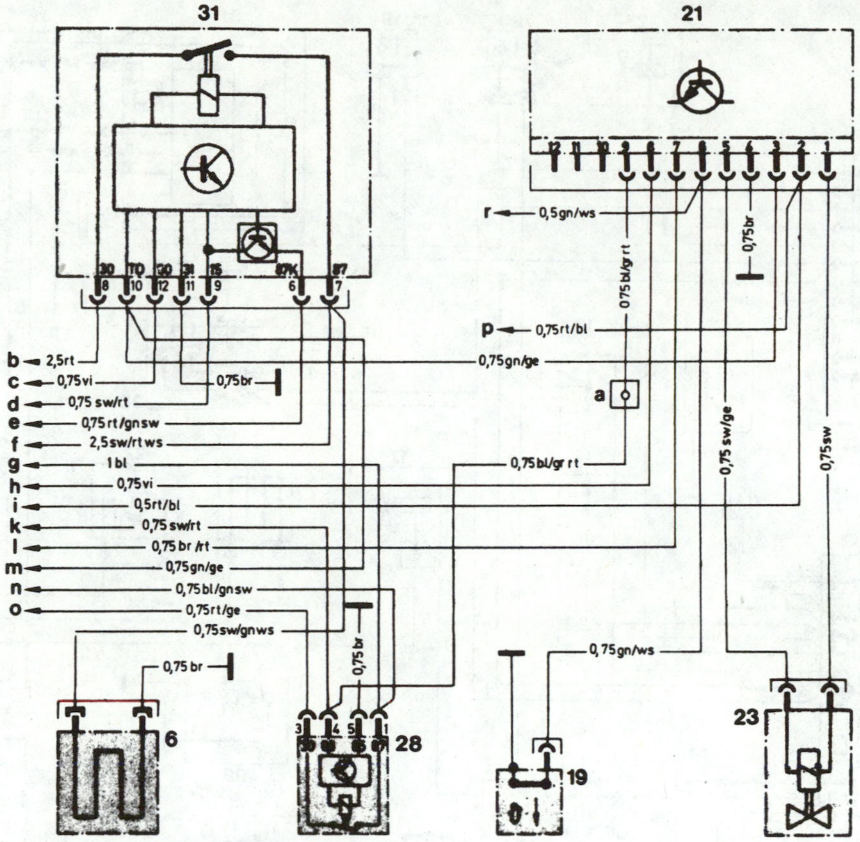

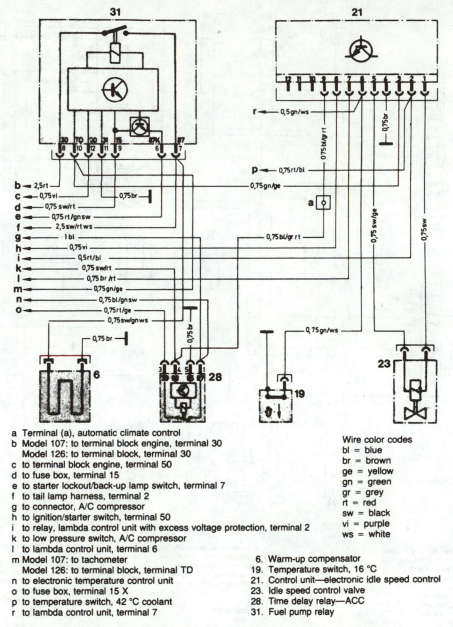

a Terminal (a), automatic climate control
b Model 107: to terminal block engine, terminal 30
  Model 126: to terminal block, terminal 30
c to terminal block engine, terminal 50
d to fuse box, terminal 15
e to starter lockout/back-up lamp switch, terminal 7
f to tail lamp harness, terminal 2
g to connector, A/C compressor
h to ignition/starter switch, terminal 50
i to relay, lambda control unit with excess voltage protection, terminal 2
k to low pressure switch, A/C compressor
l to lambda control unit, terminal 6
m Model 107: to tachometer
  Model 126: to terminal block, terminal TD
n to electronic temperature control unit
o to fuse box, terminal 15 X
p to temperature switch, 42 °C coolant
r to lambda control unit, terminal 7

Wire color codes
bl = blue
br = brown
ge = yellow
gn = green
gr = grey
rt = red
sw = black
vi = purple
ws = white

6. Warm-up compensator
19. Temperature switch, 16 °C
21. Control unit—electronic idle speed control
23. Idle speed control valve
28. Time delay relay—ACC
31. Fuel pump relay

Electronic idle speed control system wiring diagram—V8 engines

temperature. The transmission should be in P or N. Connect a multimeter to a test cable and connect the test cable between the idle speed valve and the wiring harness.

1. The reading on the meter should be above 400 mA at about 650 rpm.

2. If the reading fluctuates and the engine surges, replace the idle speed valve or the control unit.

3. If the reading is 0 mA, perform the Idle Speed Control Test.

4. Disconnect the throttle valve switch connector and check the idle speed. The idle speed should increase to about 850 rpm.

5. If the idle speed does not increase, turn off the engine and disconnect the plug from the control unit. Set the multimeter on the 0 to infinite ohms scale and connect it to bushings 4 and 7. With the throttle valve against the stop, the meter should read 0 ohms. With the throttle valve slightly opened the meter should read infinite ohms. If the readings are not present,

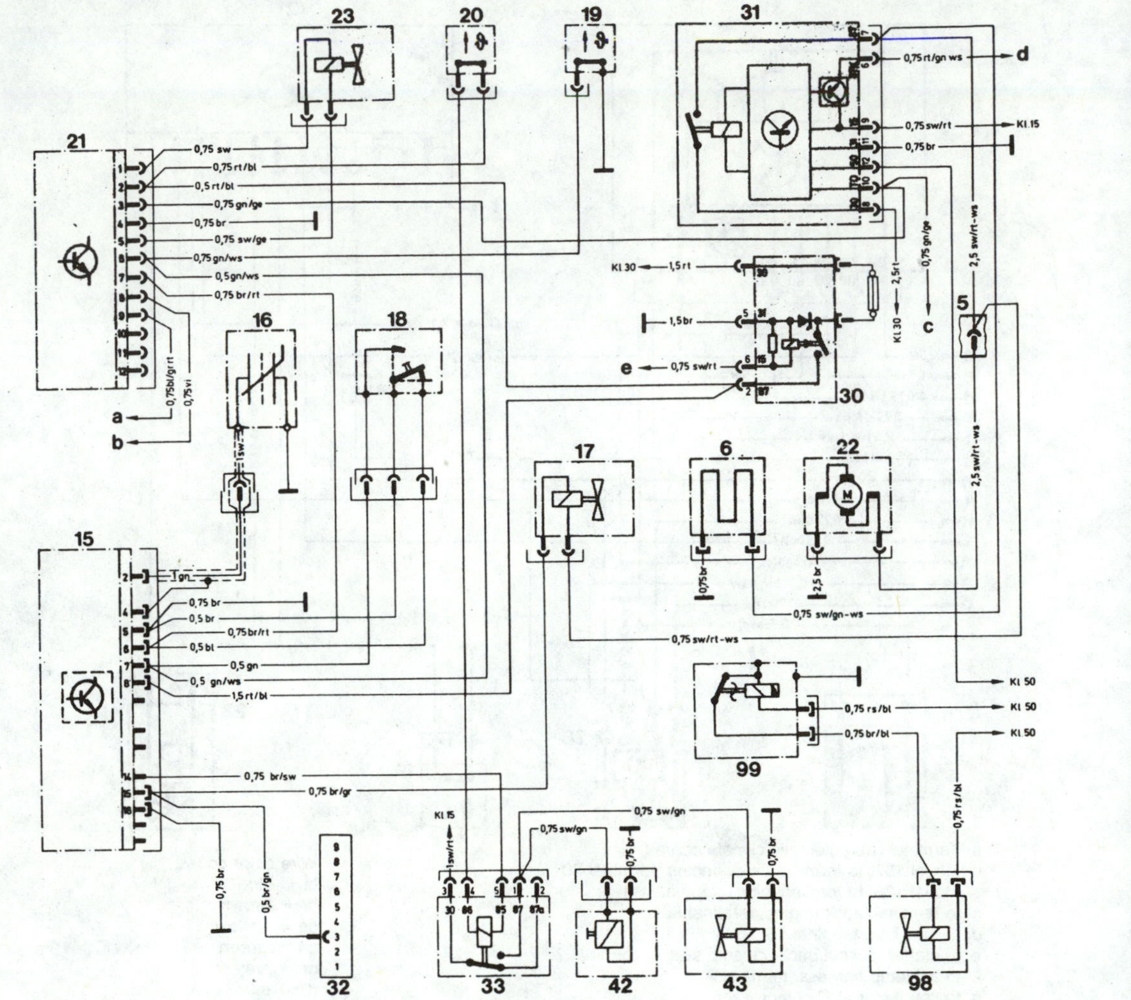

5. Connector, tail lamp harness
6. Warm-up compensator
15. Lambda control unit
16. Oxygen sensor
17. Frequency valve
18. Throttle valve switch
19. Temperature switch, 16 °C oil
20. Temperature switch, 42 °C coolant
21. Electronic idle speed control unit
22. Fuel pump
23. Idle speed control valve
30. Relay, lambda control with excess voltage protection
31. Relay, fuel pump
32. Diagnostic plug
33. Relay, air injection
42. Solenoid clutch, air pump
43. Switch-over valve, air injection
98. Cold start valve
99. Thermo time switch

a to terminal (a), automatic climate control
b to ignition/starter switch, terminal 50
c to terminal block, terminal TD
d to starter lockout/back-up light switch, terminal 7
e 380SL: to fuse Nr. 5, terminal 15
380SEL, SEC: to fuse Nr. 14, terminal 15

Wire color code
bl = blue
br = brown
ge = yellow
gn = green
gr = grey
rs = pink
rt = red
sw = black
vi = purple
ws = white

2. Frame—transverse member
5. Suspension strut
5c. Upper rubber mount
5d. Lower rubber mount
5g. Hex. bolt
5h. Spring washer
5q. Stud
B3. Pressure line (pressure hose), pressure reservoir—suspension strut

Lambda control, air injection and electronic idle speed control wiring diagram

Time delay relay—380SEC and 380SEL

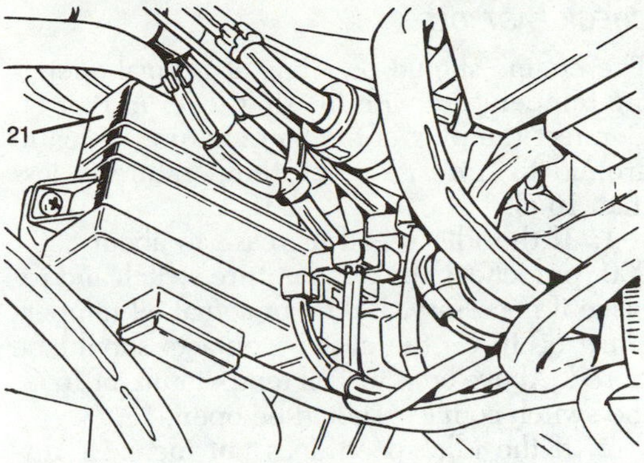

Control unit on the 380SL is under a cover on the right side of the passenger compartment

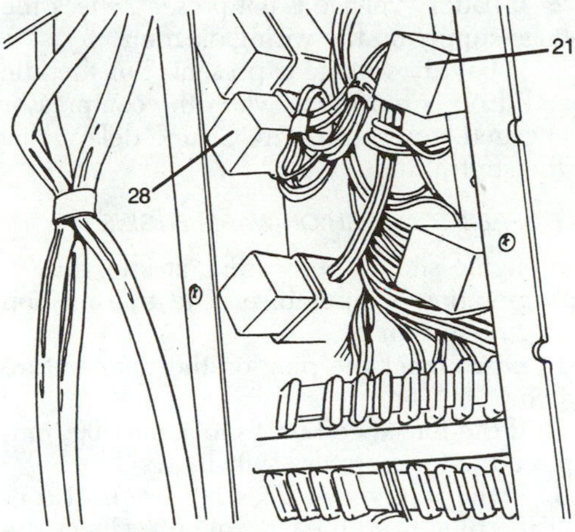

Time delay relay—380SL

Control unit location on the 380SEC and 380SEL

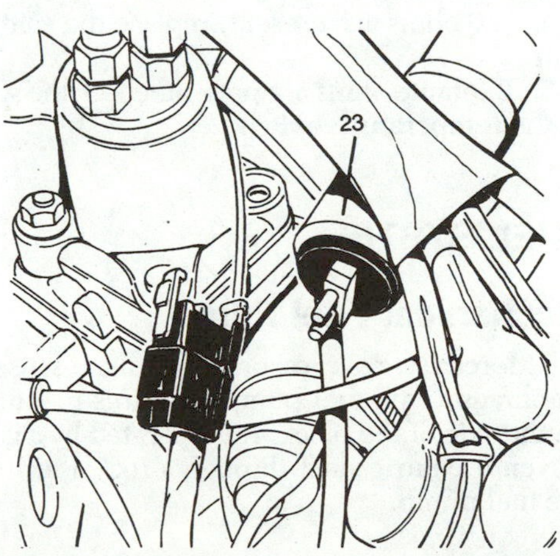

Disconnect the wiring harness (arrow) from the idle control solenoid (23)

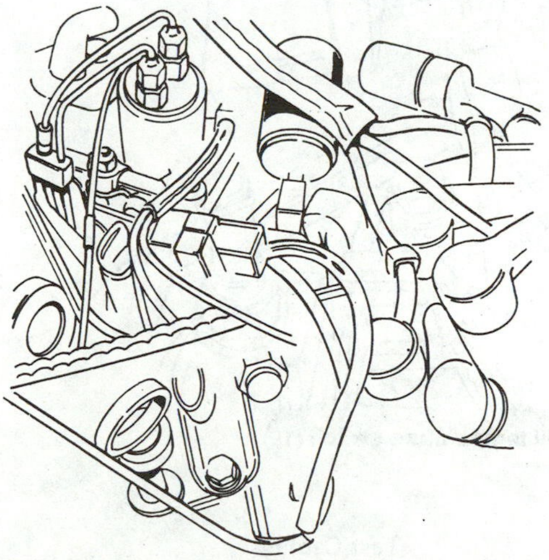

Disconnect the control unit

adjust the throttle valve switch, or if necessary replace it. Check the wires to the throttle valve switch.

6. Reconnect the plug to the control unit. Start the engine.

7. The idle speed should increase to approximately 850 rpm.

8. If not, replace the control unit.

CHECK FAST IDLE

The engine should be idling at normal operating temperature with the shift lever in P or N. Connect the plug of the temperature switch to ground to simulate an oil temperature of less than 16°C.

1. If the idle speed increase to about 800–900 rpm, check the temperature switch and replace if necessary. Below an actual oil temperature of 16°C, the switch contacts should be closed. Above an actual oil temperature of 16°C, the switch contacts should be open.
2. If the idle speed does not increase, disconnect the plug from the control unit and check the wire from pin #6 to the temperature switch for continuity. If 0 ohms are present, replace the control unit. If infinite ohms are present, check the wire to the temperature switch.

CHECK IDLE SPEED WITH AND WITHOUT THE TRANSMISSION ENGAGED

The engine should be running at idle, at normal operating temperature, and the wheels blocked.

1. Put the car in gear. The idle speed should drop to about 500 rpm.
2. If the idle speed does not drop, disconnect the plug from the control unit. Turn the engine off, then on.
3. Connect a voltmeter between pins 8 and (negative) and 2 (positive). Battery voltage should be present with the transmission in P or N.
4. If battery voltage is present, replace the control unit. If battery voltage is not present, and no voltage is present at pin #2, check the wiring according to the wiring diagram.
5. If no ground is made at pin #8, check the writing to the starter lockout/back-up light switch.

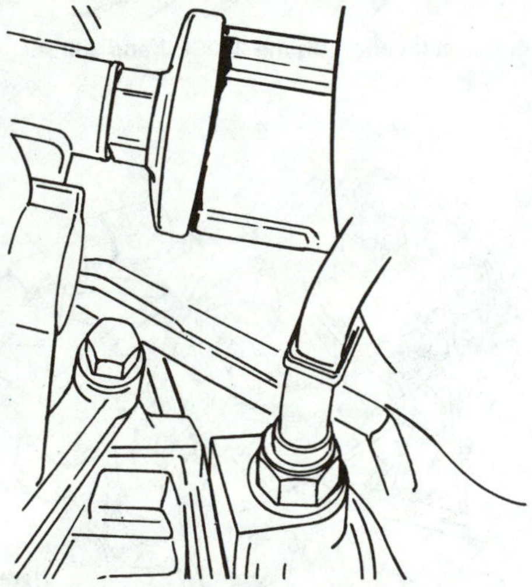

Oil temperature switch (19)

CHECK IDLE SPEED WHEN A/C COMPRESSOR IS ENGAGED

1. Turn the ignition on and engage the A/C compressor. Disconnect the plug from the control unit. Battery voltage should be present at pin #9.
2. If battery voltage is not present, check the voltage supply on the wiring diagram.
3. If battery voltage is present, but the idle speed drop is too much when the compressor is engaged, replace the ACC time delay relay or the control unit.

IDLE SPEED TOO HIGH ON WARM ENGINE

The engine should be running at idle, at normal operating temperature. The transmission should be in P or N.

1. Disconnect the plug on the temperature switch.
2. If the idle speed drops to about 500 rpm, replace the temperature switch.
3. If the idle speed does not drop, disconnect the plug from the control unit. Check the wire from pin #6 to the temperature switch for continuity.
4. If 0 ohms are present, replace the control unit.
5. If infinite ohms are present, check the wire to the temperature switch.

FUEL SYSTEM

Mechanical Fuel Pump

All Mercedes-Benz carbureted engines use a diaphragm type fuel pump, which is mounted on the side of the block. It is operated by a gear driven eccentric shaft through a rocker arm on the fuel pump.

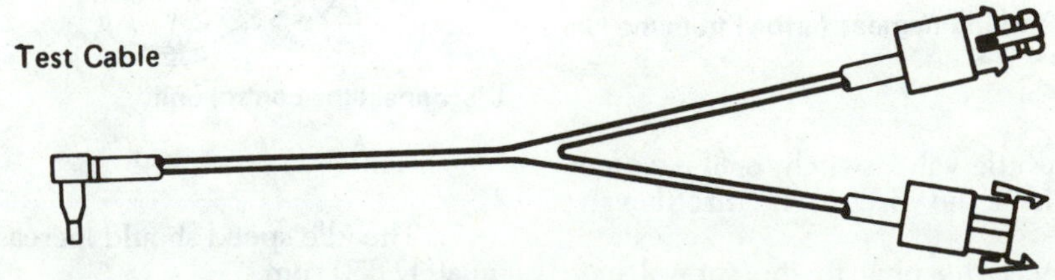

Test cable for testing electronic idle control

REMOVAL AND INSTALLATION

1. Clean the joint around the fuel pump base and cylinder block.
2. One at a time, remove and plug the intake and outlet lines from the fuel pump.
3. Unbolt the retaining bolts and remove the fuel pump and gasket from the cylinder block.
4. Clean the mating surfaces of the engine and cylinder block.
5. Install a new gasket.
6. Insert the fuel pump into the block and install the retaining bolts. Be sure that the bolts are tightened evenly.
7. Reconnect the intake and outlet lines to the fuel pump.
8. Run the engine and check for leaks.

TESTING DELIVERY PRESSURE

1. Remove the wire from the coil to prevent starting.
2. Connect a pressure gauge into the output line of the fuel pump.
3. Crank the engine and read the delivery pressure on the pressure gauge. The pressure should be a constant 1.5–2.5 psi.
4. If the pressure is not within specifications or is erratic, remove the pump for service or for replacement with a new or rebuilt unit. No adjustment is provided.

Electric Fuel Pump

NOTE: *Do not confuse the electric fuel pump with the injection pump.*

All Mercedes-Benz fuel injected engines are equipped with electric fuel pumps. The electric fuel pump is located underneath the rear floor panel. The fuel return line was also eliminated and a check ball installed in its place.

Two types of fuel pumps have been used. One, the large pump, has been replaced with a new small design which has a bypass system to prevent vapor lock.

REMOVAL AND INSTALLATION

1. Jack the left rear of the car and support it on jackstands. This will provide sufficient working clearance.
2. Remove and plug the intake, outlet, and bypass lines from the pump.
3. Disconnect the electrical leads.
4. Unbolt and remove the fuel pump and vibration pads.
5. Install the fuel pump in the reverse order of removal. Be sure that the electrical leads are connected to the proper terminals. The negative wire (brown) is connected to the negative terminal (brown plastic plate) and the positive wire (black/red) is connected to the positive terminal (red plastic plate). If the terminals are reversed, the pump will operate in the reverse direction of normal rotation and will deliver no fuel.

TESTING FUEL PUMP PRESSURE

1974–75

Temporarily reduce the pressure in the ring line by unplugging the connection at the starting valve. Connect the terminals of the starting valve to the battery for approximately 20 seconds. Reconnect the starting valve.

1. Remove the air filter and connect a pressure gauge at the branch connection at the ring line.
2. Run the engine and measure the pressure. It should be 26.5–29.5 psi.
3. Stop the engine. The fuel pressure may drop to 21 psi, after approximately 5 minutes. If the fuel pressure drops uniformly to 0, check the following points for leaks.

Starting valve—Switch on ignition and disconnect hose at starting valve. If there is no drop in pressure, the valve leaks.

Pressure regulator—Switch on the ignition and disconnect the fuel return hose, as soon as the fuel pump stops. If there is no drop in pressure, the regulator leaks.

Ball valve in delivery connection of fuel pump—Switch on the ignition and disconnect the fuel hose in front of the ring line the moment the fuel pump stops. If there is no drop in pressure, replace the fuel pump.

Injection Valves—remove the kick panel and bridge terminals 1 and 3 of the relay shown.This will energize the fuel pump with the engine stopped, and ignition ON. Check the valves for leaks.

4. Before removing the gauge, reduce the pressure in the ring line.

The fuel pressure can be adjusted on the regulator with the adjusting screw. Adjust to

Testing fuel pump pressures—1976 and later

28 psi. If a slight turn of the screw shows no change of pressure replace the regulator.

1976 and Later

Remove the fuel return hose from the fuel distributor. Connect a fuel line and hold the end in a measuring cup. Disconnect the plug from the safety switch on the mixture regulator and turn on the ignition for 30 seconds. If the delivery rate is less than 1 liter in 30 seconds, check the voltage at the fuel pump (11.5) and the fuel lines for kinks.

Disconnect the leak off line between the fuel accumulator and the suction damper. Check the delivery rate again. If it is low replace the accumulator.

Replace the fuel filter and test again. If still low, replace the fuel fump.

Carburetors

REMOVAL AND INSTALLATION

Stromberg 175CDT 1974–78

1. Remove the air cleaner.
2. Remove and plug the fuel lines.
CAUTION: *Do not pull off the fuel lines. They should be pried off along with the securing discs.*
3. Disconnect the control linkage.
4. Remove the vacuum lines.
5. Disconnect the water hoses for the automatic choke.
6. Disconnect the leads for the automatic choke and fuel shut-off valve.
7. Remove the carburetor retaining nuts and remove the carburetor.
8. Installation is the reverse of removal. Adjust the carburetor. See "Tune-Up Specifications."

Carburetor Applications

Model	Year	Carburetor
230	1974–78	1 Stromberg 175 CDT
280	1974–76	1 Solex 4A1
280C	1974–76	
280S	1975–76	

Solex 4 A 1 (280, 280C and 280S)

1. Remove the air filter.
2. Remove the electric cable from the starter cover and cut-off valves.
3. Remove the vacuum lines.
4. To prevent corrosion from leaked coolant, cover the starter housing with a rag. Release the pressure in the cooling system by cracking the radiator cap until pressure has escaped. Install and tighten the radiator cap. Remove and plug the coolant water hoses from the carburetor.

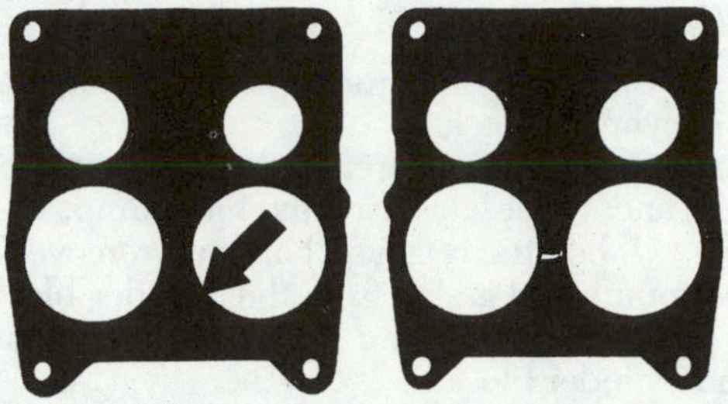

New style gasket on Solex 4A1 beginning 1974. The top is shown on the left and the bottom on the right

5. Remove and plug the fuel lines.
6. Remove the retaining nuts and remove the carburetor from the manifold.
7. Installation is the reverse of removal. Install the insulating flange on the intake manifold as shown. The paper side of the insulating flange must face UP. In 1974, a new style insulating flange was used, which can be installed on previous engines.
8. Install the retaining nuts and tighten evenly, torquing the nuts in a crossing pattern. Torque the nuts to 7–11 ft. lbs.
9. Be sure to adjust the idle speed. See "Tune-Up Specifications."

OVERHAUL

All Models

Efficient carburetion depends greatly on careful cleaning and inspection during overhaul. Since dirt, gum, water, or varnish in or on the carburetor parts are often responsible for poor performance.

Overhaul your carburetor in a clean, dust-free area. Carefully disassemble the carburetor, referring often to the exploded views. Keep all similar and lookalike parts segregated during disassembly and cleaning to avoid accidental interchange during assembly. Make a note of all jet sizes.

When the carburetor is assembled, wash all parts (except diaphragms, electric choke units, pump plunger, and any other plastic, leather, fiber, or rubber parts) in clean carburetor solvent. Do not leave parts in the solvent any longer than is necessary to sufficiently loosen the deposits. Excessive cleaning may remove the special finish from the float bowl and choke valve bodies, leaving these parts unfit for service. Rinse all parts in clean solvent and blow them dry with compressed air or allow them to air dry. Wipe clean all cork, plastic, leather, and fiber parts with a clean, lint-free cloth.

Blow out all passages and jets with com-

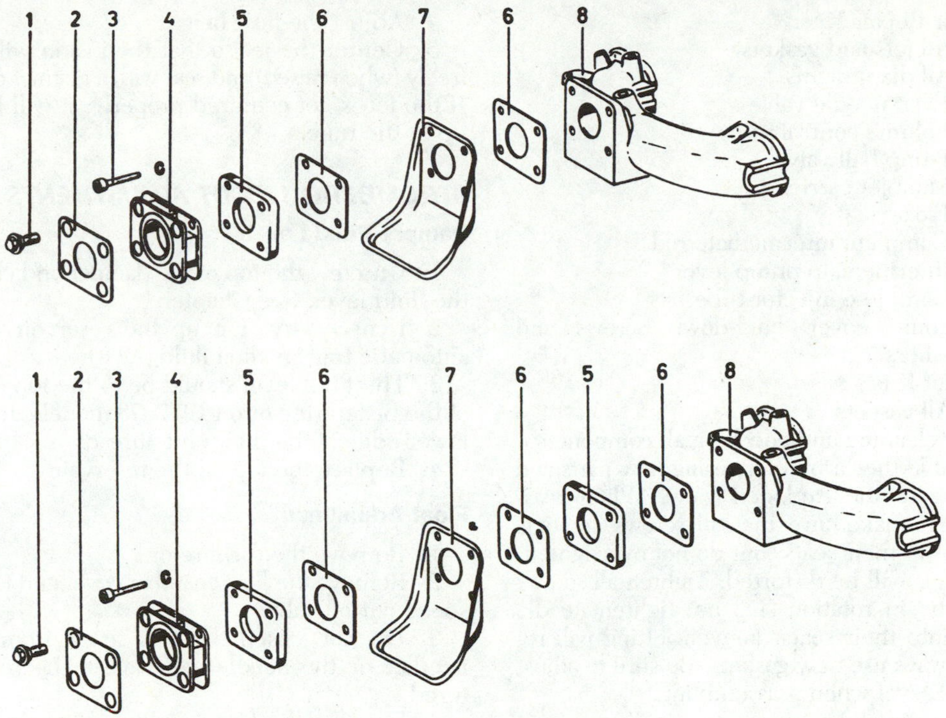

1. Carburetor attachment screw
2. Gasket
3. Rubber flange fastening screw
4. Rubber flange
5. Insulating flange
6. Gasket
7. Shielding plate
8. Intake pipe

Stromberg 175 CDT carburetor gaskets 1974 (top) and 1975 and later (bottom)

pressed air and be sure that there are no restrictions or blockages. Never use wire or similar tools to clean jets, fuel passages, or air bleeds. Clean all jets and valves separately to avoid accidental interchange.

Check all parts for wear or damage. If wear or damage is found, replace the defective parts. Especially check the following:

1. Check the float needle and seat for wear. If wear is found, replace the complete assembly.
2. Check the float hinge pin for wear and the float(s) for dents or distortion. Replace the float if fuel has leaked into it.
3. Check the throttle and choke shaft bores for wear or an out-of-round condition. Damage or wear to the throttle arm, shaft, or shaft bore will often require replacement of the throttle body. These parts require a close tolerance of fit; wear may allow air leakage, which could affect starting and idling.

NOTE: *Throttle shafts and bushings are not included in overhaul kits. They can be purchased separately.*

4. Inspect the idle mixture adjusting needles for burrs or grooves. Any such condition requires replacement of the needle, since you will not be able to obtain a satisfactory idle.
5. Test the accelerator pump check valves. They should pass air one way but not the other. Test for proper seating by blowing and sucking on the valve. Replace the valve if necessary. If the valve is satisfactory, wash the valve again to remove breath moisture.
6. Check the bowl cover for warped surfaces with a straightedge.
7. Closely inspect the valves and seats for wear and damage, replacing as necessary.
8. After the carburetor is assembled, check the choke valve for freedom of operation.

Carburetor overhaul kits are recommended for each overhaul. These kits contain all gaskets and new parts to replace those that deteriorate most rapidly. Failure to replace all parts supplied with the kit (especially gaskets) can result in poor performance later.

Some carburetor manufacturers supply overhaul kits of three basic types: minor repair; major repair; and gasket kits. Basically, they contain the following:

Minor Repair Kits:

- All gaskets
- Float needle valve
- Volume control screw
- All diaphragms
- Spring for the pump diaphragm

Major Repair Kits:
- All jets and gaskets
- All diaphragms
- Float needle valve
- Volume control screw
- Pump ball valve
- Main jet carrier
- Float
- Complete intermediate rod
- Intermediate pump lever
- Complete injector tube
- Some cover hold-down screws and washers

Gasket Kits:
- All gaskets

After cleaning and checking all components, reassemble the carburetor, using new parts and referring to the exploded view. When reassembling, make sure that all screws and jets are tight in their seats, but do not overtighten, as the tips will be distorted. Tighten all screws gradually, in rotation. Do not tighten needle valves into their seats; uneven jetting will result. Always use new gaskets. Be sure to adjust the float level when reassembling.

Stromberg 175CDT Carburetor Only

The preceding information applies to Stomberg carburetors also, but the following, additional suggestions should be followed.

1. Soak the small cork gaskets (jet gland washers) in penetrating oil or hot water for at least a half-hour prior to assembly, or they will invariably split.
2. When the jet is fully assembled, the jet tube should be a close fit without any lateral play, but it should be free to move smoothly. A few drops of oil or polishing of the tube may be necessary to achieve this.
3. If the jet sealing ring washer is made of cork, soak it in hot water for a minute or two prior to installation.
4. Adjust the float height.
5. Center the jet so that the piston will fall freely (when raised) and seat with a distinct click. If the jet is not centered properly, it will hang up in the tube.

STROMBERG 175CDT ADJUSTMENTS

Damper Fluid Level

1. Unscrew the top of the damper and check the fluid level. See Chapter 1.
2. If necessary, top up the reservoir with automatic transmission fluid (ATF).
3. The fluid level should be to the top edge of the piston ring or on 1977–78 models, to the lower edge of the filler plug threads.
4. Replace the top on the reservoir.

Float Adjustment

1. Remove the carburetor.
2. Remove the float chamber cover and idling speed cut-off valve.
3. Do not loosen the lock screw from the needle, or the needle will have to be recentered.
4. Remove the fuel nozzle and compensating element.
5. Push the float down until the float needle valve ball is fully pushed in.

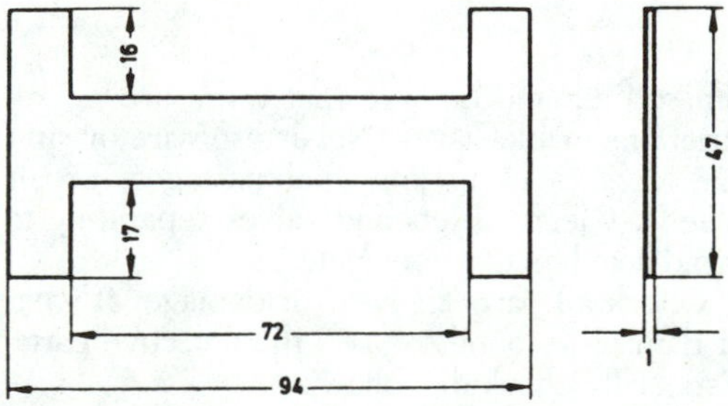

Home-made gauge for measuring Stromberg 175 CDT float level (dimensions in mm)

28. Diaphragm for fuel return valve
29. Spring plate
30. Compression spring
31. Valve cover
32. Vacuum hose
33. Countersunk head screw
34. Guide bushing for fuel nozzle (pressed-in)
35. Rubber sealing ring
36. Temperature-controlled compensating element with fuel nozzle
37. Compression spring
38. Idling speed shutoff valve
39. Float needle valve
40. Sealing ring
41. Bracket for float shaft
42. Snap ring
43. Screw
44. Float shaft
45. Float
46. Air piston
47. Screw
48. Vacuum diaphragm
49. Gasket for float chamber
50. Float chamber
51. Nozzle needle
52. Stud for attaching nozzle needle
53. Compression spring
54. Carburetor cover
55. Screw
56. Washer
57. Cheese head screw
58. Damper for air piston
59. Washer
60. Damper piston
61. Locking spring
62. Capillary pipe
63. Spring clip
64. Rubber sealing ring
65. Closing cover
66. Screw
67. Damper oil filler plug
68. Vacuum box with fastening elements
69. Vacuum hose
70. Screw
71. Snap-ring
72. Washer
73. Grounding cable
74. Rubber closing cap
75. Holding disc
76. Cheese head screw
77. Compression spring
78. Adjusting nut
79. Thrust bolt

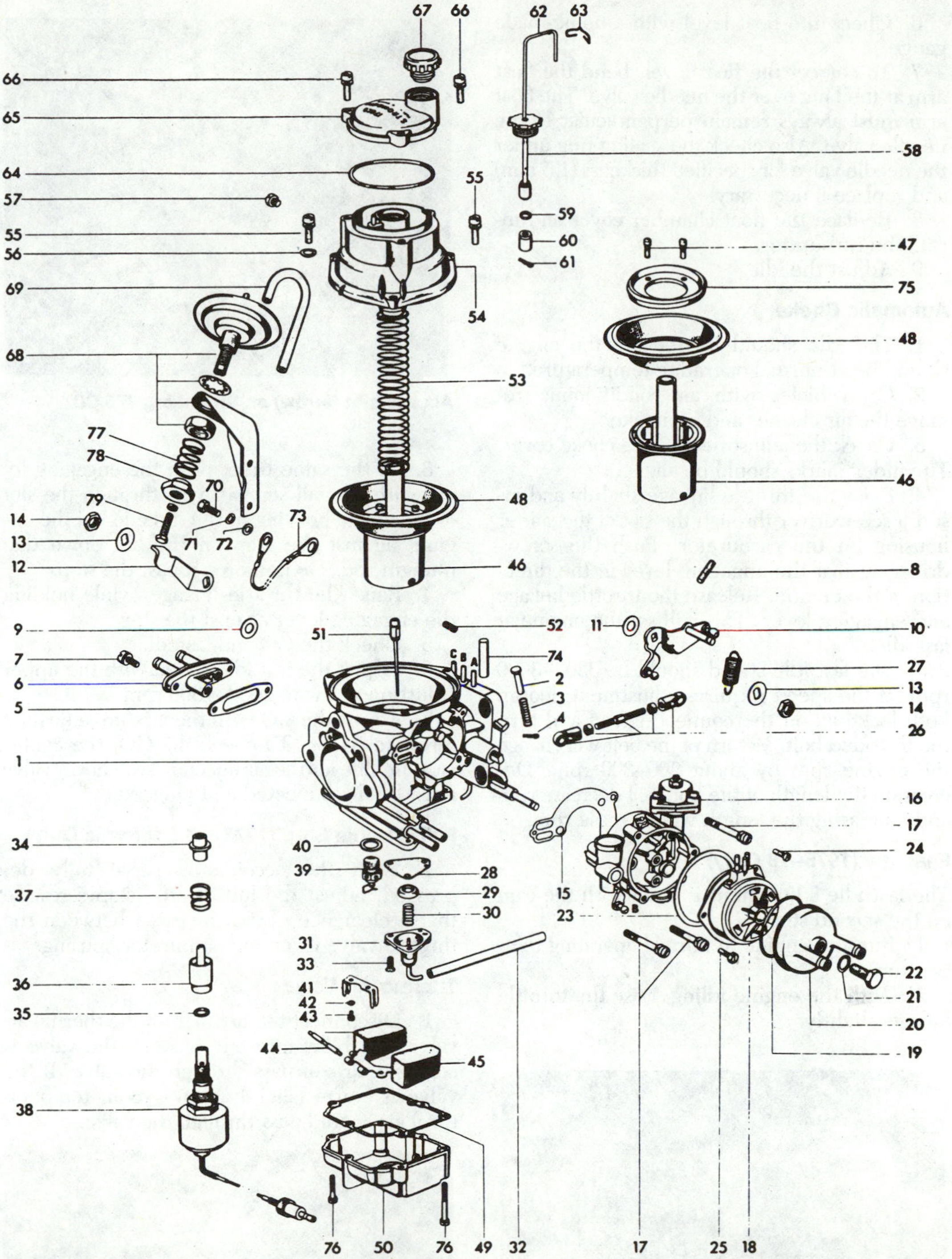

1. Carburetor housing
2. Tickler
3. Compression spring
4. Locking spring
5. Gasket
6. Water connection cover
7. Screw
8. Idling speed adjusting screw
9. Spring washer
10. Throttle valve lever
11. Spring washer
12. Actuating lever
13. Lockwasher
14. Nut
15. Gasket for starter housing
16. Starter housing
17. Screw
18. Starter cover
19. Rubber sealing ring
20. Water connection
21. Aluminum sealing ring
22. Screw
23. Insulating seal
24. Screw
25. Screw
26. Connecting rod (compl.)
27. Draw spring

Exploded view of Stromberg 175 CDT

6. Check the float level with a home-made gauge.
7. To correct the float level, bend the float arm at the tang over the needle valve. The float arm must always remain perpendicular to the needle valve. Also check the sealing ring under the needle valve for specified thickness (1.5 mm) and replace if necessary.
8. Replace the float chamber cover and install the carburetor.
9. Adjust the idle.

Automatic Choke

1. The idle should be set and the engine should be at normal operating temperature.
2. On vehicles with air conditioning, remove the air cleaner and air intake.
3. Check the adjustment of the choke cover. The index marks should be aligned.
4. Raise the throttle linkage slightly and insert a screwdriver through the slot of the starter housing on the carburetor. Push the screwdriver against the engaging lever in the direction of the engine. Release the throttle linkage and engaging lever. This will set the engine at fast idle.
5. The fast idle speed should be 3300–3600 rpm. If the speed requires adjustment, loosen both locknuts on the connecting rod and turn the threaded bolt. ½ turn of the bolt will change the engine rpm by about 200–300 rpm. Decreasing the length of the bolt will decrease rpm and increasing the length will increase rpm.

Fast Idle (1975–78 Only)

The fast idle adjustment is done with the cam on the second step.

1. Run the engine to normal operating temperature.
2. With the engine idling, raise the throttle linkage slightly.

8. Idle adjusting screw
114. Fast adjusting screw (cold start)

Fast idle adjusting screw (114) on the 1975–78 Stromberg 175 CDT

Access slot (arrow) on Stromberg 175 CDT

3. At the same time, push the engaging lever with a small screwdriver, through the slot of the choke housing in the direction of the engine, against the stop on the full down diaphragm rod. Do not force it past the stop.
4. Raise the throttle linkage, while holding the engaging lever against the stop.
5. Check the CO and fast idle.
6. Adjust the fast idle speed with the upper adjusting screw to 1600–1800 rpm.
7. Adjust the CO with the mixture adjusting screw to 5–8%. To check the CO, the center vacuum line for the air injection switchover valve must be disconnected and plugged.

Full Throttle Stop (1975–78 California Only)

1. With the accelerator pedal fully depressed, adjust the full throttle stop screw so that a clearance of .02 in. exists between the throttle valve lever and carburetor housing.

Thermo Air Valve

1. Disconnect the hoses from the thermo air valve and blow into one hose. If the valve is cold, no air can pass through the valve. If the valve is warm (slightly above room temperature) air should pass through the valve.

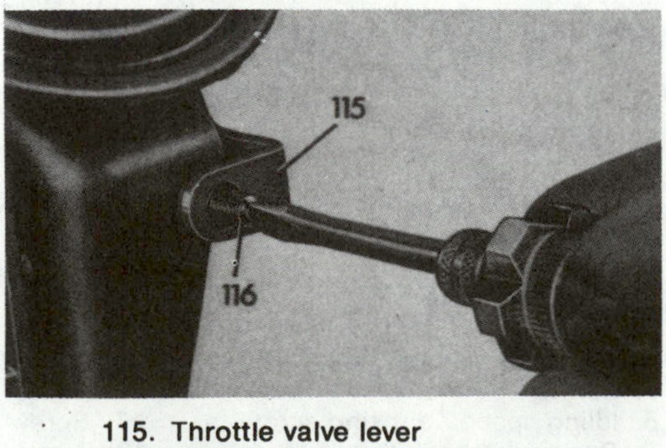

115. Throttle valve lever
116. Full throttle adjusting screw

Full throttle stop adjusting screw

SOLEX 4 A 1 ADJUSTMENTS

Fuel Level

1. There is no provision for measuring the fuel level, other than with the special Mercedes-Benz tool. It is a measuring rod which is inserted through the bore of the carburetor cover, and can be purchased from a dealer or fabricated.
2. Run the engine briefly at fast idle and shut off the ignition.
3. Insert the measuring gauge through the bore of the carburetor cover as far as it will go.
4. Remove the gauge and read the fuel level.

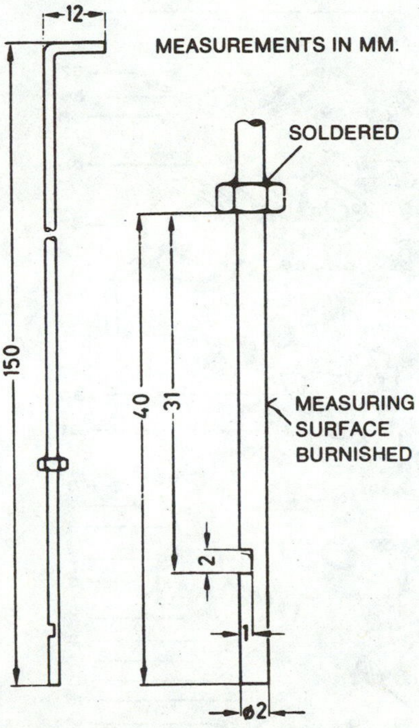

Fabricated tool for measuring fuel level on Solex 4A1 carburetor

Measuring fuel level on Solex 4A1 carburetor

The reading should be within the tolerance range marked on the stick.

5. To adjust the level, remove the carburetor cover and adjust the float by bending it on the hinge.
6. Reinstall the cover and test the level again.

Float Level

1. Remove the carburetor cover. The carburetor does not have to be removed.
2. With the float needle valve installed, push the connecting web of the float arms down until a noticeable stop. Be sure to push at the web. If not, the float shaft will lift from the bottom and result in an incorrect measurement.
3. Using a T-gauge or a homemade gauge, measure the level of the float below the carburetor housing without the gasket installed.
4. If the float level is not correct, remove the float in the desired direction.
5. Reinstall the carburetor cover.

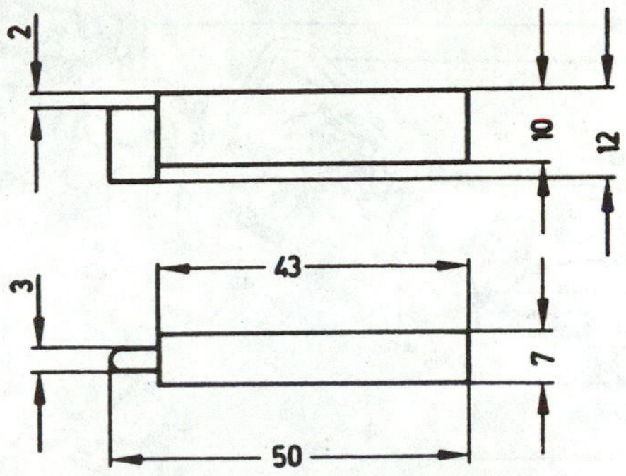

Fabricated tool for measuring float level on Solex 4A1 carburetor

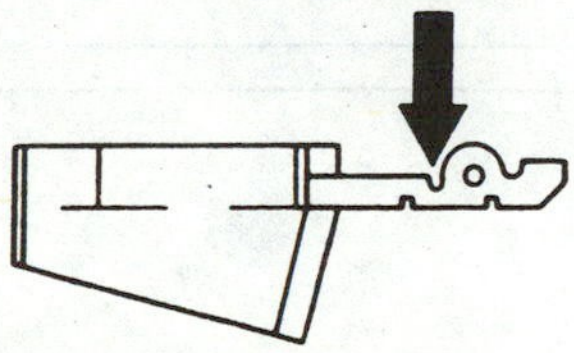

Bend the float at the arrow to adjust the float level on Solex 4A1 carburetor

Vacuum Governor

1. Set the idle speed and make sure that the engine is at normal operating temperature.
2. Run the engine at idle and pull the vacuum hose from the governor.
3. Set the engine speed to approximately 1200–1400 rpm. Loosen the locknut and adjust the rpm with the adjusting screw. Hold the diaphragm rod and turn the adjusting nut.
4. Adjust the compression spring with the transmission in gear.
5. The speed should be 600–700 rpm. If

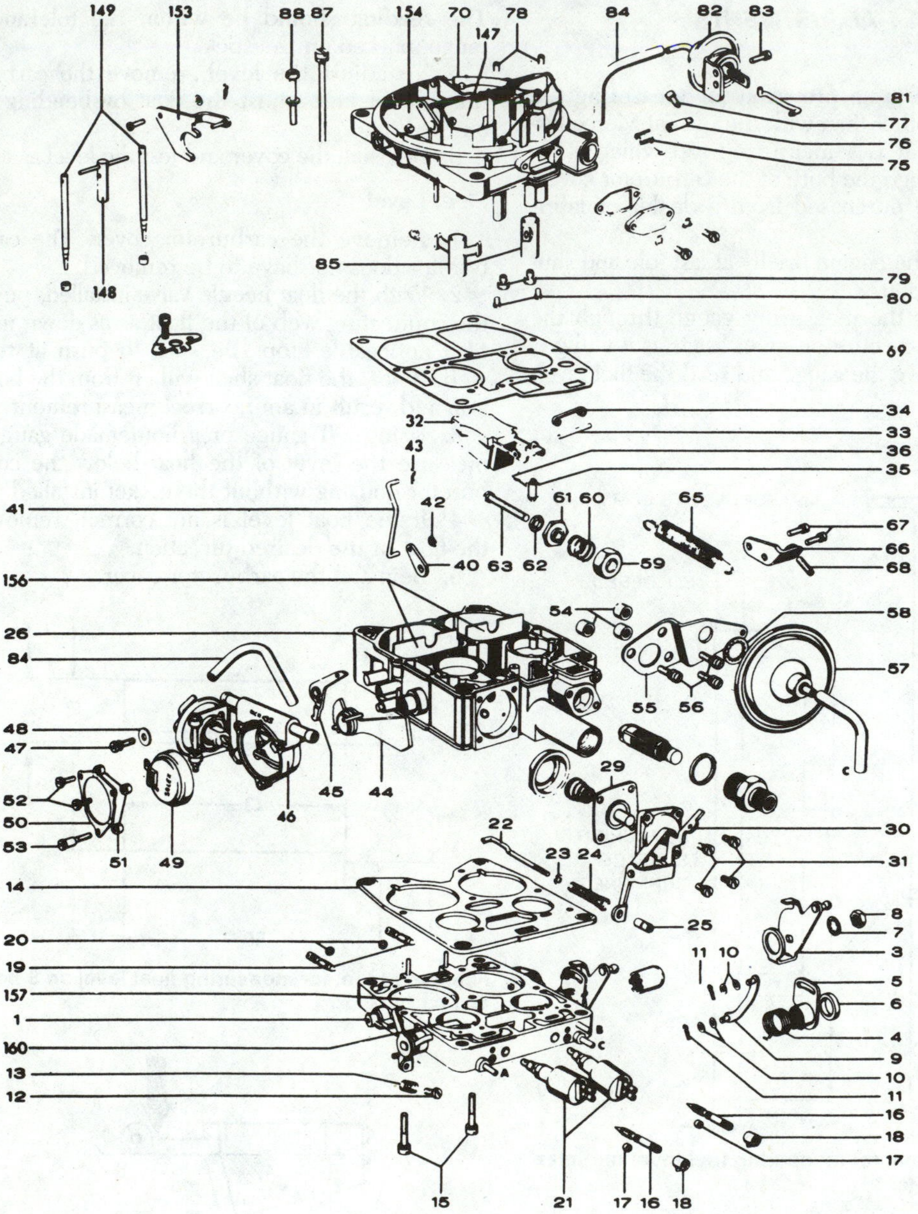

1. Throttle valve housing
3. Bracket
4. Spring
5. Cam lever
6. Bushing
7. Washer
8. Nut
9. Secondary connecting rod
10. Washer
11. Cotter pin
12. Screw
13. Spring
14. Plate
15. Screw
16. Idle mixture adjusting screws
17. Idle mixture adjusting screws
18. Idle mixture adjusting screws
19. Secondary jets
20. Secondary jets
21. Idle speed solenoid
22. Actuating levers for accelerator pump
23. Actuating levers for accelerator pump
24. Actuating levers for accelerator pump
25. Actuating levers for accelerator pump
26. Float housing
29. Diaphragm
30. Accelerator pump cover
31. Screws
32. Float
33. Float shaft
34. Hold-down clamp
35. Float needle
36. Float needle
40. Choke connecting rod
41. Choke connecting rod
42. Circlip
43. Cotter pin
44. Cam lever
45. Step lever
46. Thermostat housing
47. Screw
48. Washer
49. Thermostat cover
50. Attaching plate
51. Bushing
52. Screws (short)
53. Screw (long)

Exploded view of Solex 4A1 carburetor

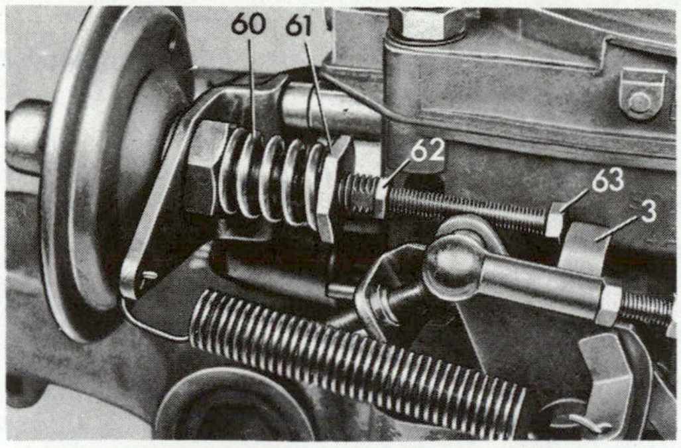

3. Throttle valve lever
60. Compression spring
61. Adjusting nut
62. Counternut
63. Adjusting screw

Vacuum governor adjustment—Solex 4A1 carburetor

necessary, adjust the compression spring with the adjusting nut.

6. Turn on the air conditioning, and turn the wheels to full lock. The engine should keep running. If it does not, adjust the speed with the adjusting nut again. See Step 3.

Automatic Choke

1. Check the choke for ease of operation.
2. Switch on the ignition and check to be sure that the choke opens after a minute or so.
3. Check the adjustment on the choke cover. The markings on the housing and cover should be aligned.

Choke Gap

1. Run the engine at idle until the diaphragm in the vacuum unit has been pulled completely against the stop.
2. Then clamp the hose to block all vacuum.
3. Be sure that the diaphragm is still against the stop and slightly raise the throttle valve lever. Position the stepped disc upward against the top stop. Release the throttle valve lever.
4. Push the lever of the bi-metallic spring until the stop is felt. The connecting rod will now be against the stop in the slot of the lever.
5. Measure the choke gap with a drill (0.060 in.—1974 Federal; 0.10″—1974 California; 0.108–0.120 in.—1975–76) between the choke plate and the wall of the air horn.
6. To adjust the gap, remove the coolant hose from the choke housing. Cover the choke housing with a rag and release the pressure in the radiator. Tighten the radiator cap again. Remove the coolant hose and clamp it shut.
7. Bend the connecting rod with a pair of pliers. On later models, the adjustment is made by turning the adjusting screw in the choke

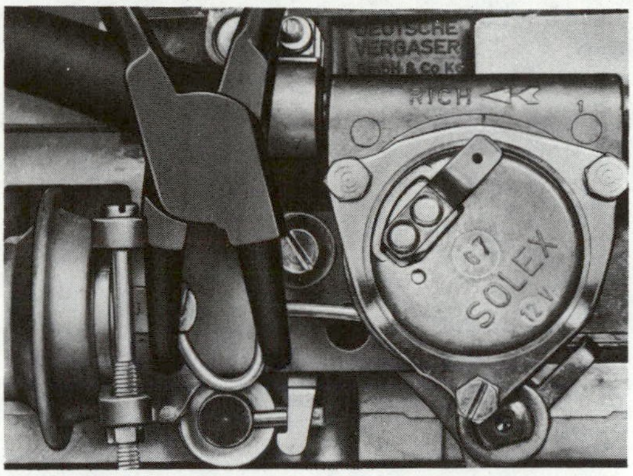

Automatic choke adjustment—Solex 4A1. If the choke gap is too large, push the bend apart; if the choke gap is too small, push the bend together

On later models, adjust the choke gap with the adjusting screw (211) located in the housing (210)

54. Vacuum regulator with bracket
55. Vacuum regulator with bracket
56. Vacuum regulator with bracket
57. Vacuum regulator with bracket
58. Vacuum regulator with bracket
59. Nut
60. Spring
61, 62. Nut
63. Screw
65. Throttle return spring
66. Idle stop screw with bracket
67. Idle stop screw with bracket
68. Idle stop screw with bracket
69. Gasket
70. Carburetor cover
75. Spring
76. Eccentric pin
77. Clamp screw
78. Primary idle air jets
79. Main jets
80. Screws
81. Vacuum diaphragm connecting rod
82. Vacuum diaphragm
83. Screw
84. Vacuum line
85. Emulsion Tube
87. Screw
88. Screw
147. Choke plate
148. Guide pin
149. Secondary needle valve
153. Lever
154. Secondary choke plate
156. Secondary baffle plates
157. Throttle valve (primary)
160. Throttle valve (secondary)

housing cover in (decrease gap) or out (increase gap).

8. While making the adjustment, be sure that the diaphragm in the vacuum unit is still against its stop.

Fast Idle

1. Adjust the idle speed and be sure that the engine is at normal operating temperature.
2. Run the engine at idle speed.
3. Raise the throttle valve lever slightly and position the stepped disc completely upward against the top stop.
4. Release the throttle valve lever.
5. Connect a tachometer and measure the engine speed. It should be 2400–2600. If required, adjust the fast idle with the fast idle speed adjusting screw.

Solex 4A1 fast idle adjustment

Accelerator Pump

1. Move the throttle valve lever several times. A strong jet of fuel should be forced out of the fuel outlets.
2. If not, remove the accelerator pump cover and check the diaphragm. Blow out the ducts with compressed air.

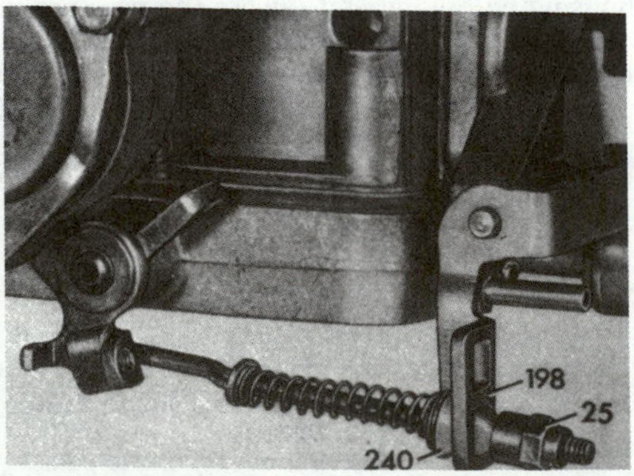

25. Accelerator pump adjusting nut
198. Actuating lever
240. Plastic guide bushing

Solex 4A1 accelerator pump adjustment

3. Install the accelerator pump cover.
4. If there still is no fuel from the injection tube, remove the carburetor cover.
5. Actuate the accelerator pump. If fuel emerges from the ball valves, blow out the injection holes in the carburetor cover with compressed air.
6. Install the carburetor cover. Tighten the screws evenly to 11 ft. lbs.

Fuel Return Valve

1. Pull the fuel return hose from the connection to the return line below the fuel pump.
2. Hold the return hose in a container and check whether a strong fuel jet comes from the line with the automatic transmission in Drive and the air conditioning on.

Bosch Electronic Fuel Injection—1974–75 V8 Engines

This system is a constant pressure, electronically controlled unit. The "brain" of the system, actually a small computer that senses the determining factors for fuel delivery, is located behind the passenger kick panel on the right-hand side.

A Bosch tester is necessary to accurately test the solid state circuitry and components, but there are a few checks that can be carried out independently of the tester.

TESTS

Delivery Pressure

See "Testing the Fuel Pump Delivery Pressure" earlier in this chapter.

ADJUSTMENTS

Fuel Pressure

The fuel pressure can be adjusted on the regulator with the adjusting screw. Adjust to 28 psi. If a slight turn of the screw shows no change of pressure replace the regulator.

Before replacing the regulator or removing the pressure gauge, reduce the pressure in the ring line by unplugging the starting valve and connecting it to battery voltage for 20 seconds.

Regulating Shaft

Step on the accelerator pedal up to the kick-down. The regulating lever should rest against the fuel throttle stop of the valve.

Loosen the hex bolt and push the linkage up to the full throttle stop if adjustment is required.

Regulating Linkage

1. Check the linkage for ease of operation.
2. Check that the throttle valve closes

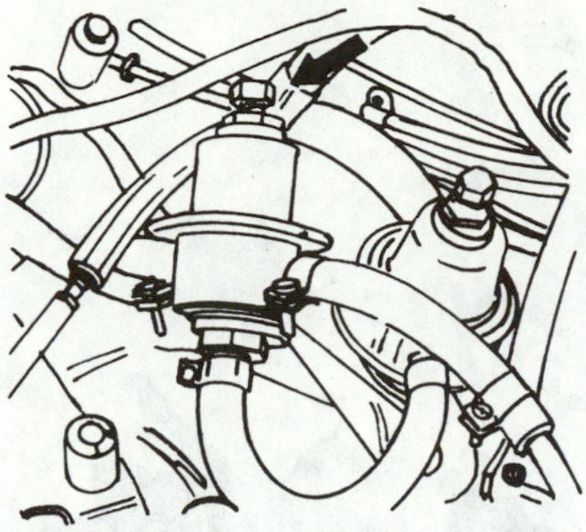

Electronic fuel injection pressure regulator adjusting screw (arrow)

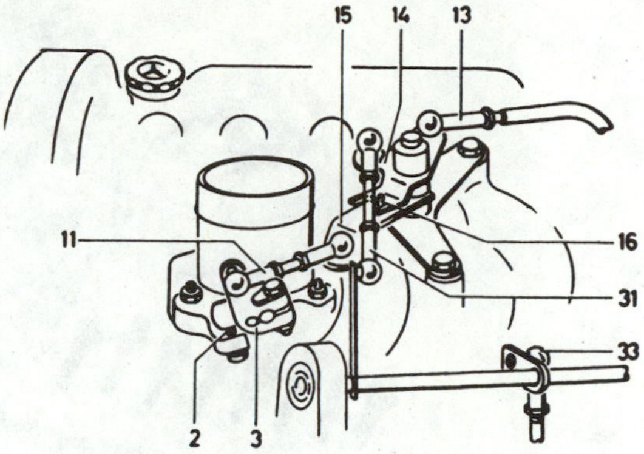

2. Idling speed stop
3. Throttle valve level
11. Connecting rod
13. Control pushrod
14. Regulating lever
15. Regulating lever
16. Stop pin
31. Connecting rod
33. Pushrod

Electronic fuel injection regulating linkage

completely. Disconnect the regulating rods.

3. Adjust the pushrod to a length of 4 in. from the center of the rubber mount to the center of the ball socket and attach.

On vehicles with manual transmission:

4. Adjust the connecting rod to a length of 3.5 in. (4.1 in. for cars with gate shift lever with bore next to ball head) and attach it.

5. Push the throttle lever against the idle speed stop. Adjust the connecting rod so that the regulating lever rests with the roller against the end stop of the gate shift lever.

On cars with automatic transmission and no gate shift lever:

6. Adjust the connecting rod (31) to 4.2 in. and the connecting rod (11) to 2.7 in. and attach.

7. Push the control rod to the rear against the stop and attach it tension free. During adjustment of the control pushrod, the ball socket must be held next to the ball head.

On cars with automatic transmission and gate shift lever:

8. Adjust the connecting rod to 4.2 in. and attach.

9. Push the throttle valve lever against the idle speed stop. Adjust the connecting rod so that the regulating lever rests with the roller against the end stop of the gate lever. Push the regulating lever to the rear against the stop pin.

10. Push the control pushrod against the stop and connect it tension free. The ball socket must be held next to the ball head.

Bosch K-Jetronic (CIS) Mechanical Fuel Injection—1976 and Later

This system replaces the electronic system of earlier years. In contrast to the intermittent type fuel injection, this system measures air volume through and air flow sensor and injects fuel continuously in front of the intake valves, regardless of firing position.

Minor running changes and improvements are made during production, but essential operation and service of the system remains alike on all vehicles equipped with the CIS injection.

The 190E utilizes an electronically controlled version of the K-Jetronic injection system called KE-Jetronic (CIS-E). This system is a further development of the mechanically controlled CIS system. The essential difference between the two is mixture correction by means of electronically controlled correction functions (CIS-E). An electronic control unit sends out impulses which effect the amount of fuel being injected. Since only the mixture corrections are controlled by this new system, the vehicle will continue to operate if there is an electronic malfunction.

CAUTION: *Even a seemingly minor adjustment, such as idle speed, can necessitate adjustments to other portions of the fuel injection system. Be extremely careful when adjusting the idle. If any difficulty at all is experienced, it will only upset the balance of an already delicate system.*

TESTING

Delivery Capacity

See "Testing the Fuel Pump Output" earlier in this chapter.

Cold Start Valve

1. Disconnect the plugs from the safety switch and mixture control regulator.
2. Remove the cold start valve with fuel line connected.

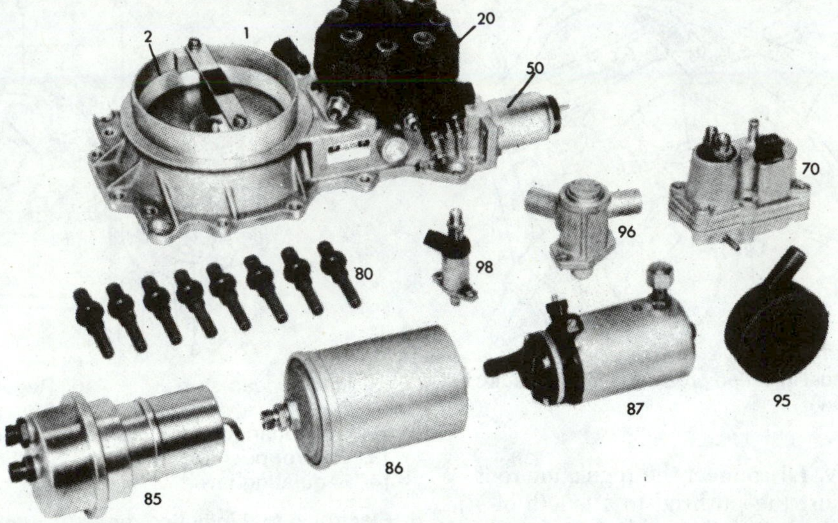

1. Mixture regulator assembly
2. Airflow sensor
20. Fuel distributor
50. Hot-start solenoid
70. Warm-up/full-load enrichment compensator
80. Injection nozzles
85. Fuel accumulator
86. Fuel filter
87. Fuel pump
95. Suction damper
96. Auxiliary air valve
98. Cold-start valve

Air flow controlled fuel injection components

3. Hold the cold start valve in a container,

4. Turn on the ignition. Connect the valve to battery voltage. It should emit a come shaped spray.

5. Dry the nozzle off. No fuel should leak out.

Hot Start System

Perform the test at coolant temperature 104°–122°F.

1. Remove the coil wire.

2. Connect a voltmeter to hot-start terminal 3 and ground.

3. Actuate the starter. In approximately 3–4 seconds, the voltmeter should read about 11 volts for 3–4 seconds.

4. If 11 volts are not indicated, check fuse 10. Connect the plug of the 104°F temperature switch and ground and repeat the test. If 11 volts are now indicated, replace the temperature switch. If 11 volts are not indicated, or if the time periods are wrong, replace the hot start relay.

Fuel Pump Safety Circuit

The pump will only run if the starter motor is actuated or if the engine is running.

1. Remove the air filter.

2. Turn on the ignition and briefly depress the sensor plate.

3. Remove the coil wire from the distributor.

4. Connect a voltmeter to the positive fuel pump terminal and ground.

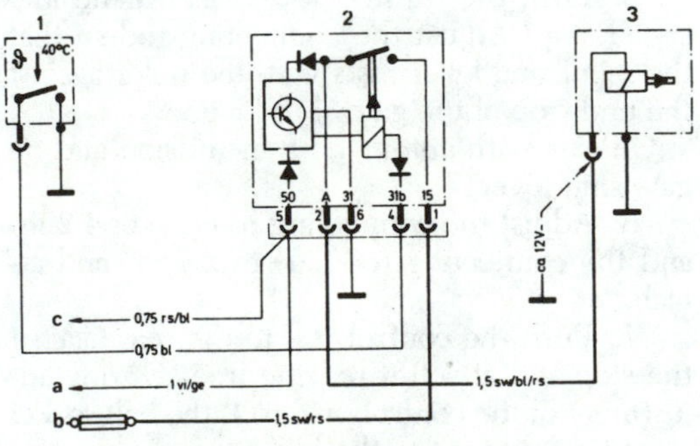

1. Temperature switch 104° F (40° C)
2. Hot-start relay
3. Hot-start solenoid

a. Terminal 50 (starter lock-out switch)
b. Fuse No. 10 (15/54)
c. To thermo-time switch

Hot start system wiring schematic

5. Actuate the starter. Voltmeter should indicate 11 volts.

6. If the fuel pump runs only when the sensor plate is depressed or only when the engine is cranked, replace the fuel pump relay. If the pump is already running when the ignition is turned ON, replace the safety switch.

ADJUSTMENTS

Control Linkage

1976–79

1. Check the control linkage for ease of operation.

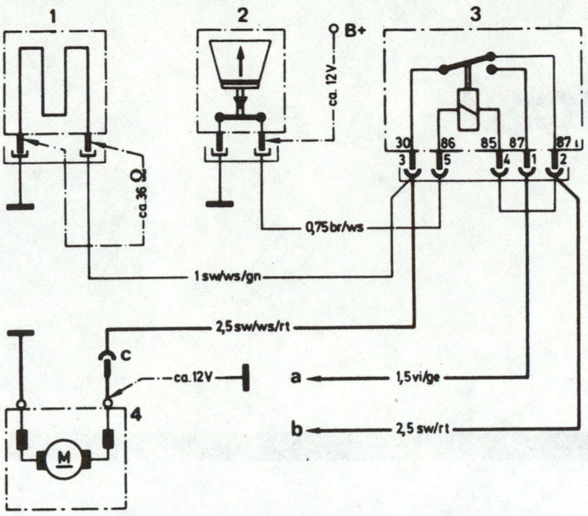

1. Heating coil, warm-up/full-load enrichment compensator
2. Safety switch, sensor plate
3. Relay, fuel pump
4. Fuel pump

a. To terminal 50 (starter)
b. To terminal 15/54 (ignition)
c. To plug connection, tail light harness

Safety circuit wiring schematic

2. Disconnect the control rod. The throttle valve should rest against the idle stop. Reconnect the control rod.

3. Adjust the control rod so that the roller rests tension free in the gate lever slot.

Full Throttle Stop

1976–69

1. With the engine stopped, press the accelerator pedal until it rests against the kick-down switch.
2. The throttle valve lever should rest against the full throttle stop. If necessary, adjust the throttle valve lever.
3. If the full throttle stop is not reached, adjust the control rod (bell crank lever to accelerator pedal) to 4.8 in. (from center to center of ball sockets).
4. Adjust the accelerator pedal linkage if necessary with the fastening screw.
5. Adjust the control pressure rod (at idle) by compressing the adjusting clip, and moving the rod completely to the rear against the stop.

Throttle Valve Switch

1980–84

1. Set an ohmmeter to 0-infinity.
2. Check the idle speed stop. Push the throttle valve against the idle speed stop. Connect the ohmmeter across terminals 1 and 2. Rotate the throttle valve switch until the ohmmeter reads 0.
3. Advance the throttle valve slightly. The ohmmeter should read 0-infinite ohms.
4. Check the full throttle stop. Push the throttle valve against the full throttle stop and connect an ohmmeter across terminals 2 and 3. The reading should be 0 ohms.
5. Turn the throttle valve back slightly. A reading of infinite ohms should result.

Chassis Electrical

5

UNDERSTANDING BASIC ELECTRICITY

Understanding the basic theory of electricity makes electrical troubleshooting much easier. Several gauges are used in electrical troubleshooting to see inside the circuit being tested. Without a basic understanding, it will be difficult to understand testing procedures.

Electricity is the flow of electrons—hypothetical particles thought to constitute the basic "stuff" of electricity. In a comparison with water flowing in a pipe, the electrons would be the water. As the flow of water can be measured, the flow of electricity can be measured. The unit of measurement is amperes, frequently abbreviated "amps." An ammeter will measure the actual amount of current flowing in the circuit.

Just as the water pressure is measured in units such as pounds per square inch, electrical pressure is measured in volts. When a voltmeter's two probes are placed on two "live" portions of an electrical circuit with different electrical pressures, current will flow through the voltmeter and produce a reading which indicates the difference in electrical pressure between the two parts of the circuit.

While increasing the voltage in a circuit will increase the flow of current, the actual flow depends not only on voltage, but on the resistance of the circuit. The standard unit for measuring circuit resistance is an ohm, measured by an ohmmeter. The ohmmeter is somewhat similar to an ammeter, but incorporates its own source of power so that a standard voltage is always present.

An actual electric circuit consists of four basic parts. These are: the power source, such as a generator or battery; a hot wire, which conducts the electricity under a relatively high voltage to the component supplied by the circuit; the load, such as a lamp, motor, resistor, or relay coil; and the ground wire, which carries the current back to the source under very low voltage. In such a circuit the bulk of the resistance exists between the point where the hot wire is connected to the load, and the point where the load is grounded. In an automobile, the vehicle's frame, which is made of steel, is used as a part of the ground circuit for many of the electrical devices.

Remember that, in electrical testing, the voltmeter is connected in parallel with the circuit being tested (without disconnecting any wires) and measures the difference in voltage between the locations of the two probes; that the ammeter is connected in series with the load (the circuit is separated at one point and the ammeter inserted so it becomes a part of the circuit); and the ohmmeter is self-powered, so that all the power in the circuit should be off and the portion of the circuit to be measured contacted at either end by one of the probes of the meter.

For any electrical system to operate, it must make a complete circuit. This simply means that the power flow from the battery must make a complete circle. When an electrical component is operating, power flows from the battery to the component, passes through the component causing it to perform its function (lighting a light bulb) and then returns to the battery through the ground of the circuit. This ground is usually (but not always) the metal part of the car on which the electrical component is mounted.

Perhaps the easiest way to visualize this is to think of connecting a light bulb with two wires attached to it to your car battery. The battery in your car has two posts (negative and positive). If one of the two wires attached to the light bulb was attached to the negative post of the battery and the other wire was attached to the positive post of the battery, you would have a complete circuit. Current from the battery would flow out one post, through the wire attached to it and then to the light bulb, where it would pass through causing it to light. It would then leave the light bulb, travel through the other wire, and return to the other post of the battery.

The normal automotive circuit differs from this simple example in two ways. First, instead of having a return wire from the bulb to the battery, the light bulb returns the current to the battery through the chassis of the vehicle. Since the negative battery cable is attached to the chassis and the chassis is made of electrically conductive metal, the chassis of the vehicle can serve as a ground wire to complete the circuit. Secondly, most automotive circuits contain switches to turn components on and off when it is turned off.

Some electrical components which require a large amount of current to operate also have a relay in their circuit. Since these circuits carry a large amount of current, the thickness of the wire in the circuit (gauge size) is also greater. If this large wire were connected from the component to the control switch on the instrument panel, and then back to the component, a voltage drop would occur in the circuit. To prevent this potential drop in voltage, an electromagnetic switch (relay) is used. The large wires in the circuit are connected from the car battery to one side of the relay, and from the opposite side of the relay to the component. The relay is normally open, preventing current from passing through the circuit. An additional, smaller, wire is connected from the relay to the control switch for the circuit. When the control switch is turned on, it grounds the smaller wire from the relay and completes the circuit. When the control switch is turned on, it grounds the smaller wire from the relay. If you were to disconnect the light bulb (from the previous example of a light bulb being connected to the battery by two wires) from the wires and touch the two wires together (please take our word for this; don't try it), the result will be a shower of sparks. A similar thing happens (on a smaller scale) when the power supply wire to a component or the electrical component itself becomes grounded before the normal ground connection for the circuit. To prevent damage to the system, the fuse for the circuit blows to interrupt the circuit—protecting the components from damage. Because grounding a wire from a power source makes a complete circuit—less the required component to use the power—the phenomenon is called a short circuit. The most common causes of short circuits are: the rubber insulation on a wire breaking or rubbing through to expose the current carrying core of the wire to a metal part of the car, or a shorted switch.

Some electrical systems on the car are protected by a circuit breaker which is, basically, a self-repairing fuse. When either of the above-described events takes place in a system which is protected by a circuit breaker, the circuit breaker opens the circuit the same way a fuse does. However, when either the short is removed from the circuit or the surge subsides, the circuit breaker resets itself and does not have to be replaced as a fuse does.

The final protective device in the chassis electrical system is a fuse link. A fuse link is a wire that acts as a fuse. It is connected between the starter relay and the main wiring harness for the car. This connection is under the hood, very near a similar fuse link which protects the engine electrical system. Since the fuse link protects all the chassis electrical components, it is the probable cause of trouble when none of the electrical components function, unless the battery is disconnected or dead.

Electrical problems generally fall into one of three areas:

1. The component that is not functioning is not receiving current.
2. The component itself is not functioning.
3. The component is not properly grounded.

Problems that fall into the first category are by far the most complicated. It is the current supply system to the component which contains all the switches, relays, fuses, etc.

The electrical system can be checked with a test light and a jumper wire. A test light is a device that looks like a pointed screwdriver with a wire attached to it. It has a light bulb in its handle. A jumper wire is a piece of insulated wire with an alligator clip attached to each end.

If a light bulb is not working, you must follow a systematic plan to determine which of the three causes is the villain.

1. Turn on the switch that controls the inoperable bulb.
2. Disconnect the power supply wire from the bulb.
3. Attach the ground wire on the test light to a good metal ground.
4. Touch the probe end of the test light to the end of the power supply wire that was disconnected from the bulb. If the bulb is receiving current, the test light will go on.

NOTE: *If the bulb is one which works only when the ignition key is turned on (turn signal), make sure the key is turned on.*

If the test light does not go on, then the problem is in the circuit between the battery and the bulb. As mentioned before, this includes all the switches, fuses, and relays in the system. Turn to the wiring diagram and find the bulb on the diagram. Follow the wire that runs back to the battery. The problem is an open circuit between the battery and the bulb. If the fuse is blown and, when replaced, immediately blows again, there is a short circuit in the system which must be located and repaired. If there is a switch in the system, bypass it with a jumper wire. This is done by connecting one end of the jumper wire to the power supply wire into the switch and the other end of the jumper wire to the wire coming out of the switch. Again, consult the wiring diagram. If the test light lights with the jumper wire installed, the switch or whatever was bypassed is defective.

NOTE: *Never substitute the jumper wire for the bulb, as the bulb is the component required to use the power from the power source.*

5. If the bulb in the test light goes on, then the current is getting to the bulb that is not working in the car. This eliminates the first of the three possible causes. Connect the power supply wire and connect a jumper wire from the bulb to a good metal ground. Do this with the switch which controls the bulb turned on, and also the ignition switch turned on if it is required for the light to work. If the bulb works with jumper wire installed, then it has a bad ground. This is usually caused by the metal area on which the bulb mounts to the car being coated with some type of foreign matter.

6. If neither test located the source of the trouble, then the light bulb itself is defective.

The above test procedure can be applied to any of the components of the chassis electrical system by substituting the component that is not working for the light bulb. Remember that for any electrical system to work, all connections must be clean and tight.

HEATER

Heater Blower

REMOVAL AND INSTALLATION

240D (thru 1976), 230 (thru 1976), 280, 280C, 300D (thru 1976)

1. Remove the heater box.
2. Back out the three retaining screws.
3. Slightly pull out the blower and remove the electrical plug and the blower.
4. Installation is the reverse of removal. To prevent leaks, install the three screws with three new special washers exactly like those removed.

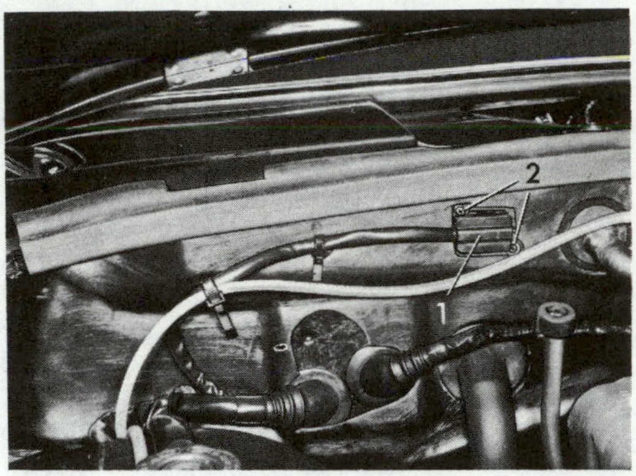

Unplug the series resistor (1) and remove it (2) before removing the heater blower on the 280S, 280SE, 300SD (1978–80), all 450 models, 380SL, 380SLC and the 6.9

230 (1977–78), 240D (1977–83), 280E, 280CE, 300D (1977 and later), 300CD and 300TD

1. Remove the cover from under the right side of the instrument panel.
2. Disconnect the plug from the blower motor.
3. Unscrew the contact plate screw, lift the contact plate and disconnect both wires to the series resistor.
4. Loosen the blower motor flange screws and lift out the blower motor.
5. Installation is in the reverse order of removal.

280S, 280SE, 300SD (1978–80), 450SE, 450SEL and 6.9

1. Disconnect the series resistor plug at the fire wall.
2. Unscrew both mounting bolts and remove the series resistor.
3. Remove the air inlet grille.
4. Remove the glove box.
5. Remove the cover from under the right side of the instrument panel.
6. Remove the hose between the center air duct and the right side ring nozzle.
7. Remove the clamp and then disconnect the cable control at the lever.
8. Unscrew both mounting nuts and remove the blower motor.

NOTE: *On installation, make sure that the rubber seal between the blower motor and the firewall is not damaged and that the rubber grommet for the connecting cable is correctly seated.*

9. Guide the connecting cable through the air duct on the firewall and into the water box.
10. Insert the blower motor into the housing, position the mounting nuts and then push

the blower motor to the left (as far as possible) while tightening.

11. Installation of the remaining components is in the reverse order of installation.

380SL, 380SLC, 450SL and 450SLC

1. Working in the engine compartment, unscrew the eight (8) mounting screws and remove the panel which covers the blower motor.
2. Disconnect the plug from the series resistor at the firewall.
3. Remove the mounting bolts and then remove the series resistor.
4. Unscrew the four (4) blower motor retaining nuts and lift out the motor.
5. Installation is in the reverse order of removal. Be sure that the rubber sealing strip is not damaged.

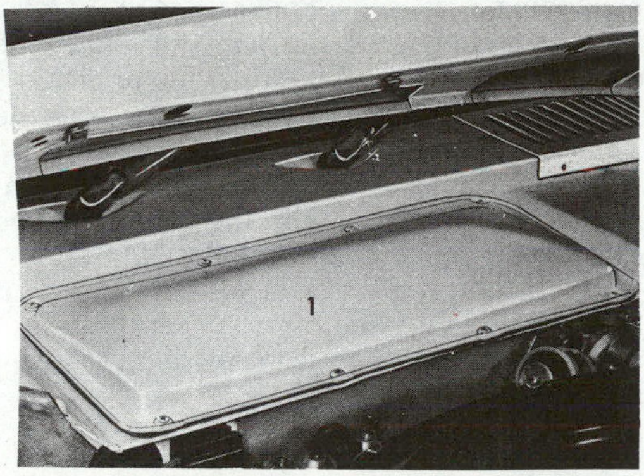

Access plate to the blower motor—380SL, 380SLC, 450SL and 450SLC

2. Collar nut
3. Plug
4. Series resistance
5. Blower

Blower motor—380SL, 380SLC, 450SL and 450SLC

300SD (1981 and later), 380SE, 380SEL, 380SEC, 500SEL and 500SEC

1. Remove the cover from under the right side of the instrument panel.
2. Remove the cover for the blower motor and disconnect the two-prong plug.
3. Remove the retaining bolts on the blower motor flange and then remove the blower motor.
4. Installation is in the reverse order of removal.

190D and 190E

1. Open the hood to a 90° position and then remove the wiper arms.
2. Disconnect the retaining clips for the air intake cover at the firewall.
3. Remove the rubber sealing strip from the cover and then remove the retaining screws. Slide the cover out of the lower windshield trim strip and remove it.
4. Disconnect the vacuum line from the heater valve.
5. Remove the heater cover retaining screws.
6. Pull up the rubber sealing strip from the engine side of the defroster plenum (firewall), unscrew the retaining screws and pull up and out on the blower motor cover.
7. Loosen the cable straps on the connecting cable and then disconnect the plug.
8. Unscrew the mounting bolts and then remove the blower motor.
9. Installation is in the reverse order of removal.

WINDSHIELD WIPERS

Wiper Arms

REMOVAL AND INSTALLATION

230 (1974–76), 240D (1974–76), 280, 280C and 300D (1975–76)

1. Unscrew the cap nut at the base of the wiper arm and remove it. Make sure that you get the spring washer.
2. Remove the wiper arm.
3. Installation is in the reverse order of removal.

NOTE: *The wiper shaft has a cone end with serrations on which the wiper arm is mounted. New wiper arms have no serrations on the inside cone. When the cap nut is tightened, the shaft serrations dig into the smooth surface of the inside of the wiper arm cone. If the serrations on the inside cone of an old wiper arm are chewed up, loosely install the wiper arm on the shaft and wiggle it back and forth until the old serrations are gone. Adjust the arm and then tighten it down; this will form new serrations.*

All Other Models

NOTE: *On the 190D and 190E, the wiper arm is removed by lifting the cover at the bottom of the arm and removing the retaining nut.*

1. Lift the wiper arm so that it is at a 90° angle to the windshield.
2. Disengage the lock on the mounting nut covering cap by lifting the cap slightly upward.
3. Continue to hold the cap in a slightly raised position and then lower the wiper arm to the windshield. This should allow the cap to pivot all the way open.
4. Unscrew the mounting nut and remove the wiper arm.
5. Installation is in the reverse order of removal.

Wiper Linkage

REMOVAL AND INSTALLATION

230 (1974–76), 240D (1974–76), 280, 280C and 300D (1975–76)

LEFT SIDE

1. Remove the wiper arm. Remove the grommet, nut, washer and seal from the wiper shaft.
2. Pop both linkage arms off of the ball joints on the wiper shaft.
3. Unscrew the mounting bolts for the wiper shaft and remove along with the linkage.
4. Installation is in the reverse order of removal.

RIGHT SIDE

1. Remove the wiper arm. Remove the grommet, nut, washer and seal from the wiper shaft.
2. Remove the covers underneath both sides of the instrument panel.
3. Remove the glove box.
4. Pop both linkage arms off of the ball joints on the wiper shaft.
5. Unscrew the mounting bolts on the wiper shaft and remove down and to the right along with the linkage.
6. Installation is in the reverse order of removal.

Wiper Motor

REMOVAL AND INSTALLATION

230 (1974–76), 240D (1974–76), 280, 280C and 300D (1975–76)

NOTE: *If only the motor is to be removed, DON'T loosen the adjusting nut on the linkage arm.*

1. Remove the cover underneath the left side of the instrument panel.
2. Disconnect the ball joint at the linkage connecting rod (it should pop right off).
3. Unscrew the three mounting nuts.
4. From the engine compartment, pull off the cable on the wiper motor and then remove the motor.
5. Installation is in the reverse order of removal. Always use new sealing rings on the wiper motor mounting nuts.

Wiper Motor and Linkage

REMOVAL AND INSTALLATION

230 (1977–78), 240D (1977–83), 280E, 280CE, 300D (1977 and later), 300CD, and 300TD

1. Remove the wiper arms.
2. Remove the air intake grille on the right side.
3. Remove the covering cap and nut on the left and right side bearing shafts.
4. Remove the four expanding rivets and then remove the left side air intake grille.
5. Remove the center air plenum cover (four expanding rivets and a Phillips screw).
6. Carefully pull the left and right side connecting rods off of the wiper motor crank.
7. Remove the water drain tube from the right side bearing shaft.
8. Disconnect the coupler plug in the engine compartment. Unclip the plug from the firewall and pull it all the way through.
9. Unbolt the wiper motor and remove it toward the right side.
10. Installation is in the reverse order of removal.

300SD (1981 and later), 380SE, 380SEC, 380SEL, 500SEC and 500SEL

1. Remove the wiper arms.
2. Remove the air intake cover. Unscrew the fastening screws and then disconnect the front plug connector.
3. Compress the mounting flange on the rear plug connector. Push the plug out of the firewall toward the front of the car, twist it and then insert it toward the rear of the car.
4. Remove the wiper motor and linkage.
5. Unscrew the nut on the wiper motor shaft.
6. Swivel the wiper linkage and then unscrew the bolts for the wiper motor underneath.
7. Remove the wiper motor.

To install:

8. Mount the wiper motor in the base plate.
9. Push the crank arm on the wiper motor shaft and position the nut. Make sure that the lever on the right hand wiper shaft is pointing down.
10. Align the crank arm so that the upper edge is parallel with the wiper motor shaft.
11. Tighten the nut on the wiper motor shaft.

12. Attach the wiper motor and linkage assembly to the vehicle.

13. Installation of the remaining components is in the reverse order of removal.

280S, 280SE, 300SD (1978–80), 450SE, 450SEL and 6.9

1. Remove the wiper arms.
2. Remove the covering caps and nuts on both wiper shafts.
3. Remove the air intake grille.
4. Unscrew the mounting bolts.
5. Disconnect the wiper motor plug under the left side of the instrument panel and then pull it into the engine compartment along with the rubber grommet in the firewall.
6. Pull off the linkage drive rod and then unscrew the crank on the wiper motor.
7. Unscrew the mounting bolts and remove the wiper motor.
8. Installation is in the reverse order of removal.

NOTE: *Remove the rubber seal around the motor housing during installation or leave it off.*

190D and 190E

1. Open the hood all the way and disconnect the battery.
2. Remove the wiper arm.
3. Remove the round cover from the wiper shaft.
4. Remove the two clips, the rubber seal and the two screws and then remove the air intake cover.
5. Pull the three-piece air intake pan from the windshield and remove it.
6. Unscrew the wiper motor/linkage assembly.
7. Remove the cover and unscrew the four mounting bolts for the fuse box. Pull the fuse box slightly forward and up and then unplug the wiper motor connection.
8. Remove the wiper motor/linkage assembly.
9. Remove the nut on the wiper motor shaft and then pull off the crank arm and linkage.
10. Unscrew and remove the wiper motor.

To install:

11. Attach the wiper motor to the base plate.
12. Press the crank arm onto the wiper motor shaft. Make sure that the crank arm and the pushrod are parallel.
13. Attach the crank arm to the wiper motor and then install the wiper motor/linkage assembly.
14. Installation of the remaining components is in the reverse order of removal.

Instrument Cluster

REMOVAL AND INSTALLATION

230 (thru 1976), 240D (thru 1976), 280, 280C, 300D (thru 1976)

1. Remove the cover plate from the left side underneath the dashboard.
2. On vehicles with automatic transmission, disconnect the Bowden cable for the gear selector lever, after engaging Park.
3. Remove the bracket holding the handbrake.
4. Unscrew the knurled nut and pull the instrument cluster slightly forward.
5. Disconnect the tachometer drive.
6. Cover the steering column to prevent scratches.
7. If only bulb replacement is desired, this is sufficient. To remove the entire cluster, continue with the remaining steps.
8. Disconnect the oil pressure line.
9. Remove the electrical plug connections.
10. Release the excess pressure in the cooling system and install the cap afterward.
11. Remove the temperature sensor from the cylinder head and plug the hole.
12. Carefully remove the instrument cluster with the capillary tube and temperature sensor.

CAUTION: *Do not bend the capillary tube.*

13. Installation is the reverse of removal.

Instrument cluster removal—early models

280S, 280SE, 300SD (1978–80), 380SL, 380SLC, 450SE, 450SEL, 450SL, 450SLC and 6.9

1. Remove the steering wheel.

NOTE: *The instrument cluster is held in the instrument panel by means of a molded rubber strip. When pulling out the cluster, the panel can be slightly raised above the cluster. NEVER force the cluster with a screwdriver or the like.*

Remove the trim emblem (18) with a small screw driver and remove the steering wheel padding

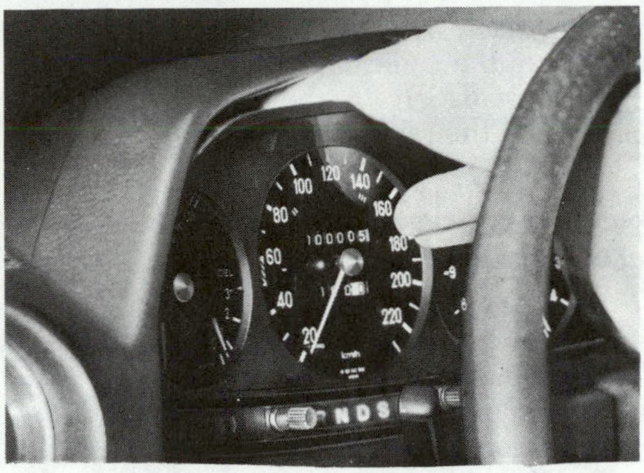

Pull the instrument cluster out by hand

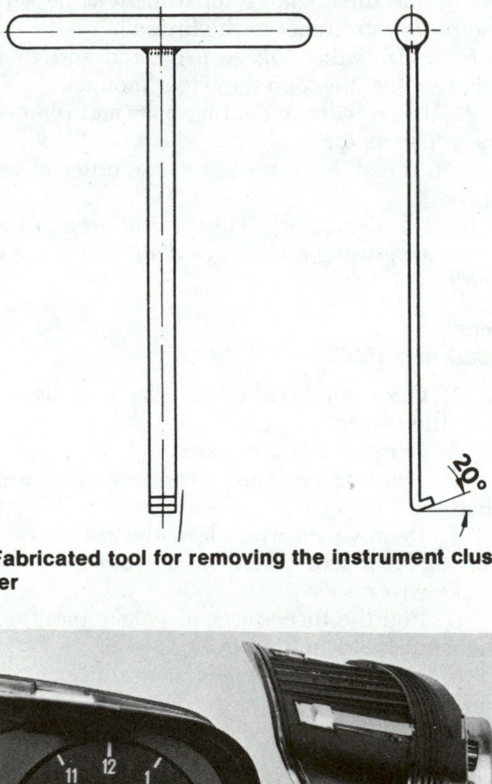

Fabricated tool for removing the instrument cluster

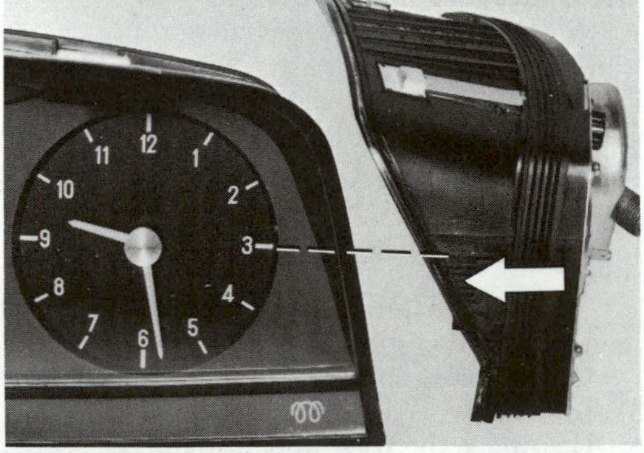

Recess slot in the instrument cluster

2. Remove the tachometer shaft from the cable strap underneath the left hand floor mat, near the jacket tube (except 380SL, SLC and 450SL, SLC).

3. Pull the instrument cluster out as much as possible and loosen or remove the tachometer shaft, all electrical connections and the oil pressure line.

4. Remove the instrument cluster to the left.

CAUTION: *Do not bend the oil pressure line.*

5. Installation is in the reverse order of removal. Make sure that the speedometer cable is not bent excessively or it will vibrate when running.

190D and 190E

1. Remove the cover under the left side of the instrument panel.

2. Disconnect the defroster ducting which runs behind the instrument cluster.

3. Unscrew the speedometer cable from below and then push the cluster out far enough to disconnect all connections on the back of the instrument cluster.

4. Remove the five clips which secure the instrument cluster and then remove it.

5. Installation is in the reverse order of removal.

230 (1977–78), 240D (1977–83), 280E, 280CE, 300D (1977 and later), 300CD, 300SD (1981 and later), 300TD, 380SE, 380SEC, 380SEL, 500SEC and 500SEL

1. Remove the steering wheel (300SD, 380SE, 380SEC, 380SEL, 500SEC and 500SEL only).

2. Remove the instrument cluster slightly by hand. Don't pull on the edge of the glass.

3. A removal hook can be fabricated and inserted between the instrument cluster and the dashboard.

4. Guide the removal hook up to the right to the recess (arrow) and pull the instrument cluster out.

5. Pull it out as far as possible and disconnect the speedometer cable, electrical connections and oil pressure line.

NOTE: *The 1981 and later 300SD, 380SE, 380SEC, 380SEL, 500SEC and 500SEL models utilize 5 clips to secure the instrument cluster in place.*

6. To install, reconnect the electrical connections, oil pressure line and speedometer cable. To avoid speedometer cable noise, guide it into the largest radius possible.

7. Push the instrument cluster firmly into the dashboard.

Combination Switch

REMOVAL AND INSTALLATION

190D, 190E, 230, 240D, 280 (all models), 300D, 300CD, 300SD (1978–80), 300TD, 380SL, 380SLC, 450 (all models) and 6.9

1. Remove the rubber sleeve on the switch and then unscrew the retaining screws.
2. Pull the switch out slightly, loosen the screws for the cable connection of the twin carbon contacts and pull out the cable.
3. Remove the cover underneath the left side of the instrument panel.
4. Disconnect the plug and then remove the switch.
5. Installation is in the reverse order of removal.

300SD (1981 and later), 380SE, 380SEC, 380SEL, 500SEC and 500SEL

1. Remove the steering wheel.
2. Remove the cover underneath the left side of the instrument panel.
3. Unscrew the switch retaining screws.
4. Disconnect the 14-prong plug underneath the instrument panel.
5. Remove the switch.
6. Installation is in the reverse order of removal.

Ignition Switch

REMOVAL AND INSTALLATION

All Models with Ignition Switch in Dashboard Except 190D And 190E

1. Remove the instrument cluster.
2. Remove the right-hand cover plate under the dashboard.
3. Remove the plug connection from the ignition switch.
4. Remove the screws which hold the ignition switch to the rear of the lock cylinder and remove the ignition switch.
5. To install the ignition switch, attach the plug connection, after fastening the switch to the steering lock.
6. Install the instrument cluster.
7. Check the switch for proper function and install the lower cover.

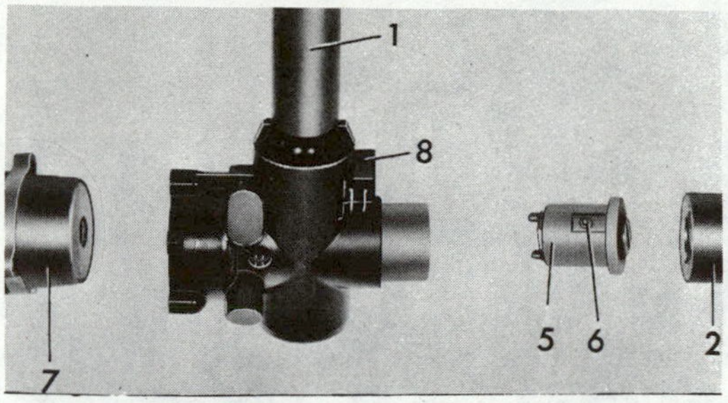

1. Steering lock
2. Cover sleeve
5. Locking cylinder
6. Locking pin
7. Ignition starting switch
8. Contact switch (USA version only)

Ignition switch—all models

190D and 190E

1. Remove the cover plate under the left side of the instrument panel.
2. Remove the steering wheel. Remove the instrument cluster.
3. Pry the cylinder rosette (trim ring) upwards and then remove it.
4. Insert the ignition key and turn it to position 1.
5. Disconnect the plug at the rear of the ignition switch.

NOTE: *The plug can only be disconnected when the key is in position 1.*

6. Loosen the screws and then remove the steering column jacket (upper and lower halves).
7. Release the clamp on the jacket tube. Press in the lock-pin in position 1 and then pull the steering lock out slightly from the jacket tube holder.
8. Pull off the ignition key at the right bottom section, slightly to the rear. Swivel the steering lock so that the lock cylinder clears its hole in the instrument panel.
9. Unscrew the retaining screws and remove the ignition switch from the back of the steering lock.
10. Installation is in the reverse order of removal. Remember to reconnect the switch to the steering lock.

Lock Cylinder (Key Can Be Removed in Position 1)

REMOVAL AND INSTALLATION

All Models Equipped as Above

1. Turn the key to position 1 and remove the key.
2. Pry the cover sleeve from the lock cylinder with a small screwdriver.
3. Using a bent paper clip, hook onto the cover sleeve and remove the sleeve. Be sure that you do not remove the rosette in the dashboard also.

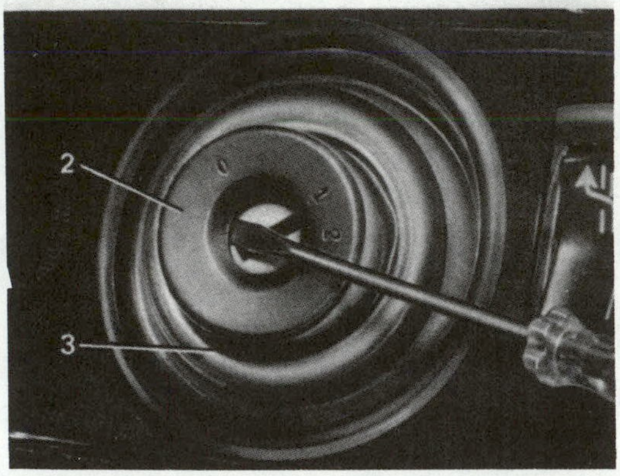

Pry the cover sleeve (2) loose with a small screwdriver. Be careful not to remove the rosette (3)

Hook the cover sleeve with a paper clip (4) to remove it

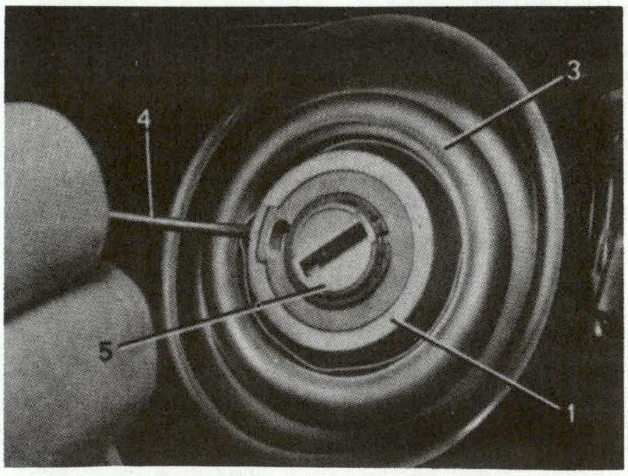

1. Steering lock
3. Rosette
4. Steel wire
5. Closing cylinder

Remove the sleeve with the paper clip

4. Insert the paper clip between the rosette and the steering lock and push in the lock pin. Remove the lock cylinder slightly with the key.
5. Insert the paper clip into the locking hole and pull the lock cylinder completely out.
6. Installation is the reverse of removal. Turn

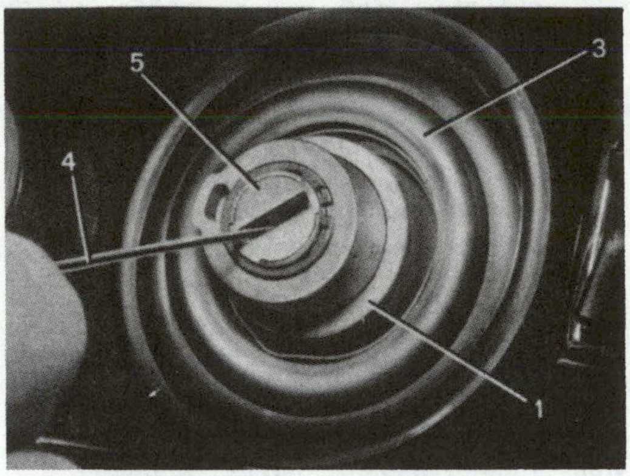

1. Steering lock
3. Rosette
4. Steel wire
5. Closing cylinder

Remove the cylinder with the paper clip

the lock cylinder to position 1 and insert it into the steering lock, making sure that the lock pin engages. Push the cover sleeve into position 1.
7. Make sure the the cylinder operates properly.

Lock Cylinder (Key Cannot Be Removed in Position 1)

REMOVAL AND INSTALLATION

All Models Except 190D and 190E

Because of legal requirements, the lock was changed from the previous version, so that the key can only be removed in position 0.

1. Turn the key to position 1.
2. Lift the cover sleeve to the edge of the key and turn the key to position 0.
3. Remove the key and cover sleeve.
4. Insert the key into the lock cylinder and turn to position 1 (90° to the right), push in the lock pin and remove the lock cylinder.
5. To install the lock cylinder, turn the lock cylinder to position 1 and insert the lock cylin-

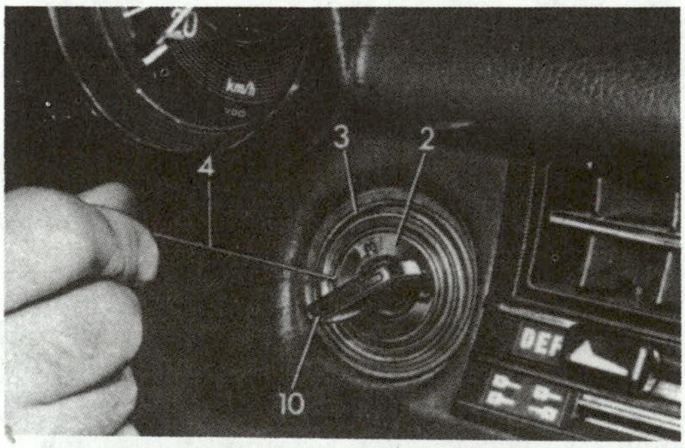

2. Cover sleeve
3. Rosette
4. Steel wire
5. Closing cylinder

Lift the cover sleeve to the edge of the key with a thin piece of wire der, making sure that the locking pin engages.

6. Turn the key to position 0 and remove the key.

7. Place the cover sleeve on the steering lock, insert and turn the key, and push in the cover sleeve at position 1.

8. Check the locking cylinder for proper function.

190D and 190E

1. Pry the cylinder rosette (trim ring) upwards and then remove it.

2. Insert the ignition key and turn it to position 1.

3. Using a bent paper clip, insert each end into the holes on either side of the lock cylinder. Press the clip ends inward; the pressure will unlock the cylinder from the steering lock.

4. Grasp the key and with pressure still on the paper clip, pull the ignition key/lock cylinder assembly out of the steering lock.

5. Remove the paper clip, turn the key to position 0 and remove it. Slide the lock cylinder out of the cover.

To install:

6. Insert the lock cylinder just enough so that the ridge on the cylinder body engages the groove in the steering lock.

7. Slide the cover onto the lock cylinder so that the detent is on the left side.

8. Insert the ignition key, turn it to position 1 and then push the lock cylinder and its cover into the steering lock.

NOTE: *When the ignition key is in position 1 and is aligned with the mark on the cover, the detent on the cover is also aligned with the ridge on the steering lock. This is the only manner in which the lock cylinder/cover can be installed in the steering lock.*

9. Check that the lock cylinder functions properly, if so, install the rosette.

Steering Lock

REMOVAL AND INSTALLATION

All Models Except 190D and 190E

1. Disconnect the ground cable from the battery.

2. Remove the instrument cluster.

3. Remove the plug connection from the ignition switch behind the dashboard.

4. Pull the ignition key to position 1.

5. Loosen the attaching screw for the steering lock.

6. Remove the cover sleeve from the steering lock.

7. On vehicles with the latest version of the steering lock, pull the connection for the warning buzzer.

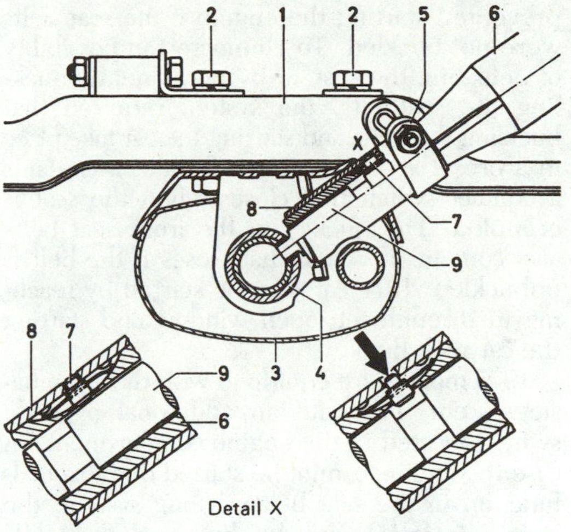

1. Cross member
2. Bolt
3. Jacket tube
4. Steering spindle
5. Fastening clip
6. Steering lock
7. Locking pin
8. Holder for steering lock
9. Locking bolt

Steering lock mechanism

8. Push in the lock pin with a small punch.

9. Turn the steering lock and remove it from the holder in the column jacket. Be sure that the rosette is not damaged.

CAUTION: *The lock pin can only be pushed in when the cylinder is in position 1.*

10. To install the steering lock, connect the warning buzzer if so equipped.

11. Place the steering lock in position 1 and insert the lock into the steering column while pushing the lockpin in. But sure that the lockpin engages.

12. Tighten the attaching clamp screw.

13. Attach the plug connection to the ignition switch.

14. Push the cover sleeve onto the lock in position 1.

15. Install the instrument cluster.

16. Check to be sure that the steering lock works properly.

190D and 190E

1. Follow Steps 1–8 of the "Ignition Switch Removal and Installation" procedure.

2. Unplug the switch and remove the steering lock.

3. Installation is in the reverse order of removal.

SEAT BELTS

Beginning in August of 1973 (1974 models), all Mercedes-Benz cars conformed to the regulation requiring a starter interlock system that prevented starting the engine if the seat belts were not buckled. To eliminate the possibility of defeating the system by permanently buckling the seatbelts, the system required that buckling the belts and starting the car take place in a preset sequence. Each front seat contains a contact switch that closes when the seat is occupied. The buckle on the front seat belts also contains a switch that closes if the belt is unbuckled. 1974 cars can be started by reaching in through the open window and starting the car with the key.

1975 models are equipped with the same basic system, but with an additional override switch, located in the engine compartment. In case the engine cannot be started due to a malfunction in the seat belt warning system, the starter interlock can be bypassed for ONE starting attempt, by pushing on the button on the switch with the ignition ON and the transmission in N or P. As soon as the transmission is shifted out of N or P, or the ignition is turned OFF, the relay in the over-ride switch is opened. To repeat the process, the switch must be depressed again.

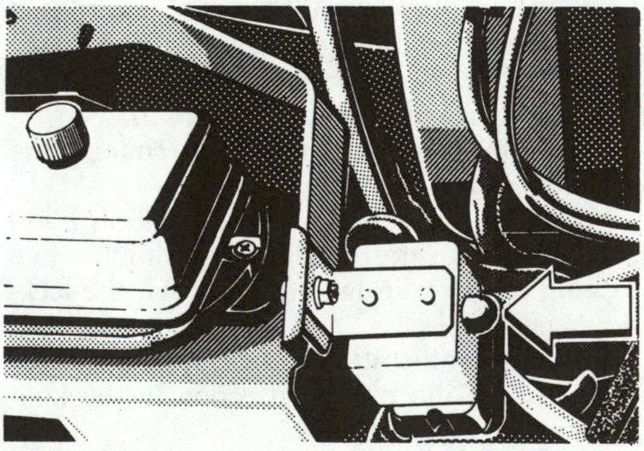

Ignition interlock over-ride switch location—1975 230

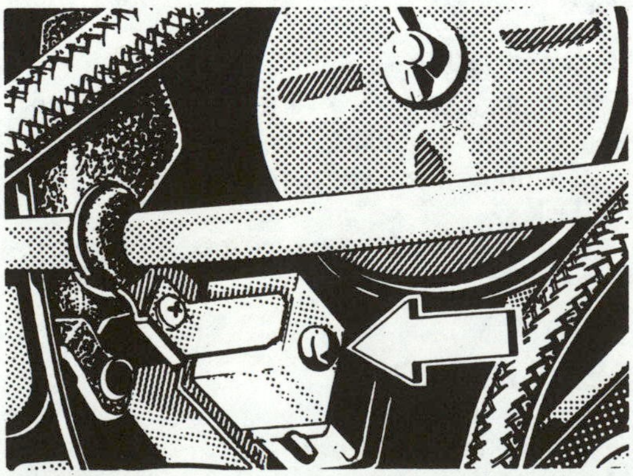

Ignition interlock over-ride switch location—1975 280, 280C

Ignition interlock over-ride switch location—1975 450SL, SLC

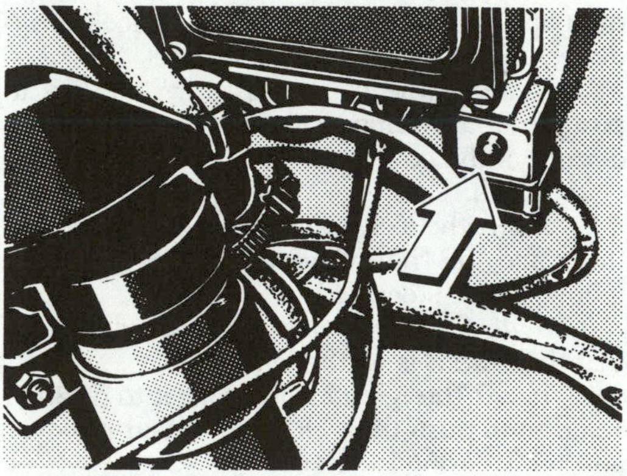

Ignition interlock over-ride switch location—1975 450SE, SEL

Disabling the Interlock System

As a result of Federal legislation, the starter interlock system used on 1974–75 cars was replaced with a light and buzzer reminder system. The new law, which took effect 12/26/74, permitted the disconnection of the starter interlock system (but not the warning light) and Mercedes-Benz does not advocate that this be done.

To bypass the interlock feature on all models so equipped (with or without an over-ride switch), replace the seatbelt logic relay (Part No. 000 545 69 32 or 000 545 68 32) with a new relay (Part No. 001 545 00 32). This will disable the interlock feature, but still allow the warning buzzer and buckle-up sequence to remain in effect.

NOTE: *Under no circumstances should the interlock system be bypassed by bridging either the over-ride switch relay or the logic relay, since this could allow the car to be started in gear.*

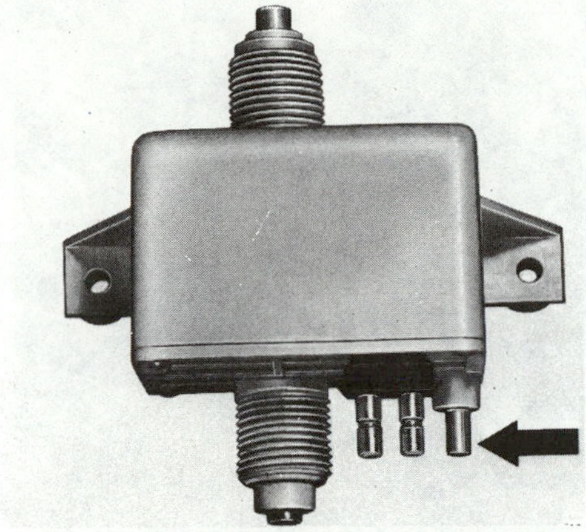

Catalyst elapsed mileage indicator reset button (arrow)

CATALYST REPLACEMENT WARNING INDICATOR

A warning light in the instrument cluster comes on at 37,500 mile intervals, indicating that the catalyst should be replaced. The catalyst mileage counter is located under the dash and is driven by the speedometer cable. To reset the mileage counter, push the reset pin on the counter.

HEADLIGHTS

REMOVAL AND INSTALLATION

230 (thru 1976), 280, 280C, 240D (thru 1976)

1. Loosen the screw on the lower portion of the unit.
2. Remove the trim ring together with the lower part of the unit.
3. Push the retaining ring in and, at the same time, turn the ring left to the stop.
4. Remove the ring, sealed beam lamp, and disconnect the plug.
5. Installation is the reverse of removal. If installing a Mercedes-Benz replacement sealed beam, be sure that the number "2" is at the top in the center. Be sure to have the headlights adjusted.

300SD (1981 and Later), 380SE, 380SEC, 380SEL, 500 SEC and 500 SEL

1. Open the hood and unscrew the 5 plastic knurled nuts.
2. Remove the assembly from the front of the car. Unplug the electrical connector.
3. Remove the headlight attaching screws.

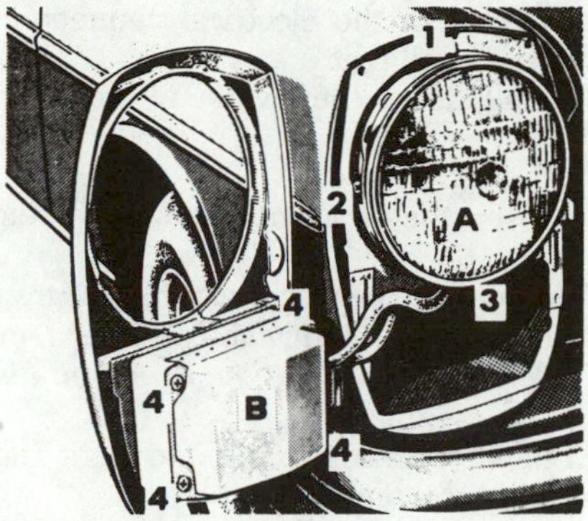

A. Sealed beam
B. Clearance lights housing
1. Vertical adjustment screws
2. Horizontal adjustment screws
3. Trim ring
4. Contact plug

Headlight removal—230, (thru '76), 280, 280C, 240D (thru '76)

1. Cover
2. Cover attaching screws
3. Horizontal aiming screws
4. Vertical aiming screws
5. High and low sealed beam
6. High sealed beam
7. Connector
8, 9. Trim ring attaching screws
10. Headlight housing

Headlight removal—except 230 and 240D (thru '76), 280, 280C

4. Disconnect the electrical connector and remove the headlight.
5. Installation is the reverse of removal.

All Other Models

1. Loosen the attaching screws and remove the cover.
2. Remove the headlight attaching screws and remove the retaining ring and light as a unit.

NOTE: *Do not disturb the headlight aiming screws.*

3. Pull the retaining ring and light slightly forward and disconnect the plug.
4. Remove the headlight and retaining ring.
5. Installation is the reverse of removal. Be sure that the plug and socket on the rear of the light are tight.

Some components (other than radio) are fused with a separate inline fuse located in the engine compartment

FUSES

A listing of the protected equipment and the amperage of the fuse is printed in the lid of the fuse box. Spare fuses and a tool for removing and installing fuses are contained in the vehicle tool kit.

Fuses cannot be repaired—they must be replaced. Always determine the cause of the blown fuse before replacing it with a new one.

Fuse Box Location

230, 240D, 300D, 300TD, 280, 280C, 280E, 280CE and 300CD

On early models, the fuse box may be found in the kick panel on the driver's side. On later models, the fuse box is located in the engine compartment on the driver's side, next to the brake master cylinder. Some models have separate fuse boxes or inline fuses for additional equipment. The radio is usually fused with a separate inline glass fuse behind the radio and the ignition is unfused.

190D, 190E, 280S, 280SE, 300SD, 380SE, 380SEL, 380SEL, 450SE, 450SEL, 500 SEC, 500 SEL and 6.9

The fuse box is located in the engine compartment, on the driver's side, next to the brake master cylinder. Some models may have separate fuse boxes or inline fuses in the engine compartment for additional equipment. The radio is usually fused with a separate inline glass

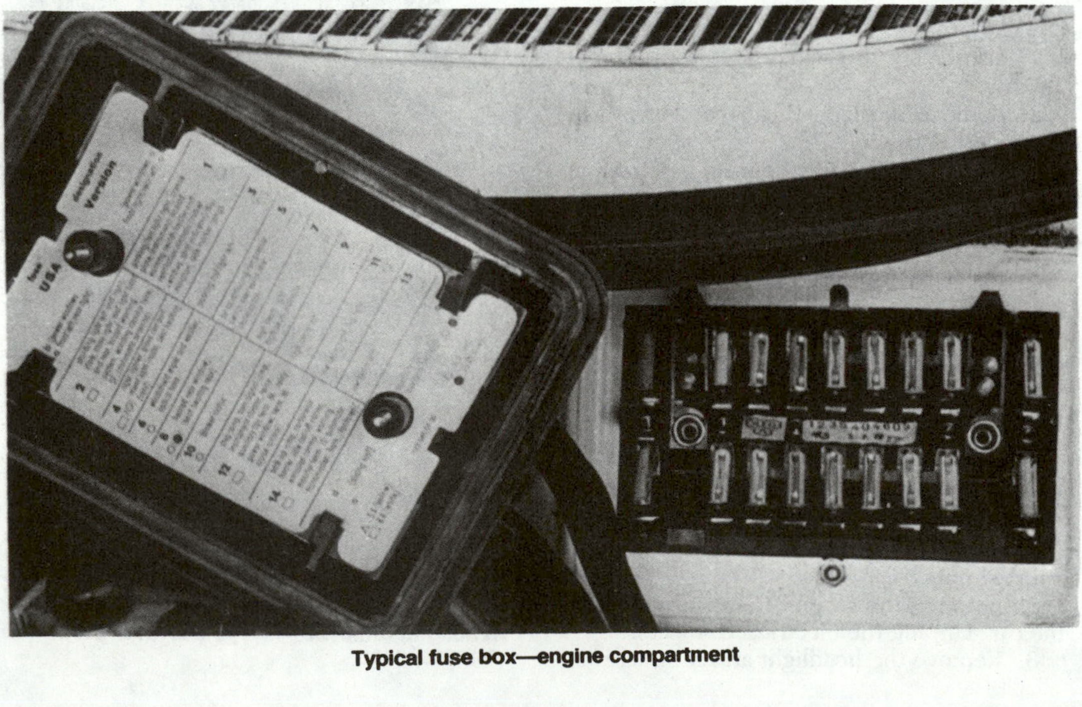

Typical fuse box—engine compartment

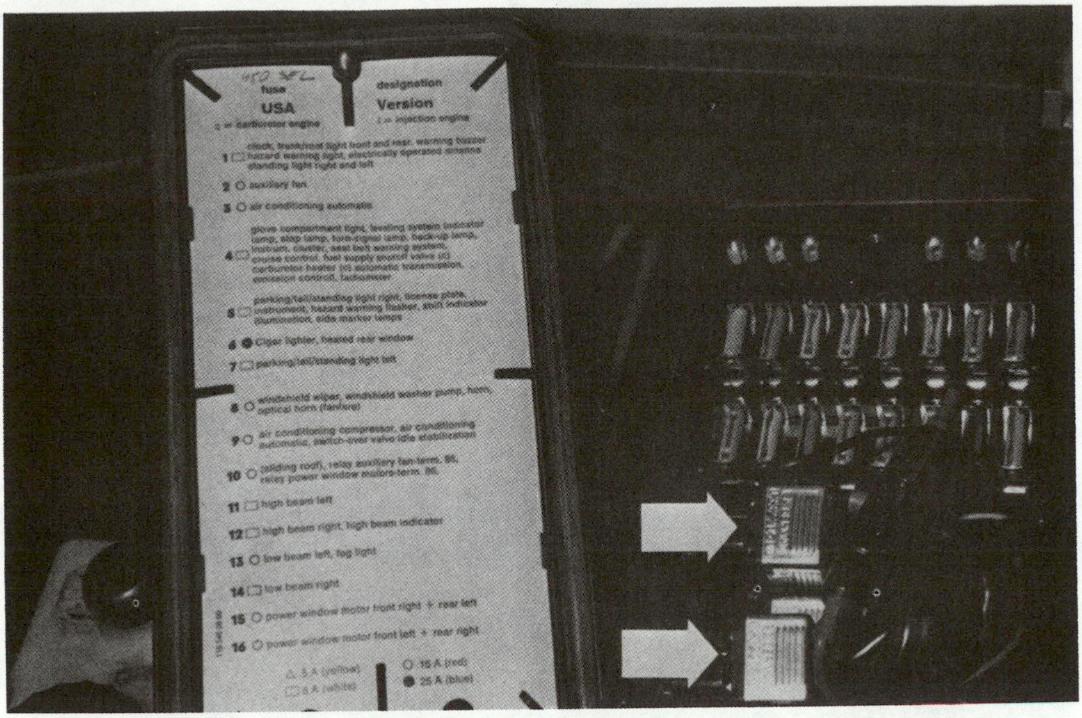

Typical fuse box (engine compartment)—this box contains various relays (arrow)

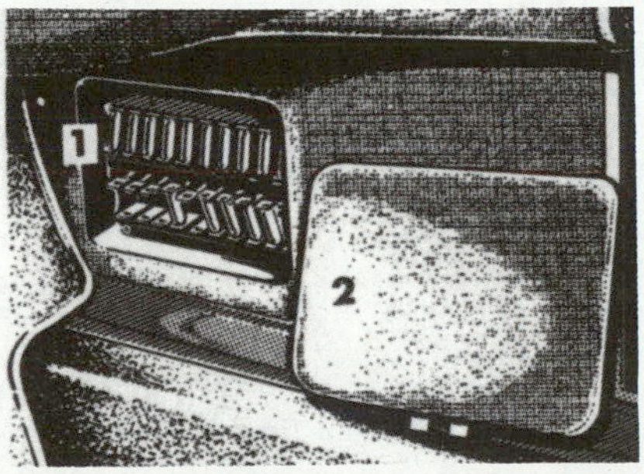

The fuse box in the 380SL, 380SLC, 450SL and 450SLC (1) is located behind an access panel (2) in the passenger-side kick panel

fuse behind the radio and the ignition is unfused. The fuse box also contains various relays.

380SL, 380SLC, 450SL and 450SLC

The fuse box is located in the right-hand (passenger's side) kick panel, behind a cover plate. There may also be separate fuse boxes or inline fuses in the engine compartment for additional equipment. The radio is usually fused with a separate inline glass fuse behind the radio and the ignition is unfused. The kick panel area also contains various relays and switches.

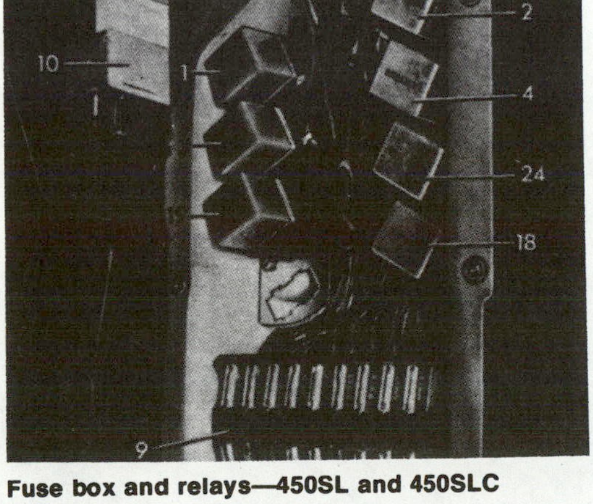

Fuse box and relays—450SL and 450SLC

1. Relay for fuel pump
2. Relay for starting valve
3. Relays for electronic control unit (early models)
4. Relay for starter terminal 50 or on USA vehicles relay for air-conditioner/starter terminal 50
9. Fuses
10. Time switch for heatable rear window
18. Relay for separating air-conditioner (supplementary fan) from exhaust cleaning (ignition changeover), on USA vehicles only
19. Relays for air-conditioning system and exhaust (two-way valve) on USA vehicles
24. Relay for supplementary fan

WIRING DIAGRAMS

Wiring diagrams have been left out of this book. As cars have become more complex, and available with longer and longer option lists, wiring diagrams have grown in size and complexity also. It has become virtually impossible to provide a readable reproduction in a reasonable number of pages. Information on ordering wiring diagrams from the vehicle manufacturer can be obtained from your dealer.

Clutch and Transmission

6

MANUAL TRANSMISSION

Only three models use a manual transmission today; the 190D, 190E and 240D. The 1974–81 240D uses a four speed, model G76/18C, the 1982–83 240D uses a four speed, model GL68/20A. The 190 series both are equipped with five speed transmissions, models GL68/20A(B)-5. All four transmissions are similar in design, operation and service.

REMOVAL AND INSTALLATION

The transmission should only be removed with the engine as a unit. The transmission-to-bell housing bolts can only be reached from inside. Once the engine/transmission unit has been removed from the vehicle, the transmission and bell housing must be separated from the engine, as follows:

With Engine

ALL MODELS

1. See Chapter 1 to remove the engine/transmission.
2. After removing the engine/transmission unit, unbolt the bellhousing from the engine. The bolts which hold the transmission to the bellhousing cannot be reached except from inside the bell housing.
3. Remove the starter. Pull the transmission and bellhousing from the engine.
4. The bolts which secure the bellhousing to the transmission are now visible and can be removed to separate the bellhousing and transmission.
5. To install, connect the engine, bellhousing, and transmission, after coating the splines of the mainshaft with grease.
6. Install the starter.
7. Further installation is the reverse of removal.

Without Engine

1974–81 240D

1. Support the car on jackstands.
2. Disconnect the battery.
3. Disconnect the exhaust pipe and/or muffler to provide clearance around the bellhousing.
4. Unhook the slave cylinder hydraulic line at the connection and plug both openings.
5. Unbolt the rear engine mount.
6. Slightly raise the transmission with a jack and remove the lower plate covering the transmission tunnel.
7. Disconnect the speedometer cable from the rear of the transmission.
8. Disconnect the shift rods from the transmission shift levers.
9. Loosen, but do not remove, the intermediate bearing bolts.
10. Matchmark the U-joint and driveshaft coupling and loosen the U-joint.
11. Matchmark the driveshaft flange and adaptor. Loosen the 3 driveshaft bolts. Remove 2 of the bolts and pivot the driveshaft around enough to reinstall the 2 bolts. Remove the 3rd bolt and position the driveshaft rearward as far as the center bearing permits. Use a piece of wood to block the driveshaft up in the driveshaft tunnel. Reinstall the 3rd bolt. The adaptor plate should remain on the 3-legged transmission flange.
12. Remove the starter.
13. Remove all bolts attaching the transmission to the intermediate flange, but remove the upper 2 bolts last.

    NOTE: *The clutch housing is heavily ribbed. Because of this, most of the bolts can only be reached with a 17 or 19 mm insert and extension.*

14. Turn the transmission 45° to the left so that the starter domes on both sides of the clutch housing do not scrape the transmission tunnel.

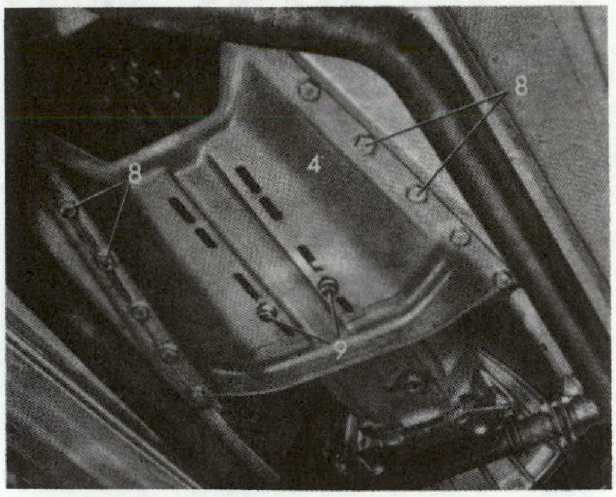

4. Tunnel plate
8. Bolts for tunnel plate
9. Bolts for rear engine rubber mount

Remove the driveshaft tunnel

10. Speedometer driveshaft
11. Fastening bolt
12. Rear engine rubber mount
13. Universal shaft bolt

Remove the driveshaft

Block the driveshaft up with a block of wood

15. Keep the transmission level and slide it out.
16. The clutch housing bolts can only be reached from inside. Unbolt the housing and remove it.
17. Installation is the reverse of removal.

1982–83 240D

1. Disconnect the battery.
2. Disconnect the regulating shaft in the engine compartment.
3. Support the transmission with a floor jack.
4. Unbolt the rear engine mount.
5. Unbolt each side of the engine carrier on the floor frame.
6. Unscrew the exhaust mounting bracket on the transmission. *Note the number and positioning of all washers.*
7. Unbolt the retaining strap and remove the exhaust pipe bracket.
8. Loosen the clamp nut on the driveshaft.
9. Loosen, but do not remove, the intermediate bearing bolts.
10. Unbolt the driveshaft on the transmission so that the companion plate remains with the driveshaft.
11. Carefully push the driveshaft as far to the rear as permitted.
12. Loosen and remove the tachometer drive shaft on the rear transmission case cover. Unclip the clip for the tachometer drive shaft from its holder.
13. Unscrew the holder for the line to the clutch housing. Unscrew the clutch slave cylinder and move it toward the rear until the pushrod is clear of the housing.
14. Push off the clip locks and then remove the shift rods from the intermediate levers on the shift bracket. *Note the position of the disc springs.*

CAUTION: *When the shift rods are disconnected, do not move the shift lever into reverse or you risk damaging the back-up light switch.*

15. Unbolt the starter and remove it.
16. Remove all transmission-to-intermediate flange screws. Remove the upper two last.
17. Carefully pull the transmission toward the rear of the vehicle and then remove it downward.

CAUTION: *Make sure that the input shaft has cleared the clutch plate before tilting the transmission.*

To install:

1. Lightly grease the centering lug and splines on the transmission input shaft.

NOTE: *Position the clutch slave cylinder and line above the transmission before beginning installation.*

2. Move the transmission into the clutch

so that one gear step engages. Rotate the mainshaft back and forth until the splines on the input shaft and clutch plate are aligned.

3. Move the transmission all the way in and then tighten the transmission-to-intermediate flange screws.
4. Install the starter.
5. Install the clutch slave cylinder with the proper plastic shims.
6. Installation of the remaining components is in the reverse order of removal. Please note the following:
   a. After installing the driveshaft, roll the car back and forth and then tighten the intermediate bearing free of tension.
   b. Tighten the driveshaft clamp nut to 22–29 ft. lbs. (30–40 Nm).
   c. Make sure of the proper positioning of all washers, spacers and shims.

190D AND 190E

1. Disconnect the battery.
2. Cover the insulation mat in the engine compartment to prevent damage.
3. On vehicles equipped with a auxiliary heater, be sure that the water hose is out of the way.
4. Support the transmission with a floor jack.
5. Unbolt the engine mounts at the rear transmission cover.
6. Unbolt the engine carrier on the floor frame.
7. Unscrew the exhaust holder at the transmission. *Note the number and positioning of all washers.*
8. Unscrew the clamping strap and remove the exhaust pipe holder.
9. Remove the intermediate bearing shield plate.
10. Repeat Steps 8–11 of the 1982–83 240D procedure.

NOTE: *On the 190E, the fitted sleeves on the universal flange must be loosened before separating the flange from the companion plate. This will require a cylindrical mandrel.*

11. Disconnect the exhaust system at the rear suspension and suspend it with wire.
12. Loosen and remove the input shaft for the tachometer.
13. Repeat Steps 12–16 of the 1982–83 240D procedure.
14. Rotate the transmission approximately 45° to the left, slide it out of the clutch plate and then remove it downward.

CAUTION: *Make sure that the input shaft has cleared the clutch plate before tilting the transmission.*

15. To install, repeat Steps 1–6 (installation) of the 1982–83 240D procedure. Remember that the transmission must be tilted approximately 45° to the left when installing.

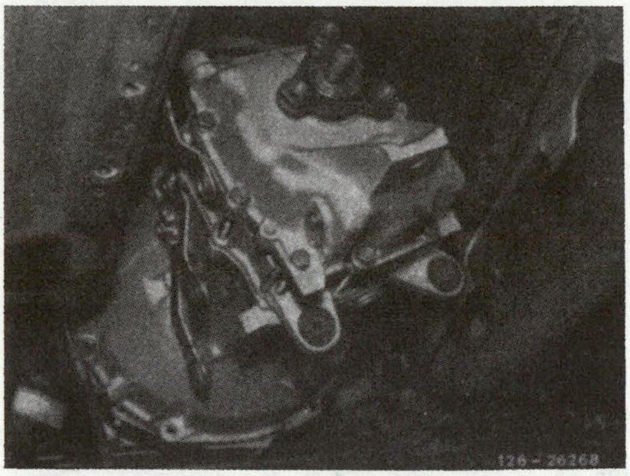

Tilt the transmission 45° to the left when removing from the 190

LINKAGE ADJUSTMENT

The only type of shifter used is a floor mounted type.

CAUTION: *On all types of transmissions, never hammer or force a new shift knob on with the shifter installed, as the plastic bushing connected to the lever will be damaged and cause hard shifting.*

Proper adjustment of the shaft linkage is dependent on both the position of the shift levers at the transmission and the length of the shift rods. The shift levers, rods and bearing block are all located underneath the floor tunnel; the driveshaft shield may have to be removed to gain access to them.

1. With the transmission in neutral and the driveshaft shield removed (if so equipped), remove the clip locks and disconnect the shift rods from the intermediate shift levers under the floor shift bearing bracket.
2. With the shifter still in the neutral position, lock the three intermediate shift levers by inserting a 0.2156 in. rod (a No. 3 drill bit will do, or any other tool of approximately the same diameter) through the levers and the holes in the bearing bracket.
3. Check the positioning of the shift levers at the transmission (see illustrations). Adjust by loosening the clamp bolts and moving the levers.
4. With the intermediate levers locked and the shift levers adjusted properly, try hooking the shift rods back onto their respective intermediate levers. The shift rods may be adjusted by loosening the locknut and turning the ball socket on the end until they are the proper length.

NOTE: *When hooking up the shift rods to*

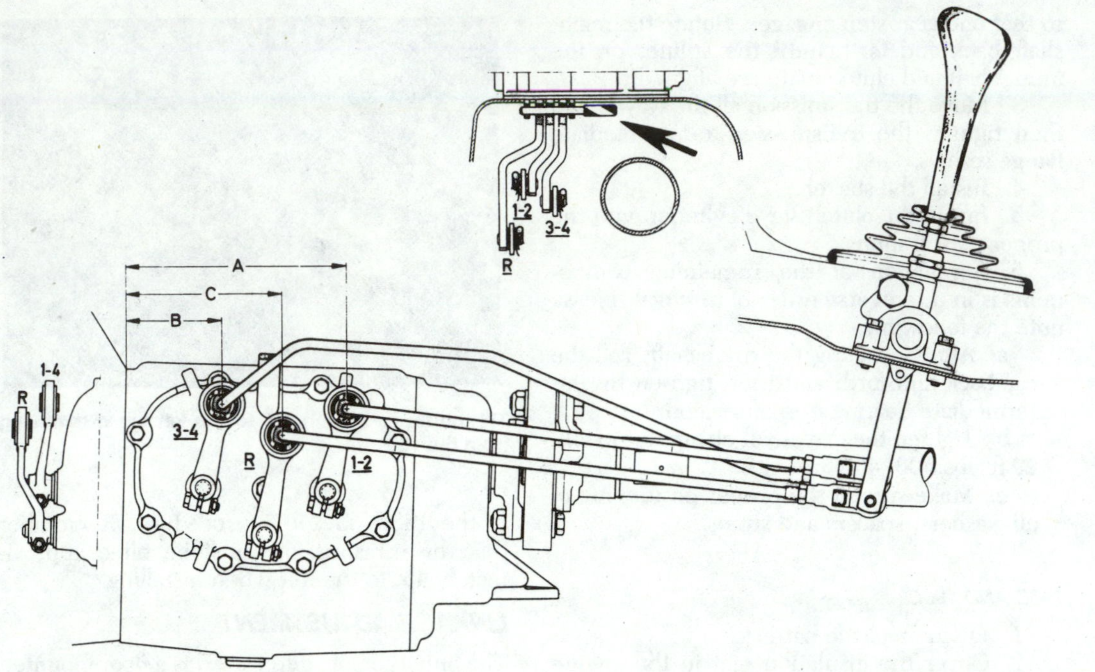

Transmission linkage—1974–81 240D. Arrow at top shows locking pin installed prior to adjustment

the intermediate levers, be very careful not to move the transmission shift levers out of their adjusted position.

NOTE: *When reattaching the shift rods on 190 models, use only clip locks which have a radiused edge. If the old style clip locks with a square edge are used, there is a possibility that the locks will pop out and the shift rods will drop down.*

5. Remove the locking rod from the bearing bracket, start the engine and then shift through the gears a few times. Occasionally slight binding may call for VERY slight further adjustments.

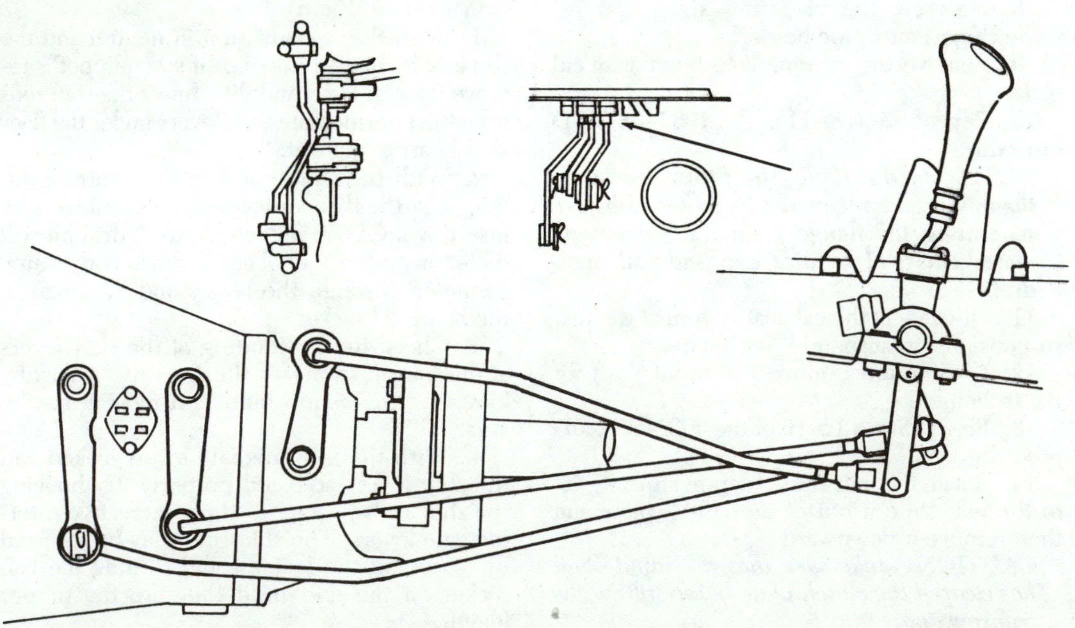
Transmission linkage—1982–83 240D. Arrow at top shows locking rod installed prior to adjustment

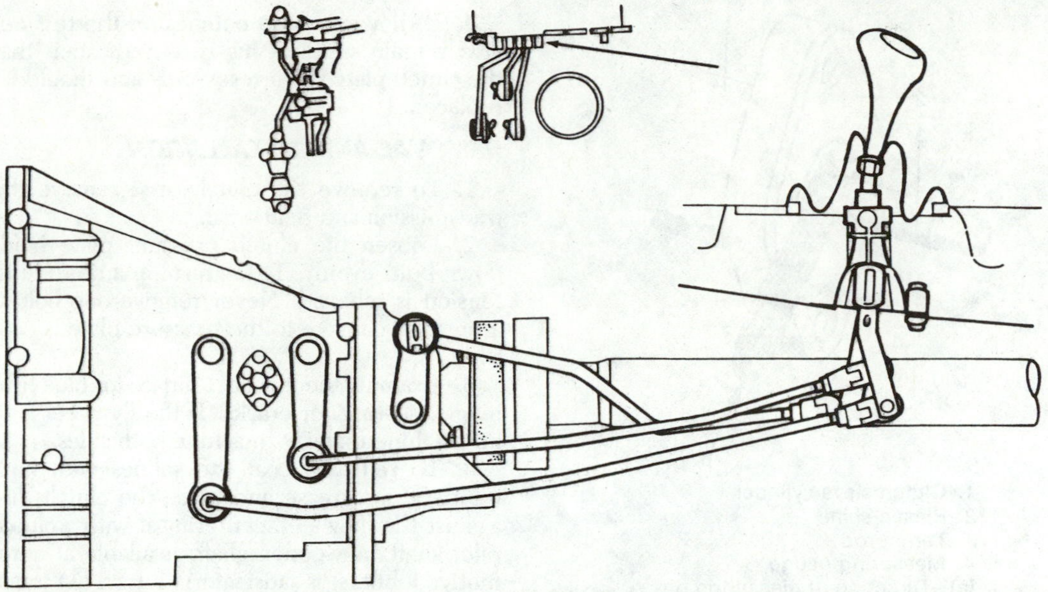

Transmission linkage—190 (4 speed shown, 5 speed similar). Arrow at top shows locking rod installed prior to adjustment

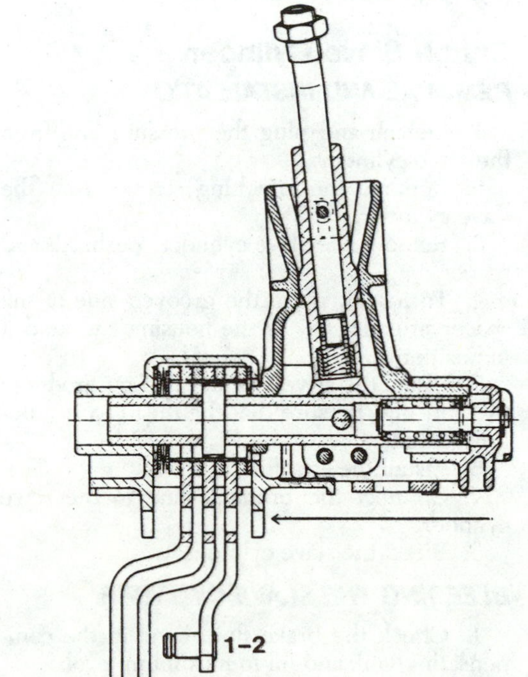

Intermediate lever positioning on the 5 speed 190. Arrow shows where locking rod goes

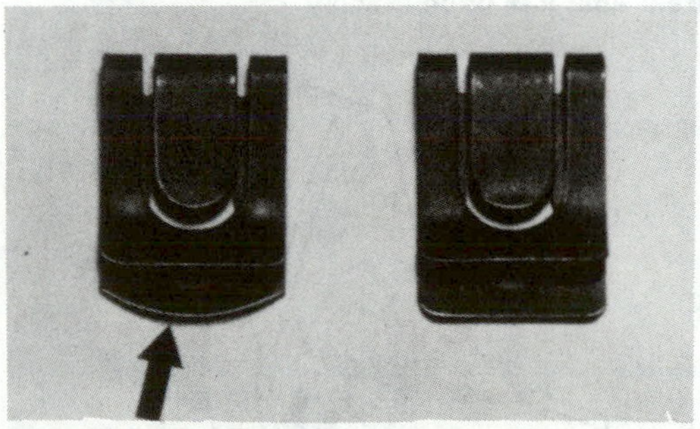

Always use clip locks with curved edges when installing the shift rods on the 190

CLUTCH

Checking for Wear

A spring plate clutch that automatically compensates for wear is used, so no periodic adjustments are required. Apart from the usual slippage which accompanies severe wear of the clutch plate or disc, Mercedes-Benz has a simple tool, which can be purchased from a dealer that measures the amount of wear on the clutch plate. Actually, it is a simple "go-no go" gauge.

1. A plastic shim is installed between the slave cylinder and the bellhousing.

2. The shim is provided with two flat grooves running diagonally from bottom to center. When

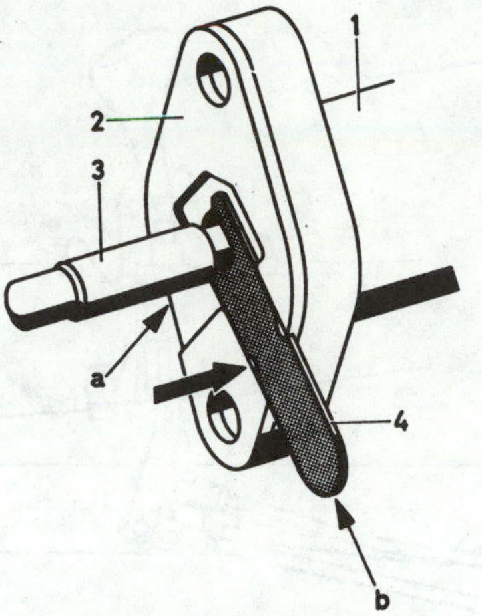

1. Clutch slave cylinder
2. Plastic shim
3. Thrust rod
4. Measuring gauge
(a)—Direction of measuring on lefthand drive vehicle with steering wheel and center shift, as well as on righthand drive vehicles with center shift
(b)—Direction of measuring on righthand drive vehicles with steering wheel shift

Wear limit has been reached

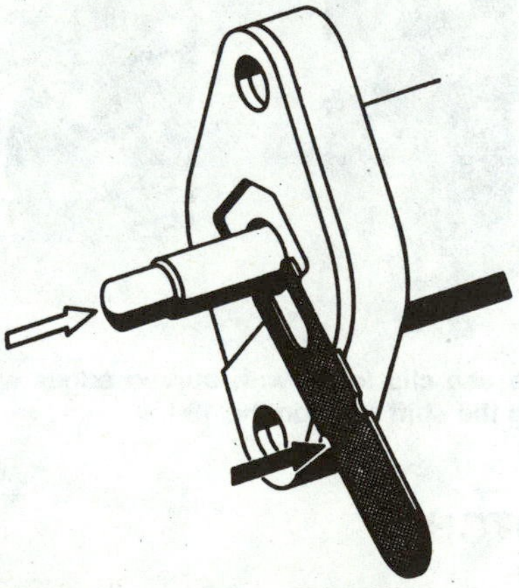

Wear limit has not been reached

the shim is installed, these grooves appear as slots. Use groove (a) for left-hand drive vehicles and groove (b) for right-hand drive vehicles.

3. The clutch slave cylinder pushrod has two different diameters. The jaw width of the test device corresponds to the smaller diameter of the pushrod. If the notches on the test device disappear when the test device is inserted as far as it will go, the clutch plate is still operational.

4. If, however, the notches on the test device remain visible, this is an indication that the clutch plate is worn severely and should be replaced.

REMOVAL AND INSTALLATION

1. To remove the clutch, first remove the transmission and bellhousing.
2. Loosen the clutch pressure plate hold-down bolts evenly, 1–1½ turns at a time, until tension is relieved. Never remove one bolt at a time, as damage to the pressure plate is possible.
3. Examine the flywheel surface for blue heat marks, scoring, or cracks. If the flywheel is to be machined, always machine both sides.
4. To reinstall, coat the splines with high temperature grease and place the clutch disc against the flywheel, centering it with a clutch pilot shaft. A wooden shaft, available at automotive jobbers, is satisfactory, but an old transmission mainshaft works best.
5. Tighten the pressure plate holddown bolts evenly 1–1½ turns at a time until tight, then remove the pilot shaft.

CAUTION: *Most clutch plates have the flywheel side marked as such (Kupplungsseite). Do not assume that the pressure springs always face the transmission.*

Clutch Slave Cylinder

REMOVAL AND INSTALLATION

1. Detach and plug the pressure line from the slave cylinder.
2. Remove the attaching screws from the slave cylinder.
3. Remove the slave cylinder, pushrod, and spacer.
4. To install, place the grooved side of the spacer in contact with the housing and hold it in position.
5. Install the slave cylinder and pushrod into the housing. Be sure that the dust cap is properly seated.
6. Install the attaching screws.
7. Connect the pressure line to the slave cylinder.
8. Bleed the slave cylinder.

BLEEDING THE SLAVE CYLINDER

1. Check the brake fluid level in the compensating tank and fill to maximum level.
2. Put a hose on the bleeder screw of the right front caliper and open the bleeder screw.
3. Have a helper depress the brake pedal until the hose is full and there are no air bubbles. Be sure the bleeder screw is closed each time the pedal is released.
4. Put the free end of the hose on the bleeder

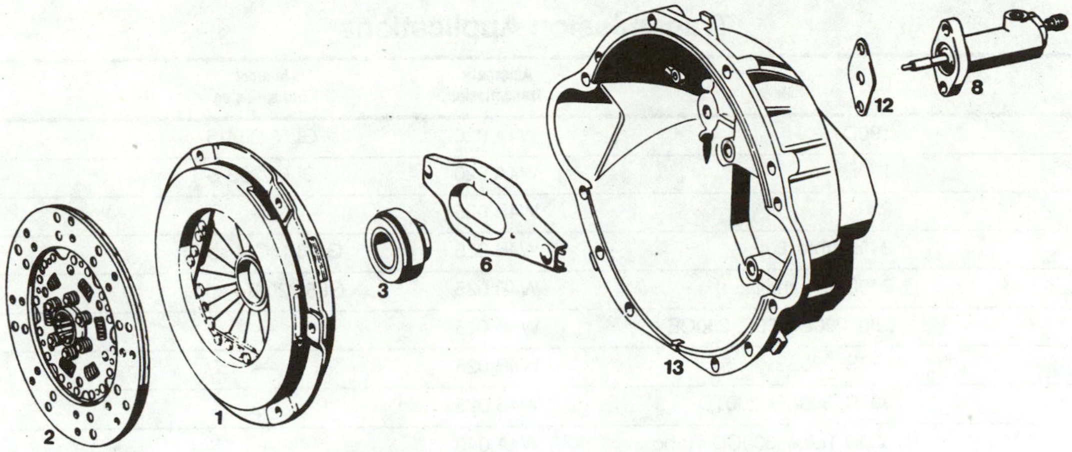

1. Plate spring clutch
2. Driven plate
3. Throwout
6. Throwout rocker
8. Slave cylinder
12. Shim
13. Clutch housing

Exploded view of clutch

screw of the slave cylinder and open the bleeder screw.

5. Keep stepping on the brake pedal. Close the bleeder screw on the caliper and release the brake pedal. Open the bleeder screw and repeat the process until no air bubbles show up at the mouth of the inlet line on the compensating tank.

Between operations, check, and, if necessary, refill the compensating tank.

6. Close the bleeder screws on the caliper and slave cylinder and remove the hose.

7. Check the clutch operation and the fluid level.

AUTOMATIC TRANSMISSION

REMOVAL AND INSTALLATION

Mercedes-Benz automatic transmissions are removed as a unit with the engine. Consult the "Engine Mechanical" section for removal and installation procedures concerning a given engine.

In-Car Service

Because automatic transmission work is mainly done by specialty shops, only in-car service procedures are given here.

Before doing any work on the automatic transmission, consult the transmission identification chart to determine which transmission you are dealing with.

PAN AND FILTER REPLACEMENT

1. Drain the transmission of all fluid by loosening the dipstick tube.
2. Remove the transmission pan.
3. Remove the bolt or bolts which retain the filter to the transmission.
4. Remove the filter and replace it with a new one.
5. Install the transmission pan, using a new gasket.
6. Refill the transmission to the proper level with the specified brand of fluid.

SELECTOR ROD LINKAGE ADJUSTMENT

NOTE: *Before performing this adjustment on any Mercedes-Benz vehicle, be sure that the vehicle is resting on its wheels. No part of the vehicle may be jacked for this adjustment.*

Bottom view of automatic transmission showing dipstick tube (1), converter drain plug (2) and pan (3)

Transmission Applications

Model	Automatic Transmission	Manual Transmission
190D	W4A 020	GL68/20A-5
190E	W4A 020	GL68/20B-5
230	W4B 025	—
240D (thru '80)	W4B 025	G-76/18C(4-spd.)
240D ('81 and later)	W4B 025	GL68/20A(4-spd.)
280, 280C, 280E, 280CE	W4B 025	—
280S, 280SE	W4B 025	—
300D, 300CD, 300TD	W4B 025	—
300D Turbo. 300CD Turbo	W4A 040	—
300TD Turbo 1981–83	W4A 040	—
300SD 1978–80	W4B 025	—
300SD 1981–84	W4A 040	—
280SL, 380SLC, 380SEL, 380SEC, 380SE	W4A 040	—
450SE, 450SEL, 450SL, 450SLC	W3A 040	—
500SEL, 500SEC	W4A 040	—
6.9	W3B 050	—

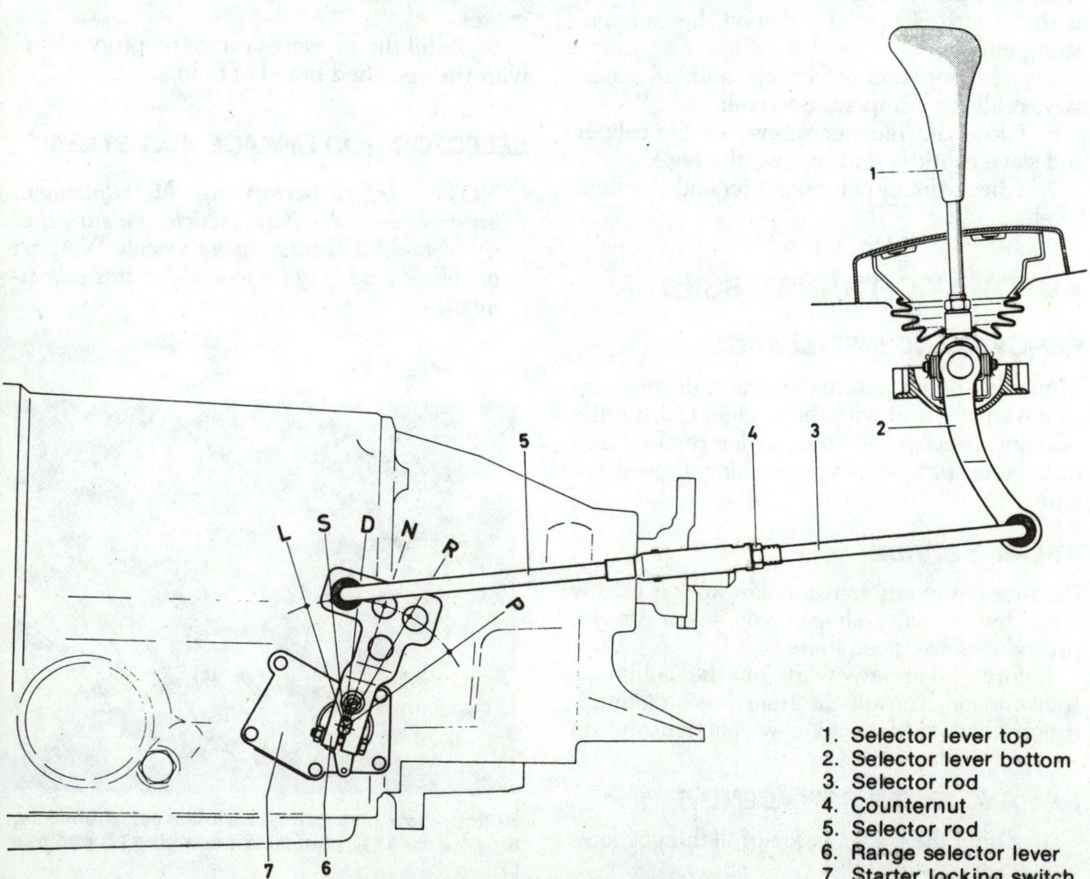

1. Selector lever top
2. Selector lever bottom
3. Selector rod
4. Counternut
5. Selector rod
6. Range selector lever
7. Starter locking switch

Floor mounted selector rod linkage

Column Mounted Linkage

See the "Transmission Application" chart in the specifications for Transmission Application.

W3A 040

1. Loosen the counternut on the ball socket.
2. Disconnect the selector rod from the shift lever bracket.
3. Set the transmission selector lever and the selector rod in Neutral.
4. Adjust the length of the selector rod until the ball socket aligns with the end of the ball on the intermediate lever.
5. Attach the ball socket to the intermediate lever, making sure that the play in the selector lever in position Three (D) and Four (S) is about equal.
6. Tighten the counternut on the ball socket.

W3A 040 (380SEL, 450SE AND 450SEL ONLY), W4B 025 AND W4A 040

1. Loosen the counternut on the rear selector rod while holding both recesses of the front selector rod with an open end wrench.
2. Disconnect the selector rod from the selector lever.
3. Set the selector lever on the transmission and on the column to Neutral.
4. Adjust the selector rod until the bearing pin is aligned with the bearing bushing in the selector lever.
5. Connect the rear selector lever to the selector rod and secure it with the lock. Be sure that the clearance of the selector lever in D and S is equal.
6. Tighten the locknut on the rear selector rod while holding the front selector rod as in Step 1.

Floor Mounted Linkage

NOTE: *The vehicle must be standing with the weight normally distributed on all four wheels. No jacks may be used.*

1. Disconnect the selector rod from the selector lever.
2. Set the selector lever in Neutral and make sure that there is approximately 1 mm clearance between the selector lever and the N stop of the selector gate.
3. Adjust the length of the selector rod so that it can be attached free of tension.
4. Retighten the counternut.

STARTER LOCKOUT AND BACK-UP LIGHT SWITCH ADJUSTMENT

All Models

1. Disconnect the selector rod and move the selector lever on the transmission to position Neutral.
2. Tighten the clamping screw prior to making adjustments.
3. Loosen the adjusting screw and insert the locating pin through the driver into the locating hole in the shift housing.
4. Tighten the adjusting screw and remove the locating pin.
5. Move the selector lever to position N and connect the selector rod so that there is no tension.
6. Check to be sure that the engine cannot be started in Neutral or Park.

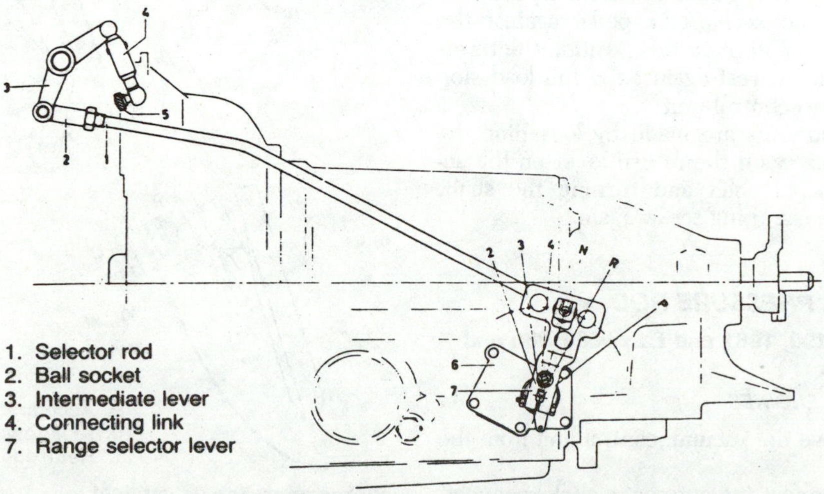

1. Selector rod
2. Ball socket
3. Intermediate lever
4. Connecting link
7. Range selector lever

Column mounted selector rod linkage—W3A 040

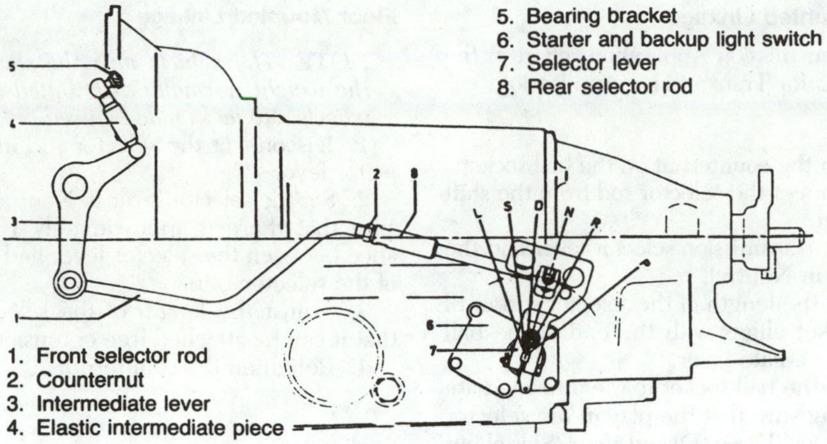

1. Front selector rod
2. Counternut
3. Intermediate lever
4. Elastic intermediate piece
5. Bearing bracket
6. Starter and backup light switch
7. Selector lever
8. Rear selector rod

Selector rod linkage on the W4A 040 and W4B 025

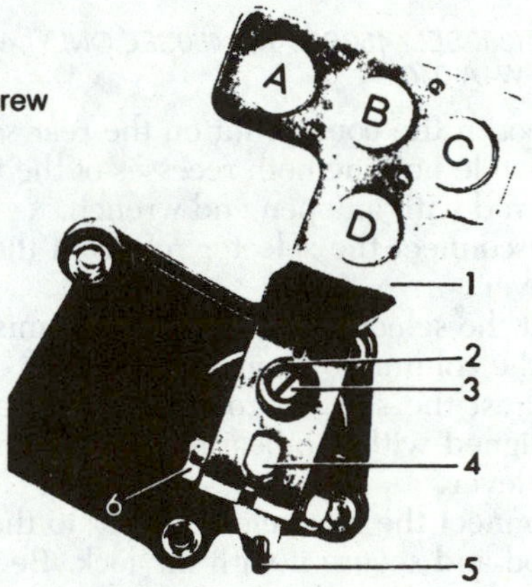

1. Selector range lever
2. Washer
3. Adjusting screw
4. Shaft
5. Locating pin
6. Clamping screw

(a)—Column shift for left-hand and right-hand drive vehicles 200/8, 220 D/8, 230/8, 280 S/8, 280 SE/8 and 300 SEL/8.

(b)—Steering wheel shift for left-hand drive vehicles (220/8, 220 D/8, 230/8, 250/8)

(c)—Steering wheel shift for right-hand drive vehicles (220/8, 220 D/8, 230/8, 250/8)

(d)—Steering wheel shift for left-hand drive vehicles (280S/8, 280 SE/8, 300 SEL/8, 280 SE/3.5 and 300 SEL/3.5)

Starter lockout and back-up light switch adjustment

KICKDOWN SWITCH

All Models

1. The kickdown position of the solenoid valve is controlled by the accelerator pedal.

2. Push the accelerator pedal against the kickdown limit stop. In this position the throttle lever should rest against the full load stop of the venturi control unit.

3. Adjustments are made by loosening the clamping screw on the return lever on the accelerator pedal shaft and turning the shaft. Tighten the clamping screw again.

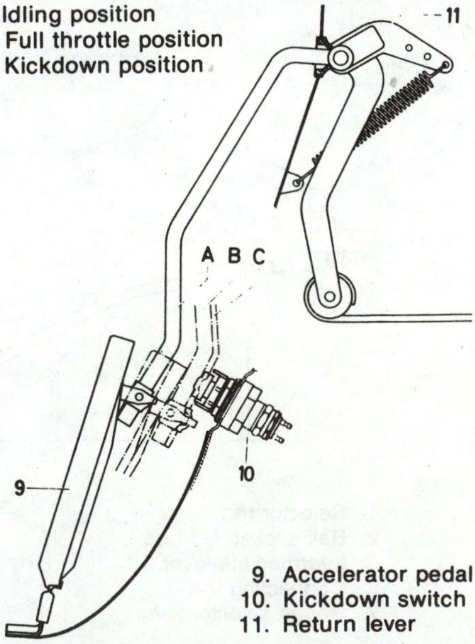

A. Idling position
B. Full throttle position
C. Kickdown position

9. Accelerator pedal
10. Kickdown switch
11. Return lever

Kickdown switch adjustment

CONTROL PRESSURE ROD

All except 190, 1981 and Later 300, 380 and 500 Models

4 CYLINDER ENGINES

1. Remove the vacuum control unit from the carburetor.

2. Disconnect the automatic choke connect-

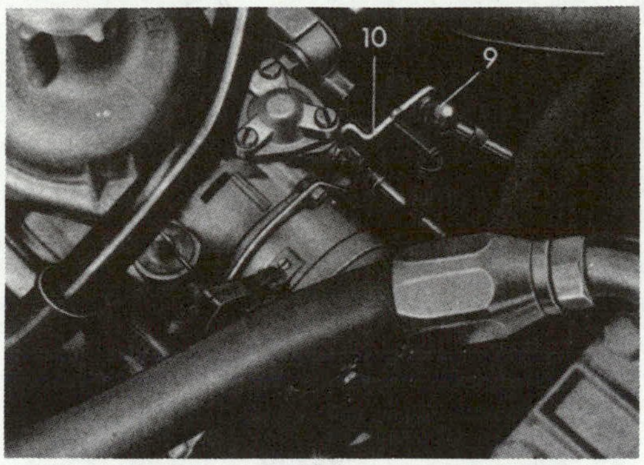

9. Ball socket 10. Throttle valve lever

Control pressure rod adjustment—230

ing rod so the throttle valve rests against the idle stop.

3. Loosen the screw and turn the levers against each other so the control rod rests against the idle stop.

4. Tighten the screw and depress the accelerator to the kickdown position. The throttle valve must rest against the full throttle stop.

5. Install the vacuum control unit on the distributor and connect the automatic choke rod.

DIESEL ENGINES

The control pressure rod can only be adjusted with a special gauge available only from Mercedes-Benz dealers.

6-CYLINDER ENGINES

1. Disconnect the control pressure rod.
2. Push the angle lever in the direction of the arrow.
3. Push the control pressure rod rearward

57. Control pressure rod
58. Ball socket
59. Counternut
120. Angle lever
144. Connecting rod

Control pressure rod adjustment—6-cylinder engine

7. Roller
11. Connecting rod
12. Bearing bracket
13. Control pressure rod
17. Regulating lever
18. Stop pin
19. Gate lever
20. Angle lever
31. Connecting rod

Control pressure rod adjustment—1974–80 V8 engines

against the stop and adjust its length so there is no binding.

4. Tighten the counter nut after adjustment.

V8 Engines

1. Remove the air filter and disconnect the control pressure linkage.
2. The throttle valve should rest against the idle speed stop.
3. Push the regulating lever and angle lever to the idle position.
4. Push the control pressure rod completely rearward against the stop and adjust the length of the rod so there is no tension.
5. When checking the rod for length, hold it to the left of the socket, not above to compensate for rotary motion of the linkage.

CONTROL PRESSURE CABLE

1981 and later

380SE, 380SEC, 380SEL, 380SL, 380SLC, 500SEC AND 500SEL

1. Remove the air cleaner.
2. Loosen the clamping screw.
3. Push the ball socket back, then carefully forward until a slight resistance is felt. At this point, tighten the clamp screw.
4. Install the air cleaner.

TURBODIESELS

1. Pry off the ball socket.
2. Push the ball socket back, then pull carefully forward until a slight resistance is felt.
3. Hold the ball socket above the ball head. The drag lever should rest against the stop.

Control pressure cable adjustment—190D

4. Adjust the cable at the adjusting screw so that the ball socket can be attached with no strain.

190D

1. Remove the ball socket (19) and extend the telescoping rod (8) to its full length.
2. Pull the control cable forward until a slight resistance is felt. Hold the ball socket over the ball head and engage tension free.

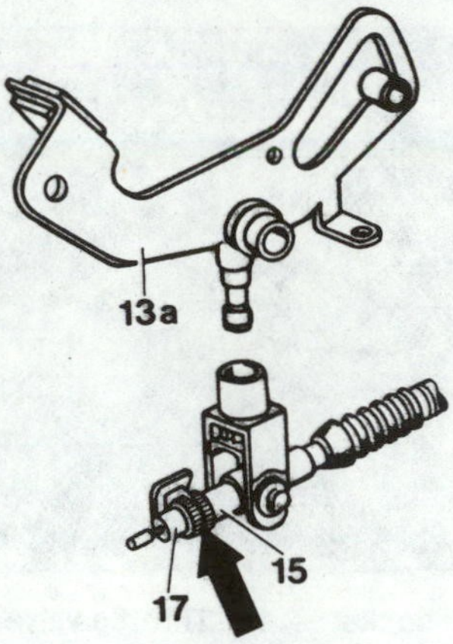

Control pressure cable adjustment—190E

3. Adjust by using the telescoping rod if so required.

190E

1. Turn the adjusting screw (15) inward until the compression nipple on the spacing sleeve (17) has approximately 1mm of play left.
2. Unscrew the adjusting screw until the tip of the pointer rests directly above the groove on the adjusting screw.

Drive Train 7

DRIVELINE

Mercedes-Benz automobiles use either two or three piece driveshafts to connect the transmission to a hypoid independent rear axle. All models covered in this book use independent rear suspension.

Understanding Rear Axles

The rear axle is a special type of transmission that reduces the speed of the drive from the engine and transmission and drives the power to the rear wheels. Power enters the rear axle from the driveshaft via the companion flange. The flange is mounted on the drive pinion shaft. The drive pinion shaft and gear which carry the power into the differential turn at engine speed. The gear on the end of the pinion shaft drives a large ring gear the axis of rotation of which is 90° away from that of the pinion. The pinion and ring gear reduce the speed and multiply the power by the gear ratio of the axle, and change the direction of rotation to turn the axle shafts which drive both wheels. The rear axle gear ratio is found by dividing the number of pinion gear teeth into the number of ring gear teeth.

The ring gear drives the differential case. The case provides the two mounting points for the ends of a pinion shaft on which are mounted two pinion gears. The pinion gears drive the two side gears, one of which is located on the inner end of each axle shaft.

By driving the axle shafts through this arrangement, the differential allows the outer drive wheel to turn faster than the inner drive wheel in a turn.

The main drive pinion and the side bearings, which bear the weight of the differential case, are shimmed to provide proper bearing preload, and to position and the pinion and ring gears properly.

NOTE: *The proper adjustment of the relationship of the ring and pinion gears is critical. It should be attempted only by those with extensive equipment and/or experience.*

Limited-slip differentials include clutches which tend to link each axle shaft to the differential case. Clutches may be engaged either by spring action or by pressure produced by the torque on the axles during a turn. During turning on a dry pavement, the effects of the clutch are overcome, and each wheel turns at the required speed. When slippage occurs at either wheel, however, the clutches will transmit some of the power to the wheel which has the greater amount of traction. Because of the presence of clutches, limited-slip units require a special lubricant.

Basic Rear Axle Problems

First, determine when the noise is most noticeable.

- Drive Noise: Produced under vehicle acceleration.
- Coast Noise: Produced while the car coasts with a closed throttle.
- Float Noise: Occurs while maintaining constant car speed (just enough to keep speed constant) on a level road.

Road Noise

Brick or rough surfaced concrete roads produce noises that seem to come from the rear axle. Road noise is usually identical in Drive or Coast and driving on a different type of road will tell whether the road is the problem.

Tire Noise

Tire noises are often mistaken for rear axle problems. Snow treads or unevenly worn tires produce vibrations seeming to originate elsewhere. Temporarily inflating the tires to 40 lbs will significantly alter tire noise, but will have

Noise Diagnosis

The Noise Is:	Most Probably Produced By
1. Identical under Drive or Coast	Road surface, tires or front wheel bearings
2. Different depending on road surface	Road surface or tires
3. Lower as the car speed is lowered	Tires
4. Similar with car standing or moving	Engine or transmission
5. A vibration	Unbalanced tires, rear wheel bearing, unbalanced driveshaft or worn U-joint
6. A knock or click about every 2 tire revolutions	Rear wheel bearing
7. Most pronounced on turns	Damaged differential gears
8. A steady low-pitched whirring or scraping, started at low speeds	Damaged or worn pinion bearing
9. A chattering vibration on turns	Wrong differential lubricant or worn clutch plates (limited slip rear axle)
10. Noticed only in Drive, Coast or Float conditions	Worn ring gear and/or pinion gear

no effect on rear axle noises (which normally cease below about 30 mph).

Engine/Transmission Noise

Determine at what speed the noise is most pronounced, then stop the car in a quiet place. With the transmission in Neurtal, run the engine through speeds corresponding to road speeds where the noise was noticed. Noises produced with the car standing still are coming from the engine or transmission.

Front Wheel Bearings

While holding the car speed steady; lightly apply the footbrake; this will often decrease bearing noise, as some of the load is taken from the bearing.

Rear Axle Noises

Eliminating other possible sources can narrow the cause to the rear axle, which normally produces noise from worn gears or bearings. Gear noises tend to peak in a narrow speed range, while bearing noises will usually vary in pitch with engine speeds.

Driveshaft and U-Joints

REMOVAL AND INSTALLATION

230, 240D, 300D, 300CD, 300TD, 280, 280C, 280E, 280CE

NOTE: *Matchmark all driveshaft connections prior to removal.*

1. Remove the equalizer and disconnect the parking brake cables.
2. Remove the bolts which secure the two brackets to the chassis at the front and rear and remove the brackets. It may be necessary to lower the exhaust system slightly to allow access to the left-hand bolts on the rear bracket.
3. Loosen the nut on the driveshaft about 2 turns without pushing the rubber sleeve back (it slides along). On a two-piece shaft, only loosen the front clamp nut.
4. Remove the nuts which secure the attaching plate to the transmission flange and rear axle.
5. Remove the bolts which secure the intermediate bearing(s) to the chassis. Push the driveshaft together and slightly down, and remove the driveshaft from the vehicle.

Troubleshooting the Driveline

The Problem	Is Caused By	What to Do
Shudder as car accelerates from stop or low speed	• Loose U-joint • Defective center bearing	• Tighten or replace U-joint • Replace center bearing
Loud clunk in driveshaft when shifting gears	• Worn U-joints	• Replace U-joints
Roughness or vibration at any speed	• Out-of-balance, bent or dented driveshaft • Worn U-joints • U-joint clamp bolts loose	• Have driveshaft serviced • Service U-joints • Tighten U-joint clamp bolts
Squeaking noise at low speeds	• Lack of U-joint lubrication	• Lubricate U-joints if problem persists, service U-joint
Knock or clicking noise	• U-joint or driveshaft hitting frame tunnel • Worn U-joint	• Correct overloaded condition • Replace U-joint

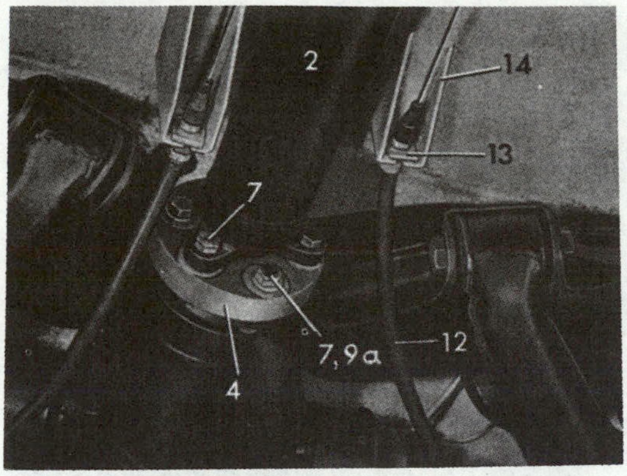

2. Rear propeller shaft
4. Companion plate
7. Hex. bolt
9a. Washer
12. Rear brake cable control
13. Spring clip
14. Holder on frame floor

Rear driveshaft mounting flange

NOTE: *If possible, do not sparate the parts of the driveshaft since each driveshaft is balanced at the factory. If separation is necessary, all parts must be marked and reassembled in the same relative positions to assure that the driveshafts will remain reasonably well balanced.*

6. Installation is the reverse of removal.
7. Pack the cavities of the two centering sleeves with special Mercedes-Benz grease.
8. Install the driveshaft and attach the intermediate bearing(s) to the chassis.
9. Rock the car backward and forward several times to be sure that the driveshaft is properly centered without forcing.
10. Prior to tightening the clamp nuts on a three piece driveshaft, be sure that the intermediate shaft does not contact either the front or rear intermediate bearing. The clearance between the intermediate shaft and the bearing should be the same at both ends.

All Other Models

NOTE: *Steps 1–3 apply to 4 cylinder and V8 models. Matchmark all driveshaft connections prior to removal.*

1. Fold the torsion bar down after disconnecting the level control linkage (if equipped).
2. Remove the exhaust system.
3. Remove the heat shield from the frame.
4. Support the transmission with a jack and completely remove the rear engine mount crossmember.
5. Without sliding the rubber sleeve back loosen the clamp nut approximately two turns (the rubber sleeve will slide along).

NOTE: *On 3 piece driveshafts, only the front clamp nut need be loosened.*

6. Unscrew the U-joint mounting flange from the U-joint plate.
7. Bend back the locktabs and remove the bolts that attach the driveshaft to the rear axle pinion yoke.
8. Remove the bolts which attach the intermediate bearing(s) to the frame. Push the driveshaft together slightly and remove it from the vehicle.
9. Try not to separate the driveshafts. If it is absolutely necessary, matchmark all components so that they can be reassembled in the same order.
10. Installation is the reverse of removal. Always use new self-locking nuts. After the driveshaft is installed, rock the car back and forth several times to settle the driveshaft. Make sure that neither intermediate shaft is binding against either intermediate bearing, and that the clearance between the intermediate bearing and the driveshaft is the same at both ends.

Axle Shaft

NOTE: *The rubber covered joints are filled with special oil. If they are disassembled for any reason they must be refilled with the special oil.*

REMOVAL AND INSTALLATION

All Except 190D, 190E, 380SEC and 500SEC

(MODELS WITHOUT TORQUE COMPENSATOR (TORSION BAR)

Most models do not use a torque compensator (torsion bar) which is actually a steel bar used to locate the rear axle under acceleration. In general only the 450 series cars and the 300SD use a torque compensator, but it is wise to check for one before servicing the axle shaft. The illustrations apply to either type.

NOTE: *On the 280, 280C, and 280E only axle shafts identified with a yellow paint dot or part no. 107 350 07 10 (left) or part no. 107 350 0810 (right) can be installed.*

1. Jack up the rear of the car and remove the wheel and center axle holddown bolt (in hub).
2. Remove the brake caliper and suspend it from a hook.
3. Drain the differential oil and place a jack under the differential housing.
4. Unbolt the rubber mount from the chassis and the differential housing, then remove the differential housing cover to expose the ring and pinion gears.
5. Press the shaft from the axle flange. If necessary, loosen the shock absorber.

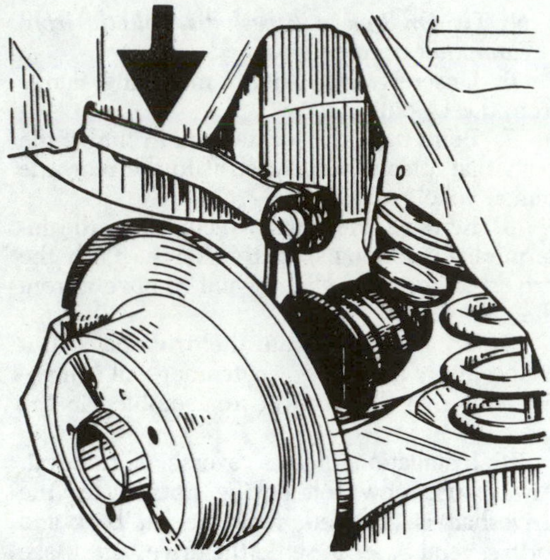

Most models do not use a torque compensator (arrow)

Suspend the brake caliper from a hook after removal

Loosen the center axle hold-down bolt in the hub

Remove the lock-ring (26) with pliers (1) or a small pick

Axle shafts are marked L (left) or R (right)

6. Using a screwdriver, remove the axle lock ring inside the differential case.

7. Pull the axle from the housing by pulling the splined end from the side gears, with the spacer.

NOTE: *Axle shafts are stamped R and L for right and left units. Always use new lock-rings.*

8. Installation is the reverse of removal. Fill the rear axle.

CAUTION: *Check end-play of the lockring in the groove. If necessary, install a thicker lock ring or spacer to eliminate all end-play, while still allowing the lock-ring to rotate. Do not allow the joints in the axleshaft to hang free or the joint bearing may be damaged and leak.*

Models with Torque Compensator (Torsion Bar)

1. Drain the oil from the rear axle.
2. Disconnect and plug the brake lines.
3. Loosen the connecting rod and unscrew the torsion bar bearing bracket. Lower the ex-

haust system slightly and remove the torsion bar.

4. Lower the shock absorber.

5. Remove the bolt which attaches the rear axle shaft to the rear axle shaft flange.

6. Disconnect the brake cable control. Remove the bracket from the wheel carrier, remove the rubber sleeve, and push back the cover.

7. Press the rear axle shaft out of the flange with a suitable tool.

8. Support the rear axle with a jack.

9. Remove the rear rubber mount.

10. Clean the axle housing and remove the cover from the housing.

NOTE: *The axle shafts are the floating type and can be compressed in the constant velocity joints.*

11. Remove the locking ring from the end of the axle shafts which engage the side gears in the differential.

12. Disengage the axle shaft from the side gear and remove the axle shaft together with the spacer.

CAUTION: *Do not hang the outer constant velocity joint in a free position (without any support) as the shaft may be damaged and the constant velocity joint housing may leak.*

13. Installation is the reverse of removal.

14. If either axle shaft is replaced, be sure that the proper replacement shaft is installed. Axle shafts are marked L and R for left and right.

15. Check the end-play between the lockring on the axle shaft and the side gear. There should be no noticeable endplay, but the lockring should be able to turn in the groove.

16. Be sure to bleed the brakes and fill the rear axle with the proper quantity and type of lubricant.

190D, 190E, 380SEC and 500SEC

1. Loosen, but do not remove, the axle shaft collar nut.

2. Raise the rear of the vehicle and support it on jackstands.

3. Disconnect the axle shaft from the hub assembly. On the 190, make sure that while loosening the locking screws, the bit is seated properly in the multi-tooth profile of the screws.

4. Remove the self-locking screws that attach the inner CV-joint to the connecting flange on the differential. Always loosen the screws in a crosswise manner.

NOTE: *Make sure that the end cover on the inner CV-joint is not damaged when separated from the connecting flange.*

5. While supporting the axle shaft, use a slide hammer or the like and press the axle shaft out of the hub assembly.

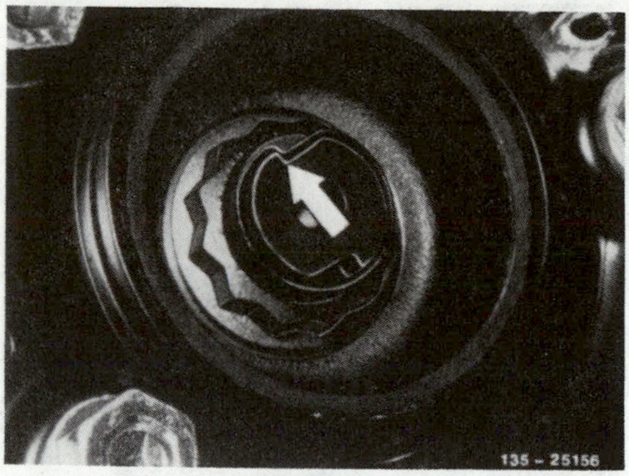

Lock the collar nut on the 190 at the crush flange (arrow)

6. Tilt the axle shaft down and remove it.

CAUTION: *Make sure that the CV-joint boots are not damaged during the removal process.*

7. Installation is in the reverse order of removal. Please note the following:

a. Always clean the connecting flanges before installation.

b. Always use new self-locking screws. On the 190, moisten the screw threads and contact faces with oil before installing. Tighten the screws to 51 ft. lbs. (70 Nm) on the 190 and 90–105 ft. lbs. (125–145 Nm) on the others. Always tighten the screws in a crosswise pattern.

c. Tighten the axle shaft collar nut to 203–230 ft. lbs. (280–320 Nm) on the 190 and 22 ft. lbs. (30 Nm) on the others. On the 190, lock the collar nut at the crush flange (see illustration).

Differential

REMOVAL AND INSTALLATION

All Models Except 190D and 190E

1. Drain the oil from the differential.

2. On cars without torque compensators, remove the brake caliper and suspend it on a hook.

3. On cars with torque compensation, (see previous procedure) disconnect the brake cable control, unbolt the holding bracket on the wheel carrier, remove the rubber sleeve and push the cover back.

4. Remove the bolt from both sides that holds the rear axle shaft to the flange.

5. Press the rear axle shaft out of the flange.

6. If required, loosen the right-hand rear shock absorber and lower the trailing arm to the stop.

7. Remove the exhaust system, if necessary.

8. Remove the heat shield if equipped.

42. Rear rubber mounting
43. Hexagon socket bolt
45. Breather
46. Plug for filler hole
47. Plug for drain hole

Differential attaching points

9. Loosen the clamp nut and remove the intermediate bearing from the floor pan. On 3-piece driveshafts, only remove the front nut.
10. Unbolt the driveshaft and remove it.
11. Support the rear axle housing.
12. Unbolt the rear rubber mount from the frame floor.
13. On the 500 series, 450, 380, 280S, 280SE and 300SD, lower the jack until the self-locking nuts are accessible.
14. Unbolt the rear axle center housing from the rear axle carrier.
15. On all other models, remove the bolt from the rubber mount on the cover of the rear axle housing. Fold back the rubber mat in the trunk and remove the rubber plugs; unbolt the rear axle center housing from the rear axle carrier.
16. Lower the rear axle center housing and remove it with the axle shafts. Do not allow the axle shafts to hang free, or the seals will be damaged, resulting in leaks.
17. Installation is the reverse of removal. Install new self-locking nuts, adjust the parking brake and fill the rear axle with the correct fluid.

190D and 190E

1. Drain the oil from the differential.
2. Remove the exhaust shielding plate.
3. Loosen the clamp nut on the driveshaft. Unscrew the intermediate bearing screws at the floor pan and remove.
4. Disconnect the driveshaft from the universal flange of the drive pinion and push it forward to remove. Position the driveshaft out of the way and support it with wire.
5. Disconnect the inner CV-joints from the differential connecting flange and wire them out of the way.
6. Support the differential with a floor jack.
7. Remove the four bolts and two locking plates at the rear differential mount.
8. Loosen and remove the screw from the front mount where it connects to the rear axle carrier.
9. Lower the jack and remove the differential.

To install:

1. Raise the differential into position.
2. Position the screw in the front mount but do not tighten it.
3. Install the rear mount screws and plates. Tighten to 29–33 ft. lbs. (40–45 Nm). Now tighten the front mount screw to 33 ft. lbs. (45 Nm).

NOTE: *Always use new self-locking screws and plates.*

4. Position the driveshaft and install the intermediate bearing. Do not tighten it yet.
5. Tighten the driveshaft clamp nut to 25–29 ft. lbs. (35–40 Nm). Now tighten the intermediate bearing screws to 19 ft. lbs. (25 Nm).
6. Installation of the remaining components is in the reverse order of removal.

Suspension and Steering

8

FRONT SUSPENSION

Springs

REMOVAL AND INSTALLATION

All Models Except 190, 1974–76 230 and 240D, 280, 280C, 1975–76 300D, 380SL, 380SLC, 450SL and 450SLC

1. Jack and support the front of the car and support the lower control arm.
2. Remove the wheel. Unbolt the upper shock absorber mount.
3. Install a spring compressor and compress the spring.
4. Remove the front spring with the lower mount.
5. Installation is the reverse of removal. Tighten the upper shock absorber suspension.

NOTE: *Tighten the eccentric bolt on the lower control arm only with the car resting on its wheels.*

1974–75 230 and 240D, 280, 280C, 1975–76 300D, 380SL, 380SLC, 450SL and 450SLC

NOTE: *Be extremely careful when attempting to remove front springs as they are compressed and under considerable load.*

1. Jack up the front of the car, put up jackstands and remove the front wheels.
2. Support the control arm and remove the lower shock absorber and disconnect the sway bar.

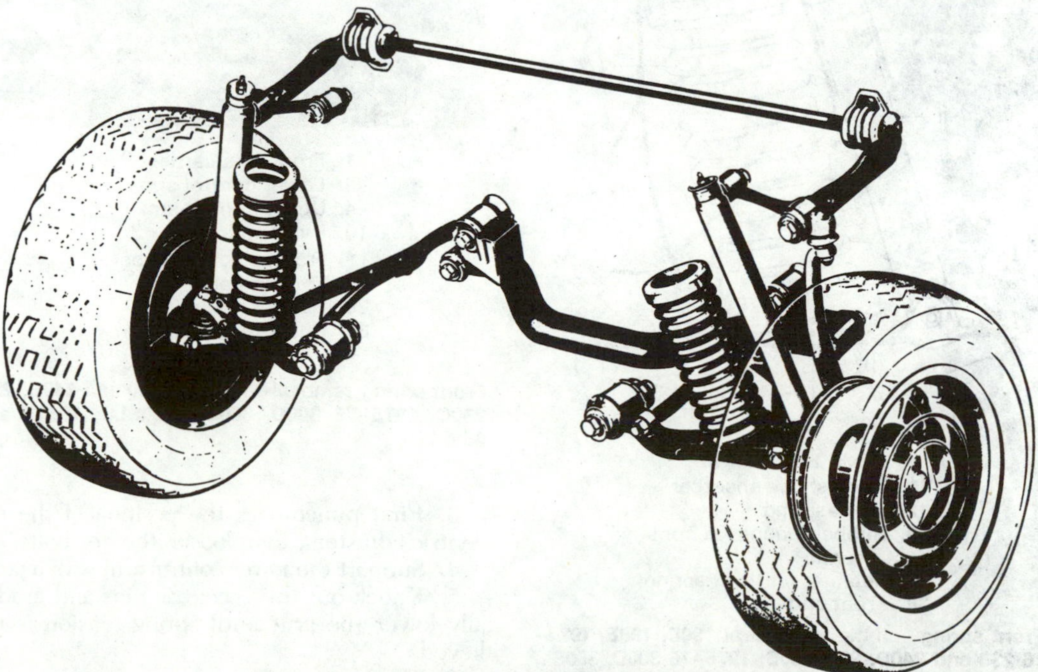

Component view of "zero offset" front suspension

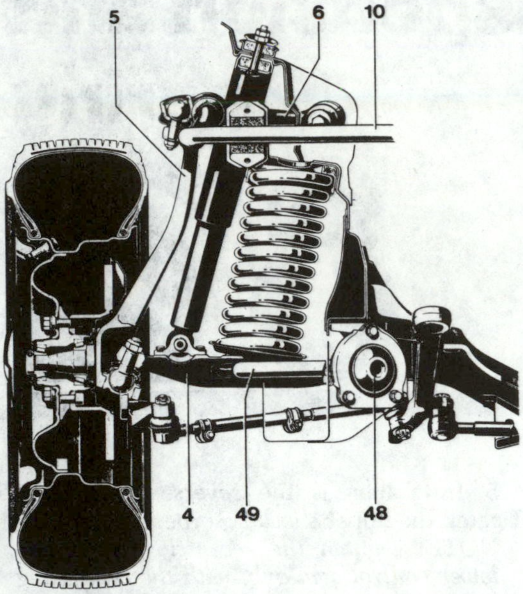

4. Lower control arm
5. Steering knuckle
6. Upper control arm
10. Torsion bar
48. Supporting joint
49. Supporting tube

Sectional view of "zero offset" front suspension

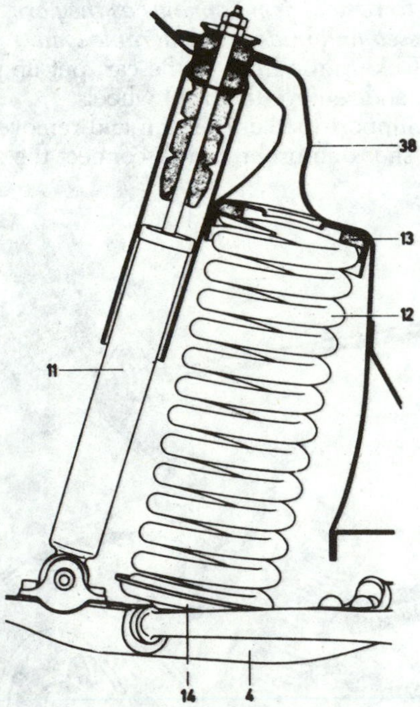

4. Lower control arm
11. Front shock absorber
12. Front spring
13. Rubber mount for front spring
14. Retainer for front spring
38. Front end

Front spring—all models except 190D, 190E, 1974–76 230 and 240D, 280, 280C, 1975–76 300D, 380SL, 380SLC, 450SL and 450SLC

1. Front axle carrier
3. Lower control arm
7. Supporting joint
27. Torsion bar connecting linkage
29. Rubber mounting
30. Cam bolt

Matchmark the position of the adjusters on all 1974–76 230 and 240D, 280, 280C, 1975–76 300D, 380SL, 380SLC, 450SL and 450SLC models

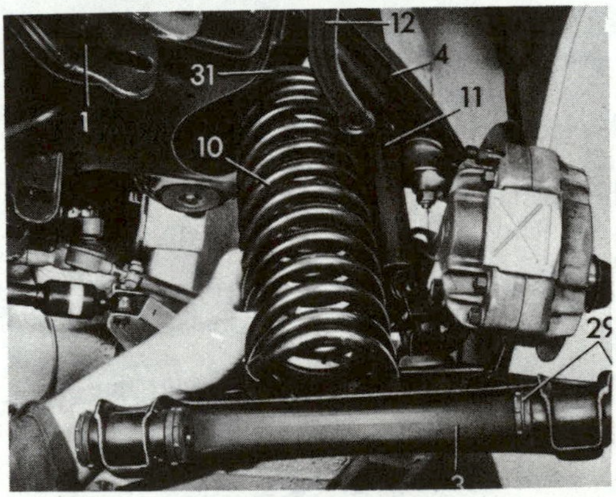

1. Front axle carrier
3. Lower control arm
4. Upper control arm
10. Front spring
11. Front shock absorber
12. Torsion bar
29. Rubber mounting
31. Rubber mounting for front spring

Front spring removal—1974–76 230 and 240D, 280, 280C, 1975–76 300D, 380SL, 380SLC, 450SL and 450SLC

3. First punchmark the position of the eccentric adjusters, then loosen the hex bolts.
4. Support the lower control arm with a jack.
5. Knock out the eccentric pins and gradually lower the arm until spring tension is relieved.
6. The spring can now be removed.

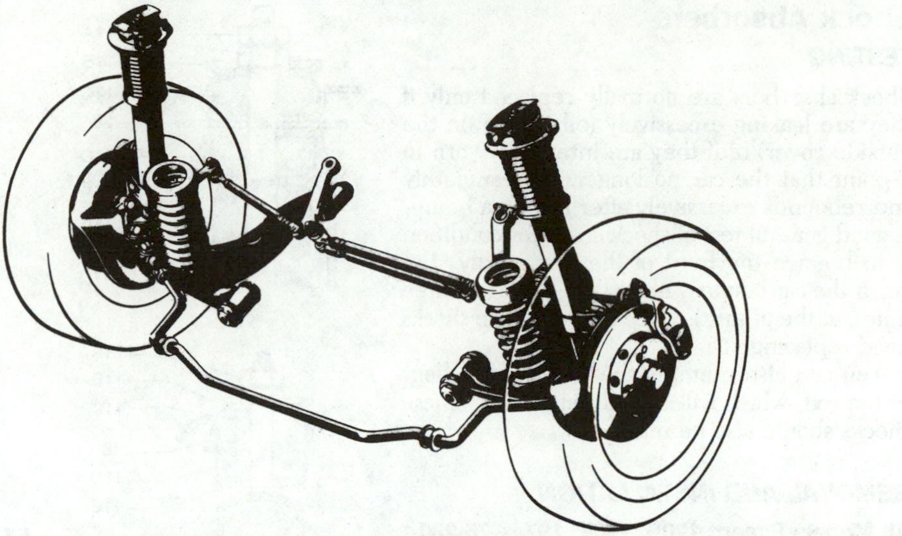

Front suspension—190D and 190E

NOTE: *Check caster and camber after installing a new spring.*

7. Installation is the reverse of removal.

8. For ease of installation, tape the rubber mounts to the springs.

9. If the eccentric adjusters were not matchmarked, install the eccentric bolts as illustrated under "Front End Alignment."

190D and 190E

1. Raise the front of the vehicle and support it with jackstands. Remove the wheel.

2. Remove the engine compartment lining underneath the vehicle (if so equipped).

3. Install a spring compressor so that at least 7½ coils are engaged.

4. Support the lower control arm with a floor jack and then loosen the retaining nut at the upper end of the damper strut.

CAUTION: *NEVER loosen the damper strut retaining nut unless the wheels are on the ground, the control arm is supported or the springs have been removed.*

5. Lower the jack under the control arm slightly and then remove the spring toward the front.

6. On installation, position the spring between the control arm and the upper mount so that when the control arm is raised, the end of the lower coil will be seated in the impression in the control arm.

7. Use the jack and raise the control arm until the spring is held securely.

8. Using a new nut, tighten the upper end of the damper strut to 44 ft. lbs. (60 Nm).

9. Slowly ease the tension on the spring compressor until the spring is seated properly and then remove the compressor.

10. Installation of the remaining components is in the reverse order of removal.

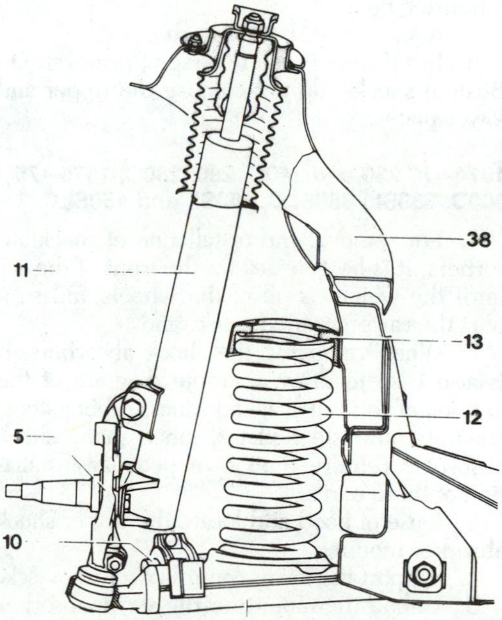

4. Wishbone (control arm)
5. Steering knuckle
10. Torsion bar
11. Damper strut
12. Front spring
13. Spring-rubber mount
38. Front end

Front spring—190D and 190E

Shock Absorbers

TESTING

Shock absorbers are normally replaced only if they are leaking excessively (oil visible on the outside cover) of if they are internally worn to a point that the car no longer rides smoothly and rebounds excessively after hitting a bump. A good general test of shock absorber condition is to bounce the front of the car rapidly. Let go. If the car bounces more than twice (or three times, at the utmost), you can assume the shocks need replacing.

You can also examine the shocks for a bent piston rod, which will bind during travel. These shocks should also be replaced.

REMOVAL AND INSTALLATION

All Models Except 190D, 190E, 1974–76 230 and 240D, 280, 280C, 1975–76 300D, 380SL, 380SLC, 450SL and 450SLC

1. Jack and support the front of the car. Support the lower control arm.
2. Loosen the nuts on the upper shock absorber mount. Remove the plate and ring.
3. Place the shock arbsorber vertical to the lower control arm and remove the lower mounting bolts.
4. Remove the shock absorber.
5. Installation is the reverse of removal. On Bilstein shocks, do not confuse the upper and lower plates.

1974–76 230 and 240D, 280, 280C, 1975–75 300D, 380SL, 380SLC, 450SL and 450SLC

1. For removal and installation of shock absorbers, it is best to jack up the front of the car until the weight is off of the wheels and support the car securely on jackstands.
2. When removing the shock absorbers, it is also wise to draw a simple diagram of the location of parts such as lock-rings, rubber stops, locknuts, and steel plates, since many shock absorbers require their own peculiar installation of these parts.
3. Raise of hood and locate the upper shock absorber mount.
4. Support the lower control arm with a jack.
5. Unbolt the mount for the shock absorber at the top. On 450SL and 450SLC, remove the coolant expansion tank to allow access to the right front shock absorber.
6. Remove the nuts which secure the shock absorber to the lower control arm.
7. Push the shock absorber piston rod in, install the stirrup, and remove the shock absorber.
8. Remove the stirrup, since this must be installed on replacement shock absorbers.

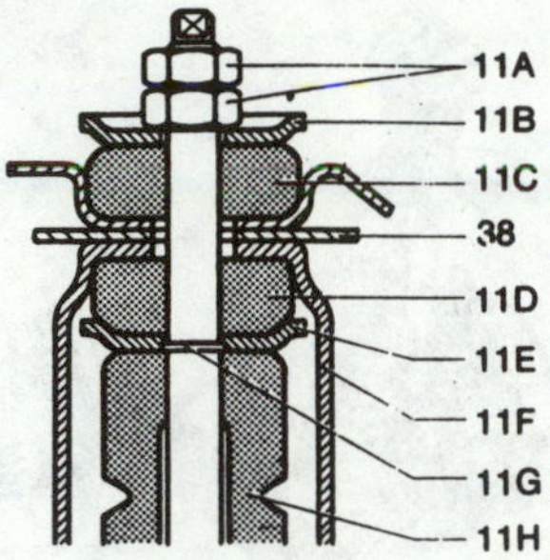

BILSTEIN SHOCK ABSORBER

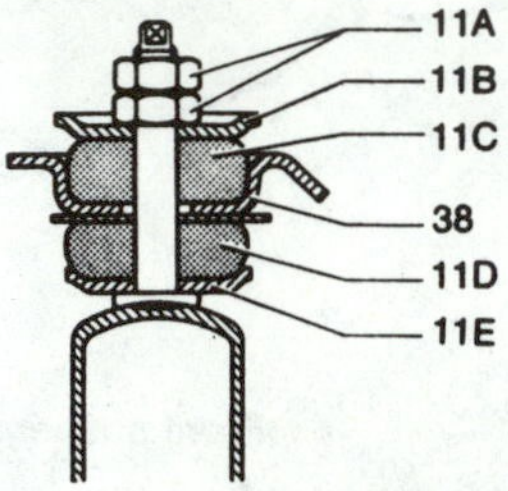

F & S SHOCK ABSORBER

11a. Hex. nuts
11b. Upper plate
11c. Upper rubber ring
11d. Lower rubber ring
11e. Lower plate
11f. Protective sleeve
11g. Locking ring
11h. Supplementary rubber spring (stop buffer)
38. Dome on frame floor

Typical upper shock absorber mounting—all models except 190D, 190E, 1974–76 230 and 240D, 280, 280C, 1975–76 300D, 380SL, 380SLC, 450SL and 450SLC

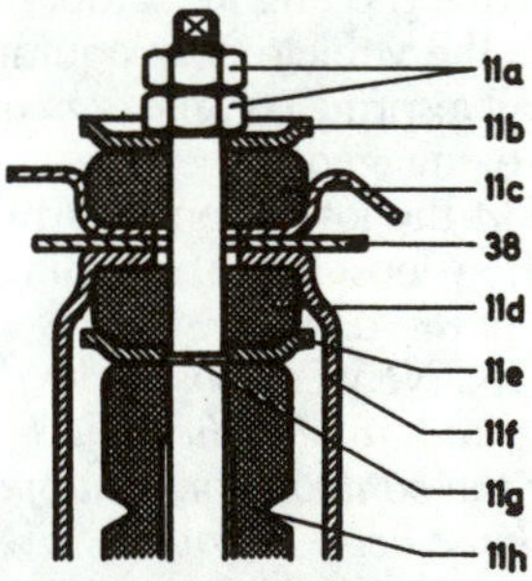

11a. Hexagon nuts
11b. Top cup
11c. Top rubber ring
11d. Bottom rubber ring
11e. Bottom cup
11f. Protective sleeve
11g. Lock ring
11h. Supplementary rubber buffer stop
38. Dome on chassis base panel

Front upper shock absorber mounting—1974–76 230 and 240D, 280, 280C, 1975–76 300D, 380SL, 380SLC, 450SL and 450SLC

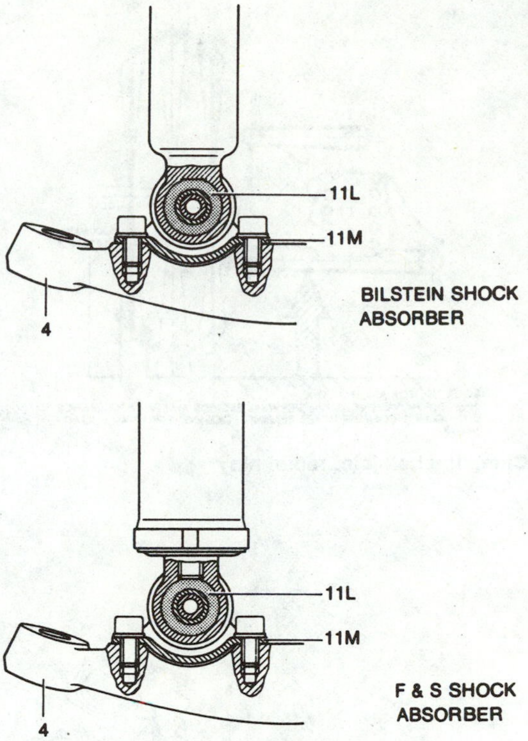

4. Lower control arm
11l. Rubber mount
11m. Fastening stirrup

Typical lower shock absorber mounting on all models except the 190D, 190E, 1974–76 230 and 240D, 280, 280C, 1975–76 300D, 380SL, 380SLC, 450SL and 450SLC

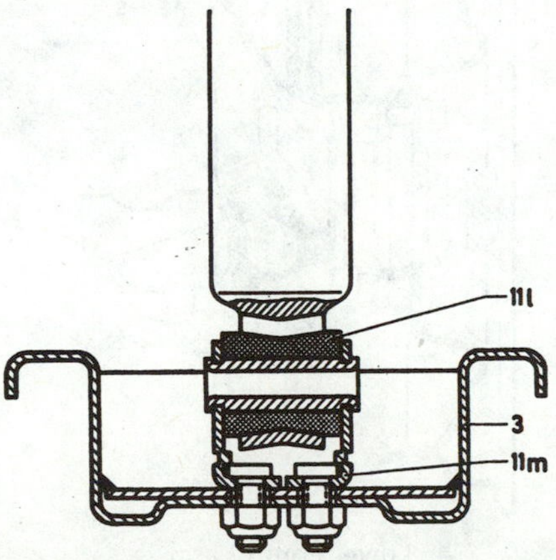

Front lower shock absorber mounting—1974–76 230 and 240D, 280, 280C, 1975–76 300D, 380SL, 380SLC, 450SL and 450SLC

NOTE: *Most models use both Bilstein and F&S shock absorbers. On Bilstein shock absorbers, never re-use the upper or lower cups.*

9. Installation is the reverse of removal. Always use new bushings when installing replacement shock absorbers.

Damper Strut

REMOVAL AND INSTALLATION

190D and 190E

1. Raise the front of the vehicle and support it with jackstands. Remove the wheel.
2. Using a spring compressor, compress the spring until any load is removed from the lower control arm.

   NOTE: *When using a spring compressor, be sure that at least 7½ coils are engaged before applying tension.*
3. Support the lower control arm with a floor jack. Loosen the retaining bolt for the upper end of the damper strut by holding the inner piston rod with an Allen wrench and then unscrewing the nut. *NEVER use an impact wrench on the retaining nut.*

   CAUTION: *Never unscrew the nut with the axle half at full rebound—the spring may fly out with considerable force, causing personal injury.*
4. Unbolt the two screws and one nut and then disconnect the lower damper strut from the steering knuckle.
5. Remove the strut down and forward. Secure the steering knuckle in position so that it won't tilt.
6. Installation is in the reverse order of removal. Please note the following:

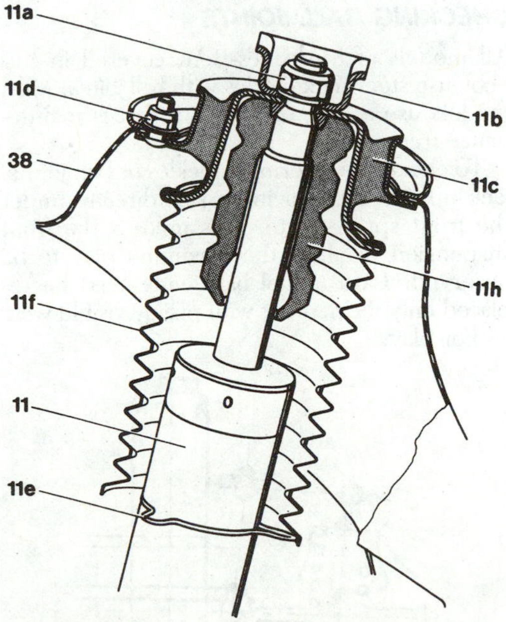

11. Damper strut
11a. Hex. nut
11b. Rebound stop
11c. Rubber mount
11d. Hex. nuts
11e. Stop ring
11f. Sleeve
11h. Additional PU spring
38. Front end

Upper damper strut mounting—190D and 190E

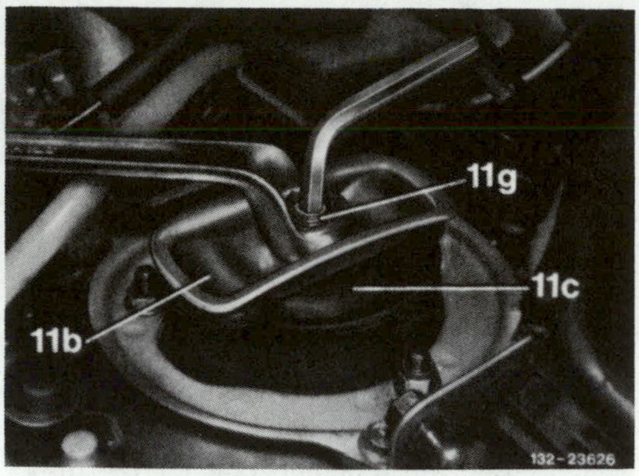
11g
11c
11b
132-23626

11b. Rebound limiter
11c. Rubber mount
11g. Piston rod

Remove the upper damper strut retaining nut by locking the piston rod with an Allen wrench—190D and 190E

a. When attaching the lower end of the damper strut to the steering knuckle, first position all three screws; next tighten the two lower screws to 72 ft. lbs. (100 Nm); finally, tighten the nut on the upper clamping connection screw to 54 ft. lbs. (75 Nm).

b. Tighten the retaining nut on the upper end of the damper strut to 44 ft. lbs. (60 Nm).

Steering Knuckle/Ball Joints

CHECKING BALL JOINTS

All models of Mercedes-Benz covered in this book use steering knuckles with ball joints. Most models use a type of ball joint that is maintenance free.

To check the steering knuckles or ball joints, jack up the car, placing a jack directly under the front spring plate. This unloads the front suspension to allow the maximum play to be observed. Late model ball joints need be replaced only if dried out with plainly visible wear and/or play.

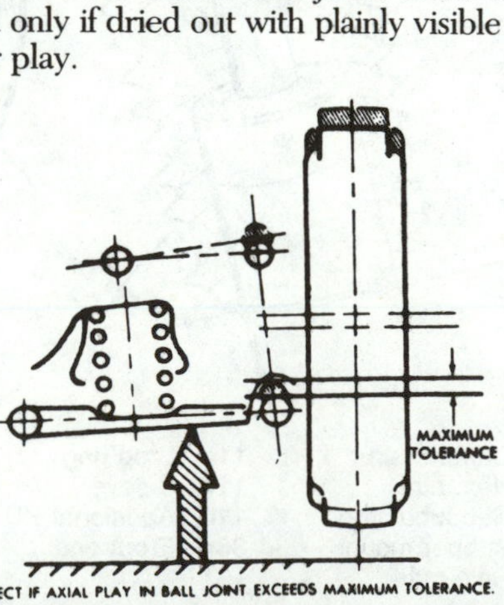
MAXIMUM TOLERANCE
REJECT IF AXIAL PLAY IN BALL JOINT EXCEEDS MAXIMUM TOLERANCE.

Checking ball joint axial play

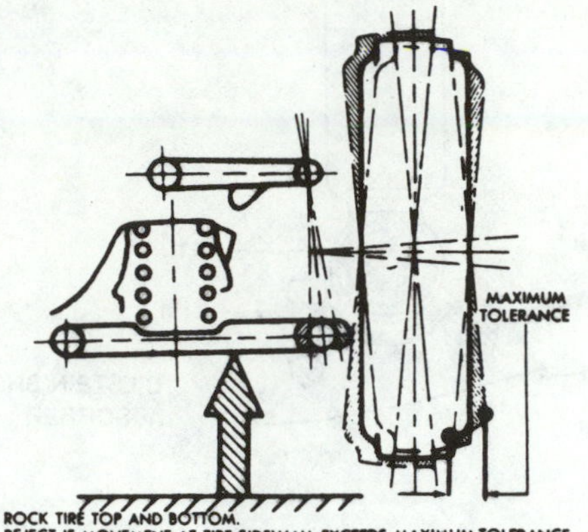
MAXIMUM TOLERANCE
ROCK TIRE TOP AND BOTTOM.
REJECT IF MOVEMENT AT TIRE SIDEWALL EXCEEDS MAXIMUM TOLERANCE, BUT DO NOT CONFUSE WHEEL BEARING LOOSENESS WITH BALL JOINT WEAR.

Checking ball joint radial play

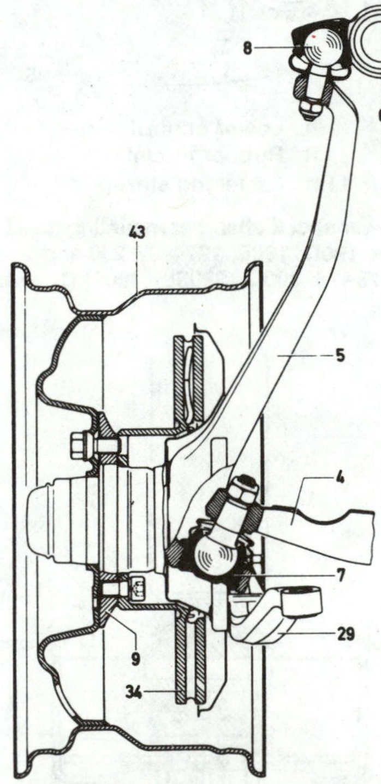
8
6
43
5
4
7
29
9
34

4. Lower control arm
5. Steering knuckle
6. Upper control arm
7. Support joint
8. Guide joint
9. Front wheel hub
29. Steering knuckle arm
34. Brake disc
43. Wheel

Steering knuckle/ball joint on all models except the 190D, 190E, 1974–76 230 and 240D, 280, 280C, 1975–76 300D, 380SL, 380SLC, 450SL and 450SLC

REMOVAL AND INSTALLATION

1974–76 230 and 240D, 280, 280C, 1975–76 300D, 380 SL, 380 SLC, 450SL land 450SLC

1. This should only be done with the front shock absorber installed. If, however, the front shock absorber has been removed, the lower control arm should be supported with a jack and the spring should be clamped with a spring tensioner. In this case, the hex nut on the guide joint should not be loosened without the spring tensioner installed.
2. Jack up the front of the car and support it on jackstands.
3. Remove the wheel.
4. Remove the brake caliper.
5. Unbolt the steering relay lever from the steering knuckle. For safety, install spring clamps on the front springs.
6. Remove the hex nuts from the upper and lower ball joints.
7. Remove the ball joints from the steering knuckle with the aid of a puller.
8. Remove the steering knuckle.
9. Installation is the reverse of removal. Be sure that the seats for the pins of the ball joints are free of grease.
10. Bleed the brakes.

190D and 190E

1. Raise the front of the vehicle and support it with jackstands. Remove the wheel.
2. Install a spring compressor on the spring.
3. Remove the brake caliper and then wire it out of the way. Be careful not to damage the brake line.
4. Remove the brake disc and wheel hub.
5. Unscrew the three socket-head bolts and then remove the brake backing plate from the steering knuckle.
6. Tighten the spring compressor until all tension and/or load has been removed from the lower control arm.
7. Disconnect the steering knuckle arm from the steering knuckle (this is the arm attached to the tie rod).

CAUTION: *There must be no tension on the lower control arm.*

8. Unscrew the three bolts and disconnect the lower end of the damper strut from the steering knuckle.
9. Remove the hex-head clamp nut at the supporting joint (lower ball joint).
10. Remove the steering knuckle.
11. Installation is in the reverse order of removal. Please note the following:
    a. Tighten the supporting joint clamp nut to 70 ft. lbs. (125 Nm).
    b. Refer to the "Damper Strut Removal and Installation" procedure when connect-

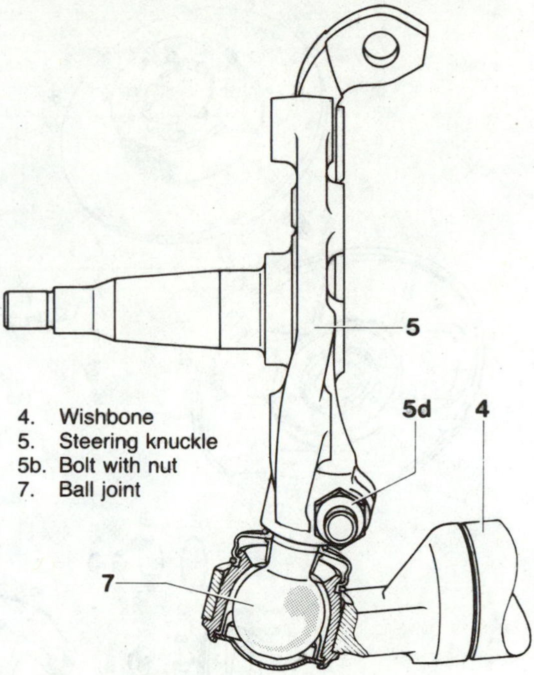

Steering knuckle/ball joint—190D and 190E

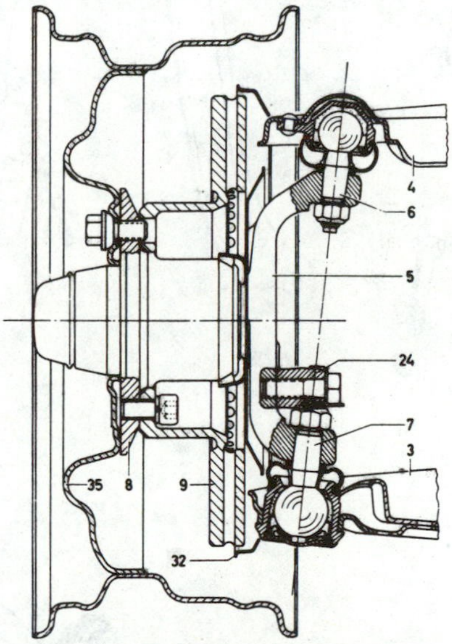

3. Lower control arm
4. Upper control arm
5. Steering knuckle
6. Guide joint
7. Supporting joint
8. Front wheel hub
9. Brake disc
24. Steering knuckle arm
32. Cover plate
35. Wheel

Steering knuckle/ball joint—1974–76 230 and 240D, 280, 280C, 1975–76 300D, 380SL, 380SLC, 450SL and 450SLC

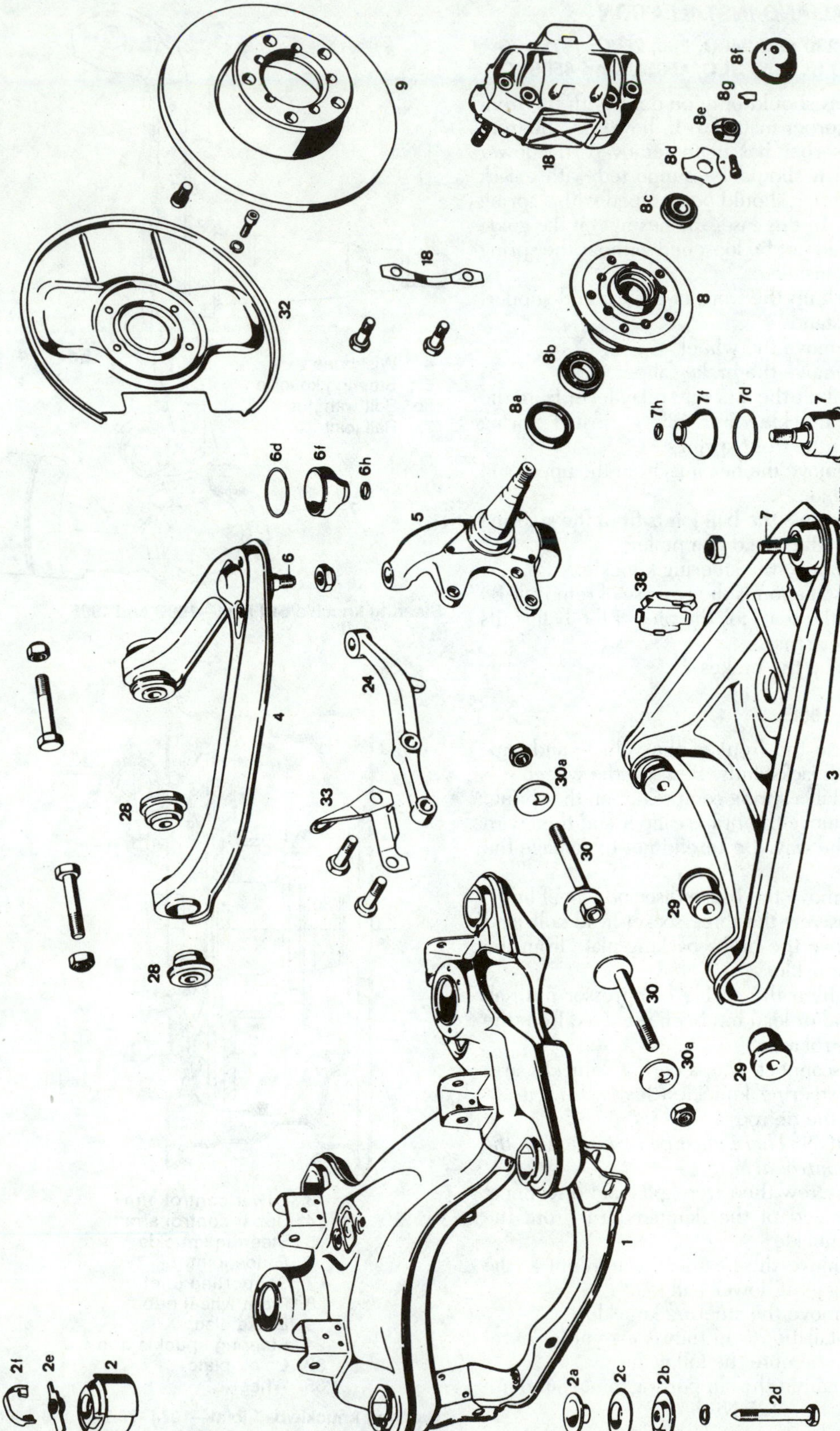

Front suspension—1974–76 230 and 240D, 280, 280C, 1975–76 300D, 380SL, 380SLC, 450SL and 450SLC

1. Front axle carrier
2. Rubber mount for suspension of front axle
2a. Stop buffer for inward deflection
2b. Stop plate
2c. Stop buffer for outward deflections
2d. Hex. bolt with snap ring
2e. Fastening nut
2f. Nut holder
3. Lower control arm
4. Upper control arm
5. Steering knuckle
6. Guide joint
6d. Circlip
6f. Sleeve
6h. Clamping ring
7. Supporting joint
7d. Circlip
7f. Sleeve
7h. Clamping ring
8. Front wheel hub
8a. Radial sealing ring
8b. Inside tapered roller bearing
8c. Outside tapered roller bearing
8d. Washer
8e. Clamp nut
8f. Wheel cap
8g. Contact spring
9. Brake disc
18. Brake caliper
18a. Lockwasher
24. Steering knuckle arm
28. Rubber slide bearing
29. Rubber bearing (torsion bearing)
30. Cam bolt
30a. Cam washer
32. Cover plate
33. Holder for brake hose
38. Protective cap for steering lock

ing the lower end of the damper strut to the steering knuckle.

All Models Except 190D, 190E, 1974–76 230 and 240D, 280, 280C, 1975–76 300D, 380SL, 380SLC, 450SL and 450SLC

1. Jack and support the car. For safety, it's a good idea to install some type of clamp on the frontspring. Position jackstands at the outside front against the lower control arms.
2. Remove the wheel.
3. Remove the steering knuckle arm from the steering knuckle.
4. Remove and suspend the brake caliper.
5. Remove the front wheel hub.
6. Loosen the brake hose holder on the cover plate.
7. Loosen the nut on the guide joint and remove the joint from the steering knuckle.
8. Loosen the nut on the support joint.
9. Swivel the steering knuckle outward and force the ball joint from the lower control arm.
10. Remove the steering knuckle.
11. If necessary, remove the cover plate from the steering knuckle.
12. Installation is the reverse of removal. Use self-locking nuts and adjust the wheel bearings.

Upper Control Arm

NOTE: *The 190D and 190E have no upper control arm.*

REMOVAL AND INSTALLATION

All Models Except 190D, 190E, 1974–76 230 and 240D, 280, 280C, 1975–76 300D, 380SL, 380SLC, 450SL and 450SLC Models

1. Jack and support the car. Position jackstands at the outside front against the lower control arms.

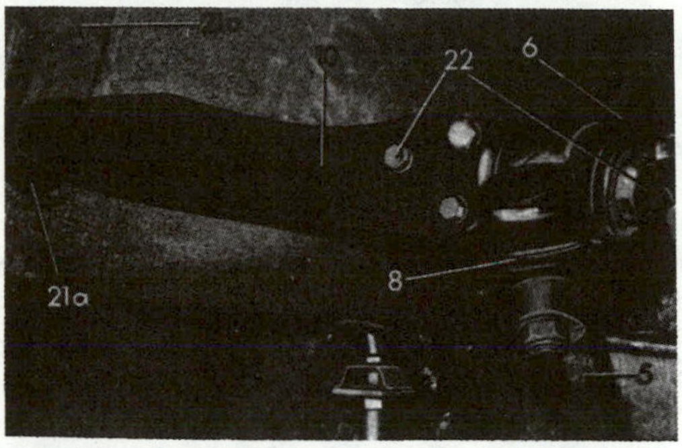

5. Steering knuckle
6. Upper control arm
8. Guide joint
10. Torsion bar
21a. Rubber mounting
21c. Cover
22. Support of upper control arms on torsion bar

Upper control arm on all models except the 190D, 190E, 1974–76 230 and 240D, 280, 280C, 1975–76 300D, 380SL, 380SLC, 450SL and 450SLC

2. Remove the wheel.
3. Loosen the nut on the guide joint.
4. Remove the guide joint from the steering knuckle.
5. Secure the steering knuckle with a hook on the upper control arm stop to prevent it from tilting.
6. Loosen the clamp screw and separate the upper control arm from the torsion bar.
7. Loosen the upper control arm bearing at the front and remove the upper control arm.
8. Installation is the reverse of removal. Use new self-locking nuts and check the front wheel alignment.

1974–76 230 and 240D, 280, 280C, 1975–76 300D, 380SL, 380SLC, 450SL and 450SLC

1. The front shock absorbers should remain installed. Never loosen the hex nuts of

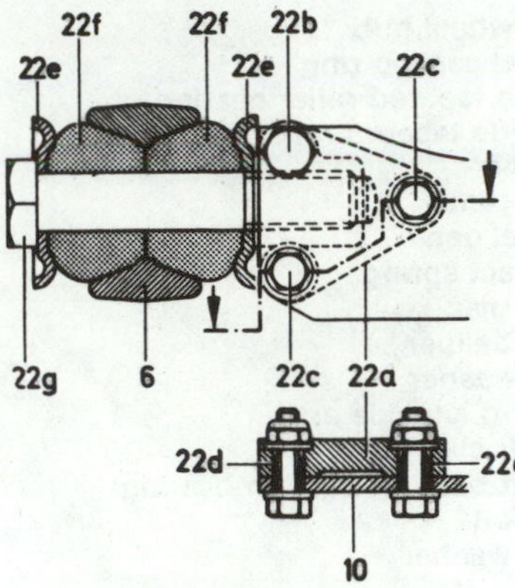

6. Upper control arm
10. Torsion bar
22a. Clamping piece
22b. Hex. head clamping screw
22c. Hex. screws with washers and self-locking hex. nuts
22d. Clamping sleeves
22e. Cup washers
22f . Rubber mounting
22g. Hex. screw

Mounting details of the upper control arm support on the torsion bar—all models except the 190D, 190E, 1974–76 230 and 240D, 280, 280C, 1975–76 300D, 380SL, 380SLC, 450SL and 450SLC

the ball joints with the shock absorber removed, unless a spring clamp is installed.

2. Jack the front of the car and remove the wheel.
3. Support the front end on jackstands.
4. Remove the steering arm from the steering knuckle.
5. Separate the brake line and brake hose from each other and plug the openings.
6. Support the lower control arm and unscrew the nuts from the ball joints.
7. Remove the ball joints from the steering knuckle.
8. Loosen the bolts on the upper control arm and remove the upper control arm.
9. Installation is the reverse of removal.

CAUTION: *Mount the front hex bolt from the rear in a forward direction, and the rear hex bolt from the front in a rearward direction.*

10. Bleed the brakes.

Lower Control Arm

REMOVAL AND INSTALLATION

All Models Except 190D, 190E, 1974–76 230 and 240D, 280, 280C, 1975–76 300D, 380SL, 380SLC, 450SL and 450SLC

The lower control arm is the same as the front axle half. For safety install a spring compressor on the coil spring.

Front axle half of zero offset suspension—all models except the 190D, 190E, 1974–76 230 and 240D, 280, 280C, 1975–76 300D, 380SL, 380SLC, 450SL and 450SLC

1. Jack and support the front of the car and remove the wheels.
2. Remove the front shock absorber. Loosen the top mount first.
3. Remove the front springs.
4. Separate and plug the brake lines.
5. Remove the track rod from the steering knuckle arm.
6. Matchmark the position of the eccentric bolts on the bearing of the lower control arm in relation to the frame cross-member.
7. Remove the shield from the cross yoke.
8. Support the front axle half.
9. Loosen the eccentric bolt on the front

3. Cross yoke
4. Lower control arm
6. Upper control arm
10. Torsion bar
24. Pitman arm
27. Drag link
28. Track rod
29. Steering knuckle arm
33. Brake caliper
39. Brake hose

Front suspension components—all models except the 190D, 190E, 1974–76 230 and 240D, 280, 280C, 1975–76 300D, 380SL, 380SLC, 450SL and 450SLC

and rear bearing of the lower control arm and knock them out.

10. Remove the bolt from the cross-yoke bearing.

11. Loosen the screw at the opposite end of the cross-yoke bearing.

12. Pull the cross-yoke bearing down slightly.

13. Loosen the support of the upper control arm on the torsion bar. Remove the clamp screw from the clamp.

14. Remove the upper control arm bearing on the front end.

15. Remove the front axle half.

16. Installation is the reverse of removal. Tighten the eccentric bolts of the lower control arm bearing with the car resting on the wheels. Bleed the brakes and check the front end alignment.

190D and 190E

1. Remove the engine compartment lining at the bottom of the vehicle (if so equipped).

2. Raise the front of the vehicle and support it with jackstands. Remove the wheel.

3. Support the lower control arm with jackstands and then disconnect the torsion bar bearing at the control arm.

4. Remove the spring as detailed earlier in this chapter.

5. Disconnect the tie rod at the steering knuckle and then press out the ball joint with the proper tool.

6. Remove the brake caliper and position it out of the way. Be sure that you do not damage the brake line.

7. Remove the brake disc/wheel hub assembly.

8. Disconnect the lower end of the damper strut from the steering knuckle and then remove the knuckle.

9. Mark the position of the inner eccentric pins, relative to the frame, on the bearing of the control arm.

10. Unscrew and remove the pins.

11. Remove the jackstands and remove the lower control arm.

12. Installation is in the reverse order of removal. Please note the following:

a. Tighten the eccentric bolts on the inner arm to 130 ft. lbs. (180 Nm).

b. To facilitate torsion bar installation, raise the opposite side of the lower control arm with a jack.

c. Tighten the clamp nut on the tie rod ball joint to 25 ft. lbs. (35 Nm).

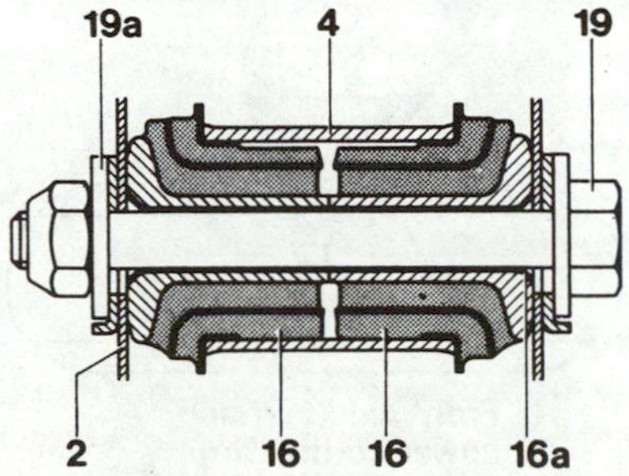

2. Frame cross member
4. Wishbone
16. Torsion rubber bushing
16a. Clamping sleeve
19. Eccentric bolt (camber adjustment)
19a. Eccentric washer

Cross section of the front lower control arm bushing on 190 models

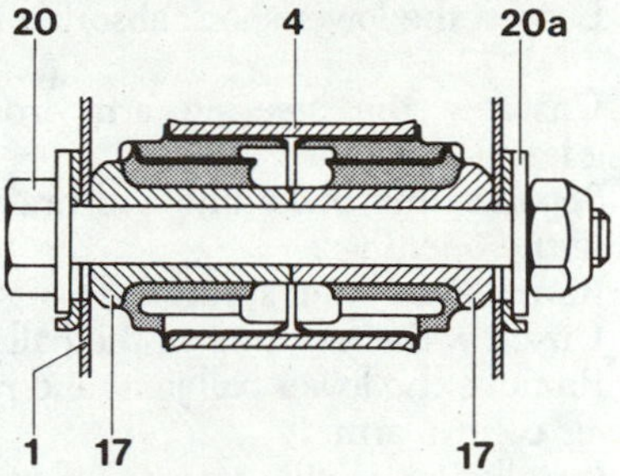

1. Frame side member
4. Wishbone
17. Torsion rubber bushing
20. Eccentric bolt (caster adjustment)
20a. Eccentric washer

Cross section of the rear lower control arm bushing on 190 models

Lower control arm—190D and 190E

1974–76 230 and 240D, 280, 280C, 1975–76 300D, 380SL, 380SLC, 450SL and 450SLC

1. Since the front shock absorber acts as a deflection stop for the front wheels, the lower shock absorber attaching point should not be loosened unless the vehicle is resting on the wheels or unless the lower control arm is supported.

2. Jack up the front of the vehicle and support it on jackstands.

3. Support the lower control arm.

4. Loosen the lower shock absorber attachment.
5. Unscrew the steering arm from the steering knuckle.
6. Separate the brake line and brake hose and plug the openings.
7. Remove the front spring.
8. Unscrew the hex nuts on the ball joints.
9. Remove the lower ball joint and remove the lower control arm.
10. Installation is the reverse of removal. Bleed the brakes and check the front end alignment.

Front End Alignment

CASTER AND CAMBER ADJUSTMENT

Caster and camber are critical to proper handling and tire wear. Neither adjustment should be attempted without the specialized equipment to accurately measure the geometry of the front end.

All Models Except 1974–76 230 and 240D, 280, 280C, 1975–76 300D, 380SL, 380SLC, 450SL and 450SLC

The front axle provides for caster and camber adjustment, but both wheel adjustments can only be made together. Adjustments are made with cam bolts on the lower control arm bearings.

The front bearing cam bolt is used to set caster, while the rear bearing cam bolt is used for camber.

1974–76 230 and 240D, 280, 280C, 1975–76 300D, 380SL, 380SLC, and 450SL and 450SLC

Caster and camber are dependent upon each other and cannot be adjusted independently. They can only be adjusted simultaneously.

Camber is adjusted by turning the lower control arm about the rear mounting, using the eccentric bolt. Bear in mind that caster will be changed accordingly.

When camber is adjusted in a positive direction, caster is changed in a negative direction, and vice versa. Adjustment of camber by 0° 15′ results in a caster change of approximately 0° 20′. Adjustment of caster by 1° results in a camber change of approximately 0° 7′.

TOE-IN ADJUSTMENT

Toe-in is the difference of the distance between the front edges of the wheel rims and the rear edges of the wheel rims.

To measure toe-in, the steering should be in the straight ahead position and the marks on the pitman arm and pitman shaft should be aligned.

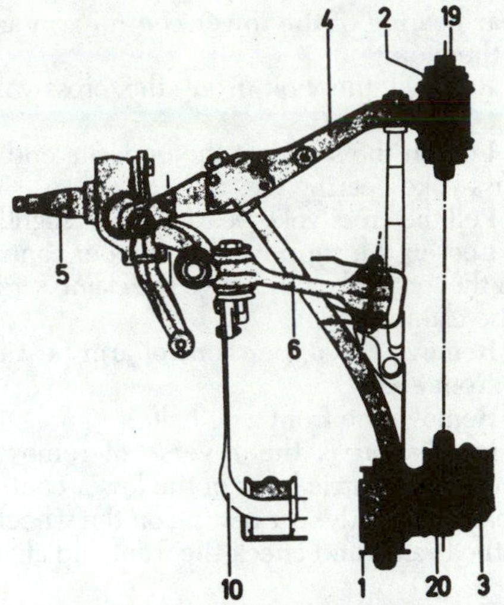

1. Frame side member
2. Frame cross member for front axle
3. Cross yoke
4. Lower control arm
5. Steering knuckle
6. Upper control arm
10. Torsion bar
19. Cam bolt of front bearing (camber adjustment)
20. Cam bolt of rear bearing (caster adjustment)

Caster and camber adjustment points on the 280S, 280SE, 1978–80 300SD, 450SE, 450SEL and 6.9

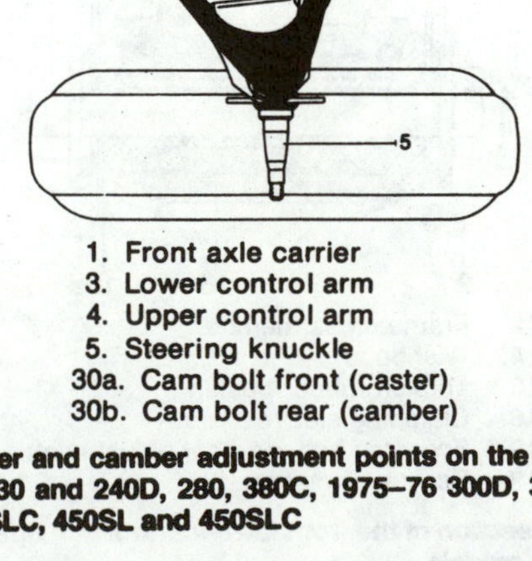

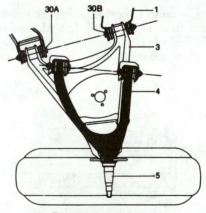

1. Front axle carrier
3. Lower control arm
4. Upper control arm
5. Steering knuckle

30a. Cam bolt front (caster)
30b. Cam bolt rear (camber)

Caster and camber adjustment points on the 1974–76 230 and 240D, 280, 380C, 1975–76 300D, 380SL, 380SLC, 450SL and 450SLC

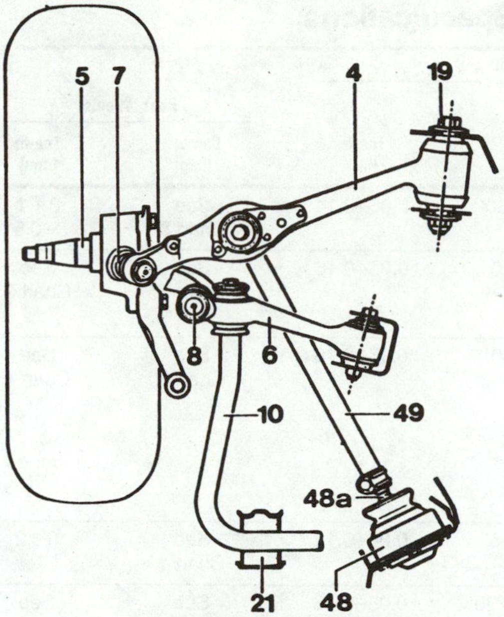

1. Frame side member
2. Frame cross member for front axle
4. Lower control arm
5. Steering knuckle
6. Upper control arm
7. Supporting joint
8. Guide joint
10. Torsion bar
19. Eccentric bolt (camber adjustment)
21. Torsion bar mounting on front end
48. Supporting joint
48a. Ball pin (caster adjustment)
49. Supporting tube

Caster and camber adjustment points on all other models

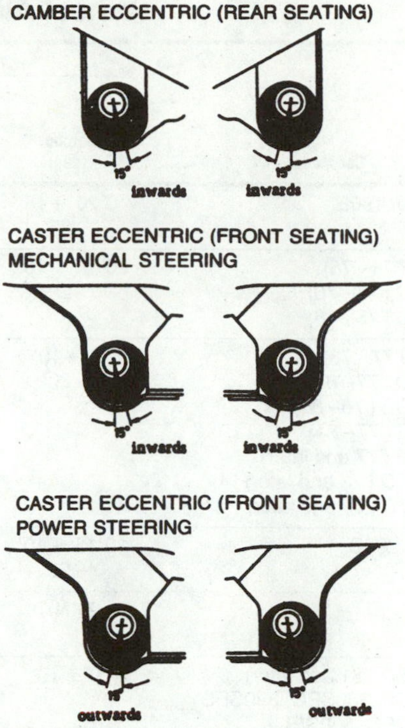

Basic caster and camber settings—1974–76 230 and 240D, 280, 280C and 1975–76 300D

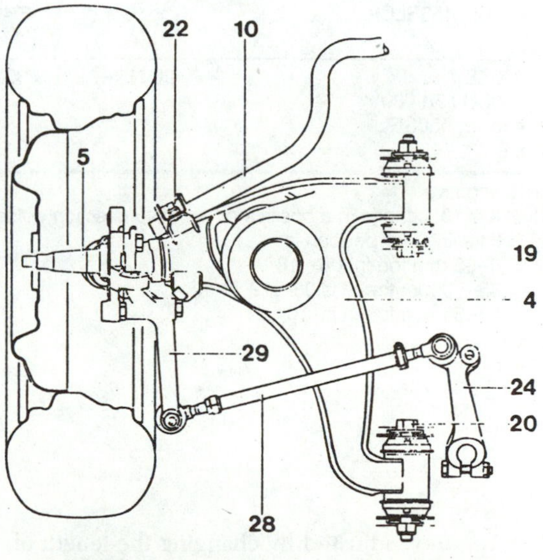

4. Wishbone
5. Steering knuckle
10. Torsion bar
19. Eccentric bolt of front bushing (camber adjustment)
20. Eccentric bolt of rear bushing (caster adjustment)
22. Torsion bar bushing on wishbone
24. Pitman arm
28. Tie rod
29. Steering knuckle arm

Caster and camber adjustment points—190D and 190E

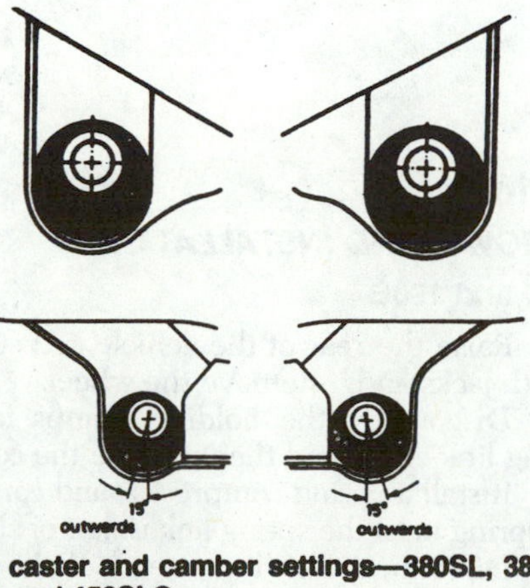

Basic caster and camber settings—380SL, 380SLC, 450SL and 450SLC

Wheel Alignment Specifications

Car Model	Front Wheels Camber (deg)	Front Wheels Caster (deg) Power Steering	Front Wheels Toe-In (in.)	Rear Wheels Camber (deg)	Rear Wheels Toe-In (mm)
190D, 190E	0°20′ +15′ −25′	10°10′ ±30′	0.06–0.14	See Chart 8	3+1 −0.5
230 ('74–'76) 240D ('74–'76) 300D ('75–'76)	0°15′ +10′ −20′	3°40′ ±20′	0.08–0.16	See Chart 1	See Chart 2
230 ('77–'78) 240D ('77–'83) 280CE ('78–'81) 280E ('77–'81) 300D ('77 and later) 300CD ('78 and later) 300TD ('79 and later)	0° + 10′ −20′	8°45′ ±30′	0.08–0.16	See Chart 3	See Chart 4
280, 280C	0°15′ +10′ −20′	3°40′ ±15′	0.04–0.12	See Chart 1	0±2
280S	20′N ①	9°30′ − 10°30′	0.08–0.16	See Chart 5	See Chart 4
300SD ('81 and later) 380SE, 380SEC, 380SEL 500SEC, 500SEL	0° ±10′	9°15′–10°15′	0.13–0.21	See Chart 6	②
380SL, 380SLC	0° + 10′ −20′	3°40 ±20′	0.04–0.12	0°10′ to 0°40′ See Chart 7	0 − 35
450SL, 450SLC	0° + 10′ −20′	3°40′ ±20′	0.04–0.12	See Chart 1	See Chart 2
280SE 300SD ('78–'80) 450SE, 450SEL 6.9	20′N	9°30′ − 10°30′	0.08–0.16	See Chart 5	See Chart 4

N Negative
① A 0°10′ change in a positive or negative direction yields a 0°10′ change in caster in the corresponding direction
② If trailing arm position is
0–35 mm toe-in .06–.18
35–50 mm toe-in is.08–.19
50–60 mm toe-in is .10–.21

Toe-in is adjusted by changing the length of the two tie-rods or track rods with the wheels in the straight ahead position.

NOTE: *Install new tie-rods so that the left-hand thread points toward the left-hand side of the car.*

REAR SUSPENSION

All Mercedes-Benz cars covered in this book use independent rear suspension, known as the diagonal swing arm type.

Springs

REMOVAL AND INSTALLATION

190D and 190E

1. Raise the rear of the vehicle and support it with jackstands. Remove the wheel.
2. Disconnect the holding clamps for the spring link cover and then remove the cover.
3. Install a spring compressor and compress the spring until the spring link is free of all load.
4. Disconnect the lower end of the shock absorber.

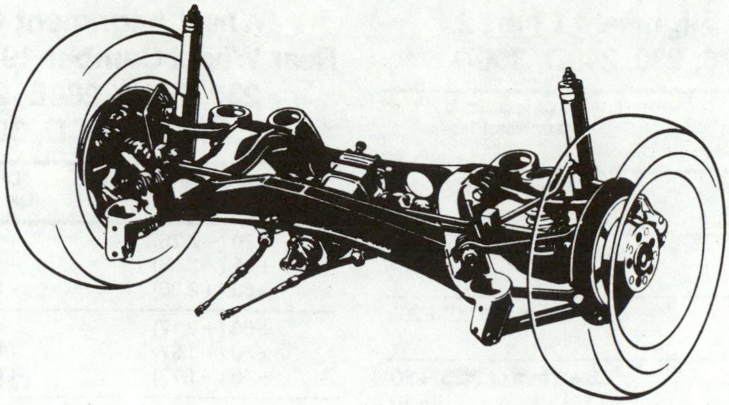

Rear suspension—190D and 190E

5. Increase the tension on the spring compressor and remove the spring.

6. Installation is in the reverse order of removal. Please note the following:

a. Position the spring so that the end of the lower coil is seated in the impression of the spring seat and the upper coil seats properly in the rubber mount in the frame floor.

b. Do not release tension on the spring compressor until the lower end of the shock absorber is connected and tightened to 47 ft. lbs. (65 Nm).

Wheel Alignment Chart 1

Control Arm Position mm (in.)	Corresponds to Rear Wheel Camber on: 230, 240D, 300D 280, 280C	450SL, 450SLC
+80 (3.17″)	+2°30′±30′	—
+75 (2.98″)	+2°15′±30′	—
+70 (2.78″)	+2°±30′	—
+65 (2.58″)	+1°45′±30′	—
+60 (2.38″)	+1°30′±30′	—
+55 (2.18″)	+1°15′±30′	—
+50 (1.99″)	+1°±30′	+0°50′±30′
+45 (1.79″)	+0°45′±30′	+0°35′±30′
+40 (1.59″)	+0°30′±30′	+0°20′±30′
+35 (1.39″)	+0°15′±30′	+0°05′±30′
+30 (1.12″)	0°±30′	−0°10′±30′
+25 (0.99″)	−0°15′±30′	−0°25′±30′
+20 (0.79″)	−0°30′±30′	−0°40′±30′
+15 (0.60″)	−0°45′±30′	−0°55′±30′
+10 (0.40″)	−1°±30′	−1°10′±30′
+5 (0.20″)	−1°15′±30′	−1°25′±30′
rf0	−1°30′±30′	−1°40′±30′
−5 (0.20″)	−1°45′±30′	−1°55′±30°
−10 (0.40″)	−2°±30′	−2°10′±30′
−15 (0.60″)	−2°15′±30′	−2°25′±30′
−20 (0.79″)	−2°30′±30′	−2°40′±30′

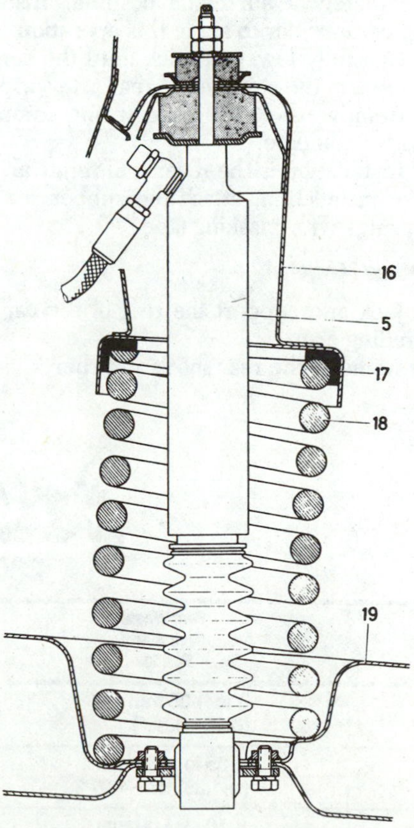

5. Spring strut
16. Dome on frame floor
17. Rubber mount
18. Rear spring
19. Semi-trailing arm

Rear spring—1974–76 230 and 240D, 280, 280C, 1975–76 300D, 380SL, 380SLC, 450SL and 450SLC

Wheel Alignment Chart 2
1974–76, 230, 240D, 300D

Rear Wheel Control Arm Position	Corresponds to Rear Wheel Toe-in of:
0 to +35 mm (0–1.39″)	1+2 mm or 0°10′+20′ −1 −10′
+35 to +50 mm (1.39″–1.99″)	1.5+2 mm or 0°15′+20′ −1 −10′
+50 to +60 mm (1.99″–2.38″)	2+2 mm or 0°20′+20′ −1 −10′
+60 to +70 mm (2.38″–2.78″)	2.5+2 mm or 0°25′+20′ −1 −10′
+70 to +80 mm (2.78″–3.17″)	3.0+2 mm or 0°30′+20′ −1 −10′

1974–76 230 and 240D, 280, 280C, 1975–76 300D, 380SL, 380SLC, 450SL and 450SLC

1. Jack up the rear of the car.
2. Remove the rear shock absorber.
3. With a floor jack, raise the control arm to approximately a horizontal position. Install a spring compressor to aid in this operation.
4. Carefully lower the jack until the control arm contacts the stop on the rear axle support.
5. Remove the spring and spring compressor with great care.
6. Installation is the reverse of removal. For ease of installation, attach the rubber seats to the springs with masking tape.

All Other Models

1. Jack and support the rear of the car and the trailing arm.
2. Remove the rear shock absorber.

Wheel Alignment Chart 3
Rear Wheel Camber 1977 and later 230, 240D, 280E, 280CE, 300D, 300CD, 300TD

Semi-trailing Arm Position mm (in.)	Corresponds to Rear Wheel Camber
+70 (+2.76) +65 (+2.56) +60 (+2.36)	+1°45′±30′ +1°30′±30′ +1°15′±30′
+55 (+2.17) +50 (+1.97) +45 (+1.77)	+1°±30′ +0°45′±30′ +0°30′±30′
+40 (+1.58) +35 (+1.37) +30 (+1.18)	+0°15′±30′ 0°±30′ −0°15′±30′
+25 (+0.98) +20 (+0.79) +15 (+0.59)	−0°30′±30′ −0°45′±30′ −1°±30′
+10 (+0.39) +5 (+0.20) +0 (0)	−1°15′±30′ −1°30′±30′ −1°45′±30′
−5 (−0.20) −10 (−0.39) −15 (−0.59)	−2°±30′ −2°15′±30′ −2°30′±30′

3. Be sure that the upper shock absorber attachment is released first.
4. Compress the spring with a spring compressor.
5. Remove the rear spring with the rubber mount.
6. Installation is the reverse of removal. When installing the shock absorber, tighten the lower mount first.

Wheel Alignment Chart 4
All Models Except 1974–76 230, 240D, 300D

Rear Wheel Control Arm Position	Corresponds to Rear Wheel Toe-in of:
0 to +35 mm (0 to +1.38″)	0°10′+20′ or 1+2 mm (0.04″+0.08″) −10′ −1 −0.04″)
+35 to +50 mm (+1.38″ to +1.97″)	0°15′+20′ or 1.5+2 mm (0.06″+0.08″) −10′ −1 −0.04″)
+50 to +60 mm (+1.97″ to +2.36″)	0°20′+20′ or 2+2 mm (0.08″+0.08″) −10′ −1 −0.04″)
+60 to +70 mm (+2.36″ to +2.76″)	0°25′+20′ or 2.5+2 mm (0.10″+0.08″) −10′ −1 −0.04″)
+70 to +80 mm (+2.76″ to +3.15″)	0°30′+20′ or 3+2 mm (0.12″+0.08″) −10′ −1 −0.04″)

Chart 5 Rear Wheel Camber 450SE, 450SEL, 300SD, 280S, 280SE, 6.9

Semi-trailing Arm Position mm (in.)	Corresponds to Rear Wheel Camber
+65 (2.58″)	+1°45′ ± 30′
+60 (2.38″)	+1°30′ ± 30′
+55 (2.18″)	+1°15′ ± 30′
+50 (1.99″)	+1° ± 30′
+45 (1.79″)	+0°45′ ± 30′
+40 (1.59″)	+0°30′ ± 30′
+35 (1.39″)	+0°15′ ± 30′
+30 (1.12″)	0° ± 30′
+25 (0.99″)	−0°15′ ± 30′
+20 (0.79″)	−0°30′ ± 30′
+15 (0.60″)	−0°45′ ± 30′
+10 (0.40″)	−1° ± 30′
+5 (0.20″)	−1°15′ ± 30′
0	−1°30′ ± 30′
−5 (0.20″)	−1°45′ ± 30′
−10(0.40″)	−2° ± 30′
−15(0.60″)	−2°15′ ± 30′
−20(0.79″)	−2°30′ ± 30′

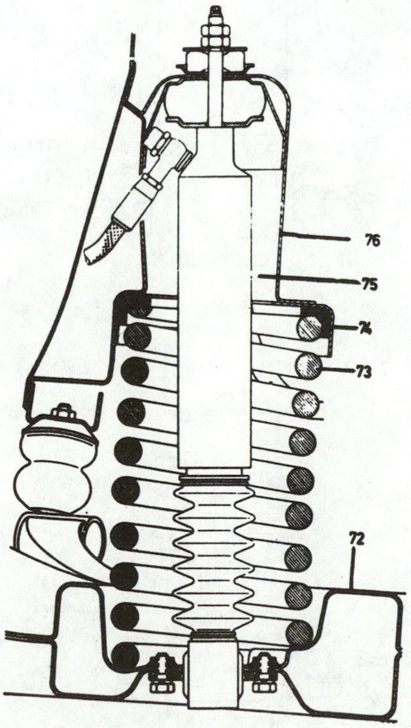

72. Semi-trailing arm
73. Rear spring
74. Rubber mounting
75. Shock absorber or spring strut
76. Dome on frame floor

Rear spring—all models except the 190D, 190E, 1974–76 230 and 240D, 280, 280C, 1975–76 300D, 380SL, 380SLC, 450SL and 450SLC

Wheel Alignment Chart 6

('81 and Later 300SD, 380SEL, 380SEC, 500SEC, 500SEL)

Semi-trailing Arm Position mm	Corresponds to Rear Wheel Camber
+65	+1°30′ ± 30′
+60	+1°15′ ± 30′
+55	+1° ± 30′
+50	+0°45′ ± 30′
+45	+0°30′ ± 30′
+40	+0°15′ ± 30′
+35	0° ± 30′
+30	−0°15′ ± 30′
+25	−0°30′ ± 30′
+20	−0°45′ ± 30′
+15	−1° ± 30′
+10	−1°15′ ± 30′
+5	−1°30′ ± 30′
0	−1°45′ ± 30′
−5	−2° ± 30′
−10	−2°15′ ± 30′
−15	−2°30′ ± 30′
−20	−2°45′ ± 30′

Rear Wheel Alignment Chart 7

(380SL, 380SLC)

Semi-trailing Arm Position mm	Corresponds to Rear Wheel Camber
35	0° ± 30′
30	−0°15′ ± 30′
25	−0°30′ ± 30′
20	−0°45′ ± 30′
15	−1° ± 30′
10	−1°15′ ± 30′
5	−1°30′ ± 30′
0	−1°45′ ± 30′
−5	−2° ± 30′
−10	−2°15′ ± 30′
−15	−2°30′ ± 30′
−20	−2°45′ ± 30′

Rear Wheel Alignment Chart 8

Spring Link Position mm	Corresponds to Rear Wheel Camber
+50	−0°15′ ± 30′
+40	−0°30′ ± 30′
+30	−0°45′ ± 30′
+20	−1° ± 30′
+10	−1°15′ ± 30′
0	−1°30′ ± 30′
−10	−1°45′ ± 30′
−20	−2° ± 30′

Shock Absorbers

REMOVAL AND INSTALLATION

190D, 190E, 1974–76 230 and 240D, 280, 280C, 1975–76 300D, 380SL, 380SLC, 450SL and 450SLC

1. Jack up the rear of the car and support the control arm.
2. From inside the trunk (sedans), remove the rubber cap, locknut, and hex nut from the upper mount of the shock absorber. On the 280SL and 450SL, the upper mount of the rear shock absorber is accessible after removing the top, top flap, rear seat, backrest, and lining. On the 380SLC and 450SLC, remove the rear seat, backrest and cover plate.
3. Unbolt the mounting for the rear shock

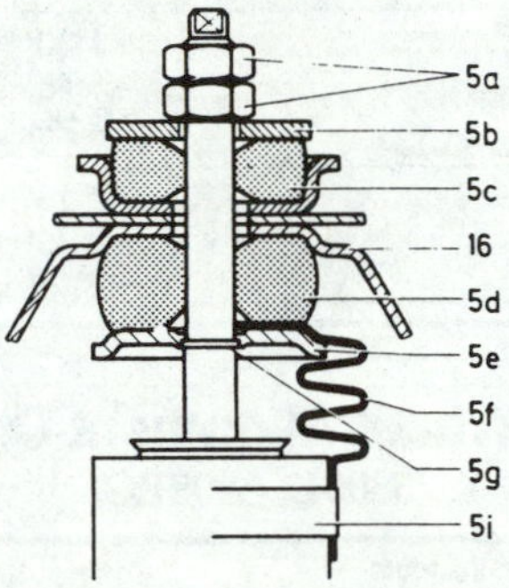

5a. Nut
5b. Washer
5c. Upper rubber ring
5d. Lower rubber ring
5e. Plate
5f . Dust protection
5g. Lockring
5i . Clamping strap
16. Dome on frame floor

Rear shock absorber upper mount—1981 and later 300SD, 380SE, 380SEC, 380SEL, 380SL, 380SLC, 450SL, 450SLC, 500SEC and 500SEL (5 not used in U.S.)

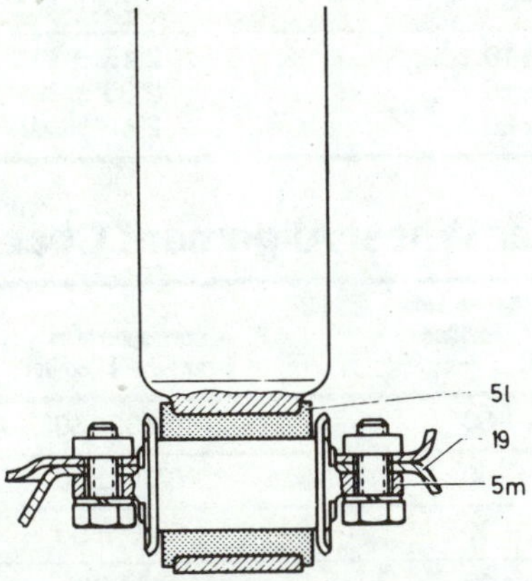

5l. Rubber mounting
5m. Fastening clip
19. Semi-trailing arm

Rear shock absorber lower mount—1974–76 230 and 240D, 280, 280C, 1975–76 300D, all 380 models, 450SL, 450SLC, 500SEC and 500SEL

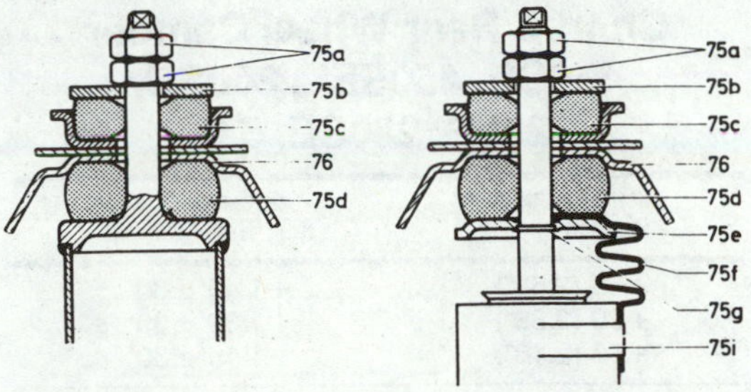

75a. Nuts
75b. Washer
75c. Upper rubber ring
75d. Lower rubber ring
75e. Plate
75f . Dust protection
75g. Locking ring
75i . Clamping strap
76. Dome on frame floor

Rear shock absorber upper mount—1977–83 230 and 240D, 280CE, 280E, 280S, 280SE, 1978–80 300SD, 1977 and later 300D, 300CD, 1979–80 300TD, 450SE, 450SEL and 6.9 (15f not used in U.S.)

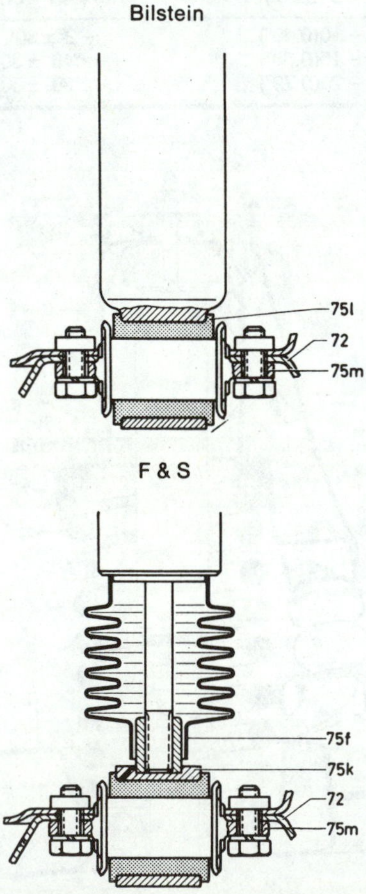

72. Semi-trailing arm
75f . Dust protection
75k. Suspension eye
75l . Rubber mounting
75m. Fastening stirrup

Rear shock absorber lower mount—1977–83 230 and 240D, 280CE, 280E, 280S, 280SE, 1978–80 300SD, 1977 and later 300D, 300CD, 1979–80 300TD, 450SE, 450SEL and 6.9

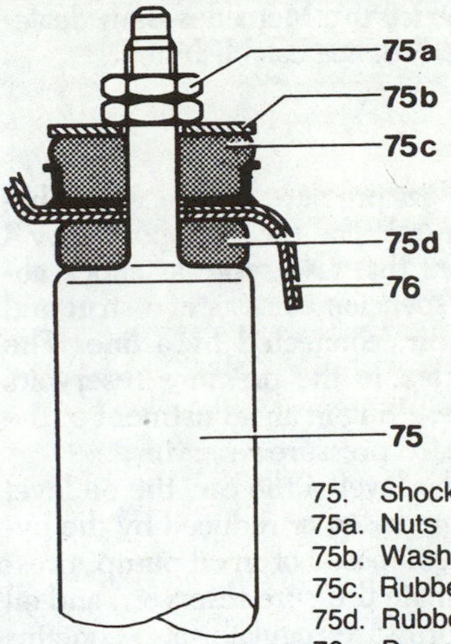

75. Shock absorber
75a. Nuts
75b. Washer
75c. Rubber mount, top
75d. Rubber mount, bottom
76. Dome on frame floor

Rear shock absorber upper mount—190D and 190E

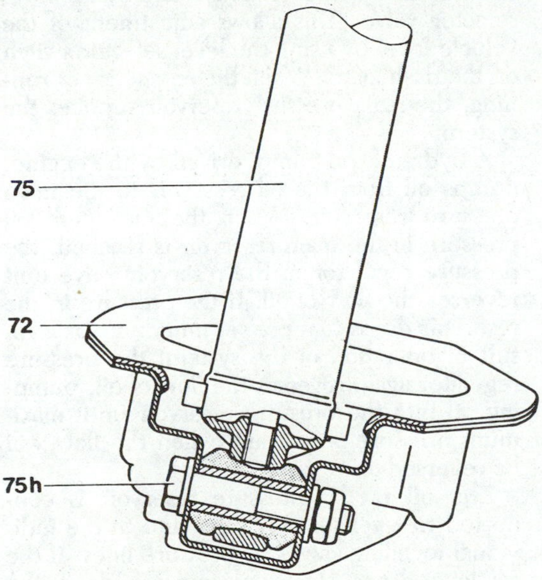

72. Spring link
75. Shock absorber
75h. Bolt with washers and self-locking nut

Rear shock absorber lower mount—190D and 190E

absorber at the bottom and remove the shock absorber.

4. Installation is the reverse of removal.

All Other Models

1. Remove the rear seat and backrest.
2. Remove the cover from the rear wall.
3. Jack and support the car and the trailing arm.
4. Loosen the nuts on the upper mount. Remove the washer and rubber ring.
5. Loosen the lower mount and remove the shock absorber downward.

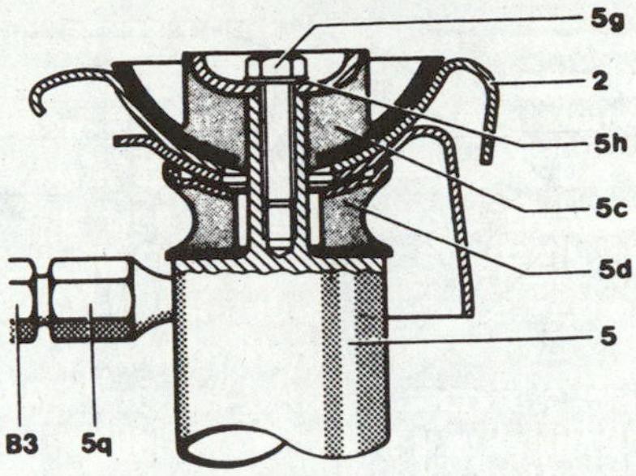

Rear shock absorber upper mount—1981–82 300TD

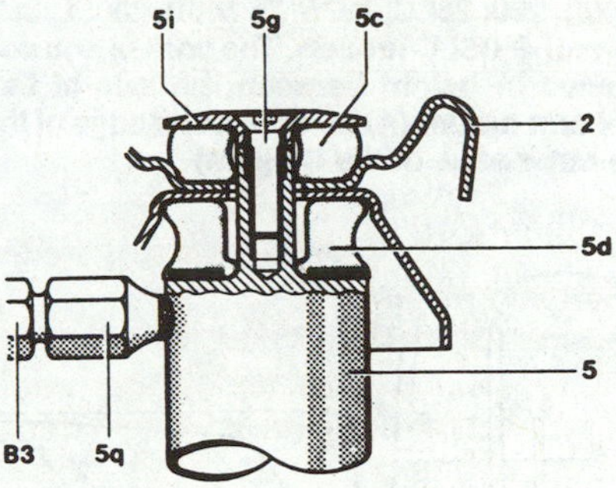

2. Frame—transverse member
5. Suspension strut
5c. Upper rubber mount
5d. Lower rubber mount
5g. Special screw
5i. Plate
5q. Stud
B3. Pressure line (pressure hose), pressure reservoir—suspension strut

Rear shock absorber upper mount—1983 and later 300TD. Retrofitting is not possible

6. Installation is the reverse of removal. Tighten the upper mounting nut to the end of the threads.

Independent Rear Suspension Adjustments

Suspension adjustments should only be checked when the vehicle is resting on a level surface and is carrying the required fluids (full tank of gas, engine oil, etc.).

CAMBER

All Models

Rear wheel camber is determined by the position of the control arm. The difference in height (a) between the axis of the control arm mounting point on the rear axle subframe and the lower edge of the cup on the constant velocity joint is directly translated in degrees of camber.

TOE-IN

Toe-in, on the rear wheels, is dependent on the camber of the rear wheels.

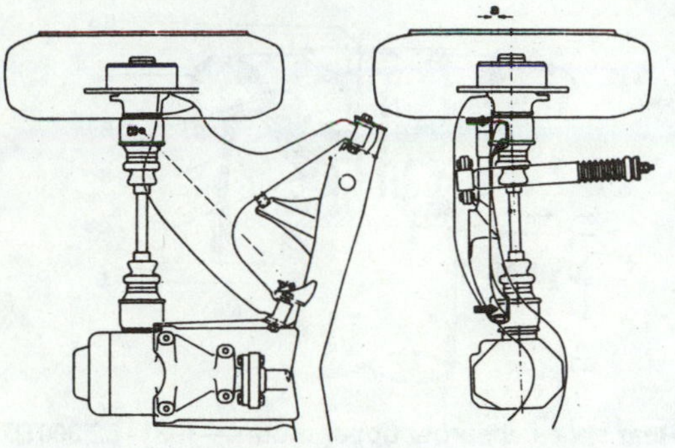

Rear wheel camber measurement on all 1974–76 230 and 240D, 280, 280C, 1975–76 300D, 380SL, 380SLC, 450SL and 450SLC models. The control arm position (difference in height between the axis of the rear control arm mount (A) and the lower edge of the cup on the outer edge of the CV-joint)

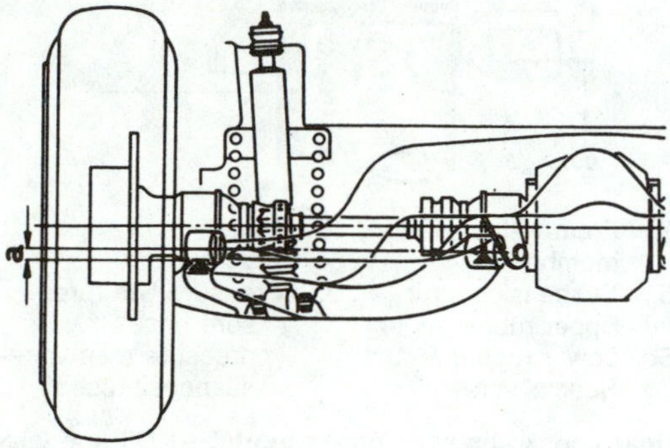

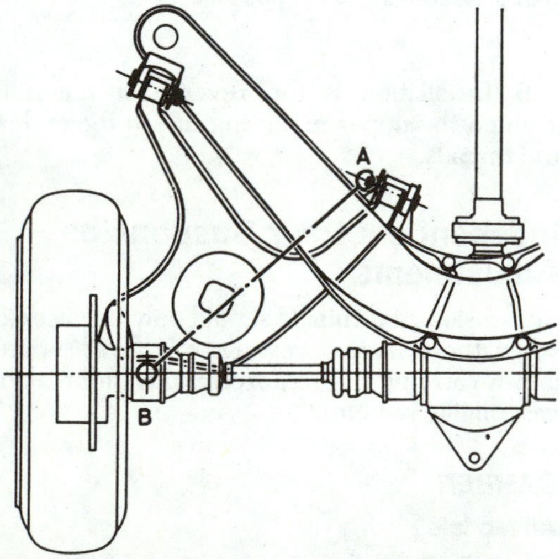

Rear wheel camber measurment on all models except the 190D, 190E, 1974–76 230 and 240D, 280, 280C, 1975–76 300D, 380SL, 380SLC, 450SL and 450SLC

HYDROPNEUMATIC SUSPENSION

The hydropneumatic suspension is used on the 380SEL, 500SEL and the 6.9. Service of this system should be left to a Mercedes-Benz dealer or other qualified service establishment.

Operation

The system is a gas pressure system with a hydraulic level control. The car is supported by 4 suspension struts that also serve as shock absorbers. The suspension consists of a strut and pressure reservoir, connected by a line. The load is transmitted to the pressure reservoirs via the struts, resulting in an adjustment of the gas cushion in each pressure reservoir.

To regulate the level of the car, the oil level in the struts is increased or reduced by the hydraulic system, composed of an oil pump, pressure regulator, main pressure reservoir, and oil reservoir. The pressure regulator also contains a level selector valve as part of the unit.

The oil volume is controlled by a levelling valve at the front and rear axle and by the level selector valve. This allows adjustment of the vehicle level by using the level selector switch on the dashboard. When the engine is not running, the main pressure reservoir supplies the system.

A hydraulic oil pump, driven by the engine, pumps oil from the oil reservoir to the main pressure reservoir. When the maximum oil pressure in the main reservoir is reached, the pressure regulator in the reservoir valve unit reverses the flow of oil. If the pressure in the reservoir drops to a pre-set minimum (as a result of operation of the system) the pressure regulator again reverses the flow of oil, pumping oil into the pressure reservoir until maximum pressure is reached, when the flow will be reversed once more.

The oil in the pressure reservoir is connected to level selector valve and to the individual levelling valves by pressure lines. If the car level drops, due to an increased load, the levelling valve opens the passage to the suspension struts, allowing the passage of oil until normal vehicle attitude is reached. If the level rises, due to a decreased load, the levelling valve opens and allows oil to flow from the suspension struts back to the oil reservoir, until the car resumes its normal level.

STEERING

Steering Wheel

REMOVAL AND INSTALLATION

All Models

1. Remove the padded plate. It is best to pull at one corner near the wheel spokes.

Hydropneumatic suspension components

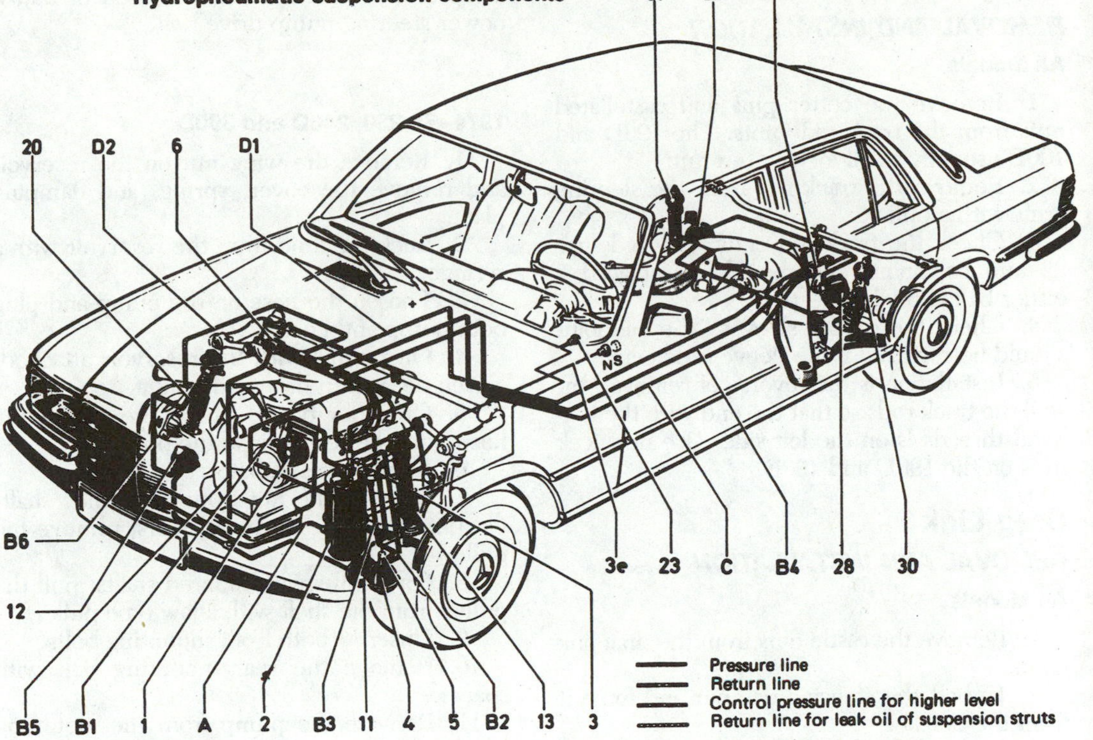

1. Hydraulic oil pump
2. Hydraulic oil reservoir
3. Valve unit (pressure regulator and level selector valve)

3a. Pressure regulator of valve unit
3b. Level selector valve of valve unit
3e. Control knob for level selector valve of valve unit

4. Main pressure reservoir
5. Electric pressure switch for warning light
6. Levelling valve, front axle
11. Pressure reservoir, front axle left
12. Pressure reservoir, front axle right
13. Suspension strut, front axle left
20. Suspension strut, front axle right
23. Warning light
24. Levelling valve, rear axle
28. Pressure reservoir, rear axle left
29. Pressure reservoir, rear axle right
30. Suspension strut, rear axle left
31. Suspension strut, rear axle right

A. Suction line, oil reservoir to hydraulic oil pump
B1. Pressure line, oil pump to pressure regulator of valve unit
B2. Pressure line, pressure regulator of valve unit to main pressure reservoir
B3. Pressure, main pressure reservoir to level selector valve
B4. Pressure line, level selector valve of valve unit to levelling valve on front and rear axle
B5. Pressure line, levelling valves to pressure reservoirs
B6. Pressure line, pressure reservoirs to suspension struts
C. Control pressure line for "higher level" level selector valve to levelling valves
D1. Return line, levelling valve to pressure regulator
D2. Return line, leak oil of suspension struts

Remove the padded plate (25) from the steering wheel

2. Unscrew the hex nut from the steering shaft and remove the spring washer and the steering wheel.

3. Installation is the reverse of removal. Be sure that the alignment mark on the steering shaft is pointing upward and be sure that the slightly curved spoke of the steering wheel is down.

Ignition Switch and Lock Cylinder

See Chapter 5.

Track Rod

REMOVAL AND INSTALLATION

All Models

1. Remove the cotter pins and castellated nuts from the track rod joints. The 190D and 190E use only a self-locking hex nut.
2. Remove the track rod from the steering arms with a puller.
3. Check the track rod ends. The rods use 22 mm ball joints and should be replaced if either ball joints is defective.
4. Check the rubber sleeves. The ball joint should be replaced if the sleeve is defective.
5. Installation is the reverse of removal. Install the track rods so that the end with the left-hand threads is on the left side. Use new lock nuts on the 190D and 190E.

Drag Link

REMOVAL AND INSTALLATION

All Models

1. Remove the castle nuts from the drag link joints.
2. Unbolt the steering damper and force it from the bracket.
3. Remove the drag link with a puller.
4. Installation is the reverse of removal.
5. Check the front wheel alignment.

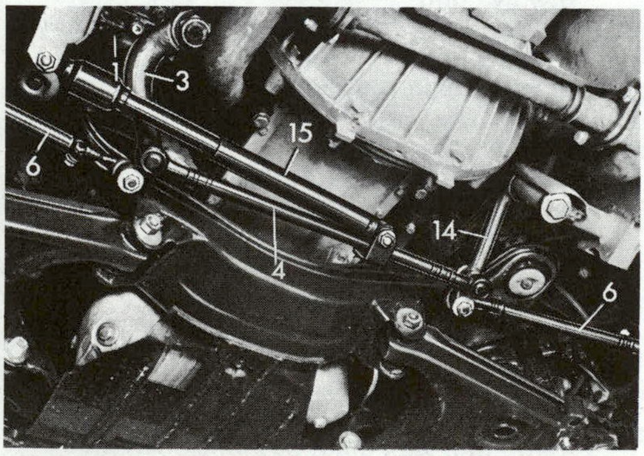

1. Steering
3. Pitman arm
4. Drag link
6. Track rod
14. Intermediate steering lever
15. Steering shock absorber

Bottom view of steering linkage showing track rod and drag link

Power Steering Pump

REMOVAL AND INSTALLATION

Many types of power steering pumps are used on Mercedes-Benz vehicles. Use only the instructions that apply to your vehicle. See Chapter 1 for procedures to loosen or adjust power steering pump drive belt.

1974–76 230, 240D and 300D

1. Remove the wing nut on the reservoir and remove the cover, spring, and damping plate.
2. Suck the fluid from the reservoir with a syringe.
3. Loosen the hose on the pump and plug both pump and hose.
4. On pumps with the reservoir attached, loosen the return hose and plug it.
5. On other types, loosen the connecting hose from the reservoir to the pump.
6. Remove the radiator.
7. Remove the nut from the pulley shaft. On pumps with cylindrical shafts, remove the pulley.
8. On pumps with tapered shafts, pull the pulley from the shaft with a jaw type puller.
9. Unscrew both front mounting bolts.
10. Remove the rear mounting bolt with spacer.
11. Remove the pump from the mounting bracket.
12. On all 4 cylinder models, remove the screws between the pump housing and the bracket. Remove the pump and pulley.
13. Installation, in all cases, is the reverse of removal.

All Models Except 1974–76 230, 240D and 300D

1. Remove the nut from the supply tank.
2. Remove the spring and damping plate.
3. Drain the oil from the tank with a syringe.
4. Loosen and remove the expanding and return hoses from the pump. Plug all connections and pump openings.
5. If necessary for clearance, loosen the radiator shell. Loosen the mounting bolts, and move the pump toward the engine by using the toothed wheel. Remove the belt. Remove the pulley, and then remove the pump.
6. Loosen the nut on the attaching plate and the bolt on the support.
7. Push the pump toward the engine and remove the belts from the pulley.
8. Unscrew the mounting bolts and remove the pump and carrier.
9. Installation is the reverse of removal.

Brakes

9

BRAKE SYSTEM

All Mercedes-Benz cars imported into the U.S. are equipped with 4-wheel disc brakes. The disc brakes are basically similar on all models, though there may be slight differences in design from model to model. The caliper bore sizes, for instance, differ depending upon application. The bore size (in mm) is usually stamped on the outside of the caliper, but occasionally, a code is used. For instance, the 14 on a Teves (ATE) caliper is really a 57 mm bore (obviously, it isn't a 14 mm bore).

Three different manufacturers make calipers for Mercedes-Benz production—Teves (ATE), Bendix or Girling—but calipers of the same manufacturer are installed on the same axle. For service, install calipers of the same manufacturer on the front axle; on the rear axle, calipers of any manufacturer can be installed.

Most models are equipped with brake pad wear indicators to indicate when the pad lining requires replacement. Beginning in 1976, a new design, step-type master cylinder is used which eliminates the need for the vacuum pump previously used on 230, 280, 280C and 280S. The brake circuits are reversed from 1974 and 1975 models; the front brakes are connected to the primary side of the master cylinder and the rear brakes to the secondary side. A pressure differential warning indicator is also used, which will immediately indicate the total loss of one part of the braking system by lighting the brake warning light on the dash. Once the warning light has come on, it will remain on until the system is repaired and the switch on the master cylinder reset. The warning light will only go out after pushing the reset pin in the switch.

Beginning with 1978 models, the pressure differential warning indicator has been eliminated from models with the step-type master cylinder. The master cylinder reservoir has 2 chambers with 2 sets of electrical contacts. Loss of brake fluid in either reservoir will light the warning light on the dash.

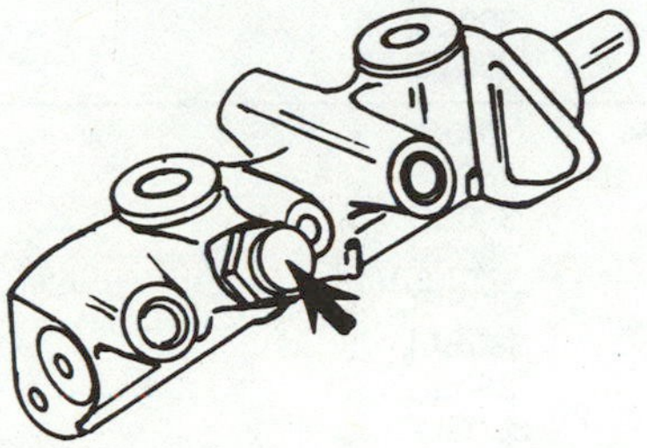

Reset pin (arrow) on the master cylinder with a pressure differential warning valve

Adjustment

Since disc brakes are used at all four wheels, no adjustments are necessary. Disc brakes are inherently self-adjusting. The only adjustment possible is to the handbrake, which is covered at the end of this section.

Master Cylinder

The dual master cylinder has a safety feature which the single unit lacks—if a leak develops in one brake circuit (rear wheels, for example), the other circuit will still operate.

Failure of one system is immediately obvious—the pedal travel increases appreciably and a warning light is activated. When the fluid falls below a certain level, a switch activates the circuit.

CAUTION: *This design was not intended to allow driving the car for any distance with, in effect, a two-wheel brake system. If one brake circuit fails, braking action is correspondingly lower. Front circuit failure is the more serious, however, since the front brake contribute up to 75% of the braking force required to stop the car.*

REMOVAL AND INSTALLATION

1. To remove the master cylinder, first open a bleed screw at one front, and one rear, wheel.

Brake Specifications

Year	Model	Lug Nut Torque (ft/lb)	Master Cylinder Bore (in.)	Front Brake Disc Minimum Thickness (in.)	Front Brake Disc Maximum Run-Out (in.)	Rear Brake Disc Minimum Thickness (in.)	Rear Brake Disc Maximum Run-Out (in.)	Thickness Minimum Lining Front▲ (in.)	Thickness Minimum Lining Rear▲ (in.)
1974–75	230 240D 280 280C 300D	75	15⁄16	①	0.0047 (max.)	0.33	0.0047 (max.)	0.08 ②	0.08 ②
1976–84	230 240D 280 280C 280CE 280E 300D 300CD 300TD	75	③	①	0.0047 (max.)	0.33	0.0047 (max.)	0.08 ②	0.08 ②
1974–84	280S 280SE 300SD 380SE 380SEC 380SEL 380SL 380SLC 450SE 450SEL 450SL 450SLC 500SEC 500SEL 6.9	75	③	④ ⑤	0.0047 (max.)	0.33	0.0047 (max.)	0.08 ②	0.08 ②
1984	190D 190E	75	⑥	0.35	0.0047 (max.)	0.30	0.0059 (max.)	0.08 ②	0.08 ②

▲New thickness of brake lining and back-up plate—0.59 in.
New thickness of backing plate—0.20 in.
New thickness of brake lining—0.39 in.
—Not Applicable

NOTE: *Minimum lining thickness is as recommended by the manufacturer. Due to variations in state inspection regulations, the minimum allowable thickness may be different than recommended by the manufacturer.*

① Caliper w/57 mm piston diameter: 0.44 in.
Caliper w/60 mm piston diameter: 0.42 in.
② 1976 and later brake pads are equipped with electric pad wear indicators
③ Pushrod circuit: 15⁄16 in.
Floating circuit: ¾ in.
④ Caliper w/57 mm piston diameter: 0.81 in.
Caliper w/60 mm piston diameter: 0.79 in.
⑤ March, 1980 and later: 0.76 in.
⑥ Pushrod circuit: ⅞ in.
Floating circuit: 11⁄16 in.

2. Pump the pedal to empty the reservoir completely. Make sure both reservoirs are completely drained.

3. Disconnect the switch connectors using a small screwdriver. Disconnect the brake lines at the master cylinder. Plug the ends with bleed screw caps or the equivalent.

4. Unbolt the master cylinder from the power brake unit and remove. Be careful you do not lose the O-ring in the flange groove of the master cylinder.

5. Installation is the reverse of removal. Be sure to replace the O-ring between the master cylinder and the power brake unit, since this must be absolutely tight. Torque the nuts to 12–15 ft. lbs. Be sure that both chambers are completely filled with brake fluid and bleed the brakes.

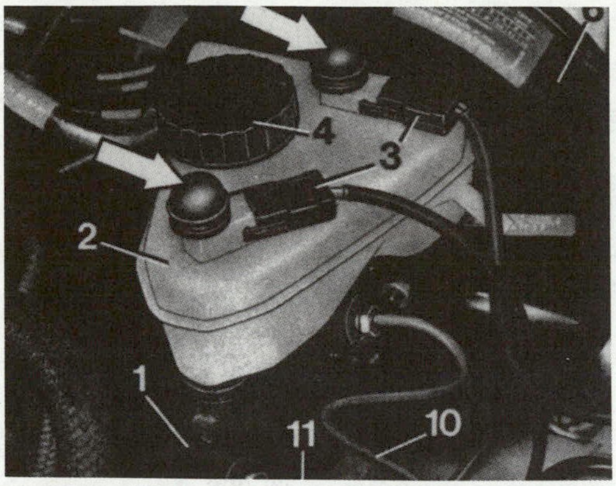

Master cylinders after 1977 do not use a pressure differential warning valve. A switch (3) in each reservoir replaces the warning valve

OVERHAUL

1. To disassemble pull the reservoir out of the top of the cylinder.
2. Remove the screw cap, strainer, and splash shield.
3. Unscrew the cover caps and take out the inserts and O-rings.
4. Push the piston inward slightly and remove the stop screws.
5. Remove the piston stop-ring in the same manner, then pull out the piston and other components.
6. The spring must be unscrewed from the piston.
7. Clean all parts in clean brake fluid.
8. Check the housing bore for score marks and rust. Do not hone the cylinder bore. If slight rust marks do not come out with crocus cloth, replace the housing.

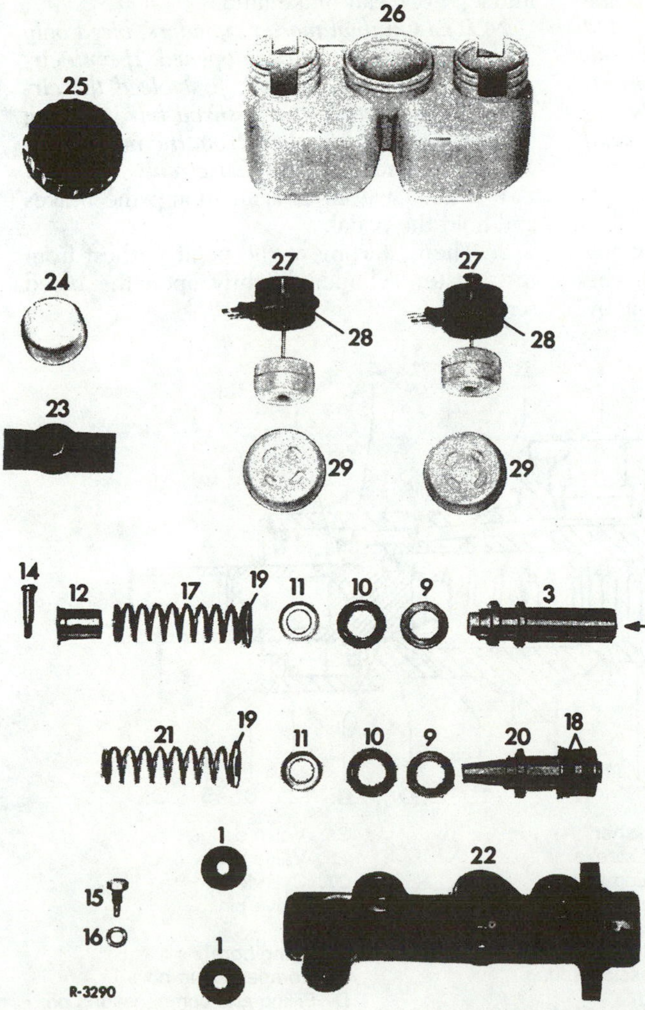

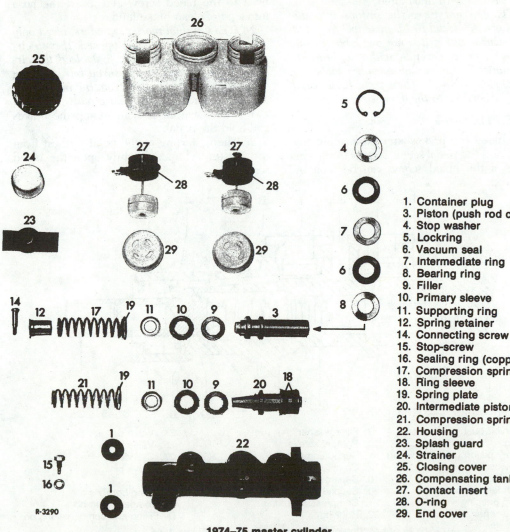

1. Container plug
3. Piston (push rod circuit)
4. Stop washer
5. Lockring
6. Vacuum seal
7. Intermediate ring
8. Bearing ring
9. Filler
10. Primary sleeve
11. Supporting ring
12. Spring retainer
14. Connecting screw
15. Stop-screw
16. Sealing ring (copper)
17. Compression spring
18. Ring sleeve
19. Spring plate
20. Intermediate piston
21. Compression spring
22. Housing
23. Splash guard
24. Strainer
25. Closing cover
26. Compensating tank
27. Contact insert
28. O-ring
29. End cover

1974–75 master cylinder

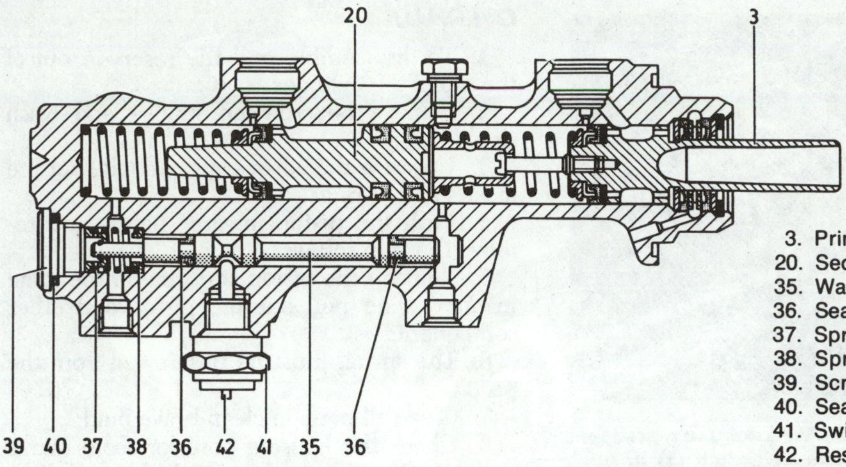

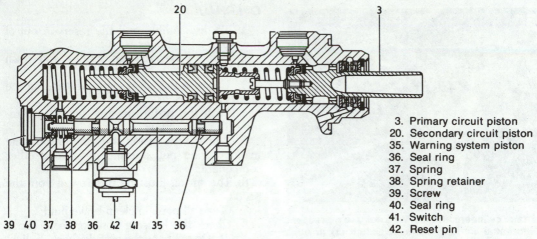

3. Primary circuit piston
20. Secondary circuit piston
35. Warning system piston
36. Seal ring
37. Spring
38. Spring retainer
39. Screw
40. Seal ring
41. Switch
42. Reset pin

Cross section of a typical step-type master cylinder (1976 and later)

9. Assembly is the reverse of disassembly. Before installing the pistons, coat the sleeves of both pistons with brake fluid.

NOTE: *Do not force the pistons into the housings. A special tool is available to install the pistons, but if it is not available, install the pistons very carefully with a slight twisting motion. The special assembly tools can be fabricated in the shop from light metal alloy, according to the dimensions given.*

BRAKE BLEEDING

Always bleed the brakes after performing any service, or if the pedal seems spongy (soft). The location of the bleed screws can be seen by consulting the illustrations throughout this section. Prior to bleeding each wheel, connect a hose to the bleed screw and insert the hose into a jar of clean brake fluid.

NOTE: *On dual master cylinders, bleed only the circuit that has been opened. If both circuits have been opened, first bleed the circuit connected to the pushrod bore starting with the wheel farthest from the master cylinder, then bleed the other circuit.*

1. First have an assistant pump the brakes and hold the pedal.
2. Then, starting at the point farthest from the master cylinder, slightly open the bleed screw.

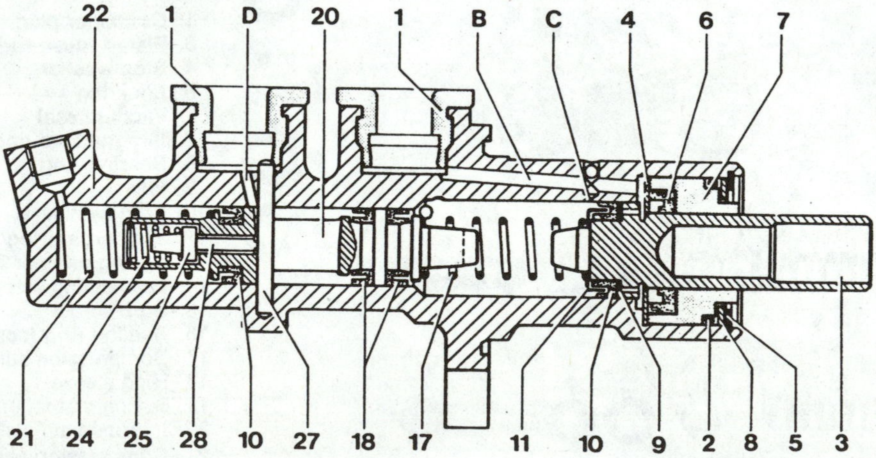

1. Reservoir bushing (rubber)
2. O-ring
3. Primary piston (primary circuit)
4. Stop washer
5. Snap ring
6. Secondary sleeve
7. Plastic bushing
8. Stop washer
9. Filler washer
10. Primary sleeve
11. Supporting ring
12. Compression spring
18. Separating sleeve
20. Secondary piston (secondary circuit)
21. Compression spring
22. Housing
24. Valve spring
25. Valve seal
27. Cylinder pin
28. Valve pin
B. Filling bore
C. Compensating bore
D. Filling and compensating bore

Cross section of the master cylinder—190D and 190E

3. When the pedal hits the floor, close the bleed screw before allowing the pedal to return (to prevent air from being sucked into the system).

4. Continue this procedure until no more air bubbles exit from the bleed screw hole, then go to the next wheel. Fluid, which has been bled from the system, is filled with microscopic air bubbles after the bleeding process is completed, therefore it should be discarded.

FRONT DISC BRAKES

Disc Brake Pads

REPLACEMENT

Fixed Calipers

NOTE: *These procedures apply to front or rear brake pads on all models, but the 190D, 190E, 300SD, 380SE, 380SEC, 380SEL, 500SEC and 500SEL which utilize floating calipers on the front wheels.*

1. Remove the cover plate (15). The cover plate is only installed on front brakes of cars with solid brake discs (not ventilated) and 57 mm calipers.

2. On models with the brake pad lining wear indicator, pull the cable sensors (25) from the plug connections (26) at the inside edge of the caliper.

3. Remove the sensors (25) from the brake lining (18) or backing plate.

NOTE: *If the contact pin insulation is worn, the clip sensor should be replaced.*

4. On models with Teves (ATE) brake calipers, use a punch to knock the retaining pins (3) out of the caliper. Remove the cross-spring (2).

5. On models with the Bendix (BX) caliper, remove the locking eyes (21), retaining pins (17) and pad retaining springs (16).

6. On models with Girling calipers (usually only at rear axle), remove the locking eyes (21), the retaining pins (17) and the pad retaining plates (16).

7. Pull the brake shoes out of the caliper. Mercedes-Benz recommends a special tool, an impact puller (033) for this, but you can carefully grab the pad backing plate ears with pliers or a piece of bent welding rod and wiggle them out. It's best to leave one pad in the caliper always.

8. Use a small brush to clean the pad guides on the inside of the brake caliper. Check the dust boots for cracks or damage. If necessary, remove and overhaul the caliper.

9. When the pads are removed, the pistons will move forward slightly, due to hydraulic pressure in the system. To install the pads, the pistons must be pushed back slightly. Mercedes-Benz recommends a special tool (31) to do this, but a flat piece of hardwood will do if used carefully. Other tools will increase the chances of damaging the piston or dust boots.

NOTE: *It should be relatively easy to push the pistons back.*

If equipped, remove the cover plate

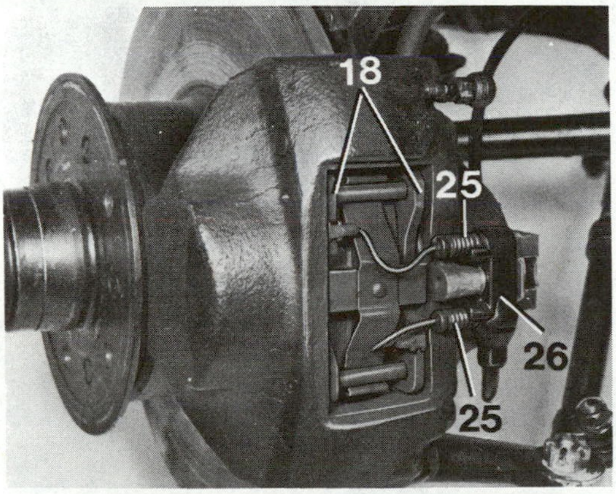

If equipped with lining wear indicator, disconnect the clip sensors

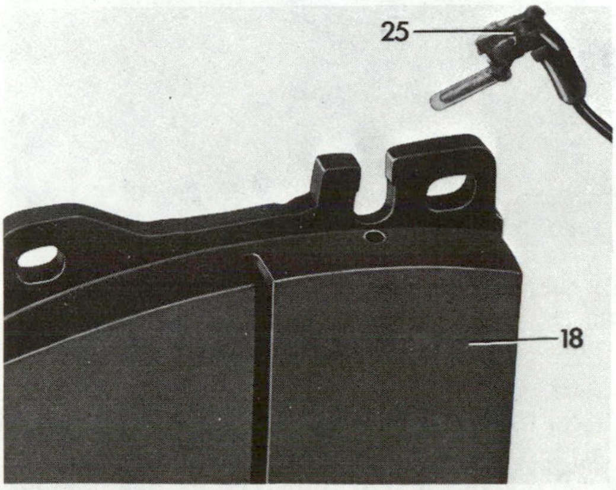

Remove the clip sensors from the backing plate

Remove the cross-spring and retaining pins from Teves (ATE) caliper

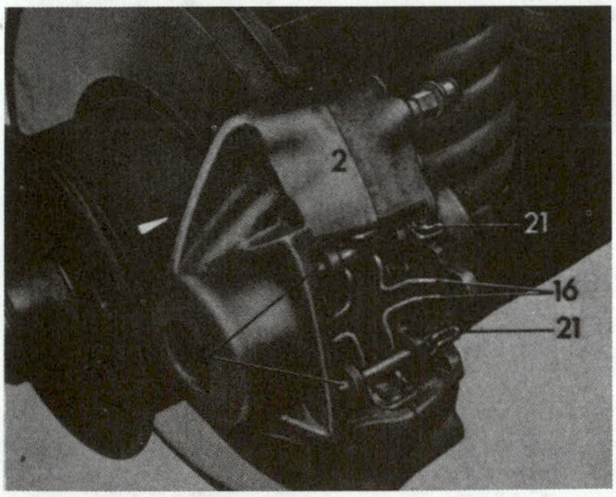

Remove the retaining pins and springs from Bendix (BX)

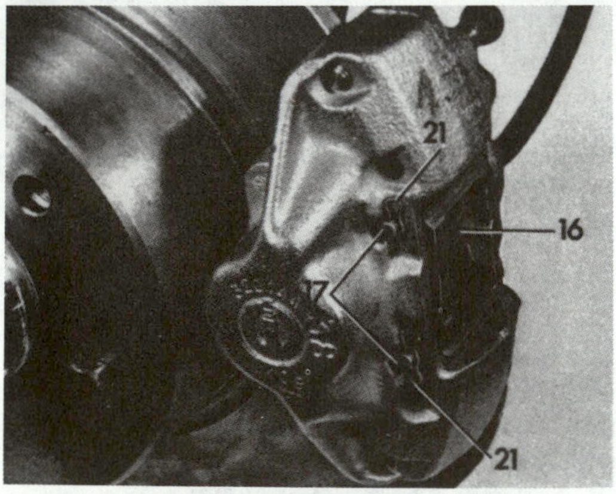

On Girling caliper, remove the retaining pins and plates

10. Check the thickness of the brake disc. Refer to the brake specifications for tolerances.

11. Check the brake discs for scoring or cracks. Score marks up to 0.02 in. deep can be accepted as normal scoring.

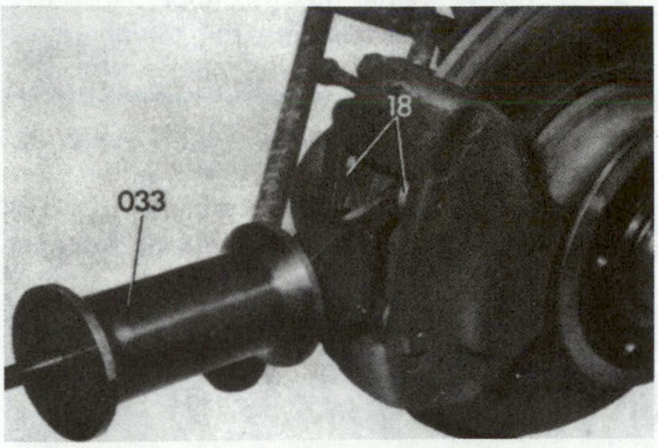

Remove the brake pads

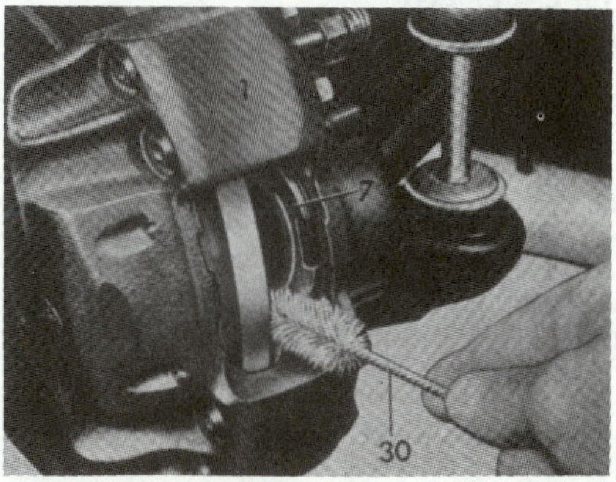

Clean the pad guides

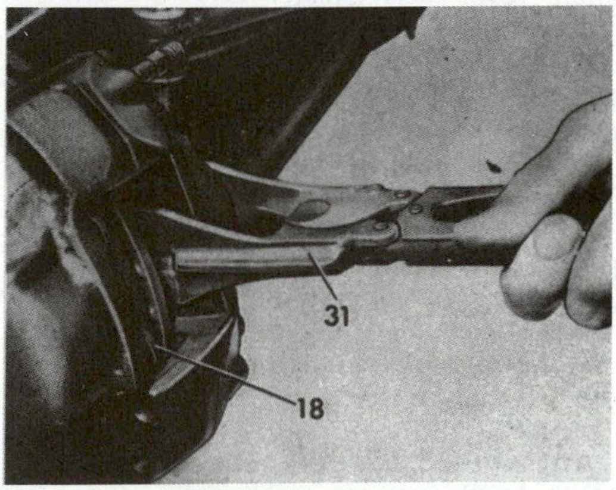

Force the pistons back into the caliper

12. Clean the air passages of ventilated discs with a thin piece of wire. Blow out all loose dirt. Do not clean with solvent unless the disc is removed from the car.

13. Clean the rain groove in the backing plate and measure the thickness of the lining. See the Brake Specifications for minimum lining thickness.

14. Apply a heat resistant, long-term lubri-

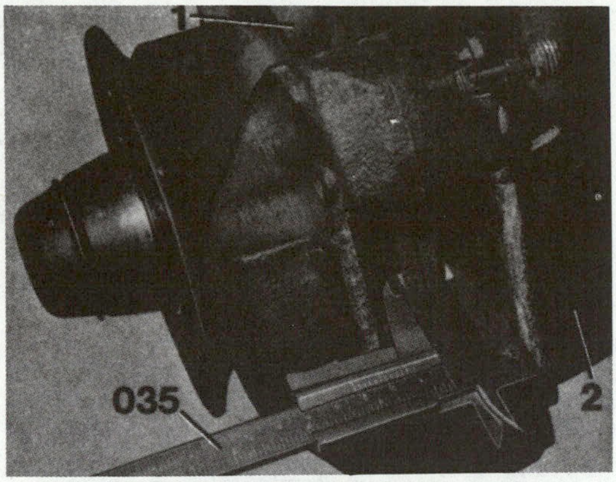

Check the thickness of brake disc

Check the surface of the brake disc

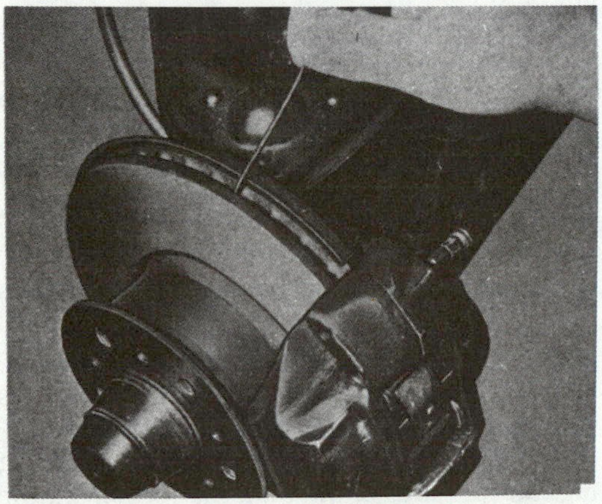
Clean the air passages in the ventilated brake discs

cant to the backing plate as shown. Install the brake pad.

15. Depending on the type of caliper, install the cross-spring, retaining plate, retaining pins and locking eyes.

16. On cars with a brake pad wear indicator, connect the sensors into the brake lining and the cable to the plug connection.

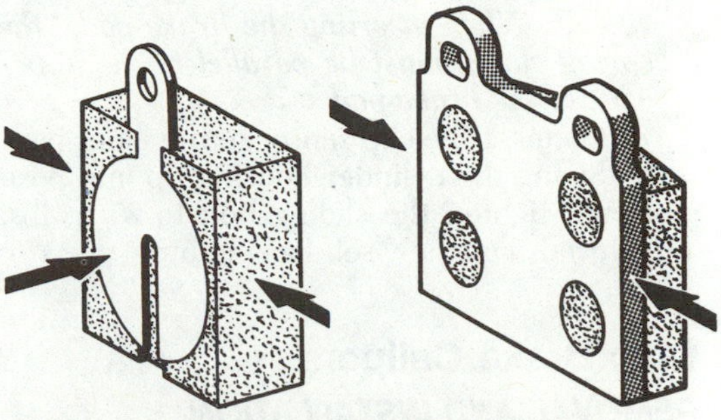
Lubricate the brake pads where shown

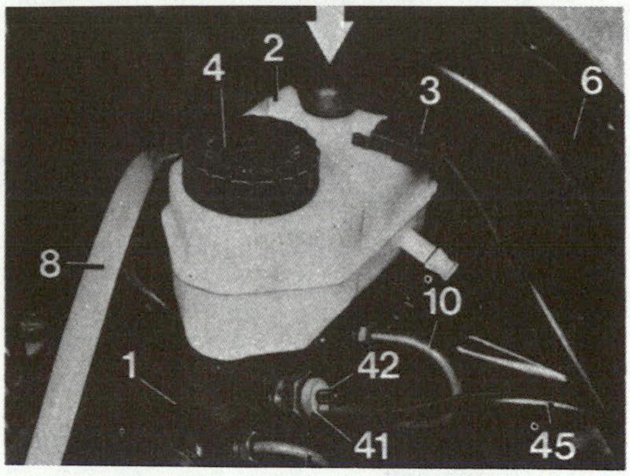

Pressure differential valve warning light reset button (42)

17. If equipped, install the cover plate.

18. On vehicles with a pressure differential warning system (1976 and 1977), the warning indicator may light when pads are replaced. To extinguish the light, push the reset pin (42) on the switch (41) after replacing the lining. The switch is located on the outboard side of the master cylinder.

Floating Calipers

NOTE: *This procedure applies only to the front brake pads on the 190D, 190E, 300SD, 380SE, 380SEC, 380SEL, 500SEC and 500SEL.*

1. Use a small pry bar to lift the two holding lugs on the sides of the plug connection (on the caliper) and then open the cover.
2. Disconnect the clip sensor cable from the plug. Do not pull on the cable.
3. Hold the sliding caliper pin and unscrew the upper hex screw.
4. Swing the cylinder housing (top of the caliper assembly) out and down. Remove the brake pads.
5. Disconnect the clip sensor from the brake pad backing plate.
6. To install, follow Steps 8–14 of the “Fixed Caliper Removal and Installation” procedure.

NOTE: *When inserting the brake pads, the spring clamp must be parallel to the upper edge of the brake pad.*

7. Connect the clip sensor to the inner pad.
8. Swing the cylinder housing up into position and tighten the sliding bolt to 25 ft. lbs. (35 Nm) using a new self-locking nut.

Disc Brake Calipers

REMOVAL AND INSTALLATION

Fixed Calipers

1. Drain brake fluid from the front brake circuit through an open bleeder screw.
2. Disconnect the brake hose from the brake line (or, on some models, disconnect the brake line from the caliper).
3. Immediately plug the lines and openings to prevent loss of fluid.
4. On models where the brake line does not connect directly to the caliper, remove the hose from the caliper.
5. Remove the brake hose from the bracket.
6. Plug the connection at the brake caliper.
7. Unlock the lockwasher and remove the hex mounting bolts.

CAUTION: *The caliper mounting bolts should not be removed unless the calipers are at approximately room temperature.*

8. Remove the calipers from the steering knuckle. As the caliper is removed, take note of any shim that may be installed and tape these (if any) in their original positions.
9. To install, use a new lockplate and attach the brake caliper to the steering knuckle. The proper torque for the mounting bolts is 82 ft. lbs.

It is extremely important that the brake disc be parallel to the caliper. Using a feeler gauge, measure the clearance at the top and bottom of the caliper (between disc and caliper) and on both sides of the disc. The clearance should not vary more than 0.15 mm. If the clearance varies, position the brake caliper by adding or subtracting shims as required. This procedure only applies to models equipped with shims, usually on the rear brake calipers.

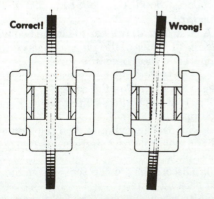

Uneven brake pad wear will result from misalignment of the caliper and the disc—fixed caliper

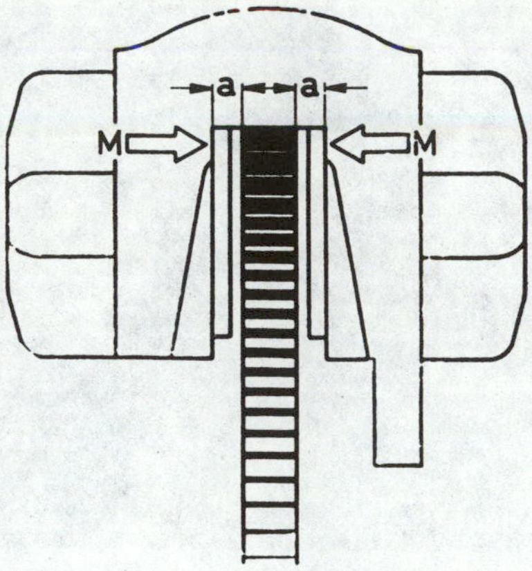

Measure the clearance (a) on each side of the disc at point M—fixed calipers

10. Insert the brake hose into the bracket, making sure that the grommet is not damaged, or connect the brake line to the calipers. If applicable, connect the brake hose to the brake line. Make sure that the hose is not twisted.
11. On some models a locking disc is attached to the brake line bracket. Install the brake hose into the disc so that the disc or hose does not bind.
12. Turn the steering lock-to-lock to make sure that the brake hose or lines do not bind.
13. Fill the master cylinder and bleed the brake system.
14. Before driving the car, depress the brake pedal hard, several times, to seat the pads.

Floating Caliper

1. Drain the brake fluid from the front brake circuit through an open bleeder screw.
2. Disconnect the brake hose from the brake line and plug each end; a golf tee usually works well for this purpose.
3. Use a small pry bar to lift the two holding lugs on the sides of the plug connection (on the caliper) and then open the cover.
4. Disconnect the brake pad wear indicator and the brake hose from the cylinder housing. Plug the open holes in the end of the brake hose and cylinder housing.
5. Unbolt the brake carrier from the steering knuckle and remove the caliper assembly.
6. On installation, use new mounting bolts and tighten them to 83 ft. lbs. (115 Nm).
7. Installation of the remaining components is in the reverse order of removal.

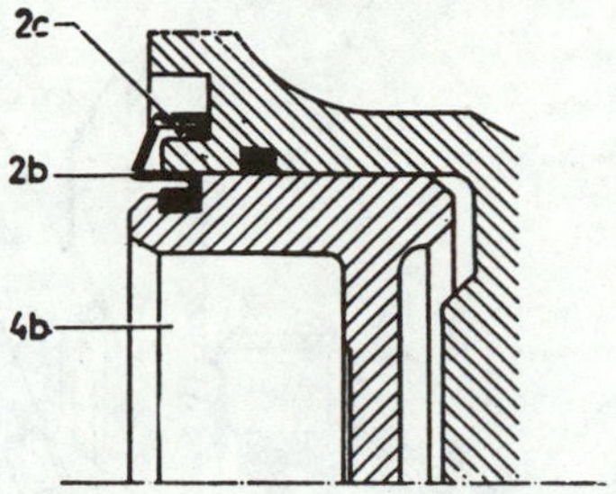

2b. Dust cap
2c. Closed clamp ring
4b. Piston

Piston dust seal installation—fixed calipers

PISTON SEAL REPLACEMENT (FRONT BRAKE CALIPER)

CAUTION: *Do not unbolt the two caliper halves for any reason. Remove the brake caliper for easier service.*

1. Remove the friction pads, brake line, and dust cap, then pry the clamp ring from the housing.

2. Using a rubber-backed piece of flat steel, hold one piston in place while blowing the other one out with compressed air (7–8 psi).

3. Remove the piston seals from the cylinder bores and examine the bores. Scored bores necessitate replacement of the entire caliper, since the inner surface is chrome plated and cannot be honed.

4. Clean the bores with crocus cloth only, never use emery paper.

5. Install the new seals, coating them with brake fluid beforehand, then install the (front) piston so that the projection points downward. The rear caliper pistons must be installed with the projection facing downward.

NOTE: *If the projection is in any other position, the brakes may squeal badly.*

NOTE: *Floating calipers have only one piston.*

6. Install the dust cap, clamp ring and heat shield.

7. The recess in the heat shield must fit the piston projection, but be above the shield level by about 0.004 in.

NOTE: *The heat shields differ for inner and outer pistons.*

8. Install the friction pads and the caliper assembly, then bleed the brakes.

Brake Disc

REMOVAL AND INSTALLATION

1. Removal for the various types is similar.

2. On all models, remove the brake caliper. On 1974–76 230, 240D, 300D, 280 and 280C models and on 380SL, SLC, 450SL and SLC models, the hub and disc can be removed by prying off the dust cap, removing the socket screw and clamp nut, and pulling off the wheel hub. Fasten the hub in a vise or holding fixture (be careful not to distort the housing), matchmark the disc and hub, then unbolt the brake disc.

3. On all other models the disc can be unbolted from the hub.

4. Inspect the disc for burning (blue color), cracks and scoring. The disc becomes scored slightly in normal service; therefore, replace it only if the depth of individual scores exceeds 0.020 in.

5. To ensure proper alignment, clean the hub and disc with emergy paper to remove all rust and/or burrs, then bolt the disc to the hub.

6. It is a wise precaution to use new lockwashers under the bolts.

7. Install the hub and disc, then check the disc for runout (wobble), using a dial indicator as illustrated.

8. If runout is excessive, it sometimes helps to remove the disc and reseat it on the hub. Install the caliper assembly and bleed the brakes.

NOTE: *If new brake discs are being installed, remove the anti-corrosion paint before installing it.*

Wheel Bearings

REMOVAL AND INSTALLATION

If the wheel bearing play is being checked for correct setting only, it is not necessary to remove the caliper. It is only necessary to remove the brake pads.

1. Remove the brake caliper.

2. Pull the cap from the hub with a pair of channel-lock pliers. Remove the radio suppression spring, if equipped.

3. Loosen the socket screw of the clamp nut on the wheel spindle. Remove the clamp nut and washer.

4. Remove the front wheel hub and brake disc.

5. Remove the inner race with the roller cage of the outer bearing.

6. Using a brass or aluminum drift, carefully tap the outer race of the inner bearing until it can be removed with the inner race, bearing cage, and seal.

7. In the same manner, tap the outer race of the bearing out of the hub.

8. Separate the front hub from the brake disc.

9. To assemble, press the outer races into the front wheel hub.

10. Pack the bearing cage with bearing grease

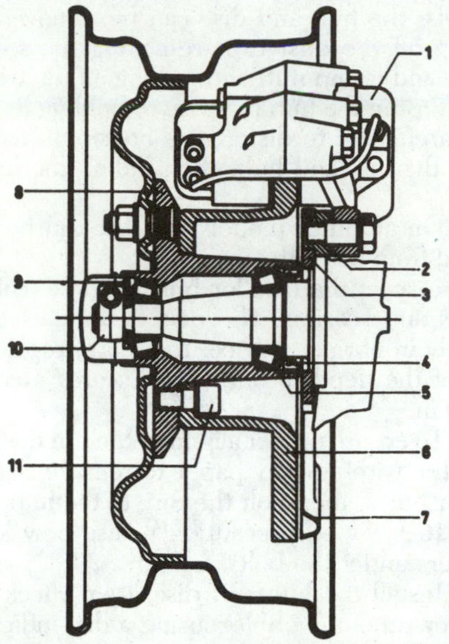

1. Brake caliper
2. Shim
3. Caliper bracket
4. Seal
5. Puller ring
6. Brake disc
7. Cover plate
8. Wheel hub
9. Washer
10. Clamp nut
11. Screw and lockwasher

Wheel bearing cutaway—1974–76 230, 240D, 280, 280C, 300D

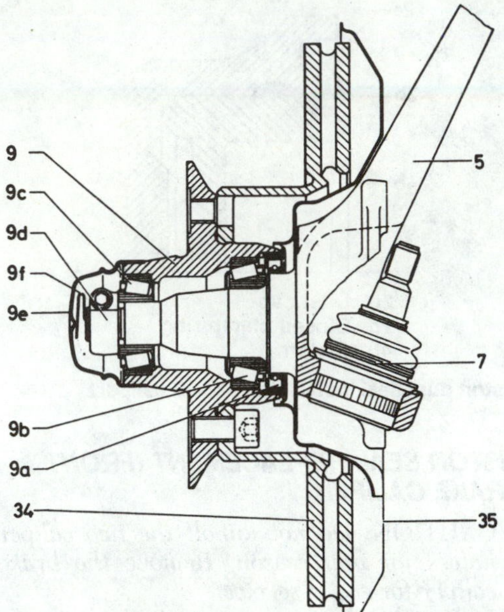

5. Steering knuckle
7. Supporting joint
9. Front wheel hub
9a. Radial sealing ring
9b. Tapered roller bearing, inside
9c. Tapered roller bearing, outside
9d. Clamping nut
9e. Wheel cap
9f . Contact spring
34. Brake disc
35. Cover plate

Wheel bearing cutaway—all models not already pictured

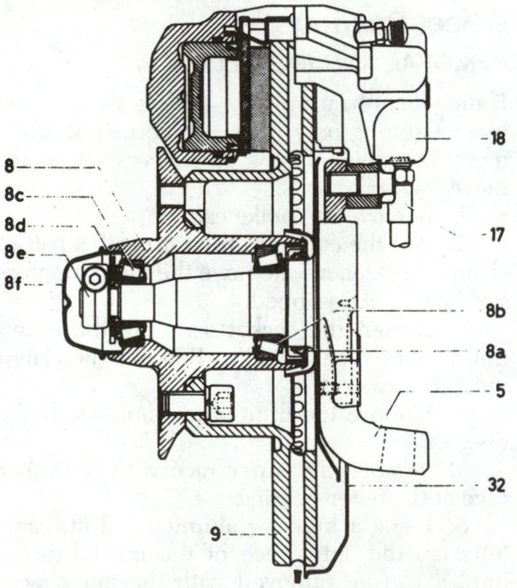

5. Steering knuckle
8. Wheel hub
8a. Radial sealing ring
8b. Tapered roller bearing, outside
8c. Tapered roller bearing, inside
8d. Washer
8e. Clamping nut
8 . Wheel cap
9. Brake disc
17. Brake hose
18. Brake caliper
32. Cover plate

Wheel bearing cutaway—380SL, 380SLC, 450SL and 450SLC

and insert the inner race with the bearing into the wheel hub.

11. Coat the sealing ring with sealant and press it into the hub.

12. Pack the front wheel hub with 45–55 grams of wheel bearing grease. The races of the tapered bearing should be well packed, also apply grease to the front faces of the rollers. Pack the front bearings with the specified amount of grease. Too much grease will cause overheating of the lubricant and it may lose its lubricity. Too little grease will not lubricate properly.

13. Coat the contact surface of the sealing ring on the wheel spindle with Molykote® paste.

14. Press the wheel hub onto the wheel spindle.

15. Install the inner race and cage of the outer bearing.

16. Install the steel washer and the clamp nut.

ADJUSTMENT

1. Tighten the clamp nut until the hub can just be turned.

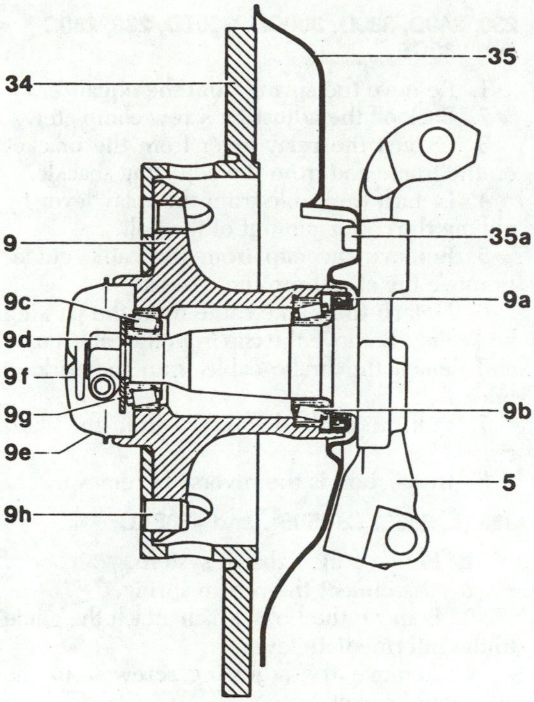

5. Steering knuckle
9. Front wheel hub
9a. Radial seal ring
9b. Tapered roller bearing, inner
9c. Tapered roller bearing, outer
9d. Clamping nut
9e. Greasco cap
9f. Contact spring
9g. Washer
9h. Clamping sleeve
34. Brake disk
35. Brake backing plate
35a. Allen screws

Wheel bearing cutaway—190D and 190E

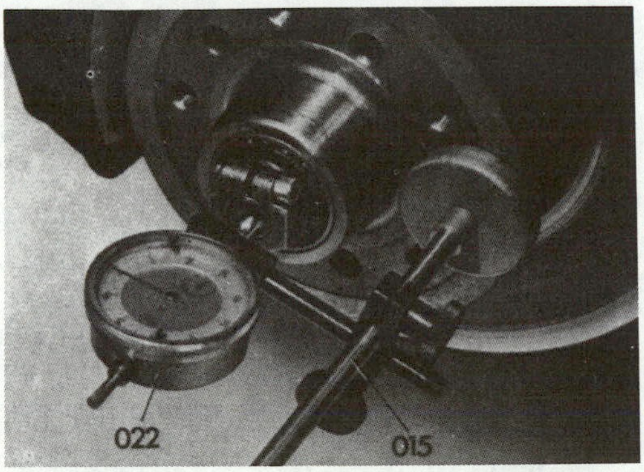

Dial indicator set-up for checking wheel bearing play

2. Slacken the clamp nut and seat the bearings on the spindle by rapping the spindle sharply with a hammer.

3. Attach a dial indicator, with the pointer indexed, onto the wheel hub.

8. Front wheel hub 8e. Locking nut
8d. Disc

Wheel hub—190D, 190E, 1974–76 230 and 240D, 280, 280C, 1975–76 300D, 380SL, 380SLC, 450SL and 450SLC

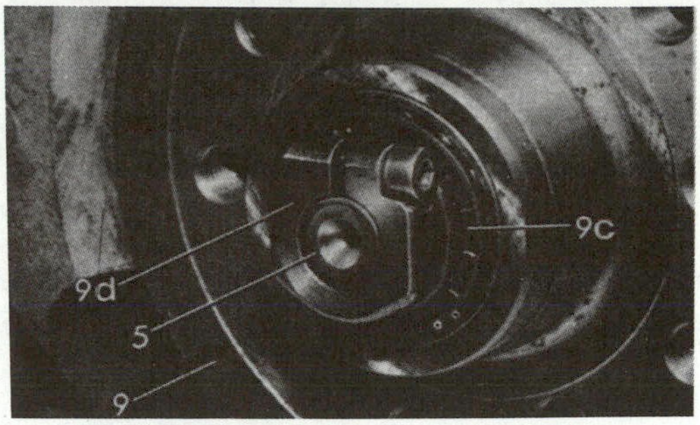

5. Wheel spindle
9. Front wheel hub
9c. Outer tapered roller bearing
9d. Clamping nut

Wheel hub—all other models

4. Check the end-play of the hub by pushing and pulling on the flange. The end-play should be approximately 0.0004–0.0008 in.

5. Make an additional check by rotating the washer between the inner race of the outer bearing and the clamp nut. It should be able to be turned by hand.

6. Check the position of the suppressor pin in the wheel spindle and the contact spring in the dust cap.

7. Pack the dust cap with 20–25 grams of wheel bearing grease and install the cap.

8. Install the brake caliper and bleed the brakes.

REAR DISC BRAKES

Disc Brake Pads

REMOVAL AND INSTALLATION

NOTE: *Floating calipers are used only on the front brakes of certain models. All models use fixed calipers on the rear brakes.*

The procedure for removing the rear disc brake pads is the same as for front disc brake pads. Use the instructions given under "Front Disc Brake Pad Removal and Installation," with the accompanying illustrations.

Disc Brake Calipers

REMOVAL AND INSTALLATION

NOTE: *Floating calipers are used only on the front brakes of certain models. All models use fixed calipers on the rear brakes.*

Use the procedure given under "Front Brake Caliper Removal and Installation." Some rear brake calipers have no disc run-out compensating feature. These calipers can only be installed on vehicles where the rear axle shaft is supported on grooved ball bearings. Calipers with a compensating feature may be installed on axles with grooved ball bearings or self-aligning bearings.

OVERHAUL

NOTE: *Floating calipers are used only on the front brakes of certain models. All models use fixed calipers on the rear brakes.*

Rear disc brake caliper overhaul procedures are the same as those given for front disc brake caliper overhaul.

Brake Discs

REMOVAL AND INSTALLATION

1. Remove the brake caliper.
2. Remove the brake disc from the rear axle shaft flange. Jammed brake discs can be loosened from the axle shaft flanges by light taps with a plastic hammer. Be sure that the parking brake is fully released.
3. Installation is the reverse of removal.
4. Inspection procedures are the same as those for front brake discs.

HANDBRAKE

Front Cable

REMOVAL AND INSTALLATION

190D and 190E

1. Disconnect the return spring at the cable control compensator.
2. Unbolt the brake cable from the intermediate lever and pull the cable away.
3. Remove the parking brake lever.
4. Loosen the brake cable at the lever and then pull it out toward the rear, through the floor.
5. Installation is in the reverse order of removal.

230, 240D, 300D, 300CD, 300TD, 280, 280C and 280CE

1. Remove the spring from the equalizer.
2. Back off the adjusting screw completely.
3. Detach the relay lever from the bracket on the frame and from the adjusting shackle.
4. Detach the cable from the relay lever by pulling the cotter pin out of the bolt.
5. Remove the clip from the cable guide. Remove the clips from the chassis.
6. Detach the brake cable from the parking brake link. Remove the clip from the cable guide and detach the brake cable from the parking brake.
7. Pull the cable downward from the chassis.
8. Installation is the reverse of removal

380SL, 380SLC, 450SL and 450SLC

1. Remove the exhaust system.
2. Disconnect the return spring.
3. Remove the bolts which attach the guide to the intermediate lever.
4. Remove the adjusting screw from the adjusting bracket.
5. Loosen the brake control cables on the intermediate lever and pull the cotter pin from the flange bolt. Remove the flange bolt.
6. Remove the spring clamp from the cable guide and remove the cable control from the bracket.
7. Remove the tunnel cover.
8. Disconnect the brake control from the parking brake and remove the spring clamp from the cable guide. Remove the cable control from the parking brake.
9. Remove the brake control cable out of the frame toward the rear.
10. Installation is the reverse of removal.

All Others

1. Remove the floor mat.
2. Remove the legroom cover (upper and lower).
3. Remove the air duct.
4. Disconnect the 4 rubber rings and lower and support the exhaust system.
5. Remove the shield above the exhaust pipes.
6. Disconnect the return spring from the bracket.
7. Back off the adjusting screw on the bracket.
8. Disconnect the intermediate lever from the adjusting bracket.
9. Loosen the brake cable controls on the intermediate lever while pulling the cotter pin from the flange bolt. Remove the flange bolt.
10. Remove the spring clip from the cable guide on on the floor pan.

11. Disconnect the brake cable control from the parking brake bracket.

12. Remove the spring clip from the cable guide and remove the cable control from the parking brake.

13. Pull the cable away upward.

14. Installation is the reverse of removal. Adjust the parking brake.

Rear Brake Cable

REMOVAL AND INSTALLATION

230, 240D, 280, 280C, 280CE, 280E, 300D, 300CD, 300TD

1. Remove the parking brake shoes after removing the wheel.
2. Remove the screw from the wheel support and detach the brake cable.
3. Back off the adjusting screw from the adjusting shackle.
4. Remove the spring clips, detach the cable, and remove the equalizer.
5. Installation is the reverse of removal.

All Other Models

1. Remove the parking brake shoes.
2. Remove the bolt from the wheel carrier and remove the cable.
3. Remove the exhaust system. On some models the exhaust system can be lowered and supported after removing the rubber rings. If equipped, remove the heat shield from above the exhaust pipes.
4. Disconnect the draw spring from the holder.
5. Detach the guide from the intermediate lever.
6. Remove the adjusting screw from the bracket.
7. Disconnect the intermediate lever on the bearing and remove it from the adjusting bracket.
8. Remove the holder, compensating lever, cable control plates, and intermediate lever from the tunnel.
9. Remove the spring clamps and disconnect the cable from the plate.
10. Installation is the reverse of removal.

ADJUSTMENT

All Models

1. If the floor pedal can be depressed more than two notches before actuating the brakes, adjust by jacking up the rear of the car, then removing one lug bolt and adjusting the star wheel with a screwdriver.
2. Move the screwdriver upward on the left (driver's) side, downward on the right (passenger's) side to tighten the shoes.

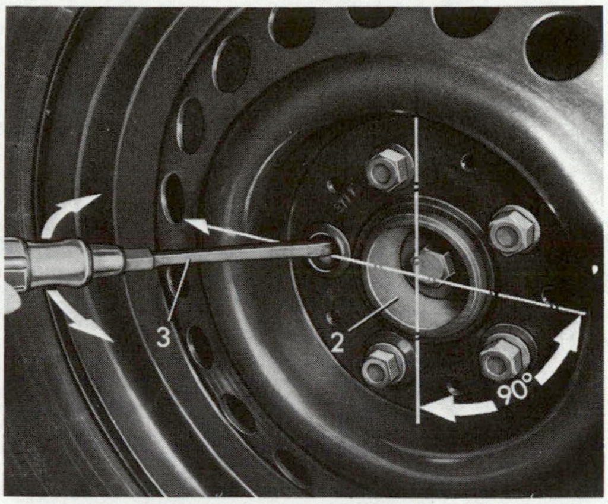

The rear wheels have an access hole to adjust the parking brake shoes

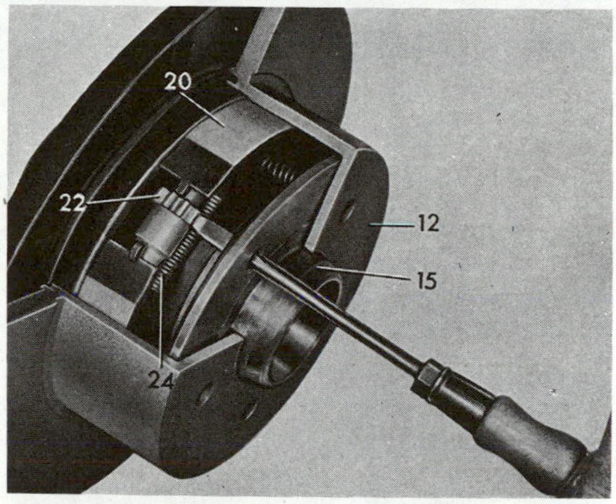

Cut-away view of rear brake shoe adjustment

3. When the wheel is locked, back off about 2–4 clicks.
4. With this type system, the adjusting bolt on the cable relay lever only serves to equalize cable length; therefore, do not attempt to adjust the brakes by turning this bolt.

Parking Brake Shoes

REMOVAL AND INSTALLATION

1. Remove the brake caliper.
2. Remove the brake disc.
3. Disconnect the lower spring with brake pliers.
4. Turn the rear axle shaft flange so that one hole faces the spring. With brake spring removal pliers, disconnect and remove the spring from the cover plate.
5. Remove the spring on the other brake shoe in a similar manner.
6. Pull both brake shoes apart so that they can be removed past the rear axle shaft flange.

7. Disconnect the upper return spring from the brake shoes and remove the adjuster.

8. Force the pin out of the expanding lock and remove the expanding lock from the brake cable.

9. Remove the brake shoes.

10. Installation is the reverse of removal. Coat all bearing and sliding surfaces with Molykote® prior to installation. Attach the lower spring with the small eye to the brake shoes.

11. Adjust the parking brakes.

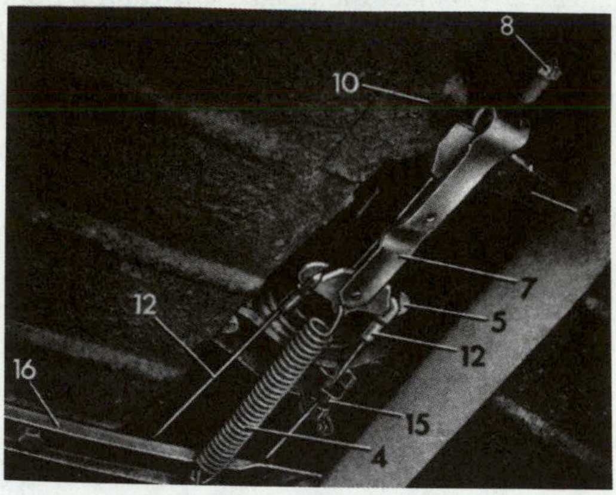

Use the adjusting screw (8) to adjust the hand brake adjustment

Troubleshooting

10

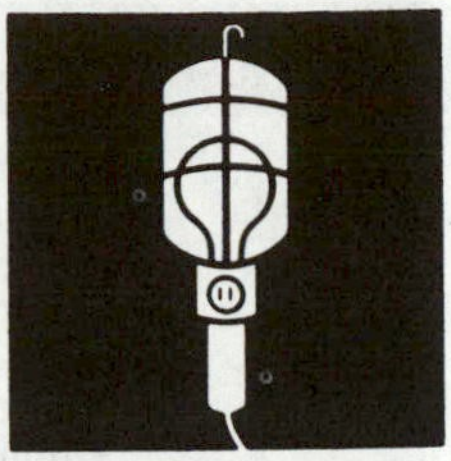

This section is designed to aid in the quick, accurate diagnosis of automotive problems. While automotive repairs can be made by many people, accurate troubleshooting is a rare skill for the amateur and professional alike.

In its simplest state, troubleshooting is an exercise in logic. It is essential to realize that an automobile is really composed of a series of systems. Some of these systems are interrelated; others are not. Automobiles operate within a framework of logical rules and physical laws, and the key to troubleshooting is a good understanding of all the automotive systems.

This section breaks the car or truck down into its component systems, allowing the problem to be isolated. The charts and diagnostic road maps list the most common problems and the most probable causes of trouble. Obviously it would be impossible to list every possible problem that could happen along with every possible cause, but it will locate MOST problems and eliminate a lot of unnecessary guesswork. The systematic format will locate problems within a given system, but, because many automotive systems are interrelated, the solution to your particular problem may be found in a number of systems on the car or truck.

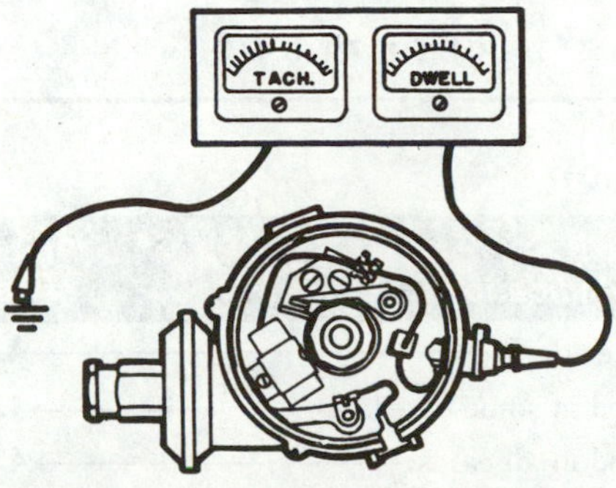

Tach-dwell hooked-up to distributor

USING THE TROUBLESHOOTING CHARTS

This book contains all of the specific information that the average do-it-yourself mechanic needs to repair and maintain his or her car or truck. The troubleshooting charts are designed to be used in conjunction with the specific procedures and information in the text. For instance, troubleshooting a point-type ignition system is fairly standard for all models, but you may be directed to the text to find procedures for troubleshooting an individual type of electronic ignition. You will also have to refer to the specification charts throughout the book for specifications applicable to your car or truck.

TOOLS AND EQUIPMENT

The tools illustrated in Chapter 1 (plus two more diagnostic pieces) will be adequate to troubleshoot most problems. The two other tools needed are a voltmeter and an ohmmeter. These can be purchased separately or in combination, known as a VOM meter.

In the event that other tools are required, they will be noted in the procedures.

Troubleshooting Engine Problems

See Chapters 2, 3, 4 for more information and service procedures.

Index to Systems

System	To Test	Group
Battery	Engine need not be running	1
Starting system	Engine need not be running	2
Primary electrical system	Engine need not be running	3
Secondary electrical system	Engine need not be running	4
Fuel system	Engine need not be running	5
Engine compression	Engine need not be running	6
Engine vacuum	Engine must be running	7
Secondary electrical system	Engine must be running	8
Valve train	Engine must be running	9
Exhaust system	Engine must be running	10
Cooling system	Engine must be running	11
Engine lubrication	Engine must be running	12

Index to Problems

Problem: Symptom	Begin at Specific Diagnosis, Number ___
Engine Won't Start:	
Starter doesn't turn	1.1, 2.1
Starter turns, engine doesn't	2.1
Starter turns engine very slowly	1.1, 2.4
Starter turns engine normally	3.1, 4.1
Starter turns engine very quickly	6.1
Engine fires intermittently	4.1
Engine fires consistently	5.1, 6.1
Engine Runs Poorly:	
Hard starting	3.1, 4.1, 5.1, 8.1
Rough idle	4.1, 5.1, 8.1
Stalling	3.1, 4.1, 5.1, 8.1
Engine dies at high speeds	4.1, 5.1
Hesitation (on acceleration from standing stop)	5.1, 8.1
Poor pickup	4.1, 5.1, 8.1
Lack of power	3.1, 4.1, 5.1, 8.1
Backfire through the carburetor	4.1, 8.1, 9.1
Backfire through the exhaust	4.1, 8.1, 9.1
Blue exhaust gases	6.1, 7.1
Black exhaust gases	5.1
Running on (after the ignition is shut off)	3.1, 8.1
Susceptible to moisture	4.1
Engine misfires under load	4.1, 7.1, 8.4, 9.1
Engine misfires at speed	4.1, 8.4
Engine misfires at idle	3.1, 4.1, 5.1, 7.1, 8.4

Sample Section

Test and Procedure	Results and Indications	Proceed to
4.1—Check for spark: Hold each spark plug wire approximately ¼″ from ground with gloves or a heavy, dry rag. Crank the engine and observe the spark.	→ If no spark is evident: →	**4.2**
	→ If spark is good in some cases: →	**4.3**
	→ If spark is good in all cases: →	**4.6**

Specific Diagnosis

This section is arranged so that following each test, instructions are given to proceed to another, until a problem is diagnosed.

Section 1—Battery

Test and Procedure	Results and Indications	Proceed to
1.1—Inspect the battery visually for case condition (corrosion, cracks) and water level.	If case is cracked, replace battery:	1.4
	If the case is intact, remove corrosion with a solution of baking soda and water (**CAUTION:** ***do not get the solution into the battery***), and fill with water:	1.2

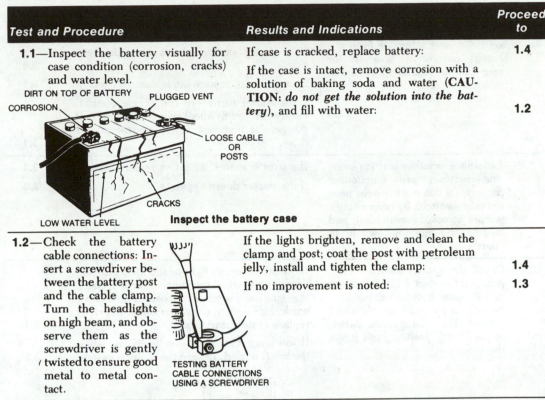

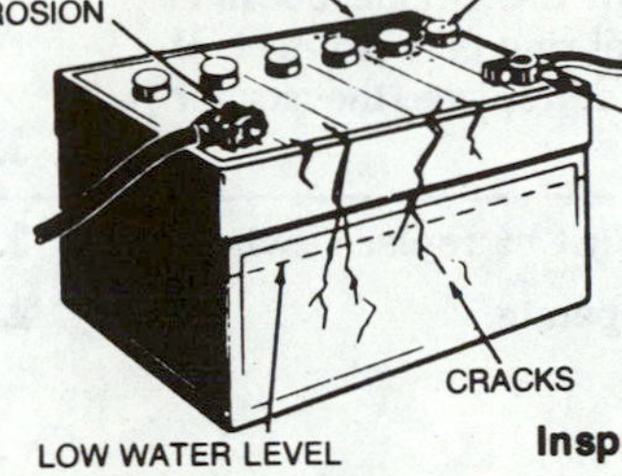

Inspect the battery case

Test and Procedure	Results and Indications	Proceed to
1.2—Check the battery cable connections: Insert a screwdriver between the battery post and the cable clamp. Turn the headlights on high beam, and observe them as the screwdriver is gently twisted to ensure good metal to metal contact.	If the lights brighten, remove and clean the clamp and post; coat the post with petroleum jelly, install and tighten the clamp:	1.4
	If no improvement is noted:	1.3

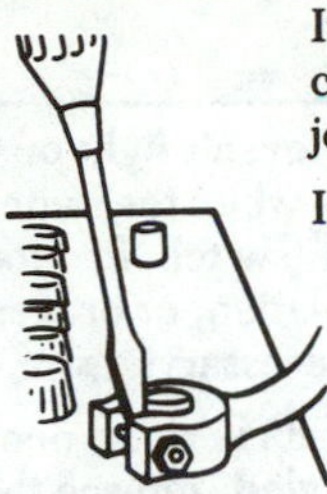

TESTING BATTERY CABLE CONNECTIONS USING A SCREWDRIVER

Test and Procedure	Results and Indications	Proceed to
1.3—Test the state of charge of the battery using an individual cell tester or hydrometer.	If indicated, charge the battery. **NOTE:** ***If no obvious reason exists for the low state of charge (i.e., battery age, prolonged storage), proceed to:***	1.4

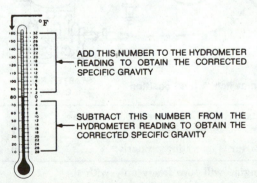

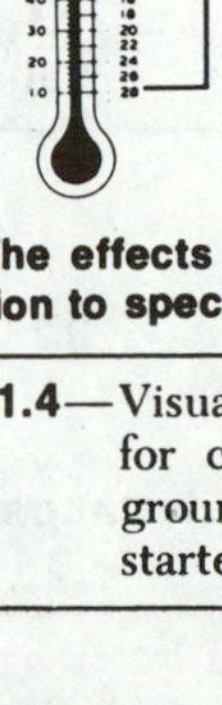

Specific Gravity (@ 80° F.)

Minimum	*Battery Charge*
1.260	100% Charged
1.230	75% Charged
1.200	50% Charged
1.170	25% Charged
1.140	Very Little Power Left
1.110	Completely Discharged

The effects of temperature on battery specific gravity (left) and amount of battery charge in relation to specific gravity (right)

Test and Procedure	Results and Indications	Proceed to
1.4—Visually inspect battery cables for cracking, bad connection to ground, or bad connection to starter.	If necessary, tighten connections or replace the cables:	2.1

Section 2—Starting System

See Chapter 3 for service procedures

Test and Procedure	Results and Indications	Proceed to
Note: Tests in Group 2 are performed with coil high tension lead disconnected to prevent accidental starting.		
2.1—Test the starter motor and solenoid: Connect a jumper from the battery post of the solenoid (or relay) to the starter post of the solenoid (or relay).	If starter turns the engine normally:	2.2
	If the starter buzzes, or turns the engine very slowly:	2.4
	If no response, replace the solenoid (or relay).	3.1
	If the starter turns, but the engine doesn't, ensure that the flywheel ring gear is intact. If the gear is undamaged, replace the starter drive.	3.1
2.2—Determine whether ignition override switches are functioning properly (clutch start switch, neutral safety switch), by connecting a jumper across the switch(es), and turning the ignition switch to "start".	If starter operates, adjust or replace switch:	3.1
	If the starter doesn't operate:	2.3
2.3—Check the ignition switch "start" position: Connect a 12V test lamp or voltmeter between the starter post of the solenoid (or relay) and ground. Turn the ignition switch to the "start" position, and jiggle the key.	If the lamp doesn't light or the meter needle doesn't move when the switch is turned, check the ignition switch for loose connections, cracked insulation, or broken wires. Repair or replace as necessary:	3.1
	If the lamp flickers or needle moves when the key is jiggled, replace the ignition switch.	3.3

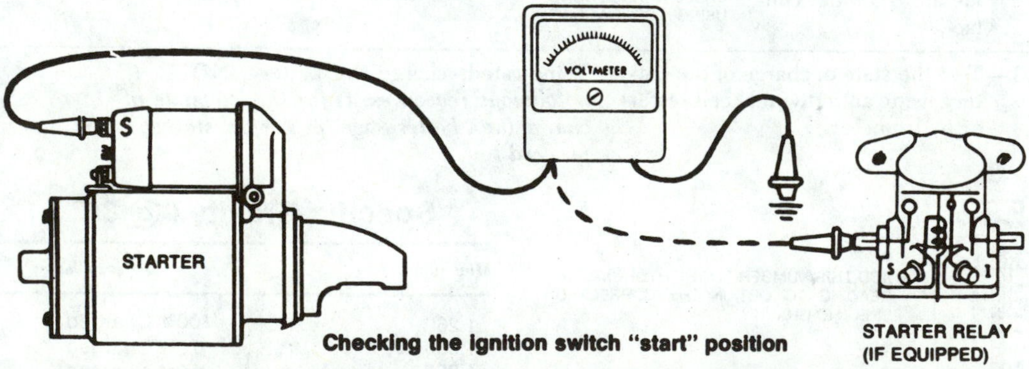

Checking the ignition switch "start" position

Test and Procedure	Results and Indications	Proceed to
2.4—Remove and bench test the starter, according to specifications in the engine electrical section.	If the starter does not meet specifications, repair or replace as needed:	3.1
	If the starter is operating properly:	2.5
2.5—Determine whether the engine can turn freely: Remove the spark plugs, and check for water in the cylinders. Check for water on the dipstick, or oil in the radiator. Attempt to turn the engine using an 18" flex drive and socket on the crankshaft pulley nut or bolt.	If the engine will turn freely only with the spark plugs out, and hydrostatic lock (water in the cylinders) is ruled out, check valve timing:	9.2
	If engine will not turn freely, and it is known that the clutch and transmission are free, the engine must be disassembled for further evaluation:	Chapter 3

Section 3—Primary Electrical System

Test and Procedure	Results and Indications	Proceed to
3.1—Check the ignition switch "on" position: Connect a jumper wire between the distributor side of the coil and ground, and a 12V test lamp between the switch side of the coil and ground. Remove the high tension lead from the coil. Turn the ignition switch on and jiggle the key.	If the lamp lights:	3.2
	If the lamp flickers when the key is jiggled, replace the ignition switch:	3.3
	If the lamp doesn't light, check for loose or open connections. If none are found, remove the ignition switch and check for continuity. If the switch is faulty, replace it:	3.3
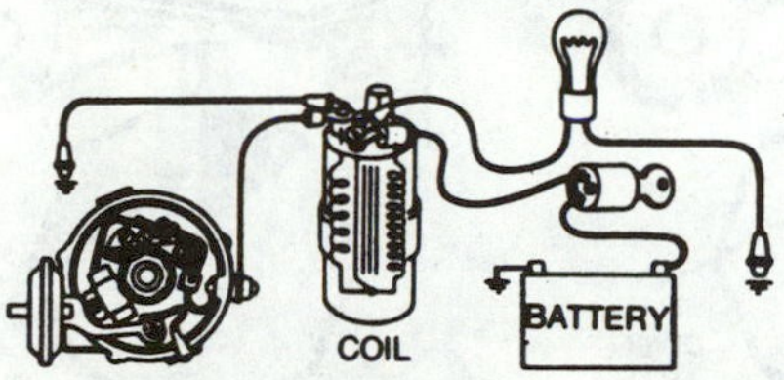 **Checking the ignition switch "on" position**		
3.2—Check the ballast resistor or resistance wire for an open circuit, using an ohmmeter. See Chapter 3 for specific tests.	Replace the resistor or resistance wire if the resistance is zero. **NOTE:** ***Some ignition systems have no ballast resistor.***	3.3
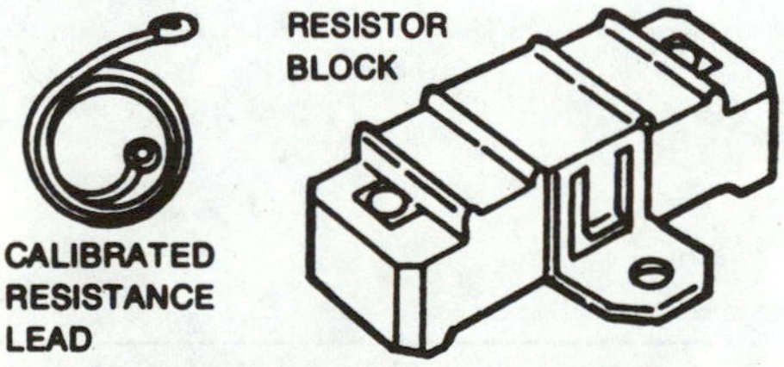 **Two types of resistors**		
3.3—On point-type ignition systems, visually inspect the breaker points for burning, pitting or excessive wear. Gray coloring of the point contact surfaces is normal. Rotate the crankshaft until the contact heel rests on a high point of the distributor cam and adjust the point gap to specifications. On electronic ignition models, remove the distributor cap and visually inspect the armature. Ensure that the armature pin is in place, and that the armature is on tight and rotates when the engine is cranked. Make sure there are no cracks, chips or rounded edges on the armature.	If the breaker points are intact, clean the contact surfaces with fine emery cloth, and adjust the point gap to specifications. If the points are worn, replace them. On electronic systems, replace any parts which appear defective. If condition persists:	3.4

Test and Procedure	Results and Indications	Proceed to
3.4—On point-type ignition systems, connect a dwell-meter between the distributor primary lead and ground. Crank the engine and observe the point dwell angle. On electronic ignition systems, conduct a stator (magnetic pickup assembly) test. See Chapter 3.	On point-type systems, adjust the dwell angle if necessary. **NOTE:** ***Increasing the point gap decreases the dwell angle and vice-versa.***	3.6
	If the dwell meter shows little or no reading;	3.5
	On electronic ignition systems, if the stator is bad, replace the stator. If the stator is good, proceed to the other tests in Chapter 3.	

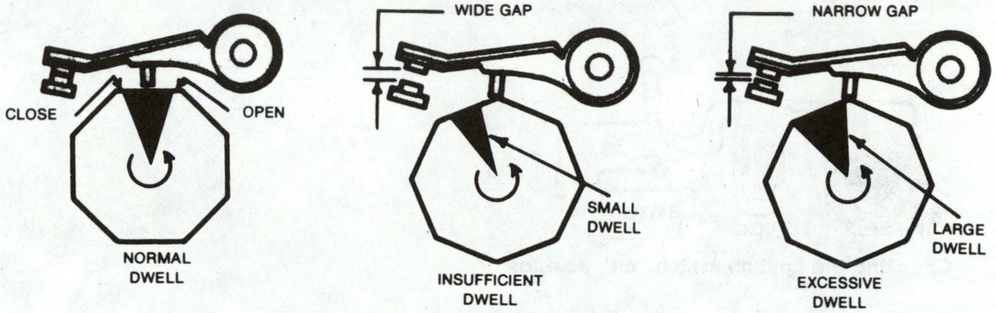

Dwell is a function of point gap

Test and Procedure	Results and Indications	Proceed to
3.5—On the point-type ignition systems, check the condenser for short: connect an ohmeter across the condenser body and the pigtail lead.	If any reading other than infinite is noted, replace the condenser	3.6

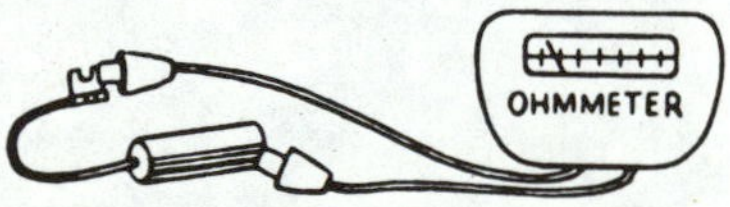

Checking the condenser for short

Test and Procedure	Results and Indications	Proceed to
3.6—Test the coil primary resistance: On point-type ignition systems, connect an ohmmeter across the coil primary terminals, and read the resistance on the low scale. Note whether an external ballast resistor or resistance wire is used. On electronic ignition systems, test the coil primary resistance as in Chapter 3.	Point-type ignition coils utilizing ballast resistors or resistance wires should have approximately 1.0 ohms resistance. Coils with internal resistors should have approximately 4.0 ohms resistance. If values far from the above are noted, replace the coil.	4.1

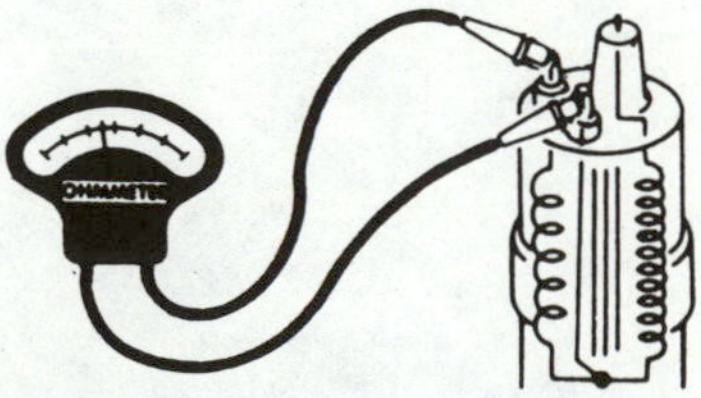

Check the coil primary resistance

Section 4—Secondary Electrical System

See Chapters 2–3 for service procedures

Test and Procedure	Results and Indications	Proceed to
4.1—Check for spark: Hold each spark plug wire approximately ¼″ from ground with gloves or a heavy, dry rag. Crank the engine, and observe the spark.	If no spark is evident:	4.2
	If spark is good in some cylinders:	4.3
	If spark is good in all cylinders:	4.6

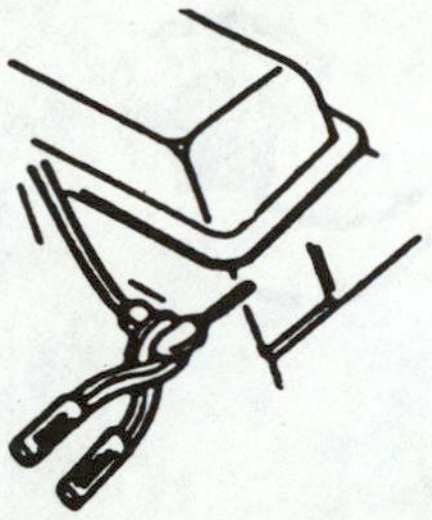

Check for spark at the plugs

Test and Procedure	Results and Indications	Proceed to
4.2—Check for spark at the coil high tension lead: Remove the coil high tension lead from the distributor and position it approximately ¼″ from ground. Crank the engine and observe spark. **CAUTION:** ***This test should not be performed on engines equipped with electronic ignition.***	If the spark is good and consistent:	4.3
	If the spark is good but intermittent, test the primary electrical system starting at 3.3:	3.3
	If the spark is weak or non-existent, replace the coil high tension lead, clean and tighten all connections and retest. If no improvement is noted:	4.4
4.3—Visually inspect the distributor cap and rotor for burned or corroded contacts, cracks, carbon tracks, or moisture. Also check the fit of the rotor on the distributor shaft (where applicable).	If moisture is present, dry thoroughly, and retest per 4.1:	4.1
	If burned or excessively corroded contacts, cracks, or carbon tracks are noted, replace the defective part(s) and retest per 4.1:	4.1
	If the rotor and cap appear intact, or are only slightly corroded, clean the contacts thoroughly (including the cap towers and spark plug wire ends) and retest per 4.1:	
	If the spark is good in all cases:	4.6
	If the spark is poor in all cases:	4.5

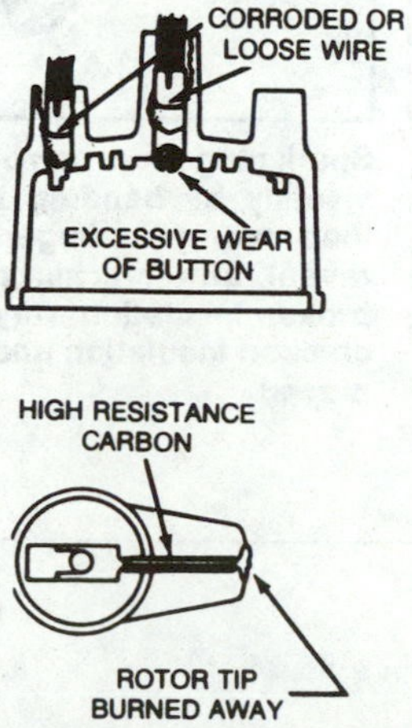

Inspect the distributor cap and rotor

Test and Procedure	Results and Indications	Proceed to
4.4—Check the coil secondary resistance: On point-type systems connect an ohmmeter across the distributor side of the coil and the coil tower. Read the resistance on the high scale of the ohmmeter. On electronic ignition systems, see Chapter 3 for specific tests.	The resistance of a satisfactory coil should be between 4,000 and 10,000 ohms. If resistance is considerably higher (i.e., 40,000 ohms) replace the coil and retest per 4.1. **NOTE:** ***This does not apply to high performance coils.***	

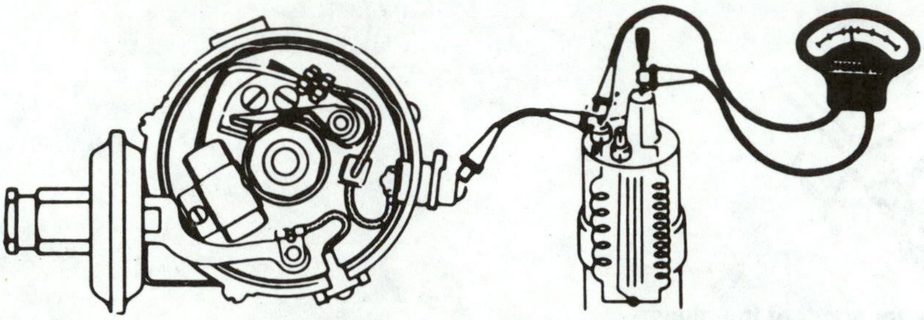

Testing the coil secondary resistance

Test and Procedure	Results and Indications	Proceed to
4.5—Visually inspect the spark plug wires for cracking or brittleness. Ensure that no two wires are positioned so as to cause induction firing (adjacent and parallel). Remove each wire, one by one, and check resistance with an ohmmeter.	Replace any cracked or brittle wires. If any of the wires are defective, replace the entire set. Replace any wires with excessive resistance (over 8000 Ω per foot for suppression wire), and separate any wires that might cause induction firing.	**4.6**

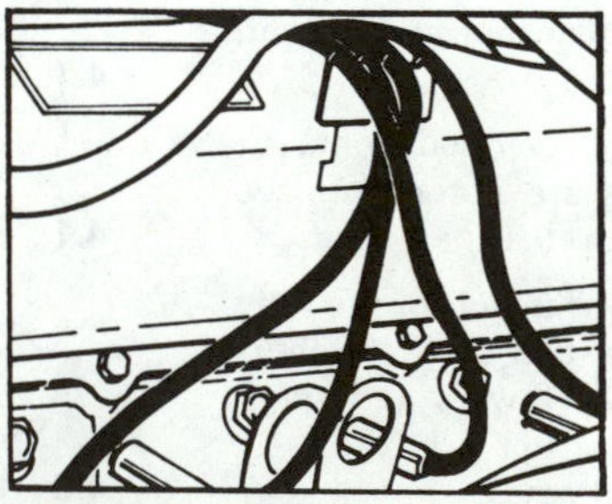

Misfiring can be the result of spark plug leads to adjacent, consecutively firing cylinders running parallel and too close together

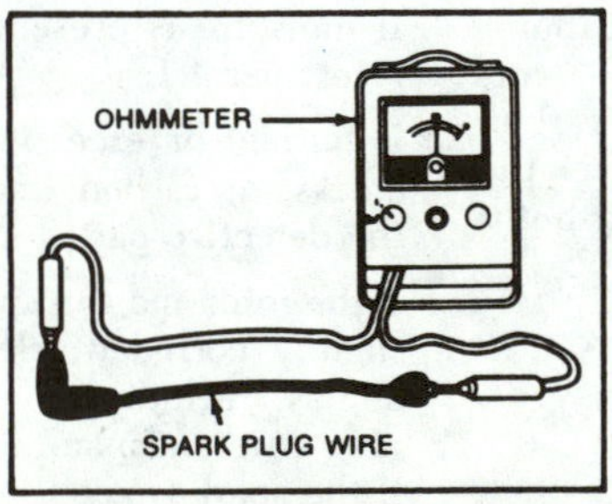

On point-type ignition systems, check the spark plug wires as shown. On electronic ignitions, do not remove the wire from the distributor cap terminal; instead, test through the cap

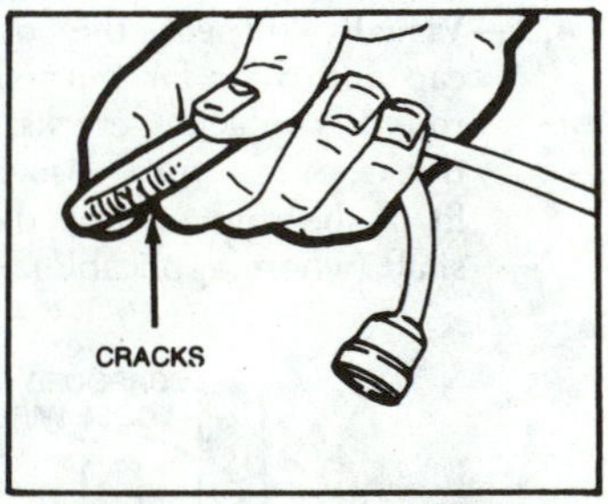

Spark plug wires can be checked visually by bending them in a loop over your finger. This will reveal any cracks, burned or broken insulation. Any wire with cracked insulation should be replaced

Test and Procedure	Results and Indications	Proceed to
4.6—Remove the spark plugs, noting the cylinders from which they were removed, and evaluate according to the color photos in the middle of this book.	See following.	**See following.**

Test and Procedure	Results and Indications	Proceed to
4.7—Examine the location of all the plugs.	The following diagrams illustrate some of the conditions that the location of plugs will reveal.	**4.8**

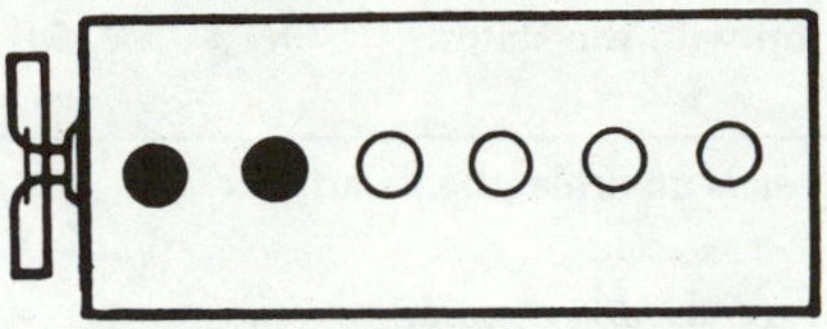

Two adjacent plugs are fouled in a 6-cylinder engine, 4-cylinder engine or either bank of a V-8. This is probably due to a blown head gasket between the two cylinders

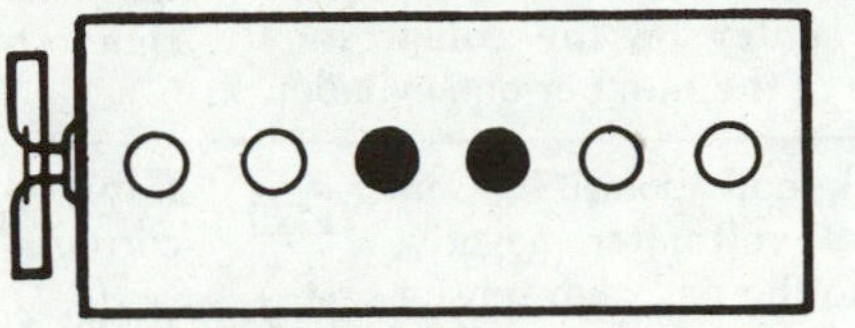

The two center plugs in a 6-cylinder engine are fouled. Raw fuel may be "boiled" out of the carburetor into the intake manifold after the engine is shut-off. Stop-start driving can also foul the center plugs, due to overly rich mixture. Proper float level, a new float needle and seat or use of an insulating spacer may help this problem

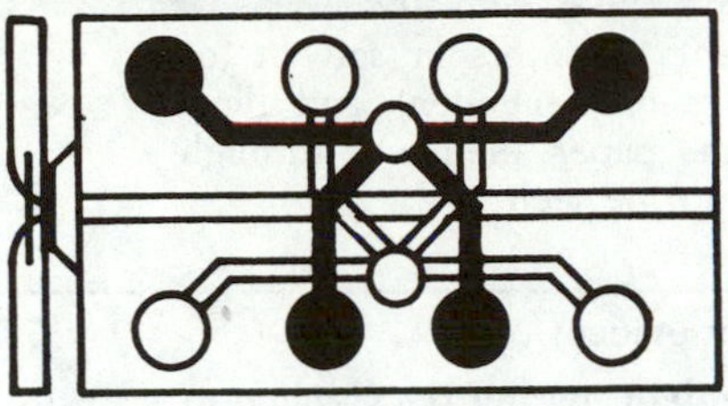

An unbalanced carburetor is indicated. Following the fuel flow on this particular design shows that the cylinders fed by the right-hand barrel are fouled from overly rich mixture, while the cylinders fed by the left-hand barrel are normal

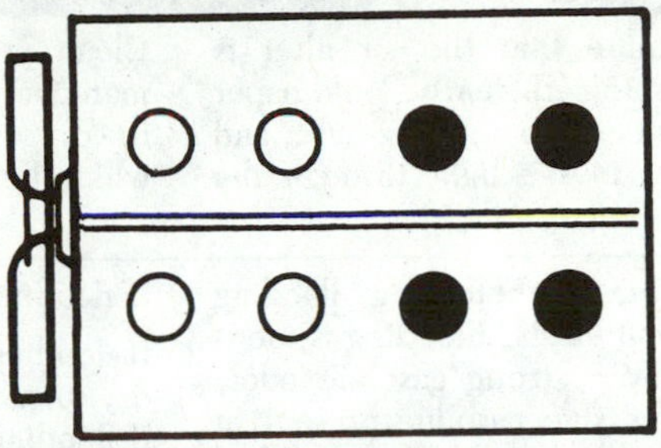

If the four rear plugs are overheated, a cooling system problem is suggested. A thorough cleaning of the cooling system may restore coolant circulation and cure the problem

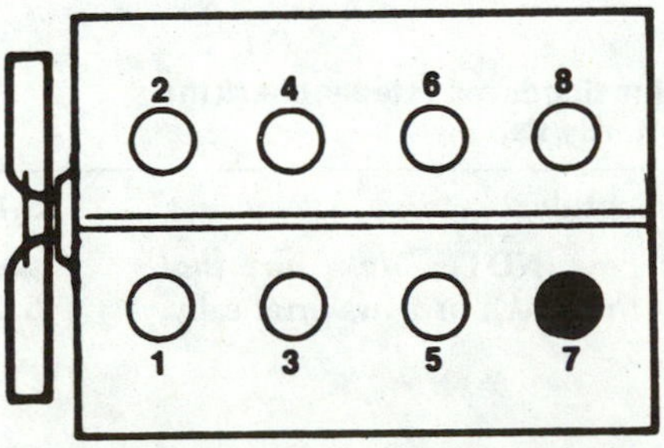

Finding one plug overheated may indicate an intake manifold leak near the affected cylinder. If the overheated plug is the second of two adjacent, consecutively firing plugs, it could be the result of ignition cross-firing. Separating the leads to these two plugs will eliminate cross-fire

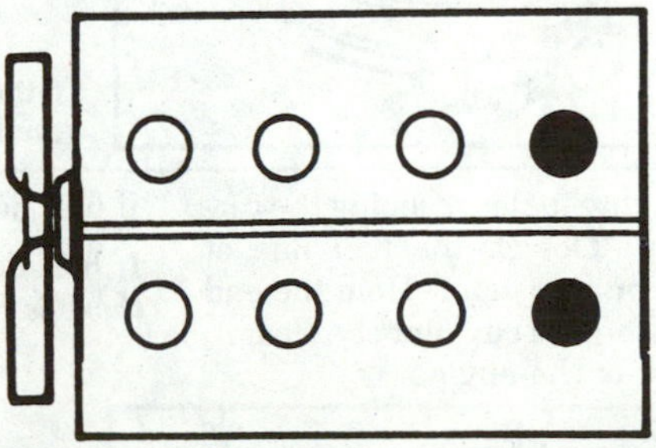

Occasionally, the two rear plugs in large, lightly used V-8's will become oil fouled. High oil consumption and smoky exhaust may also be noticed. It is probably due to plugged oil drain holes in the rear of the cylinder head, causing oil to be sucked in around the valve stems. This usually occurs in the rear cylinders first, because the engine slants that way

Test and Procedure	Results and Indications	Proceed to
4.8—Determine the static ignition timing. Using the crankshaft pulley timing marks as a guide, locate top dead center on the compression stroke of the number one cylinder.	The rotor should be pointing toward the No. 1 tower in the distributor cap, and, on electronic ignitions, the armature spoke for that cylinder should be lined up with the stator.	**4.8**
4.9—Check coil polarity: Connect a voltmeter negative lead to the coil high tension lead, and the positive lead to ground (**NOTE:** ***Reverse the hook-up for positive ground systems***). Crank the engine momentarily. 	If the voltmeter reads up-scale, the polarity is correct:	**5.1**
	If the voltmeter reads down-scale, reverse the coil polarity (switch the primary leads):	**5.1**
	Checking coil polarity	

Section 5—Fuel System

See Chapter 4 for service procedures

Test and Procedure	Results and Indications	Proceed to
5.1—Determine that the air filter is functioning efficiently: Hold paper elements up to a strong light, and attempt to see light through the filter.	Clean permanent air filters in solvent (or manufacturer's recommendation), and allow to dry. Replace paper elements through which light cannot be seen:	**5.2**
5.2—Determine whether a flooding condition exists: Flooding is identified by a strong gasoline odor, and excessive gasoline present in the throttle bore(s) of the carburetor.	If flooding is not evident:	**5.3**
	If flooding is evident, permit the gasoline to dry for a few moments and restart. If flooding doesn't recur:	**5.7**
	If flooding is persistent:	**5.5**
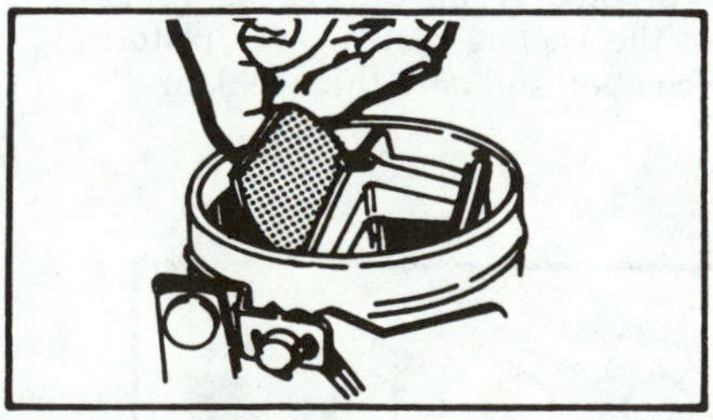	**If the engine floods repeatedly, check the choke butterfly flap**	
5.3—Check that fuel is reaching the carburetor: Detach the fuel line at the carburetor inlet. Hold the end of the line in a cup (not styrofoam), and crank the engine.	If fuel flows smoothly:	**5.7**
	If fuel doesn't flow (**NOTE:** ***Make sure that there is fuel in the tank***), or flows erratically:	**5.4**
	**Check the fuel pump by disconnecting the output line (fuel pump-to-carburetor) at the carburetor and operating the starter briefly**	

Test and Procedure	Results and Indications	Proceed to
5.4—Test the fuel pump: Disconnect all fuel lines from the fuel pump. Hold a finger over the input fitting, crank the engine (with electric pump, turn the ignition or pump on); and feel for suction.	If suction is evident, blow out the fuel line to the tank with low pressure compressed air until bubbling is heard from the fuel filler neck. Also blow out the carburetor fuel line (both ends disconnected):	**5.7**
	If no suction is evident, replace or repair the fuel pump:	**5.7**
	NOTE: ***Repeated oil fouling of the spark plugs, or a no-start condition, could be the result of a ruptured vacuum booster pump diaphragm, through which oil or gasoline is being drawn into the intake manifold (where applicable).***	
5.5—Occasionally, small specks of dirt will clog the small jets and orifices in the carburetor. With the engine cold, hold a flat piece of wood or similar material over the carburetor, where possible, and crank the engine.	If the engine starts, but runs roughly the engine is probably not run enough.	
	If the engine won't start:	**5.9**
5.6—Check the needle and seat: Tap the carburetor in the area of the needle and seat.	If flooding stops, a gasoline additive (e.g., Gumout) will often cure the problem:	**5.7**
	If flooding continues, check the fuel pump for excessive pressure at the carburetor (according to specifications). If the pressure is normal, the needle and seat must be removed and checked, and/or the float level adjusted:	**5.7**
5.7—Test the accelerator pump by looking into the throttle bores while operating the throttle. 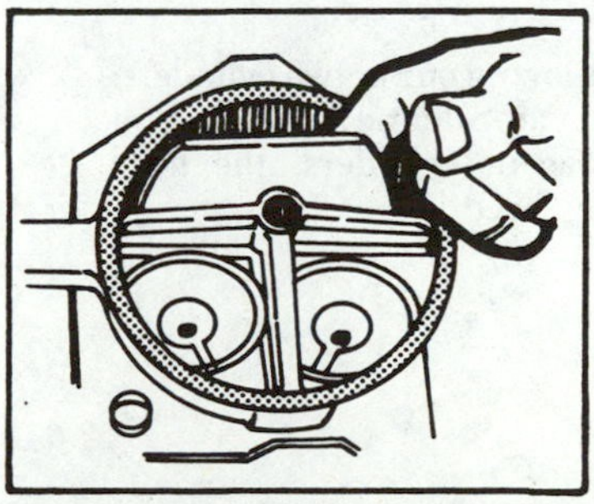 **Check for gas at the carburetor by looking down the carburetor throat while someone moves the accelerator**	If the accelerator pump appears to be operating normally:	**5.8**
	If the accelerator pump is not operating, the pump must be reconditioned. Where possible, service the pump with the carburetor(s) installed on the engine. If necessary, remove the carburetor. Prior to removal:	**5.8**
5.8—Determine whether the carburetor main fuel system is functioning: Spray a commercial starting fluid into the carburetor while attempting to start the engine.	If the engine starts, runs for a few seconds, and dies:	**5.9**
	If the engine doesn't start:	**6.1**

Test and Procedure	Results and Indications	Proceed to
5.9—Uncommon fuel system malfunctions: See below:	If the problem is solved:	**6.1**
	If the problem remains, remove and recondition the carburetor.	

Condition	Indication	Test	Prevailing Weather Conditions	Remedy
Vapor lock	Engine will not restart shortly after running.	Cool the components of the fuel system until the engine starts. Vapor lock can be cured faster by draping a wet cloth over a mechanical fuel pump.	Hot to very hot	Ensure that the exhaust manifold heat control valve is operating. Check with the vehicle manufacturer for the recommended solution to vapor lock on the model in question.
Carburetor icing	Engine will not idle, stalls at low speeds.	Visually inspect the throttle plate area of the throttle bores for frost.	High humidity, 32–40° F.	Ensure that the exhaust manifold heat control valve is operating, and that the intake manifold heat riser is not blocked.
Water in the fuel	Engine sputters and stalls; may not start.	Pump a small amount of fuel into a glass jar. Allow to stand, and inspect for droplets or a layer of water.	High humidity, extreme temperature changes.	For droplets, use one or two cans of commercial gas line anti-freeze. For a layer of water, the tank must be drained, and the fuel lines blown out with compressed air.

Section 6—Engine Compression

See Chapter 3 for service procedures

Test and Procedure	Results and Indications	Proceed to
6.1—Test engine compression: Remove all spark plugs. Block the throttle wide open. Insert a compression gauge into a spark plug port, crank the engine to obtain the maximum reading, and record.	If compression is within limits on all cylinders:	**7.1**
	If gauge reading is extremely low on all cylinders:	**6.2**
	If gauge reading is low on one or two cylinders: (If gauge readings are identical and low on two or more adjacent cylinders, the head gasket must be replaced.)	**6.2**

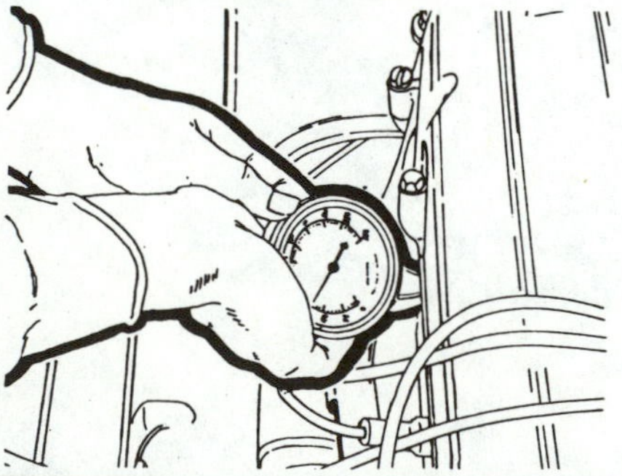

Checking compression

Test and Procedure	Results and Indications	Proceed to
6.2—Test engine compression (wet): Squirt approximately 30 cc. of engine oil into each cylinder, and retest per 6.1.	If the readings improve, worn or cracked rings or broken pistons are indicated:	**See Chapter 3**
	If the readings do not improve, burned or excessively carboned valves or a jumped timing chain are indicated: **NOTE:** ***A jumped timing chain is often indicated by difficult cranking.***	**7.1**

Section 7—Engine Vacuum

See Chapter 3 for service procedures

Test and Procedure	Results and Indications	Proceed to
7.1—Attach a vacuum gauge to the intake manifold beyond the throttle plate. Start the engine, and observe the action of the needle over the range of engine speeds.	See below.	**See below**

INDICATION: normal engine in good condition

Proceed to: 8.1

Normal engine

Gauge reading: steady, from 17–22 in./Hg.

INDICATION: sticking valves or ignition miss

Proceed to: 9.1, 8.3

Sticking valves

Gauge reading: intermittent fluctuation at idle

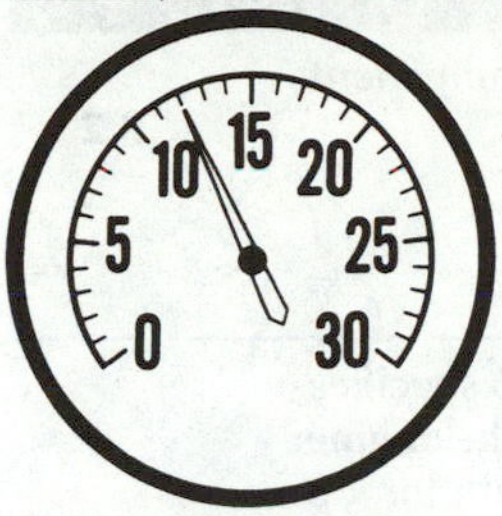

INDICATION: late ignition or valve timing, low compression, stuck throttle valve, leaking carburetor or manifold gasket

Proceed to: 6.1

Incorrect valve timing

Gauge reading: low (10–15 in./Hg) but steady

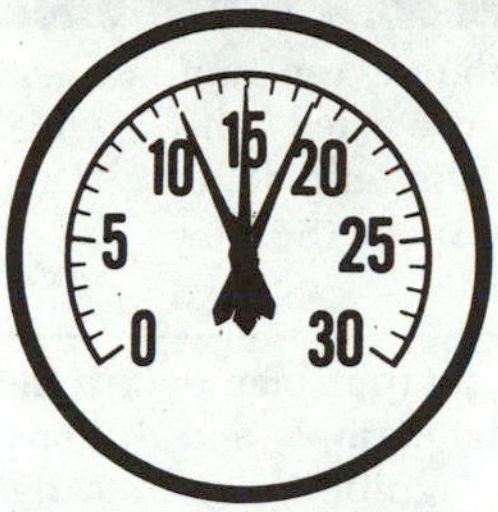

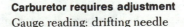

INDICATION: improper carburetor adjustment or minor intake leak.

Proceed to: 7.2

Carburetor requires adjustment

Gauge reading: drifting needle

INDICATION: ignition miss, blown cylinder head gasket, leaking valve or weak valve spring

Proceed to: 8.3, 6.1

Blown head gasket

Gauge reading: needle fluctuates as engine speed increases

INDICATION: burnt valve or faulty valve clearance. Needle will fall when defective valve operates

Proceed to: 9.1

Burnt or leaking valves

Gauge reading: steady needle, but drops regularly

INDICATION: choked muffler, excessive back pressure in system

Proceed to: 10.1

Clogged exhaust system

Gauge reading: gradual drop in reading at idle

INDICATION: worn valve guides

Proceed to: 9.1

Worn valve guides

Gauge reading: needle vibrates excessively at idle, but steadies as engine speed increases

White pointer = steady gauge hand

Black pointer = fluctuating gauge hand

Test and Procedure	Results and Indications	Proceed to
7.2—Attach a vacuum gauge per 7.1, and test for an intake manifold leak. Squirt a small amount of oil around the intake manifold gaskets, carburetor gaskets, plugs and fittings. Observe the action of the vacuum gauge.	If the reading improves, replace the indicated gasket, or seal the indicated fitting or plug:	**8.1**
	If the reading remains low:	**7.3**
7.3—Test all vacuum hoses and accessories for leaks as described in 7.2. Also check the carburetor body (dashpots, automatic choke mechanism, throttle shafts) for leaks in the same manner.	If the reading improves, service or replace the offending part(s):	**8.1**
	If the reading remains low:	**6.1**

Section 8—Secondary Electrical System

See Chapter 2 for service procedures

Test and Procedure	Results and Indications	Proceed to
8.1—Remove the distributor cap and check to make sure that the rotor turns when the engine is cranked. Visually inspect the distributor components.	Clean, tighten or replace any components which appear defective.	**8.2**
8.2—Connect a timing light (per manufacturer's recommendation) and check the dynamic ignition timing. Disconnect and plug the vacuum hose(s) to the distributor if specified, start the engine, and observe the timing marks at the specified engine speed.	If the timing is not correct, adjust to specifications by rotating the distributor in the engine: (Advance timing by rotating distributor opposite normal direction of rotor rotation, retard timing by rotating distributor in same direction as rotor rotation.)	**8.3**
8.3—Check the operation of the distributor advance mechanism(s): To test the mechanical advance, disconnect the vacuum lines from the distributor advance unit and observe the timing marks with a timing light as the engine speed is increased from idle. If the mark moves smoothly, without hesitation, it may be assumed that the mechanical advance is functioning properly. To test vacuum advance and/or retard systems, alternately crimp and release the vacuum line, and observe the timing mark for movement. If movement is noted, the system is operating.	If the systems are functioning:	**8.4**
	If the systems are not functioning, remove the distributor, and test on a distributor tester:	**8.4**
8.4—Locate an ignition miss: With the engine running, remove each spark plug wire, one at a time, until one is found that doesn't cause the engine to roughen and slow down.	When the missing cylinder is identified:	**4.1**

Section 9—Valve Train

See Chapter 3 for service procedures

Test and Procedure	Results and Indications	Proceed to
9.1—Evaluate the valve train: Remove the valve cover, and ensure that the valves are adjusted to specifications. A mechanic's stethoscope may be used to aid in the diagnosis of the valve train. By pushing the probe on or near push rods or rockers, valve noise often can be isolated. A timing light also may be used to diagnose valve problems. Connect the light according to manufacturer's recommendations, and start the engine. Vary the firing moment of the light by increasing the engine speed (and therefore the ignition advance), and moving the trigger from cylinder to cylinder. Observe the movement of each valve.	Sticking valves or erratic valve train motion can be observed with the timing light. The cylinder head must be disassembled for repairs.	See Chapter 3
9.2—Check the valve timing: Locate top dead center of the No. 1 piston, and install a degree wheel or tape on the crankshaft pulley or damper with zero corresponding to an index mark on the engine. Rotate the crankshaft in its direction of rotation, and observe the opening of the No. 1 cylinder intake valve. The opening should correspond with the correct mark on the degree wheel according to specifications.	If the timing is not correct, the timing cover must be removed for further investigation.	See Chapter 3

Section 10—Exhaust System

Test and Procedure	Results and Indications	Proceed to
10.1—Determine whether the exhaust manifold heat control valve is operating: Operate the valve by hand to determine whether it is free to move. If the valve is free, run the engine to operating temperature and observe the action of the valve, to ensure that it is opening.	If the valve sticks, spray it with a suitable solvent, open and close the valve to free it, and retest.	
	If the valve functions properly:	10.2
	If the valve does not free, or does not operate, replace the valve:	10.2
10.2—Ensure that there are no exhaust restrictions: Visually inspect the exhaust system for kinks, dents, or crushing. Also note that gases are flowing freely from the tailpipe at all engine speeds, indicating no restriction in the muffler or resonator.	Replace any damaged portion of the system:	11.1

Section 11—Cooling System

See Chapter 3 for service procedures

Test and Procedure	Results and Indications	Proceed to
11.1—Visually inspect the fan belt for glazing, cracks, and fraying, and replace if necessary. Tighten the belt so that the longest span has approximately ½″ play at its midpoint under thumb pressure (see Chapter 1).	Replace or tighten the fan belt as necessary: 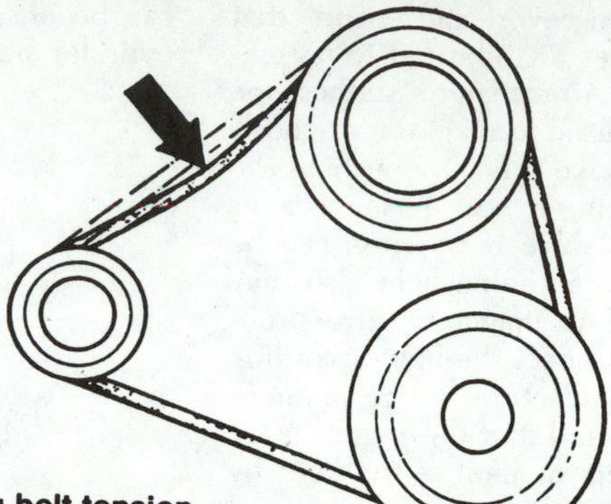 **Checking belt tension**	**11.2**
11.2—Check the fluid level of the cooling system.	If full or slightly low, fill as necessary:	**11.5**
	If extremely low:	**11.3**
11.3—Visually inspect the external portions of the cooling system (radiator, radiator hoses, thermostat elbow, water pump seals, heater hoses, etc.) for leaks. If none are found, pressurize the cooling system to 14–15 psi.	If cooling system holds the pressure:	**11.5**
	If cooling system loses pressure rapidly, reinspect external parts of the system for leaks under pressure. If none are found, check dipstick for coolant in crankcase. If no coolant is present, but pressure loss continues:	**11.4**
	If coolant is evident in crankcase, remove cylinder head(s), and check gasket(s). If gaskets are intact, block and cylinder head(s) should be checked for cracks or holes. If the gasket(s) is blown, replace, and purge the crankcase of coolant:	**12.6**
	NOTE: ***Occasionally, due to atmospheric and driving conditions, condensation of water can occur in the crankcase. This causes the oil to appear milky white. To remedy, run the engine until hot, and change the oil and oil filter.***	
11.4—Check for combustion leaks into the cooling system: Pressurize the cooling system as above. Start the engine, and observe the pressure gauge. If the needle fluctuates, remove each spark plug wire, one at a time, noting which cylinder(s) reduce or eliminate the fluctuation. **Pressurizing the cooling system**	Cylinders which reduce or eliminate the fluctuation, when the spark plug wire is removed, are leaking into the cooling system. Replace the head gasket on the affected cylinder bank(s). 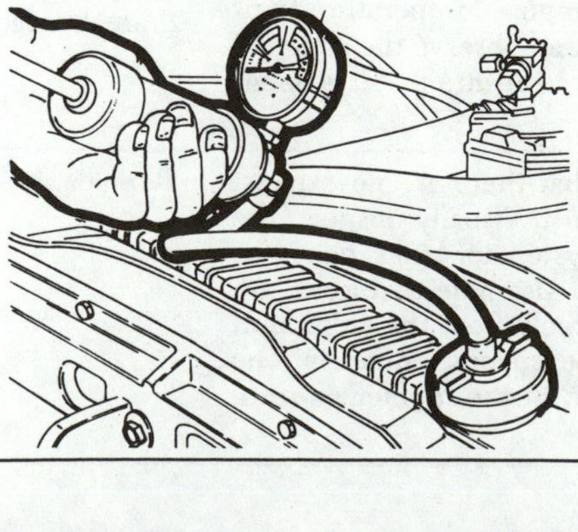	

Test and Procedure	Results and Indications	Proceed to
11.5—Check the radiator pressure cap: Attach a radiator pressure tester to the radiator cap (wet the seal prior to installation). Quickly pump up the pressure, noting the point at which the cap releases.	If the cap releases within ± 1 psi of the specified rating, it is operating properly:	**11.6**
	If the cap releases at more than ± 1 psi of the specified rating, it should be replaced:	**11.6**

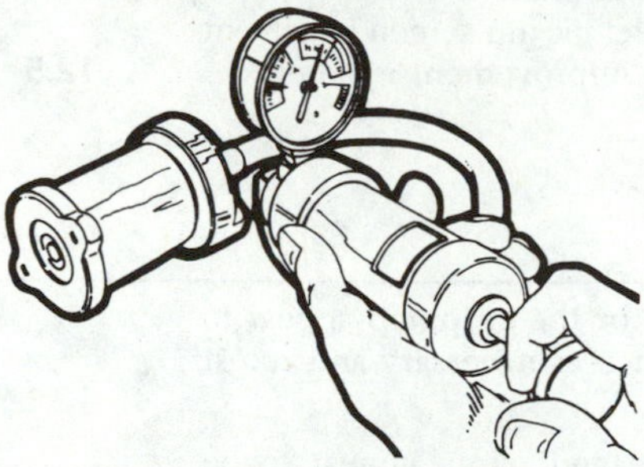

Checking radiator pressure cap

Test and Procedure	Results and Indications	Proceed to
11.6—Test the thermostat: Start the engine cold, remove the radiator cap, and insert a thermometer into the radiator. Allow the engine to idle. After a short while, there will be a sudden, rapid increase in coolant temperature. The temperature at which this sharp rise stops is the thermostat opening temperature.	If the thermostat opens at or about the specified temperature:	**11.7**
	If the temperature doesn't increase: (If the temperature increases slowly and gradually, replace the thermostat.)	**11.7**
11.7—Check the water pump: Remove the thermostat elbow and the thermostat, disconnect the coil high tension lead (to prevent starting), and crank the engine momentarily.	If coolant flows, replace the thermostat and retest per 11.6:	**11.6**
	If coolant doesn't flow, reverse flush the cooling system to alleviate any blockage that might exist. If system is not blocked, and coolant will not flow, replace the water pump.	

Section 12—Lubrication

See Chapter 3 for service procedures

Test and Procedure	Results and Indications	Proceed to
12.1—Check the oil pressure gauge or warning light: If the gauge shows low pressure, or the light is on for no obvious reason, remove the oil pressure sender. Install an accurate oil pressure gauge and run the engine momentarily.	If oil pressure builds normally, run engine for a few moments to determine that it is functioning normally, and replace the sender.	—
	If the pressure remains low:	**12.2**
	If the pressure surges:	**12.3**
	If the oil pressure is zero:	**12.3**
12.2—Visually inspect the oil: If the oil is watery or very thin, milky, or foamy, replace the oil and oil filter.	If the oil is normal:	**12.3**
	If after replacing oil the pressure remains low:	**12.3**
	If after replacing oil the pressure becomes normal:	—

Test and Procedure	Results and Indications	Proceed to
12.3—Inspect the oil pressure relief valve and spring, to ensure that it is not sticking or stuck. Remove and thoroughly clean the valve, spring, and the valve body.	If the oil pressure improves:	—
	If no improvement is noted:	**12.4**
12.4—Check to ensure that the oil pump is not cavitating (sucking air instead of oil): See that the crankcase is neither over nor underfull, and that the pickup in the sump is in the proper position and free from sludge.	Fill or drain the crankcase to the proper capacity, and clean the pickup screen in solvent if necessary. If no improvement is noted:	**12.5**
12.5—Inspect the oil pump drive and the oil pump:	If the pump drive or the oil pump appear to be defective, service as necessary and retest per 12.1:	**12.1**
	If the pump drive and pump appear to be operating normally, the engine should be disassembled to determine where blockage exists:	**See Chapter 3**
12.6—Purge the engine of ethylene glycol coolant: Completely drain the crankcase and the oil filter. Obtain a commercial butyl cellosolve base solvent, designated for this purpose, and follow the instructions precisely. Following this, install a new oil filter and refill the crankcase with the proper weight oil. The next oil and filter change should follow shortly thereafter (1000 miles).		

TROUBLESHOOTING EMISSION CONTROL SYSTEMS

See Chapter 4 for procedures applicable to individual emission control systems used on specific combinations of engine/transmission/model.

TROUBLESHOOTING THE CARBURETOR

See Chapter 4 for service procedures

Carburetor problems cannot be effectively isolated unless all other engine systems (particularly ignition and emission) are functioning properly and the engine is properly tuned.

Condition	Possible Cause
Engine cranks, but does not start	1. Improper starting procedure 2. No fuel in tank 3. Clogged fuel line or filter 4. Defective fuel pump 5. Choke valve not closing properly 6. Engine flooded 7. Choke valve not unloading 8. Throttle linkage not making full travel 9. Stuck needle or float 10. Leaking float needle or seat 11. Improper float adjustment
Engine stalls	1. Improperly adjusted idle speed or mixture **Engine hot** 2. Improperly adjusted dashpot 3. Defective or improperly adjusted solenoid 4. Incorrect fuel level in fuel bowl 5. Fuel pump pressure too high 6. Leaking float needle seat 7. Secondary throttle valve stuck open 8. Air or fuel leaks 9. Idle air bleeds plugged or missing 10. Idle passages plugged **Engine Cold** 11. Incorrectly adjusted choke 12. Improperly adjusted fast idle speed 13. Air leaks 14. Plugged idle or idle air passages 15. Stuck choke valve or binding linkage 16. Stuck secondary throttle valves 17. Engine flooding—high fuel level 18. Leaking or misaligned float
Engine hesitates on acceleration	1. Clogged fuel filter 2. Leaking fuel pump diaphragm 3. Low fuel pump pressure 4. Secondary throttle valves stuck, bent or misadjusted 5. Sticking or binding air valve 6. Defective accelerator pump 7. Vacuum leaks 8. Clogged air filter 9. Incorrect choke adjustment (engine cold)
Engine feels sluggish or flat on acceleration	1. Improperly adjusted idle speed or mixture 2. Clogged fuel filter 3. Defective accelerator pump 4. Dirty, plugged or incorrect main metering jets 5. Bent or sticking main metering rods 6. Sticking throttle valves 7. Stuck heat riser 8. Binding or stuck air valve 9. Dirty, plugged or incorrect secondary jets 10. Bent or sticking secondary metering rods. 11. Throttle body or manifold heat passages plugged 12. Improperly adjusted choke or choke vacuum break.
Carburetor floods	1. Defective fuel pump. Pressure too high. 2. Stuck choke valve 3. Dirty, worn or damaged float or needle valve/seat 4. Incorrect float/fuel level 5. Leaking float bowl

Condition	Possible Cause
Engine idles roughly and stalls	1. Incorrect idle speed 2. Clogged fuel filter 3. Dirt in fuel system or carburetor 4. Loose carburetor screws or attaching bolts 5. Broken carburetor gaskets 6. Air leaks 7. Dirty carburetor 8. Worn idle mixture needles 9. Throttle valves stuck open 10. Incorrectly adjusted float or fuel level 11. Clogged air filter
Engine runs unevenly or surges	1. Defective fuel pump 2. Dirty or clogged fuel filter 3. Plugged, loose or incorrect main metering jets or rods 4. Air leaks 5. Bent or sticking main metering rods 6. Stuck power piston 7. Incorrect float adjustment 8. Incorrect idle speed or mixture 9. Dirty or plugged idle system passages 10. Hard, brittle or broken gaskets 11. Loose attaching or mounting screws 12. Stuck or misaligned secondary throttle valves
Poor fuel economy	1. Poor driving habits 2. Stuck choke valve 3. Binding choke linkage 4. Stuck heat riser 5. Incorrect idle mixture 6. Defective accelerator pump 7. Air leaks 8. Plugged, loose or incorrect main metering jets 9. Improperly adjusted float or fuel level 10. Bent, misaligned or fuel-clogged float 11. Leaking float needle seat 12. Fuel leak 13. Accelerator pump discharge ball not seating properly 14. Incorrect main jets
Engine lacks high speed performance or power	1. Incorrect throttle linkage adjustment 2. Stuck or binding power piston 3. Defective accelerator pump 4. Air leaks 5. Incorrect float setting or fuel level 6. Dirty, plugged, worn or incorrect main metering jets or rods 7. Binding or sticking air valve 8. Brittle or cracked gaskets 9. Bent, incorrect or improperly adjusted secondary metering rods 10. Clogged fuel filter 11. Clogged air filter 12. Defective fuel pump

TROUBLESHOOTING FUEL INJECTION PROBLEMS

Each fuel injection system has its own unique components and test procedures, for which it is impossible to generalize. Refer to Chapter 4 of this Repair & Tune-Up Guide for specific test and repair procedures, if the vehicle is equipped with fuel injection.

TROUBLESHOOTING ELECTRICAL PROBLEMS

See Chapter 5 for service procedures

For any electrical system to operate, it must make a complete circuit. This simply means that the power flow from the battery must make a complete circle. When an electrical component is operating, power flows from the battery to the component, passes through the component causing it to perform its function (lighting a light bulb), and then returns to the battery through the ground of the circuit. This ground is usually (but not always) the metal part of the car or truck on which the electrical component is mounted.

Perhaps the easiest way to visualize this is to think of connecting a light bulb with two wires attached to it to the battery. If one of the two wires attached to the light bulb were attached to the negative post of the battery and the other were attached to the positive post of the battery, you would have a complete circuit. Current from the battery would flow to the light bulb, causing it to light, and return to the negative post of the battery.

The normal automotive circuit differs from this simple example in two ways. First, instead of having a return wire from the bulb to the battery, the light bulb returns the current to the battery through the chassis of the vehicle. Since the negative battery cable is attached to the chassis and the chassis is made of electrically conductive metal, the chassis of the vehicle can serve as a ground wire to complete the circuit. Secondly, most automotive circuits contain switches to turn components on and off as required.

Every complete circuit from a power source must include a component which is using the power from the power source. If you were to disconnect the light bulb from the wires and touch the two wires together (don't do this) the power supply wire to the component would be grounded before the normal ground connection for the circuit.

Because grounding a wire from a power source makes a complete circuit—less the required component to use the power—this phenomenon is called a short circuit. Common causes are: broken insulation (exposing the metal wire to a metal part of the car or truck), or a shorted switch.

Some electrical components which require a large amount of current to operate also have a relay in their circuit. Since these circuits carry a large amount of current, the thickness of the wire in the circuit (gauge size) is also greater. If this large wire were connected from the component to the control switch on the instrument panel, and then back to the component, a voltage drop would occur in the circuit. To prevent this potential drop in voltage, an electromagnetic switch (relay) is used. The large wires in the circuit are connected from the battery to one side of the relay, and from the opposite side of the relay to the component. The relay is normally open, preventing current from passing through the circuit. An additional, smaller, wire is connected from the relay to the control switch for the circuit. When the control switch is turned on, it grounds the smaller wire from the relay and completes the circuit. This closes the relay and allows current to flow from the battery to the component. The horn, headlight, and starter circuits are three which use relays.

It is possible for larger surges of current to pass through the electrical system of your car or truck. If this surge of current were to reach an electrical component, it could burn it out. To prevent this, fuses, circuit breakers or fusible links are connected into the current supply wires of most of the major electrical systems. When an electrical current of excessive power passes through the component's fuse, the fuse blows out and breaks the circuit, saving the component from destruction.

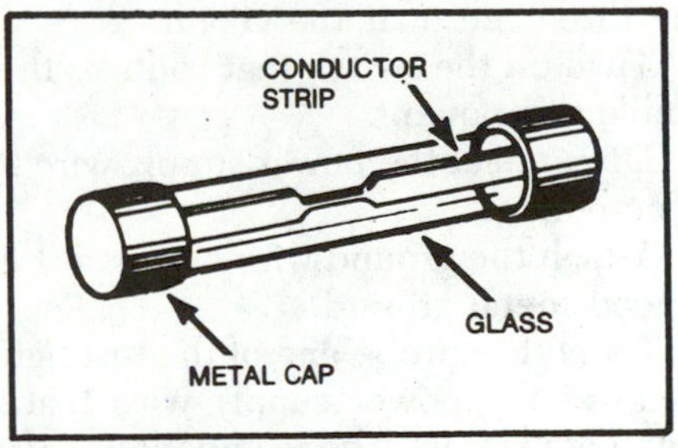

Typical automotive fuse

A circuit breaker is basically a self-repairing fuse. The circuit breaker opens the circuit the same way a fuse does. However, when either the short is removed from the circuit or the surge subsides, the circuit breaker resets itself and does not have to be replaced as a fuse does.

A fuse link is a wire that acts as a fuse. It is normally connected between the starter relay and the main wiring harness. This connection is usually under the hood. The fuse link (if installed) protects all the

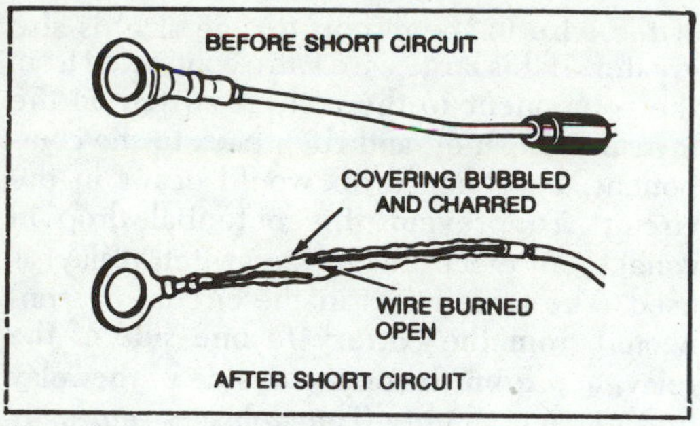

Most fusible links show a charred, melted insulation when they burn out

chassis electrical components, and is the probable cause of trouble when none of the electrical components function, unless the battery is disconnected or dead.

Electrical problems generally fall into one of three areas:

1. The component that is not functioning is not receiving current.
2. The component itself is not functioning.
3. The component is not properly grounded.

The electrical system can be checked with a test light and a jumper wire. A test light is a device that looks like a pointed screwdriver with a wire attached to it and has a light bulb in its handle. A jumper wire is a piece of insulated wire with an alligator clip attached to each end.

If a component is not working, you must follow a systematic plan to determine which of the three causes is the villain.

1. Turn on the switch that controls the inoperable component.
2. Disconnect the power supply wire from the component.
3. Attach the ground wire on the test light to a good metal ground.
4. Touch the probe end of the test light to the end of the power supply wire that was disconnected from the component. If the component is receiving current, the test light will go on.

NOTE: ***Some components work only when the ignition switch is turned on.***

If the test light does not go on, then the problem is in the circuit between the battery and the component. This includes all the switches, fuses, and relays in the system. Follow the wire that runs back to the battery. The problem is an open circuit between the

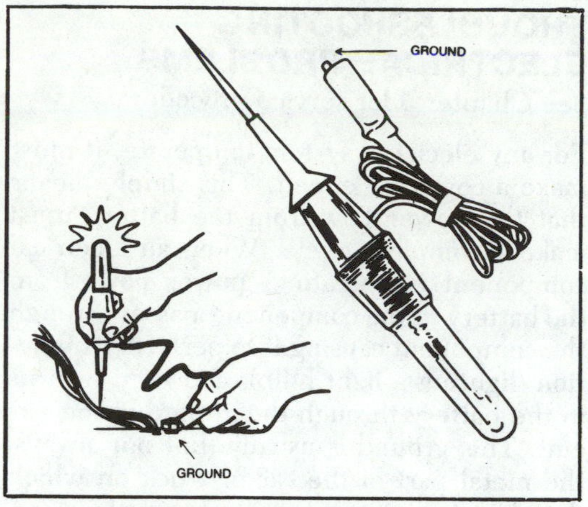

The test light will show the presence of current when touched to a hot wire and grounded at the other end

battery and the component. If the fuse is blown and, when replaced, immediately blows again, there is a short circuit in the system which must be located and repaired. If there is a switch in the system, bypass it with a jumper wire. This is done by connecting one end of the jumper wire to the power supply wire into the switch and the other end of the jumper wire to the wire coming out of the switch. If the test light lights with the jumper wire installed, the switch or whatever was bypassed is defective.

NOTE: ***Never substitute the jumper wire for the component, since it is required to use the power from the power source.***

5. If the bulb in the test light goes on, then the current is getting to the component that is not working. This eliminates the first of the three possible causes. Connect the power supply wire and connect a jumper wire from the component to a good metal ground. Do this with the switch which controls the component turned on, and also the ignition switch turned on if it is required for the component to work. If the component works with the jumper wire installed, then it has a bad ground. This is usually caused by the metal area on which the component mounts to the chassis being coated with some type of foreign matter.
6. If neither test located the source of the trouble, then the component itself is defective. Remember that for any electrical system to work, all connections must be clean and tight.

Troubleshooting Basic Turn Signal and Flasher Problems

See Chapter 5 for service procedures

Most problems in the turn signals or flasher system can be reduced to defective flashers or bulbs, which are easily replaced. Occasionally, the turn signal switch will prove defective.

F = Front R = Rear ● = Lights off ○ = Lights on

Condition		*Possible Cause*
Turn signals light, but do not flash	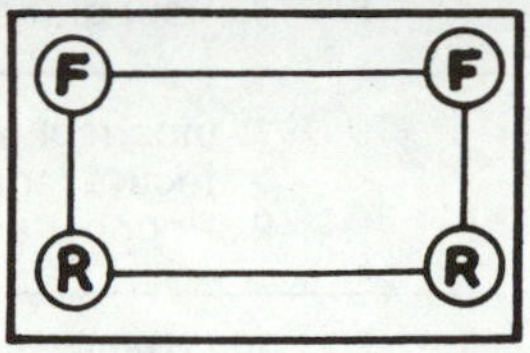	Defective flasher
No turn signals light on either side	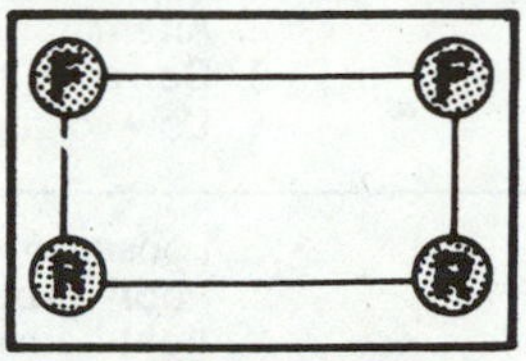	Blown fuse. Replace if defective. Defective flasher. Check by substitution. Open circuit, short circuit or poor ground.
Both turn signals on one side don't work	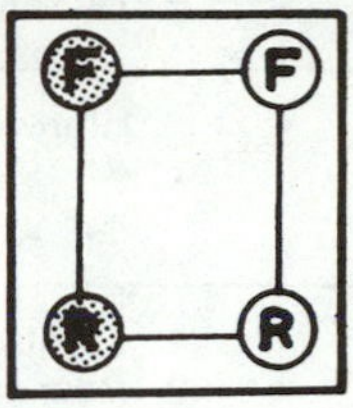	Bad bulbs. Bad ground in both (or either) housings.
One turn signal light on one side doesn't work	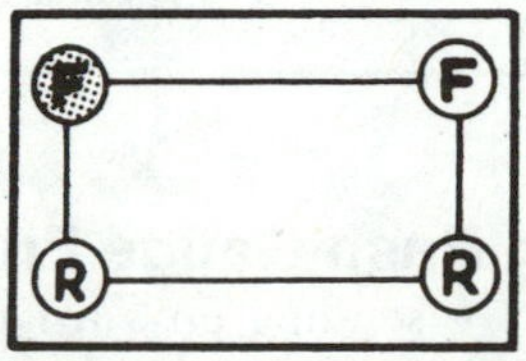	Defective bulb. Corrosion in socket. Clean contacts. Poor ground at socket.
Turn signal flashes too fast or too slowly	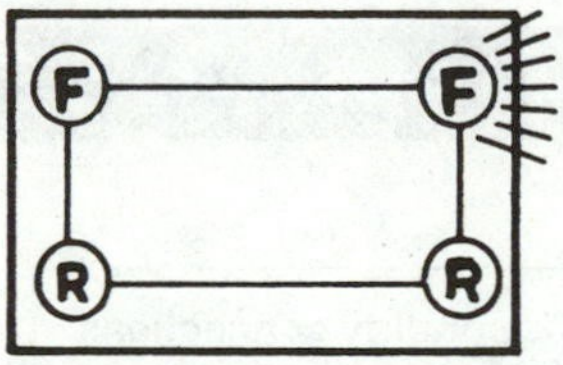	Check any bulb on the side flashing too fast. A heavy-duty bulb is probably installed in place of a regular bulb. Check the bulb flashing too slowly. A standard bulb was probably installed in place of a heavy-duty bulb. Loose connections or corrosion at the bulb socket.
Indicator lights don't work in either direction	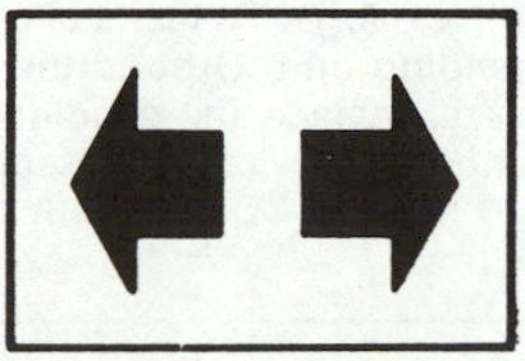	Check if the turn signals are working. Check the dash indicator lights. Check the flasher by substitution.
One indicator light doesn't light		On systems with one dash indicator: See if the lights work on the same side. Often the filaments have been reversed in systems combining stoplights with taillights and turn signals. Check the flasher by substitution. On systems with two indicators: Check the bulbs on the same side. Check the indicator light bulb. Check the flasher by substitution.

Troubleshooting Lighting Problems

See Chapter 5 for service procedures

Condition	Possible Cause
One or more lights don't work, but others do	1. Defective bulb(s) 2. Blown fuse(s) 3. Dirty fuse clips or light sockets 4. Poor ground circuit
Lights burn out quickly	1. Incorrect voltage regulator setting or defective regulator 2. Poor battery/alternator connections
Lights go dim	1. Low/discharged battery 2. Alternator not charging 3. Corroded sockets or connections 4. Low voltage output
Lights flicker	1. Loose connection 2. Poor ground. (Run ground wire from light housing to frame) 3. Circuit breaker operating (short circuit)
Lights "flare"—Some flare is normal on acceleration—If excessive, see "Lights Burn Out Quickly"	High voltage setting
Lights glare—approaching drivers are blinded	1. Lights adjusted too high 2. Rear springs or shocks sagging 3. Rear tires soft

Troubleshooting Dash Gauge Problems

Most problems can be traced to a defective sending unit or faulty wiring. Occasionally, the gauge itself is at fault. See Chapter 5 for service procedures.

Condition	Possible Cause
COOLANT TEMPERATURE GAUGE	
Gauge reads erratically or not at all	1. Loose or dirty connections 2. Defective sending unit. 3. Defective gauge. To test a bi-metal gauge, remove the wire from the sending unit. Ground the wire for an instant. If the gauge registers, replace the sending unit. To test a magnetic gauge, disconnect the wire at the sending unit. With ignition ON gauge should register COLD. Ground the wire; gauge should register HOT.
AMMETER GAUGE—TURN HEADLIGHTS ON (DO NOT START ENGINE). NOTE REACTION	
Ammeter shows charge Ammeter shows discharge Ammeter does not move	1. Connections reversed on gauge 2. Ammeter is OK 3. Loose connections or faulty wiring 4. Defective gauge

Condition	Possible Cause
OIL PRESSURE GAUGE	
Gauge does not register or is inaccurate	1. On mechanical gauge, Bourdon tube may be bent or kinked. 2. Low oil pressure. Remove sending unit. Idle the engine briefly. If no oil flows from sending unit hole, problem is in engine. 3. Defective gauge. Remove the wire from the sending unit and ground it for an instant with the ignition ON. A good gauge will go to the top of the scale. 4. Defective wiring. Check the wiring to the gauge. If it's OK and the gauge doesn't register when grounded, replace the gauge. 5. Defective sending unit.
ALL GAUGES	
All gauges do not operate All gauges read low or erratically All gauges pegged	1. Blown fuse 2. Defective instrument regulator 3. Defective or dirty instrument voltage regulator 4. Loss of ground between instrument voltage regulator and frame 5. Defective instrument regulator
WARNING LIGHTS	
Light(s) do not come on when ignition is ON, but engine is not started Light comes on with engine running	1. Defective bulb 2. Defective wire 3. Defective sending unit. Disconnect the wire from the sending unit and ground it. Replace the sending unit if the light comes on with the ignition ON. 4. Problem in individual system 5. Defective sending unit

Troubleshooting Clutch Problems

It is false economy to replace individual clutch components. The pressure plate, clutch plate and throwout bearing should be replaced as a set, and the flywheel face inspected, whenever the clutch is overhauled. See Chapter 6 for service procedures.

Condition	Possible Cause
Clutch chatter	1. Grease on driven plate (disc) facing 2. Binding clutch linkage or cable 3. Loose, damaged facings on driven plate (disc) 4. Engine mounts loose 5. Incorrect height adjustment of pressure plate release levers 6. Clutch housing or housing to transmission adapter misalignment 7. Loose driven plate hub
Clutch grabbing	1. Oil, grease on driven plate (disc) facing 2. Broken pressure plate 3. Warped or binding driven plate. Driven plate binding on clutch shaft
Clutch slips	1. Lack of lubrication in clutch linkage or cable (linkage or cable binds, causes incomplete engagement) 2. Incorrect pedal, or linkage adjustment 3. Broken pressure plate springs 4. Weak pressure plate springs 5. Grease on driven plate facings (disc)

Troubleshooting Clutch Problems (cont.)

Condition	Possible Cause
Incomplete clutch release	1. Incorrect pedal or linkage adjustment or linkage or cable binding 2. Incorrect height adjustment on pressure plate release levers 3. Loose, broken facings on driven plate (disc) 4. Bent, dished, warped driven plate caused by overheating
Grinding, whirring grating noise when pedal is depressed	1. Worn or defective throwout bearing 2. Starter drive teeth contacting flywheel ring gear teeth. Look for milled or polished teeth on ring gear.
Squeal, howl, trumpeting noise when pedal is being released (occurs during first inch to inch and one-half of pedal travel)	Pilot bushing worn or lack of lubricant. If bushing appears OK, polish bushing with emery cloth, soak lube wick in oil, lube bushing with oil, apply film of chassis grease to clutch shaft pilot hub, reassemble. NOTE: Bushing wear may be due to misalignment of clutch housing or housing to transmission adapter
Vibration or clutch pedal pulsation with clutch disengaged (pedal fully depressed)	1. Worn or defective engine transmission mounts 2. Flywheel run out. (Flywheel run out at face not to exceed 0.005″) 3. Damaged or defective clutch components

Troubleshooting Manual Transmission Problems

See Chapter 6 for service procedures

Condition	Possible Cause
Transmission jumps out of gear	1. Misalignment of transmission case or clutch housing. 2. Worn pilot bearing in crankshaft. 3. Bent transmission shaft. 4. Worn high speed sliding gear. 5. Worn teeth or end-play in clutch shaft. 6. Insufficient spring tension on shifter rail plunger. 7. Bent or loose shifter fork. 8. Gears not engaging completely. 9. Loose or worn bearings on clutch shaft or mainshaft. 10. Worn gear teeth. 11. Worn or damaged detent balls.
Transmission sticks in gear	1. Clutch not releasing fully. 2. Burred or battered teeth on clutch shaft, or sliding sleeve. 3. Burred or battered transmission mainshaft. 4. Frozen synchronizing clutch. 5. Stuck shifter rail plunger. 6. Gearshift lever twisting and binding shifter rail. 7. Battered teeth on high speed sliding gear or on sleeve. 8. Improper lubrication, or lack of lubrication. 9. Corroded transmission parts. 10. Defective mainshaft pilot bearing. 11. Locked gear bearings will give same effect as stuck in gear.
Transmission gears will not synchronize	1. Binding pilot bearing on mainshaft, will synchronize in high gear only. 2. Clutch not releasing fully. 3. Detent spring weak or broken. 4. Weak or broken springs under balls in sliding gear sleeve. 5. Binding bearing on clutch shaft, or binding countershaft. 6. Binding pilot bearing in crankshaft. 7. Badly worn gear teeth. 8. Improper lubrication. 9. Constant mesh gear not turning freely on transmission mainshaft. Will synchronize in that gear only.

Condition	Possible Cause
Gears spinning when shifting into gear from neutral	1. Clutch not releasing fully. 2. In some cases an extremely light lubricant in transmission will cause gears to continue to spin for a short time after clutch is released. 3. Binding pilot bearing in crankshaft.
Transmission noisy in all gears	1. Insufficient lubricant, or improper lubricant. 2. Worn countergear bearings. 3. Worn or damaged main drive gear or countergear. 4. Damaged main drive gear or mainshaft bearings. 5. Worn or damaged countergear anti-lash plate.
Transmission noisy in neutral only	1. Damaged main drive gear bearing. 2. Damaged or loose mainshaft pilot bearing. 3. Worn or damaged countergear anti-lash plate. 4. Worn countergear bearings.
Transmission noisy in one gear only	1. Damaged or worn constant mesh gears. 2. Worn or damaged countergear bearings. 3. Damaged or worn synchronizer.
Transmission noisy in reverse only	1. Worn or damaged reverse idler gear or idler bushing. 2. Worn or damaged mainshaft reverse gear. 3. Worn or damaged reverse countergear. 4. Damaged shift mechanism.

TROUBLESHOOTING AUTOMATIC TRANSMISSION PROBLEMS

Keeping alert to changes in the operating characteristics of the transmission (changing shift points, noises, etc.) can prevent small problems from becoming large ones. If the problem cannot be traced to loose bolts, fluid level, misadjusted linkage, clogged filters or similar problems, you should probably seek professional service.

Transmission Fluid Indications

The appearance and odor of the transmission fluid can give valuable clues to the overall condition of the transmission. Always note the appearance of the fluid when you check the fluid level or change the fluid. Rub a small amount of fluid between your fingers to feel for grit and smell the fluid on the dipstick.

If the fluid appears:	It indicates:
Clear and red colored	Normal operation
Discolored (extremely dark red or brownish) or smells burned	Band or clutch pack failure, usually caused by an overheated transmission. Hauling very heavy loads with insufficient power or failure to change the fluid often result in overheating. Do not confuse this appearance with newer fluids that have a darker red color and a strong odor (though not a burned odor).
Foamy or aerated (light in color and full of bubbles)	1. The level is too high (gear train is churning oil) 2. An internal air leak (air is mixing with the fluid). Have the transmission checked professionally.
Solid residue in the fluid	Defective bands, clutch pack or bearings. Bits of band material or metal abrasives are clinging to the dipstick. Have the transmission checked professionally.
Varnish coating on the dipstick	The transmission fluid is overheating

TROUBLESHOOTING DRIVE AXLE PROBLEMS

First, determine when the noise is most noticeable.

Drive Noise: Produced under vehicle acceleration.

Coast Noise: Produced while coasting with a closed throttle.

Float Noise: Occurs while maintaining constant speed (just enough to keep speed constant) on a level road.

External Noise Elimination

It is advisable to make a thorough road test to determine whether the noise originates in the rear axle or whether it originates from the tires, engine, transmission, wheel bearings or road surface. Noise originating from other places cannot be corrected by servicing the rear axle.

ROAD NOISE

Brick or rough surfaced concrete roads produce noises that seem to come from the rear axle. Road noise is usually identical in Drive or Coast and driving on a different type of road will tell whether the road is the problem.

TIRE NOISE

Tire noise can be mistaken as rear axle noise, even though the tires on the front are at fault. Snow tread and mud tread tires or tires worn unevenly will frequently cause vibrations which seem to originate elsewhere; *temporarily, and for test purposes only,* inflate the tires to 40–50 lbs. This will significantly alter the noise produced by the tires, but will not alter noise from the rear axle. Noises from the rear axle will normally cease at speeds below 30 mph on coast, while tire noise will continue at lower tone as speed is decreased. The rear axle noise will usually change from drive conditions to coast conditions, while tire noise will not. Do not forget to lower the tire pressure to normal after the test is complete.

ENGINE/TRANSMISSION NOISE

Determine at what speed the noise is most pronounced, then stop in a quiet place. With the transmission in Neutral, run the engine through speeds corresponding to road speeds where the noise was noticed. Noises produced with the vehicle standing still are coming from the engine or transmission.

FRONT WHEEL BEARINGS

Front wheel bearing noises, sometimes confused with rear axle noises, will not change when comparing drive and coast conditions. While holding the speed steady, lightly apply the footbrake. This will often cause wheel bearing noise to lessen, as some of the weight is taken off the bearing. Front wheel bearings are easily checked by jacking up the wheels and spinning the wheels. Shaking the wheels will also determine if the wheel bearings are excessively loose.

REAR AXLE NOISES

Eliminating other possible sources can narrow the cause to the rear axle, which normally produces noise from worn gears or bearings. Gear noises tend to peak in a narrow speed range, while bearing noises will usually vary in pitch with engine speeds.

Noise Diagnosis

The Noise Is:	*Most Probably Produced By:*
1. Identical under Drive or Coast	Road surface, tires or front wheel bearings
2. Different depending on road surface	Road surface or tires
3. Lower as speed is lowered	Tires
4. Similar when standing or moving	Engine or transmission
5. A vibration	Unbalanced tires, rear wheel bearing, unbalanced driveshaft or worn U-joint
6. A knock or click about every two tire revolutions	Rear wheel bearing
7. Most pronounced on turns	Damaged differential gears
8. A steady low-pitched whirring or scraping, starting at low speeds	Damaged or worn pinion bearing
9. A chattering vibration on turns	Wrong differential lubricant or worn clutch plates (limited slip rear axle)
10. Noticed only in Drive, Coast or Float conditions	Worn ring gear and/or pinion gear

Troubleshooting Steering & Suspension Problems

Condition	Possible Cause
Hard steering (wheel is hard to turn)	1. Improper tire pressure 2. Loose or glazed pump drive belt 3. Low or incorrect fluid 4. Loose, bent or poorly lubricated front end parts 5. Improper front end alignment (excessive caster) 6. Bind in steering column or linkage 7. Kinked hydraulic hose 8. Air in hydraulic system 9. Low pump output or leaks in system 10. Obstruction in lines 11. Pump valves sticking or out of adjustment 12. Incorrect wheel alignment
Loose steering (too much play in steering wheel)	1. Loose wheel bearings 2. Faulty shocks 3., Worn linkage or suspension components 4. Loose steering gear mounting or linkage points 5. Steering mechanism worn or improperly adjusted 6. Valve spool improperly adjusted 7. Worn ball joints, tie-rod ends, etc.
Veers or wanders (pulls to one side with hands off steering wheel)	1. Improper tire pressure 2. Improper front end alignment 3. Dragging or improperly adjusted brakes 4. Bent frame 5. Improper rear end alignment 6. Faulty shocks or springs 7. Loose or bent front end components 8. Play in Pitman arm 9. Steering gear mountings loose 10. Loose wheel bearings 11. Binding Pitman arm 12. Spool valve sticking or improperly adjusted 13. Worn ball joints
Wheel oscillation or vibration transmitted through steering wheel	1. Low or uneven tire pressure 2. Loose wheel bearings 3. Improper front end alignment 4. Bent spindle 5. Worn, bent or broken front end components 6. Tires out of round or out of balance 7. Excessive lateral runout in disc brake rotor 8. Loose or bent shock absorber or strut
Noises (see also "Troubleshooting Drive Axle Problems")	1. Loose belts 2. Low fluid, air in system 3. Foreign matter in system 4. Improper lubrication 5. Interference or chafing in linkage 6. Steering gear mountings loose 7. Incorrect adjustment or wear in gear box 8. Faulty valves or wear in pump 9. Kinked hydraulic lines 10. Worn wheel bearings
Poor return of steering	1. Over-inflated tires 2. Improperly aligned front end (excessive caster) 3. Binding in steering column 4. No lubrication in front end 5. Steering gear adjusted too tight
Uneven tire wear (see "How To Read Tire Wear")	1. Incorrect tire pressure 2. Improperly aligned front end 3. Tires out-of-balance 4. Bent or worn suspension parts

HOW TO READ TIRE WEAR

The way your tires wear is a good indicator of other parts of the suspension. Abnormal wear patterns are often caused by the need for simple tire maintenance, or for front end alignment.

Excessive wear at the center of the tread indicates that the air pressure in the tire is consistently too high. The tire is riding on the center of the tread and wearing it prematurely. Occasionally, this wear pattern can result from outrageously wide tires on narrow rims. The cure for this is to replace either the tires or the wheels.

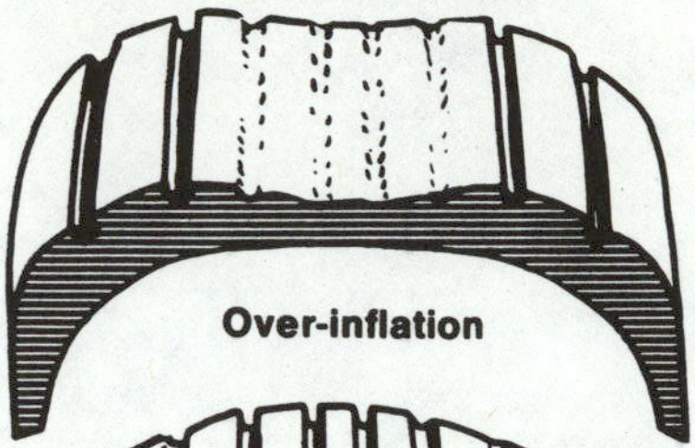
Over-inflation

This type of wear usually results from consistent under-inflation. When a tire is under-inflated, there is too much contact with the road by the outer treads, which wear prematurely. When this type of wear occurs, and the tire pressure is known to be consistently correct, a bent or worn steering component or the need for wheel alignment could be indicated.

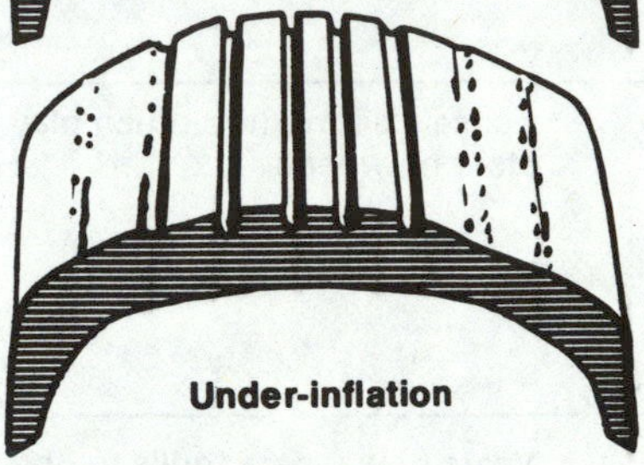
Under-inflation

Feathering is a condition when the edge of each tread rib develops a slightly rounded edge on one side and a sharp edge on the other. By running your hand over the tire, you can usually feel the sharper edges before you'll be able to see them. The most common causes of feathering are incorrect toe-in setting or deteriorated bushings in the front suspension.

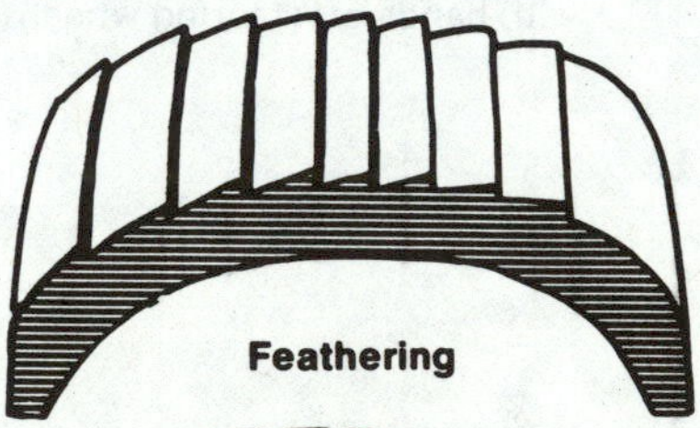
Feathering

When an inner or outer rib wears faster than the rest of the tire, the need for wheel alignment is indicated. There is excessive camber in the front suspension, causing the wheel to lean too much putting excessive load on one side of the tire. Misalignment could also be due to sagging springs, worn ball joints, or worn control arm bushings. Be sure the vehicle is loaded the way it's normally driven when you have the wheels aligned.

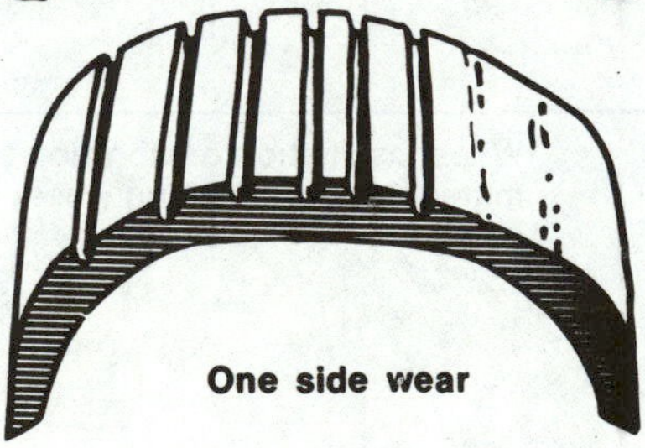
One side wear

Cups or scalloped dips appearing around the edge of the tread almost always indicate worn (sometimes bent) suspension parts. Adjustment of wheel alignment alone will seldom cure the problem. Any worn component that connects the wheel to the suspension can cause this type of wear. Occasionally, wheels that are out of balance will wear like this, but wheel imbalance usually shows up as bald spots between the outside edges and center of the tread.

Cupping

Second-rib wear is usually found only in radial tires, and appears where the steel belts end in relation to the tread. It can be kept to a minimum by paying careful attention to tire pressure and frequently rotating the tires. This is often considered normal wear but excessive amounts indicate that the tires are too wide for the wheels.

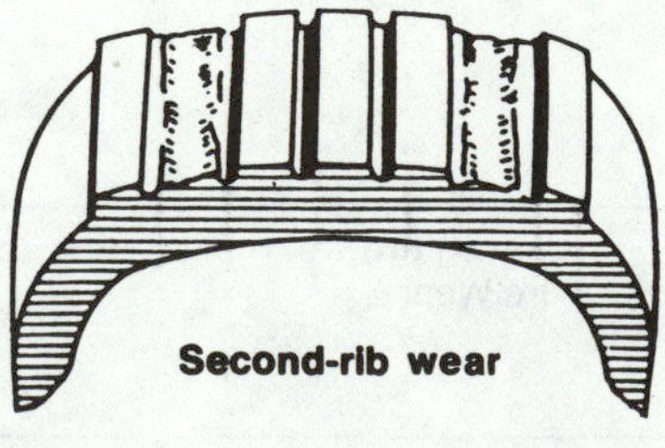
Second-rib wear

Troubleshooting Disc Brake Problems

Condition	Possible Cause
Noise—groan—brake noise emanating when slowly releasing brakes (creep-groan)	Not detrimental to function of disc brakes—no corrective action required. (This noise may be eliminated by slightly increasing or decreasing brake pedal efforts.)
Rattle—brake noise or rattle emanating at low speeds on rough roads, (front wheels only).	1. Shoe anti-rattle spring missing or not properly positioned. 2. Excessive clearance between shoe and caliper. 3. Soft or broken caliper seals. 4. Deformed or misaligned disc. 5. Loose caliper.
Scraping	1. Mounting bolts too long. 2. Loose wheel bearings. 3. Bent, loose, or misaligned splash shield.
Front brakes heat up during driving and fail to release	1. Operator riding brake pedal. 2. Stop light switch improperly adjusted. 3. Sticking pedal linkage. 4. Frozen or seized piston. 5. Residual pressure valve in master cylinder. 6. Power brake malfunction. 7. Proportioning valve malfunction.
Leaky brake caliper	1. Damaged or worn caliper piston seal. 2. Scores or corrosion on surface of cylinder bore.
Grabbing or uneven brake action—Brakes pull to one side	1. Causes listed under "Brakes Pull" 2. Power brake malfunction. 3. Low fluid level in master cylinder. 4. Air in hydraulic system. 5. Brake fluid, oil or grease on linings. 6. Unmatched linings. 7. Distorted brake pads. 8. Frozen or seized pistons. 9. Incorrect tire pressure. 10. Front end out of alignment. 11. Broken rear spring. 12. Brake caliper pistons sticking. 13. Restricted hose or line. 14. Caliper not in proper alignment to braking disc. 15. Stuck or malfunctioning metering valve. 16. Soft or broken caliper seals. 17. Loose caliper.
Brake pedal can be depressed without braking effect	1. Air in hydraulic system or improper bleeding procedure. 2. Leak past primary cup in master cylinder. 3. Leak in system. 4. Rear brakes out of adjustment. 5. Bleeder screw open.
Excessive pedal travel	1. Air, leak, or insufficient fluid in system or caliper. 2. Warped or excessively tapered shoe and lining assembly. 3. Excessive disc runout. 4. Rear brake adjustment required. 5. Loose wheel bearing adjustment. 6. Damaged caliper piston seal. 7. Improper brake fluid (boil). 8. Power brake malfunction. 9. Weak or soft hoses.

Troubleshooting Disc Brake Problems (cont.)

Condition	Possible Cause
Brake roughness or chatter (pedal pumping)	1. Excessive thickness variation of braking disc. 2. Excessive lateral runout of braking disc. 3. Rear brake drums out-of-round. 4. Excessive front bearing clearance.
Excessive pedal effort	1. Brake fluid, oil or grease on linings. 2. Incorrect lining. 3. Frozen or seized pistons. 4. Power brake malfunction. 5. Kinked or collapsed hose or line. 6. Stuck metering valve. 7. Scored caliper or master cylinder bore. 8. Seized caliper pistons.
Brake pedal fades (pedal travel increases with foot on brake)	1. Rough master cylinder or caliper bore. 2. Loose or broken hydraulic lines/connections. 3. Air in hydraulic system. 4. Fluid level low. 5. Weak or soft hoses. 6. Inferior quality brake shoes or fluid. 7. Worn master cylinder piston cups or seals.

Troubleshooting Drum Brakes

Condition	Possible Cause
Pedal goes to floor	1. Fluid low in reservoir. 2. Air in hydraulic system. 3. Improperly adjusted brake. 4. Leaking wheel cylinders. 5. Loose or broken brake lines. 6. Leaking or worn master cylinder. 7. Excessively worn brake lining.
Spongy brake pedal	1. Air in hydraulic system. 2. Improper brake fluid (low boiling point). 3. Excessively worn or cracked brake drums. 4. Broken pedal pivot bushing.
Brakes pulling	1. Contaminated lining. 2. Front end out of alignment. 3. Incorrect brake adjustment. 4. Unmatched brake lining. 5. Brake drums out of round. 6. Brake shoes distorted. 7. Restricted brake hose or line. 8. Broken rear spring. 9. Worn brake linings. 10. Uneven lining wear. 11. Glazed brake lining. 12. Excessive brake lining dust. 13. Heat spotted brake drums. 14. Weak brake return springs. 15. Faulty automatic adjusters. 16. Low or incorrect tire pressure.

Condition	Possible Cause
Squealing brakes	1. Glazed brake lining. 2. Saturated brake lining. 3. Weak or broken brake shoe retaining spring. 4. Broken or weak brake shoe return spring. 5. Incorrect brake lining. 6. Distorted brake shoes. 7. Bent support plate. 8. Dust in brakes or scored brake drums. 9. Linings worn below limit. 10. Uneven brake lining wear. 11. Heat spotted brake drums.
Chirping brakes	1. Out of round drum or eccentric axle flange pilot.
Dragging brakes	1. Incorrect wheel or parking brake adjustment. 2. Parking brakes engaged or improperly adjusted. 3. Weak or broken brake shoe return spring. 4. Brake pedal binding. 5. Master cylinder cup sticking. 6. Obstructed master cylinder relief port. 7. Saturated brake lining. 8. Bent or out of round brake drum. 9. Contaminated or improper brake fluid. 10. Sticking wheel cylinder pistons. 11. Driver riding brake pedal. 12. Defective proportioning valve. 13. Insufficient brake shoe lubricant.
Hard pedal	1. Brake booster inoperative. 2. Incorrect brake lining. 3. Restricted brake line or hose. 4. Frozen brake pedal linkage. 5. Stuck wheel cylinder. 6. Binding pedal linkage. 7. Faulty proportioning valve.
Wheel locks	1. Contaminated brake lining. 2. Loose or torn brake lining. 3. Wheel cylinder cups sticking. 4. Incorrect wheel bearing adjustment. 5. Faulty proportioning valve.
Brakes fade (high speed)	1. Incorrect lining. 2. Overheated brake drums. 3. Incorrect brake fluid (low boiling temperature). 4. Saturated brake lining. 5. Leak in hydraulic system. 6. Faulty automatic adjusters.
Pedal pulsates	1. Bent or out of round brake drum.
Brake chatter and shoe knock	1. Out of round brake drum. 2. Loose support plate. 3. Bent support plate. 4. Distorted brake shoes. 5. Machine grooves in contact face of brake drum (Shoe Knock). 6. Contaminated brake lining. 7. Missing or loose components. 8. Incorrect lining material. 9. Out-of-round brake drums. 10. Heat spotted or scored brake drums. 11. Out-of-balance wheels.

Troubleshooting Drum Brakes (cont.)

Condition	Possible Cause
Brakes do not self adjust	1. Adjuster screw frozen in thread. 2. Adjuster screw corroded at thrust washer. 3. Adjuster lever does not engage star wheel. 4. Adjuster installed on wrong wheel.
Brake light glows	1. Leak in the hydraulic system. 2. Air in the system. 3. Improperly adjusted master cylinder pushrod. 4. Uneven lining wear. 5. Failure to center combination valve or proportioning valve.

Mechanic's Data

General Conversion Table

Multiply By	To Convert	To	
	LENGTH		
2.54	Inches	Centimeters	.3937
25.4	Inches	Millimeters	.03937
30.48	Feet	Centimeters	.0328
.304	Feet	Meters	3.28
.914	Yards	Meters	1.094
1.609	Miles	Kilometers	.621
	VOLUME		
.473	Pints	Liters	2.11
.946	Quarts	Liters	1.06
3.785	Gallons	Liters	.264
.016	Cubic inches	Liters	61.02
16.39	Cubic inches	Cubic cms.	.061
28.3	Cubic feet	Liters	.0353
	MASS (Weight)		
28.35	Ounces	Grams	.035
.4536	Pounds	Kilograms	2.20
—	To obtain	From	Multiply by

Multiply By	To Convert	To	
	AREA		
.645	Square inches	Square cms.	.155
.836	Square yds.	Square meters	1.196
	FORCE		
4.448	Pounds	Newtons	.225
.138	Ft./lbs.	Kilogram/meters	7.23
1.36	Ft./lbs.	Newton-meters	.737
.112	In./lbs.	Newton-meters	8.844
	PRESSURE		
.068	Psi	Atmospheres	14.7
6.89	Psi	Kilopascals	.145
	OTHER		
1.104	Horsepower (DIN)	Horsepower (SAE)	.9861
.746	Horsepower (SAE)	Kilowatts (KW)	1.34
1.60	Mph	Km/h	.625
.425	Mpg	Km/1	2.35
—	To obtain	From	Multiply by

Tap Drill Sizes

National Coarse or U.S.S.

Screw & Tap Size	Threads Per Inch	Use Drill Number
No. 5	40	39
No. 6	32	36
No. 8	32	29
No. 10	24	25
No. 12	24	17
1/4	20	8
5/16	18	F
3/8	16	5/16
7/16	14	U
1/2	13	27/64
9/16	12	31/64
5/8	11	17/32
3/4	10	21/32
7/8	9	49/64

National Coarse or U.S.S.

Screw & Tap Size	Threads Per Inch	Use Drill Number
1	8	7/8
1 1/8	7	63/64
1 1/4	7	1 7/64
1 1/2	6	1 11/32

National Fine or S.A.E.

Screw & Tap Size	Threads Per Inch	Use Drill Number
No. 5	44	37
No. 6	40	33
No. 8	36	29
No. 10	32	21

National Fine or S.A.E.

Screw & Tap Size	Threads Per Inch	Use Drill Number
No. 12	28	15
1/4	28	3
6/16	24	1
3/8	24	Q
7/16	20	W
1/2	20	29/64
9/16	18	33/64
5/8	18	37/64
3/4	16	11/16
7/8	14	13/16
1 1/8	12	1 3/64
1 1/4	12	1 11/64
1 1/2	12	1 27/64

Index

A

Air cleaner, 14
Air conditioning
  Sight glass inspection, 27
Alternator, 85
Antifreeze, 44
Automatic transmission
  Adjustment, 199
  Filter change, 199
  Pan removal, 199
Axle
  Fluid recommendations, 34
  Lubricant level, 44
Axle shaft, 207

B

Ball joints, 216
Battery
  Jump starting, 50
  Maintenance, 15
Belt tension adjustment, 18
Brakes
  Adjustment, 233
  Bleeding, 236
  Caliper, 240, 244
  Fluid level, 46
  Fluid recommendations, 34
  Front brakes, 237
  Master cylinder, 233
  Parking brake, 244
  Rear brakes, 243

C

Camber, 222, 229
Camshaft and bearings, 119
Capacities, 37
Carburetor
  Adjustment, 168
  Overhaul, 166
  Replacement, 166
Caster, 222
Catalytic converter, 135
Chassis lubrication, 48
Clutch
  Adjustment, 197
  Replacement, 198
Compression, 101, 110
Condenser, 60
Connecting rod and bearings, 122
Control arm
  Upper, 219
  Lower, 220
Cooling system, 44, 131
Crankcase ventilation (PCV), 135
Crankshaft, 122
Cylinder head
  Removal and installation, 97
  Torque sequence, 97

D

Differential
  Fluid change, 44
  Ratios, 209
Distributor
  Removal and installation, 84
  Breaker points, 60
Drive axle, 207
Driveshaft, 206
Dwell angle, 64
Dwell meter, 64

E

Electrical
  Chassis, 178
  Engine, 84
Electronic ignition, 84
Emission controls, 135
Engine
  Camshaft, 119
  Cylinder head torque sequence, 97
  Exhaust manifold, 95
  Front cover, 122
  Identification, 7
  Intake manifold, 94
  Oil recommendations, 34
  Pistons and rings, 122
  Rebuilding, 122
  Removal and installation, 86
  Rocker arm (or shaft), 93
  Specifications, 87
  Timing chain (or gears), 118
  Tune-up, 54
Evaporative canister, 135
Exhaust manifold, 95

F

Fan belt adjustment, 18
Firing order, 60
Fluid level checks
  Battery, 15
  Coolant, 44
  Engine oil, 37
  Master cylinder, 46, 47
  Power steering pump, 46
  Rear axle, 44
  Steering gear, 47
  Transmission, 41
Fluid recommendations, 34
Front suspension
  Ball joints, 216
  Lower control arm, 220
  Upper control arm, 219
  Wheel alignment, 222
Front wheel bearing, 241
Fuel injection, 174
Fuel filter, 31
Fuel pump, 164

Fuel system, 164
Fuses and flashers, 190
Fusible links, 190

G

Gearshift linkage adjustment
  Automatic, 199
  Manual, 195

H

Hand brake, 244
Headlights, 189
Heater, 180
History, 5
Hoses, 27

I

Identification
  Vehicle, 7
  Engine, 7
  Transmission, 7
Idle speed and mixture, 72
Ignition switch, 185
Instrument cluster, 183
Intake manifold, 94

J

Jacking points, 51
Jump starting, 50

L

Lower control arm, 220
Lubrication
  Chassis, 48
  Differential, 48
  Engine, 48
  Transmission, 48

M

Maintenance intervals, 16
Manifolds
  Intake, 94
  Exhaust, 95
Manual transmission, 193
Master cylinder, 233

N

Neutral safety switch, 200

O

Oil and fuel recommendations, 34
Oil change, 38
Oil filter (engine), 38
Oil pan, 119
Oil pump, 119
Oil level (engine), 37

P

Parking brake, 244
Pistons and rings
  Installation, 122
  Positioning, 122
PCV valve, 135
Points, 60
Power steering, 232
Power steering pump, 232

R

Radiator, 132
Rear axle, 207
Rear suspension, 224
Rear main oil seal, 122
Rings, 122
Rocker arm (or shaft), 93
Routine maintenance, 11

S

Seat belts, 187
Serial number location, 7
Shock absorbers
  Front, 214
  Rear, 228
Spark plugs, 54
Specifications
  Battery and starter, 87
  Brakes, 234
  Capacities, 37
  Crankshaft and connecting rod, 91
  General engine, 87
  Torque, 92
  Tune-up, 56
  Valve, 89
  Wheel alignment, 224
Springs
  Front, 211
  Rear, 224
Starter, 86
Steering
  Linkage, 232
  Wheel, 230

T

Thermostat, 133
Timing (ignition), 65
Timing chain, 118
Timing chain tensioner, 115
Tires, 29
Toe, 222, 229

Tools, 2
Towing, 48
Transmission
  Automatic, 199
  Manual, 193
  Fluid change, 43
Troubleshooting, 247
Tune-up
  Procedures, 54
  Specifications, 56
Turn signal switch, 183
Turbocharger, 96

U

U-joints, 206

V

Valves
  Adjustment, 67
  Service, 111
  Specifications, 89
Vehicle identification, 7

W

Water pump, 132
Wheel alignment, 222, 229
Wheel bearings, 241
Windshield wipers
  Arm, 181
  Blade, 33
  Linkage, 182
  Motor, 182